Technology in the Law Office
Second Edition

Thomas F. Goldman, JD
Attorney at Law
Thomas Edison State College
Professor Emeritus
Bucks County Community College

Prentice Hall
Boston Columbus Indianapolis New York San Francisco Upper Saddle River
Amsterdam Cape Town Dubai London Madrid Milan Munich Paris Montreal Toronto
Delhi Mexico City Sao Paulo Sydney Hong Kong Seoul Singapore Taipei Tokyo

Editor in Chief: Vernon Anthony
Senior Acquisitions Editor: Gary Bauer
Editorial Assistant: Megan Heintz
Director of Marketing: David Gesell
Marketing Manager: Leigh Ann Sims
Marketing Assistant: Les Roberts
Project Manager: Christina Taylor
Senior Operations Supervisor: Pat Tonneman
Art Director: Diane Ernsberger
Manager, Rights and Permissions, Image Resource Center: Zina Arabia

Image Permission Coordinator: Kathy Gavilanes
Cover Designer: Jeff Vanik
Cover Art: istock
Full-Service Project Management: Mary Jo Graham, S4Carlisle Publishing Services
Composition: S4Carlisle Publishing Services
Printer/Binder: Edwards Brothers, Inc.
Cover Printer: Lehigh-Phoenix Color/Hagerstown
Text Font: Goudy

Microsoft® and Windows® are registered trademarks of the Microsoft Corporation in the U.S.A. and other countries. Screen shots and icons reprinted with permission from the Microsoft Corporation. This book is not sponsored or endorsed by or affiliated with the Microsoft Corporation.

Photo Credits: Ariadna de Raadt/Dreamstime LLC, p. 2; Thethirdma/Dreamstime LLC, p. 26; Satyr/Dreamstime LLC, p. 54; G. Schuster/Masterfile Corporation, p. 82; Orangeline/Dreamsline LLC, p. 114; Getty Images-Stockbyte, p. 146; Jack Star/Photolink/Getty Images, Inc.-Photodisc, p. 188; David Raymer/Corbis/Bettman, p. 210; Prebranac/Dreamstime, LLC, p. 228; Photolibrary.com, 262; Zimmytws/Dreamstime LLC, 284; Endostock/Dreamstime LLC, 310; Getty Images-Stockbyte, 340; Endostock/Dreamstime LLC, 368; Corbis Royalty, 390; Steve Mason/Getty Images, Inc.-Photdisc, 416

Library of Congress Cataloging-in-Publication Data

Goldman, Thomas F.
  Technology in the law office/Thomas F. Goldman.—2nd ed.
       p. cm.
  Includes bibliographical references and index.
  ISBN 978-0-13-505682-0 (alk. paper)
1. Law offices—United States—Automation—Popular works. I. Title.
KF320.A9G645 2010
340.068—dc22

2008050334

10 9 8 7 6 5

Prentice Hall
is an imprint of

PEARSON
www.pearsonhighered.com

ISBN-10:   0-13-505682-9
ISBN-13:   978-0-13-505682-0

DEDICATION

To the children
who have blessed my life with joy
who have allowed me to be part of their journey
who have opened my eyes and shown me the world
who are always in my thoughts and in my heart.

BRIEF CONTENTS

CONTENTS

CHAPTER 4

The Internet and Electronic Mail 83

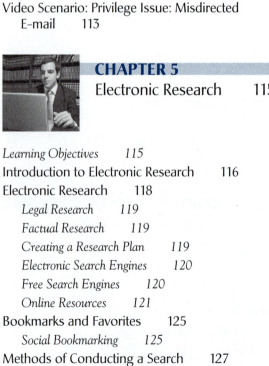

CHAPTER 5

Electronic Research 115

CHAPTER 6
Word Processing 147

CHAPTER 7
Electronic Spreadsheets 189

CHAPTER 8
Electronic Databases 211

CHAPTER 9

The Paperless Office   229

CHAPTER 10

Office Management Software   263

CHAPTER 11

Case Organization and Management Software   285

CHAPTER 15
Presentation and Trial Graphics 391

CHAPTER 16
The Electronic Courthouse 417

APPENDIX 1
Case Studies 437

APPENDIX 2
Frequently Asked Questions (FAQs) about Installing Software 471

LEARNING OBJECTIVES

The following list describes the outcomes you should expect from completing the course or reading this book.

1. Explain the functions of the components of a computer system in the law office.
2. Describe the different classes of software and the functions they perform in a law office.
3. Understand the application of legal ethics in the use of technology.
4. Understand the impact of court rules on the use of software and trial practice.
5. Describe the features of the electronic courtroom and the paperless office.
6. Describe how a computer network is used by a law firm.
7. Explain the importance of maintaining computer and network security and the steps that may be taken to do so.
8. Understand the use of legal-specific applications programs.
9. Describe how the computer is used to conduct factual and legal research.
10. Locate and use the resources for learning how to use specific software programs.
11. Understand how the courts use technology.
12. Be able to communicate with others in a support or user position about technology as it relates to the legal community.

PREFACE

FROM THE AUTHOR

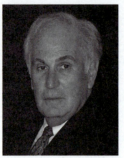 "Certainty?" That is how I started the preface to the first edition, with comments about the need to find a way to handle the constant change that happens in the world of technology and in the law. In the very short period of time since the release of the first edition, all of the software programs used in the legal community have undergone updates, been enhanced, patched, or had features added. In the first edition, we included a DVD with demonstration software packaged with the text; however, problems occurred when instructors and students had different versions of the software or tried to use them in different operating systems. To resolve these issues, we have worked with the software vendors to allow extended-period downloads directly from special websites that are accessible from the new Technology Resources Website. The ability to download these resources will enable users to access the latest versions of these programs, eliminating the need for the DVD.

I am deeply grateful to the software companies that have worked with us to extend their standard demonstration time-out periods and allowed me to link to their software, tutorials, and other training material from my companion website. As with the first edition, this edition focuses on learning how to use the training tutorials and help functions in the software, rather than on executing rote keystroke instructions. Many of the instructors and readers of the first edition have told us that learning how to find and use help programs is the most important skill that they developed while using this text.

The practice of law is evolving more quickly than ever before as electronic tools provide new methods of creation, storage, production, and access to information by clients, lawyers, and the courts. The courts are imposing greater responsibilities on the legal team to understand technology applications and to monitor use not only internally but by clients as well. Even the smallest law firms must be aware of the new rules of procedure and evidence to avoid court sanctions and ethical violations. In this edition I have greatly expanded material on the ethical implications of using technology in legal practice in response to the increased ethical violations reported in cases and the press. Hopefully, references throughout the text to the potential ethical impact of each application will help students avoid major problems in practice.

Change in the law is also inevitable. We were introduced to the "new" federal rules in December 2006. Since that time we have experienced a restatement of the "new" rules, actually a re-stylized writing of the rules, and the passage of the new rules of evidence, section 502. These changes are the result of the increased importance of electronic discovery in practice, not only in the federal system but also in the state courts as they adopt their own rules and procedures. Consequently, I have expanded the coverage of electronic discovery from one chapter to two. Case law continues to evolve in this area, so while there is no absolute set of rules to follow, there are some well-reasoned opinions that can be used as a starting point for further research and guidance. In addition, I have also addressed the growing field of litigation support, as it becomes a major area of practice support.

This second edition continues to provide a basic foundation in legal technology applications. Sources of help and references for learning about new programs, features, and changes in the law relating to electronic applications are provided in every chapter. You will also find a wealth of support online at the new Technology Resources Website at www.pearsonhighered.com/goldman.

Thomas F. Goldman

ORGANIZATION OF THE BOOK

The book is divided into four units:

UNIT ONE—THE FUNDAMENTALS is a review of the concepts learned in computer courses. In these chapters, issues facing the legal team such as ethical concerns are presented. For the new paralegal, the information technologist, or the lawyer quickly trying to come up to speed with the use of technology and computers, this unit will present an overview and introduction to the use of computers and technology in the law office and corporate and government law departments.

Chapter 1: Technology in the Law Office
Chapter 2: Legal Ethics in a Technology Age
Chapter 3: Computer Hardware and Software
Chapter 4: The Internet and Electronic Mail

UNIT TWO—THE BUILDING BLOCKS shows the uses of law-related applications software that are the software building blocks on which all other specialty applications software is built: the database, the word processor, the spreadsheet, and computer search engines. The IT people reading this say that that is an oversimplification and that there are other important components as well. But from over thirty years teaching, writing, and lecturing on this subject, I have found that with these conceptual building blocks in mind, students, paralegals, and lawyers have a better understanding about how to use the more complex software applications.

Chapter 5: Electronic Research
Chapter 6: Word Processing
Chapter 7: Electronic Spreadsheets
Chapter 8: Electronic Databases
Chapter 9: The Paperless Office

UNIT THREE—SPECIALTY APPLICATIONS SOFTWARE offers an introduction to some of the classes of specialty applications software in use in the law office and the court system. Specialty applications software for the legal community is constantly evolving. What was once a field of single-application software programs, like stand-alone calendar programs or single-purpose timekeeping programs, is now a marketplace of integrated programs performing some, most, or all of the automation needs of the law office.

Chapter 10: Office Management Software
Chapter 11: Case Organization and Management Software
Chapter 12: Electronic Discovery—The Fundamentals
Chapter 13: Electronic Discovery—Rules and Procedures

UNIT FOUR—COMPUTER APPLICATIONS IN LITIGATION presents the ways in which technology is being used by the courts and by litigators. As one of the evolving areas of practice and court administration, it cannot be definitive. The unit attempts to demonstrate how the technology is being used and suggests how it may be used in the future.

Appropriate representative programs are presented, with a learning module for that software, demonstrating the use of the learning resources available to understand the program and to provide a resource for future use of the rarely used features. With an understanding of the use of the Help resources, it is hoped that the user will not need to go back to school, and call technical support.

Chapter 14: Litigation Support
Chapter 15: Presentation and Trial Graphics
Chapter 16: The Electronic Courthouse

NEW TO THE SECOND EDITION

The applications of technology in the law office continue to evolve at a rapid pace. Changes to the second edition are numerous, reflecting changes in the technology, software applications, legal software applications, and changes in law relating to its usage. In addition, many users of the book provided feedback that led to refinement in coverage, presentation, and exercises. Here is a list of some of the most important changes:

VIDEO INTRODUCTIONS TO EACH CHAPTER

- In videos located at this book's companion website, students can watch the author introduce the chapter topics reinforcing the importance of the topic for paralegal students.

MORE EXERCISES AND EXAMPLES

- More exercises and examples were added throughout the textbook to provide students with more hands-on experiences with technology concepts and applications.

NEW ETHICS AND TECHNOLOGY CHAPTER (CHAPTER 2)

- A full chapter on ethics was added, reflecting the importance of being aware of ethical issues related to technology applications in practice.
- Ethical perspectives and guideline notes are also integrated throughout the text.

EXPANDED COVERAGE OF MICROSOFT OFFICE APPLICATIONS

- Coverage and exercise of law-related Office Suite functions has been expanded.
- A new Law Office Case Study has been added with data to be used in new Office application exercises.

TWO NEW CHAPTERS ON E-DISCOVERY

- Chapter 12: Electronic Discovery—The Fundamentals covers an overview of the fundamental concepts of e-discovery.
- Chapter 13: Electronic Discovery—Rules and Procedures covers the latest rules of court and of evidence and case law applications.

NEW VIDEO CASE STUDY SCENARIOS

- Eleven Case Study Videos dealing with technology topics have been added to the textbook as end-of-chapter assignments. The videos are available to students on the companion website.

NEW CASE STUDY APPENDIX

- A second case has been added in a new appendix, providing two case studies to use in end-of-chapter assignments.

CHAPTER FEATURES

Chapter 13 Digital Resources at www.prenhall.com/goldman
- Author Video Introduction
- Case Study Video
- Comprehension Quizzes and Glossary
- Video Interview: Role of Paralegal in Litigation with Charlotte Riser Harris

◀**NEW LISTING OF DIGITAL ASSETS ON CHAPTER OPENING PAGE**—On the bottom of the chapter opening page is a listing of the digital resources available for use in conjunction with the chapter. Digital resources include an online video introduction to the chapter by the author, video overviews of software applications, video case studies, links to helpful online resources, and quizzes to help students gauge their mastery of the material.

▶**OPENING SCENARIOS**—Each chapter contains a scenario designed to focus the reader on the relationship of the chapter content to law office practice. The scenarios follow the career of a fictional law office starting from scratch.

OPENING SCENARIO

Attorneys Owen Mason and Ariel Marshall weighed filing the lawsuit involving multiple plaintiffs injured as a result of what appeared to be defective brakes in the various courts with jurisdiction and venue. Procedurally they wanted the case to get to a jury as quickly as possible. A concern was the time it might take in state court where they felt the rules were not as rigid as in the federal system. It was hoped the new discovery rules in federal court would bring out all the discoverable evidence that might be used in court. After attending a continuing legal education program, the partners came away with a number of questions about the time lines and actual implementation of the rules on discovery. They worked out what they thought was a discovery timetable for the case and had an uneasy feeling about the apparent shortness in time for taking action before meeting with the judge assigned to the case. Since neither of them had ever taken part in a meet and confer under the new federal rules, they were uncertain as to what would happen and how to prepare. No one in the office had any extensive technology training and there were some doubts about the requests for electronically stored documents and the production of documents to the other side.

▪ LEGAL SOFTWARE COVERAGE

Material covered in the book has been divided into chapters representing functional aspects of the use of the technology. The core programs found in other legal specialty applications software, including word processing, electronic spreadsheets, and databases, are covered from the view of the law office application and the specific features and applications commonly used in the legal environment.

Specialty applications software is divided into classifications and covered by class, including law office applications, case management, litigation support, and presentation graphics.

Emerging topics covered are use of the Internet, the paperless office, electronic courtroom, and electronic research.

Contemporary legal software programs are presented, where applicable, with an overview of the software and end-of-chapter exercises utilizing real-world software. Tutorial learning modules are provided for download from the companion website to ensure that the latest versions are covered and taught.

A primary learning objective of the end-of-chapter software exercises is to teach the user how to use the built-in Help features in software programs and to locate and use the training materials available from the software vendor, to learn new or rarely used features of the program, and to know when to call for outside assistance.

■ END-OF-CHAPTER EXERCISES AND MATERIALS

End-of-chapter practice materials, continuing case studies, and two comprehensive case studies reflect the actual information and documents frequently found in legal practice and utilize the appropriate application software.

■ CHAPTER-ENDING VIDEO CASE STUDIES

New to this edition are 11 scenario-based video case studies dealing with technology issues in the law office. Located on the companion website, these videos introduce students to the use of technology in workplace settings and pose thought-provoking questions regarding ethical and legal issues that arise from the usage.

VIDEO SCENARIO: LEGAL RESEARCH–ARE BOOKS OBSOLETE?

 In the middle of a trial in another state, the trial attorney sends his paralegal to the courthouse law library to find a case that has been cited as precedent. The local courthouse has both traditional books and electronic research services available. A password not available to visiting legal teams is needed to use the electronic system.

Go to the Companion Website, select Chapter 5 from the pull down menu, and watch this video: Legal Research—Are Books Obsolete?

1. Should members of the legal team be skilled in using alternative methods for conducting research?
2. If a password were available would the paralegal be able to conduct the research if the legal research service is not one in which she had been trained?
3. How could this lack of research tools have been avoided? What hardware or software should the legal team take with them when they are trying cases away from their normal jurisdiction?

VIDEO SCENARIO: SIGNING DOCUMENTS

 The statute of limitation will run out at the close of the day, and the court office for filing documents is closing in minutes. The paralegal taking action to avoid missing the deadline asks if there is an alternative. Electronic filing is suggested by the clerk as a way to avoid having to rush to the court to file documents.
Go to the Companion Website, select Chapter 9 from the pull down menu, and watch this video.

1. Are there dangers in using electronic filing at the last minute?
2. Are there preliminary steps that must be taken to be able to use electronic filing?
3. What are the rules on electronic filing in your local state and federal courts?

VIDEO SCENARIO: SCHEDULING CONFERENCE

 The trial attorneys are meeting with the Judge assigned to the case in a scheduling conference. Significant discovery issues are raised by both sides and a request for sanctions. The judge mentions violation of the hold order as a reason for granting sanctions.

Go to the Companion Website, select Chapter 13 from the pull down menu, and watch this video.

1. Is the granting of sanctions a real threat?
2. What would be the impact of a negative inference instruction to the jury?
3. How important is a liti gation hold" under the Federal Rules of Civil Procedure?

■ GETTING READY TO USE SOFTWARE

To prepare your computer for some of the software learning modules, you will need to select "plug-ins" and "viewers." OK, so I started with the geek talk already. These and the other technical terms are explained in the text itself, in the Frequently Asked Questions appendix (Appendix 2), and in the technical Glossary.

For some of the advanced software learning topics, you will need Microsoft Internet Explorer. To view the Webinars in certain software learning modules, you will need the Webex Player. To hear the sound files will require one of the sound programs, such as SoundRec, iTunes, MS Media Player, or similar program. Again, all of these will be explained in Appendix 2. You may want to take a moment to check your computer for these plug-ins and viewers and download them before starting the first chapter.

Lessons in the chapters on word processing, spreadsheets, databases, and presentation graphics require the user to have a copy of Microsoft Office to access the Microsoft Internet site. Microsoft makes available a "Test Drive" version of Office 2007 at http://www.microsoft.com/office/trial/default.mspx. Microsoft recommends this for broadband users only. When you log on to the Microsoft site, it will check your computer for the needed plug-in. You may need to install the Test Drive browser plug-in.

STUDENT WARNING   Do not download software until told to do so by your instructor. Some of the programs are time-limited, meaning that you can only download them once and they will be active for a period of 30, 90, or 120 days. Download too early and you may not have access to the software when it is time to use the software in the course.

■ EDUCATIONAL DEMONSTRATION SOFTWARE

From the Technology Resources Website you can link to software vendors to download demonstration software from the following companies. These companies have graciously agreed to provide demonstration versions of their software for educational use with this text. Each of these programs share common elements, they are leading programs used in law offices, government agencies, courts, and corporate legal departments. Each provides resources for learning and using the software in the form of extensive help features and learning tutorials.

The programs may be installed on personal portable, home, school, or work computers. Most have a timing feature that allows generally for 90–120 days of use to provide access for the entire semester; others limit the number of total entries allowed or are the traditional 30-day software demos. Exercises are provided throughout the book, which use these programs to demonstrate the features and provide a foundation in the use of current technology in the law office. The programs can be used with exercises and case studies throughout the text but are introduced and explained in the chapters that correspond with discussion of the class of software into which each fits.

WORD PROCESSING   Today the most commonly used software program in the law office is the word processor.

Microsoft Word

OFFICE MANAGEMENT SYSTEMS   There are a number of office or practice management software programs available, of which AbacusLaw and Tabs3 are two of the most popular. These programs offer a number of *integrated functions* in a common package, like Office Suites.

AbacusLaw and Abacus Accounting
Tabs3 and Practice Master

CASE ORGANIZATION AND MANAGEMENT SOFTWARE   Case management software can be used to organize the cast of characters in a case, the documents, the relevant time table, issues, legal authority, and other desired information. Good case management software does all of these organization functions and provides the information in an organized manner for everyone working on the case.

LexisNexis CaseMap
LexisNexis TimeMap

LITIGATION SUPPORT   Litigation support software such as CT Summation provides a specialty application software program for managing these electronic documents.

CT Summation

PRESENTATION AND TRIAL GRAPHICS   Graphic creation programs are used to create graphics for presentations either as stand-alone graphics or as part of a graphics presentation, such as part of a PowerPoint presentation. The obvious advantage to this class of software is the ability of the legal team to create their own graphics without the need of graphic artists and outside consultants.

SmartDraw

THE ELECTRONIC COURTHOUSE   Litigation support software is used in trial to display documentary evidence, graphic presentations, and simulations of accident cases. Relevant portions of documents can be displayed as the witness testifies and identifies the document for everyone in the courtroom to see at the same time, without passing paper copies to everyone.

Sanction

NEED MORE OFFICE 2007 COVERAGE?

Package chapters from the acclaimed GO! Microsoft Office 2007 Series with *Technology in the Law Office* Second Edition to meet your needs. The Pearson Learning Solutions custom book program allows you to select chapters from the Office 2007 series to create your own custom book. Contact your local Pearson representative for more information.

TECHNOLOGY RESOURCES

■ COMPANION WEBSITE: WWW.PEARSONHIGHERED.COM/GOLDMAN

In the textbook, students will be directed to this companion website to access a wealth of online resources:

- Video introduction to the chapter for each chapter
- Video overviews of software applications
- Video case studies links to online resources
- Quizzes to help students gauge their mastery of the material in the chapter
- Link to the Technology Resources Website

Welcome to the Companion Website for Technology in the Law Office.

This **Companion Website** contains a wealth of study and application resources for each chapter of the textbook and a variety of legal software applications.

Please select a chapter above to access the following resources:

- Author Video Introduction to the Chapter
- Video Overview of Software Applications
- Video Cases studies
- Links to Online Resources
- Quizzes to Gauge Student Mastery of Topics

Tom Goldman's Technology Resource Website
Click here to go access the Technology Resource Website where you will find:

- Software Download Instructions
- Software Tutorials
- Case Study Resources
- Instructional Videos
- Link to Instructor's Resource Center for downloadable:
- Instructor's Manual
- Test Generator
- PowerPoint Lecture Presentation Package.

Find your Prentice Hall Sales Representative.

■ TECHNOLOGY RESOURCES WEBSITE: WWW.PEARSONHIGHERED.COM/GOLDMAN

From the Goldman textbook's home page or from the companion website, you can link to the Technology Resources Website. Online resources include the following:

- Links to download demonstration software
- Links to online tutorials and Webinars for each software application
- Video overviews of software applications
- Instructor notes for each software application
- Case study materials
- Link to the Instructor's Resource Center to download instructor materials

INSTRUCTOR RESOURCES

■ INSTRUCTOR NOTES FOR INDIVIDUAL SOFTWARE APPLICATIONS

Notes relating to installation and instruction for each software application are located on the Technology Resources Website at www.pearsonhighered.com/goldman.

The following instructor supplements are available for download from the Pearson Instructor's Resource Center. To access supplementary materials online, instructors need to request an instructor access code. Go to **www.pearsonhighered. com/irc**, where you can register for an instructor access code. Within 48 hours of registering you will receive a confirming e-mail including an instructor access code. Once you have received your code, locate your text in the online catalog and click on the Instructor Resources button on the left side of the catalog product page. Select a supplement and a log-in page will appear. Once you have logged in, you can access instructor material for all Prentice Hall textbooks.

■ INSTRUCTOR'S MANUAL

The instructor's manual, written by Thomas Goldman and Marissa Moran and updated by Steven Dayton, contains sample syllabi, chapter outlines and summaries, WWW Mini Exercise results, answers to questions and exercises, and software teaching notes.

■ TEST GENERATOR

The Test Generator revised by Steven Dayton allows you to generate quizzes and tests composed of questions from the Test Item File, modify them, and add your own.

■ POWERPOINT LECTURE PRESENTATION

The PowerPoint Lecture Presentation revised by Steven Dayton includes key concept screens and exhibits from the textbook.

ACKNOWLEDGMENTS

■ REVIEWERS

The following individuals were very helpful in their review of this text. I am grateful for their insights and contributions.

John Bradley,
Bucks County Community College

Matthew Cornick,
Clayton State University

Katherine Currier,
Elms College

Stephanie Delaney,
Edmonds Community College

Veronica Dufresne,
Finger Lakes Community College

Dora Dye,
City College of San Francisco

David Freeman,
Community College of Philadelphia

Louise Gussin,
University of Maryland University College

Cathy Kennedy,
Minnesota School of Business

Bryce Letterman,
Coastline Community College

Marissa Moran,
New York City College of Technology

William Mulkeen,
Thomas Edison State College

Kathryn L. Myers,
Saint Mary-of-the-Woods College

Deborah K. Periman,
University of Alaska

Jennifer Severson,
University of California San Diego

Kathleen Smith,
Community College of Philadelphia

Robert Van Der Velde,
Eastern Michigan University

William Weston,
Kaplan University

■ SOFTWARE COMPANIES

Thanks also go out to the software companies who contributed and reviewed material for this text.

Abacus

Judd Kessler
Bob Elliott

CaseSoft

Robert Wiss
Greg Kehel
Ivan Browning

Lexis Nexis

Dianne Callahan

Sanction

Mike Hahn

SmartDraw

Paul Stannard
Todd Savitt

Summation

Kate Paslin

Tabs3

Kent Merkl

WordPerfect

Gillian Darby
Cynthia Howard

ABOUT THE AUTHOR

THOMAS F. GOLDMAN, JD, is Professor Emeritus of Bucks County Community College where he was a professor of Law and Management and Director of the Center for Legal Studies and the Paralegal Studies Program. He is currently a member of the Paralegal Studies Advisory Board and mentor at Thomas Edison State College, where he has developed the Advanced Litigation Support and Technology Certificate Program in the School of Professional Studies.

He is an author of textbooks in paralegal studies and technology, including The *Paralegal Professional*, Second Edition; *Accounting and Taxation for Paralegals*; *Civil Litigation: Process and Procedures*; and *SmartDraw: A Hands-On Tutorial and Guide*.

An accounting and economics graduate of Boston University and of Temple University School of Law, Professor Goldman has an active international law, technology law, and litigation practice. He has worked extensively with paralegals and received the award of the Legal Support Staff Guild. He was elected the Legal Secretaries Association Boss of the Year for his contribution to cooperative education by encouraging the use of paralegals and legal assistants in law offices. He also received the Bucks County Community College Alumni Association Professional Achievement Award. He has been an educational consultant on technology to educational institutions and major corporations and a frequent speaker and lecturer on educational, legal, and technology issues.

Technology in the Law Office

Second Edition

Chapter 1 Digital Resources at www.prenhall.com/goldman

- Author Video Introduction
- Case Study Video: Videoconferencing
- Comprehension Quizzes and Glossary

Technology in the Law Office | CHAPTER 1

OPENING SCENARIO

Mrs. Hannah had worked in large center-city law firms for twenty years, rising to the level of senior paralegal. In the course of working on a case for which she was responsible for technical support, she met Owen Mason, an attorney fresh out of law school, who, having just passed the bar, was clerking for a federal judge. After many months of sitting in on the judge's cases and watching the trial attorneys in action, he confided to Mrs. Hannah that he had decided he wanted to open his own firm and try cases. Candidly he acknowledged to her that his greatest reluctance about going out on his own was that he didn't know how much he *didn't* know about setting up a law office until he started looking around at actual law offices in the area. He said, "I can do the law part, but the internal operations of a law office are something I never thought about or had to worry about when I was clerking for the judge. It certainly wasn't something they taught in law school."

He asked Mrs. Hannah if she would help him, offering her employment with his new firm. She agreed to leave the law firm—not only for the challenge of establishing a new office, but also for a chance to work closer to home, reducing her commute time.

The attorney's first question to her was, "What do I need at the minimum, and what is essential if I am frequently out of the office trying cases?"

LEARNING OBJECTIVES

After studying this chapter you should be able to:

1. Explain the use of technology in the law office.

2. Discuss the impact of the Federal Rules of Civil Procedure on electronic documents and the use of technology in the law.

3. Explain the role of the technology support staff.

4. Describe the need to understand the language of technology.

5. Identify technologies that can help the legal team.

INTRODUCTION TO TECHNOLOGY IN THE LAW OFFICE

The increased use of technology and computers in the law office, the court system, and the courtroom has changed the way many traditional procedures are performed. The computer and the Internet are increasingly used, not just for traditional document preparation, but also for maintaining client databases, keeping office and client accounting records, engaging in electronic communications, research and filing documents with the court, and trial presentation as shown in Exhibit 1.1.

Computer technology is used in the following ways in the law office:

Word processing—Prepare documents
Electronic spreadsheets—Perform financial calculations and financial presentations
Time and billing programs—Record accurate client time and billing
Accounting programs—Manage firm financial records, payroll, and client escrow accounts
Calendaring—Track deadlines, appointments, and hearing dates
Graphic presentation software—Prepare persuasive presentations
Trial presentation software—Organize trial presentations
Internet search engines—Search for accurate and current legal information and factual information to support a case
Databases—Maintain records and documents
Document scanning—Convert documents to electronic format
Document search features—Locate relevant material in documents and exhibits
E-mail and document delivery—Communicate electronically
Online Collaboration—Use the Internet to work collaboratively
Online electronic document repositories—Use for remote storage and access to documents

WWW MINI EXERCISE

Compare the results of the latest survey information with the data listed to the right. The full survey may be viewed at the International Paralegal Management Association website at http://www.paralegal management.org/ipma/

Exhibit 1.1 IPMA survey results

Technology Most Often Used by Paralegals

In a survey by the International Paralegal Management Association (IPMA), the most frequently used programs as reported by respondents were:

General

Microsoft Word	99%
Document management programs	83%
General Internet research	74%
Spreadsheets	57%
Databases	57%
Billing applications	53%

Litigation

Litigation support	75%
Electronic court filing	42%
Online docket programs	33%
Trial preparation	25%

Source: 2005 Utilization Survey IPMA.

Computers are also being used with greater frequency to share information in **digital format** between remote offices, courthouses, government agencies, and clients. Computer files are shared today more and more by the use of the Internet as well as in the form of CDs, DVDs, and as **attachments** to e-mails. In the past, paper had to be physically copied and sent, frequently by costly messenger service or express mail service. Today large files can be quickly, almost instantaneously, exchanged electronically, anywhere in the world, without any paper **(hardcopy)**. Whereas formerly the physical safety of the delivery of paper documents was a concern, today the security and **confidentiality** of documents sent in electronic format are increasing concerns.

The legal team is increasingly using the Web and the Internet for more than just pure legal research. Access to most government information is obtained online through Internet websites. Finding businesses and individuals through private service providers, such as the yellow pages and white pages, is now handled most efficiently through Web search engines such as Google and Yahoo!. Though legal firms are increasingly developing and using websites for their own businesses as shown in Exhibit 1.2, only the best of these sites are created in a way that effectively helps to retain clients and attract new clients.

The implementation of new federal court rules on electronic discovery, the use of electronically stored documents in litigation, and emerging electronic discovery case law is creating increased demand for skills and knowledge in the use of technology in civil litigation. Increasingly the legal team must be able to interface with technology professionals in maximizing the efficiency of internal computer usage, and in obtaining and handling client and trial data electronically. Everyone on the legal team must now have a working familiarity with computers and the

Digital Format
A computerized format utilizing a series of 0's and 1's.

Attachments
A popular method of transmitting text files and occasionally graphic images, by attaching the file to an e-mail.

Hardcopy
Paper copies of documents.

Confidentiality
In the law, any information with regard to a client, learned from whatever sources, that is to be kept in confidence by the legal team.

Exhibit 1.2 A typical law firm website, the new yellow pages

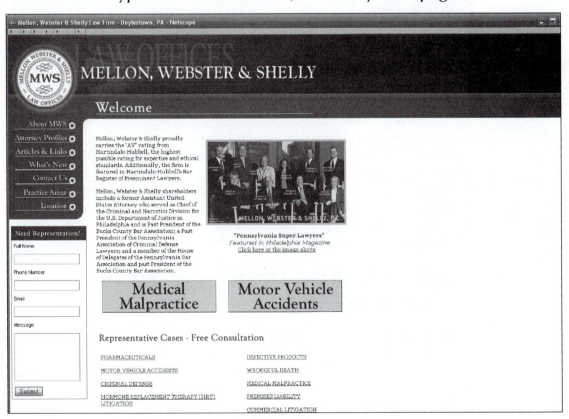

Reprinted with permission from Mellon, Webster, & Shelly Law Offices.

Exhibit 1.3 Secure remote access for the legal profession

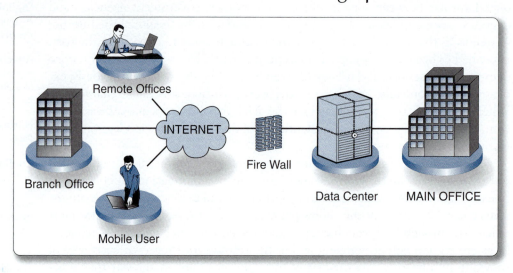

Remote Offices

INTERNET

Fire Wall

Branch Office

Mobile User

Data Center   MAIN OFFICE

types of computer programs used in the law office. Not too many years ago, the average law office had a typewriter, an adding machine, and a duplicating machine of some type. Paper was king, with every document typed, edited, retyped—and frequently retyped again. In each instance, a paper copy was produced and delivered to the supervising attorney for review and additional changes. It then was returned for retyping and eventually sent to the client, to the opposing counsel, or filed with the court. File cabinets abounded in the law office, and the storage of paper files created back rooms, warehouses, and other storage locations filled with box after box of paper. The trend is toward eliminating paper in the law office through the use of computer technology and software.

Members of the legal team frequently find themselves working from locations outside the traditional office. In some cases, the legal team is composed of members who are located in different offices of the firm or from different firms located in different parts of the country or world. Each member of the team may need access to the case data or electronic files. One solution is to have all of the files stored electronically in an **electronic repository** on a secure, protected file server to which everyone authorized has access over the Internet.

Members of the team may use the Internet to work collaboratively using **online collaboration** software that allows each person to see the documents and, in some cases, each other, and make on-screen notes and comments. A number of companies provide services and software for converting case documents to electronic format and storing of the documents on a secure server. Collaboration software is provided for the individual members of the legal or litigation team. Exhibit 1.3 shows a typical secure remote litigation network.

Electronic Repository
An off-site computer used to store records that may be accessed over secure Internet connections.

Online Collaboration
Using the Internet to conduct meetings and share documents.

THE IMPACT OF THE FEDERAL RULES OF CIVIL PROCEDURE

The revision to the Federal Rules of Civil Procedure that became effective December 2006 has had a major impact on the thinking about technology in the practice of law. Members of the legal team who had ignored or only given passing notice to the inroads of computers and electronic documents replacing paper realized they could no longer ignore the impact of technology on the practice of law. For many it appeared that there were suddenly new rules in both the state and federal courts. What had been a patchwork of court rules and some case law was now in an organized form, formalized in the new federal rules on electronic discovery.

The new rules specifically address the issue of the increased use of electronic stored documentation regularly found in all aspects of business and personal life. Where people formerly used pen or typewriter and ink to write letters, today the method of choice is more likely e-mail or text message. The federal courts have, with the adoption of the new rules of civil procedure, acknowledged the role of electronically stored information and the impact it has on litigation. The state courts are also looking at the issue and many have or are implementing their own rules, frequently fashioned after the federal rules.

For the legal team, technology and its impact on the documents created and stored by clients must be addressed in litigation, but they must also address the impact potential litigation has on the rules for document retention. The retention of paper documents has frequently been a function of the available storage space. The more space available, the greater the number of documents that can be stored for longer periods of time. For the litigator this represents a source of a potential **"smoking gun"** document—a document on which the case hinges that may be introduced into evidence. For example, this could be a document that admits a course of conduct, such as removing a safety feature for the sake of saving money (even after netting out the costs of paying the costs of lawsuits for injuries), which is the cause of injury to a plaintiff. A document potentially "hiding" in a maze of potentially thousands of pieces of paper, if the other parties can find it, is a risky proposition at best. In some classic litigation cases, tractor-trailer loads of documents were produced in product liability and antitrust cases. In a case against Ford, the smoking gun was a report of the cost trade-off of the savings from eliminating a gasket and the potential monetary damage from lawsuits found by the plaintiffs' team—some might say found serendipitously, like finding a needle in a haystack.

With technology and a big enough budget for discovery, all of the paper documents in a case can be scanned electronically in a form that allows an electronic search for the smoking gun. Even easier is the ability to search electronic files of the opposing side when delivered in a searchable electronic format as the result of a proper discovery request.

With the potentially massive delivery of documents in electronic form comes the concern that these electronic documents may have privileged or confidential information. These documents may be delivered to the opposing side in compliance with an electronic discovery request without the opportunity to check each document before delivery for the privileged or confidential material.

No longer can the legal team ignore the role of technology in use by clients or in litigation, whether the legal team is a sole practitioner with just a legal secretary, or a mega-member international law firm with in-house technical support. Everyone on the legal team must understand the role of the various technologies in counseling and representing clients.

Smoking Gun
Document, such as an e-mail, hidden in the old files that would conclusively impeach or destroy the credibility of a witness or be evidence that conclusively determines an issue.

TECHNOLOGY SUPPORT IN THE LAW OFFICE

In larger law offices, corporate legal departments, and government offices, there is usually a technical support staff (frequently called the **IT**, or information technology, department). The IT staff handles questions and issues about the use and implementation of technology in general, and computers and software in particular. Smaller offices may have a person who is unofficially responsible for the same

IT
Information technology, the technology support staff within organizations.

ADVICE FROM THE FIELD

TAKING YOUR CAREER IN A NEW DIRECTION—AN INSIDE GLIMPSE AT LIT SUPPORT CAREERS
by Sally Kane, J.D.

Advances in technology, the growth of electronically stored information and amendments to federal and state e-discovery rules have transformed litigation support into one of the hottest careers in today's legal market. The e-discovery/litigation support industry is predicted to experience double-digit growth in the next three years, reaching $21.8 billion by the year 2011.

As the market heats up, new positions are opening within law firms, litigation support vendors, the government and corporate legal departments across the globe. The unprecedented number of opportunities in the litigation support marketplace has created a new market dynamic as supply/demand economics fuel salary growth and lateral hiring. As a result, "litigation support professionals are moving with increasing frequency between what I call the three silos of the litigation support market: law firms, litigation support vendors and corporate legal departments," says David Cowen of The Cowen Group, a global provider of e-discovery and litigation support staffing services.

These three market silos differ significantly in terms of benefits, challenges, professional development opportunities, career paths, work/life balance, compensation and career growth (government employment will be discussed separately in an upcoming issue). So, how does employment in a law firm compare with employment with litigation support vendor or corporate legal department? Who is paying top dollar? What is the best career move for you right now?

Below, attorneys, recruiting experts and litigation support professionals share their insight into the pros and cons of working in the three silos of litigation support.

LAW FIRM LIFE

Employment within a law firm offers litigation support professionals many distinct advantages including a well-defined career path, extensive firm resources, access to the latest technology, a large support staff, well-developed training programs, challenging work and a diverse client base.

As the profession evolves, law firms are creating more well-defined career paths in order to attract and retain talented litigation support professionals. The

typical path at a major firm with a large litigation support department progresses from analyst level one, analyst level two and specialist to coordinator, project manager, senior project manager, supervisor, manager and director, according to Cowen. Many of these positions did not exist five years ago and, as the industry evolves, law firms continue to offer significant advancement opportunities.

Brian Stempel, firm wide litigation services manager for Kirkland & Ellis, LLP, notes that one of the primary advantages of working for a law firm over other practice environments is the big-picture perspective and insight into the entire litigation life cycle. "It's where the rubber meets the road," Stempel says. "You see the actual legal representation in terms of what the issues are and what the client's needs are."

Scott Cohen, Director of Practice Support at Proskauer Rose, agrees. "The breadth and diversity of the work is substantially greater than what I experienced in a corporation," notes Cohen who has spent his twenty-year litigation support career in law firms, corporations and vendors. "In a corporation, you are only working for one client. In a law firm, you could be working on a white collar crime matter today, a complex commercial litigation tomorrow and everything in between."

Salaries paid to litigation support professionals in law firms are among the highest in the industry. Project managers in top markets such as New York earn between $95,000 and $125,000 in a law firm; managers and directors are making between $150,000 and $200,000, Cowen says.

Since law firms pay top dollar, they can afford to recruit the most skilled and experienced professionals. Litigation support professionals in law firms are surrounded by and benefit from knowledgeable, well-credentialed colleagues. The large pool of qualified candidates within a firm may also fuel competition as a number of high-caliber candidates compete for the best assignments and advancement opportunities.

Law firms also offer ample opportunities for professional development ranging from in-house training sessions to certification in specific software programs. Stempel's firm sends employees to industry training programs and certification classes on litigation support technology.

Law firm life as a litigation professional also presents challenges. The hours can be long and evening and weekend work is often required. The "support" aspect of litigation support requires that services be available when the client—firm partners, associates and outside clients—need them. Law firm litigation support departments may need 24/7 capabilities as the firm gears up for trial or another large matter. "It is a delicate balancing act," says Gyorgy Pados, director of litigation support at Hughes Hubbard & Reed, LLP. "You may have multiple cases going on at the same time, each with competing demands... You must measure the triangle of scope, time and money [and staff the matter accordingly]."

Moreover, litigation support professionals are required to track and bill time, both billable and administrative. This requirement seems to be fairly universal, whether the law firm treats its litigation support department as a capital expense with the goal of cost-recovery or as a profit center with the goal of raising revenue. Stempel reports that his level one through level three employees are required to be 70% billable (about 35 to 40 hours a week) while managers are expected to bill 50% of their work week.

Litigation support professionals looking to transition to a law firm generally need several years of experience. "Law firms, for the most part, are not willing to train," says Cowen. "Firms want experience—any combination of hands-on technical skills, project management experience and high level communication skills. Litigation support professionals must have the ability to interact with IT, litigation support, attorneys and, in some cases, clients," Cowen says.

CORPORATE LEGAL DEPARTMENTS

Compared to the frenzied environment of law firms and vendor, professionals employed in the corporate legal environment often enjoy a more relaxed work pace. Large corporations (i.e., those that typically employ litigation support and e-discovery professionals) are notoriously slower to embrace change, purchase new technological tools, implement new processes and make hiring decisions....

LITIGATION SUPPORT VENDORS

Employment with a litigation support vendor offers a different landscape and perspective than the law firm and corporate environment. Spending on e-discovery software technologies and services is forecasted to grow more than 35% annually through 2011, fueling growth in the vendor space.

While law firms and corporations are often characterized as linear, traditional and conventional, the vendor environment is entrepreneurial, flexible, informal, innovative and fast-paced. These qualities may stem from the recent arrival of many vendors to the litigation support arena. Most litigation support vendors have been established within the last five to ten years and are in the nascent stages of development, boasting smaller workforces, dynamic growth and a more informal business environment....

THE PERFECT FIT

Every law firm, corporation and vendor boasts its own unique structure, business practices and culture. Determining the perfect fit for you is "a combination of timing, luck and personal career goals," Cowen says. When preparing to transition from one practice environment to another, it is important to understand the differences within each organization. By conducting a thorough due diligence and considering how the move will impact your future career, you will more surely find personal fulfillment in today's competitive job market....

About the Author: Sally A. Kane is an attorney and writer specializing in legal and career topics. Visit Sally's legal careers website at www.legalcareers.about. com/ or post questions and comments about this article on her forum at www.legalcareers.about.com/ mpboards.htm.

Source: Originally published in *Litigation Support Today* May/July 2008.

type of support. In many small offices, the IT person is usually the more knowledgeable member of the staff—a lawyer, paralegal, secretary, a "friend" of the office, or a relative or child, sometimes referred to affectionately as the office "geek."

Technology Usage in the Law

The role of technology in the law has evolved in a very few years from a minor function, such as the stand-alone word processor, to a ubiquitous element in the management of law offices of all sizes. Computers are now being used for everything from word processing to computerized timekeeping, payroll productions, and tax return preparation. In some offices computerized telephone systems even use a computerized attendant to answer the phone without human intervention. The use of technology in litigation was once limited to large law firms working on large cases for wealthy clients who could pay the cost of the technology. Today even the smallest law firm and litigator must use technology. Some courts are demanding computerized filing. Records previously available in paper form, such as medical records in litigation cases, are now provided electronically. The result is that offices of all sizes need to have computer or technology support, in some cases with dedicated technologists or support of the computerized infrastructure and others dedicated to providing litigation support.

Working with In-House Technology Support Staff

Support issues in the past were limited to in-house support of on-site computer systems and software. The advances in portable computers and wireless technologies have expanded the demand placed on IT departments to support the legal team outside the office. What is the range of services that *can* be supported outside the office? Litigation teams may require support for videotaping depositions at out-of-office or out-of-town locations. Trials may require the use of sophisticated presentation equipment. And all members of the legal team may need access to the home office files on the office file servers from remote locations on their wireless laptops.

The IT department may not have the resources in people or in the specialty hardware or software to support every demand. The IT staff is frequently called in at the last moment, and may not have the time to gear up to support the immediate needs of the legal team. When the support staff has time to prepare, it can usually find a way to support potential applications, whether they are **remote access** issues or graphic-intense litigation needs. IT may be able to offer support and training to the legal team if it is clear what the legal team needs in technical support or what the legal team needs to accomplish. For instance, calling in the IT person in the early stage of litigation, when the use of graphics for simulation is considered for trial, may save time and money. Outside consultants may offer a simulation that seems to the legal team as the way to present and win a case. To the IT staff, providing the same solution may be an issue of whether the courthouse has the necessary equipment to show the simulation or if specialty equipment must be obtained or used, or if the graphics will be delivered in a format compatible with the law firm's trial presentation software or the courtroom's equipment.

Remote Access
Accessing a file server or computer from a remote location using the Internet.

Issues in Working with Outside Technology Consultants

There are many independent computer, software, and multimedia consultants. Selecting the correct consultant is a matter of understanding what is needed from the consultant. It may be to fix a computer or other computer peripheral like a printer. Many outside companies are retained on a maintenance contract basis to provide coverage as needed for a period of time, or for a fixed rate for hardware issues or to support software used in the office. Others are hired as needed at an hourly rate for support or maintenance.

Media consultants are frequently called to assist in specific cases. Some are called upon to prepare graphic presentations ranging from individual exhibits to multimedia simulations; others to operate equipment and assist in trial presentations.

To obtain the service needed from the consultant, the legal team must speak the same language as the technical consultant in defining the scope and desired results. Hiring a consultant (no matter how good he or she is) who works on a system that is incompatible with the system used by the legal team can be a costly mistake, or even a disaster—one sometimes not discovered until the actual day of trial. For example, if the legal team is using PC-based hardware and software and the consultant is using a Mac platform (jargon for an Apple Macintosh system), the consultant might produce the final product in a version that works only on an Apple computer. Although such a gross oversight might seem unlikely, it has been known to happen. The ownership of graphic presentation must also be addressed. Is it a work for hire to be owned by the law firm or client, or is it a creative work owned by the consultant that the consultant may use in any way he or she wishes for other purposes?

Outsourcing

Outsourcing has become a buzzword for shipping work out of the office or overseas to save money. Some of the services that can be performed in-house may, in fact, be better outsourced. For years, many law firms have outsourced the payroll function instead of preparing payroll checks and tax returns in-house. The confidentiality of information about salaries may dictate that an outside firm handle the payroll process so that only a few people in the office have access to the critical payroll information. In a similar vein, the accounting functions may be outsourced to an outside bookkeeping or accounting firm.

Using an outside computer consultant to help with support for the hardware and software of the office is a form of outsourcing and may involve a help desk located in a foreign location to answer questions.

Outsourcing
Use of persons or services outside of the immediate office staff.

Information Technologists as Members of the Legal Team

The legal team can no longer depend only on the skill and time of lawyers and paralegals in preparing and executing a discovery plan, or for that matter advising clients on maintenance and methods of document retention. The technology of electronically maintained records requires the input of information technology specialists. IT members of the legal team understand the electronic format of the documentation, the efforts required in producing or reproducing it, and the problems involved.

Electronically stored data is created and stored in many formats using many different software programs. While there are some commonly used protocols, formats, and methods for creation and storage, the lawyers and paralegals on the legal team cannot be expected to have the specialized technical knowledge of an **information technologist**. Even the IT specialist may need to engage the assistance of additional specialists in rarely used methods, software, or hardware. In some cases, like those involving erased data or damaged storage media, a forensic expert may have to be called in.

Information Technologist
A member of the legal team who has legal and technology skills and primarily supports electronic discovery activities.

TRAINING FOR HARDWARE AND SOFTWARE SUPPORT

To be efficient each user of the office computer system must be trained in the features and procedures of that system. The starting point may be the security features, including the password system used by the office. Each office tends to

WWW MINI EXERCISE

Look at the latest survey information at the ILTA website at
www.iltanet.org

International Legal Technology Association (ILTA) IT Staffing Survey

Outsourcing

"There are simply too many IT functions to be performed in today's law firm and too many different skill sets required to go it alone; outsourcing some IT function, either in whole or in part, is the norm for firms of all sizes.

The most commonly outsourced function, regardless of firm size, is printer maintenance. Across the board, eight out of ten firms report outsourcing all or part of this function.

Outsourcing the help desk function is more commonly seen at Very Large firms than at their smaller counterparts, not so much for providing the basic services during office hours, but for providing extended coverage after-hours, on weekends and on holidays. A quarter of Very Large firms employ third-party help desk providers compared to only 5% of Small firms.

A significant amount of Web and application development is outsourced by firms large and small. 60% of Small firms outsource their Web development, as do 40% of Very Large firms. Application development work is outsourced at 24% of Small firms and 22% of Very Large firms."

Source: ILTA 2006 Staffing Survey, December 2006.

have its own method of filing documents, either on individual personal computer workstations or on the office computer network file server. In the ideal world a reference guide is available to each employee, where everything is documented, easy to read, and completely understandable. But in the real world, people need instruction in everything from the basics, like where the on-off switch is located, to the more sophisticated how to connect with a remote office file server and download a file. In between are questions like, how do I use this specialty software program?

Someone must do the training. Again, in the ideal world there is an IT person in-house to do that job. In the real world few offices have this resource. Often, some of the basics are taught by other, more-experienced people in the office. In most law practices one or more outside sources are used. The person or company who sold or installed the hardware or software may also offer training. The manufacturers may offer online help or telephone support. In some cases classes may be offered at local educational institutions for credit or as noncredit offerings. Many specialty software vendors also offer training from basic level through certified trainer levels.

How Much Do I Really Need to Know

No one can be an expert in everything. What is important is to know enough to know what you do not know and be able to find someone who does. The need is to understand the basic concepts and be able to communicate with those who are the experts. Having a basic understanding of what different programs are used for in the legal environment is a starting point. What are the programs used in daily support of the legal team, word processors, spreadsheets, databases, and the like. Understand the differences in the software and computer tools used by the litigation specialist from those used by the in-house legal support team. Most important is the ability to communicate with the legal side and the technology side of a firm. Learn the language of the other, what some refer to as "geek talk." Keep current by

ETHICAL Perspective

WEST VIRGINIA RULES OF PROFESSIONAL CONDUCT
Rule 1.1. Competence.

A lawyer shall provide competent representation to a client. Competent representation requires the legal knowledge, skill, thoroughness and preparation reasonably necessary for the representation.

Web Exploration

Contrast and compare West Virginia Rules of Professional Conduct Rule 1.1. Competence at http://www.wvbar.org/ BARINFO/ rulesprofconduct/rules 1. htm with the American Bar Association Model Rules of Professional Responsibility at http://www.abanet.org/cpr/ mrpc/mrpc_toc.html, and the ethical rule in your jurisdiction.

reading the professional journals and legal papers for new tools and services being offered to make the job of legal and litigation teams more efficient. Attend the local, regional, and national technology shows for the legal industry to see the products and services and ask questions to learn enough to make the suggestions for updating and changing the tools of your profession.

UNDERSTANDING THE LANGUAGE OF TECHNOLOGY

An understanding of the terminology of technology is a prerequisite to understanding the technology found in the law office, the courthouse, and the clients' business. Law has developed its own lexicon of terms that enables those in the legal community to communicate effectively and with precision. The technology world also has developed its own lexicon. The legal team and the technology support team must learn the language of the other to communicate the needs and solutions to each other. Each group thinks it is communicating, but the meaning of the words used sometimes overlap with different meanings.

For example, the word *protocol*. To the legal team protocol is defined as "a summary of a document or treaty; or, a treaty amending another treaty, or the rules of diplomatic etiquette" (*Black's Law Dictionary*—West Group).

To the technology specialist, *protocol* is defined as "A set of formal rules describing how to transmit data, especially across a network. Low level protocols define the electrical and physical standards to be observed, bit- and byte-ordering and the transmission and error detection and correction of the bit stream. High level protocols deal with the data formatting, including the syntax of messages, the terminal to computer dialogue, character sets, sequencing of messages etc." (Free On-Line Dictionary of Computing [http://foldoc.org/]).

Another example is the word *cell*. To the criminal lawyer, a cell is a place where clients are held in jail. To the computer support staff, it is a space on a spreadsheet where a piece of data is displayed. Lawyers, paralegals, and other members of the legal team, and the members of the technology support team must learn each other's language in order to effectively meet the needs of clients and work together effectively.

FUTURE TRENDS IN LAW OFFICE TECHNOLOGY

The pressure is on law offices to be more productive. The increased cost of operating law offices is a major factor in law office managers looking for new ways to use technology to increase productivity. Clients and the courts are not willing to approve fees and costs where more cost-effective methods are available. The demand for speedy justice in the courts has resulted in less time to prepare and present cases, requiring the legal team to use technology to become faster and more productive with less time in which to do it. Advances in computer technology are providing solutions to the productivity and cost issues.

Looking ahead to what's on the technological horizon is imperative to the smooth and profitable functioning of the law office. Anticipating change and incorporating it requires IT knowledge and savvy, whether it comes in the form of in-house staff or external technology consultants. Corporate law firms might have a chief information officer or chief technology officer whose role includes anticipating change and planning for it in concrete as well as visionary ways. Those responsible for IT at smaller firms, as well, have the responsibility to be well-informed of technology trends in order to assess when a new tool should be added to their technology repertoire— and when it should be avoided.

The legal team is an increasingly mobile workforce. Working out of the office is a fact of life for trial attorneys and their support staff. The litigation team may spend much of their time in courthouses and outside the office taking depositions as close as across the street or across the country and around the globe. Increasingly the support staff is also located or working outside the traditional law office. In some cases it is because of outsourcing of activity to other firms or companies in remote locations, such as the legal support firms in India. It is also lawyers, paralegals, and litigation support members of the legal team who, for various reasons, work from home. With advances in technology it is possible to connect with the traditional office and access all the needed files and electronic resources on a computer at home; these workers are sometimes referred to as **teleworkers**.

The following section describes emerging technology that is available now and in use at some law firms and technology that is available but not fully deployed. The list is not exhaustive but rather illuminative of what businesses might expect in the near and distant future. How soon is a matter of conjecture, but we know from recent technology trends that it will be sooner than we could have expected even a few years ago. As Raymond Kurzweil writes in his essay, "The Law of Accelerating Returns" (2001),

> An analysis of the history of technology shows that technological change is exponential, contrary to the common-sense "intuitive linear" view. So we won't experience 100 years of progress in the 21st century—it will be more like 20,000 years of progress (at today's rate). The "returns," such as chip speed and cost-effectiveness, also increase exponentially. There's even exponential growth in the rate of exponential growth.

Videoconferencing

Videoconferencing is the use generally of the Internet, or in some cases telephone lines or special satellite systems, to transmit and receive video and audio signals in real time to allow parties to see and hear each other. It is defined in the Wisconsin court rules (subchapter III of Wis. Stat. chapter 885) as; *Videoconferencing*, as defined in section 885.52(3) of the new rule, means an interactive technology that sends video, voice, and data signals over a transmission circuit so that two or more individuals or groups can communicate with each other simultaneously using video monitors. It is a live, real-time, interactive form of communication and does not include the presentation of prerecorded video testimony pursuant to subchapter II of Wis. Stat. chapter 885. The definition is intended to encompass emerging technologies such as Web-based solutions, as they appear, so long as the functional requirements of the definition are met.

The Wisconsin Supreme Court adopted a rule effective July 1, 2008 entitled "Use of Videoconferencing in the Circuit Courts," one of the most advanced rules on the use of this technology in the country. Videoconferencing has been used in

Teleworkers
People who work from remote locations, typically from home.

Videoconferencing
Conferencing from multiple locations using high-speed Internet connections to transmit sound and images.

many courts for criminal proceedings at various stages of the process, usually at the beginning of the process. The Wisconsin rule advances the use to all aspects of criminal and civil litigation.

Many law firms and their clients use videoconferencing on a regular basis as a method of "face-to-face" communication when parties are at remote sites. With Wisconsin leading the way it can be expected to be an important new tool in the litigation practice.

VoIP

Voice over Internet Protocol **(VoIP)** is a protocol for using the Internet as a method of communication instead of traditional telephone company services. A computer with a microphone and headset or speaker is used to complete a call to another computer or telephone over the Internet. It may be a voice connection or voice and image. Software is installed on the computer that facilitates the desired activity. An example of a popular service for VoIP is Yahoo Messenger, which has provisions for traditional telephone calling and short message service to cell phone and other portable devices. Exhibit 1.4 shows the on-screen dialing window in process. The initial limitation of VoIP was the inability to call a traditional phone or receive a call. Services like Yahoo Messenger provide options that permit calling traditional phones at a very nominal rate, sometimes as low as one cent per minute.

The relative ease of use of these services and the low cost make conferencing, including videoconferencing, a reality. The days of going to a special location and paying substantial fees to conduct a videoconference are gone. Anyone with an Internet connection, a laptop with built-in microphone and speakers, and an inexpensive video camera can set up a videoconference from almost anywhere there is an Internet connection.

Voice Recognition

Voice recognition software has been around for a number of years. Many will remember trying out an earlier version of a speech recognition program as a possible alternative to typing. More computer technology has brought this software to the point of accuracy approaching, and in some cases exceeding, the accuracy of typing. Speech-enabled devices include cell phones, personal digital assistants (PDAs), and other handheld devices. It is now possible with programs like Dragon Naturally Speaking Legal Version to dictate working drafts of legal documents directly into almost any program, including word processors, spreadsheets, and databases, without touching a computer keyboard, and send the document to another member of the legal team electronically over a network or by e-mail, as shown in Exhibit 1.5. So advanced have the systems become, portable dictation devices can be used out of the office and then connected to the office computer, on which the speech recognition program has been installed, and the documents transcribed without the intervention of a typist. At up to 160 words a minute for speech input, for the average typist on the legal team the savings are significant. The underlying technology that enables voice technology to perform is now being used in automated response systems, like automatic call attendants that replace operators and receptionists in some firms. It is also a technology that permits those with physical disabilities that prevent using a keyboard, such as carpal tunnel syndrome, to remain or become productive in a world of word processors.

Miniaturization and Portability

The trend in computers and related computer devices has been toward miniaturization and portability. Smaller devices are becoming more powerful than some of

Web Exploration

Read an article on the use of videoconferencing in Wisconsin in the *Wisconsin Lawyer* Vol. 81, No. 7, July 2008, at http://www.wisbar.org/AM/Template.cfm?Section=Wisconsin_Lawyer&template=/CM/ContentDisplay.cfm&contentid=73013

VoIP
Voice over Internet Protocol is a computer Internet replacement for traditional telephone connections.

Voice Recognition
Computer programs for converting speech into text or commands without the use of other input devices such as keyboards.

Exhibit 1.4 Yahoo Messenger VoIP voice SMS window

the older desktop systems and laptops. Even the telephone has been reduced to a pocket-sized wireless communication device that is also capable of taking and displaying photo images, video, documents, and e-mails and accessing the Internet—many functions that formerly were reserved to large hardwired computer devices. The Apple I-Phone is an example of a device that can perform many functions formerly requiring a computer. Laptops have been reduced in size, with some weighing less than 3 pounds. They include all of the features previously mentioned together with built-in Web camera for videoconferencing and have built-in and removable memory greater than many file servers in some small offices.

Wireless Technology

Hardware in many offices today includes the wireless telephone and the laptop computer with built-in wireless Internet capability. The worldwide availability of inexpensive high-speed Internet connections has expanded the availability and

Exhibit 1.5 A paralegal using The Boom from UmeVoice, a high quality noise reduction microphone with Dragon Naturally Speaking to achieve high accuracy speech recognition

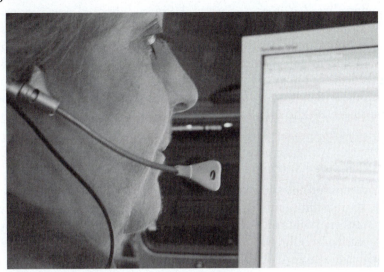

use of new technologies. These tools allow constant communication and enable work to be performed virtually anywhere—home, courthouse, airport lounge, or coffee shop. The connection to the office may be by wireless network using the cell phone, or by a wireless connection with built-in wireless network hardware on the computer, or using an adapter card plugged into the computer that uses a wireless Internet connection.

Unlike a few years ago, wires are not necessary to access networks or to set up network connections. Today they may be set up using wireless technology in a wireless network. Just as the cell phone has enabled communications without wires, so has wireless technology allowed networks to be set up where workstations, servers, and peripherals connect over a wireless connection. Remote access is also possible by the use of wireless Internet connection using laptops and other personal computing devices including cell phones with built-in Web or Internet access.

Remote Access

Remote access allows members of the legal team working on cases out of the office to connect with the office file server to retrieve documents, work on them, and send them to other members of the team anywhere in the world. If hardcopy is needed, documents may be printed on any printer accessible over the Internet, including printers in remote office locations, public access points in airports, clients' offices, and courthouses. Exhibit 1.3 shows a typical remote access configuration that provides security for the data and limits access to authorized users.

Remote Collaboration

Remote collaboration means that members of the team can work collaboratively from multiple locations as if in the same physical location. This is possible through software conferencing programs that allow the sharing of files while communicating

Remote Collaboration
Working on a common document utilizing remote access by two or more parties.

and seeing each other on the same screen using small desktop cameras or cameras built-in to laptop computers. The same remote access technology allows for the taking of witness statements from remote locations while the parties can see each other or view exhibits on the computer screen.

With higher-speed Internet connections the reality of true real-time video-conferencing has become a reality. Formerly, limited-speed connections restricted how much information could be transmitted. In the simplest form, slower speed increased the time to send a document. If not fast enough it prevented full-motion, full-screen video. With the introduction of fiber optic and cable Internet services in offices and in homes, videoconferencing from multiple locations, which requires a high-speed Internet connection to simultaneously transmit both the sound and the images, is now available on-site at many offices.

Wireless Computer Networks

Wireless Computer Networks
A wireless network uses wireless technology instead of wires for connecting to the network.

Wireless computer networks are like cell phone networks in that both use radio waves to transmit signals to a receiver. Cell phone systems use cell towers located at strategic points all over the world to receive the signals from the cell phone subscriber's cellular device. The wireless network uses wireless access points, which are essentially receivers of radio signals that convert them so they can be transmitted over a connecting wire to a computer or other connection to the Internet.

Unlike cell phone towers, these access points are more limited. With the exception of a few cities that have access points over a large portion of the city these access points are local, often with a range limited to a few hundred feet. Many of these access points are provided in coffee shops, airport lounges, hotels, libraries, and bookstores without charge or at a nominal fee to encourage customers to use the facility instead of a competitor's.

Hot Spot
A wireless access point, generally in a public area.

With the growth of wireless **"hot spot"** locations, the wire connection has been cut. Lawyers and their paralegals may be connected anywhere in the world and send documents electronically back and forth with the same ease as sending them within the same building. With the growth of Internet connections to portable devices over cell phone connections, computers with built-in devices or with the use of plug-in devices can access the Internet over wide areas not previously possible.

Wireless Laptop Connections

Laptops may be used wirelessly to connect to the Internet without the limitation of use of a "hot spot" by using plug-in devices such as the AT&T LaptopConnect Card, Sierra WirelessAirCard, and a subscription to the service provided by most major providers like AT&T, Verizon, and Sprint. These services essentially provide service virtually anywhere there is a cellular connection. The popularity of these wireless services has resulted in many newer-generation laptops having the feature built-in, eliminating the need for the external cards.

Thin Client

Thin Client
A computer system where programs and files are maintained on a centralized server.

A trend called **"thin client"** or cloud computing is emerging where programs and files are maintained on a centralized server and each user has access through a dumb terminal (one without programs or data). The thin client model offers some additional level of control and prevents loss of information through the loss of a computer. This general concept also includes Software as a Service (SaaS) and Web 2.0.

Checklist ✔

Use the following checklist as a tool to assess how your firm uses technology and to discover areas you might want to address in the future.

- Which functions are automated now; which additional functions do you wish to automate?
- Are existing pieces of equipment mutually compatible?
- Does everyone in the office use the same software?
- Are word processing procedures standardized?
- Is the billing system interfaced with accounting?
- Are the accounts payable checks computer-generated or prepared manually?
- Are you keeping track of client expenses (e.g., copies, fax, long distance, postage)?
- Are you getting telephone messages delivered accurately and in a timely manner?
- Does the office get flooded with interoffice memoranda?
- Is the payroll prepared in-house? Manually?
- Do the attorneys carry boxes to the courthouse?
- Do the paralegals spend hours preparing manual document index systems?
- How do you check for conflicts of interest?
- What type of calendaring system do you use for docket control purposes?

Source: http://www.texasbar.com/lomp/links.htm

SUMMARY

CHAPTER *1*
TECHNOLOGY IN THE LAW OFFICE

Introduction to Technology in the Law Office	Computer technology is used in many ways in the law office: Word processing Electronic spreadsheets Time and billing programs Accounting programs Calendaring Graphic presentation software Trial presentation software Internet search engines Databases Document scanning Document search features E-mail and document delivery Online collaboration Online electronic document repositories
Impact of the Federal Rules of Civil Procedure	New Federal Rules that became effective December 2006 specifically address the issue of the increased use of electronically stored documentation. The implementation of new federal court rules on electronic discovery, electronically stored documents use in litigation, and emerging electronic discovery case law is creating increased demand for skills and knowledge in the use of technology in civil litigation.

(Continued)

Technology Support in the Law Office	In larger law offices, corporate legal departments, and government offices there is usually a technical support staff.
Technology Usage in the Law	The role of technology in the law has evolved in a very few years from a minor function, such as the stand-alone word processor, to a ubiquitous element in the management of law offices of all sizes.
Working with In-House Technology Support Staff	Litigation teams may require support for videotaping depositions at out-of-office or out-of-town locations. Trials may require the use of sophisticated presentation equipment. All members of the legal team may need access to the home office files on the office file servers from remote locations on their wireless laptops.
Issues in Working with Outside Technology Consultants	Outside companies are retained on a maintenance contract basis to provide coverage as needed for a period of time, or for a fixed rate for hardware issues or to support software used in the office. Others are hired as needed at an hourly rate for support or maintenance.
Outsourcing	Shipping work out of the office or overseas to save money.
Information Technologists as Members of the Legal Team	Members of the legal team who combine legal skills and technology skills working primarily in the area of electronic discovery.
Training for Hardware and Software Support	To be efficient each user of the office computer system must be trained in the features and procedures of that system.
How Much Do I Really Need to Know	What is important is to know enough to know what you do not know and be able to find someone who does.
Understanding the Language of Technology	An understanding of the terminology of technology is a prerequisite to understanding the technology found in the law office, the courthouse, and the client's business.
Future Trends in Law Office Technology	The pressure on the legal team is to be more productive. Advances in computer technology are providing solutions to the productivity issue.
Videoconferencing	Videoconferencing allows remote conferences, hearings and the taping of depositions with video and sound on real time between parties at remote sites.
VoIP	Voice over Internet Protocol is a computer substitute for the use of traditional telephone connections.
Voice Recognition	Speech-enabled devices include cell phones, personal digital assistants (PDAs), and other handheld devices.
Miniaturization and Portability	The trend in computers and related computer devices has been toward miniaturization and portability.
Wireless Technology	Wires are not necessary to access networks or to set up network connections. Today they may be set up using wireless technology in a wireless network.
Remote Access	The legal team working on cases out of the office can connect with the office file server.

Remote Collaboration	The legal team can work collaboratively from multiple locations as if in the same physical location through software conferencing programs that allow the sharing of files while communicating and seeing each other on the same screen using small desktop cameras or cameras built-in to laptop computers.
Wireless Computer Networks	Wireless computers use radio waves to transmit signals to wireless access points, which are essentially receivers of radio signals that convert them so they can be transmitted over a connecting wire to a computer or other connection to the Internet.
Wireless Laptop Connections	Laptops may access the Internet using built-in or plug-in devices with a subscription service which provides access anywhere there is a cellular connection.
Thin Client	Programs and Files are maintained on a centralized server and each user has access through a dumb terminal. A general concept also sometimes referred to as Cloud Computing, Software as a Service (SaaS) on Web 2.0.

KEY TERMINOLOGY

Attachments 5	IT 7	Thin client 18
Confidentiality 5	Online collaboration 6	Videoconferencing 14
Digital format 5	Outsourcing 11	Voice recognition 15
Electronic repository 6	Remote access 10	VoIP 15
Hardcopy 5	Remote collaboration 17	Wireless computer network 18
Hot spot 18	Smoking gun 7	
Information technologist 11	Teleworkers 14	

CONCEPT REVIEW QUESTIONS AND EXERCISES

1. Test your knowledge and comprehension of the topics in this chapter by completing the multiple-choice questions on the textbook Companion Website.
2. Test your knowledge and comprehension of the topics in this chapter by completing the True-False questions on the textbook Companion Website.
3. Prepare a detailed list of the ways technology is used in the law office and courts.
4. How can law offices use computers to share information?
5. How can the Internet be used to attract new business for the law office?
6. How has the use of technology changed the skills needed to work in a law office?
7. How can the computer help members on a legal team work together when they are not in the same physical location?
8. Explain, with examples, how the Internet is used today by law offices and the courts.
9. Why does the legal team need to have a working familiarity with computers and the different types of computer software programs? Give examples.
10. How have the new Federal Rules of Civil Procedure impacted the legal profession?
11. What is the role of the Information Technology department in a law office?
12. What role do passwords play in computer security?
13. Why is it necessary for the members of the legal team to be able to communicate with others in a support or user position about technology as it relates to the legal community? Give examples.
14. Why is the quantity of documents increasing in litigation?

15. How has technology changed the roles of the members of the legal team?
16. Why would a law firm use an outside technology support firm?
17. What are the underlying reasons for the difficulty some legal team members may have in communicating with the IT staff?
18. Do the members of the legal team need to know everything about the computers and software they are using?
19. How can a member of the legal team learn about the technology used in a law office? Give specific examples.
20. How will videoconferencing change the way law is practiced in the future?
21. Is it realistic for members of a legal team to work from home?

Create a companion website profile

A profile lets you store the names and e-mail addresses of the people to whom you send your quiz results from this website so that you don't have to type that information for every quiz. A profile is stored on your computer, not at the website, so your profile won't be available if you take a quiz while using a different computer. Also, on a shared computer (as in a computer lab), all or part of a profile may be replaced if another user creates a profile.

To create a new profile, when you first use the Companion Website enter your information in the PROFILE on the Companion Website at: http://wps.prenhall.com/chet_goldman_technology_1/

INTERNET EXERCISES

1. Find an article on the use of outsourcing in the legal community.
2. Review the latest version of the technology survey of the International Paralegal Management Association.
3. Locate at least three legal technology resources on the Internet and save the Internet addresses for future reference.

PORTFOLIO ASSIGNMENTS

1. Prepare a memo in the form of a job description for the different members of a legal team in the age of technology.
2. Prepare a memo on how the IT department can aid the paralegal support staff.

SCENARIO CASE STUDY

Use the opening scenario for this chapter to answer the following questions. The setting is the discussion between a new attorney and an experienced paralegal who has agreed to help him open an office.
1. What are office and legal functions for which technology can be used in a start-up law office?
2. Are the functions and technology needs different if the attorney is frequently out of the office trying cases?
3. What issues are there in using an outside software, hardware, or Internet consultant in setting up a law office?
4. Prepare a checklist of *minimum* software and hardware requirements and a second of *recommended* technology needs for the start-up office. Be specific. Print out and save a copy for future reference.
5. What, if any, additional minimum or recommended items should be added to the list in question 4 for a trial attorney regarding office set-up?
6. Use the Internet to find the prices for the equipment and software on the checklists in questions 4 and 5.

CONTINUING CASES AND EXERCISES

1. Internet Resources
   Start a list of resources available on the Internet as you progress through the chapters and complete assignments. To get you started, the Internet resources from Chapter 1 have been inserted. Remember that Web addresses change; update your list regularly.

Subject	Source	Topic	URL	Date of entry
Ethics	ABA	Model rules of professional conduct	www.abanet.org/cpr/ mrpc/home.html	
Computer utilization	IPMA	Survey	www.paralegalmanagement. org/ipma	
Dictionary	FOLDOC	Computing	http://foldoc.org	
Federal Court Rules–Civil	Legal Information Institute	FRCP	www.law.cornell.edu/ rules/frcp	
Federal Court Rules–Criminal		FRCRMP	www.law.cornell.edu/ Rules/FRCRMP	

2. Keep a log of the time you spend in this course. Use the following format:

	Time				
Date	Start	Stop	Elapsed	Code	Description

Record the actual time spent (you can round to 1/10 of an hour) for:
   a. Class attendance (Conference with supervising attorney)
   b. Travel to and from class (Travel)
   c. Time reading and researching material (Research)
   d. Time preparing assignments (Drafting documents)
   e. Time spent preparing for tests (Preparation)
   f. Time taking tests (Trial)
   g. Other miscellaneous items (Miscellaneous)

3. Prepare a list of calendar items for the course including times and locations for class, library sessions, tests, assignment deadlines, and other class-related calendar items.

4. Design a personal Web page.

5. Owen Mason, Esq., a young technology-aware attorney, just starting out in a new legal practice, thought the World Wide Web was a good source of potential business. As a clerk in the Federal Court he had not had an opportunity to look at many law office websites. He asks your help in designing his Web page.

   a. Locate the websites of law firms in your area as well as around the country using the Internet search tools available to you. Make a list of the best and the worst features of these websites.

   b. Prepare your recommendations for Mr. Mason, including details and, if possible, screen printouts. Make a list of the Web addresses for each of the sites that you feel demonstrate the good, the bad, and the ugly.

   c. Prepare a list of website designers in your immediate area.

d. What are the ethical issues and potential UPL issues in the use of a website in your jurisdiction?

e. ADVANCED STUDENTS. Create a website using available resources and software.

Note: A number of lawyers use the Web to promote their specialty practices. Use the generic terminology—civil litigation—to locate other Web pages of attorneys specializing in civil litigation.

VIDEO SCENARIO

 A small multioffice law firm has been retained in a case involving a large number of passengers who were injured on a bus involved in a collision with a large truck. The case has been filed in federal court. The legal team has decided to conduct in-house conferences, using videoconferencing. Go to the Companion Website, select Chapter 1 from the pull down menu, and watch this video.

1. Are there any confidentiality issues in using videoconferencing?
2. Is the cost of videoconferencing justified by the travel time saved?
3. Is there any advantage to using videoconferencing instead of telephone conference calling?
4. Does the legal team working on a case have a duty to remain silent when information about the case has been made public?

Chapter 2 Digital Resources at www.prenhall.com/goldman

- Author Video Introduction
- Case Study Video: Confidentiality: Public Information
- Comprehension Quizzes and Glossary

Legal Ethics in a Technology Age

OPENING SCENARIO

Each lawyer in the firm was required to attend a minimum number of continuing legal education programs as part of the licensing requirements for lawyers in their jurisdiction, at least one hour of which had to be on ethics. To maximize the effort and share the knowledge it was the firm's practice to have those attending CLE programs review the program materials and any special issues they learned in the seminar at the morning staff meetings. Ethan had just taken a litigation update seminar with the required ethics hour. His recounting of the advice from the seminar that only those with a "need to know" have access to client information and files raised a question from his paralegal, Caitlin. She and her twin sister Emily, the paralegal in the firm's other office, often discussed cases that were interesting but with which they individually had no connection. Caitlin remarked that she and her sister routinely accessed files using their personal access codes to look at these files over the Internet connection the firm maintained. Ethan cautioned them that no one in the firm had the right to use their personal access code to access files unless they were personally directed to do so by the supervising attorney. Caitlin suggested everyone in the firm needed to be instructed in the "need to know" ethical guidelines and wondered aloud who was going to do that or if it really mattered.

LEARNING OBJECTIVES

After studying this chapter you should be able to:

1. Define the term legal ethics in terms of duties owed to the client and the legal system.

2. Explain the difference between the duty of confidentiality and attorney–client privilege.

3. Explain the function of the work product doctrine.

4. Explain the potential consequences of an inadvertent disclosure of confidential information.

5. Discuss the reasons for conflict of interests rules.

6. Discuss the duty of competency in a technology age.

7. Explain the rationale for the obligations of candor and fairness in litigation.

8. Describe the ethical obligation of appropriate hiring, delegating, and supervising owed by managing and supervising attorneys.

INTRODUCTION TO ETHICS IN TECHNOLOGY

Ethics
Minimally acceptable standards of conduct in a profession.

Model Rules of Professional Conduct
The American Bar Association set of proposed ethical standards for the legal profession.

Every profession has a set of rules that members of that profession are expected to follow. These rules typically set forth the minimum in ethical behavior—the very least each professional should do. In the field of law, these rules are referred to as "the rules of **ethics**" or "the rules of professional responsibility." Each state controls the right to practice law and, therefore, each state has adopted its own "rules of ethics." The supreme court or legislature of each state has created a committee or board that is authorized to enforce state rules of professional responsibility. States typically use a "bar association" to receive and investigate complaints against lawyers. With only a few exceptions, most states have adopted some form of the current or former version of the American Bar Association's **Model Rules of Professional Conduct**. This provides a high degree of consistency in the ethical guidelines for the legal profession across the country. Exhibit 2.1 shows the ethics links and resources provided by the American Bar Association to the profession and

Exhibit 2.1 A portion of the American Bar Association Center for Professional Responsibility website

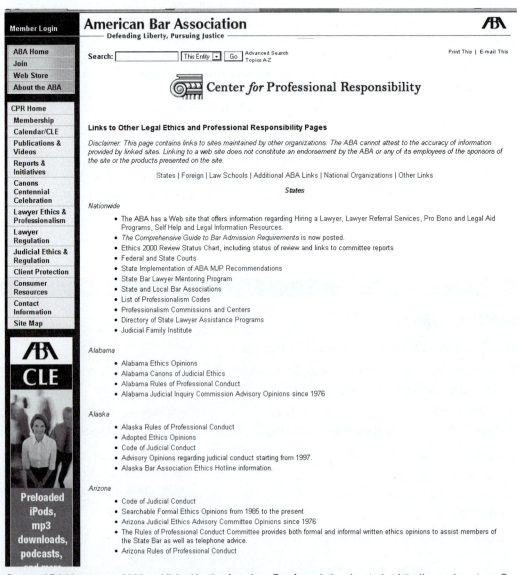

Source: ABA Homepage, 2008, published by the American Bar Association, located at http://www.abanet.org © 2008 by the American Bar Association. Reprinted with permission.

users of legal services. Members of national paralegal associations, such as NALA, the National Association of Legal Assistants, and NFPA, the National Federation of Paralegal Associations, have ethics guidelines. These organizations require members to conduct themselves in accordance with these guidelines, observance of which by its members is a condition of continued membership in the organization. One of the resources of the ABA is its report on the status of individual state review of the ethical rules (Exhibit 2.2).

Ethical behavior is expected and required of every member of the legal team, attorney, paralegal, litigation support, information technologist, and outside consultant. What is not clear in the minds of many members of the nonlawyer members of the legal team is what ethical obligations they have and how the ethics rules are to be followed and enforced. Ethical guidelines are enforced by the court in the jurisdiction where the attorney is practicing or where the case is being tried. The supervising attorney of every legal team must follow the ethics rules and ensure the members of the legal team follow the same rules as the supervising attorney. These rules are as much a part of the administration of justice as the rules of civil or criminal procedure and the rules of evidence. The bigger issue, in the

Exhibit 2.2 Portion of the ABA Status of State Review of Professional Conduct Rules 5–15–2008

STATUS OF STATE REVIEW OF PROFESSIONAL CONDUCT RULES (5/15/08)

34 states and the District of Columbia have adopted revised rules (AZ, AR, CO, CT, DE, DC, FL, ID, IN, IA, KS, LA, MD, MN, MS, MO, MT, NE, NV, NH, NJ, NC, ND, OH, OK, OR, PA, RI, SC, SD, UT, VA, WA, WI, WY).
10 states have circulated proposed rules (AK, CA, IL, KY, ME, MI, NY, TX, VT, WV).
Five states have committees that have not yet issued a report (GA, HI, MA, NM, TN).
One state is not considering the recent revisions (AL).

State	Committee Reviewing Rules	Committee Issued Report	Supreme Court Approved Rule Amendments	Notes
Alabama				No current review. Revised 5.5 effective 9/1/06. http://www.alabar.org/rulechanges/ Rule%205.5_Rules%20of%20Professional %20Code_Unauthorized%20Practice%20of %20Law_Supreme%20Court%20order.pdf
Alaska		X		State Bar Board of Governors sent proposed rules to Supreme Court.
Arizona			X	Revised rules effective 12/1/03. http://www.supreme.state.az.us/media/pdf/ test%20ule%2042%20%2043.pdf
Arkansas			X	Revised rules effective 5/1/05. http://courts.state.ar.us/opinions/2005a/ 20050303/arpc2005.html

technology age, is who has the responsibility to instruct the nonlawyer members of the legal or trial team and who is responsible for ensuring their compliance. While it is ultimately the responsibility of the lawyer to supervise these non-lawyers, in many cases this obligation falls to the paralegal or litigation manager.

The obligation to ensure ethical conduct is that of the **supervising attorney** under the ethical obligation to supervise all who work on the case for the attorney, under Rules 5.1 and 5.3. Each person working for or supervised by the attorney is in fact the **agent** of the attorney. Under fundamentals of agency law, the agent and the **principal**—the attorney—have a **fiduciary relationship** to each other. The agent must obey the reasonable instructions of the principal and the principal is presumed to know everything the agent learns in the ordinary course of working for the attorney on the case. The attorney is ultimately responsible for the ethical conduct of the agent.

Among the ethical obligations of the attorney and the legal team acting as agent of the attorney are:

Rule 1.1, Competency,
Rule 1.6(A), Confidentiality,
Rule 1.7, Conflicts Of Interest,
Rule 3.3, Candor,
Rule 3.4, Fairness To Opposing Party And Counsel, and
Rules 5.1 and 5.3, Duty to Supervise.

Related to the issues of ethical conduct are the related rules of evidence that bar the legal team from having to testify under the attorney–client privilege and protect the **work product** of the legal team prepared for trial from disclosure (**Federal Rules of Evidence** 501.)

Levels of ability and competency are important in choosing and using technical consultants and support staff. Also important are the confidentiality issues in adding technical staff to the legal team. The technical staff and computer consultant are nonlegal staff who may have access to files that contain privileged or confidential client information and trial strategy. Technology staff must understand the ethical obligations and the confidential nature of the files on which they are working.

As more members are added to the legal team who do not fit within the traditional roles of lawyer, paralegal, legal assistant, clerk or legal secretary, the concern as to how the rules of confidentiality and privilege will be applied and enforced broadens. The courts have recognized that the lawyer must engage others to help in the representation of clients, and numerous cases have explored the use of legal support staff like paralegals and investigators. The use of technology or computer consultants, however, may not be as clear. Certainly they are frequently essential where large volumes of e-discovery are involved. Most computer consultants are not adequately educated in the ethical rules of the legal profession.

CONFIDENTIALITY AND PRIVILEGE

Technical support personnel and computer consultants must understand the nature and obligations of the legal profession with regard to the duty of confidentiality and the attorney–client privilege. The differences and obligations imposed by these concepts can be confusing even to members of the legal team, let alone to IT staff whose training and education were not in the law profession. There are two sets of rules, ethical rules and rules of evidence. Confidentiality is an ethical obligation. **Privilege** is a rule of evidence.

Supervising Attorney
The attorney managing or supervising the legal team members.

Agent
A person authorized to act on behalf of another.

Principal
One who authorizes another to act on his or her behalf.

Fiduciary Relationship
A relationship where one is under a duty to act for the benefit of another under the scope of the relationship.

Work Product
In the law, material prepared in preparation for trial that is protected from disclosure.

Federal Rules of Evidence
The rules governing the admissibility of evidence in federal court.

Privilege
A rule of evidence that protects certain forms of communication from disclosure at trial. The attorney–client privilege provides that communication between the attorney and client in obtaining legal advice may not be required to be revealed in court.

Subchapter I Client–Lawyer Relationship

SCR 20:1.1 Competence

A lawyer shall provide competent representation to a client. Competent representation requires the legal knowledge, skill, thoroughness and preparation reasonably necessary for the representation.

History: Sup. Ct. Order No. 04–07, 2007 WI 4, 293 Wis. 2d xv.

ABA Comment: Legal Knowledge and Skill

[1] In determining whether a lawyer employs the requisite knowledge and skill in a particular matter, relevant factors include the relative complexity and specialized nature of the matter, the lawyer's general experience, the lawyer's training and experience in the field in question, the preparation and study the lawyer is able to give the matter and whether it is feasible to refer the matter to, or associate or consult with, a lawyer of established competence in the field in question. In many instances, the required proficiency is that of a general practitioner. Expertise in a particular field of law may be required in some circumstances.

[2] A lawyer need not necessarily have special training or prior experience to handle legal problems of a type with which the lawyer is unfamiliar. A newly admitted lawyer can be as competent as a practitioner with long experience. Some important legal skills, such as the analysis of precedent, the evaluation of evidence and legal drafting, are required in all legal problems. Perhaps the most fundamental legal skill consists of determining what kind of legal problems a situation may involve, a skill that necessarily transcends any particular specialized knowledge. A lawyer can provide adequate representation in a wholly novel field through necessary study. Competent representation can also be provided through the association of a lawyer of established competence in the field in question.

[3] In an emergency a lawyer may give advice or assistance in a matter in which the lawyer does not have the skill ordinarily required where referral to or consultation or association with another lawyer would be impractical. Even in an emergency, however, assistance should be limited to that reasonably necessary in the circumstances, for ill–considered action under emergency conditions can jeopardize the client's interest.

[4] A lawyer may accept representation where the requisite level of competence can be achieved by reasonable preparation. This applies as well to a lawyer who is appointed as counsel for an unrepresented person. See also Rule 6.2.

Thoroughness and Preparation

[5] Competent handling of a particular matter includes inquiry into and analysis of the factual and legal elements of the problem, and use of methods and procedures meeting the standards of competent practitioners. It also includes adequate preparation. The required attention and preparation are determined in part by what is at stake; major litigation and complex transactions ordinarily require more extensive treatment than matters of lesser complexity and consequence. An agreement between the lawyer and the client regarding the scope of the representation may limit the matters for which the lawyer is responsible. See Rule 1.2(c).

Maintaining Competence

[6] To maintain the requisite knowledge and skill, a lawyer should keep abreast of changes in the law and its practice, engage in continuing study and education and comply with all continuing legal education requirements to which the lawyer is subject.

http://www.legis.state.wi.us/rsb/scr/5200.pdf2006

ADVICE FROM THE FIELD _____

THE INTERNET: COMPLICATING LEGAL ETHICS, BUT FULL OF RESOURCES TO HELP YOU UNDERSTAND THE COMPLICATIONS

Maureen A. Cahill J.D., M.L.I.S.
Student Services Librarian
The University of Georgia
School of Law
Alexander Campbell King Law Library
(http:// www.law.uga.edu/library)
Athens, Georgia

I. INTRODUCTION

First, it became almost impossible to practice law without a computer. Then, you almost *had* to have email, which meant that you had to have Internet service. Then, some courts began encouraging electronic filing. Then, it was all but malpractice not to use computerized citation checking. And on, and on, and on.... Face it, electronic data production, storage, and communication broke the flood gates long ago. Today, many lawyers own domain names, publish a Web page, participate in online forums or chat rooms, use on-line referral services, and transmit and store all documents electronically. Surely, this monumental shift in the mechanics of law practice has changed all the rules. Not quite; but many of the Rules of Professional Conduct *are* impacted by the use of computers and the Internet. The Georgia rules require competence and diligence (Rules 1.1 and 1.3), confidentiality of information (Rule 1.6), candor toward the tribunal (Rule 3.3), and fairness to opposing party and counsel (Rule 3.4). They forbid the unauthorized practice of law (Rule 5.5). Finally, they govern closely the manner in which lawyers may disseminate information about their services (Rules 7.1–7.5). Each and every one of these rules is more complex in the electronic age.

In the first portion of this paper, I will try to give you an idea of a few of the specific ethical complications that have arisen or are anticipated because of electronic information production, storage, and communication. My search of the Georgia ethics decisions and opinions did not turn up instances where the Georgia Supreme Court or the State Disciplinary Board (which issued opinions prior to 1986) have ruled explicitly on any of these issues, but in today's climate it is only a matter of time before at least some of these questions come up in Georgia. I will summarize what some other jurisdictions have decided when confronted with some of the complications of electronic information. The second part of the paper is an annotated list of some of the Internet resources that will help you stay up to date on the latest wrinkles in professional ethics.

II. PROFESSIONAL ETHICS IN AN AGE OF DIGITAL INFORMATION AND COMMUNICATION

A. Overview of Ethical Concerns that Arise

What duty does an attorney have to ensure the confidentiality of an electronically transmitted document? If you decide to digitize your files, do you have an obligation to retain any paper documents? What safeguards would you have to put in place if you outsourced the electronic conversion and storage of your files? Can you make use of information you discover by viewing the metadata associated with an electronic document sent to you by opposing counsel? Do you have a duty to strip out all metadata associated with documents you create that could possibly be shared with opposing counsel? Can you participate in Internet discussion groups that address legal issues? If you do, what dangers must you stay alert to?

These are only a few of the novel issues that are arising because of the intersection of electronic data and the practice of law. In the paragraphs that follow, I will run through the Rules of Professional Conduct that I cited above and give examples of issues that have arisen within the scope of those rules. In addition, I will try to show how some jurisdictions have resolved these issues. However, please keep in mind that the positions of many jurisdictions on these issues have altered, sometimes rapidly. As both technology and our understanding of its capacities change, the response of bodies governing the conduct of lawyers will remain fluid. Never rely on what you knew was the rule last year; both the rule and the technology probably will have changed.

ETHICAL Perspective

Read the entire article at:
http://digitalcom
mons.law.uga.edu/cgi/
viewcontent.cgi?article=
1036&context=speeches

PENNSYLVANIA BAR ASSOCIATION
PROFESSIONALISM COMMITTEE—WORKING RULES

1. Treat with civility the lawyers, clients, opposing parties, the Court, and all the officials with whom we work. Professional courtesy is compatible with vigorous advocacy and zealous representation.
2. Communications are life lines. Keep the lines open. Telephone calls and correspondence are a two-way channel; respond to them promptly.
3. Respect other lawyers' schedules as your own. Seek agreement on meetings, depositions, hearings and trial dates. A reasonable request for a scheduling accommodation should never be unreasonably refused.
4. Be punctual in appointments, communications and in honoring scheduled appearances. Neglect and tardiness are demeaning to others and to the judicial system.
5. Procedural rules are necessary to judicial order and decorum. Be mindful that pleadings, discovery processes and motions cost time and money. They should not be heedlessly used. If an adversary is entitled to something, provide it without unnecessary formalities.
6. Grant extensions of time when they are reasonable and when they will not have a material, adverse effect on your client's interest.
7. Resolve differences through negotiation, expeditiously and without needless expense.
8. Enjoy what you are doing and the company you keep. You and the world will be better for it.

Beyond all this, the respect of our peers and the society which we serve is the ultimate measure of responsible professional conduct.

I hereby endorse the PBA Working Rules for Professionalism.

Signature _____
Date _____
Attorney ID Number _____
Firm/Office _____
Address _____

Confidentiality

The ethical obligation to keep client information confidential is founded on the belief that clients should be able to tell their attorneys everything about their case so the attorney can give proper legal advice to the client. **Confidentiality** is an ethical obligation. For the attorney, the American Bar Association (ABA) Model Rules require, in Rule 1.6, that lawyers "not reveal information relating to representation of a client" until the client gives informed consent to the disclosure after being advised of the consequences of disclosure, except for disclosures that are "impliedly authorized." Everything the lawyer or the members of the legal team learn about the case from every possible source is to be kept confidential. For example, the client's case is written up in the local daily newspaper and that sets out details of the case. Even though these details are made

Confidentiality
An obligation to not reveal information which is based on a relationship of trust placed in one person by the other.

public the members of the legal team are not free to discuss them. They are still to be kept confidential. They may not be discussed with someone else who has read the newspaper who is not on the team.

Implied Attorney–Client Relationship

Implied attorney–client relationship may result when a prospective client divulges confidential information during a consultation with an attorney for the purpose of retaining the attorney, even if actual employment does not result.

Trust v. Monthei, 49 P.3d 56, 59 (Mont. 2002).

Privilege

Attorney–Client Privilege
A rule of evidence permitting an attorney to refuse to testify as to confidential client information.

All communication between the client and the lawyer for the purpose of obtaining legal advice is protected by the attorney–client privilege. The **attorney–client privilege** is a rule of evidence that protects the client from the attorney being required to reveal the information. (Note that the information is also confidential, but the privilege is different from the duty of confidentiality.) The privilege only applies when the lawyer is questioned under oath. At that point, the attorney must invoke the privilege, saying, "*I refuse to answer because that is confidential information covered by the attorney–client privilege.*" This could happen any time the attorney is under oath. Some examples are responses to interrogatories or requests for production of documents, testimony in court, in a deposition, or before a grand jury. Only the client can waive the privilege and allow the attorney to reveal protected information. The privilege may not be waived by the attorney; it is the client's right to preserve the privilege except in limited circumstances such as when the information is about a crime of violence that the client is about to commit.

> "The attorney–client privilege is founded on the assumption that encouraging clients to make the fullest disclosure to their attorneys enables the latter to act more effectively. We have recognized that an attorney's effectiveness depends upon his ability to rely on the assistance of various aides, be they secretaries, file clerks, telephone operators, messengers, clerks not yet admitted to the bar, and aids of other sorts. The privilege must include all the persons who act as the attorney's agents." (*Von Bulow v. Von Bulow*, 811 F. 2d 136 (2d Cir. 1987))

If the client reveals the same information to someone outside of the attorney or legal staff, the privilege is lost. Thus, the client must really keep the information secret for the privilege to apply.

The concept of privilege also extends to persons while acting within certain roles such as:

1. Spouse
2. Clergy–penitent
3. Doctor–patient
4. Psychotherapist–patient
5. Participants in settlement negotiations

IN THE WORDS OF THE COURT . . .

Trammell v. United States, 445 U.S. 40 (1980)[i]

Burger C. J.

"The privileges between priest and penitent, attorney and client, and physician and patient limit protection to private communication. These privileges are rooted in the imperative need for confidence and trust. The priest-penitent privilege recognizes the human need to disclose to a spiritual counselor, in total and absolute confidence, what are believed to be flawed acts or thoughts and to receive priestly consolation and guidance in return. The lawyer-client privilege rests on the need for the advocate and counselor to know all that relates to the client's reasons for seeking representation if the professional mission is to be carried out. Similarly, the physician must know all that a patient can articulate in order to identify and to treat disease; barriers to full disclosure would impair diagnosis and treatment."

In this case, the court confirmed that the principle of privileged communications extends not just to the attorney, but to legal support staff who work on the team as well.

Claim of Privilege

The attorney–client privilege is not automatically invoked. The person claiming the privilege—usually the client—has the burden to establish its existence, called **claim of privilege**.

> "To sustain a claim of privilege, the party invoking it must demonstrate that the information at issue was a communication between client and counsel or his employee, that it was intended to be and was in fact kept confidential, and that it was made in order to assist in obtaining or providing legal advice or services to the client" *SR International Bus. Ins. Co v. World Trade Center* Prop No 01 Civ 9291 (S.D.N.Y. 2002), quoting *Browne of New York City, Inc. v. Ambase Corp.*[ii]

Claim of Privilege
Preventing the disclosure of confidential communications as evidence based on a recognized privilege.

Extension of Attorney–Client Privilege to Others

It is now accepted that the efficient administration of justice requires lawyers to engage others, such as legal assistants, accountants, and other experts. This would not be possible if the privilege did not extend to these agents of the attorney including, most recently, public relations firms.

The U.S. District Court for the Southern District of New York summarized the law, stating:

> ". . . the privilege in appropriate circumstances extends to otherwise privileged communications that involve persons assisting the lawyer in the rendition of legal services. This principle has been applied universally to cover office personnel, such as secretaries and law clerks, who assist lawyers in performing their tasks. But it has been applied more broadly as well. For example, In *United States v. Kovel*, the Second Circuit held that a client's communication with an accountant employed by his attorney were privileged where made for the purpose of enabling the attorney to understand the client situation in order to provide legal advice." (IN RE Grand Jury Subpoenas dated March 24, 2003 directed to (A) Grand Jury Witness Firm and (B) Grand Jury Witness, M11-188 (USDC, S.D.N.Y.) (June 2, 2003)).

WWW MINI EXERCISE
ETHICAL Perspective
Review the most current version and comments to Rule 1.6 on Confidentiality of Information of the American Bar Association Model Rules of Professional Conduct at the American Bar Association website:
http://www.abanet.org/cpr/mrpc/rule_1_6.html

IN THE WORDS OF THE COURT...

Extension of Attorney–Client Privilege to Others

IN RE Grand jury subpoenas dated March 24, 2003, directed to (A) Grand Jury Witness Firm and (B) Grand Jury Witness, M11-188 (USDC, S.D.N.Y.) (June 2, 2003).

The U.S. District Court for the Southern District of New York summarized the law stating:

> "... the privilege in appropriate circumstances extends to otherwise privileged communications that involve persons assisting the lawyer in the rendition of legal services. [fn17] This principle has been applied universally to cover office personnel, such as secretaries and law clerks, who assist lawyers in performing their tasks. [fn16] But it has been applied more broadly as well. For example. In United States v. Kovel. [fn19] the Second Circuit held that a client's communication with an accountant employed by his attorney were privileged where made for the purpose of enabling the attorney to understand the client situation in order to provide legal advice. [fn20]"

In the modern practice of law, the attorney must rely on others, such as paralegals, legal secretaries, investigators, law clerks, and the like, to assist in the vigorous representation of the client. These "agents" must also be covered by the attorney–client privilege; to do otherwise would obligate the attorney to guard every document, exhibit, and pretrial memorandum from the eyes of everyone on the legal team and perform every task personally, from interviews of clients and witnesses, to the typing of reports and memorandum of law, to the conduct of fact and legal research, to the preparation of trial exhibits and documents. This is clearly not desirable or cost effective for the client or the administration of justice.

Self-Defense Exception

Due Process
An established course of judicial proceedings or other activity designed to ensure the legal rights of an individual.

Self-Defense Exception
The right to reveal a client confidence when necessary to defend oneself against a claim of wrongful conduct.

The rules concerning the duty of confidentiality and the attorney–client privilege are not absolute. Lawyers who are accused of wrongdoing (either intentional or negligent) by their clients must be able to defend themselves. This defense may require the use of confidential and/or privileged information. Therefore, lawyers will not be bound by the rules of confidentiality and privilege in this instance because of an inherent right to **due process**. This is frequently referred to as the **"self-defense exception."**

Web Exploration

Contrast and compare Rule 1.6(c)(4) **of the Pennsylvania Rules** at http://www .padisciplinaryboard/ board.org/documents/PA 9.2.Rpc.pdf, with the American Bar Association Model Rules of Professional Responsibility at http://www.abanet.org/ cpr/mrpc/mrpc_toc.html, and the ethical rule in your jurisdiction.

The Pennsylvania Rules of Professional Conduct Rule 1.6(c)(4) Provides

(c) A lawyer may reveal such information to the extent that the lawyer reasonably believes necessary:
...(4) to establish a claim or defense on behalf of the lawyer in a controversy between the lawyer and the client, to establish a defense to a criminal charge or civil claim or disciplinary proceeding against the lawyer based upon conduct in which the client was involved, or to respond to allegations in any proceeding concerning the lawyer's representation of the client; or

One of the most significant technology cases involving the self-defense exception is *Qualcomm, Inc. v. Broadcom Corp.* In this case, substantial sanctions were assessed against the client. In response, the client made accusations of wrongdoing by outside counsel as part of its attempt to exonerate itself.

IN THE WORDS OF THE COURT …

UNITED STATES DISTRICT COURT
SOUTHERN DISTRICT OF CALIFORNIA
Case No. 05CV1958-RMB (BLM)
Qualcomm, Inc, Plaintiff
Vs
Broadcom Corp, Defendant
ORDER REMANDING PART OF ORDER OF MAGISTRATE COURT RE MOTIONS FOR SANCTIONS DATED 1/07/08

… Qualcomm filed four declarations of employees, in spite of the fact it had maintained its position of invoking attorney-client privilege. All four declarations were exonerative of Qualcomm and critical of the services and advice of their retained counsel. None were filed under seal.

This introduction of accusatory adversity between Qualcomm and its retained counsel regarding the issue of assessing responsibility for the failure of discovery changes the factual basis which supported the court's earlier order denying the self-defense exception to Qualcomm's attorney-client privilege. *Meyerhofer v. Empire Fire & Marine Ins. Co.,* 497 F.2d 1190, 1194-95 (2d Cir. 1974); *Hearn v. Rhay,* 68 F.R.D. 574, 581 (E.D. Wash. 1975); *First Fed. Sav. & Loan Ass'n v. Oppenheim, Appel, Dixon & Co.,* 110 F.R.D. 557, 560-68 (S.D.N.Y. 1986); A.B.A. Model Rules of Prof. Conduct 1.6(b)(5) & comment 10.

Accordingly, the court's order denying the self-defense exception to the attorney-client privilege is vacated. The attorneys have a due process right to defend themselves under the totality of circumstances presented in this sanctions hearing where their alleged conduct regarding discovery is in conflict with that alleged by Qualcomm concerning performance of discovery responsibilities. See, e.g., *Miranda v. So. Pac. Transp. Co.,* 710 F.2d 516, 522-23 (9th Cir. 1983). …

The full opinion of the court may be viewed at www.ediscoverylaw.com/ Brewster.pdf

Work Product Doctrine
The rule of evidence that allows the attorney to treat as confidential and not make available work product to the opposing side.

WORK PRODUCT DOCTRINE

The **work product doctrine** provides a limited protection for material prepared by the attorney, or those working for the attorney, in anticipation of litigation or for trial. The work product doctrine is different from both the attorney–client privilege and the duty of confidentiality. The attorney–client privilege and the duty of confidentiality relate to the information provided by the clients regardless of whether they involve potential litigation.

Exceptions and Limitations to the Work Product Doctrine

The work product doctrine has some exceptions. For example, it does not cover documents prepared in the normal operation of the client's business, such as sales reports, data analysis, or summaries of business operations.

"The work product doctrine does not extend to documents in an attorney's possession that were prepared by a third party in the ordinary course of

WWW MINI EXERCISE
Review the current language of the Federal Rules of Civil Procedure Rule 26. One source of the rule may be found on the website of Cornell Law School Legal Information Institute at http://www .law.cornell.edu/rules/ frcp/Rule26.htm and the related Federal Rules of Criminal Procedure Rule 16 at http://www .law.cornell.edu/rules/ frcrmp/Rule16.htm

IN THE WORDS OF THE COURT . . .

Work Product Doctrine

Electronic Data Systems Corporation v. Steingraber
Case 4:02 CV 225 USDC, E.D. Texas, 2003.

The work product doctrine is narrower than the attorney–client privilege in that it only protects materials prepared "in anticipation of litigation [Fed. R. Civ. P. 26(b) (3)], whereas the attorney–client privilege protects confidential legal communications between an attorney and client regardless of whether they involve possible litigation."

IN THE WORDS OF THE COURT . . .

Work Product Doctrine

Hickman v. Taylor 329 U.S. 496 (1947), page 511.

The U.S. Supreme Court recognized the work product doctrine and its importance, saying:

> "Proper preparation of a client's case demands that he assemble information, sift what he considers to be the relevant from the irrelevant facts, prepare his legal theories and plan his strategy without undue and needless interference. That is the historical and the necessary way in which lawyers act within the framework of our system of jurisprudence to promote justice and to protect their clients' interests. This work is reflected, of course, in interviews, statements, memoranda, correspondence, briefs, mental impressions, personal beliefs, and countless other tangible and intangible ways—aptly though roughly termed by the Circuit Court of Appeals in this case as the 'work product of the lawyer.' Were such materials open to opposing counsel on mere demand, much of what is now put down in writing would remain unwritten. An attorney's thoughts, heretofore inviolate, would not be his own. Inefficiency, unfairness and sharp practices would inevitably develop in the giving of legal advice and in the preparation of cases for trial. The effect on the legal profession would be demoralizing. And the interests of the clients and the cause of justice would be poorly served... '...where relevant and non-privileged facts remain hidden in an attorney's file and where production of those facts is essential to the preparation of one's case, discovery may be properly had.'"

business and that would have been created in essentially similar form irrespective of any litigation anticipated by counsel." In Re Grand Jury Subpoenas, 318 F.3d 379 (2nd Cir. 2002) at 3851.

In other words, the client cannot obtain protection for internal business documents by giving them to the attorney. Giving them to the attorney does not make them work product so they are not protected from discovery by the other side simply because they are in the possession of the attorney.

Internal Investigations and Evidentiary Privileges

Businesses, and particularly corporations with publicly traded securities, are under state and federal law and regulation requirements to take a proactive approach to determine wrongdoing and identify violations of statutes and regulations. These investigations and "audits" create a body of documents all, some, or none of which may be subject to evidentiary privilege. Without the protection of the privilege, businesses would be hesitant to conduct audits for fear of prosecution. Therefore, the courts have extended the privilege to these documents. The privilege will apply differently in each jurisdiction.

INADVERTENT DISCLOSURE OF CONFIDENTIAL INFORMATION

Inadvertent disclosure of confidential or privileged information does happen. It may be the slip of the finger in sending an e-mail, an accidental pushing of the wrong number on the speed dial of a fax machine, or the sending of a misaddressed envelope.

The admissibility of the inadvertently disclosed documents may hinge on the steps the firm takes before and after the disclosure. Having a proper privilege review process in place and monitoring this policy may prevent a claim of negligence.[iii]

The treatment will depend on the individual jurisdiction. The courts follow no single policy.

Judicial Views

There are three judicial views on handling the inadvertent disclosure of confidential and privileged information: (1) Automatic waiver; (2) no waiver; and (3) balancing test.[iv]

> *Automatic waiver*—These cases hold that once the confidentiality is breached, the privilege is automatically waived. There is nothing that will redeem the privilege and therefore, the documents may be used by the party that received them by accident.
> *No waiver*—Under this theory, the privilege is only destroyed when a client makes a knowing voluntary waiver of the privilege. Therefore, the attorney's inadvertent disclosure does not constitute a waiver.
> *Balancing test*—The courts using the balancing test looked to several factors: (1) the nature of the methods taken to protect the information, (2) efforts made to correct the error, (3) the extent of the disclosure, and (4) fairness. Remedies under this test range from unlimited use of the disclosed materials, to court-ordered return of documents, to disqualification of attorneys who have reviewed inadvertently disclosed privileged documents.

ABA Ethics Opinion

The American Bar Association has issued a formal opinion modifying the long-standing opinion 92-368, which advocated for confidentiality of privileged materials to protect the client, and imposing a burden upon receiving attorneys not to review privileged material and return it following instructions given to them by the disclosing attorney, issuing a clarifying formal opinion 05-437, which states:

> A lawyer who receives a document from opposing parties or their lawyers and knows or reasonably should know that the document was inadvertently sent should promptly notify the sender in order to permit the sender to take protective measures. To the extent that Formal Opinion 92-368 opined otherwise, it is hereby withdrawn.

What the ABA wrote, however, is not enough of the opinion to answer the questions: "what should happen to the attorney who reads the inadvertently disclosed document?" and "can the information be used by the other side?" Each jurisdiction may have a different rule. The California courts have addressed these questions in *Rico v. Mitsubishi Motors Corp.*

IN THE WORDS OF THE COURT . . .

Rico v. Mitsubishi Motors Corp., 42 Cal.4th 807 (2007)
171 P.3d 1092, 68 Cal.Rptr.3d 758

. . . Here we consider what action is required of an attorney who receives privileged documents through inadvertence and whether the remedy of disqualification is appropriate. We conclude that, under the authority of State Comp. Ins. Fund v. WPS, Inc. (1999) 70 Cal. App. 4th 644 (State Fund), an attorney in these circumstances may not read a document any more closely than is necessary to ascertain that it is privileged. Once it becomes apparent that the content is privileged, counsel must immediately notify opposing counsel and try to resolve the situation. . . .

Moreover, we agree with the Court of Appeal that, "when a writing is protected under the absolute attorney work product privilege, courts do not invade upon the attorney's thought processes by evaluating the content of the writing. Once [it is apparent] that the writing contains an attorney's impressions, conclusions, opinions, legal research or theories, the reading stops and the contents of the document for all practical purposes are off limits. In the same way, once the court determines that the writing is absolutely privileged, the inquiry ends. Courts do not make exceptions based on the content of the writing." Thus, "regardless of its potential impeachment value, Yukevich's personal notes should never have been subject to opposing counsel's scrutiny and use."

Web Exploration

Contrast and compare the **Arizona Ethics Rules** at http://www.myazbar.org/ Ethics/ruleview.cfm?id=27, with the American Bar Association Model Rules of Professional Responsibility at http://www.abanet.org/cpr/ mrpc/mrpc_toc.html, and the ethical rules in your jurisdiction.

ETHICAL Perspectives

ARIZONA ETHICS RULES

ER 1.6. Confidentiality of Information.

(a) A lawyer shall not reveal information relating to the representation of a client unless the client gives informed consent, the disclosure is impliedly authorized in order to carry out the representation or the disclosure is permitted or required by paragraphs (b), (c) or (d), or ER 3.3(a)(3).

(b) A lawyer shall reveal such information to the extent the lawyer reasonably believes necessary to prevent the client from committing a criminal act that the lawyer believes is likely to result in death or substantial bodily harm.

(c) A lawyer may reveal the intention of the lawyer's client to commit a crime and the information necessary to prevent the crime.

(d) A lawyer may reveal such information relating to the representation of a client to the extent the lawyer reasonably believes necessary:

(1) to prevent the client from committing a crime or fraud that is reasonably certain to result in substantial injury to the financial interests or property of another and in furtherance of which the client has used or is using the lawyer's services;

(2) to mitigate or rectify substantial injury to the financial interests or property of another that is reasonably certain to result or has resulted from the client's commission of a crime or fraud in furtherance of which the client has used the lawyer's services;

(3) to secure legal advice about the lawyer's compliance with these Rules;

(4) to establish a claim or defense on behalf of the lawyer in a controversy between the lawyer and the client, to establish a defense to a criminal charge or civil claim against the lawyer based upon conduct in which the client was involved, or to respond to allegations in any proceeding concerning the lawyer's representation of the client; or

(5) to comply with other law or a final order of a court or tribunal of competent jurisdiction directing the lawyer to disclose such information.

CONFLICT OF INTEREST

The basis of the **conflict of interest** rule is the belief that a person cannot be loyal to two clients. Lawyers cannot represent two clients with potentially conflicting interests, such as a husband and wife in a domestic relations case, nor represent a client when the attorney has a financial interest in the subject matter of the case, such as being a partner in a real estate transaction. It is clearly an issue for the lawyer on the legal team. But, what about the nonlawyer members, the paralegals, and the computer and technology consultants? The line is not clear. If both sides of a case use the same paralegal, the answer to the conflict of interest question is probably the same as the lawyer's: do not do it. For technology consultants, however, the distinction is less clear. Consultants are not offering legal advice. But they are privy to trial strategy and confidential information. To whom is the obligation to keep the confidences owed? If the consultant is an agent of the lawyer-principal, what about the agent's duty to advise of information learned as an agent of the principal? Does the consultant have a duty to tell one principal what was learned while working for another principal? The legal team should be certain the client's rights are not jeopardized and obtain the same assurance from the outside consultants as they would demand of in-house staff.

Loyalty to the client is the essence of ethics Rule 1.7 on Conflict of Interest. A lawyer should not represent another client if "representation of one client will be directly adverse to another client" (ABA Model Rules of Professional Conduct Rule 1.7), unless both clients give their informed consent to the dual representation, and the consent is confirmed in writing. The lawyer's personal interests or that of third parties who are not clients, such as family members, may also create a risk of a conflict that must be avoided.

Clearly, a lawyer should not accept the engagement if the lawyer's personal interests or desires will, or if there is a reasonable probability that they will, adversely affect the advice to be given or services to be rendered to the prospective client. The client is entitled to independent advice from members of the legal team. In this instance, "independent" means free from concern for personal gain. The information that may be considered to create a conflict of interest is not limited solely to that of the attorney representing a client. It also includes the information held by another member of the legal team, including the legal assistant—and yes, the technology consultant.

Conflict of Interest
Representing one client that will be directly adverse to the interest of another client, the attorney, or another third party not a client.

WWW MINI EXERCISE
ETHICAL Perspective
Review the most current version and comments to Rule 1.7 on Conflict of Interest of the American Bar Association Model Rules of Professional Conduct at the American Bar Association website at http://www.abanet.org/cpr/mrpc/rule_1_7.html

Web Exploration

Contrast and compare the
**Arkansas Rules of
Professional Conduct** at
http://courts.state.ar.us/
rules/current_ark_prof_
conduct/index.cfm, with the
American Bar Association
Model Rules of Professional
Responsibility at http://
www.abanet.org/cpr/mrpc/
mrpc_toc.html, and the
ethical rules in your
jurisdiction.

ETHICAL Perspectives

ARKANSAS RULES OF PROFESSIONAL CONDUCT
Rule 1.7. Conflict of Interest: Current Clients.

(a) Except as provided in paragraph (b), a lawyer shall not represent a client if the representation involves a concurrent conflict of interest. A concurrent conflict of interest exists if:
  (1) the representation of one client will be directly adverse to another client; or
  (2) there is a significant risk that the representation of one or more clients will be materially limited by the lawyer's responsibilities to another client, a former client or a third person or by a personal interest of the lawyer.
(b) Notwithstanding the existence of a concurrent conflict of interest under paragraph (a), a lawyer may represent a client if:
  (1) the lawyer reasonably believes that the lawyer will be able to provide competent and diligent representation to each affected client;
  (2) the representation is not prohibited by law;
  (3) the representation does not involve the assertion of a claim by one client against another client represented by the lawyer in the same litigation or other proceeding before a tribunal; and
  (4) each affected client gives informed consent, confirmed in writing.

COMPETENCE

Competent
Having the requisite knowledge and skill thoroughness and preparation necessary for representation.

Rules of Court
Rules governing the practice or procedure in a specific court.

ABA Model Rule of Professional Conduct 1.1 requires that lawyers provide competent representation to a client. **Competent** representation requires the legal knowledge, skill, thoroughness, and preparation reasonably necessary for the representation. Few ethics opinions have been written on the subject of competent representation required under Rule 1.1 as it relates to nonspecific legal issues of workload and legal knowledge. However, the minimum standards clearly require an understanding of the **rules of court**. These rules continue to grow in number and complexity including the adoption of rules regarding electronic discovery. New rules require a new level of knowledge to competently represent clients. Further, lawyers must be able to communicate with clients in the language of technology about methods of creation and sources of electronic documents and the methods for retrieving them and processing them for submission to opposing counsel and the court. Consider the need to use "interpreters of the language of technology" as similar to the use of language interpreters as explained in the Formal Opinion of the Association of the Bar of the City of New York in the following Ethical Perspective.

ETHICAL Perspective

**THE ASSOCIATION OF THE BAR OF THE CITY OF NEW YORK
FORMAL OPINION 1995-12
COMMITTEE ON PROFESSIONAL AND JUDICIAL ETHICS
JULY 6, 1995
ACTION: FORMAL OPINION**

... DR 6-101(A)(2) mandates that "[a] lawyer shall not ... [h]andle a legal matter without preparation adequate in the circumstances." Adequate preparation requires, not only that a lawyer conduct necessary legal research, but also that he or she gather information material to the claims or defenses of the client. See Mason v. Balcom, 531 F.2d 717, 724 (5th Cir. 1976). The lawyer's inability, because of a language barrier, to understand fully what the client is telling him or her may unnecessarily impede the lawyer's ability to gather the information from the client needed to familiarize the lawyer with the circumstances of the case. This makes communication via the interpreter vital since it may be the only practical way that a free-flowing dialogue can be maintained with the client, and the only means by which the lawyer can actually and substantially assist the client.

The duty to represent a client competently, embodied in DR 6-101(A)(1), requires a lawyer confronted with a legal matter calling for legal skills or knowledge outside the lawyer's experience or ability, to associate with lawyers with skills or knowledge necessary to handle the legal matter. When a lawyer is confronted with a legal matter requiring non-legal skills or knowledge outside the lawyer's experience or ability and these skills or knowledge are necessary for the proper preparation of the legal matter, DR 6-101(A)(2) appears to require that the lawyer associate with professionals in other disciplines who possess the requisite skills or knowledge needed by the lawyer to prepare the legal matter. The interpreter appears to be the type of professional envisioned by EC 6-3's observation that "[p]roper preparation and representation may require the association by the lawyer of professionals in other disciplines." When the need for an interpreter is apparent or it is reasonable to conclude that an interpreter is required for effective communication, failure to take steps with the client to secure an interpreter may be a breach of the duty to represent the client competently. . . .

REVIEW

The complete version of the Formal Opinion at: http://www. abcny.org/Publications/ reports/show_html.php? rid=168

Wisconsin Rules of Professional Conduct for Attorneys

SCR 20:1.1 Competence

A lawyer shall provide competent representation to a client. Competent representation requires the legal knowledge, skill, thoroughness and preparation reasonably necessary for the representation.

Web Exploration

Contrast and compare the **Wisconsin Rules of Professional Conduct for Attorneys** at http://www.legis.state.wi.us /rsb/scr/5200.pdf2006, with the American Bar Association Model Rules of Professional Responsibility at http:// www.abanet.org/cpr/mrpc/ mrpc_toc.html, and the ethical rules in your jurisdiction.

CANDOR AND FAIRNESS IN LITGATION

Litigation is the practice of advocacy, advocating a legal position to the court or trying to persuade a trier of facts to accept the facts as presented. It is the duty of the advocate to avoid any conduct that undermines the integrity of the process. The duty to the client to persuasively present the case is a qualified duty, qualified by the ethical obligation (**candor**) to not mislead the court or opposing counsel with false statements of law or of facts which the lawyer knows to be false. Without mutual respect, honesty, and fairness the system cannot function properly.

It may be a simple ethical duty to competently research and present the current case and statutory law, even when the most current version is not favorable to the position taken. In the technology age, this duty requires making a complete search for ALL the law, statutory enactments and case law, and not just the part that is favorable to the client's position. In an age of vast numbers of electronic cases, it is easy to lose a few or not run the search as professionally as possible. Not making the proper inquiry of the client's staff to find all of the law may lead to sanctions and potentially worse, disbarment.

Candor
Ethical obligation to not mislead the court or opposing counsel with false statements of law or of facts which the lawyer knows to be false.

ETHICAL Perspective

PROPOSED MICHIGAN STANDARDS FOR IMPOSING LAWYER SANCTIONS
[WITHOUT COMMENTARY]
(SUBMITTED IN JUNE 2002 BY THE ATTORNEY DISCIPLINE BOARD)

"Preface

These Michigan Standards for Imposing Lawyer Sanctions were adopted by the State of Michigan Attorney Discipline Board (ADB or Board) on [date] under the authority granted by the Michigan Supreme Court in its order dated [date], and are intended for use by the Attorney Discipline Board and its hearing panels in imposing discipline following a finding or acknowledgment of professional misconduct. Pursuant to the Court's order, these standards may be amended by the Board from time to time. The Court may at any time modify these standards or direct the Board to modify them.

. . . 6.0 *Violations of Duties* Owed to the Legal System

6.1   False Statements, Fraud, and Misrepresentation to a Tribunal. The following sanctions are generally appropriate in cases involving conduct that is prejudicial to the administration of justice or that involves dishonesty, fraud, deceit, or misrepresentation to a tribunal:

6.11   Disbarment is generally appropriate when a lawyer, with the intent to deceive the tribunal, makes a false statement, submits a false document, or improperly withholds material information, and causes serious or potentially serious injury.

6.12   Suspension is generally appropriate when a lawyer knows that false statements or documents are being submitted to the tribunal or that material information is improperly being withheld, and takes no remedial action, and causes injury or potential injury.

6.13   Reprimand is generally appropriate when a lawyer is negligent either in determining whether statements or documents submitted to a tribunal are false or in taking remedial action when material information is being withheld and causes injury or potential injury. . . ."

REVIEW

The entire set of Michigan proposed standards for imposing lawyer sanctions at: http://courts.michigan .gov/supremecourt/ Resources/Administrative/ 2002-29-ADB-proposal.pdf

Rhode Island Rules of Professional Conduct

Rule 3.3 Candor Toward The Tribunal

(a)   A lawyer shall not knowingly:

(1)   make a false statement of fact or law to a tribunal or fail to correct a false statement of material fact or law previously made to the tribunal by the lawyer;

(2)   fail to disclose to the tribunal legal authority in the controlling jurisdiction known to the lawyer to be directly adverse to the position of the client and not disclosed by opposing counsel; or

(3)   offer evidence that the lawyer knows to be false. If a lawyer, the lawyer's client, or a witness called by the lawyer, has offered material evidence and the lawyer comes to know of its falsity, the lawyer shall take reasonable remedial measures, including, if necessary, disclosure to the tribunal. A lawyer may refuse to offer evidence, other than the testimony of a defendant in a criminal matter, that the lawyer reasonably believes is false.

(b)   A lawyer who represents a client in an adjudicative proceeding and who knows that a person intends to engage, is engaging or has engaged in criminal or fraudulent conduct related to the proceeding shall take reasonable remedial measures, including, if necessary, disclosure to the tribunal.

Web Exploration

Contrast and compare the **Rhode Island Rules of Professional Conduct** at http://www.courts.ri.gov/ supreme/pdf-files/ Rules_Of_Professional_ Conduct.pdf, with the American Bar Association Model Rules of Professional Responsibility at http://www.abanet.org/cpr/ mrpc/mrpc_toc.html, and the ethical rules in your jurisdiction.

(c) The duties stated in paragraphs (a) and (b) continue to the conclusion of the proceeding, and apply even if compliance requires disclosure of information otherwise protected by Rule 1.6.

(d) In an ex parte proceeding, a lawyer shall inform the tribunal of all material facts known to the lawyer that will enable the tribunal to make an informed decision, whether or not the facts are adverse.

Fairness to Opposing Party and Counsel

Fairness in the practice of law has been an issue probably as long as there has been an adversarial justice system. A number of states have established professionalism centers such as that of the Pennsylvania Bar Association shown in Exhibit 2.3. Attorneys are advocates for their clients and occasionally forget that the purpose of

Exhibit 2.3 Pennsylvania Bar Association Professionalism Committee website

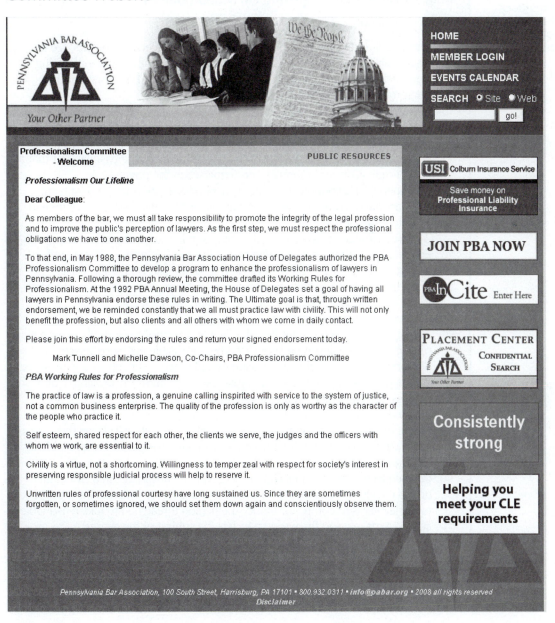

the legal system is justice for all. The ethical rule of fairness to opposing counsel and parties is an attempt to set the guidelines to ensure justice is done even if one's client loses the case. Each side is expected to use its best skills and knowledge and present fairly their position in the form of evidence for the trier of fact to determine where the truth lies. Destroying, falsifying, or tampering with evidence destroys the fabric of the system. If people lose confidence in the system because of these unfair tactics society loses confidence in the system and it breaks down. Just consider the criminal cases where the prosecutor does not turn over, as required, exculpatory evidence that might show the defendant innocent.

Web Exploration

Contrast and compare the **Oregon Rules of Professional Conduct** at http://www.osbar.org/_docs /rulesregs/orpc.pdf, with the American Bar Association Model Rules of Professional Responsibility at http://www.abanet.org/cpr/ mrpc/mrpc_toc.html, and the ethical rules in your jurisdiction.

Oregon Rules of Professional Conduct (12/01/06)

Rule 3.4 Fairness to Opposing Party and Counsel

A lawyer shall not:

(a) knowingly and unlawfully obstruct another party's access to evidence or unlawfully alter, destroy or conceal a document or other material having potential evidentiary value. A lawyer shall not counsel or assist another person to do any such act;

(b) falsify evidence; counsel or assist a witness to testify falsely; offer an inducement to a witness that is prohibited by law; or pay, offer to pay, or acquiesce in payment of compensation to a witness contingent upon the content of the witness's testimony or the outcome of the case; except that a lawyer may advance, guarantee or acquiesce in the payment of:

   (1) expenses reasonably incurred by a witness in attending or testifying;

   (2) reasonable compensation to a witness for the witness's loss of time in attending or testifying; or

   (3) a reasonable fee for the professional services of an expert witness.

(c) knowingly disobey an obligation under the rules of a tribunal, except for an open refusal based on an assertion that no valid obligation exists;

(d) in pretrial procedure, knowingly make a frivolous discovery request or fail to make reasonably diligent effort to comply with a legally proper discovery request by an opposing party;

(e) in trial, allude to any matter that the lawyer does not reasonably believe is relevant or that will not be supported by admissible evidence, assert personal knowledge of facts in issue except when testifying as a witness, or state a personal opinion as to the justness of a cause, the credibility of a witness, the culpability of a civil litigant or the guilt or innocence of an accused;

(f) advise or cause a person to secrete himself or herself or to leave the jurisdiction of a tribunal for purposes of making the person unavailable as a witness therein; or

(g) threaten to present criminal charges to obtain an advantage in a civil matter unless the lawyer reasonably believes the charge to be true and if the purpose of the lawyer is to compel or induce the person threatened to take reasonable action to make good the wrong which is the subject of the charge.

Adopted 01/01/05

http://www.osbar.org/_docs/rulesregs/orpc.pdf

ETHICAL Perspective

Web Exploration

COLORADO SUPREME COURT

Rule 3.4. Fairness to Opposing Party and Counsel.

Annotations

Comment

[1]The procedure of the adversary system contemplates that the evidence in a case is to be marshalled competitively by the contending parties. Fair competition in the adversary system is secured by prohibitions against destruction or concealment of evidence, improperly influencing witnesses, obstructive tactics in discovery procedure, and the like.

[2]Documents and other items of evidence are often essential to establish a claim or defense. Subject to evidentiary privileges, the right of an opposing party, including the government, to obtain evidence through discovery or subpoena is an important procedural right. The exercise of that right can be frustrated if relevant material is altered, concealed or destroyed. Applicable law in many jurisdictions makes it an offense to destroy material for purpose of impairing its availability in a pending proceeding or one whose commencement can be foreseen. Falsifying evidence is also generally a criminal offense. Paragraph (a) applies to evidentiary material generally, including computerized information.

http://www.coloradosupremecourt.com/Regulation/Rules/appendix20/statdspp88f6.html

Contrast and compare the **COLORADO SUPREME COURT Rules of Professional Conduct** at http://www.coloradosupremecourt.com/Regulation/Rules/appendix20/statdspp88f6.html, with the American Bar Association Model Rules of Professional Responsibility at http://www.abanet.org/cpr/mrpc/mrpc_toc.html, and the ethical rules in your jurisdiction.

 IN THE WORDS OF THE COURT . . .

UNITED STATES DISTRICT COURT SOUTHERN DISTRICT OF CALIFORNIA
QUALCOMM INCORPORATED, Plaintiff, v. BROADCOM CORPORATION, Defendant.
and RELATED COUNTERCLAIMS.
Case No. 05cv1958–B (BLM)

ORDER GRANTING IN PART AND DENYING IN PART DEFENDANT'S MOTION FOR SANCTIONS AND SANCTIONING QUALCOMM, INCORPORATED AND INDIVIDUAL LAWYERS

. . . b. Referral to the California State Bar

As set forth above, the Sanctioned Attorneys assisted Qualcomm in committing this incredible discovery violation by intentionally hiding or recklessly ignoring relevant documents, ignoring or rejecting numerous warning signs that Qualcomm's document search was inadequate, and blindly accepting Qualcomm's unsupported assurances that its document search was adequate. The Sanctioned Attorneys then used the lack of evidence to repeatedly and forcefully make false statements and arguments to the court and jury. As such, the Sanctioned Attorneys violated their discovery obligations and also may have violated their ethical duties. See e.g., The State Bar of California, Rules of Professional Conduct, Rule 5–200 (a lawyer shall not seek to mislead the judge or jury by a false statement of fact or law), Rule 5–220 (a lawyer shall not suppress evidence that the lawyer or the lawyer's client has a legal obligation to reveal or to produce) . . .

DUTY TO SUPERVISE

The duty of supervision is required of partners, and lawyers with managerial authority in the firm to ensure other lawyers' conduct conforms to the ethical code. Rule 5.1. Direct supervising attorneys with authority over nonlawyers have an ethical obligation to ensure those persons' conduct is compatible with the obligations of the lawyer. Rule 5.3(b). What happens in the handling and processing of a case by the legal team is ultimately the responsibility of the supervising attorney. Any ethical breaches or lapses are ultimately the responsibility of the attorney under the ethical guidelines and under common law principles of agency law. (The principal is responsible for the acts of the agent when the agent is acting within the scope of their employment.) The attorney is the one to whom the client looks for professional advice and the outcome of the case. The attorney will suffer any sanctions that result from a failure to follow and enforce the ethical rules by members of the legal team. As noted in the *Qualcomm v. Broadcom* case, the obligation to the court and to the other side may extend to the attorney supervising the client and its staff to ensure full compliance with the rules of court. Sanctions can come from two sources: the court hearing the underlying action (as in the Qualcomm case above) and the attorney disciplinary agency. The court typically punishes this sort of misbehavior with monetary sanctions, the purpose of which is to recompense the other side for the time and effort they have expended or will expend because of the discovery abuse. The attorney disciplinary agency's punishment can include, in extreme cases, disbarment or suspension from practice before the court for a period of time, or in less extreme cases public or private censure. In addition, under some circumstances "unfair" litigation tactics may result in a suit for malpractice by the client against the attorney and the law firm.

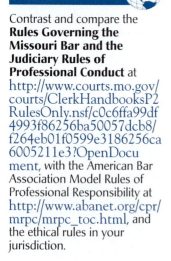

Web Exploration

Contrast and compare the **Rules Governing the Missouri Bar and the Judiciary Rules of Professional Conduct** at http://www.courts.mo.gov/courts/ClerkHandbooksP2RulesOnly.nsf/c0c6ffa99df4993f86256ba50057dcb8/f264eb01f0599e3186256ca6005211e3?OpenDocument, with the American Bar Association Model Rules of Professional Responsibility at http://www.abanet.org/cpr/mrpc/mrpc_toc.html, and the ethical rules in your jurisdiction.

Rules Governing the Missouri Bar and the Judiciary Rules of Professional Conduct

Rule 4-5.3: Responsibilities Regarding Nonlawyer Assistants

With respect to a nonlawyer employed or retained by or associated with a lawyer:

(a) a partner, and a lawyer who individually or together with other lawyers possesses comparable managerial authority in a law firm, shall make reasonable efforts to ensure that the firm has in effect measures giving reasonable assurance that the person's conduct is compatible with the professional obligations of the lawyer;

(b) a lawyer having direct supervisory authority over the nonlawyer shall make reasonable efforts to ensure that the person's conduct is compatible with the professional obligations of the lawyer; and

(c) a lawyer shall be responsible for conduct of such a person that would be a violation of the Rules of Professional Conduct if engaged in by a lawyer if:

   (1) the lawyer orders or, with the knowledge of the specific conduct, ratifies the conduct involved; or

   (2) the lawyer is a partner, or has comparable managerial authority in the law firm in which the person is employed, or has direct supervisory authority over the person and knows of the conduct at a time when its consequences can be avoided or mitigated but fails to take reasonable remedial action.

Source: http://www.courts.mo.gov/courts/ClerkHandbooksP2RulesOnly.nsf/c0c6ffa99df4993f86256ba50057dcb8/f264eb01f0599e3186256ca6005211e3?OpenDocument

Temporary Attorneys

It has become a common practice to hire attorneys to do "privilege reviews" of documents as part of the electronic discovery process. Model Rule 7.5(d) states that clients are entitled to know who or what entity is providing their legal services, the Rule only requires notice when a temporary lawyer is providing work for a client without the close supervision of a lawyer associated with the law firm. See ABA Op. 88-356 (1988). If the temporary lawyer is working under the direct supervision of a lawyer associated with the firm, there may be no duty of disclosure.

SUMMARY

CHAPTER 2
LEGAL ETHICS IN A TECHNOLOGY AGE

Introduction To Ethics In Technology	Ethics is the minimally acceptable standards of conduct in a profession. Ethical guidelines are enforced by the court in the jurisdiction where the attorney is practicing or where the case is being tried. The supervising attorney of every legal team must follow the ethics rules and ensure the members of the legal team follow the same rules as the supervising lawyer.
Confidentiality and Privilege	Every member of the legal team including technical support personnel and computer consultants must understand the nature and obligations of the legal profession with regard to confidentiality and the attorney–client privilege.
Confidentiality	Confidentiality is an ethical obligation. Attorneys have a duty to treat client information obtained in the course of representation of a client in confidence under ABA Rule 1.6.
Privilege	Privilege is a rule of evidence. The attorney–client privilege is a rule of evidence that protects the client from the attorney revealing the confidential information. The concept of privilege also applies to: 1. Spouses 2. Clergy–penitent 3. Doctor–patient 4. Psychotherapist–patient 5. Participants in settlement negotiations
Claim of Privilege	Privilege is not automatic. The person claiming the privilege has the burden of establishing the privilege, called claim of privilege.
Extension of Attorney–Client Privilege to Others	"… the privilege in appropriate circumstances extends to otherwise privileged communications that involve persons assisting the lawyer in the rendition of legal services…." (U.S. District Court for the Southern District of New York) Common Interest Privilege allows sharing of information with an attorney for another who shares a common legal interest.

(Continued)

Self-Defense Exception	Lawyers who are accused of wrongdoing by their clients must be able to defend themselves and not be bound by the rules of confidentiality and privilege.
Work Product Doctrine	Limited protection for material prepared by the attorney, or those working for the attorney, in anticipation of litigation or for trial.
Exceptions and Limitations to the Work Product Doctrine	The work product doctrine does not apply to documents created in the normal course of a client's business, nor to some materials prepared as part of a government case preparation or internal investigation required by law.
Internal Investigations and Evidentiary Privileges	Internal business investigations required by Statute on Regulation that would not be performed properly if court did not extend privilege to documents created during these audits.
Inadvertent Disclosure of Confidential Information	The admissibility will depend on the judicial view in a particular jurisdiction. There are three judicial views: Automatic waiver: Once divulged there is no confidentiality. No Waiver: Only a waiver if knowingly made. Balancing Test: Depends on steps taken to prevent disclosure and efforts to retrieve information after disclosure.
Conflict of Interest	A lawyer should not accept the engagement (representation) if the lawyer's personal interests or desires will, or if there is a reasonable probability that they will, adversely affect the advice to be given or services to be rendered to the prospective client.
Competence	Ethical guidelines require lawyers to provide competent representation. In the technology age, lawyers need to be able to communicate with clients about methods of creation and sources of electronic documents and methods used to retrieve them.
Candor and Fairness in Litigtion	A lawyer has an ethical duty (candor) to not mislead the court even when the most current version of the law is not favorable to the client's legal position. It requires all members of the legal team to make accurate inquiry and present the most current information.
Fairness to Opposing Party and Counsel	Lawyers are expected to use their best skills on presenting a case but avoid destruction or tampering with evidence or ignoring rules of court.
Duty to Supervise	All lawyers and partners in law firms are required to supervise everyone over whom they have supervisory authority. All ethical breaches by members of the legal team are ultimately those of the supervising attorney.
Temporary Attorneys	Attorneys hired for a specific case on a temporary basis must be supervised by the responsible supervising attorney on the case.

KEY TERMINOLOGY

Agent   30
Attorney–client privilege   34
Candor   43
Claim of privilege   35
Competent   42
Confidentiality   33
Conflict of interest   41

Due process   36
Ethics   28
Federal Rules of Evidence   30
Fiduciary relationship   30
Model Rules of Professional
  Conduct   28
Principal   30

Privilege   30
Rules of court   42
Self-defense exception   36
Supervising attorney   30
Work product   30
Work product doctrine   37

CONCEPT REVIEW QUESTIONS AND EXERCISES

1. Test your knowledge and comprehension of the topics in this chapter by completing the multiple-choice questions on the textbook Companion Website.
2. Test your knowledge and comprehension of the topics in this chapter by completing the True-False questions on the textbook Companion Website.
3. What is ethics?
4. What is the purpose of the confidentiality rule in the legal setting?
5. What is the difference between the duty of confidentiality and the attorney–client privilege?
6. Can the confidentiality between attorney and client be lost?
7. Can the attorney–client privilege be lost?
8. What are the judicial approaches to the inadvertent disclosure of confidential information?
9. What ethical guidelines, if any, does your state follow?
10. What is the ethical obligation of a paralegal to the firm's client?
11. What is the ethical obligation of the paralegal to the court?
12. What is the ethical obligation of a litigation support staff member to the client? To the court? Of a litigation support person from an outside firm or consultant? Explain.
13. In addition to the attorney–client relationship are there others where there is a privilege? Why

would it apply to others not in an attorney–client relationship?
14. How is a claim of privilege made?
15. Why is the attorney–client privilege extended to others working for the attorney?
16. What is the purpose of the self-defense exception to the confidentiality rule?
17. Why is conflict of interest an issue for the legal team?
18. What are the ethical issues for a law firm using outside computer or technology consultants?
19. What is required to invoke the attorney–client privilege? Explain sufficiently for a nonlegal team member to be able to understand.
20. What is protected by the work product doctrine?
21. Should a technology consultant be considered an "other representative" under the Federal Rules of Civil Procedure, Rule 26? Why or why not?
22. Describe some of the applications of legal ethics in the use of technology.
23. How has technology changed the concept of competence for lawyers?
24. Do the ethical rules of "fairness" prevent lawyers from aggressively advocating their client's position?
25. Why would a partner in a law firm be required to supervise the other lawyers in the firm?
26. How can members of the legal team demonstrate they have been adequately supervised?

INTERNET EXERCISES

1. Find a copy of the most current version of the Model Rules of Professional Conduct as published by the American Bar Association.
2. Use the Internet to locate the most current version of the ethical rules as used in your jurisdiction. Save the Internet address for future reference.
3. Find ethics opinions or sources of information on ethics in your jurisdiction.

PORTFOLIO ASSIGNMENTS

1. Prepare a memo for distribution to members of the legal team on their obligations to obey the ethical rules.
2. Prepare a memo to a supervising attorney on methods for insuring proper ethical conduct by the members of the attorney's staff.
3. Prepare a brief note to a supervising attorney on why a failure to supervise properly could result in a problem for the attorney and the firm.
4. Prepare a memo to the supervising attorney who has just been admitted to practice in your jurisdiction about the continuing legal education requirements in your jurisdiction including any ethical education elements.

SCENARIO CASE STUDY

Use the opening scenario for this chapter to answer the following questions. The setting is the daily meeting of the partners after they had been asked questions about ethical obligations.

1. What policy should the firm institute with regard to discussion of cases among the litigation team, and others in the law firm not working on a particular case?
2. Should the firm have a firmwide policy independent of any jurisdictional requirement for ethics training on a regular basis and who should be covered by that policy?
3. What guidelines should the partners institute to ensure all staff members are properly supervised?
4. What steps should the firm take to ensure that the attorneys and staff are competent?
5. What policies or procedures should be instituted to protect confidential information and litigation work product?

CONTINUING CASES AND EXERCISES

1. Internet Resources. Update your list of Internet resources with those of the ABA Ethics rules, your local jurisdiction rules, and sources for ethics opinions.
2. Locate and save information on sources of continuing education including ethics updates in your jurisdiction.
3. Continue to maintain a time log of your activity in the course.

ENDNOTES

i   *Trammell v. U.S.*, 445 U.S. 40 (1980).

ii *SR International Bus. Ins. Co. v. World Trade Center* Prop No 01 Civ 9291 (S.D.N.Y. 2002), quoting *Browne of New York City, Inc. v. Ambase Corp.*

iii *VLT Inc. Lucent Technologies*, No 00–11049-PBS (D. Mass. 01/21/03).

iv Inadvertent Disclosure: Approaches and Remedies, *The Practical Lawyer*, Philadelphia, April 2001, by Kevin M. McCarthy.

VIDEO SCENARIO: CONFIDENTIALITY: PUBLIC INFORMATION

 The law firm has a case that has received coverage by the local press. Two paralegals from the same firm are on a coffee break at a public coffee shop. One of the paralegals is working on the case and the other is not assigned to the case but has some interest in it.

Go to the Companion Website, select Chapter 2 from the pull down menu, and watch this video.

1. Does the legal team working on a case have a duty to remain silent when information about the case has been made public?

2. If incorrect information about a case has been made public, can the members of the legal team correct any misinformation?

3. Can confidential information about cases be shared between members of the same law firm?

4. What is the difference between confidentiality and attorney-client privilege?

Chapter 3 Digital Resources at www.prenhall.com/goldman

- Author Video Introduction
- Case Study Video: Video Depositions
- Comprehension Quizzes and Glossary

Computer Hardware and Software

OPENING SCENARIO

It was obvious to Mrs. Hannah that the attorney she had left the large center-city law firm to work for had no experience in setting up a law office. His experience as a law clerk in federal court did nothing to show him the realities of getting a practice off the ground. His immediate inclination was to just buy one inexpensive desktop computer with a very basic word processing program. With a little help from Mrs. H, he realized they needed a computer for both of them and more than a basic word processor program. He quickly began to depend on her advice as she explained the problems she and other members of her paralegal association encountered in their offices. She explained the issue of buying a system that could not grow as the practice expanded. She wanted to make sure that when they added a secretary and an associate, they would not have to start over again with new computers and software. Her old firm had had to make a lot of changes when they added more people. As one of the associates at that firm confirmed to him, when they added more computers to the network to handle the additional workload, "everything fell apart, slowed down, and crashed around us."

She reminded him that they would be subletting one of the rooms in their office suite to a friend of his, Ariel Marshall, Esq., defense attorney, for enough to make a dent in covering the overhead costs. His very efficient paralegal reminded him that they would need to get another computer hooked up to their system so she could do the work for Ms. Marshall as well as Mr. Mason. It was agreed that he would hire a part-time secretary and paralegal to help out when he had a busy trial schedule.

It had been clear that Mr. Mason's trial work came first. Her concern was the possible conflict with her boss, a plaintiff attorney, and Ms. Marshall, a defense attorney. In a small town it was possible they would be on opposite sides of a

LEARNING OBJECTIVES

After studying this chapter you should be able to:

1. Discuss the different types of computer systems used in a law office.

2. Describe the different computer operating systems.

3. Explain the differences between applications and specialty applications software.

4. Understand basic issues in installing and using software.

5. Understand how a network functions and the issues of network security.

case. She expressed her concern to both attorneys, telling them she would feel a little awkward. She especially wanted to know how to prevent each side and their respective staff from looking at the other lawyer's confidential and privileged client files—or maybe that wasn't a problem?

They finally decided that it would be a good idea to attend the legal technology show and see what was available.

INTRODUCTION TO COMPUTER HARDWARE AND SOFTWARE

Computer Hardware
A tangible or physical part of a computer system.

Computer System
A combination of an input device, a processor, and an output device.

Mainframe
A large computer system used primarily for bulk processing of data and financial information.

EXPLORE
The components inside your computer at:
http://www.videojug
.com/film/what-com
ponents-are-inside-my
-computer

Central Processing Unit (CPU)
Central processor unit, the computer chip, and memory module that performs the basic computer functions.

Random Access Memory (RAM)
Temporary computer memory that stores work in progress.

Operating System
The software that the rest of the software depends on to make the computer functional. On most PCs this is Windows or the Macintosh OS. Unix and Linux are other operating systems often found in scientific and technical environments.

Computer hardware is the term used to describe the tangible or physical parts of a computer system; a **computer system** includes at least one input device, a computer processor, and at least one output device. A system may be as small and portable as a digital watch or as large as a **mainframe** computer requiring a large room to house it.

Older models of computers, many of which are still found in many law offices, are large, ugly metal boxes connected to large, bulky, and heavy desktop monitors, sometimes taking up half of a desk top. Newer models are smaller and less obtrusive. In some offices the computer system consists of a portable laptop computer, weighing as little as three to four pounds, the size of a large book, used at the user's desk with a docking station to connect it to a flat-screen monitor, external keyboard and mouse, Internet connection, and network.

With the reduction in size have come increased speed and functionality. On older models, opening more than one document uses most of the computer system resources, slowing them down or even "freezing" or stopping the processing of data. The newer models typically run well while allowing the display of multiple documents from multiple applications all running at the same time—Word files, Excel spreadsheets, calendaring programs, and timekeeping applications. Exhibit 3.1 shows a monitor display of four programs running at the same time.

The ability to perform multiple functions simultaneously is in part the result of the increase in processing speed permitted by newer **central processing units (CPUs)**, also called simply processors, and the availability of inexpensive dynamic or volatile computer memory, **random access memory (RAM).** A CPU is the computer "chip" that interprets computer instructions and processes data, and RAM is the temporary computer memory that stores work in progress.

Hardware of all sizes requires software instructions to run and perform desired functions. **Operating system** software provides the basic instructions for starting up the computer and processing the basic input and output activity. The processing of data requires additional applications software such as that used for word processing and financial data processing.

All computer components must have a power source (electrical outlet or battery) to operate, including the basic CPU, the dynamic memory modules used for temporary storage of data (RAM or random access memory), and output devices like the computer monitor, and printer.

Just as an automobile depends on fuel to continue to operate, so is the computer dependent on a power source to operate. Computers cannot remember data or information that appears on the computer screen (work in progress) after the power is turned off—unless it has been saved to a permanent memory device. The transfer of the information in the form of electrical signals also requires power to

Exhibit 3.1 A monitor display of four programs running at the same time

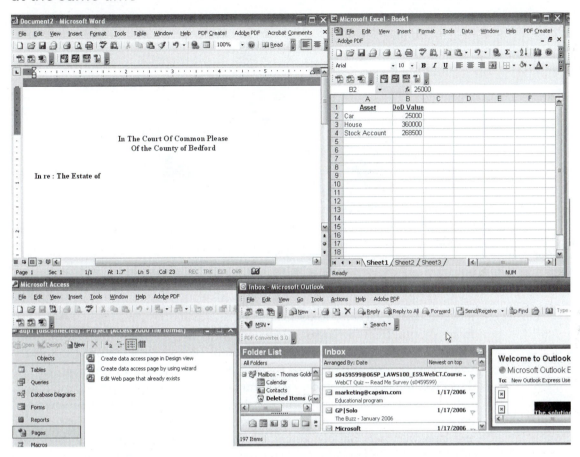

write the information on devices such as magnetic tape, floppy disks, or hard disk drives, or to portable memory devices like USB memory devices, or removable memory cards such as the popular secure digital (SD) cards, CDs or DVDs. These permanent memory devices do not require power to retain data—only to write or read the data to or from a computer.

Uninterruptible power supply (UPS) battery backup systems for the computer are used frequently to guard against loss of the "work-in-process" files when there is a short-term power loss or long-term outage. A UPS is a battery system that can supply power to a computer or computer peripheral for a short period of time. The length of time the computer will continue to work after loss of its permanent power supply depends on the size of the battery in the UPS, and may be as short as a few minutes or as long as an hour or more. The UPS is designed to allow time to save the current work-in-process files and shut down the computer normally in the event of a major power outage.

Uninterruptible Power Supply (UPS)
A battery system that can supply power to a computer or computer peripheral for a short period of time.

COMPUTER SYSTEMS

Most small and medium size offices use personal computers **(PCs)**. But some larger firms, corporations, and governmental offices use large centralized computer systems referred to as mainframes. The terminology comes from the original computer systems, which were large, complicated machines, and usually required a temperature- and humidity-controlled environment for operational stability. While this is not necessarily true of large-scale systems today, there has been a substantial

PC
Personal computer.

Exhibit 3.2 A small office or home computer: a file server, and two workstations

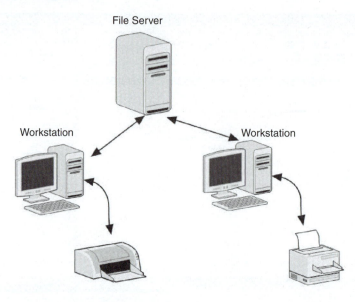

move in most legal firms to personal-computer–based systems, some of which are more powerful than the largest original mainframes. Mainframes are typically used by organizations to handle bulk data processing such as census information, statistical computations, and financial transaction processing. Early mainframes had no direct user interface and processed information in batches using paper punch cards. Later versions allowed user interface and were used as timesharing computers supporting up to thousands of simultaneous users through specialized user terminals and later with personal computers. Those working in government legal departments may still find mainframes being used within their organizations.

The scope of this book is limited to the personal computer system.

Typical systems in use today are the stand-alone computer or the networked computer. The **stand-alone computer** is one on which all the software used is installed and on which all the data or files are electronically stored. The **networked computer** may be any combination of **workstations** (stand-alone computers) electronically connected, usually with a central computer that acts as a **server** on which files and data are stored for access to all other computers and shared software programs. Exhibit 3.2 shows an example of a small office or home network.

The server acts as the traffic cop for the connected computers, allowing or denying access as needed. Advanced systems may include multiple networks of workstations-servers connected with each other in the same physical location or in remote locations such as offices in other cities.

All computers, from the smallest digital watch to the largest mainframe, have some form of device for input, for output, and internal hardware for processing. Some devices are used only for input like the keyboard, mouse, and scanner. Others are used only for output like the monitor or printer. Other memory storage devices may be used for storage of information and processed information, including tape backup drives, rewritable CDs, and USB memory cards.

Some of the components of a computer system are inside the computer; others are external devices that "plug in" to the computer. The devices that plug in use one of a number of standardized connectors or plugs. Part of the confusion for users is that there is no standard location for some of these connections; ones shown in Exhibit 3.3 are on the front, and others are on the back of the computer.

Stand-alone Computer
A computer on which all of the software used is installed and on which all of the data or files are electronically stored.

Networked Computer
Any combination of workstations (stand-alone computers) electronically connected, usually with a central computer that acts as a server on which files and data are stored for access to all other computers and shared software programs.

Workstation
A computer connected to a network that is used for access consisting of a monitor, input device, and computer.

Server
Any computer on a network that contains data or applications shared by users of the network on their client PCs.

Exhibit 3.3 Connectors on a personal computer (PC)

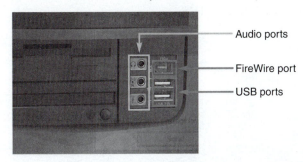

Audio ports

FireWire port

USB ports

Exhibit 3.4 Sample computer plugs and connectors

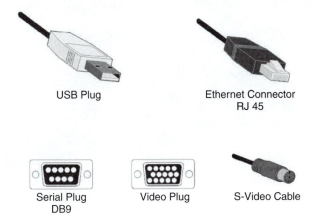

USB Plug

Ethernet Connector
RJ 45

Serial Plug
DB9

Video Plug

S-Video Cable

Some of the typical standard plugs and connectors are shown in Exhibit 3.4.

Understanding the differences in the types of plugs, **adapters**, and connectors should reduce some of the mystery of how things connect. But more importantly, being able to communicate the differences will enable you to advise the support staff or computer store of your need with less confusion and time lost trying different parts or waiting for a service call.

The inside of a computer should not be any more of a mystery than the connectors. The largest item in a computer is the motherboard. The motherboard is the printed circuit on which components are installed permanently or may be added or removed, with connectors and sockets into which items like memory modules are plugged. Desktop computers are easily opened for access to the main components on the motherboard parts, as shown in Exhibit 3.5.

Most desktops are designed to allow the user to add additional components or replace existing components. The component most commonly added to desktops is additional memory modules. New or updated versions of software programs frequently require more memory for efficiently processing the information. Adding additional memory is as simple as plugging in a new memory module of the speed, type, and size specified for the particular computer in an available memory slot. Exhibit 3.6 shows a memory module in a motherboard.

Since each add-on device has its own type of slot and a system of notches to prevent improper installation, the process is fairly simple.

Adding components or memory is usually a function of the support staff, but in smaller offices members of the legal team may find that they themselves *are* the support staff and should at least understand the process. It should be noted that the

Adapters
Devices for changing the connection on a connector to a different configuration.

Caution should always be taken to prevent static electricity by grounding oneself, by touching a metal part of the case before touching the components or the inside of the computer.

Exhibit 3.5 Inside of a typical desktop PC showing the motherboard and components

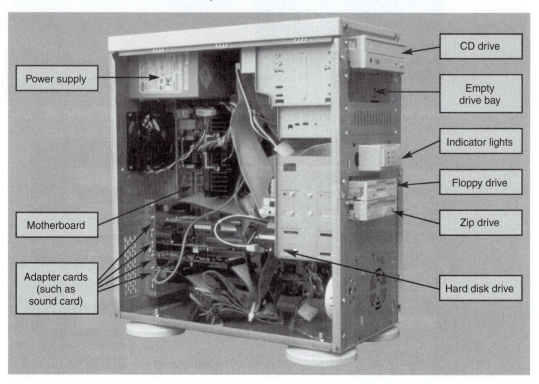

Exhibit 3.6 A PC memory module in a motherboard

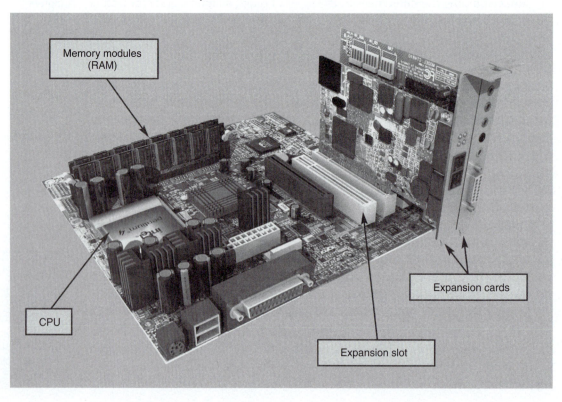

only services users may perform on most laptops are adding memory modules or replacing a hard disk drive. All other components are part of the motherboard and are not replaceable except by factory authorized repair facilities.

PORTABLE COMPUTER SYSTEMS

With the increase in electronic access and improved communications, the contemporary legal team has become more mobile. The legal team frequently will work outside the traditional office, in clients' places of business, government offices, and courthouses locally or across the state, the country, or the world. The personal computer is no longer limited to the large, practically immovable computer and monitor combination; it is highly portable in the form of a laptop computer.

New battery and CPU technology has reduced power consumption, allowing the newest generation of laptops to run faster and for longer periods of time, as long as twelve hours. Some laptops weigh less than four pounds, with full keyboard, large screen, and the ability to plug in all the same peripherals as the desktop system, including external keyboard, mouse, monitor, printer, scanner, and projection unit.

Laptops

The modern **laptop** is a powerful full-function wireless device. Laptop computers can support multiple input and output devices, such as document scanners and projection devices for making courtroom presentations. Most of the newer generations of laptop computers also have built-in wireless Internet and network connections.

Laptop
Smaller, portable computer.

One issue with laptops is battery life. Older models of laptops used CPUs that required more power, resulting in shorter battery usage before recharging. Newer CPUs, in addition to being faster and more powerful, use less battery power, resulting in longer work sessions before charging or looking for an electrical outlet to plug in the AC power adapter.

Being able to connect with the peripherals found outside the office may require a setup procedure to add the necessary software programs, called drivers, that allow the computer to communicate with these devices.

Security is a major concern with laptops. The advantage of the laptop is portability and reduced size. The disadvantage is the ease of it being stolen from checked luggage, hotel rooms, and unattended automobiles. The news is filled with the stories of lost, stolen, or "missing" laptops containing confidential information.

Tablet PC

A **tablet PC** is a laptop that allows input from a pen device instead of a mouse or keyboard. The screens on tablets become the writing surface, like a pad of paper. A special pen, called a stylus, is used instead of ink to write on the tablet. With appropriate software, the input in the form of handwriting can be converted to traditional typed format and inputted into word processing documents or saved as graphic images.

Tablet PC
Laptop that allows input from a pen device instead of a mouse or keyboard.

Mobile Devices

The contemporary mobile device is usually a multifunction device. It may be the laptop or tablet PC just described, or it may be a smaller handheld device like a personal digital assistant (PDA), or a smartphone like the Blackberry or Apple iPhone. A PDA or smartphone may be of almost any size, though small is usually

preferred, and the smaller the better. They perform any number of functions—telephone, camera, e-mail receipt and sending, text messaging, playing music, playing videos, connecting to the Internet with a browser, maintaining calendars, telephone directories, and reminder notes, and new features are introduced every day. It is not unusual to see attorneys, even in court, receive e-mails and text messages on their PDAs. They have become, for many, the portable office assistant, replacing the small combination pocket-calendar/phone book. Many features of the laptop are now found in the PDA, like e-mail and Internet functions, in many cases replacing the need to carry a portable or laptop computer just to send and receive e-mail when out of the office.

Personal digital assistants (PDAs) are handheld computers combining elements of computing, telephone/fax, Internet, and networking in a single device. The PDA can be used as a cellular phone, fax sender, Web browser, and personal organizer. Examples of PDA devices include the popular Palm Pilot.

Smartphones combine both mobile phone and handheld computer functions into a single device. For many people, smartphones have replaced PDAs, as the functions performed by each have been combined, such as the very popular Blackberry, which can be used to make and receive calls, send and receive e-mail and text messages, browse the Web, and to keep a personal calendar, telephone contact list, and task list that can be synchronized with a desktop containing a copy of all the same information. Some also have built-in maps, global positioning system (GPS) capability, and, for the bored, computer games and a built-in camera, all usable wirelessly almost anywhere in the world. Examples of smartphones include the Treo, Blackberry, Nokia, and T-Mobile Sidekick.

SOFTWARE

Software programs provide instructions to the computer hardware for internal operations and to perform specific tasks, such as preparing documents, sorting information, performing computations, and creating and presenting graphic displays. These are the software programs used in the management of the law office and the management of client cases.

OPERATING SYSTEMS

The operating system is a basic set of instructions to the computer on how to handle basic functions, such as how to process input from "input devices" such as the keyboard and the mouse, the order in which to process information, and what to show on the computer monitor. The operating system is like the ringmaster of a circus, directing the flow of performers and the timing of the performance. A portion of the basic operating instruction set needed to start up the CPU is contained in **read only memory (ROM)**. This is a type of nonvolatile memory that does not require power to retain its contents. This basic information set instructs the CPU to look for the main operating system on the designated device, usually a hard disk drive or CD. This setup allows a computer to start and the user to use the CD to install the new operating system.

PC, Apple, and Linux Operating Systems

The two most popular computer systems are the PC, or personal computer, and the Apple. The original designs of these two systems were built around different central processor system chips manufactured by different companies—Intel in the case of the PC, and Motorola in the case of Apple. Each computer system requires its own unique operating system.

Although both computer systems have advocates, the PC has a dominant position in the legal and business communities where the main use is text and mathematical computations in the form of word processing and spreadsheets. The Apple system achieved the dominant position in the graphic and artistic communities, and to some extent among computer game players. New models of both systems have software that permits the other computer system software to run on the competitive machine.

Apple in 2006 started to utilize the same CPU manufacturer as the PC manufacturers use, allowing the new Apple computers to use software for both systems on its computers without any additional software to interpret the software instruction of the other system.

Microsoft Windows is the most commonly used computer operating system for the personal computer. A number of different versions of the Windows operating system are found in the workplace with the latest versions, such as Windows XP and Vista, designed to take advantage of increased computer operating speeds and to better display screen graphics. The original PC operating systems did not provide for the **graphic user interface (GUI)**, which everyone has now come to expect. Exhibit 3.7 shows a command line interface and a graphic user interface.

Graphic User Interface (GUI)
A set of screen presentations and metaphors that utilize graphic elements such as icons in an attempt to make an operating system easier to use.

Exhibit 3.7 A Windows screen showing the command line within a GUI interface

Over time the PC and the Apple systems have come to have similar appearances, and software is generally provided by most software companies for both systems, sometimes on the same CD.

Among the newer computer operating systems gaining followers is the Linux operating system, a popular version supplied by Sun Microsystems. This is an operating system offered by its developer as an alternative to the Microsoft operating system, provided without a licensing or royalty fee, with the agreement that any improvements will be made available without a fee to anyone using the Linux operating system.

Mobile Operating Systems (Mobile OS)

Mobile Operating System
The software that controls the functions of mobile operating devices.

Like a computer *operating system*, a **mobile operating system** is the software platform on top of which other programs run. The operating system is responsible for determining the functions and features available on the device. The mobile operating system will also determine which third-party applications can be used on the device. Some of the more common and well-known mobile operating systems include the following:

Symbian OS is a standard operating system for smartphones, licensed by most of the world's smartphone manufacturers.

Windows mobile operating system from Microsoft is used on a variety of devices from manufacturers like Dell, HP, Motorola, and Palm.

Palm OS
A proprietary computer operating system for personal digital assistants and smartphones.

Palm OS, introduced in 1996, provides mobile devices with essential business tools, as well as capability to access the Internet.

Utility Software

Utility Software
Programs that perform functions in the background related to the operation of the computer.

Utility software, or simply utilities, are programs that perform functions in the background related to the operation of the computer. Perhaps the most commonly used utility program is the antivirus software, like Norton AntiVirus or PC-cillin Antivirus from Trend Micro that blocks, searches for, and isolates or eliminates computer viruses. Utility programs are used for viewing documents like Adobe Reader for PDF files, Quicktime or Realplayer for videos or Webex for viewing online Webinars. Other utility programs are used to compress or uncompress program and data files (commonly referred to as zip or unzip programs), create backups of programs and hard drives, and limit access to computers and computer systems such as firewall and parental blocking programs.

Applications Software

Applications Software
A collection of one or more related software programs that enables a user to enter, store, view, modify, or extract information from files or databases. The term is commonly used in place of "program" or "software." Applications may include word processors, Internet browsing tools, and spreadsheets.

Applications software is a term used to describe the class of software used generically by most users for basic functions such as word processing, preparing presentations or electronic spreadsheets. These are the generic programs that are used across different industries and not designed specifically for a particular profession or industry.

Office Suite Software

Office Software Suites
The software consists of commonly used office software programs that manage data and database programs; manipulate financial or numeric information, spreadsheet programs; or displayed images and presentation graphics programs.

Office software suites are sets of commonly used office applications software programs like word processing programs, database programs, spreadsheet programs, and graphics and presentation graphics programs. Each of the programs can be used alone, such as Microsoft Word or Corel WordPerfect, but are packaged together with other stand-alone programs. Some of the programs in the two most common office suites, Microsoft Office and Corel WordPerfect, are shown in Exhibit 3.8.

Exhibit 3.8 Software suite comparison chart

	Microsoft Office	**Corel WordPerfect Office X3**
Word processor	Word	WordPerfect
Spreadsheet	Excel	Quattro Pro
Database	Access	Paradox
Presentation graphics	PowerPoint	Presentation X3
Graphics	Visio	Presentation Graphics X3

The software suites usually are delivered on one CD or as a set of CDs, enabling all the programs to be loaded at one time, which simplifies and saves installation time. With common features and appearance, it is easier to switch between programs and copy information between the programs, like copying part of a spreadsheet into a word processing document.

Software Integration

Software suites provide a direct **integration** between the different software programs in the suite. Charts, graphs, and spreadsheets are easily copied and inserted between word processor, spreadsheet, and graphics programs in the MS Office or Corel Office suites. The same integration also exists between many programs of different software companies. Some programs allow direct export to other programs such as NoteMap from CaseSoft into Word by Microsoft or, to make it even easier, adding a button to the program toolbar such as the Adobe Acrobat button on the MS Word screen.

During the life cycle of a case or trial the legal team frequently will use different programs to serve specific needs. At the beginning of a case, CaseMap might be used to organize the factual issues. With a complete understanding of the issues, the organization of the documents may be most efficiently handled using a litigation support tool like Summation or Concordance, and finally the trial presentation may be done using TrialDirector or Sanction. With all the programs designed to allow the integration of the data from the others, a seamless workflow is possible, saving time and ultimately money for the client.

Specialty Applications Programs

Specialty applications programs are software programs that are industry specific. It is software created to perform functions for the specific industry, like case management in the law office. Computers are becoming more and more powerful, operating at faster speeds and with more operating and storage memory. Software programs are getting more powerful and capable of performing more complex functions on more data. In the past many companies had to have software custom written to perform the desired functions, functions others in the same industry also needed performed. Contemporary off-the-shelf specialty applications software frequently performs all the desired functions and sometimes more, at a substantial savings in cost and time in installing and testing the custom software before actual use. To some extent, at least in the legal community, the customization is limited, such as customized input screens or specialized reports.

Whereas older models of computers can perform only basic word processing and data management, newer, more powerful computers can perform complex functions seamlessly, thereby permitting management of law office functions and management of cases and litigation.

Software Integration
Direct input from one program into another program.

Specialty Applications Programs
Specialty programs combine many of the basic functions found in software suites, word processing, database management, spreadsheets, and graphic presentations to perform law office case and litigation management.

Specialty application programs combine many of the basic functions found in software suites, word processing, database management, spreadsheets, and graphic presentations to perform law office case and litigation management. They simplify the operation with the use of customized input screens and preset report generators designed for the law office.

Legal specialty software programs fall generally into the following categories:

Legal Specialty Software
Programs that combine functions found in software suites for performing law office management functions.

- Office management
- Case management
- Litigation support
- Transcript management
- Trial presentation

Of the office management specialty application programs, the most basic are the time and billing programs. These provide a standard input screen to record and store the time spent on a client's case, and, with a simple request, an invoice for a given client, automatically sorting the data, applying the billing rates, and printing out an invoice.

Popular programs in this group are:

- Tabs3 from Software Technology, Inc.
- AbacusLaw from Abacus Data Systems, Inc.
- ProLaw from Thomson Elite
- PCLaw from LexisNexis
- Timeslips from Sage

Early versions of time reporting software were limited to timekeeping. With faster computers and greater memory capacity, most of these programs today have other features integrated into them, such as accounting functions to track costs and expenses, and practice management functions such as calendar and contact management.

SOFTWARE INSTALLATION

Installing software should be easy. Most software is provided in a format that provides automatic installation. Just insert the CD and the program launches its own installation or setup program—at least that is the ideal situation. Achieving automatic installations requires a little preliminary effort to determine compatibility and capacity.

Compatibility
In software usage, designed to work on a particular type of computer or operating system.

Detailed instruction for installing programs can be found in Appendix 2.

Software Compatibility
Software for the type of computer on which it is to be used.

Capacity, with Regard to Computers
The technical specifications such as CPU speed and computer memory.

Compatibility is usually a matter of buying software for the type of computer used.

PC or Apple: Some programs are provided in both formats, but many are not. Advertisements for software typically specify the "platform" as PC or Apple. Software packages also offer the same information on a side panel.

Compatibility is not the only issue. Just as important is one of **capacity** or ability of the particular computer to run the software. Capacity in this regard refers to the technical specification of the computer. How fast is the CPU, does it have enough memory to hold the program (hard drive space), enough random access memory (RAM) to run the program, and the necessary input device, such as a scanner for a scanning program, or the necessary output device, such as a color printer or high resolution graphics system?

Minimum requirements can change as software is revised and upgraded. Exhibit 3.9 shows how the requirements have changed from version 2003 to version 2007 of the Microsoft Office Professional Suite. In addition to the *minimum*

Exhibit 3.9 Comparison of requirements for the 2003 and 2007 versions of Microsoft Office Professional Suite software systems

	Microsoft Office Professional Edition 2003	Microsoft Office Professional Edition 2007
Computer and processor	PC with an Intel Pentium 233-MHz or faster processor (Pentium III recommended); optional installation of Business Contact Manager for Outlook 2003 requires a 450-MHz or faster processor (Pentium III recommended)	500 megahertz (MHz) processor or higher[1]
Memory	128 megabytes (MB) of RAM or higher; optional installation of Business Contact Manager for Outlook 2003 requires 256 MB of RAM	256 megabyte (MB) RAM or higher[1,2]
Hard disk	420 MB of available hard disk space; optional installation files cache (recommended) requires an additional 200 MB of available hard disk space; optional installation of Business Contact Manager for Outlook 2003 requires an additional 190 MB of available hard disk space	2 gigabyte (GB); a portion of this disk space will be freed after installation if the original download package is removed from the hard drive
Drive	CD-ROM or DVD drive	CD-ROM or DVD drive
Display	Super VGA (800 × 600) or higher-resolution monitor	1024 × 768 or higher-resolution monitor
Operating system	Microsoft Windows 2000 with Service Pack 3 (SP3), Windows XP, or later	Microsoft Windows XP with Service Pack (SP2), Windows Server 2003 with SP1, or later operating system[3]
Sound card	Speech recognition requires close talk Microphone and audio output device	Speech recognition requires close talk Microphone and audio output device

Footnotes: Microsoft information is available at: http://office.microsoft.com/enus/products/HA101668651033.aspx

[1]gigahertz (GHz) processor or higher and 512 MB RAM or higher recommended for **Business Contact Manager.** Business Contact Manager not available in all languages.

[2]512 MB RAM or higher recommended for **Outlook Instant Search.** Grammar and contextual spelling in **Word** is not turned on unless the machine has 1 GB memory.

[3]Office Clean-up wizard not available on 64 bit OS. Internet fax not available on 64 bit OS.

and *recommended* computer requirements, there are also requirements for optimal use of software as shown in Exhibit 3.10 for Sanction II by Verdict Systems trial presentation software. The difference between minimum and recommended requirements is that **minimum requirements** will allow the computer to function with one program open at a time, but it may not run as fast as desired, or as it would if there were more computer resources such as more memory and a faster processor.

Minimum Requirements
The minimum computer requirements in terms of memory, speed, and other characteristics necessary for software to run properly.

Exhibit 3.10 Sanction Trial Presentation Software minimum, recommended, and optimal system requirements

Minimum System Requirements	Recommended Configuration	Optimal System Configuration
1. Windows 98-XP 2. Pentium III 3. 128 MB RAM 4. 1024 × 768 (XGA) 5. 16-Bit Color Depth 6. Sound Card Enabled 7. Internet Explorer 5.5+ 8. CD-ROM Drive	1. Windows 2000, XP 2. Pentium III 1.0 Ghz 3. 256 MB RAM 4. 1024 × 768 (XGA) 5. 24-Bit Color Depth 6. Sound Card Enabled 7. Internet Explorer 6 8. CD-ROM Drive	1. Windows XP 2. Pentium 4 2.4 Ghz+ 3. 512 MB + RAM 4. 1024 × 768 (XGA) 5. 32-Bit Color Depth 6. Sound Card Enabled 7. Internet Explorer 6+ 8. CD-ROM or DVD-ROM Drive
Additional Notes: • You will want to run your digital video from the hard drive if possible. CD-ROMs cannot read the information as fast as your hard drive, so you will see lagging performance if you view the video from the CD-ROM. • Hard drive capacity is critical when using digital video. Because each 2 hr video is approximately 640 MB, hard drive capacity becomes more and more important as you use video. • Sound cards are needed for Audio/Video Playback. **Additional information is available at:** http://www.verdictsystems.com/		

Recommended Computer Requirements
Computer system configuration of memory, speed, and other characteristics for the maximum utilization of the software.

The **recommended requirements** specifications allow for the full utilization of the software. Again, running multiple programs at the same time will cause a slowdown in overall performance and may result in a computer "crash" if there are conflicts in sharing the memory and CPU resources.

LICENSE ISSUES

Software is rarely sold outright to the end user. It is usually licensed for use by the end user subject to certain limitations and restrictions. These are found in the end user license agreement that the user must, as part of the installation process, accept to continue the installation.

End User License Agreement (EULA)
The contract between the software company and the user authorizing the use and setting limitations for use of the program.

End User License Agreement (EULA)

An **end user license agreement (EULA)** is the agreement with the software vendor that authorizes and specifies the terms for the legal use of the software. For example, an end user license for an educational version of software is violated when used for commercial purposes. A license for one user is violated when used by multiple simultaneous users. Types of software licenses include:

Single-User License

A **single-user license** authorizes installation of the software on one computer. Some companies permit installation on one main or desktop computer and one secondary computer like a home or portable computer that is used by the same person but not at the same time.

Single-User License
Authorizes the installation of software on one computer.

Multi-User License

A **multi-user license** authorizes installation on multiple computers. Software is authorized for the number of computers for which a license is purchased, typically 3, 5, 10, 25 or more simultaneous users.

Multi-User License
Authorizes the installation of software on multiple computers.

Network License

A **network license** authorizes the use of the software on a computer network with a specified number of simultaneous users on the network. In some network environments such as schools, corporate settings, and large law firms the number of simultaneous licensed users may be in the hundreds or thousands.

Network License
Authorizes the use of the software on a computer network with a specified number of simultaneous users on the network.

Demo Version

Demo versions or trial versions of software are for making a determination of suitability for purchase. Most trial or demo versions restrict the use of the software in the EULA. Continued use beyond the scope of the trial or demonstration period is usually a violation of the EULA.

Shareware or Freeware

Shareware or **freeware** is generally software that the author has chosen to make available free to the using public on the honor system. Some restrict its use to noncommercial applications; others set no limitations. Shareware has become a term used to describe the "try it before buying" software that can be downloaded from the Internet. In some cases a request for contribution may be made or a fixed payment required to continue to use or receive updates and full feature use. Some freeware is widely used and relied upon. Others are not reliable and may in fact have a negative impact on the computer. Before using freeware it is wise to check with a respected reviewer of software like *PC Magazine* or ZDNet.com for reviews and experience reported by users.

Shareware
Software that the author has chosen to make available free to the using public on the honor system.

Freeware
Software distributed, generally over the Internet, at no charge to the user.

INSTALLATION AND ANTIVIRUS PROGRAMS

It is generally a good idea to turn off or close all other programs when installing a new software program. This avoids potential conflicts in the use of common program elements. In some cases the computer antivirus software must also be turned off to allow the program to install the necessary files and install the necessary entries in the operating system. Antivirus programs see these efforts as a potential attack on the integrity of the computer system and may ask if it is OK to proceed or block the entry needed for the new program to run. Antivirus programs like Norton will allow the antivirus function to be stopped temporarily, showing a screen with a suggested time period during which it will not be protecting the computer. Once the time has elapsed the program resumes automatically. The danger in turning the antivirus program off is that the Internet connection may still be active during the installation period. The safest procedure is to disconnect from the network completely before installing the new software. Reconnection with the virus protection active can be resumed if necessary to allow the new program to connect with the software vendor for registration or activation.

Making a Backup of the Program

It is a good idea to have an archive version of your programs for that one time when you are facing a deadline and the entire computer crashes, catches on fire, or is struck by lightning.

If your computer has a CD drive that allows you to make CDs the process is simple. Insert the appropriate CD media and you can generally just copy and paste the program to the CD and burn a copy.

Checklist ✓   TECHNOLOGY NEEDED FOR YOUR OFFICE

- Computers
   One for each attorney and secretary/legal assistant
- Backup system: tapes, external hard drives, Internet storage
- Printer
- Copier
- Scanner
- All-in-one printer/scanner/copier
- Telephone system
- Fax machine
- Digital dictation software and transcription equipment
- Access to online legal research service (e.g., Westlaw, Lexis)
- Software
   Network operating software (e.g., Novell, Windows, Linux)
   Desktop operating software (e.g., Windows XP)
   Office suite: word processing, spreadsheet, database, presentation software (Microsoft or Corel)
   Calendaring, docket control
   Time and billing
   Accounting, payroll
   Case management
   Conflict of interest checking
   Practice-area-specific (e.g., real estate, bankruptcy, estate planning, probate, foreclosure, tax, etc.)
- Electronics
   Television set with VCR
   Video camera
   35 mm camera
   Instant camera/digital camera
   Stereo system

Source: The Practice Management Assistance Program South Carolina State Bar, www.scbar.org

NETWORKS

The first computers in law offices, as said earlier, generally consisted of a computer, a monitor, and a printer. In the contemporary law office this is called a **workstation**. A **network** is a group of workstations connected together. This may be as little as two workstations, or in large law firms, hundreds of workstations and other peripheral devices such as shared printers and fax machines all connected through a **network file server**. Every computerized device, like a computer, printer, or fax machine that is connected to a network is also referred to as a **host**. A host that shares its resources is also called a server. Exhibit 3.11 shows a typical computer network system in a small law office.

A network **file server** is generally a separate computer that acts as the traffic cop of the system, controlling the flow of information between workstations and the file server and other peripheral devices, and requests to use the resources of the system or access data stored on the system.

Like the computer that requires an **operating system** to run, the server requires network operating software that tells it how to communicate with the connected workstations and peripheral devices. These computers and devices are referred to as **connections**.

Networks come in all sizes, from the smallest home or office network of two computers to very large networks in schools, businesses, and government. And, combinations of networks come in all sizes, from the two connected networks of a main office and a branch office, to the largest combinations of networks, the Internet.

Network
A group of computers or devices that is connected together for the exchange of data and sharing of resources.

Network File Server
A computer that controls the flow of information over the network.

Host
Every computerized device, like a computer, printer, or fax machine that is connected to a network.

File Server
A computer in a network that controls the flow of information in the network.

Network Operating System
Computer software that controls the functions and flow of information over the network.

Connections
The way in which workstations, file servers, and other peripheral devices are joined to the network.

Exhibit 3.11 A small office network with a file server and workstations connected through a hub

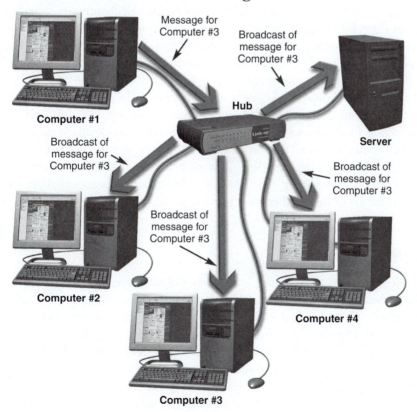

Checklist ✓   PURCHASING HARDWARE OR SOFTWARE

- Determine the need to automate a function.
- Is the computer or technology the best way to solve the problem?
- Is this a function best performed in-house or by using a consultant?
- What will the software and implementation cost, including training?
- What software or hardware is available?
- Is there a demo version to try out before buying?
- How many licensed copies will be needed?
- How many hardware items will need to be acquired?
- Who will install and support it?
- Can it be supported by the in-house team?
- How much will an outside maintenance contract cost?
- Will computers currently in place support the new software or hardware?

Local Area Networks

Local Area Network (LAN)
Usually refers to a network of computers in a single building or other discrete location.

A **local area network (LAN)** is a computer network covering a local area like an office, home, or a building or a group of buildings.

Wide Area Networks

Wide Area Network (WAN)
Network generally covering a large geographic area and is made up of other networks; a network of networks.

A **wide area network (WAN)** is a network generally covering a large geographic area and is made up of other networks, a "network of networks." The largest WAN is the Internet. Time can be saved by electronically sharing information instead of personally or by having a courier deliver paper copies of documents, whether on a different floor, building, or city. Many firms—some as small as two people—maintain multiple office sites, such as a center-city and a suburban office location, or a main office and a satellite office across from the courthouse. Each of these offices may have a separate computer network.

Exhibit 3.12 shows a WAN of three office networks connected using the Internet. With high-speed communications lines, these separate networks may be connected to form a network of networks. Access to a workstation on one of the networks allows access to the other networks in the system and the peripherals attached to the network, including network printers. This allows a person in one office to print documents on a printer in another office. Files may be shared among all the members of the legal team regardless of the office in which they are physically located.

Wireless Networks

Wireless Network
Computers on the network communicate over the airwaves wirelessly instead of through wired connections.

A **wireless network** is the same as any other network except that the computers on the network communicate over the airwaves wirelessly instead of through wired connections. The advantages are ease of setup and freedom to work without a cable or wire connection. Wireless laptops are seen everywhere using wireless technology to connect to the Internet. This may be a connection to the company or firm through the Internet to access company or firm files. Within the large office environment it may be a wireless connection to the network without an Internet intermediary. In both cases the cautions are the same. If you can connect using

Exhibit 3.12 Typical WAN of three office locations using the Internet

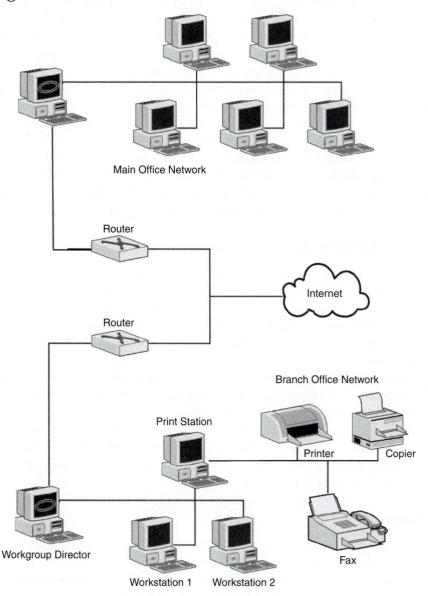

Main Office Network

Router

Internet

Router

Branch Office Network

Print Station

Printer   Copier

Workgroup Director

Fax

Workstation 1   Workstation 2

wireless tools, so can others unless appropriate precautions are taken to limit access to authorized personnel.

Municipal Area Network

A **municipal area network (MAN)** is a network in a specific geographic municipality, usually a wireless network. The cities of Philadelphia and New Orleans provide MANs.

Municipal Area Network (MAN)
A network in a specific geographic municipality, usually a wireless network.

COMPUTER AND NETWORK SECURITY ISSUES

Security has become a critical issue as law offices, courts, and clients become more dependent upon the use of the computer and the Internet. When there is only a single computer, the security concern is limited to introducing a program that does not work properly. With computer networks, there is the potential to adversely impact every workstation on the network and the network file server itself. On a network, any workstation is a potential input source of problems in the form of software programs that could corrupt the system or the files stored on the system. While not common, there are instances of employees introducing annoying or potentially harmful programs as a method of getting even with an employer.

Part of the solution to these kinds of issues is to limit access to the network, including limiting the ability to access the file server from workstations and limiting the ability or right to make changes to operating systems and limit other activity to the saving of documents. Limiting access to files on a file server is one method to ensure confidentiality in a large office. File access can be limited by password-protecting files and granting password access only to those with a need to access and work on those specific files. Because each file or set of files, called folders, can be password-protected, ethical walls can be established by restricting access to just those on the legal team who are working on a case.

Network Rights and Privileges

Security Protocols
Software programs that limit access to the file server and peripherals such as printers or other workstations.

Network Rights and Privileges
Rights to access the different information on the network.

Network Administrator
The person with the highest level of access or authority to the network.

Network software programs have **security protocols,** methods used to limit the right to access the file server and peripherals such as printers or other workstations. These rights to access the server and the other devices are sometimes called **network rights and privileges.** The rights or privileges determine who has access to the server, the data stored on the server, and the flow of information between connections.

Generally the person with the highest level access is called the **network administrator**. Law offices that use network servers generally use these servers as the central repository for all electronic files.

Although an individual workstation can store documents or data on the workstation, it is usually stored centrally. This offers a level of protection by limiting access to those who have the proper authorization, most often requiring a password for access. It also makes backing up data easier.

Passwords

Passwords
Combinations of letters, numbers, and symbols to restrict access to files and computers.

Network connection can be restricted in a number of ways. **Passwords,** frequently letter and number combinations, offer some degree of protection. But protection is lost when passwords are left in open view on the sides of computer monitors or keyboards because they are hard to remember, or are obvious like using the word *password* as the password, the person's birthday, pet name, or a child's name.

More secure is a limitation that allows access only to preapproved computerized devices on which a special code has been entered. But, anyone with access to the computer who can figure out the password can gain access. Newer methods to limit access include thumbprint devices that scan the thumbprint of the user and allow only those preapproved for access. The "science fiction" retinal scan is also becoming a reality in some security systems.

Unauthorized Network Access

The use of the Internet from workstations has introduced the security concern about unauthorized parties gaining access to the computer network; this is sometimes referred to as "hacking." In some instances the unauthorized party wants to gain access to information in files stored on the network. In other cases, the purpose of the unauthorized access is to undermine the integrity of the system by causing modification to files and programs or to introduce computer viruses that can cause minor inconvenience or even destroy entire systems by deleting files, programs, and operating systems.

A concern of many network administrators is the use of the network by authorized users to access and bring into the network unauthorized material. Businesses and schools do not want their networks and Internet connections used for certain kinds of activity, such as accessing pornography or gambling sites or sites used for personal business, like monitoring the stock market. The display and storage of illegal material can have liability issues for the owner of the network. More frequently is that the use for things like online gaming and stock market access puts a burden on the resources of the system, slowing it down and in some cases causing a complete shutdown of the system.

Firewalls

A **firewall** is a program designed to limit access to a computer or to a computer network system. Depending upon the complexity of the program, it may restrict total access without proper validation in the form of passwords or limit all access to the system for certain kinds of programs or sources not deemed to be acceptable to the network or system administrator. For example, many parents use a form of a firewall designed to limit children's access to certain kinds of programs and certain sites on the Internet that are deemed to be unacceptable. A firewall can be a two-edged sword: it prevents unauthorized access to the network, such as hackers accessing files on the firm's computer or other Internet connection, but it may also prevent working at an off-site location like a courthouse or client's office, or connecting with an educational institution to take an online course. It is important to check a connection to be sure it will allow data to be accessed from a remote location and sent as planned before it is needed for trial, depositions, or presentations. With enough time, any issue may be resolved with the local system administrator.

Firewalls
Programs designed to limit access to authorized users in an application.

Computer Viruses

Unfortunately, some computer-knowledgeable people take sadistic pleasure in developing and disseminating programs that attack and destroy computer programs, internal computer operating systems, and occasionally even the hard disk drives of computers. These programs are known as **computer viruses**. Viruses range from those that create minor inconvenience to those that can destroy data and cause computer shutdowns.

Some simple precautions can prevent disaster. Virus protection programs, such as those sold by Norton, McAfee, and others, are as important to have on your computer as the computer operating system itself. This should be the first program loaded on a new computer.

Computer Virus
A program that attacks and destroys computer programs, internal computer operating systems, and occasionally the hard drive of computers.

Antivirus Software

Antivirus software programs scan the computer to identify the presence of viruses, and the better programs eliminate the virus. The software does this by scanning the computer for software code of patterns of known viruses. Most of the major antivirus software companies are constantly checking on reports of new viruses and downloading the new patterns to subscribers on a daily or sometimes more frequent basis. Users of computers must accept the fact that if they are the first one to be sent the new virus or if they do not have a current version of the antivirus software, there is no protection available.

Antivirus Software
Programs that scan the computer to identify the presence of viruses; the better programs eliminate the virus.

Preventing viruses is not easy, but there are some preliminary precautions that can be taken. Files or attachments in e-mails from an unknown source should not be opened or installed. Every disk should be scanned with an antivirus program before being used. Files that are downloaded from other computers or over the Internet also should be checked. As good as these programs are, they quickly go out of date as new viruses are created and unleashed. Therefore, these virus checking programs should be updated regularly.

Backing Up Data

Backup
To create a copy of data as a precaution against the loss or damage of the original data.

With everything on one file server, the **backup** of data can be automated to make copies of everyone's files and not just the files on workstations of those who remember to back up their computers. Backing up data regularly is an essential function to prevent loss of critical files and office data in the event of a disaster such as a flood, fire, earthquake, or tornado.

Good backup policy is to back up the file server daily and store the duplicate copy in a safe location away from the server location, such as a fireproof safe or a bank safe deposit box. Imagine trying to reconstruct files, court-filed documents, and other essential information after a devastating hurricane and resultant flood that destroys a law firm and courthouse paper records, as occurred in New Orleans in 2005 as a result of Hurricane Katrina!

SUMMARY

CHAPTER 3
COMPUTER HARDWARE AND SOFTWARE

Introduction to Computer Hardware and Software	Computer hardware is the term used to describe the tangible or physical parts of a computer system that must have a power source. Operating system software provides the basic instructions for starting up the computer and processing the basic input and output activity.
Computer Systems	Most small and medium size offices use personal computers (PCs). A typical system is a workstation connected to a network. The stand-alone computer is one on which all the software used is installed and on which all the data or files are electronically stored. The networked computer may be any combination of workstations (stand-alone computers) electronically connected, usually with a central computer that acts as a server on which files and data are stored for access to all other computers and shared software programs.
Portable Computer Systems	The personal computer today is highly portable in the form of a laptop computer. The modern laptop is a powerful full-function device that can support multiple input and output devices and is frequently capable of wireless access to computer networks. A tablet PC is a laptop that allows input from a pen device instead of a mouse or keyboard. Some devices like the Blackberry Smartphone and the Apple iPhone have many of the features of the laptop including Internet connectivity.

Mobile Devices	The contemporary mobile device is also usually a multifunction device, allowing use as a telephone, camera, and permitting e-mail receipt and sending, text messaging, playing music, playing videos, connecting to the Internet with a browser, maintaining calendars, telephone directories, and reminder notes.
Software Operating Systems	Software programs provide instructions to the computer hardware for internal operations and to perform specific tasks, such as preparing documents, sorting information, performing computations, and creating and presenting graphic displays. The operating system is a basic set of instructions to the computer on how to handle basic functions, such as how to process input from "input devices" such as the keyboard and the mouse, the order in which to process information, and what to show on the computer monitor.
PC, Apple, and Linux Operating Systems	Microsoft Windows is the most commonly used computer operating system for the personal computer. The PC and the Apple systems have come to have similar appearances, and software is generally provided by most software companies for both systems. Among the newer computer operating systems gaining followers is Sun Microsystems' Linux operating system.
Mobile Operating Systems	Software platform used for mobile devices, such as Symbian OS, Windows Mobile OS, and the Palm OS.
Utility Software	Programs that perform background functions related to the operation of the computer.
Applications Software	Applications software is a term used to describe the class of software used generically by most users for basic functions such as word processing, preparing presentations or electronic spreadsheets. Office suite software refers to sets of commonly used office software programs. Specialty application programs combine many of the basic functions found in software suites.
Software Integration	Programs designed to allow the integration of the data from one program into another frequently between software applications of different vendors. Software suites typically provide a direct integration between the different software programs in the suite.
Software Installation Issues	Most software is provided in a format that provides automatic installation. Compatibility refers to choosing software for the type of computer used. Capacity in this regard refers to the technical specification of the computer. License issues: An end user license agreement (EULA) is the agreement with the software vendor that authorizes and specifies the terms for the legal use of the software. Making a backup of the program; it is a good idea to have an archive version of your programs.

Installation and Antivirus Programs	It is generally a good idea to turn off or close all other programs when installing a new software program. This avoids potential conflicts in the use of common program elements.
Networks	A network is a group of workstations connected together.
File Server	A separate computer that acts as the traffic cop for the system controlling the flow of information and on which files are frequently stored.
Local Area Network	A small network in a location like a home or office.
Wide Area Network	Separate networks may be connected to form a "network of networks."
Wireless Network	The computers on the network communicate over the airwaves wirelessly instead of through wired connections.
Municipal Area Network	A network provided in a town or city, usually wireless.
Computer And Network Security Issues	With computer networks, there is the potential to adversely impact every workstation on the network and the network file server itself. On a network, any workstation is a potential input source of problems.
Network Rights and Privileges	Security protocols that limit access to the file server.
Network Administrator	Generally the person with the highest level security access.
Unauthorized Network Access	The use of the Internet from workstations has introduced the security concern about unauthorized parties gaining access to the computer network; this is sometimes referred to as "hacking."
Firewall	A program designed to limit access to a computer or to a computer network system.
Computer Viruses	Programs that attack and destroy computer programs, internal computer operating systems, and occasionally even the hard disk drives of computers.
Antivirus Software	Antivirus software programs scan the computer to identify the presence of viruses, and the better programs eliminate the virus.
Backing Up Data	Backing up data regularly is an essential function to prevent loss of critical files and office data in the event of a disaster such as a flood, fire, earthquake, or tornado.

KEY TERMINOLOGY

CONCEPT REVIEW QUESTIONS AND EXERCISES

1. Test your knowledge and comprehension of the topics in this chapter by completing the multiple-choice questions on the textbook Companion Website.
2. Test your knowledge and comprehension of the topics in this chapter by completing the True-False questions on the textbook Companion Website.
3. Discuss the different types of computer systems used in a law office.
4. Describe the different computer hardware used by the legal team.
5. Explain the differences between applications and specialty applications software.
6. Explain the difference between a suite of programs and integrated software.
7. Why should passwords be changed on a regular basis?
8. Describe how a computer network may be used by a law firm.
9. Explain the importance and the steps that may be taken to maintain computer and network security.
10. Explain the difference in operation of a computer with the minimum requirements and the recommended requirements. How can the user determine if his or her computer meets the minimum or recommended requirements?
11. What are the ethical issues of using unlicensed software?

12. Prepare a list of computer hardware components, including name and model numbers, of the system you use at:
    a. home
    b. work
    c. school
    d. other (e.g., public library or Internet café)
13. If you are using a PC, using the Control Panel in the Start Menu, find the System icon. Prepare a detailed description of:
    a. general information on the *system*
    b. the *registered* party
    c. the type of *processor* and its speed and memory
    d. the *computer name* of the computer as shown in System Properties
    e. the *full computer name* and the *workgroup*
14. Prepare a list of the applications software on your personal computer:
    a. manufacturers
    b. program names
    c. version
    d. registered owner
15. What ethical issues might be raised in a review of a list of applications software programs on computers in the law office?
16. Explain the functions of the components of a computer system in the law office.

17. Describe the different classes of software and the functions they perform in a law office.
18. What law office functions can be performed with the use of legal-specific applications programs?
19. What, if any, policies should be in place in the law office regarding the use of personal computers by the members of the legal team? Explain why or why not policies should be created.
20. What does the end user license for one of the Office Suite programs say about multiple uses of the software?

INTERNET EXERCISES

1. a. Use the list from Chapter 1 or prepare a checklist of *minimum* software and hardware requirements and a second of *recommended* technology needs for the start-up office. Be specific. What, if any, additional minimum or recommended items should be added to the list for a trial attorney regarding office setup?

   b. Use the Internet to find prices on the items in the checklist you prepare.

2. Use the Internet to find information on backup software and hardware. Use the Internet to locate a copy of at least one of the EULAs for a software program on your personal computer. Does it permit use on multiple machines at the same time?

PORTFOLIO ASSIGNMENTS

1. Based on the opening scenario, prepare a plan for setting up the technology systems for the new firm that can be presented to the attorney that he can share with others who are working in the office or subletting space. Explain the reasons for the plan.

2. Prepare an office policy on the use of passwords in the law office. Explain the reasons and methods to be used for the most and the least secure passwords.

SCENARIO CASE STUDY

Use the opening scenario for this chapter to answer the following questions. The setting is a new attorney in solo practice discussing with his newly hired paralegal, who has experience working in a large firm, how to set up the technology systems for the new firm.

1. What procedure or protocol should be established for adding users to the office network?
2. How can access to confidential files be limited?
3. What are the advantages of attending a technology show for the legal profession?
4. What questions should the paralegal and attorney be prepared to ask at the show?
5. What role does the future office expansion have in the initial technology decisions?
6. What hardware should be initially purchased? Be specific regarding functions and capabilities. Is this different from the list prepared in Chapter 1?
7. What software should be purchased first? Prepare a list in order of priority with essential software at the top. Explain your reasons for the selections and priority.

CONTINUING CASES AND EXERCISES

1. Update the Internet resources list from Chapter 1.
2. Download the latest version of Adobe Reader from the Adobe website: www.Adobe.com.
3. Download a new Internet browser different from the one you usually use. You may use any search engine available to locate the new browser.
4. Continue to maintain a time record as outlined in Chapter 1.

ADVANCED EXERCISES

The detailed tutorials for AbacusLaw and Tabs3 can be found on the Companion Website: www.prenhall.com/goldman.

1. Install the AbacusLaw Software and complete the tutorial for AbacusLaw.

2. Install the Tabs3 software and complete the tutorial for Tabs3.

VIDEO SCENARIO: VIDEO DEPOSITIONS

 The parent of one of the victims of the bus truck accident is not available locally for deposition. It has been agreed that his deposition may be taken by videoconferencing. To save cost and time the trial attorneys have agreed to take the deposition by videoconference.

Go to the Companion Website, select Chapter 3 from the pull down menu, and watch this video.

1. What computer hardware and software does the law firm need to have in order to conduct a deposition by videoconference?
2. What are the advantages and disadvantages of using videoconferencing technology for taking depositions?
3. What arrangement will the legal team need to make in order to take a deposition by videoconferencing?

Exhibit 4.3 The Windows search companion on a workstation

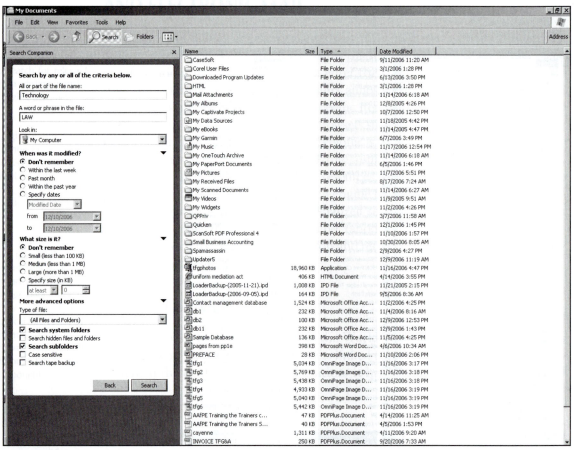

connections are made through local or national Internet service providers (ISPs) who themselves connect to a higher level national service, as shown in Exhibit 4.4.

Internet service providers (ISPs) are companies that provide users access to the World Wide Web. ISPs provide local or toll-free access numbers that many people use to connect to their service. In many communities this is a service provided by the local cable company or telephone service provider. In the past only larger offices, schools, and companies had a direct connection (hardwired, cable, fiber optic line, or dedicated telephone line, such as a **digital subscriber line [DSL]**) that eliminated the need to dial up the ISP. Increasingly, small offices and homes are able to obtain the same dedicated service from their cable or telephone company, eliminating the need to **dial up** a connection.

There are special computerized devices, such as modems and routers, and software that enable computers to "talk" with each other and send and receive messages over networks and the Internet. Exhibit 4.5 shows a modem in a network connection to the Internet, of the devices.

Modem

A **modem** is a device used to translate the electrical signals for transmission over these connections so the computers can "talk" to each other. The modem converts (modulates) the information from the keyboard and computer into a form that can

Exhibit 4.4 Typical network connected to the Internet

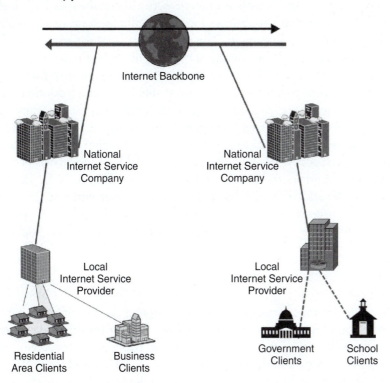

Exhibit 4.5 Modem connection

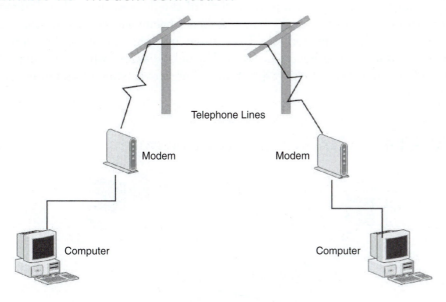

be transferred electronically over telephone lines, cable connections, fiber optic cable, and radio waves.

MO	DEM
Modulate	Demodulate

At the receiving end of the signal is another modem that reconverts (demodulates) the signal into a form usable by the computer. Depending on the modem and the ISP service, speeds of transmission vary widely. The slower the

WWW MINI EXERCISE

Use the Internet to find your local cable company and telephone company website and compare the levels of service and the prices for the Internet connection they provide.

connection provided by the modems and the service, the longer it takes to transmit and receive information. As with most services, the higher the speed, the higher the cost. It is easy to see that a multipage document will take longer to transmit or receive than a single-page document. The reasonableness of the cost of a high-speed connection depends upon the volume of pages regularly sent or received.

Perhaps less obvious is the size of the files and the number of files that are in graphic format. Most government forms are available in a graphic form rather than a text form. A single one-page form in graphic format may be the equivalent of a ten-page text document. Depending upon the frequency of downloads of forms, it might be advisable to upgrade to a high-speed line or higher speed service level.

Higher speed access is rapidly becoming available in most parts of the country and in many parts of the world at relatively affordable prices. In the past most connections depended on the limited capacity copper wires of the telephone company. Cable and telephone companies are installing higher speed infrastructures using fiber optics and satellite technologies to deliver higher speeds and capacity.

Hubs

Hub
A device used for sharing a signal among multiple computer devices.

A **hub** is a device for connecting multiple computer devices. If you have a single computer, you plug your Internet connection directly into the computer. With two computers in a small office or home network, the computers can be connected directly with one wire and they can send information back and forth. When there are more than two computers or computerized devices, like printers or fax machines on a network, a hub is used as a central connection so all the devices that are plugged into the hub can communicate with each other. One of the connections can be an Internet connection that all the devices share. The Internet connection is connected to the hub and then separate wires or connections are made to the other computers or devices. Whatever comes in one of the connections is sent to all the other connections. The hub broadcasts what comes in to all the other connections. Exhibit 4.6 shows a hub broadcasting to and from each connection.

Exhibit 4.6 A hub in a small office network

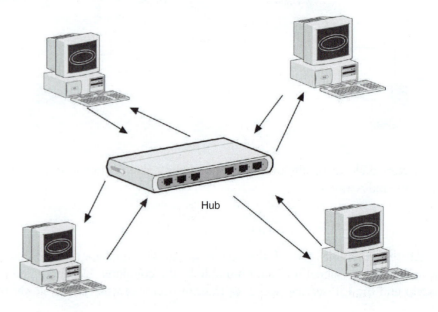

Hub

Switches

A **switch** is a high-performance alternative to a hub. Where a hub broadcasts every signal to every other connection, a switch determines the destination of each message and selectively forwards it to the computer or device for which it is intended. In smaller systems like a home network with less than four connections, a hub may be just as efficient as and less costly than a switch. In a network of more than four connections, the switch is more efficient. By directing the message to the intended recipient and not the entire network there is less total traffic, resulting in higher speed connections.

Routers

In its most basic function a **router** is a specialized computing device that routes messages, like a coin sorter sorts and sends coins to the proper slot or bin. Each message sent over a network has an address where it is to be delivered. Some messages are directed to other computerized devices in the local office network. Others are destined for some computerized device located out of the local network somewhere on the Internet. Routers use software to make the decision where to send the message by interpreting the address and "looking" at the devices attached to the hardware containing the routing software to see if the message is to be sent to a device in the local network or sent to a higher level router outside the local network somewhere on the Internet. The routing software may be on a computer or in a separate stand-alone device called a router. When you send a message, the routing software in your computer looks at the address to see if the address of the device to which it is to be sent is of one of the devices attached to your computer or if it should be sent to another device for additional routing, like forks in a road with directions to another fork in the road with more directions, and so forth.

The first decision the router makes is whether the message stays inside the local network or goes outside the network. If the decision is that it does stay inside the local network, the router sends it to the intended device. If it is not intended for a local device, the message is then sent or passed to a router further along the Internet, where the decision is made again whether to send the message to another router or to a device that is attached to the current router's network. The process is repeated until the message gets to a network with a router that has the intended recipient device attached to it.

You are probably thinking that a router sounds much like a switch. The reality is that a switch does perform some routing functions, sending traffic from one device to the intended device connected to the switch. Modern switches may contain the necessary software to act as modem, router, and high-performance hub all in one device.

Addresses

Routing software found on computers, routers, and switches uses addresses for delivering messages the same way as the post office or parcel delivery service uses the state, city, and street name and number to locate and deliver the mail or parcel. This is a **logical address;** it gives information on how to find the place. This is different than the **physical address**.

Every computerized device has a unique physical address that is stored in a special memory location in the device. This physical address is called the **media access control (MAC) address**. Since each device has a different MAC or physical address, the router can direct the incoming message to the particular device intended.

Switch
A high-performance alternative to a hub.

Router
A piece of hardware that routes data from a local area network (LAN) to a phone line.

WWW Mini Exercise
Find the MAC address of a Windows PC using Windows XP:

Go to the Start menu
Click on Run
Type cmd
When the window opens, type IPCONFIG/all

Logical Address
Addresses for delivering messages.

Physical Address
The physical address is the media access control, or MAC, address.

Media Access Control (MAC) Address
A physical address that is unique; that is stored in a special memory location in a computerized device.

Internet Addresses

IP
Internet protocol address. A string of four numbers separated by periods used to represent a computer on the Internet.

The Internet uses an address to deliver data to a specific computer or computerized device like a printer, just as a mail carrier uses an address to deliver a letter to a specific post office box. Each computerized device that connects to the Internet or is part of a network is assigned a numeric address; this is called the IP address. The **IP** address contains a set of numbers separated by periods. For example, the numeric address for the website for *Technology in the Law Office* is 192.111.222.2.2.

Most people do not remember or use the numeric IP address. Each location on the World Wide Web also has a text version of the address to access the website; this is called the domain name. An interpretation service on the Internet called a domain name service (DNS) converts the text name to the numeric IP address. For example, the domain name for the *Technology in the Law Office* website is www. technologyinthelawoffice.com.

The domain is the entryway to the computers and devices in that particular website.

In addition to the Internet service provider that maintains and provides access to the Internet, in the local office of the author, there is a server, a router, three workstations and several computerized devices. Each of these computerized devices is assigned an IP address when it connects to the Internet.

Each computerized device also has a physical address, the MAC address. The routing software in the router, switch, or computer takes the IP address and translates it into the MAC address of the devices connected to that routing device. In short, every device, whether connected or not to the Internet, has a MAC address. When it is connected to the Internet it is assigned an IP address. The router stores this information in a look-up table and translates the IP address of the Internet to the physical MAC address of the particular device. Each address assigned is as unique as the post office box in the local post office. Exhibit 4.7 shows a network with IP address and MAC address that is connected to the Internet through an Internet service provider.

Internet Browsers

Browser
A software program that allows a person to use a computer to access the Internet.

An Internet or Web **browser** is a software program that allows a person to use a computer to access the Internet. The two most popular Web browsers are Microsoft Internet Explorer and Netscape, both of which provide content as well as tools for searching the Internet.

WWW Mini Exercise

Review the information about Firefox and its features at www.firefox userguide.com and download a copy if desired. Or, visit the website of the Mozilla Foundation, a nonprofit corporation established to promote innovation on the Internet that also provides a version of Firefox at www.mozilla.org.

These browsers are typically used with Internet service providers that do not themselves provide any content but, rather, act as an intermediary, or connection, between the user and the World Wide Web. Some services, such as America Online (AOL), Netscape, and MSN, in addition to providing the traditional Internet connections and e-mail, provide content, such as news and weather and specialty sections for sharing information.

Firefox is another Internet browser that is gaining rapid acceptance. The principal advantage claimed is that it is more secure than the Internet Explorer browser. The developers claim the additional security comes from the fact that it is, unlike Internet Explorer, not attached to the operating system and therefore malicious code in the form of viruses and similar computer code cannot enter the operating system from the browser and cause problems with the operating system on the computer.

All browsers basically provide two main screens—one to display e-mail (see Exhibit 4.8) and one to display content and Internet search results (see Exhibit 4.9).

Exhibit 4.7 Network with IP and MAC addresses

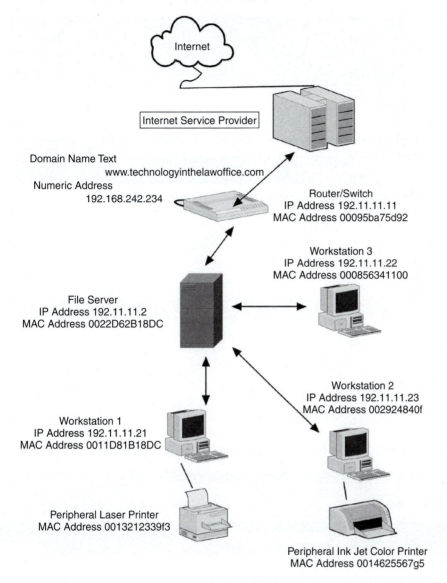

Locating Information

Obviously, finding something requires knowing where it is located. We find people by looking for their home or business address or by their telephone number. The modern equivalent of a telephone number is the e-mail address. A Web page also has an address, known as a **URL (uniform resource locator).**

The URL is made up of three parts, separated by the symbols shown:

Protocol://Computer/Path

The protocol is usually http (hypertext transfer protocol). The computer is the Internet computer name, such as www.bucks.edu. And the path is the directory or subdirectory on the computer where the information can be found.

The URL may be thought of as a file cabinet, in which the protocol is the name of the file cabinet, the computer is the drawer in the file cabinet, and the path is the file folder in the drawer. Not all URLs have a path as part of the address.

URL (Uniform Resource Locator)
The Internet address for a website.

Exhibit 4.8 Example of e-mail display

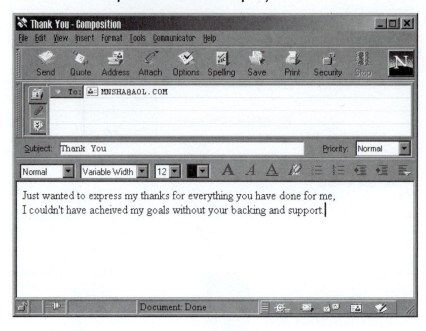

Exhibit 4.9 Example of Internet search results screen

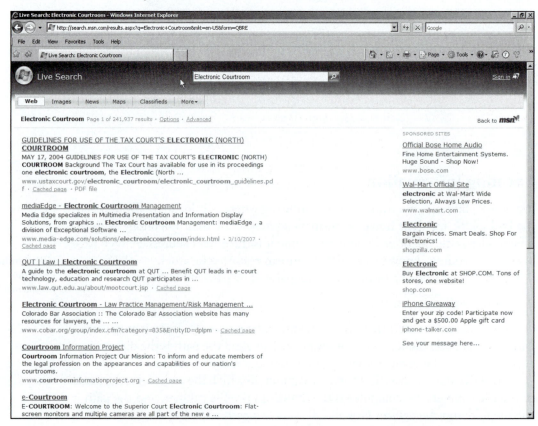

Part of the naming protocol is the **domain nomenclature**, with extensions such as the "edu" in www.TESC.edu. Common domain extensions are:

Domain Nomenclature
Part of the URL naming protocol.

.org	organizations
.edu	educational institutions
.com	commercial operations
.gov	government agencies
.bus	business
.mil	military

In addition, there are extensions such as

.jp	Japan
.fr	France
.uk	United Kingdom

These designations refer to the country where the computer is located.

In determining the authenticity of information found on the Internet, knowing if the computer is a commercial site (.com or .bus) or a government site (.gov) is sometimes useful. Some websites may appear to be official government websites or may appear to contain official information but actually are private sites.

For example, the official URL for the Internal Revenue Service is www.irs.gov. This is not to be confused with the unofficial private website, www.irs.com. To obtain the official Internal Revenue Service forms and information, you must use the official site, www.irs.gov.

Potentially, one of the biggest time-savers for the legal team is the ready availability of information, forms, and files on the Internet or World Wide Web. Public information that would have required a trip to the courthouse or other government office is instantly available, 24 hours a day, 7 days a week, without leaving the office. This information may come from public or private sources. Government information typically is available without cost or at minimum cost. Private information may be free to all, or at a cost per use, per page, or per time period (such as a minute, hour, day, or month). These charges are like the cost of cell phone usage, by the minute, month, or other prepaid plan.

E-MAIL

E-mail has become a standard method of communication across the globe and not just for the legal team. Legal teams face issues that other businesses do not face. Most obvious are the issues of confidentiality and privilege. Who will see it and who will read it? Will it be sent only to the correct person or will it be accidentally sent to a large list of recipients, or to a single recipient that should never get it?

According to a survey by the International Legal Technology Association (ILTA), 91 percent of firms have not disabled the automatic **type-ahead feature** in their e-mail program. This feature completes the address after a few letters of the address are typed. For example, you type Jones, and the program finishes it by adding the @ sign and any e-mail address in your address book with Jones as part

Type-ahead Feature
This feature completes the address after a few letters of the address are typed.

WWW Mini Exercise

ILTA is a peer networking organization providing information resources to members in order to make technology work for the legal profession. The full ILTA's 2006 E-Mail Survey is available at www.ILTA net.org, or check for the latest e-mail white paper at www.iltanet.org.

Mailbox
An electronic storage location for e-mail messages.

Attachment
An attachment is a record or file associated with another record for the purpose of storage or transfer.

of the address. If you have more than one Jones in your e-mail address book, accidentally hitting the Enter or the Send key could send the message to the wrong Jones, like attorney Jones, the opposing attorney, instead of client Jones. And according to the survey, 92 percent do not give the user a prompt to warn users about "Reply to All" being selected for sending an e-mail (i.e., "Are you sure you want to Reply to All?").

E-mail documents are a large part of the discoverable documentation in cases. How long they should be retained becomes an important question for the firm and for the client, particularly when attachments are part of the e-mail. As e-mail becomes easier to use on all types of devices, more files are sent with attachments of larger and larger files. The issue of size limitations becomes an issue depending on the devices used. With the exploding use of e-mails is the tendency to save everything.

E-mail is saved on a computer or a file server in a file or folder called a mailbox. **Mailbox** size limits may restrict how much may be saved. This is a double-edged sword. With e-mail as the standard for correspondence, larger mailboxes are needed to store the e-mails unless some other offline storage is provided, together with the training to perform the task.

One of the issues for the legal team is the question of making the e-mails part of the file. In the days of paper letters, copies routinely were printed and filed with the file. With an e-mail management program they may also be made a part of the electronic file and potentially part of the discoverable record in case of trial.

File Attachments

A popular method for transmitting text files and graphic images is by including the file as part of an e-mail. An **attachment** is a file that is sent with an e-mail. This is much easier than it sounds. Today, almost everyone has an e-mail address, whether at home or at work, or both. To send or receive e-mails requires the use of an Internet service provider and a browser such as Internet Explorer, Netscape, or one of the other specialty e-mail programs. In traditional e-mail, text is entered on the keyboard and transmitted to the e-mail account of a recipient, who reads it online. Virtually any file can be attached (linked) and sent with an e-mail. The receiver needs only to double-click the mouse on the attachment, which may appear as an icon. In most cases, the file will open using the same program from which it was created, such as Microsoft Word, Corel WordPerfect, or Adobe Acrobat. Occasionally a file may be transmitted in a format that the receiver does not have the software to open. This is particularly true with regard to graphic images, pictures, and drawings.

Receiving and Downloading Files and Attachments

The method for downloading files and attachments is the same. Users must first determine the directory (folder) into which they will be downloading these files. In Windows this usually is a folder called My Download Files or My Files. If there is no existing folder, Windows Explorer can be used to create a folder with a name such as Download. Windows Explorer is a program in the Start directory under Programs. (This is not the same as Windows Internet Explorer, which is an Internet browser.)

Most of the files attached as part of e-mail will be document files created and saved as either Microsoft Word documents or WordPerfect documents. The user may want to save these files directly into the Word or WordPerfect directory. Saving them in the computer download folder is one option, as is opening the file on the screen immediately instead of saving it for later use.

Normally, text files and graphic images are **static files**; that is, by themselves they do not perform any function but are merely data-usable within another program such as a word processor or graphic image viewer. It has become common, however, to send as attachments, files that have within them mini-programs such as **macros** that perform functions when activated, such as those used to calculate sums in spreadsheets. Others are self-contained software programs such as screensavers containing animation and animated cartoons.

Some program files have an extension of either ".exe" or ".com." Files with these extensions may run automatically after downloading. Therefore, greater caution must be taken in downloading any file, particularly files with these or other unknown file extensions, which may contain macros (mini-files), such as Excel files, which may contain formulas that run automatically and may contain computer viruses, as discussed later in this chapter. Remember that it is not enough to rely on the sender being a reliable source, as even the most reliable source can have a security breach that allows a virus to be attached to a file, or the source may be forwarding files from other, less reliable sources without checking the files before sending them to you.

Static Files
A file that contains only data.

Macros
Small programs that execute software functions when activated.

Printing

Most of the items that are displayed can be sent to a printer attached to a computer. At the top of most Web browsers is a printer icon or a Print command in the File selection in the menu or toolbar at the top of the page. Clicking on the printer icon or on the word Print in the File pulldown menu will initiate the print process. Patience may be necessary, as the computer may have to take some time to access the original source of the information. Clicking several times will not speed up the process and actually may result in several copies of the same information being printed.

Sending Files

Some Internet service providers (ISPs) limit the amount of information that may be sent at one time depending on the speed of the connection and how busy the system is at different times of the day. This may limit the number of pages that may be sent at one time. With increased transmission speed, also referred to as bandwidth, comes the ability to transmit much larger files and more pages in the same time.

Increasingly, large-size graphics files and images such as photographs are sent or attached to e-mails. The larger files being transmitted require more bandwidth (the pipeline) to avoid slowing down the system. Bandwidth may be thought of as the amount of data that can be sent in a given timeframe.

For example:

Dial-up access—uses a modem connected to a PC to connect to the Internet by dialing a phone number provided by the Internet service provider. Typical dial-up connection speeds range from 2400 bps to 56 Kbps.
ISDN (integrated services digital network)—uses digital telephone lines or normal telephone wires to transmit typically at 64 Kbps to 128 Kbps.
DSL (digital subscriber line)—is always connected using existing telephone lines.
ADSL (asymmetric digital subscriber line)—is the most common type of DSL. Typical speeds range from 1.5 to 9 Mbps for receiving data and 16 to 640 Kbps when sending data.

ISDN
Integrated services digital network, uses digital telephone lines.

Cable
Operates over cable TV lines.

WWW Mini Exercise
Full description and information on types of service available can be found at: http://www .webopedia.com/quick_ _ref/internet_ _connectiontypes.asp

ZIP File
An open standard for compression and decompression used widely for PC download archives. ZIP is used on Windows-based programs such as WinZip and Drag and Zip. The file extension given to ZIP files is .zip.

Cable—uses a modem that operates over cable TV lines. Typical cable speeds range from 512 Kbps to 20 Mbps.

T-1 lines (T for terrestrial, as opposed to satellite)—are leased, dedicated phone connections. Typical speed is 1.544 Mbps.

Satellite or Internet over Satellite (IoS)—allows a user to access the Internet via a satellite. Typical Internet over satellite connection speeds range from 492 to 512 Kbps.

FIOS (fiber optic service)—uses a dedicated fiber optic connection with typical speed up to 30 megabits (Mbps) download (receiving) speed and 5 Mbps upload (sending) speed.

As with any pipeline, only a limited amount of product can be transmitted at any one time. To more equitably share the limited pipeline resource, ISPs and network operators may permanently or temporarily during peak usage times, limit the number of files or the size of files that one user may transmit. In some offices, the same limitations may be imposed to overcome the size limitation; files may be transmitted in a compressed format, frequently referred to as **ZIP files**. Large files are run through a program that compresses them before being sent. The recipient of the compressed file then must uncompress the file before being able to read it.

A number of programs are available to compress and decompress files. Some of these require several steps, and other programs perform the task automatically. For occasional use, the manual method is acceptable, but with the increasing number of compressed files, it may be more time-efficient to purchase one of the automatic programs. Limited time-trial versions of some of these decompression programs may be downloaded without charge over the Internet from software companies who are encouraging users to buy the full version after the trial period expires. One of the most used zip/unzip programs is WinZip. WinZip provides an extensive help menu for learning and using the program and a Wizard to help the user step through the process as shown in Exhibit 4.10.

In the Supreme Court of Appeals of West Virginia

January 2008 Term

No. 33256

LAWYER DISCIPLINARY BOARD, Petitioner v. MICHAEL P. MARKINS, A MEMBER OF THE WEST VIRGINIA STATE BAR, Respondent

LAWYER DISCIPLINARY PROCEEDING TWO-YEAR SUSPENSION, WITH ADDITIONAL SANCTIONS

Submitted: April 1, 2008

Filed: May 23, 2008

The Opinion of the Court was delivered PER CURIAM. SYLLABUS BY THE COURT

(1) "A *de novo* standard applies to a review of the adjudicatory record made before the [Lawyer Disciplinary Board] as to questions of law, questions of application of the law to the facts, and questions of appropriate sanctions; this Court gives respectful consideration to the [Board's] recommendations while ultimately exercising its own independent judgment. On the other hand, substantial deference is given to the [Board's] findings of fact, unless such findings are not supported by reliable, probative, and substantial evidence on the whole record." Syl. Pt. 3, *Committee on Legal Ethics v. McCorkle*, 192 W.Va. 286, 452 S.E.2d 377 (1994).

WWW Mini Exercise
Read the entire report of the disciplinary action at http://www.state.wv.us/ wvsca/docs/Spring08/ 33256.htm.

(2) "This Court is the final arbiter of legal ethics problems and must make the ultimate decisions about public reprimands, suspensions or annulments of attorneys' licenses to practice law." Syl. Pt. 3, *Committee on Legal Ethics v. Blair*, 174 W.Va. 494, 327 S.E.2d 671 (1984).

(3) "'"In deciding on the appropriate disciplinary action for ethical violations, this Court must consider not only what steps would appropriately punish the respondent attorney, but also whether the discipline imposed is adequate to serve as an effective deterrent to other members of the Bar and at the same time restore public confidence in the ethical standards of the legal profession.' Syllabus point 3, *Committee on Legal Ethics v. Walker*, 178 W.Va. 150, 358 S.E.2d 234 (1987)." Syl. Pt. 5, *Committee on Legal Ethics v. Roark*, 181 W.Va. 260, 382 S.E.2d 313 (1989).' Syllabus point 7, *Office of Lawyer Disciplinary Counsel v. Jordan*, 204 W.Va. 495, 513 S.E.2d 722 (1998)." Syl. Pt. 4, *Lawyer Disciplinary Bd. v. Wade*, 217 W.Va. 58, 614 S.E.2d 705 (2005).

(4) "'Rule 3.16. of the West Virginia Rules of Lawyer Disciplinary Procedure enumerates factors to be considered in imposing sanctions and provides as follows: "In imposing a sanction after a finding of lawyer misconduct, unless otherwise provided in these rules, the Court [West Virginia Supreme Court of Appeals] or Board [Lawyer Disciplinary Board] shall consider the following factors: (1) whether the lawyer has violated a duty owed to a client, to the public, to the legal system or to the profession; (2) whether the lawyer acted intentionally, knowingly or negligently; (3) the amount of the actual or potential injury caused by the lawyer's misconduct; and (4) the existence of any aggravating or mitigating factors."' Syl. pt. 4, *Office of Lawyer Disciplinary Counsel v. Jordan*, 204 W.Va. 495, 513 S.E.2d 722 (1998)." Syl. Pt. 2, *Lawyer Disciplinary Bd. v. Lakin*, 217 W.Va. 134, 617 S.E.2d 484 (2005).

. . . Finally, we recognize that with the widespread use of computer e-mail as an important method of communication between and among attorneys and their clients comes the potentiality that the communication might be improperly infiltrated. This Court does not take lightly the fact that, in this case, it was an attorney who repeatedly accessed the confidential e-mails of other attorneys without their knowledge or permission. Thus, the imposition of a suitable sanction in a case such as this is not exclusively dictated by what sanction would appropriately punish the offending attorney, (See footnote 13) but, just as importantly, this Court must ensure that the discipline imposed adequately serve as an effective deterrent to other attorneys, (See footnote 14) "to protect the public, to reassure it as to the reliability and integrity of attorneys and to safeguard its interest in the administration of justice." *Battistelli*, 206 W.Va. at 201, 523 S.E.2d at 261, quoting *Lawyer Disciplinary Board v. Taylor*, 192 W.Va. at 144, 451 S.E.2d at 445. Accordingly, based upon the foregoing, we are compelled to adopt the recommendation of discipline tendered by the Board.

IV. Conclusion

For the reasons stated above, we adopt the Board's recommendations and hereby impose the following sanctions upon Respondent: (1) Respondent is suspended from the practice of law in West Virginia for a period of two years; (2) upon reinstatement, Respondent's private practice shall be supervised for a period of one year; (3) Respondent is ordered to complete twelve hours of CLE in ethics in addition to such ethics hours he is otherwise required to complete to maintain his active license to practice, said additional twelve hours to be completed before he is reinstated; and (4) Respondent is ordered to pay the costs of these proceedings.

License suspended, with additional sanctions.

WWW Mini Exercise
Download an evaluation copy of WinZip from the Companion Website at www .prenhall.com/goldman.

Exhibit 4.10 WinZip® 11.2 Pro Tool Bar and Help menu

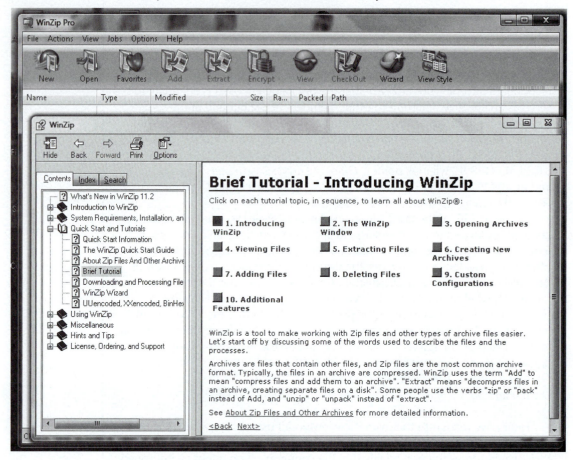

ETHICAL Perspective

WEST VIRGINIA STATE BAR

Rule 8.4. Misconduct.

It is professional misconduct for a lawyer to:

(a) violate or attempt to violate the Rules of Professional Conduct, knowingly assist or induce another to do so, or do so through the acts of another;

(b) commit a criminal act that reflects adversely on the lawyer's honesty, trustworthiness or fitness as a lawyer in other respects;

(c) engage in conduct involving dishonesty, fraud, deceit or misrepresentation;

(d) engage in conduct that is prejudicial to the administration of justice;

(e) state or imply an ability to influence improperly a government agency or official;

(f) knowingly assist a judge or judicial officer in conduct that is a violation of applicable rules of judicial conduct or other law; or

(g) have sexual relations with a client whom the lawyer personally represents during the legal representation unless a consensual sexual relationship existed between them at the commencement of the lawyer/client relationship. For purposes of this rule, "sexual relations" means sexual intercourse or any touching of the sexual or other intimate parts of a client or causing such client to touch the sexual or other intimate parts of the lawyer for the purpose of arousing or gratifying the sexual desire of either party or as a means of abuse. (Amended by order entered July 12, 1995, effective September 1, 1995.)

Web Exploration

Contrast and compare Rule 8.4 **of the West Virginia State Bar** at http://www.wvbar .org/BARINFO/rulesprof conduct/rules8.htm with the American Bar Association Model Rules of Professional Responsibility at http://www .abanet.org/cpr/mrpc/mrpc _toc.html, and the ethical rule in your jurisdiction.

E-mail Archiving

E-mail archiving is the continuous saving of e-mail data. Traditional computer data backups only save what is on the computer at the time of the backup. Archiving is a technology of continuous saving of data. A traditional e-mail backup would not capture the e-mails received and deleted between the backups. An archiving of e-mails saves every incoming and outgoing message and not just the ones that remain after the deleting activity has been performed to remove e-mails and their responses. Clients in some industries are required by federal or state law to preserve records including e-mails for a period of time. Initial archiving software was a response to the regulatory environment and compliance requirements of such laws as the Sarbanes-Oxley Act, also known as the Public Company Accounting Reform and Investor Protection Act of 2002, and the Securities and Exchange Commission rule on electronic storage, and the Health Insurance Portability and Accountability Act (HIPAA) that requires archiving of e-mails in some cases for two years following the death of a patient.

Law firms are not immune to claims of malpractice by clients where e-mail may offer a defense. In all cases, the rules of confidentiality and privilege must be maintained. However, if the client makes a claim against the firm, the firm may be released from the ethical privilege of confidentiality and of privilege to defend it. In these cases an archive of properly kept e-mails may be a source of documents of the defense.

E-mail Archiving
The continuous saving of e-mail data.

ADVICE FROM THE FIELD

E-MAIL ARCHIVING FOR DUMMIES

FOREWARD

What's in That E-mail and Why Does It Matter?
By Laura Dubois, Research Director,
Storage Software IDC

Today's businesses are focused on managing valuable information while at the same time mitigating potential risk from it. Corporate information needs to be protected from compromise, retained according to regulatory requirements, and be available in the event of audits or legal discovery or for general business use. The pervasiveness of e-mail in today's corporate environment to communicate and conduct business continues to fuel e-mail growth. However, today's businesses must be able to manage e-mail growth while satisfying requirements for e-mail availability, retention, and content-oriented retrieval. Content-oriented retrieval is of particular relevance in regulatory audits or electronic discovery, in which e-mails associated with a particular keyword or relevant to a specific topic are frequently sought. E-mail archiving applications and solutions address both of these technical and business requirements.

E-mail archiving applications provide an automated and efficient way of storing, indexing, and retrieving individual e-mail messages and file attachments in real time by individual users, IT staff, and other authorized parties from both inside and outside the firm. E-mail archiving differs from backup and retrieval solutions in that the latter are designed only to provide regularly scheduled copies of an e-mail server or disk. Backup and retrieval solutions enable e-mail to be brought back up and running after an e-mail server or disk fails, but these solutions don't maintain copies of e-mails exchanged between backups, retain copies of e-mails deleted by users after the backup is replaced with a newer one, or move e-mail content off primary e-mail servers to more efficient storage systems. Today's e-mail archiving applications, on the other hand, are designed to handle these tasks, and can be delivered as an on-premises software solution, preinstalled on an appliance, or as a hosted service.

According to IDC, the e-mail archiving applications market was a $477 million market in 2006, realizing 45 percent growth over 2005. The e-mail archiving applications market continues to be fueled by litigation and electronic discovery, regulatory requirements for record retention, as well as overall

(Continued)

mailbox management. In comparison, the overall IT industry has been hovering around 5 percent growth year over year. The phenomenal growth of e-mail archiving applications is driven by electronic discovery, in particular by amendments to the Federal Rules of Civil Procedure, regulatory compliance, and the overall need for storage and e-mail application performance optimization.

Because e-mail users tend to express themselves in an informal manner, and because metadata is associated with email, these communications are often sought during the discovery phase of corporate litigation. E-mail archiving solutions can help companies more quickly find relevant e-mail and reduce the cost of electronic discovery. Regulations in different industries may stipulate that related content contained in electronic records be retained for specified time periods or outline rules to secure the privacy, security, and lack of compromise to sensitive information. E-mail archiving supports records retention requirements and also enables content indexing for easy search and retrieval of relevant messages and attachments based on audit requests. In addition, e-mail archiving can be used to manage mailbox size by regularly archiving older or infrequently accessed data. Archiving saves space by moving messages from the email server into an archive repository, thus improving performance while giving users access to their archived e-mail.

E-mail is a core component of business communications today, and firms need to ensure that they have adequate controls in place to protect, retain, and preserve relevant e-mail content. With the volume of e-mail increasing annually, firms also need to find a way to manage growth with relatively flat budgets and limited IT administration. Today's e-mail archiving applications provide a solution to meet these legal, regulatory, and business needs. Through e-mail archiving, companies have an automated and efficient way to store, index, and retrieve individual e-mail messages and file attachments by individual users, IT staff, and other authorized parties.

Obtaining Software on the Internet

Software may be purchased locally, by mail order, or from an Internet source. Many software vendors sell their software directly from their Internet websites in immediately downloadable form or on a CD mailed to the buyer. The advantage of the downloadable version is immediate delivery and the ability to use it without waiting for the mail or express package delivery service.

Downloading software can be a simple operation. Select the option to download and, after payment with a credit card, the software is downloaded to a computer over the Internet. The software usually allows the recipient to designate where on the user's computer the software file should be downloaded, in a particular folder location or on a specific disk drive. Those with a download manager will find the software downloaded to the default location for downloads, usually a location on the main hard drive in a folder labeled as Downloads. These programs are usually not in usable form but must still be installed on the computer. One of the options in a download manger is to launch the software. Prudent practice is to make a backup copy of the program before installing it.

Download Issues

Enough Memory for the Program. Does the computer have enough random access memory (RAM) to run the program as well as the other programs normally opened and used at the same time?

Speed of the Internet Connection. If large numbers of documents or graphic-intense files or programs are to be downloaded from another location over the Internet, is the Internet connection fast enough to accomplish the job in a reasonable period of time?

Continual Connection. Downloading long documents may take time. If the connection is interrupted or terminated the download may have to be started over.

Firewalls. Firewalls are installed to prevent unauthorized access to computer systems and networks. In some cases they are set up to block everything that is not preauthorized or not recognized as coming from an allowed source. This type of firewall restriction is like the parental blocking of undesirable Internet content.

Trusted Sources. Downloading anything from a website has dangers. The document or program may have intended or unintended viruses, Trojan horses, or other spyware attached or embedded. Downloading from strangers only increases the potential for problems. Downloading from a trusted site may not eliminate the potential for problems but it does minimize the risk. For example, viruses may be attached to a document from a trusted site like another law firm. They may be trusted but someone may have sent the virus to them and they may not have checked their incoming documents for viruses and other problems.

METADATA

Metadata is frequently referred to as data about data. Every electronic document has information about that document attached to the electronic file. Metadata is the information about the document, such as who created it, the date it was created, modified, or accessed, and other information related to its existence and location.

Metadata is divided into two areas: the resource or **system metadata**, or information, and the content or application information. The resource metadata is used to track or locate the file containing the data such as file names, size, and location. **Content metadata** is in the file itself such as who the author of the document is, any tracked changes, and the version.

Each time a file is sent as an e-mail or an attachment to an e-mail, metadata is part of the transmission. The recipient can frequently see the content or application metadata like the author and version by use of the properties function in the program used to view the documents such as in Word or WordPerfect for word processing documents.

Metadata
Information about a particular data set, which may describe, for example, how, when, and by whom it was received, created, accessed, and/or modified, and how it is formatted.

System Metadata
The data such as file names, size, and location.

Content Metadata
Information about the contents of a document.

WWW Mini Exercise
For a more detailed description of metadata, see http://en.wikipedia.org/wiki/Metadata#Types_of_metadata

ADVICE FROM THE FIELD

PRODUCING METADATA IN E-DISCOVERY—WHAT YOU NEED TO KNOW
By Leonard Deutchman and Brian Wolfinger

As e-discovery requests and productions increase exponentially, many of those requests will, implicitly or explicitly, seek the production of metadata. This article will help you understand metadata production by discussing what "metadata" is, how to preserve and gather metadata, what form of production e-discovery with metadata should take, and issues regarding its production. By understanding the technical and legal issues regarding metadata, you can diminish the occasions upon which you will have to produce metadata and insure that when it is produced it is done so properly.

WHAT IS METADATA?

The Committee Note to amended F.R.Civ.P. 26(f) defines "metadata" as "information describing the history, tracking, or management of an electronic document." In the influential opinion, Williams v. Sprint, 230 F.R.D. 640, 646-647 (D. Kan. 2005), the court cited with favor the description of metadata in The Sedona Guidelines (The Sedona Conference Working Group Series, Sept. 2005 Version) as "information about a particular data set which describes how, when and by whom it was collected, created,

(Continued)

accessed, or modified and how it is formatted (including data demographics such as size, location, storage requirements and media information.)" The Sedona Guidelines noted that metadata included "all of the contextual, processing, and use information needed to identify and certify the scope, authenticity, and integrity of active or archival electronic information or records."

FILE- AND APPLICATION-LEVEL METADATA

It is important to distinguish between two types of metadata a file could have associated to it, "File-Level" metadata ("FLM") and "Application-Level" metadata ("ALM"). All files have FLM, while certain files, such as Microsoft Word documents, Excel spreadsheets, etc. will have both. While there are some exceptions, FLM is generally stored separately from where the actual file content is stored on a hard drive, while ALM is commingled with the file content.

"FILE-LEVEL" METADATA

"File-level" (or "file system") metadata about a computer file may include its size, the date/time of its creation or modification, if it is able to be written to further (as opposed to being read-only) and other information. File-level metadata is created by the computer's file system and changed due to end-user interactions with the file on that computer. Some FLM file attributes include Last Modified, Last Accessed and Creation dates and times ("MAC times"), File Physical and Logical Size, File Name and File Path.

Different user or system actions will "trip" the MAC times, causing them to be updated. Opening a new MS Office document, typing something and then saving the file to a disk or server will stamp the Created attribute with the date/ time of this first save, and the Accessed and Modified attributes will show the same, since the user did all of these things to the file. On the other hand, when files are transferred between drive volumes and/or between pieces of computer media (i.e., saved from one location to another without modification) the Created date of the file is normally changed to reflect the time of the creation of the copy, but the Modified date will remain the same. This will often result in the counterintuitive situation of having file-level metadata that shows a file was modified before it was created.

"APPLICATION-LEVEL" METADATA

In addition to FLM, certain files contain "Application-Level" metadata, that is, additional metadata within themselves. Microsoft Office documents such as PowerPoint, Excel, and Word have ALM, as do other files such as PDF files. The following is a list of some ALM file attributes that are tracked by Microsoft Office: Track changes, comments and deleted text; Author—assigned during installation of the application software (e.g., Microsoft Office) on the computer; Company—same type of value as Author, assigned during installation of the software; Revision Number—a count of every instance where the file was opened, edited and saved; Creation date and time—the Date/Time a document was first saved by a user with the stored value in the "Author" field; and, Last Save date and time—the Date/Time a document was last saved by a user with the stored value in the "Last Author" field.

DATA GATHERING TO PRESERVE METADATA

As the discussion above about copying files to other media makes clear, if data is not gathered properly, metadata such as the dates of file creation, last access and last modification can be changed. If that happens, you simply cannot produce accurate metadata.

Forensic data gathering avoids this problem by gathering all data initially, and exactly as it was on the media imaged. Even if only a handful of files are sought from a hard drive, for example, an exact, "bit stream" image of the hard drive should be made and, later, forensically searched. The image would be verified by submitting both it and the original to a complex algorithm to generate identical "hash values." Bit stream imaging with hash value verification is the standard practice of law enforcement and widely accepted by peer groups and courts as scientifically reliable.

Forensic data gathering through a vendor is more expensive than in-house copying of files by the client. However, if metadata must be produced, the data has to be gathered properly, period.

So, what do you do if you are handed some DVDs produced by the client, you have no idea how the data was copied to the DVDs and you have to produce file creation and last accessed and modified dates? You must make clear that you cannot do that—that is, your firm cannot discharge its discovery duties—unless the data is properly collected.

This will not make you the most popular person at the firm, but you will be doing your job properly.

THE FORM OF PRODUCTION

Form of production will dictate access to metadata. If you produce the data in TIFF or PDF form, the only access to any metadata will be what is found in the fields for each record in the database. If, however, the data is produced with a link to the file in its native form, then the user, i.e. your opponent, can view the metadata as found in the file. . . .

Note: The conclusion of the article may be found in Chapter 13.

Leonard Deutchman, Esquire is General Counsel and Managing Partner, and Brian Wolfinger, CIFI is Vice President of Electronic Discovery and Forensic Services LegisDiscovery, LLC, a firm based in Fort Washington, PA and McLean, VA that specializes in electronic digital discovery and digital forensics. You may contact them at ldeutchman@legisdiscovery.com and bwolfinger@ legisdiscovery.com

The full article originally appeared in May/July 2007 • *Litigation Support TODAY.*

LIST SERVES

List serves, or as they are more commonly referred to, "list servs" are, according to webopedia (www.webopedia.com):

> *An automatic mailing list server developed by Eric Thomas for BITNET in 1986. When e-mail is addressed to a LISTSERV mailing list, it is automatically broadcast to everyone on the list. The result is similar to a newsgroup or forum, except that the messages are transmitted as e-mail and are therefore available only to individuals on the list.*
>
> *LISTSERV is currently a commercial product marketed by L-Soft International. Although LISTSERV refers to a specific mailing list server, the term is sometimes used incorrectly to refer to any mailing list server. Another popular mailing list server is Majordomo, which is freeware.*

The Internet has spawned the creation of communities of people with common interests who use the Internet to exchange information. There are list serves for most of the sections of the American Bar Association, the American Trial Lawyers Association, and many other special interest groups. Exhibit 4.11 for example, shows list serve guidelines of the National Lawyers Guild. Some of these groups are moderated by a list manager. These are members who screen the postings to be sure they comply with the rules or the guidelines of the list. Others are opened with no limitation on what is posted other than the list members' own sense of propriety. Exhibit 4.12 shows the ABA's **netiquette** guidelines when using list serves.

The ABA hosts over 1,900 e-mail lists (both discussion and broadcast distribution) (see Exhibit 4.13). Subscription to the majority of these is a benefit of ABA/Section Membership.

List Serves
An automatic mailing list, usually for specific topics.

Netiquette
Rules of behavior for using the Internet.

WWW Mini Exercise
For full text of the guidelines of the National Lawyers Guild, go to http://www.nlg.org/members/listserv.htm

ENCRYPTION TECHNOLOGY

Encryption technology permits a computer user to basically put a lock around his or her computer information to protect it from being discovered by others. Encryption technology is like a lock on a house. Without the lock in place, unwanted persons can easily enter the house and steal its contents; with the lock in place, it is more difficult to enter and take the house's contents. Encryption software serves a similar function in that it lets computer users scramble information so only those who have the encryption code can enter the database and discover the information.

Encryption
Scrambling documents using algorithms (mathematical formulas).

Exhibit 4.11 ListServ guidelines of the National Lawyers Guild

National Lawyers Guild Listserv Guidelines

The following guidelines are designed to help ensure that we maintain a productive, professional, (albeit informal) and enjoyable discussion forum.

Purpose: these list servs are for current members of the National Lawyers Guild. Its purpose is to provide a forum for the exchange of information of interest to Guild members and their work. Personal information is not generally posted unless it pertains to someone well known in the Guild, such as an obituary, an award, or a newsworthy event.

In order to ensure that these list servs remains (sic) an effective mean of sharing Guild-related information, we ask that you adhere to the following guidelines. Disregarding these guidelines may distract from the overall effectiveness and will be enforced through the following process:

Guidelines:

1. Present postings in a professional and courteous manner.
2. Subject lines should be clear and descriptive.
3. Messages should be brief and to the point.
4. If posting a reply to a message, include original subject line or reference it briefly at the beginning of the message.
5. Respect the rights of others to have different opinions.
6. Do not forward or 'copy' interact postings to non-Guild members or organizations without first obtaining permission from the poster and any individual(s) mentioned by name in the text.
7. Refrain from sending messages that say "I agree" unless there is a poll of opinion. These messages add little to the content of the list.
8. When you are forwarding information that you have received in an email please format the message so it will be easy to read.

Examples of postings that may be deemed inappropriate include:

- Offensive or profane language
- Hateful, racially or ethnically objectionable content
- Advertising or solicitation
- Misleading or intentionally erroneous information
- Disruptive activity, such as sending multiple messages in an effort to monopolize the forum
- Frivolous, or non-informational content
- Spam

On the first instance of disregarding the guidelines, the subscriber will be notified and cautioned by the listserv administrator via private email. If the subscriber continues to post in violation of the guidelines, he or she may be immediately and permanently removed from the list serv.

Any conflicts about the list serv will be dealt with by the leadership of the appropriate NLG entity such as a committee, chapter, and region. Any national conflicts will be dealt with by the national executive director or the officers.

Source: http://www.nlg.org/members/listserv.htm. Reprinted with permission from the National Lawyers Guild.

Encryption

Confidential or privileged information sent over the Internet is frequently encrypted by the sender and unencrypted by the receiver because of the concerns that it will be intercepted when transmitted over the Internet. Encryption programs use

Exhibit 4.12 ABA's list serve guidelines

ABA Netiquette for List Serve Users

List Serves or electronic mailing lists are one of the most useful means of communication, since they enable their members to instantly transmit or receive information and opinions on matters of common interest. When a message is sent to a mail list the List Server immediately distributes it to all subscribers. Conversely, when replies to that message are "mailed," they too, are broadcast to the entire list of subscribers in a matter of minutes or seconds, making this a highly interactive form of communication.

The following brief set of suggested guidelines is intended to make the use of electronic mail lists as valuable and productive as possible, for all subscribers.

1. Be germane.
2. Know your audience.
3. Brevity is important.
4. Identify yourself.
5. Provide a subject line.
6. If possible avoid attachments.
7. Be careful with replies.
8. Please do not use auto-reply.
9. Keeping it simple is your best bet.

Source: Netiquette for List Serve Users, 2006, published by the American Bar Association, located at http://www.abanet.org/discussions/netiquette.html. © 2006 by the American Bar Association. Reprinted with permission.

Source: Netiquette for ListServe Users, 2008, published by the American Bar Association, located at http://www.abanet.org/discussion/netiquette.html © 2008 by the American Bar Association. Reprinted with permission.

Exhibit 4.13 Home page of the ABA's discussion board and e-mail list information

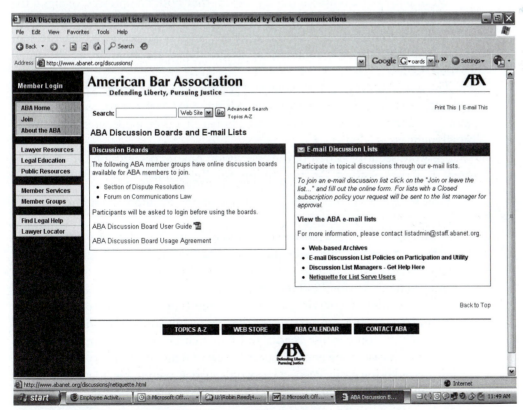

Source: © 2007 by the American Bar Association. Reprinted with permission.

algorithms (mathematical formulas) to scramble documents. Without the proper password or encryption key, unauthorized persons are not able to read the files and determine their content.

To understand the levels of protection offered by the different encryption programs, think of the protection offered by a combination lock. The least security is provided by the type of two-number combination lock frequently found with inexpensive luggage. As the numbers required for opening the lock increase to two, three, four, or more numbers, the security also increases. It is not hard to see how the two-digit combination lock can be quickly opened while the four-digit lock requires more time and effort. For an amateur computer hacker with a simple encryption-breaking program, a basic encryption program might be thought to be the equivalent of a two- or three-number combination lock. The higher-level program, with tougher algorithms designed to thwart a professional code-breaker, would require the four or more number combinations. As computers become faster, more sophisticated methods will be required.

E-mail Encryption

The use of e-mail for communication in the legal environment presents one of the biggest potentials for breach of confidentiality. E-mails between attorney and client frequently contain confidential information. Clients provide details necessary for the attorney to give legal advice and answer legal questions. Attorneys reply with legal advice intended solely for the client. A misdirected or intercepted e-mail with confidential content may be a breach of attorney–client confidentiality and void the attorney–client privilege.

One of the ways to protect confidential e-mail is to use a program, such as Mail it Safe, that can encrypt the e-mail and authenticate both parties. As shown in Exhibit 4.14, Mail it Safe provides options that allow notification of messages on cell phones, Blackberry, or to an alternative e-mail address.

WinZip E-Mail Companion is a program that both compresses, or zips a file as discussed above, and encrypts documents that are attached to e-mails. While this does not eliminate all risks, it does offer a level of protection for the attachment that may contain confidential or privileged information as shown in Exhibit 4.15.

The e-mail itself is still readable and potentially open to others having access without the password. The recipient, who is provided with the agreed password in another communication in person, telephone, or other method, can open the attachment.

Password security as part of the encryption process depends on the quality or strength of the password. As stated in the WinZip manual:

> "You should keep the following considerations in mind when choosing passwords for your files:
>
> In general, longer passwords are more secure than shorter passwords. In fact, taking maximum advantage of the full strength of AES encryption requires a password of approximately 32 characters for 128-bit encryption and 64 characters for 256-bit encryption.
>
> Passwords that contain a mixture of letters (upper and lower case), digits, and punctuation are more secure than passwords containing only letters.
>
> Because you can use spaces and punctuation, you can create "pass phrases" that are long enough but still easy to remember and type.
>
> Avoid using easily guessed passwords such as names, birthdays, Social Security numbers, addresses, telephone numbers, etc.

Exhibit 4.14 Mail it Safe Send options

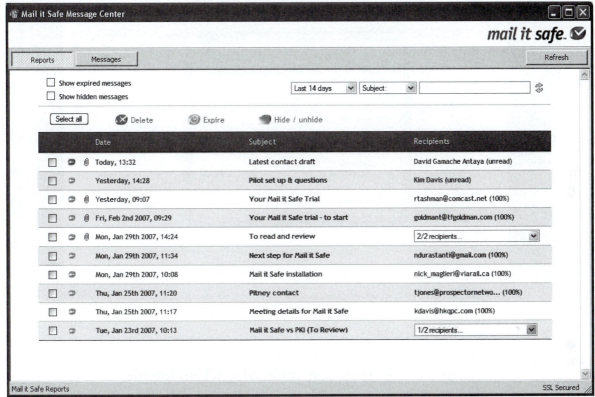

Source: Reprinted with permission from MailitSafe.com.

> Be sure to keep a record of the passwords you use and to keep this record in a secure place. WinZip has no way to access the contents of an encrypted file unless you supply the correct password. Before storing your only copies of critical information in encrypted form, you should carefully consider the risks associated with losing or forgetting the passwords involved."

ETHICAL Perspective

REVISION OF SOUTH DAKOTA RULES OF PROFESSIONAL RESPONSIBILITY

Rule 1.6. Confidentiality of Information.

(a) A lawyer shall not reveal information relating to the representation of a client unless the client gives informed consent except for disclosures that are impliedly authorized in order to carry out the representation or the disclosure is permitted by, and except as stated in paragraph (b).

Web Exploration

Contrast and compare Rule 1.6 of the Revision of South Dakota Rules of Professional Responsibility at http://www .sdbar.org/Rules/Rules/PC_ Rules.htm with the American Bar Association Model Rules of Professional Responsibility at http://www.abanet.org/cpr/ mrpc/mrpc_toc.html, and the ethical rule in your jurisdiction.

Exhibit 4.15 WinZip E-Mail Companion encryption of an e-mail attachment

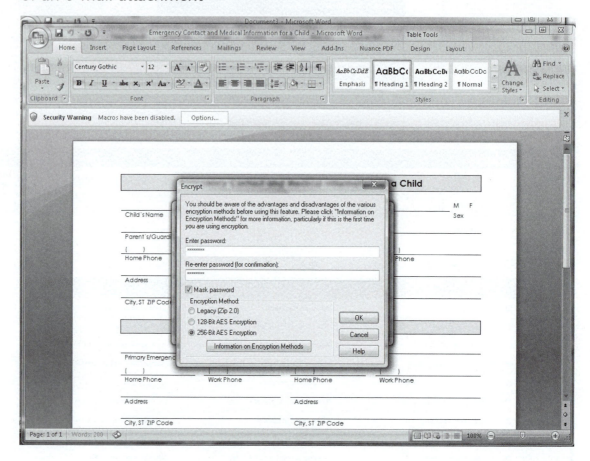

Export of Encryption Technology Worldwide

Software companies in the United States led the development of encryption technology. For years, the U.S. government permitted American software companies to sell its encryption software domestically but prohibited export of the most powerful encryption technology to foreigners. The U.S. government worried that powerful encryption and data scrambling technology would fall into the hands of criminals and terrorists who would use it to protect their illegal and clandestine activities.

Based on this fear, President Bill Clinton issued an executive order prohibiting the export of much of the most powerful encryption technology developed in the United States. These export restrictions remained in effect during most of the 1990s. In September 1999, after much lobbying by software companies located in the United States, the Administration changed its export policy to allow the export of the most powerful American-made encryption technology. The export rule was changed because criminals and terrorists could obtain similar data scrambling technology from software producers in other countries.

SUMMARY

CHAPTER 4
THE INTERNET AND ELECTRONIC MAIL

The Internet	A group of computers linked together with the added ability to search all the connections for information: a network of networks.
Internet Fundamentals	*Internet backbone:* The highest level connection. *ISP:* Internet service providers who provide access to the Internet at a local level for users. *Modem:* A device that translates electrical signals so computers can communicate over public connections like telephone, cable, and satellites. *Hubs:* Devices for sharing signals in a local network. *Switch:* A high efficiency hub. May also include software that allows it to act as a modem and router. *Router:* Software and computerized devices that translate Internet addresses and route signals by translating IP addresses into MAC addresses using a look-up table of the conversions. *Computer and Internet addresses:* Each computerized device has an address for use in getting messages, referred to as the logical address. *Media access control:* Each computerized device has an imbedded address called a MAC address, referred to as the physical address. *Internet protocol:* Each computerized device is assigned an Internet protocol (IP) address when it accesses the Internet. *Domain name service:* Translates the numbers of an IP address into more familiar word names. *Internet browsers:* Software programs that allow a person to use a computer to access the Internet. *Uniform resource locator (URL):* The Internet equivalent of a phone number that identifies the protocol used, the computer, and the extension called the domain nomenclature.
Locating Information	Local networks are searched with Windows Explorer. The Internet is searched with Internet browsers.
E-Mail	Electronic communication that raises issues of confidentiality and privilege for the legal team.
Type-Ahead Feature	A feature of e-mail that anticipates the desired remaining letters based on entries in an address book. May result in wrong party receiving confidential information.
Mailbox	E-mail is received and stored in an electronic mailbox. The number of items is determined by the available memory.
File Attachments	A popular method for transmitting text files and graphic images is by attachment of the file to an e-mail.
Receiving and Downloading Files and Attachments	Users must first determine the directory (folder) into which they will be downloading these files. Most of the files attached as part of e-mail will be document files created and saved as either Microsoft Word documents or WordPerfect documents.

Printing	Most of the items that are displayed can be printed by a printer attached to a computer.
Sending Files	Some Internet service providers (ISPs) limit the amount of information that may be sent at one time. A number of programs are available to compress and decompress files.
E-mail Archiving	A traditional e-mail backup would not capture the e-mails received and deleted between the backups.
Obtaining Software on the Internet	Software may be obtained and downloaded over the Internet.
Download Issues	1. Having enough memory for the program. 2. Speed of the connection will determine how long it takes to download. Large files may take a long time with slow connection. 3. Interruption in connection will require a restart of the download. 4. Will the firewall allow the download to come into the network? 5. Is it from a trusted source?
Metadata	Data about data. Information about a document attached to the electronic file.
Resource or System Metadata	Used to track or locate the file containing the data such as file names, size, and location.
Content or Application Metadata	Content metadata is in the file itself such as who the author of the document is, any tracked changes, and the version.
List Serves	Communities of people with common interests who use the Internet to exchange information.
Encryption Technology	Permits a computer user to basically put a lock around his or her computer information to protect it from being discovered by others.
Encryption	Encryption programs use algorithms (mathematical formulas) to scramble documents.
E-mail Encryption	One of the ways to protect confidential e-mail is to use a program that encrypts the e-mail and authenticates the parties before transmission.
Export of Encryption Technology Worldwide	The U.S. government worried that powerful encryption and data scrambling technology would fall into the hands of criminals.

KEY TERMINOLOGY

CONCEPT REVIEW QUESTIONS AND EXERCISES

1. Test your knowledge and comprehension of the topics in this chapter by completing the multiple-choice questions on the textbook Companion Website.

2. Test your knowledge and comprehension of the topics in this chapter by completing the True-False questions on the textbook Companion Website.

3. Why should passwords be changed on a regular basis?

4. Describe how a computer network may be used by a law firm.

5. Explain the importance and the steps that may be taken to maintain computer and network security.

6. What are some of the ways the Internet can be used in the law office?

7. What is an Internet browser? Give several examples.

8. Describe the use of Internet browsers for finding information on the World Wide Web.

9. Explain some of the issues in obtaining and installing software.

10. What is a list serve?

11. Why are list serve etiquette rules important?

12. How can list serves benefit the legal team?

13. What is the difference between the functions of the network server and the users' workstations?

14. Give examples of how network security can be breached and the possible ways to prevent the breach of network security in the future.

INTERNET EXERCISES

1. Conduct a search on the following topics using four different Internet or search browsers for the same term or item. Are all results shown in the same order? Why or why not?

   Search topics
   a. Legal ethics
   b. Law office technology
   c. Presentation graphics
   d. Internet security
   e. Metadata
   f. Encryption technology in the law office

2. Use the Internet to locate a definition of the term *metadata*; what is its importance to the legal team?

3. Find list serves available for lawyers through the American Bar Association.

4. Use an Internet search engine to find organizations involved with technology in the law.

5. Use the Internet to find and download a free firewall program.

6. Use the Internet to find Internet service providers in your area and prepare a list of available services and prices.

7. Use the Internet to locate a list of the ABA list serves that might be of value to a litigator.

8. Use a file compression program to "zip" a file and send it as an attachment to an e-mail. You may send it to your own e-mail address and then unzip the file on receipt.

PORTFOLIO ASSIGNMENTS

1. Prepare an office policy on the use of passwords in the law office. Explain the reasons and methods to be used for the most and the least secure passwords.

2. Prepare an office policy on the use of the Internet for sending and receiving electronic communications and documents.

SCENARIO CASE STUDY

Use the opening scenario for this chapter to answer the following questions. The setting is the attorney and paralegal discussing renting space to another attorney who is not a member of the same firm.

1. What additional hardware or software will be required to support a new person in the office? Does it matter if it is a lawyer or a paralegal or secretary?
2. Prepare a memo requesting a faster-than-dial-up Internet connection and explain why the cost is justified.
3. What procedures should be set up to protect data but allow use of the Internet by others in the office?
4. Is there any additional hardware that should be considered or purchased? Is this different from the list prepared in Chapter 3?
5. What are the ethical issues in sharing a common Website to attract clients for the plaintiff and defense attorney in this office? See the firm Website exhibit (1.2) in Chapter 1 for reference.
6. Are there any ethical issues in unrelated attorneys sharing an Internet connection?
7. Are there any ethical issues in sharing a Web page for attracting clients?

CONTINUING CASES AND EXERCISES

1. Update the Internet resources list from Chapter 1.
2. Continue to maintain a time record as outlined in Chapter 1.
3. Review the information presented in Advanced Exercises for the First Client.
   a. Set up a file for the client for use in answering the questions and preparing the documents.
   b. This exercise will require information found in future chapters and is a continuing exercise.
   c. Your instructor may give you additional instructions.

ADVANCED EXERCISES

1. Use Tabs3 to enter and maintain the time records assigned in Chapter 1.
   a. You will need to add yourself as a timekeeper and set a rate. For this continuing exercise, list yourself as timekeeper 30, at a rate of $40 per hour.
   b. Create a list of functions to be billed.
   c. Enter a client for billing purposes; you may use your instructor with the college information as the client.
2. Enter all of the calendar information for the course (see the list of suggested items in the exercise in Chapter 1) in the calendar functions in AbacusLaw.

First Client

The first client for a young attorney is always someone who will be remembered. Suddenly all the textbook theory comes face-to-face with reality. In a modern law office a series of decisions must also be made on law office management issues.

1. The client has requested information on preparing an advance medical directive, also referred to as a living will. What is the applicable law in your jurisdiction?
2. Are forms available from the Internet for your state? Locate any free forms available and download a copy to use as a template.
3. Use the following information to create a new client interview form that can be saved as a template in a word processing program.

4. How should the office files be set up? Some of the options include filing by client's name, by type of documents prepared, or a combination of both. What recommendations would you make to Mr. Mason?
5. How should time records be maintained for billing individual clients?
6. Should the office be a paperless environment, with copies of all client materials maintained electronically, or should paper copies be retained?

Note: As a reference, a sample Advance Medical Directive brochure is available from the University of Arkansas for Medical Sciences at http://www.uams.edu/patienteducation/Handouts/advance_medical_directives.pdf.

Client Information

Adam First
1 Major Road
New Hope, Your State and Zip
Phone 555 123-4567

Mr. Mason spends thirty minutes interviewing the client.
Mr. Mason reviews information with the client and disburses $5.00 to have the document notarized.

VIDEO SCENARIO: PRIVILEGE ISSUE: MISDIRECTED E-MAIL

The paralegal has accidentally sent an e-mail to opposing counsel containing a confidential memo to the client. The supervising attorney is obviously upset and instructs the paralegal on the steps the paralegal must take.

Go to the Companion Website, select Chapter 4 from the pull down menu, and watch this video.

1. Who has the ultimate responsibility for the mistakenly sent e-mail?

2. How does your jurisdiction treat the accidental sending of confidential material to opposing counsel? What are the steps that should be taken?
3. Should there be an office policy on the use of e-mail to communicate with clients about confidential material?
4. How safe is the use of the Internet for sending e-mail?

Chapter 5 Digital Resources at **www.prenhall.com/goldman**

- Author Video Introduction
- Case Study Video: Legal research: Are Books Obsolete?
- Comprehension Quizzes and Glossary

Electronic Research | CHAPTER 5

OPENING SCENARIO

Caitlin Gordon had been flattered at being offered a job as a litigation support paralegal with the promise of travel as a bonus. Her twin sister worked for Ariel Marshall in the same office suite as Owen Mason. Owen Mason had mentioned earlier in the year to Caitlin that he had admired her ability and skill when she was on the opposite side of a case in federal court that involved thousands of pages of electronic discovery. She seemed to be able to pull paper "out of the air" and have it on the large-screen projector instantly. What she had never imagined, when she accepted the new position, was supporting the firm in litigation two thousand miles from home in a small country courtroom without access to a real library, in a complex medical device malpractice case. All that was available were two laptops and a high-speed Internet connection at the motel across the street from the courthouse.

In the middle of trial the other side was being permitted by the court to use a surprise expert to testify based on an obscure local decision. Caitlin calmed Mr. Mason, assuring him that with the Internet connection from the motel, her laptop, and the wireless network she installed back at the motel, everything needed was available and accessible on the World Wide Web. It was just a matter of creating the right query, and the obscure case decision and any appellate updates of it, the information on the expert, and anything else needed was available.

LEARNING OBJECTIVES

After studying this chapter, you should be able to:

1. Describe the goal of research.

2. Describe the online resources available for conducting legal and factual research.

3. Explain the use of the terms *bookmarks* and *favorites* and the value of social bookmarking.

4. Construct a search query and complete an Internet search.

5. Explain how to update legal research electronically.

INTRODUCTION TO ELECTRONIC RESEARCH

The goal of all research is finding information. Traditional legal research consisted of looking through books, usually in a law library, to find cases, statutes, court rules, procedures, and forms. Other traditional research efforts involved manually searching for relevant material in paper documents or microfilm in courthouses, government offices, and clients' offices.

Computers and the Internet have changed the way research is performed. What used to take hours or days to manually search can now be completed in seconds or minutes using computers and a high-speed Internet connection. New sources of information of all types are being made available from print sources that are being converted to digital format, to live web cameras, showing activity in real time like those used to show traffic on the highways in many cities, or the satellite and street level views of many areas of the world. Exhibit 5.1 shows the street view of the entrance to the Boston Commons and the traffic flow around Boston.

Information of all kinds is being created and stored electronically all over the world. Traditional records, like courthouse records, old editions of newspapers and periodicals, and even famous and not so famous artwork are daily being converted into electronic form accessible over the Internet (see Exhibits 5.2 and 5.3). Manual research methods, techniques, and the skills necessary for finding traditional forms of information must give way to new computer research methods and skills.

WWW MINI EXERCISE

Use Google Maps to see the street view of Boston or San Francisco and the live traffic reports at http://maps.google.com.

Exhibit 5.1 Google Maps street view and real-time traffic report of Boston, Massachusetts

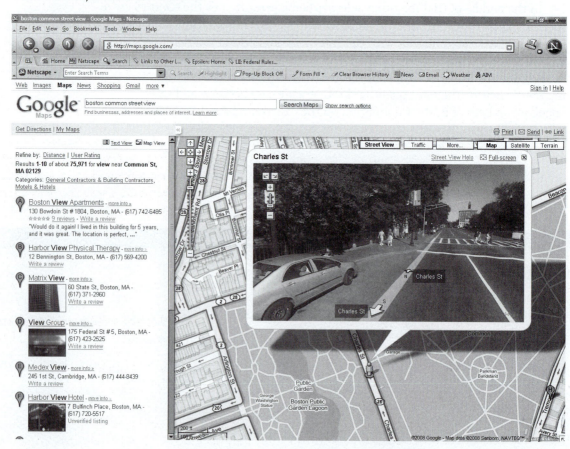

What has not changed is that the researcher must still have a grasp of basic concepts of the subject matter of the search. Legal research still requires an understanding of the goal of the specific research assignment, the legal concepts and terminology, and an understanding of the resources available. Factual research requires an understanding of what is relevant, for example, photographs and newspaper accounts of an accident. Document searches in an e-discovery process requires a list of key terms, dates of inquiry, and parties involved. Effective, efficient, traditional computerized research requires the ability to create (write) **search query** (questions) that will find what is needed. The researcher using a computer must know the language of the subject being searched and the words used to index that subject in the computer database being used.

Search Query
Specific words used in a computerized search.

Exhibit 5.2 NewspaperARCHIVE.com is an archive of newspapers from many areas

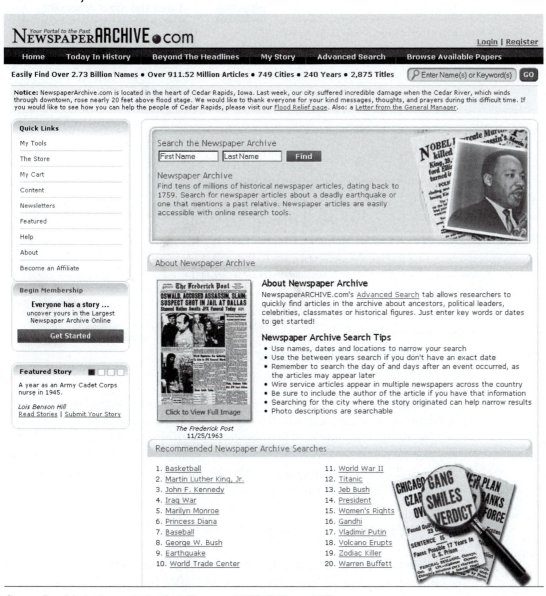

Source: Reprinted with permission from NewspaperARCHIVE.com 2008.

Exhibit 5.3 Archives of the New York Times offers the complete backfiles of over 13 million articles

The same methods apply to the searching of electronic materials of all sorts, law related, factual case related, client files, and non-law related general information. The researcher must be able to fashion a query of the right words and phrases to be searched by the computer. This is true of legal databases, like Westlaw, Lexis, Loislaw, and Internet search engines like Google, Yahoo!, Ask, and free services like the Legal Information Institute and FindLaw.

WWW MINI EXERCISE

Find a satellite view of your home at www.earth .google.com.

ELECTRONIC RESEARCH

A very few years ago conducting electronic research meant finding information on the CDs that contained documents and images copied from hardcopy sources. The rapid advances in computer technology and the development of the Internet has changed the nature of research. Documents and images are being copied and added to electronic archives daily. Major art collections are being digitally copied and added to museum websites. Newspapers, magazines, and historical documents are similarly being digitized and added to Web-based archives. Sometimes it seems everything is available on the Internet. This is not far from the truth. Live cameras (webcams) are continually broadcasting images from everywhere on the planet, including street corners, parks, schools, and in some cases courtrooms. Satellites are used to capture images that are available to anyone with a connection to popular sites like Google. Factual research in many cases can also be conducted with a computer and an Internet connection from anywhere without leaving home or the office.

Legal Research

The three primary **full-service online providers** of computer research services—Lexis, Loislaw, and Westlaw—provide a broad range of legal materials including cases, statutes, and regulations. In addition, **limited-service search providers**, such as VersusLaw, specialize in providing cases and limited access to additional items, such as the Code of Federal Regulations.

In using a limited-service provider, it is important to check the coverage dates and content. In some cases the same information, such as United States Code and the Code of Federal Regulations, is available at other online sources, for example, the U.S. Government Printing Office through the GPO Access website, www. GPO.gov. In all cases, researchers must be certain they have checked all the latest updates to information provided.

Factual Research

Factual research is learning all the facts about a case and finding case-related resources. There is a great value in conducting on-site factual investigation. Seeing firsthand what the client or other witnesses saw offers a perspective for understanding a case from the point of view of the parties involved. Before computerized research, almost everything about the case had to be done in the field by the members of the legal team, lawyers, paralegals, expert witnesses, and investigators. With the resources available over the Internet, some of the on-site work can be done with a computer. Instead of hiring an aerial photographer to fly over an area to get a photo of the scene, Google Earth can be used to find and download a satellite image of almost any place on the planet. Police, fire, building inspection, and similar reports can frequently be downloaded from government agencies 24 hours a day, 7 days a week. Suppliers of professional services, including experts, in all areas can be located over the Internet through online directories and by searching newspapers, periodicals, and specialty journals.

Creating a Research Plan

The first step in research is setting up a research plan. The research plan helps to focus on the issues, sources, and methods for finding the desired information. A few basic questions should be considered in setting up the research plan, as shown in the following checklist:

Full-service Online Providers
Those providing a broad range of legal materials, including cases, statutes, and regulations.

Limited-service Search Providers
Those specialized in providing limited access to cases and additional items.

WWW MINI EXERCISE

- Read the latest U.S. Supreme Court opinion at http://www.su premecourtus.gov
- Visit the home page of the Legal Information Institute at Cornell University Law School to see the information provided at http:// www.law.cornell.edu
- Search and view full text of Supreme Court decisions issued between 1937 and 1975 at www.fedworld .gov/supcourt
- Find the list of available material from the Government Printing Office at www.GPO .gov.

Factual Research
Determining the facts about a case.

Checklist ✓   CREATING A RESEARCH PLAN

1. What is the issue, legal question, or information needed?
   a. a statute or regulation
   b. case law
   c. document
   d. an expert witness
   e. a picture or map
2. What is the appropriate search terminology?
   a. words
   b. phrases
   c. legal terms
3. Where is the material located?
   a. courthouse
   a. government agency
   c. newspapers
   d. client records
   e. private database
   f. in-house traditional materials
   g. fee-based legal services
   h. free Web-based remote libraries
4. What jurisdiction, locality, country is involved?
   a. country
   b. federal
   c. state
   d. local
5. What is the controlling law?
   a. statutory
   b. regulatory
   c. case law
6. What are the types of resources to be used?
   a. primary
   b. secondary finding tools
7. Where is the needed research material located?
   a. in-house traditional materials
   b. fee-based legal services
   c. free Web-based remote libraries

WWW MINI EXERCISE

To conduct a search of the IRS public database, go to http://search.irs.gov/web/advanced-search.htm

---

Search Engines
Services for searching the World Wide Web using words or phrases.

Electronic Search Engines

A **search engine** is a program designed to take a word or set of words and search websites on the Internet. Of the available Internet search engines, each searches in a different fashion. The same search request may generate totally different results on different search engines. The number of search engines is expanding constantly. Some search engines are more suitable than others for legal searches or fact-finding. Many search engines are designed for use by children and families, so they may not return the results needed in the professional arenas. For example, the IRS advanced search window (Exhibit 5.4) is usable by anyone but is most effectively used by tax practitioners or those with an understanding of the terminology used in the tax field.

Free Search Engines

Among the more popular free Internet search engines in common use are Google.com, Yahoo.com, and Ask.com (formerly Askjeeves.com) (see Exhibit 5.5). Each of these free services searches for information using the terms provided by the researcher,

Exhibit 5.4 Internal Revenue Service advanced search engine window

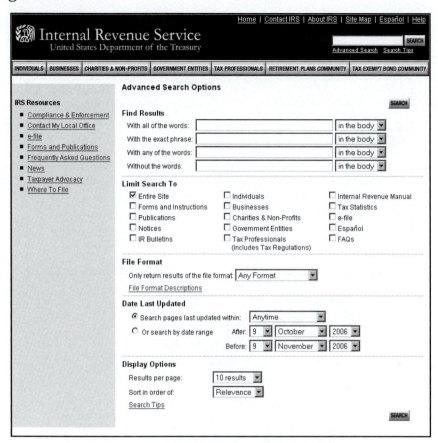

and each service uses a different formula for searching and reporting the results of the search. Results may be many pages long, with hundreds or thousands of results. Some services rank the results in order of popularity of the terms used, with the most popularly searched sites reported first. Others report findings in a chronological order. Still others allow a refinement of the search with the researcher selecting the type of search desired (e.g., general, encyclopedia, dictionary, etc.). It is often helpful or necessary to use more than one search engine with the same query to find the desired information.

Online Resources

Online resources for finding information of all kinds are added to the Web on a daily basis. Virtually anything can be found on the Web if you use the right search engine, website address (URL), and an accurately created search query. Large collections of paper records of all kinds are being converted to electronic form and the material available electronically. Some projects include: immigration records of the United States, newspapers, magazines, land records, graphic images of art collections from museums, research papers, and all form of court records.

FindLaw

FindLaw, a Thomson business, is a free legal-oriented website. It provides both a side for the Public and a side for the Legal Profession. The legal side search engine provides for a single query (see Exhibit 5.6).

The public side provides for a search of a legal issue and a place to aid in finding a lawyer, a source of referrals for subscribing attorneys (see Exhibit 5.7).

Exhibit 5.5 Windows of the most commonly used search engines

Source: Reproduced with permission of Yahoo! Inc. © 2007 by Yahoo! Inc. YAHOO! and the YAHOO! logo are trademarks of Yahoo! Inc. Ask.com screen reprinted with permission of IAC Search & Media, Inc. Google.com screen capture © Google Inc., reprinted with permission.

Exhibit 5.6 FindLaw search window for legal professionals

Source: © 2007 FindLaw, a Thomson business. Reprinted with permission.

Legal Information Institute (LII)

The Legal Information Institute (LII) is a research and electronic publishing activity of the Cornell Law School (http://www.law.cornell.edu/) (see Exhibit 5.8).

The information available is extensive and offers an easy, free method for researching a number of legal topics. It also is a good source of links to other

Exhibit 5.7 FindLaw search window for the public

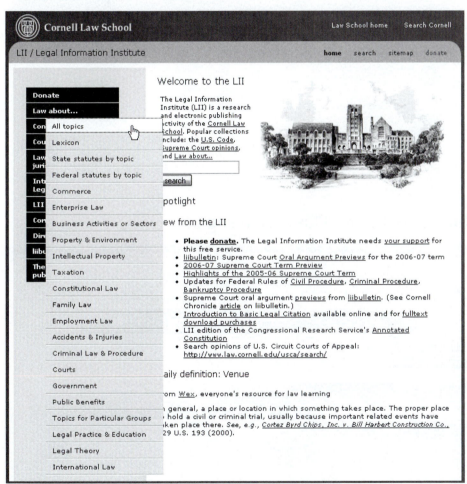

Source: © 2007 FindLaw, a Thomson business. Reprinted with permission.

Exhibit 5.8 Home page of Cornell Law School's Legal Information Institute (LII)

Source: Reprinted with permission from Cornell Law School.

WWW MINI EXERCISE

Find additional resources at the National Institutes of Health at http://www.nih.gov/science/library.html

WWW MINI EXERCISE

LocatorPlus may be found at http://locatorplus.gov/

law-related materials such as the ABA, the official website of the Supreme Court of the United States, and others.

Factual Research. The legal team must frequently find nonlegal-related information to research a case or prepare for trial, such as medical research and information. One of the leading sources is the website of the National Library of Medicine (see Exhibit 5.9) and the National Institutes of Health.

The Collections of the National Library of Medicine may be searched using the LocatorPlus search engines as shown in Exhibit 5.10.

Exhibit 5.9 Home page of the National Library of Medicine

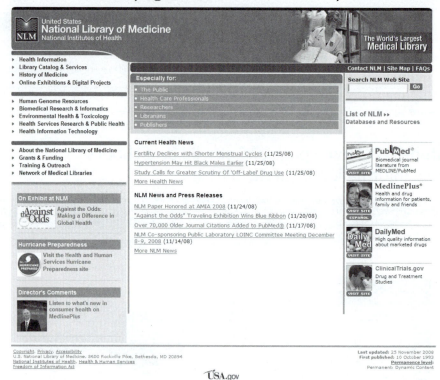

Exhibit 5.10 LocatorPlus Search Engine

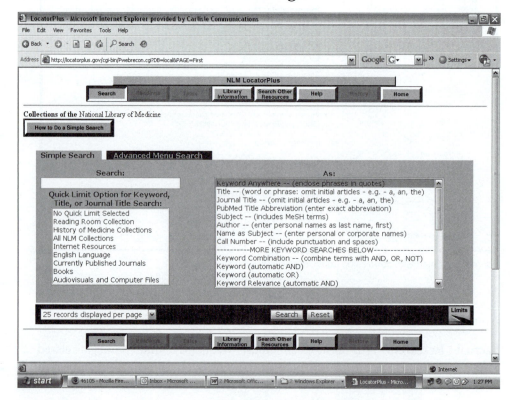

Exhibit 5.11 Netscape Bookmarks

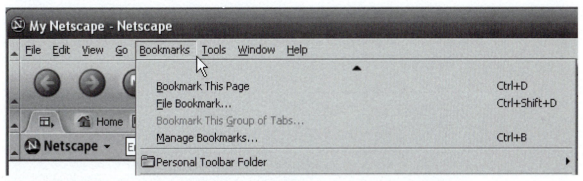

Source: Netscape Communicator browser window © 2005 Netscape Communications Corporation. Used with permission. Netscape Communications has not authorized, sponsored, endorsed, or approved this publication and is not responsible for its content.

Exhibit 5.12 Internet Explorer Favorites menu

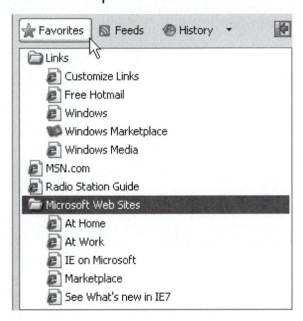

BOOKMARKS AND FAVORITES

Each of the major Internet browsers has a feature for saving the URL or Internet addresses of frequently used sites. In Netscape it is called **Bookmarks** and in Internet Explorer it is called **Favorites** (see Exhibits 5.11 and 5.12).

Bookmarks
Netscape term for saved URLs.

After typing in a Web address it may be added to favorites or bookmarks by selecting the option in the toolbar. A bookmark or favorite may also be added at any time in the course of a Web session when you find a particular page that you want to return to or use on a regular basis (see Exhibit 5.13).

Favorites
Internet Explorer term for saved URLs.

Social Bookmarking

Social bookmarking is a term used for the sharing of favorites or bookmarks. Users save lists of Web sites they find useful. A number of social bookmarking services have been available since 1999. Most of the earlier sites failed for lack of a viable way to make money. New sites have developed and more can be expected to

Social Bookmarking
Sharing of bookmarks or favorites.

Exhibit 5.13 Example of bookmarks and favorites checklist

Topic	Item	URL
Personal Bookmarks	MySpace	www.myspace.com
Free Legal Search Sites	Legal information Institute (LII)	http://www.law.cornell.edu/
Subject (Tags) Maps	Google Earth	http://earth.google.com/
Freedom of Information Act	U.S. Consumer Product Safety Commission	http://www.cpsc.gov/ LIBRARY/FOIA/foia.html
Ethics	ABA Model Rules of Professional Conduct	http://www.abanet.org/ crp/mrpc/mrpc_toc.html

Checklist ✔

RESEARCH SEARCH TERMS

Identify relevant terms to use before starting the research. Think of words, legal terms, and phrases. Consider alternatives, synonyms, antonyms, and related terms.

Persons
- Status
- Relationship
- Occupation
- Group

Jurisdiction
- Federal
- State
- City
- Locality

Type of Action
- Tort
- Contract
- Uniform Commercial Code

Source
- Public records
- Print media (online)
- Public archives or database
- Private archives or database

become available as the concept takes hold as a time-saving method of Internet usage. Commercial sites frequently sort the Internet links (URLs) by category so those with similar interests can access them.

On a local level in an office, a legal team working on a particular case may be working independently, searching for information on the Internet. Each person may find a particular set of sites that is useful and that may be of interest or use to others in the group. By sharing the bookmarks, the team may save time finding the same sites on their own. Collectively, a pattern may be evident of which sites are the most useful by virtue of their use by others. Within a large organization the potential exists to share these URLs and sort them in a manner that gives others a hint as to what others thought were good locations for research for a particular topic or issue—much like a list of cases that is circulated for a particular topic, such as electronic discovery sanctions cases.

METHODS OF CONDUCTING A SEARCH

Database Searches

A **database** is a repository of all kinds of information or data. Client records and those of opposing parties may be thought of as a large database containing e-mails, correspondence, invoices, records, reports, and every manner of electronic document created or stored in the system. Finding the right electronic document (remember the smoking gun documents) requires a search method and query like any other electronic or computer search.

Database
A collection of similar records.

Constructing a Computer Search Query

Finding information on a computer, in a database, or on a website requires a search query, which is a combination of appropriate words and terms that identify the information desired.

Appropriate Search Terminology

Knowing the legal terminology used in the indexes of the available research materials is critical. Publishers of legal materials do not always use the same words or legal terms to index the same rules of law. For example, one publisher uses the term "infant" to identify people under the age of majority that another publisher indexes under "minor." Consider the legal question: "What are the contract rights of a person under the age of majority?" Using "minor" will not produce the desired results in some published materials where the information is listed under "infant." Print research materials require finding material based on a printed index of individual words as selected by the editors of the service.

Computer research is not as dependent on an index of terms and may require a completely different set of words or legal terms. Most computer research allows for searches of words found in the documents using a text search of requested words in the search query, in which the computer looks through the entire document for every instance of the desired words.

Computer research requires the use of appropriate search words to complete a successful search. As with any profession, the legal profession has its own vocabulary. These include words defined by the courts over the years to have specific meaning when used in a legal sense. For example, the legal definition of the term "holder" is "a person to whom a negotiable instrument has been properly negotiated." To the layperson, it may mean people holding something in their hands—not necessarily a negotiable instrument, or relating to any legal formality. Other words have a different meaning to different groups. For example, to the medical community, the word "head" means the top of a person's body; to the sailor it means a bathroom; and to a bartender it means the top of a beer.

People in all areas of life develop words and phrases that help them understand their fields of interest. Conducting a search in a specialty area or particular profession requires an understanding of the terminology and nomenclature of that area. For example, search for information in a medical malpractice case requires the use of medical terms. Exhibit 5.14 shows an example of the topics that are searchable in the West Digest, West Digest Topics and Their Numerical Designations.

Exhibit 5.14 List of West Digest Topics and their numerical designations

1	Abandoned and Lost Property	59	Boundaries	103	Counterfeiting	160	Exchanges
2	Abatement and Revival	60	Bounties	104	Counties	161	Execution
4	Abortion and Birth Control	61	Breach of Marriage Promise	105	Court Commissioners	162	Executors and Administrators
5	Absentees	62	Breach of the Peace	106	Courts (see also Topic 170b Federal Courts)	163	Exemptions
6	Abstracts of Title	63	Bribery	107	Covenant, Action of	164	Explosives
7	Accession	64	Bridges	108	Covenants	165	Extortion and Threats
8	Accord and Satisfaction	65	Brokers	108a	Credit Reporting Agencies	166	Extradition and Detainers
9	Account	66	Building and Loan Associations	110	Criminal Law	167	Factors
10	Account, Action on	67	Burglary	111	Crops	168	False Imprisonment
11	Account Stated	68	Canals	113	Customs and Usages	169	False Personation
11a	Accountants	69	Cancellation of Instruments	114	Customs Duties	170	False Pretenses
12	Acknowledgment	70	Carriers	115	Damages	170a	Federal Civil Procedure
13	Action	71	Cemeteries	116	Dead Bodies	170b	Federal Courts
14	Action on the Case	72	Census	117	Death	171	Fences
15	Adjoining Landowners	73	Certiorari	117g	Debt, Action of	172	Ferries
15a	Administrative Law and Procedure	74	Champerty and Maintenance	117t	Debtor and Creditor	174	Fines
16	Admiralty	75	Charities	118a	Declaratory Judgment	175	Fires
17	Adoption	76	Chattel Mortgages	119	Dedication	176	Fish
18	Adulteration	76a	Chemical Dependents	120	Deeds	177	Fixtures
19	Adultery	76h	Children Out-of-Wedlock	122a	Deposits and Escrows	178	Food
20	Adverse Possession	77	Citizens	123	Deposits in Court	179	Forcible Entry and Detainer
21	Affidavits	78	Civil Rights	124	Descent and Distribution	180	Forfeitures
23	Agriculture	79	Clerks of Courts	125	Detectives	181	Forgery
24	Aliens	80	Clubs	126	Detinue	183	Franchises
25	Alteration of Instruments	81	Colleges and Universities	129	Disorderly Conduct	184	Fraud
26	Ambassadors and Consuls	82	Collision	130	Disorderly House	185	Frauds, Statute of
27	Amicus Curiae	83	Commerce	131	District and Prosecuting Attorneys	186	Fraudulent Conveyances
28	Animals	83h	Commodity Futures Trading Regulation	132	District of Columbia	187	Game
29	Annuities	84	Common Lands	133	Disturbance of Public Assemblage	188	Gaming
30	Appeal and Error	85	Common Law	134	Divorce	189	Garnishment
31	Appearance	88	Compounding Offenses	135	Domicile	190	Gas
33	Arbitration	89	Compromise and Settlement	135h	Double Jeopardy	191	Gifts
34	Armed Services	89a	Condominium	136	Dower and Curtesy	192	Good Will
35	Arrest	90	Confusion of Goods	137	Drains	193	Grand Jury
36	Arson	91	Conspiracy	138	Drugs and Narcotics	195	Guaranty
37	Assault and Battery	92	Constitutional Law	141	Easements	196	Guardian and Ward
38	Assignments	92b	Consumer Credit	142	Ejectment	197	Habeas Corpus
40	Assistance, Writ of	92h	Consumer Protection	143	Election of Remedies	198	Hawkers and Peddlers
41	Associations	93	Contempt	144	Elections	199	Health and Environment
42	Assumpsit, Action of	95	Contracts	145	Electricity	200	Highways
43	Asylums	96	Contribution	146	Embezzlement	201	Holidays
44	Attachment	97	Conversion	148	Eminent Domain	202	Homestead
45	Attorney and Client	98	Convicts	148a	Employers' Liability	203	Homicide
46	Attorney General	99	Copyrights and Intellectual Property	149	Entry, Writ of	204	Hospitals
47	Auctions and Auctioneers	100	Coroners	150	Equity	205	Husband and Wife
48	Audita Querela	101	Corporations	151	Escape	205h	Implied and Constructive Contracts
48a	Automobiles	102	Costs	152	Escheat	206	Improvements
48b	Aviation			154	Estates in Property	207	Incest
49	Bail			156	Estoppel	208	Indemnity
50	Bailment			157	Evidence	209	Indians
51	Bankruptcy			158	Exceptions, Bill of		
52	Banks and Banking			159	Exchange of Property		
54	Beneficial Associations						
55	Bigamy						
56	Bills and Notes						
58	Bonds						

Exhibit 5.14 Continued

210	Indictment and Information	269	Names	320	Railroads	369	Sunday
211	Infants	270	Navigable Waters	321	Rape	370	Supersedeas
212	Injunction	271	Ne Exeat	322	Real Actions	371	Taxation
213	Innkeepers	272	Negligence	323	Receivers	372	Telecommunications
216	Inspection	273	Neutrality Laws	324	Receiving Stolen Goods	373	Tenancy in Common
217	Insurance	274	Newspapers			374	Tender
218	Insurrection and Sedition	275	New Trial	325	Recognizances	375	Territories
		276	Notaries	326	Records	376	Theaters and Shows
219	Interest	277	Notice	327	Reference	378	Time
220	Internal Revenue	278	Novation	328	Reformation of Instruments	379	Torts
221	International Law	279	Nuisance			380	Towage
222	Interpleader	280	Oath	330	Registers of Deeds	381	Towns
223	Intoxicating Liquors	281	Obscenity	331	Release	382	Trade Regulation
224	Joint Adventures	282	Obstructing Justice	332	Religious Societies	384	Treason
225	Joint-Stock Companies and Business Trusts	283	Officers and Public Employees	333	Remainders	385	Treaties
				334	Removal of Cases	386	Trespass
226	Joint Tenancy	284	Pardon and Parole	335	Replevin	387	Trespass to Try Title
227	Judges	285	Parent and Child	336	Reports	388	Trial
228	Judgment	286	Parliamentary Law	337	Rescue	389	Trover and Conversion
229	Judicial Sales	287	Parties	338	Reversions	390	Trusts
230	Jury	288	Partition	339	Review	391	Turnpikes and Toll Roads
231	Justices of the Peace	289	Partnership	340	Rewards		
232	Kidnapping	290	Party Walls	341	Riot	392	Undertakings
232a	Labor Relations	291	Patents	342	Robbery	393	United States
233	Landlord and Tenant	292	Paupers	343	Sales	394	United States Magistrates
234	Larceny	294	Payment	344	Salvage		
235	Levees and Flood Control	295	Penalties	345	Schools	395	United States Marshals
		296	Pensions	346	Scire Facias		
236	Lewdness	297	Perjury	347	Seals	396	Unlawful Assembly
237	Libel and Slander	298	Perpetuities	348	Seamen	396a	Urban Railroads
238	Licenses	299	Physicians and Surgeons	349	Searches and Seizures	398	Usury
239	Liens			349a	Secured Transactions	399	Vagrancy
240	Life Estates	300	Pilots	349b	Securities Regulation	400	Vendor and Purchaser
241	Limitation of Actions	302	Pleading	350	Seduction		
242	Lis Pendens	303	Pledges	351	Sequestration	401	Venue
245	Logs and Logging	304	Poisons	352	Set-Off and Counterclaim	402	War and National Emergency
246	Lost Instruments	305	Possessory Warrant				
247	Lotteries	306	Postal Service	353	Sheriffs and Constables	403	Warehousemen
248	Malicious Mischief	307	Powers	354	Shipping	404	Waste
249	Malicious Prosecution	307a	Pretrial Procedure	355	Signatures	405	Waters and Water Courses
250	Mandamus	308	Principal and Agent	356	Slaves		
251	Manufactures	309	Principal and Surety	356a	Social Security and Public Welfare	406	Weapons
252	Maritime Liens	310	Prisons			407	Weights and Measures
253	Marriage	311	Private Roads	357	Sodomy		
255	Master and Servant	313	Process	358	Specific Performance	408	Wharves
256	Mayhem	313a	Products Liability	359	Spendthrifts	409	Wills
257	Mechanics' Liens	314	Prohibition	360	States	410	Witnesses
257a	Mental Health	315	Property	361	Statutes	411	Woods and Forests
258a	Military Justice	316	Prostitution	362	Steam	413	Workers' Compensation
259	Militia	316a	Public Contracts	363	Stipulations		
260	Mines and Minerals	317	Public Lands	365	Submission of Controversy	414	Zoning and Planning
265	Monopolies	317a	Public Utilities			450	Merit Systems Protection (Merit Systems Protection Board Reporter)
266	Mortgages	318	Quieting Title	366	Subrogation		
267	Motions	319	Quo Warranto	367	Subscriptions		
268	Municipal Corporations	319h	Racketeer Influenced and Corrupt Organizations	368	Suicide		

Source: West Digest Topics. Reprinted with permission of Thomson/West Publishing.

Search Query Usage

It is useful to create a search query and run the query through a number of different search engines, then compare the results. For example, you may wish to search the topic "regulation of paralegals." Each of the following search engines may be accessed by entering its URL (uniform resource locator) in your Web browser:

Alta Vista	www.altavista.com
Ask	www.ask.com
Dogpile	www.dogpile.com
Excite	www.excite.com
Google	www.google.com
MetaCrawler	www.metacrawler.com
Netscape	www.netscape.com
Yahoo!	www.yahoo.com

A WORD OF CAUTION
Addresses of websites tend to change frequently. It is a good idea to keep a list of frequently used websites handy and update it regularly.

Some of the information is shown on the screen and will not require any more searching. The data—such as a phone number, address, or other limited information—will appear and may be copied manually or printed out to capture the displayed page. Other information may be in the form of large text or graphics files. These may be many pages long or involve the use of graphics display programs such as the popular Adobe Reader. Typical of the graphics images are the tax forms available from the Internal Revenue Service, which are available in PDF format, which may be filled in on the computer screen and then printed out. Exhibit 5.15 shows the W-9 form partially completed, ready for printing.

Conducting a Computer Search

Conducting a search requires one to select a computer search index, then to create the query. Each of the online providers uses words to find and retrieve documents. As part of the publication process, indexes are prepared of every

Exhibit 5.15 Example of filable PDF IRS form W-9 available on the Internet

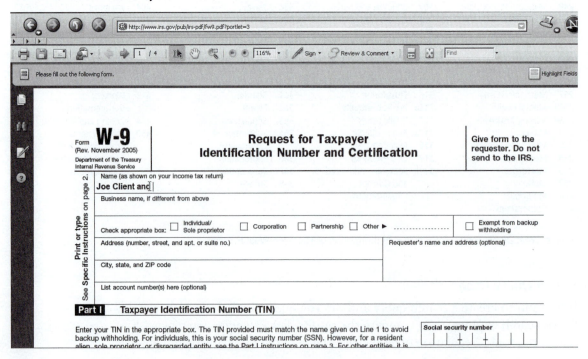

word in the document, the words are tabulated for frequency, and a word index is prepared. The search you create searches this index. VersusLaw uses a **full-text retrieval** method that searches every word except **"stop words"**—words that are used too commonly in documents to be used in a search, such as *the, not, of,* and *and.*

Full-Text Retrieval
A search of every word except "stop words."

Stop Words
Words used too commonly to be used in a search.

Creating the Query

When you conduct a search, you are asking the search engine to find the indexed words you have chosen. These may be legal specialty words or common English words. Single words may be in any of the Internet or legal search engines. Frequently you will be looking for more detailed information. Using combinations of words in the search can narrow the search results. Usually, the most productive search contains a combination of words, which may consist of terms such as "strict liability," "legal malpractice," "automobile accident," or "reckless indifference."

Using Connectors

Connectors are instructions to the search engine to look for documents containing combinations of words. Connectors may be thought of as instructions to the search engine: "Find me documents in which the words 'strict' AND 'liability' appear." The word AND is a connector that instructs the search not to return documents in which only one of the words is found. Exhibit 5.16 shows a Loislaw search with the AND connector.

Connectors
Instructions in a search query on how to treat the combinations of words in the query.

The connector OR instructs the search engine to find either term—the word "strict" OR the word "liability"—and retrieve the documents. Exhibit 5.17 depicts a Lexis search with the OR connector.

Exhibit 5.16 Loislaw search with the AND connector

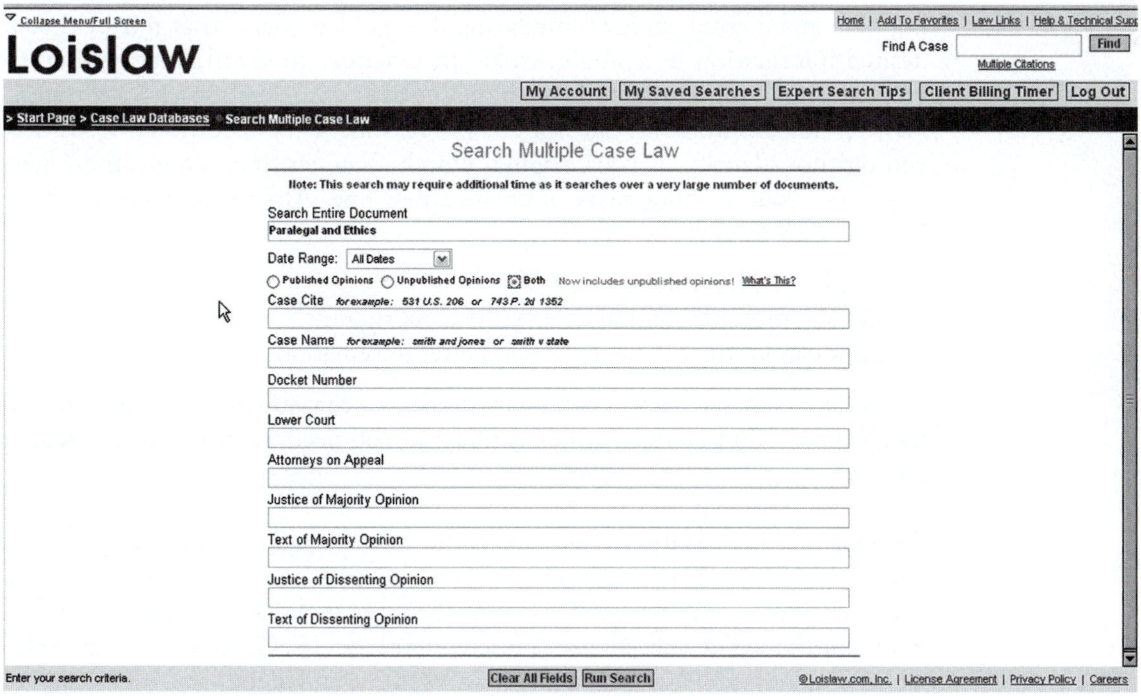

Source: From www.Loislaw.com. Reprinted with the permission of Aspen Publishers.

Exhibit 5.17   LexisNexis search with the OR connector

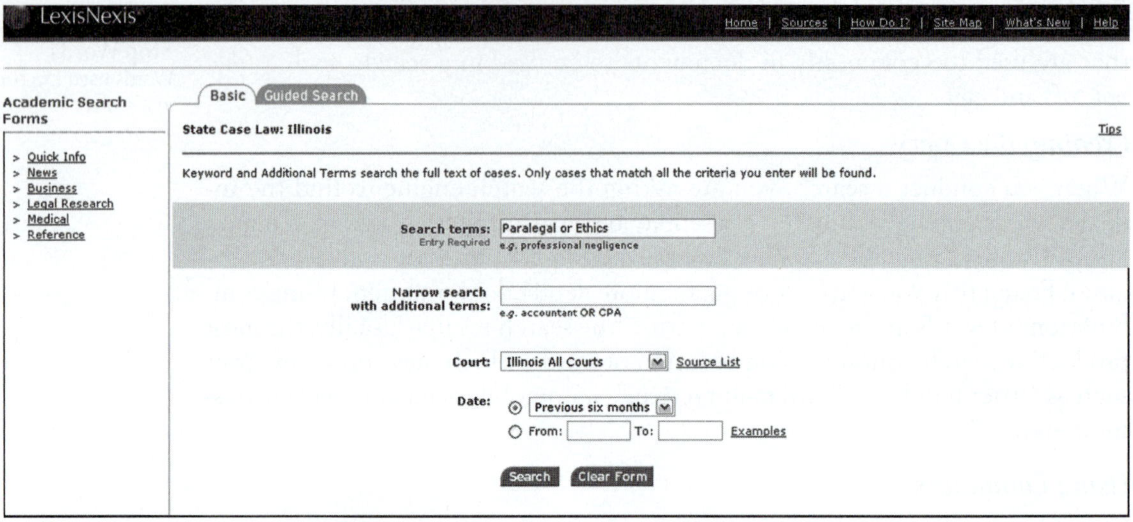

Source: LexisNexis® screen shots used with the permission of LexisNexis, a division of Reed Elsevier Inc. LexisNexis is a registered trademark of Reed Elsevier Properties Inc.

The NOT connector instructs the search to eliminate certain words. For example, you may wish to review documents in which the word "malpractice" is found but NOT those with the word "medical."

In some cases it might be assumed that there will be other words between the desired terms, such as in the phrase "Paralegals are bound by the ethics of their profession." The NEAR connector helps to locate documents where the terms are near each other; for example: find "paralegal" NEAR "ethics." The NEAR connector allows the search for words near each other by specifying the number of words apart that is acceptable.

Searching is a process, not an event. Searching a library is not about spending time and mental energy formulating the "golden query" that retrieves your desired information in a single stroke. In practice, good online searching involves formulating a succession of queries until you are satisfied with the results. As you view results from one search, you'll come across additional leads that you did not identify in your original search. You can incorporate these new terms into your existing query or create a new one. After each query, evaluate its success by asking:

Did I find what I was looking for?
What better information could still be out there?
How can I refine my query to find better information?

Issuing multiple queries can be frustrating or rewarding, depending on how long it takes you to identify the key material you need to answer your research problem.

Search the United States Code.   One of the more frequently searched documents is the U.S. Code. The office of the Law Revision Counsel provides an online search engine that allows searching using the more traditional methods, as shown in Exhibit 5.18. The U.S. House of Representatives U.S. Code search engine also allows searches using concept, related words, fuzzy, and dictionary word searches, as shown in Exhibit 5.19.

Exhibit 5.18 U.S. Code search page

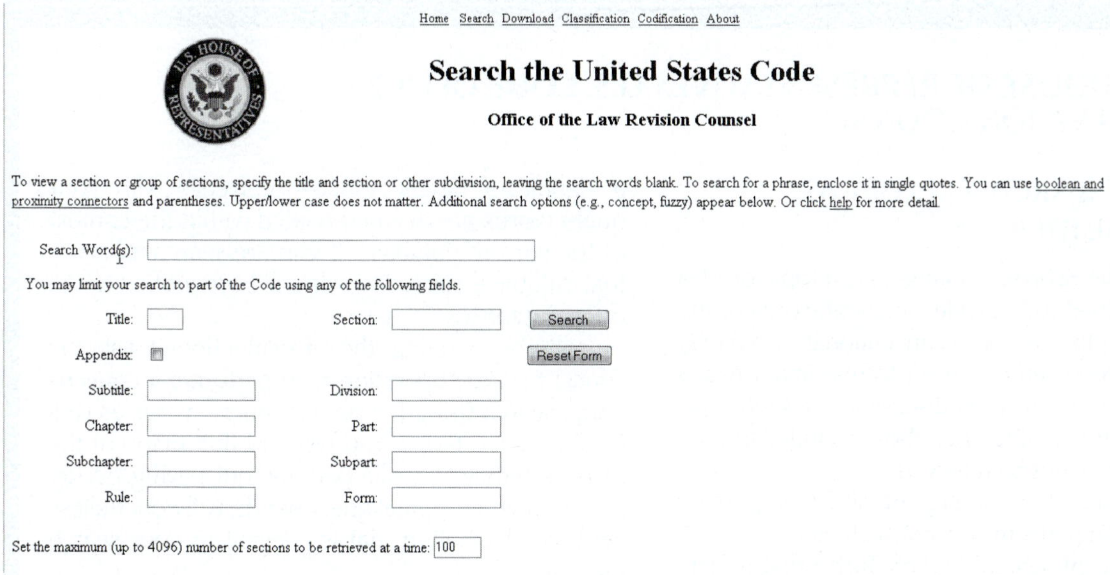

Home Search Download Classification Codification About

Search the United States Code

Office of the Law Revision Counsel

To view a section or group of sections, specify the title and section or other subdivision, leaving the search words blank. To search for a phrase, enclose it in single quotes. You can use boolean and proximity connectors and parentheses. Upper/lower case does not matter. Additional search options (e.g., concept, fuzzy) appear below. Or click help for more detail.

Search Word(s): [   ]

You may limit your search to part of the Code using any of the following fields.

Title: [ ]		Section: [ ]		[Search]
Appendix: ☐				[Reset Form]
Subtitle: [ ]		Division: [ ]		
Chapter: [ ]		Part: [ ]		
Subchapter: [ ]		Subpart: [ ]		
Rule: [ ]		Form: [ ]		

Set the maximum (up to 4096) number of sections to be retrieved at a time: [100]

Source: http://USCODE.house.gov/search/criteria.shtml

Exhibit 5.19 U.S. House of Representatives U.S. Code search engine

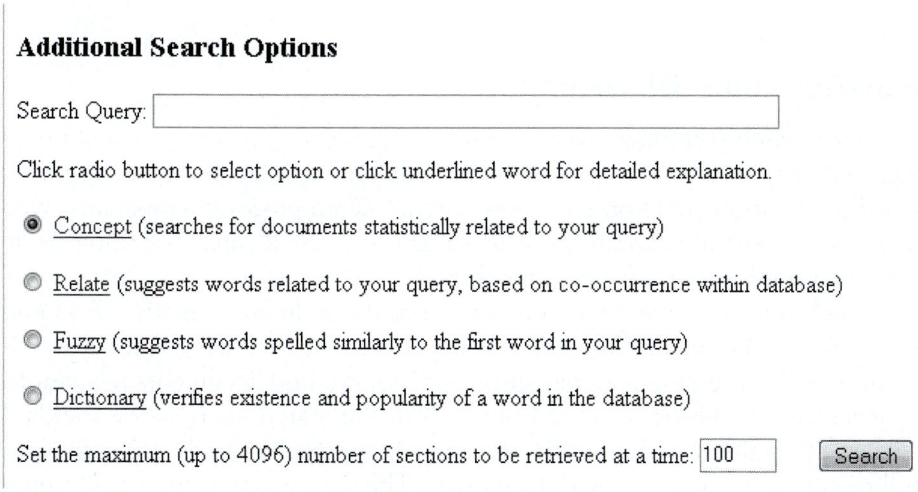

Additional Search Options

Search Query: [   ]

Click radio button to select option or click underlined word for detailed explanation.

◉ Concept (searches for documents statistically related to your query)

◎ Relate (suggests words related to your query, based on co-occurrence within database)

◎ Fuzzy (suggests words spelled similarly to the first word in your query)

◎ Dictionary (verifies existence and popularity of a word in the database)

Set the maximum (up to 4096) number of sections to be retrieved at a time: [100]   [Search]

Concept Search

A topic or idea can be described with a wide variety of words or expressions. For this reason, a conventional search may be too limiting when you want to research a broad topic area. If other records discuss the desired topic but do so in terms other than those included in your query, they may not be retrieved. **Concept searches** broaden the search by including similar or related terms.

An example of a concept search of terms using the Stanford University concept search engine is shown in Exhibit 5.20.

Concept Searching
Using a list of terms statistically related to the words in a query.

ADVICE FROM THE FIELD

THE U.S. HOUSE OF REPRESENTATIVES U.S. CODE OFFICE OF THE REVISION COUNSEL

CONCEPT SEARCH: EXPLORING A GENERAL IDEA

Because of the richness of language, a topic or idea can be described with a wide variety of words or expressions. For this reason, a conventional search may be too limiting when you want to research a broad topic area. If other records discuss the desired topic but do so in terms other than those included in your query, they may not be retrieved.

Rather than formulating an all-encompassing query, you can perform concept searching.

In a concept search, PLWeb Turbo first generates a list of terms that are statistically related to the words in your query. This list is similar to the operation of the Relate Advisor. Those words that have a significant degree of co-occurrence with your query words are deemed related within the context of the current database. If you are searching a virtual database, related words will be identified for all open databases.

After generating the aforementioned list, the concept search operation then performs a conventional search using the original query words as well as the related terms. You will find that many of the records retrieved, while perhaps not having occurrences of your original query words, will nonetheless contain information that is relevant to your search interests.

Source: http://uscode.house.gov/search/help/htmlsrc/consrch.html

Searches and E-Discovery

The same search techniques that are used for conducting searches of traditional legal and factual databases are also used in conducting searches of electronically stored information (ESI) on computer systems. Word processing programs, Web browsers, and e-mail programs provide a simplified search capability using single words or a combination of words and phrases.

Searches for documents in corporate records, including e-mails, Word and financial documents, and records can also be conducted using similar search techniques. In litigation it is frequently necessary to find documents relevant to a particular case. Using selected key words in the search query is the standard method of finding the desired documents among the hundreds, thousands, or millions of electronically stored documents. The danger is that these traditional methods may not produce the needed or the relevant documents. One approach to searches is the concept search mentioned above. Finding documents using these word or terminology methods also presumes that the documents are in searchable format, like Word or WordPerfect format or standard e-mail format. Images and picture versions such as those produced with a photocopier that digitizes the image for electronic storage are generally not searchable by computer. These may need to be manually reviewed or converted to a searchable format using a conversion program like Nuance PDF Converter 5 ond OmniPage 16 to create text-searchable files. In some cases the relevant documents are searched again for documents that may need special handling such as those that contain confidential, trade secret, work product, or privileged communication between attorney and client.

Exhibit 5.20 Concept search of terms using the Stanford University concept search engine

Welcome to the Infomap demo and search engine.

To start, enter one or more search terms in the form and click *"Send"*.
If *"Related Words"* is chosen, you will be given other words that are similar to the ones you put in and might help build your query. In effect, Infomap automatically builds a thesaurus from each collection of documents.

On the other hand, some of the results might be words you definitely do not want in your query. For example, if you want to buy a suit to wear for an interview, you don't want to know anything about lawsuits. In this case, you can *remove* the unwanted meaning from your query. This can be a big help when trying to represent the correct meaning for ambiguous words.

When you are satisfied that your query correctly reflects the underlying *meaning* of your information need, you can choose to *"Retrieve Documents"*, just like a traditional search engine.

The most general model currently available is built from the British National Corpus, a diverse collection of some 100 million words of British English from the end of the twentieth century. You can also investigate models built from specialist medical documents and newspapers, including the New York Times (from the mid 1990's), AP-newswire (from the late 1980's) and the Wall Street Journal.

Keywords: Entry of Judgement

Visualize these Results

Add to query	Subtract from query	Term	Similarity
☐	☐	entry	0.701481
☐	☐	judgment	0.701481
☐	☐	judge	0.555152
☐	☐	court	0.548642
☐	☐	appeal	0.537122
☐	☐	court's	0.534708
☐	☐	judgments	0.515508
☐	☐	jj	0.487848

☐	☐	quashed	0.483223
☐	☐	sheriff	0.480906
☐	☐	application	0.480342
☐	☐	jurisdiction	0.470904
☐	☐	case	0.461804
☐	☐	injunction	0.460742
☐	☐	ord	0.459453
☐	☐	proceedings	0.449337
☐	☐	applicant	0.447948
☐	☐	judge's	0.447682
☐	☐	trial	0.445354
☐	☐	applicants	0.439007

Source: www.Infomap.stanford.edu

IN THE WORDS OF THE COURT . . .

VICTOR STANLEY, INC., PLAINTIFF VS. CREATIVE PIPE, INC., ET AL., DEFENDANT

CIVIL ACTION NO. MJG-06-2662

UNITED STATES DISTRICT COURT FOR THE DISTRICT OF MARYLAND

2008 U.S. Dist. LEXIS 42025

May 29, 2008, Decided

<u>JUDGES:</u> Paul W. Grimm, United States Magistrate Judge

The plaintiff, Victor <u>Stanley, Inc.</u> ("VSI" or "Plaintiff") filed a motion seeking a ruling that five categories of electronically stored documents produced by defendants Creative. Pipe, Inc. ("CPI") and Mark and Stephanie Pappas ("M. Pappas", "S. Pappas" or "The Pappasses") (collectively, "Defendants") in October, 2007, are not exempt from discovery because they are within the protection of the attorney-client privilege and work-product doctrine, as claimed by the Defendants. VSI argues that the electronic records at issue, which total 165 documents, are not privileged because their production by Defendants occurred under circumstances that waived any privilege or protected status. . . .

. . . The foregoing affidavits create the impression that the keyword search Turner conducted [*14] on the text-searchable ESI files, using the seventy keywords developed by M. Pappas and his attorneys, successfully culled out the privileged/protected documents; and this status was confirmed by Monkman's review, and they were withheld from production. . . .

. . . First, the Defendants are regrettably vague in their description of the seventy keywords used for the text-searchable ESI privilege review, how they were developed, how the search was conducted, and what quality controls were employed to assess their reliability and accuracy. While it is known that M. Pappas (a party) and Mohr and Schmid (attorneys) selected the keywords, nothing is known from the affidavits provided to the court regarding their qualifications for designing a search and information retrieval strategy that could be expected to produce an effective and reliable privilege review. As will be discussed, while it is universally acknowledged that keyword searches are useful tools for search and retrieval of ESI, all keyword searches are not created equal; and there is a growing body of literature that highlights the risks associated with conducting [*16] an unreliable or inadequate keyword search or relying exclusively on such searches for privilege review. Additionally, the Defendants do not assert that any sampling was done of the text searchable ESI files that were determined not to contain privileged information on the basis of the keyword search to see if the search results were reliable. Common sense suggests that even a properly designed and executed keyword search may prove to be over-inclusive or under-inclusive, resulting in the identification of documents as privileged which are not, and non-privileged which, in fact, are. The only prudent way to test the reliability of the keyword search is to perform some appropriate sampling of the documents determined to be privileged and those determined not to be in order to arrive at a comfort level that the categories are neither over-inclusive nor under-inclusive. There is no evidence on the record that the

Defendants did so in this case. Rather, it appears from the information that they provided to the court that they simply turned over to the Plaintiff all the text-searchable ESI files that were identified by the keyword search Turner performed as non-privileged, as well as the [*17] non-text searchable files, that Monkman and M. Pappas' limited title page search determined not to be privileged....

UPDATING LEGAL RESEARCH

The legal team always must use the most current statutory and case law in advising clients and arguing cases to the court. One of the features of the American legal system is its constant change. Courts attempt to meet the needs of a changing society by reviewing prior case law and, when appropriate, overruling or modifying it as the contemporary American view of justice dictates. The American legal system concept of *stare decisis* provides that we use prior case law as precedent but change the law as American society changes. Occasionally, existing case law may be held unconstitutional, such as happened with the landmark case of *Roe v. Wade*.

Knowing if the case law being used in a legal argument is the current case law is a vital part of the lawyer's obligation to the client and to the court. Up to the moment before the arguments are made to the court or the brief is submitted, a case that the attorney or the opponent is using as a basis for a legal argument may be overturned. The ethical obligation of candor to the court and of professional competency requires the use of current case law.

Kansas Rules of Professional Conduct

3.3 Advocate: Candor Toward the Tribunal

(a) A lawyer shall not knowingly:
   (1) make a false statement of fact or law to a tribunal or fail to correct a false statement of material fact or law previously made to the tribunal by the lawyer;
   (2) fail to disclose to the tribunal legal authority in the controlling jurisdiction known to the lawyer to be directly adverse to the position of the client and not disclosed by opposing counsel; or
   (3) offer evidence that the lawyer knows to be false. If a lawyer, the lawyer's client, or a witness called by the lawyer has offered material evidence and the lawyer comes to know of its falsity, the lawyer shall take reasonable remedial measures, including, if necessary, disclosure to the tribunal. A lawyer may refuse to offer evidence, other than the testimony of a defendant in a criminal matter, that the lawyer reasonably believes is false.

(b) A lawyer who represents a client in an adjudicative proceeding and who knows that a person intends to engage, is engaging or has engaged in criminal or fraudulent conduct related to the proceeding shall take reasonable remedial measures, including, if necessary, disclosure to the tribunal.

(c) The duties stated in paragraphs (a) and (b) continue to the conclusion of the proceeding and apply even if compliance requires disclosure of information otherwise protected by Rule 1.6.

(d) In an ex parte proceeding, a lawyer shall inform the tribunal of all material facts known to the lawyer which will enable the tribunal to make an informed decision, whether or not the facts are adverse.

Web Exploration

Contrast and compare **Kansas Rules of Professional Conduct** 3.3 Advocate: Candor Toward the Tribunal at http://www.ks courts.org/rules/Rule-In fo.asp?r1=Rules+ Relating+to+Discipline+ of+Attorneys&r2=32 with the American Bar Association Model Rules of Professional Responsibility at http:// www.abanet.org/cpr/mrpc/ mrpc_toc.html, and the ethical rule in your jurisdiction

WWW MINI EXERCISE
Check the decisions of the U.S. Supreme Court for the current day at http://www .supremecourtus.gov.

Thus, an essential part of legal research for the legal team is to verify that they have the latest case or statute. The process is complicated by the method by which changes in statutes or case law are released to the public. Ultimately, new statutes and new case law are reported in a published form, both in paper and electronically, but not all publications are able to disseminate the information daily. Paper versions take time to print and distribute. Not all electronic versions are posted immediately. Therefore, it becomes important to know how quickly the reporting or electronic services used by the law firm or practice distribute poststatutory changes and new cases. More and more courts have their own websites and release case opinions electronically along with the print versions to the public and publishing companies.

What is difficult is knowing if the new cases or new statutes affect the case being researched. When the court specifically mentions a case being cited in a memo of law or a court brief, the paralegal has to know if the new case follows the older case law, reverses it, or in some way differs from the older case.

As soon as a case is entered into an electronic case law database, such as Westlaw, Lexis, Loislaw, or VersusLaw, a general search can be made for references to the case name or citation. Before it is entered, the same search will not show the newest reference. Even a reference to the case will not tell whether the case law has changed; only that another case has referred to it. Someone must actually read the case to see how the court has used it or referred to it in the opinion.

Law-Related Search Resources

The resources described in this section are specific to the legal profession. Most of these require a subscription fee except for general public use, which of course is not as detailed as that usually required by the legal team.

Shepard's

Long a standard tool of legal research in law libraries, *Shepard's Citations* is a multivolume set of books listing cases and statutes by their respective citations and giving the citation of every other case in which the listed case was mentioned. The listings originally were compiled by editors who physically read through every case reported, to find citations. These then were reported by case citation, with every other mention of the case reported by its citation in chronological fashion, with notations indicating if the opinion was reversed, affirmed, followed, overruled, and so on. The process of using Shepard's to check legal citations came to be called **"Shepardizing"**—a term that many legal assistants still use, even when using other citation-checking services such as Westlaw's KeyCite. An advantage to the Shepard's Citator is the editorial symbol system used to indicate how the new case affects the case being checked.

Sheparding
The process of using Shepard's, an electronic compilation of legal citations, to update research.

The problem with the traditional paper form of Shepard's is the lag in time for the print version to be prepared and sent out to subscribers. Shepard's now provides the same service online through the Lexis service; subscribers can obtain the latest case information, to the day, by calling a toll-free number. Another of the difficulties in using the print version of Shepard's is the number of hardbound volumes and paperback updates required to be consulted, and finding the latest update pamphlet if someone has misfiled it in the law library.

Many educational institutions and public libraries subscribe to the Web-based LexisNexis Academic Universe. Shepard's citation service usually is available for the U.S. Supreme Court as part of the service, but other federal and state Shepard's citation services may not be included because of the cost of the additional license fees involved.

GlobalCite

Loislaw's GlobalCite provides a reverse chronological list of the case law, the statutes in the order of the highest number of citation occurrences, the regulations listed in relevancy order, and reference to other databases in the Loislaw library.

KeyCite

KeyCite is the Westlaw online citation update service. The Westlaw KeyCite is a combination citator and case finder. Unlike other similar services, KeyCite uses the West Key number system and West Headnotes.

V.Cite

V.Cite, VersusLaw's citation tool, will produce a list of all cases within the selected jurisdictions that have cited the case being searched. The list that a V.Cite search produces will include cases that have cited the initial case, which most likely will discuss similar issues.

SUMMARY

CHAPTER 5

Introduction to Electronic Research	Goal of research: Finding information. Traditional methods: Paper records and books.
Electronic Research	Information accessible over the Internet.
Legal Research	Full-service providers: Provide range of materials including cases, statutes, and regulations; examples Lexis, Loislaw, Westlaw. Limited-service providers: Offer a limited range of materials, other limitations may include limited range of dates of available cases.
Factual Research	Factual investigation: Determine the facts of a case. Internet factual research: Using the Internet to obtain items such as aerial photographs, reports, and periodical accounts.
Creating a Research Plan	Set up the research plan. Write accurate search queries. Use a checklist to analyze the case.
Electronic Search Engines	Search engine: A program designed to take a word or set of words and search websites. Free search engines: Examples include Google.com, Ask.com, Yahoo.com, Netscape.com.
Law-Related Search Resources	Generally charge a fee except for very limited access.
Online Resources	Availability of information: New sources of information are added daily. Legal-oriented: Examples include FindLaw.com, Legal Information Institute at Cornell University School of Law. Nonlegal-oriented: One example is the National Institutes of Health—National Library of Medicine website.

Bookmarks and Favorites	Bookmarks and favorites: Lists of frequently used Web addresses that are saved within an Internet browser, called bookmarks by Netscape and favorites by Internet Explorer. Social bookmarking: The sharing of frequently used websites among a group.
Methods of Conducting a Search	
Database Searches	Databases are repositories of data requiring a search query.
Conducting a Search	Requires selecting a computer search index and creating a query. Requires a combination of words and phrases of the appropriate words and legal terms as used in the index by the publisher of the material where the information is stored.
Creating a Computer Search Query	Requires a combination of words and phrases of the appropriate words and legal terms as used in the index by the publisher of the material where the information is stored; most productive searches contain a combination of words.
Using Connectors	Connectors are instructions to the search engine to look for documents containing combinations of words. Connectors include *and*, *or*, and *not*.
Updating Legal Research	
Use of Current Law	The legal team must always use the most current statutory and case law.
Tools for Updating Legal Research	Electronic methods include the use of Loislaw's GlobalCite, Westlaw's KeyCite, VersusLaw's V.Cite, and LexisNexis' Shepard's.

KEY TERMINOLOGY

Bookmarks   125
Candor   137
Concept searching   133
Connectors   131
Database   127
Factual research   119

Favorites   125
Full-service online providers   119
Full-text retrieval   131
Limited-service search providers   119
Search engines   120

Search query   117
Shepardizing   138
Social bookmarking   125
Stop words   131

CONCEPT REVIEW QUESTIONS AND EXERCISES

1. Test your knowledge and comprehension of the topics in this chapter by completing the multiple-choice questions on the textbook Companion Website.
2. Test your knowledge and comprehension of the topics in this chapter by completing the True-False questions on the textbook Companion Website.
3. Describe how the computer is used to conduct factual and legal research.
4. Describe the goal of research.
5. Prepare a list of online sources of legal information, including URLs.
6. List and describe the use of Web search engines.
7. Describe the use of search connectors in a search query.

8. What is the difference in using an Internet search engine for factual research and a legal search engine for legal research?
9. What are the different methods for updating legal research electronically vs. manually? Explain the differences.
10. What differences are there in using a legal search engine with natural language and one with legal terms? Use the Internet to find the answer, and list the URLs of the sources you used.
11. Explain the use of the terms *bookmarks* and *favorites*.
12. Explain the value of social bookmarking.
13. How does the duty of candor to the tribunal impact the duties of the legal researcher?
14. How does a concept search differ from a Boolean search?

INTERNET EXERCISES

1. Construct and run a computer search query for the following factual searches:
   a. A map of the flooded areas of New Orleans from the last hurricane
   b. Recalls of three-wheeled vehicles
   c. Experts on textiles used in firefighter equipment
   d. Locations offering flu shots in your area
   e. An aerial view of the location of the accident in Appendix 1.
2. Use the Government Printing Office website (http://www.GPO.gov/) to find and print out the summary purpose of 21 CFR 404, or any other section assigned by your instructor.
3. Make a list of the available federal primary sources available on the Government Printing Office website.
4. From the site map of the VersusLaw website, print out for your future computer searches the printable version of the VersusLaw Research Manual.
5. Use the Legal Information Institute at Cornell University website to find title 44 CFR 201 and print out the list of key responsibilities of FEMA, state, and local/tribal governments. Does this site provide direct access or a link to another source? Explain. What primary federal sources does this site offer?
6. Conduct a search for information on paralegal ethics using two different search engines and print out a copy of the first page of each result. Are they the same, and what is the difference in results and order of presentation? Possible search engines include: Google, Yahoo!, Ask, and FindLaw.
7. If you have access to Loislaw, NexisLexis, Westlaw, or VersusLaw, conduct a search for paralegal ethics cases for your jurisdiction. Prepare a list of authorities cited in the search.
8. Print out the current list of opinions of the U.S. Supreme Court.
9. Print out the complete version of Rule 3.3, Candor toward the Tribunal, of the ABA Model Rules of Professional Conduct. Use a Web browser search engine to locate Web addresses of the courts in your jurisdiction. Prepare a list by court and URL for future reference.
10. Use a Web browser search engine to locate Web addresses of the governmental resources available in your local town or city and for your state, including the availability of online forms. Prepare a list of resources by URL for future reference.
11. Find a fee agreement letter on the Web.
12. Find information on a publicly traded corporation from the government website and from the company website.

PORTFOLIO ASSIGNMENT

Prepare an office policy and procedure for out-of-office technical issues including use of computers when traveling, support in trial in distant locations, and other security and procedural steps, including a timetable where appropriate.

SCENARIO CASE STUDY

Use the opening scenario for this chapter to answer the following questions. The setting is a paralegal sitting alone in her temporary office in a small suburban town after normal working hours.

1. Prepare a list of technology requirements for the trial team that will be trying a case at a remote courthouse in another state. Rank the list in the order of priority and explain the reasons.
2. Use a search engine to find prices for the items included on the list in question 1.
3. What are the ethical issues involved in using the wireless Internet connection mentioned in the opening scenario?
4. What advance planning is required before leaving the office to travel to the trial location?
5. Use the Internet to find the coverage area maps for the major wireless carriers that might be used in remote courthouses. Print out a copy of each.

CONTINUING CASES AND EXERCISES

1. Update the Internet resources list from Chapter 1. Prepare and distribute a list of social bookmarks to the class.
2. Continue to maintain a time record as outlined in Chapter 1.
3. Review the information on First Will—Husband and Wife client shown at the end of the chapter. Review the information presented for the client. Set up a file for the client for use in answering the questions and preparing the documents. This exercise will require information found in future chapters and is a continuing exercise. Your instructor may give you additional instructions.
4. Use the Internet to locate the information on the following question for the client. "What are the requirements to obtain passports for my two children?"
5. Use the Internet to obtain the needed form to apply for the passports. Save a copy for future use and print out a copy.
6. Where can the client go to apply for the passports in your area?
7. Keep track of the time spent working on the client's case. Track the date, time spent, and activity.
8. Locate an aerial photo of the scene of the accident in the case study in Appendix 1.

ADVANCED EXERCISES

1. Continue to document time spent in the course using Tabs3.
2. Add calendar information for your other courses.
3. Prepare a search query to locate information about any defects, recalls, or other information that may be useful in processing the accident described in the case study in Appendix 1.
4. Execute the search query and save the applicable URLs and the summary of the documents or locations found.
5. Research any applicable legal issues involved in the case study including sources of applicable regulations or laws.
6. Law Office Management
   Opening and operating a law office, or any business, involves a number of issues: Setting up the legal structure, hiring employees, paying taxes and keeping financial records. Each type of business has its peculiarities. For the lawyer it includes special obligations with regard to holding and disbursing client's funds, ethical obligations of confidentiality, and protection of client records.

   Based on information in the opening chapter scenarios, complete the following assignments.

   a. Obtain the necessary forms from the Internal Revenue Service:
      i. to request a business tax payer identification number (W-9)
      ii. for employee withholding information (W-4)
      iii. for employee tax withholding tables (Circular E)

b. Download information on forming a professional corporation in your jurisdiction, including necessary forms.

c. Obtain a template for an employment application for future hires.

d. Set up a spreadsheet for tracking and calculating client bills.

e. Set up a spreadsheet for calculating payroll.

f. Set up a client contact database that can also be used to check for conflicts of interest when new clients come in.

g. As a paralegal office manager, set up a list of qualifications and criteria you would use to hire a paralegal, a litigation support paralegal, a secretary, and an information technology specialist.

First Will—Husband and Wife

Mr. Mason is well on his way to a successful law practice.

The new clients, a husband and wife, are requesting the preparation of a simple will before they go on their first vacation out of the country to Canada with their children.

1. Do they need passports?
2. What are the rules with regard to obtaining a passport for children?
3. Download the appropriate passport application. Save the form as a template for future use.
4. In your immediate area, where is the closest location for applying for a passport?
5. What are the rules on executing a will in your jurisdiction?
6. In your jurisdiction, what are the rules for distributing an estate if there is no will?
7. What are the ethical and practice issues involved in using a form downloaded from the Internet?
8. Create a form for a new client that can be used in cases like this involving a family and a will request.
9. Complete the client form.
10. Set up the new client information using the information provided below and track the time you spent in working on this client's case and generate an invoice.

Client Information

Duane Matthew: date of birth 09/01/1960
Tanya Matthew: date of birth 11/15/1961
321 Michelle Court
Ashville, Your State and Zip
555 998-7777
Children:
Patricia: date of birth 7/26/1994
Pasquale: date of birth 3/19/1996

Mr. Mason spends one hour and thirty minutes interviewing the clients.
Mr. Mason spends two hours drafting documents.
Mr. Mason spends one hour reviewing information with the clients.
Mr. Mason spends one-half hour with clients executing wills.

VIDEO SCENARIO: LEGAL RESEARCH—ARE BOOKS OBSOLETE?

In the middle of a trial in another state, the trial attorney sends his paralegal to the courthouse law library to find a case that has been cited as precedent. The local courthouse has both traditional books and electronic research services available. A password not available to visiting legal teams is needed to use the electronic system.

Go to the Companion Website, select Chapter 5 from the pull down menu, and watch this video: Legal Research—Are Books Obsolete?

1. Should members of the legal team be skilled in using alternative methods for conducting research?
2. If a password were available would the paralegal be able to conduct the research if the legal research service is not one in which she had been trained?
3. How could this lack of research tools have been avoided? What hardware or software should the legal team take with them when they are trying cases away from their normal jurisdiction?

Chapter 6 Digital Resources at **www.prenhall.com/goldman**

■ Author Video Introduction
■ Comprehension Quizzes and Glossary

Word Processing

OPENING SCENARIO

Ethan Benjamin had worked for many years at a law firm that relied on an older version of WordPerfect, not out of personal choice but because the senior partners said they did not want to spend the money to upgrade or change to a new program that would require buying multiple licenses. The reality was that many of the older partners, secretaries, and paralegals were comfortable with the current program and did not like change, and did not want to learn a new program.

In his first day at the Newtown office of a small, very progressive law firm he discovered that everyone had the latest software, but not the version of WordPerfect with which he was familiar. When he arrived the first morning he saw on his computer that they were using Microsoft Word and not Corel WordPerfect. In a casual conversation in the coffee room he learned they were going to upgrade shortly to the newest version of the Microsoft Office Suite. It was obvious to him after many hours of trying to prepare documents that there were substantial improvements and differences in the word processor used in the new office. He was getting frustrated at not being as efficient as he had been with the old program, but at the same time thrilled with many of the new features that, with a few mouse clicks, he could quickly perform that required a lot of additional time and effort with the word processing program at the old firm. With the news of the new version that would be installed soon, his anxiety increased. Part of his frustration and resulting stress was not being able to ask anyone for help because, as he was discovering, the legal team of Mr. Mason and Mrs. Hannah were constantly in court with no one left in the office except him. Unlike his old office in the large city, there was no corner bookstore to run down to where he could get a non-geek guide to using programs.

LEARNING OBJECTIVES

After studying this chapter you should be able to:

1. Explain why the ability to adapt to changes in software is an important job skill.

2. Find desired functions and navigate in word processors.

3. Find online and program resources for learning how to use the program and its features.

4. Create and save a document in a word processor.

5. Discuss security issues and solutions in saving word processing documents.

6. Use some of the special features in word processors in creating documents.

7. Recognize changes in updates to major word processor software programs.

INTRODUCTION TO WORD PROCESSING

Written communication and document preparation are at the heart of every law office. It may be preparation of letters, contracts, agreements, and pleadings for clients, other counsel, or the court. Written clarity and accuracy frequently means writing, rewriting, and correcting the same document, sometimes multiple times by a number of different members of the legal team.

The ability to easily make even minor changes in document language has a direct impact on the willingness of those reviewing the document to suggest changes and make them in the final version. Computerized word processing makes this possible. Word processing files are sent electronically to the appropriate members of the legal team for review. Changes or revisions are frequently made to the electronic file copy by the reviewer. Where multiple parties may be working on a document, changes made to the original document, by each person on the legal team, may be monitored by using built-in features such as MS Word's Track Changes tool. This feature shows the original text, the deleted text, and the new text, by a series of lines that show as a line strike through the deleted text, and by margin notes on the document. When the final document is completed it may be sent by e-mail, fax (frequently directly from the computer without any intermediate paper), and in some jurisdictions filed electronically with the court.

Today the most commonly used software program in the law office is the word processor. Although many different word processing programs are available, the legal community most commonly uses either Corel WordPerfect or Microsoft Word. Exhibit 6.1 shows a comparison between the menus and tool bars of WordPerfect X4 and MS Word 2003. In addition to the usual typing functions, these programs have built-in software tools that check spelling and grammar and allow customized formatting using a variety of type sizes and font styles in the same document—functions that have not been possible with a typewriter.

All word processing programs have a set of basic word processing functions, like format, style, and saving options. Some programs offer additional features like document comparison, mail merge, and automated creation of tables of authorities using built-in mini programs called **macros**. Each new version of WordPerfect and Word has offered additional functions and improved features. Microsoft Word 2007, and the companion programs, Excel 2007, Access 2007, and PowerPoint 2007, in the 2007 Microsoft Office system offer the same traditional functions plus new features and a new user interface called the **Ribbon**. The Ribbon interface for Word 2007 is shown in Exhibit 6.2.

Macro
A set of instructions or keystrokes (a program within a program).

Ribbon
A term used to describe the new user interface in Microsoft Office 2007 suite of products.

Exhibit 6.1 Comparison of Corel WordPerfect X4 and Microsoft Word 2003 menus and toolbars

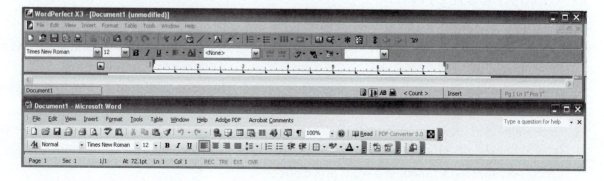

Exhibit 6.2 The Ribbon user interface for Word 2007

CHANGE

No one really likes change, but change is inevitable in almost everything. How we adapt to change is what is important. For the paralegal, legal assistant, lawyer, and members of the legal team, change is constant. We expect the courts to change case law and legislators to change statutory law. For many, job mobility is part of the change that has come to be expected. Many members of the legal team work as independent professionals, members of firms change jobs for better positions, and firms merge and get absorbed into other organizations. With these changes are changes in the software used in the workplace. It may be a different program like WordPerfect instead of Word. Or it may be a different version of the same program like Word 2007 instead of Word 2003. What is important is the ability to adapt, to recognize the common features and functions, and quickly learn, generally on one's own, the differences, the new features, and the new user interface. The following material addresses the common elements that apply to all programs of the same type, word processing, spreadsheets, and other common law office applications. As you look at the different programs, and new versions of existing programs, look for the common elements and the ways of navigating to familiar tools and features. Finally, learn how to use the built-in help features to learn the use of the new features and tools.

Word processing programs are usually purchased as part of an office suite of integrated programs like the Microsoft Office Suite or the Corel WordPerfect Office. The Help features of the programs included in the individual suites are presented in a consistent format such as those of the Microsoft Office Suite shown in Exhibit 6.3.

Help features are available in Microsoft Office both offline, on your computer as part of the program, and online, using a connection to an Internet site, such as Microsoft Office Online, as shown in Exhibit 6.4. The online content includes an extensive group of self-paced tutorials. It cannot be emphasized enough that unless software features, such as creating a table of authorities, are used on a regular basis, a refresher may be needed. If a new feature or one not previously utilized must be used, such as mail merge, help is available offline and online at the desktop workstation. No one is expected to know every feature of every program that they will use. What is expected is the ability to learn the new feature or find the necessary help when a deadline looms or there is no support line available.

One of the issues with change is the ability of the new software to support old file formats from earlier versions. For example, documents saved in the new Word 2007 are not compatible with the earlier Word 2003. If the older and newer versions are being used by people sharing documents, they must be saved in the older version format or they cannot be opened by users of the old version. In some cases very early version formats are not supported when newer versions are released. WordPerfect Office X4 does support the older version of file formats, including

Exhibit 6.3 Microsoft Office Suite programs offline Help screens

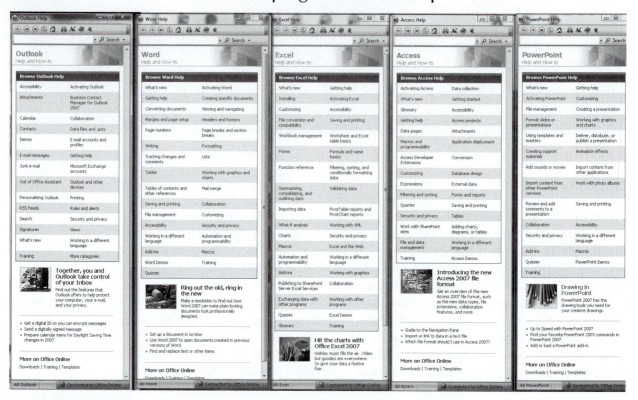

some of the oldest version of Microsoft Word, which Word may not support. This becomes an issue when documents prepared using the older version format are needed, such as contracts, wills, or briefs that contain language that requires modification and retyping the whole document is not desirable.

Exhibit 6.5 shows a representative word processor screen, Word 2003.

NAVIGATING IN WORD PROCESSOR PROGRAMS

The initial reaction of users of Microsoft Office 2003 and earlier versions is that there is a major change from the appearance of Word 2003 as shown in Exhibit 6.5 and the new Ribbon view in Word 2007 as shown in Exhibit 6.2. The initial feeling is that everything must be relearned about the use of the program. In reality all of the same functions are still available; only the location and method of selection has changed. For example, to open a new file in Word 2003, the File pulldown menu was selected and New selected from within that menu. In the Ribbon, the Office Button (a new feature) is selected and New chosen from that listing as shown in Exhibit 6.6.

The New option in these, and most programs, opens a blank document. Existing files are opened with the Open command, and the desired file selected using the Open File window, similar to the Windows Explorer window.

Menus and Toolbars

Menus and toolbars are the traditional ways to access the features and information about the program, including help in using the program and in learning about the program. Exhibit 6.7 shows the information available in Microsoft Office 2003 for learning about the program and its features by using the Help menu, in this case explaining the relationship between menus and toolbars.

Exhibit 6.4 Microsoft Office online training site

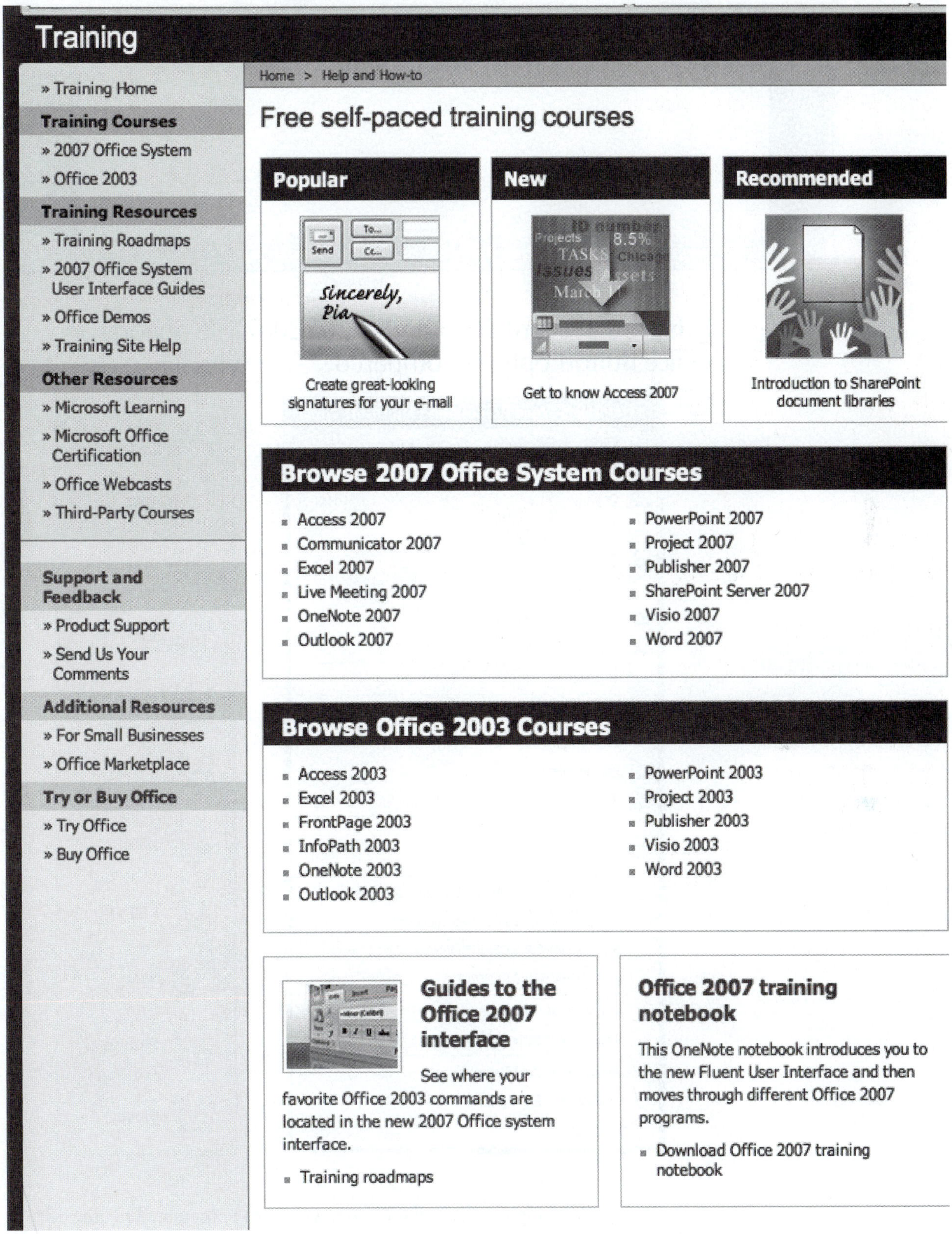

Training

» Training Home

Training Courses

» 2007 Office System

» Office 2003

Training Resources

» Training Roadmaps

» 2007 Office System
User Interface Guides

» Office Demos

» Training Site Help

Other Resources

» Microsoft Learning

» Microsoft Office
Certification

» Office Webcasts

» Third-Party Courses

**Support and
Feedback**

» Product Support

» Send Us Your
Comments

Additional Resources

» For Small Businesses

» Office Marketplace

Try or Buy Office

» Try Office

» Buy Office

Home > Help and How-to

Free self-paced training courses

Popular

Create great-looking
signatures for your e-mail

New

Get to know Access 2007

Recommended

Introduction to SharePoint
document libraries

Browse 2007 Office System Courses

- Access 2007
- Communicator 2007
- Excel 2007
- Live Meeting 2007
- OneNote 2007
- Outlook 2007

- PowerPoint 2007
- Project 2007
- Publisher 2007
- SharePoint Server 2007
- Visio 2007
- Word 2007

Browse Office 2003 Courses

- Access 2003
- Excel 2003
- FrontPage 2003
- InfoPath 2003
- OneNote 2003
- Outlook 2003

- PowerPoint 2003
- Project 2003
- Publisher 2003
- Visio 2003
- Word 2003

**Guides to the
Office 2007
interface**

See where your
favorite Office 2003 commands are
located in the new 2007 Office system
interface.

- Training roadmaps

**Office 2007 training
notebook**

This OneNote notebook introduces you to
the new Fluent User Interface and then
moves through different Office 2007
programs.

- Download Office 2007 training
notebook

Exhibit 6.5 Microsoft Word 2003 new document screen

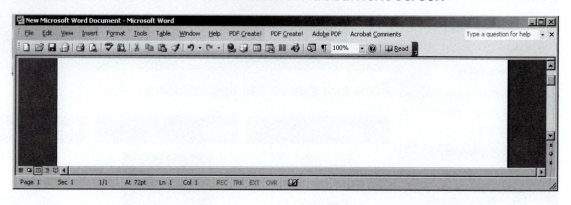

Exhibit 6.6 Word 2003 and Word 2007 File options and Office Button options compared

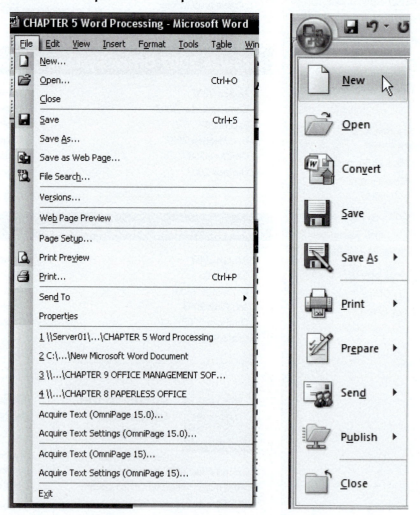

In Word 2007 help is still available from within the program. The new icon is a "?" on the right side of the Ribbon screen. Selecting this option opens a screen with links directly to the Microsoft website as shown in Exhibit 6.8.

The principal difference in the traditional interface and the new Ribbon interface is the grouping of commands by tasks most frequently used in a Tab format for the Groups as shown in Exhibit 6.9 from the Microsoft tutorial website.

Exhibit 6.7 Microsoft Office 2003 Word Help—About menus and toolbars

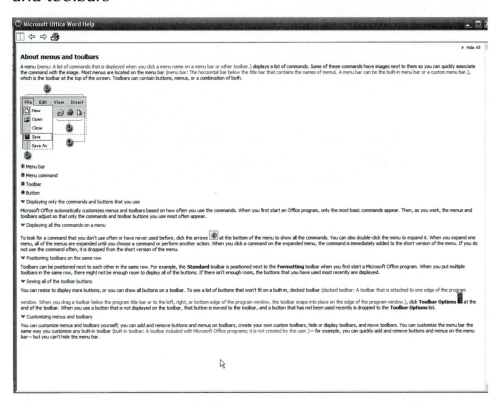

Exhibit 6.8 Word 2007 Help screen with online connection

Exhibit 6.9 Ribbon interface showing the Tabs, Groups, and Command buttons

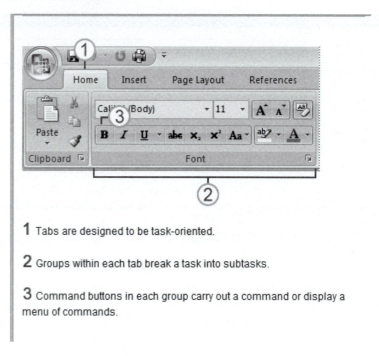

1 Tabs are designed to be task-oriented.

2 Groups within each tab break a task into subtasks.

3 Command buttons in each group carry out a command or display a menu of commands.

Exhibit 6.10 Menu comparison between programs Microsoft Office 2003 and Corel WordPerfect X.4

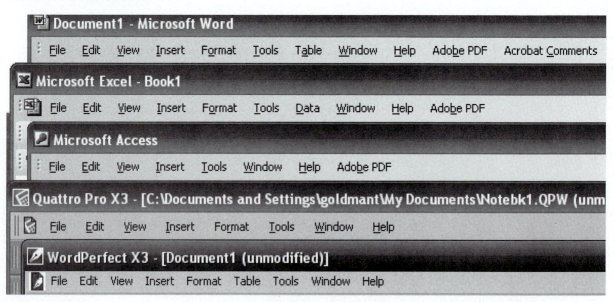

There has been a consistency in menus and toolbar options in the different programs in the same office suite of programs, like Microsoft Office or WordPerfect Office. As shown in Exhibit 6.10, there is also a surprising similarity in location and menu options in most other software used in the legal community. For example, the first menu item on most traditional program menu toolbars is File and one of the last in the row on the menu toolbar is Help.

Exhibit 6.11 Comparison of Ribbon Interface in the 2007 versions of Word, Access, Excel, and PowerPoint

Word

Access

Excel

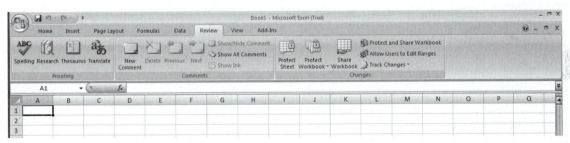

PowerPoint

The use of similar terminology and nomenclature makes switching between programs easier. For example, the menu and toolbar items within each of the programs in a suite perform the same functions.

What is the difference between a menu and a toolbar? Menus display a list of commands and are located on the menu bar, also called a toolbar, at the top of the page in the program. Toolbars can contain menus, buttons, or a combination of both. Microsoft Office 2007 does change the traditional appearance, but the basic functions of the programs are the same as in the previous version.

As with the traditional interface similarity across the suite of programs, the new Ribbon interface is the same with the new program versions. For comparison purposes, the new Ribbon interface for Word, Excel, Access, and PowerPoint 2007 is shown in Exhibit 6.11.

As with all the Microsoft programs, online tutorials (Exhibit 6.12 and Exhibit 6.13) are available to help learn about the feature of the Ribbon.

WWW MINI EXERCISE

To learn more about the Ribbon and take the tutorial lesson, go to http://office.microsoft.com/training/Training.aspx?AssetID=RP101563591033&CTT=6&Origin=RC101562731033

Exhibit 6.12 Microsoft online tutorial "What's on the Ribbon?"

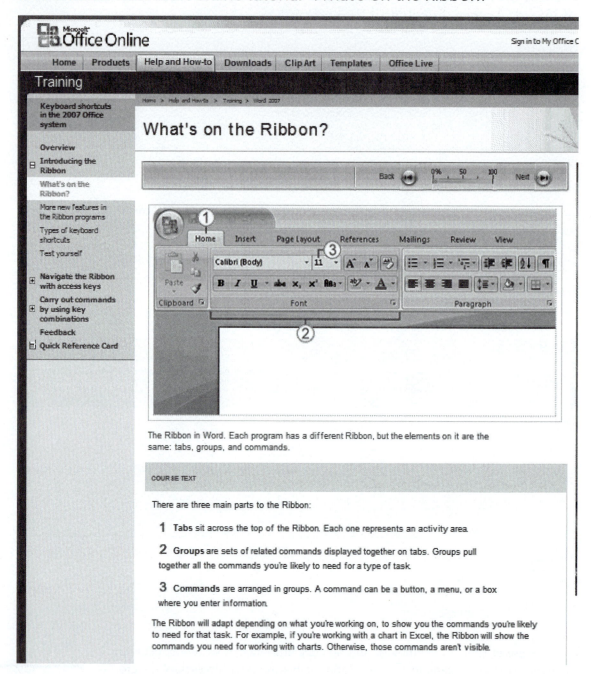

The Ribbon in Word. Each program has a different Ribbon, but the elements on it are the same: tabs, groups, and commands.

COURSE TEXT

There are three main parts to the Ribbon:

1 **Tabs** sit across the top of the Ribbon. Each one represents an activity area.

2 **Groups** are sets of related commands displayed together on tabs. Groups pull together all the commands you're likely to need for a type of task.

3 **Commands** are arranged in groups. A command can be a button, a menu, or a box where you enter information.

The Ribbon will adapt depending on what you're working on, to show you the commands you're likely to need for that task. For example, if you're working with a chart in Excel, the Ribbon will show the commands you need for working with charts. Otherwise, those commands aren't visible.

RESOURCES FOR LEARNING AND USING WORD PROCESSOR SOFTWARE

Every program has some level of instruction or help available for using the program. It may be online resources, such as information available over the Internet, including updates, tutorials, and answers to frequently asked questions. All programs have built-in help resources. These may be in the form of guides, instructions, or formal documentation. Most word processing software vendors provide help in learning and using the software.

Exhibit 6.13 Microsoft Office online tutorial "Introducing the Ribbon."

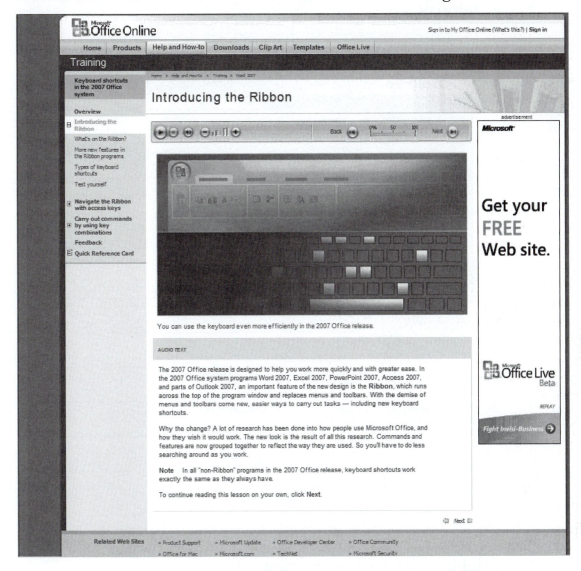

Online Resources

Online Web-based resources may be in the form of Internet-based access to the software vendor's website. Exhibit 6.14 shows a sample of the available tutorials for Word 2003. Exhibit 6.15 shows available tutorials for Word 2007. It must be mentioned that these tutorials, as many software vendors' tutorials, require an Internet connection that allows connection with the vendor website. Some programs, such as those for Word, require the user to have a copy of the same version of the program installed, for example Word 2003 or Word 2007. Many tutorials are interactive and allow the user to take part in the tutorial in some fashion; such as the introduction to the Word tutorial shown in Exhibit 6.14 and Exhibit 6.15, and also have a sound component for those with speakers or headsets.

Program Resources

All programs have some form of built-in help function, information to help the user use the functions of the program from within the program itself. Traditionally

WWW MINI EXERCISE

The Word 2003 courses from Microsoft available online may be accessed at http://office.microsoft .com/training/training .aspx?AssetID=RC010 425851033
The Word 2007 courses from Microsoft available online may be accessed at http://office.microsoft .com/en-us/training/ CR100654561033.aspx

Exhibit 6.14 Partial list of Microsoft Word 2003 online tutorials

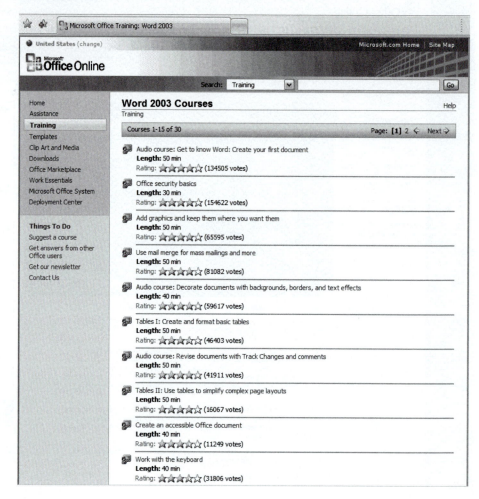

Exhibit 6.15 Word 2007 online tutorials

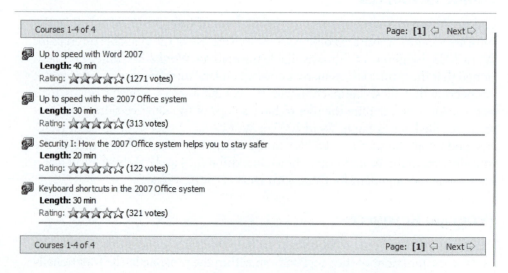

Exhibit 6.16a Microsoft Office 2007 Overview

Exhibit 6.16b WordPerfect program Help resources menu and index

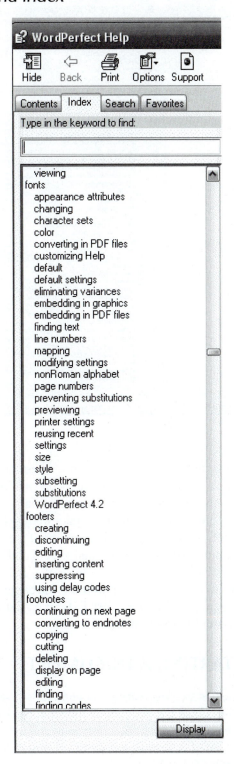

a pulldown Help menu was found on the menu bar or toolbar of the program, as shown in Exhibit 6.16.

Some standardized features are found in all programs. Some programs offer additional specialized help features. Basic to all programs is a guide in the form of a table

WWW MINI EXERCISE

The Word 2007 overview training course may be accessed on the Microsoft website at http://office .microsoft.com/training/ training.aspx?AssetID= RC100664431033

Exhibit 6.17 Microsoft Word Help contents display

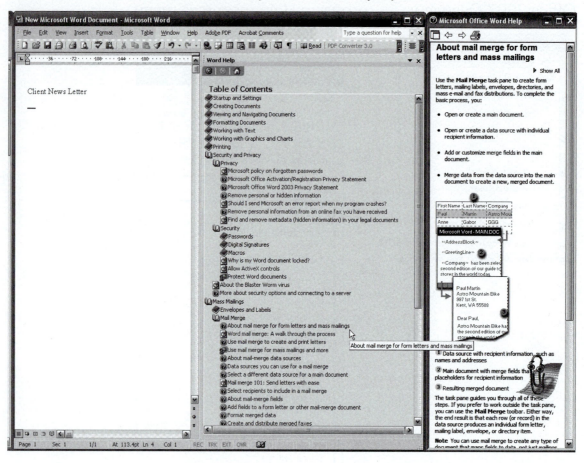

WWW MINI EXERCISE
The complete list of
Microsoft Office online
training can be viewed at
http://office.microsoft
.com/en-us/training/
CR061958171033.aspx

of contents showing the features. These tables of contents usually expand to show details of the particular feature when selected. Exhibit 6.17 shows the Word contents, and Exhibit 6.18 shows the similar version of WordPerfect. In addition, all offer some connection to the vendor website for update information and a connection to access online help and tutorials. For many topics the information is presented in expanded form with additional screens and details that can be followed step-by-step.

Word and WordPerfect both offer help in using the other program. For example, Word provides help in using the commands used in WordPerfect in the Word program (see Exhibit 6.19). Exhibit 6.20 shows the help available for WordPerfect users in Microsoft Word.

STARTING A DOCUMENT

The first step in creating a document is to select and start (launch) the desired program. Once the program is running, the next step, in most cases, is opening the File menu or the Office Button in the new Office Suite 2007.

The File menus for Word 2003 and 2007 and WordPerfect X4 are shown in Exhibit 6.21. A feature of some menus is the initial presentation of a short list of options, with the ability to expand the option by selecting the arrows at the bottom of the list as shown in the Word Document menu in Exhibit 6.21. The Word File menu also shows the last document opened, Chapter 5 Word Processing, allowing quick access to prior work without searching for the file location.

Exhibit 6.18 WordPerfect Help contents display

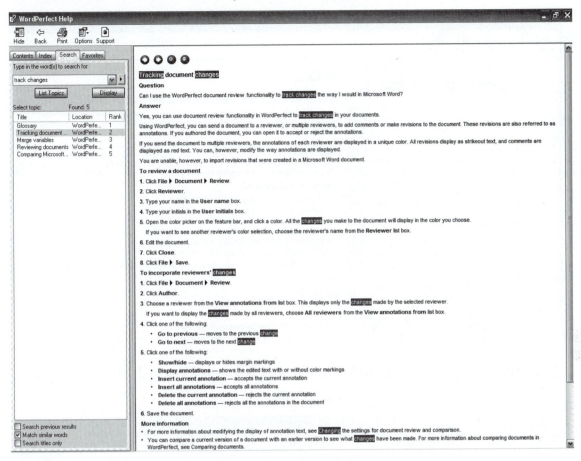

Exhibit 6.19 Welcome to Help for WordPerfect Users

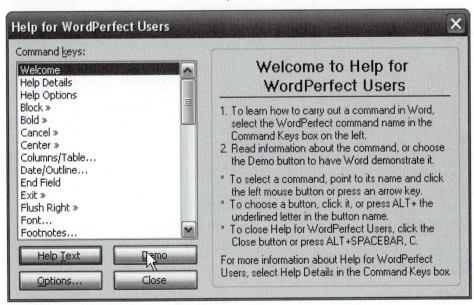

The New option in these, and most, programs opens a blank document. Existing files are opened with the Open command, and the selection of the desired file using the Open File window, similar to the Windows Explorer window.

Exhibit 6.20 WordPerfect compatibility Help screen

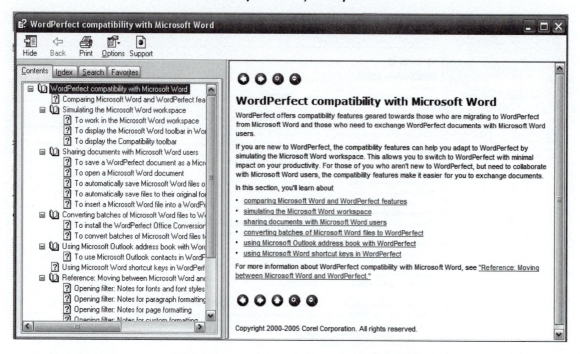

Exhibit 6.21 File menus in WordPerfect X4 and Word 2003 and Office Button in Word 2007 for comparison

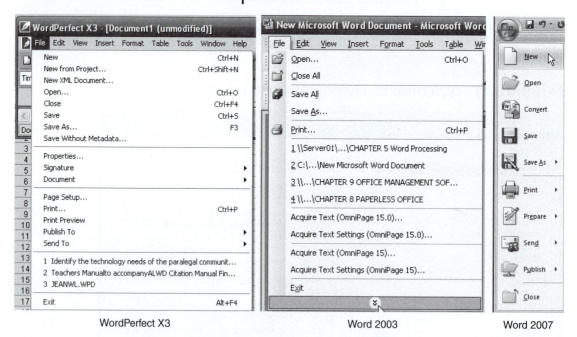

WordPerfect X3   Word 2003   Word 2007

FILE SEARCH FUNCTION

Opening an existing file is easy enough when you know the file name and the location on your computer or on the network file server. Sometimes, however, it is necessary to find a file located on a computer or file server when you may only know a part of the file name, or just a few of the words that are in the file itself. As shown in Exhibit 6.22, both WordPerfect and Word have a search tool that

Exhibit 6.22 Search for file options in WordPerfect and in Word

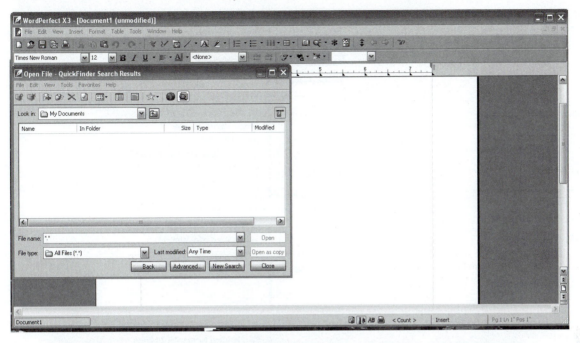

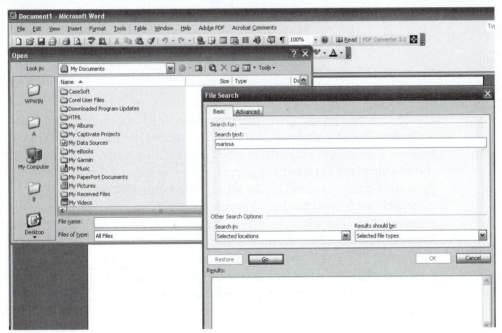

performs a search of your computer and the file server for files with the designated terms or words.

TEMPLATES

Templates are a special and commonly found feature of many programs. Some are found in the program itself as part of the program; others, like those from Microsoft Office, are accessed and downloaded from a website.

When you open a new document in Word, you are given the option to open a blank document, a Web page, an e-mail message, or an existing document. You are

Exhibit 6.23 Online Word template for download

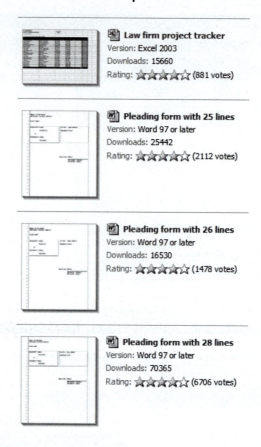

Law firm project tracker
Version: Excel 2003
Downloads: 15660
Rating: ★★★★☆ (881 votes)

Pleading form with 25 lines
Version: Word 97 or later
Downloads: 25442
Rating: ★★★★☆ (2112 votes)

Pleading form with 26 lines
Version: Word 97 or later
Downloads: 16530
Rating: ★★★★☆ (1478 votes)

Pleading form with 28 lines
Version: Word 97 or later
Downloads: 70365
Rating: ★★★★☆ (6706 votes)

Template
A form or standard document.

also offered the opportunity to use a **template**—a preset, predesigned page, such as a pleading layout with line numbers. These are available from the Office online Internet connection and offer a quick way to start a new project. Exhibit 6.23 shows a sample of the available templates for download. Even the new blank word processing page is a template, in Word a file labeled Normal.doc. This is a template with predefined borders, margins, type font, and size. Changes to the blank document can be made and saved as the normal opening page or with special setting and setups used for different applications. For example, a template for correspondence with single spacing and Times Roman 12-point type font. A contract template might be saved with a different format using a 10-point Arial type font with a 3-inch left margin and half-inch right margin. Word 2007 provides a quick access to the saved templates when the New option is selected from the Office Button menu as shown in Exhibit 6.24.

SAVING THE FILE

Saving the new document requires the selection of an appropriate name for the file, a location in which it is to be filed or stored, and the selection of the format in which it is to be saved.

Most programs offer a choice of methods for saving files. The Save command saves the file with the same name and in the same location from which it was opened. The Save command effectively erases the previous file with the same name without any warning. The Save As command prompts the user to indicate the name and the location in which the file is to be saved before saving the file.

Exhibit 6.24 My Templates in Word 2007

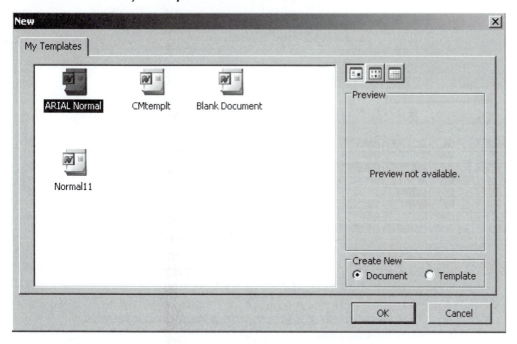

Which is better? If you are using a file previously saved as a template, such as the typical **boilerplate** document, a standard language document, from another case, you probably do not want to save the new file with the changes made, using the same name and filing it in the same location, at least not if anyone else will want to use the same boilerplate or template again. The safer method is to use the Save As option and allow the popup Save As screen to warn you before saving it.

Boilerplate
Standard language used in other documents.

File Formats

Most word processing programs allow the opening and saving of files in the file formats of other word processing programs. A **file format** is the way the word processor files are saved with the document properties such as type font and type size, and document formatting details. The saved files also include instructions to the computer on how to display the document, security features, and hidden information such as the Track Changes information.

When a file is saved, a **file extension** (a period followed by characters) is added to the end of the file name that identifies the program or format in which the file has been saved. For example:

File Format
The internal structure of a file, which defines the way it is stored and used.

File Extension
A tag of three or four letters, preceded by a period, which identifies a data file's format or the application used to create the file.

Program	Name.ext
Microsoft Word	filename.doc
WordPerfect	filename.wpd
Microsoft Works	filename.wps
Web documents	filename.htm
Generic (rich text file) word processing format	filename.rtf
Generic (text file) word processing format	filename.txt

Exhibit 6.25 Save As—File Type options in Word 2007

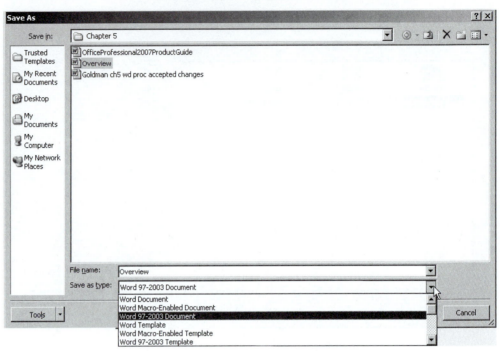

The newer version of WordPerfect even permits, as one option, simulation of the Microsoft Word workspace when starting the program. As previously mentioned, files saved using the newer version of programs such as Word 2007 may not be usable opened in other versions. Almost all programs allow files to be saved in different file formats. Some of the new features in Word 2007 are new to that version and not available in older versions of Word and, as a result, files saved in the Word 2007 format may not work in older versions like Word 2003. Word does allow files to be saved in generic formats like rich text file (RTF) or plain text format that may be imported into other programs, but it does not provide for saving in WordPerfect format. Word 2007 does permit files to be saved in formats usable in the older format if selected as the file format option when using the Save As feature as shown in Exhibit 6.25.

WordPerfect allows files to be saved in a number of formats as shown in the Save As—File Type screen shown in Exhibit 6.26. WordPerfect will convert most documents from other formats into the WordPerfect format, but as with Word 2003 and older Word versions, it will not open files saved in Word 2007 format. If files are going to be shared among users of different word processing programs, like Word 2007 and WordPerfect, a compatible format, like RTF format, should be agreed upon as the format for all exchanged files. Alternatively, users may agree to save files using an older Word format such as Word 2003, but not use the features of Word 2007 format that require files to be saved in Word 2007 format.

SECURITY FEATURES

All programs allow for some degree of security in the process of saving the file or sharing the file.

Exhibit 6.26 Save As–File Type Screen in WordPerfect X4

Protect Documents

When you send or share a file you may not want the other party to have the unrestricted ability to make changes to the original document. The Protect Document option restricts how people may access the document. This feature enables the protection of the document against changes in formatting or editing. Exhibit 6.27 shows the Protect Document options and the specific choices possible in Word 2003. The Protect Document Group is located in the Review Tab in Word 2007.

Document Properties

Document properties are a part of the metadata for word processor documents. Metadata is the data or information about the document. One of the most basic items in the metadata is the date of creation and the author. A denial of knowledge of certain facts by a specific person can be the smoking gun if knowledge of something like harassment in the workplace before a specific time frame is claimed when the writer has written a document or sent an e-mail about the conduct where the metadata date is before the date of the claimed knowledge. If the document is going to opposing counsel, you may not want them to be able to see any of the

Exhibit 6.27 Protect Document options in Word 2003

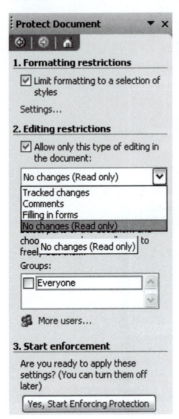

Exhibit 6.28 Sample metadata from a word processor file

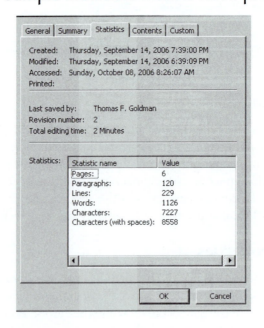

details about the document. The basic details about the document are shown in the Properties option in the File menu in Word 2003, as shown in Exhibit 6.28. In Word 2007 it is part of the Office Button options, Prepare. In Word 2007 additional options are provided to inspect documents and remove metadata as shown in Exhibit 6.29.

Exhibit 6.29 Metadata and Properties options in Word 2007

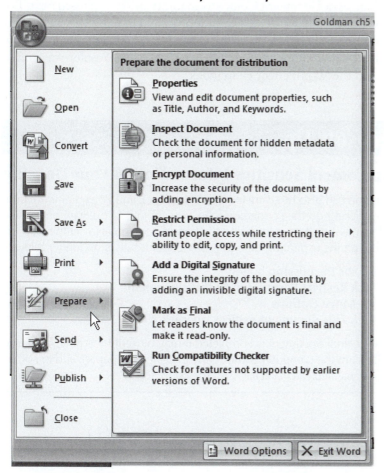

Exhibit 6.30 Password security and encryption options menus for Word 2003

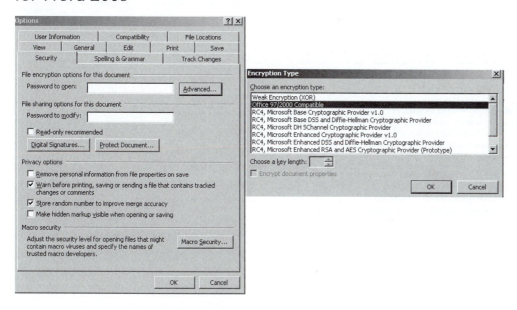

The security options also allow the creator of the document to restrict the access to the document or the functions that may be performed. A password can be used to totally restrict access or to limit the ability to edit or change the document. The options for password security and encryption for Word 2003 are shown in Exhibit 6.30.

Additional information that the creator may want to restrict include any Track Changes or Document Comparison information, discussed next. Both Word and WordPerfect offer specific instructions for removing the metadata or other hidden information. Exhibit 6.31 shows the MS Word Help Remove for removing personal or hidden information. Exhibit 6.32 shows the results of a word search for metadata in the WordPerfect Help index.

Microsoft Tip

Help Control Sensitive Information in Your Documents

Permission can also be restricted on Word, Excel, and PowerPoint documents.
By clicking on the Permission icon, you choose if you want people to read the document or have permission to change. You can also set the level of control and the expiration date to expire content that is no longer relevant.

Click the **Permission** button.
Check **Restrict Permission to this document.**
Click **More Options.**
Check **This document expires on (pick a date).**

When the final document is completed it may be sent by e-mail, fax (frequently directly from the computer without any intermediate paper), and in some jurisdictions filed electronically with the court.

Exhibit 6.31 Microsoft Word Remove personal or hidden information Help

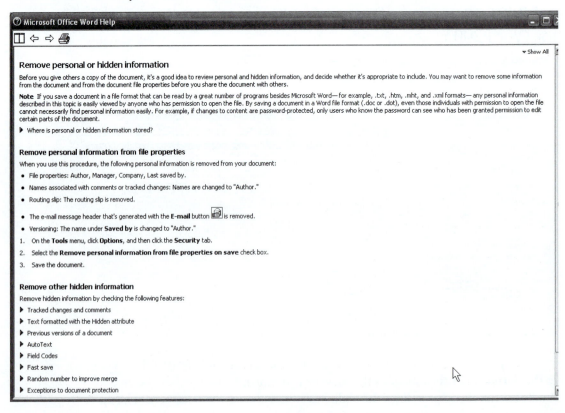

Exhibit 6.32 WordPerfect saving without metadata information

ETHICAL Perspective

DOCUMENT COMPARISON SOFTWARE ISSUE

When using Track Changes, or similar comparison programs, be sure to remove the history of the changes and other information from the document before sending it to the opposing counsel, the client, or the court.

The history of the changes may offer a reader insight to the strategy of the case—for example, showing the final price the client was willing to pay, which appeared in the original draft, and not the first offer that appeared in the final version sent to the opposing side. MS Word Help offers instruction on how to remove this information. WordPerfect allows documents to be saved without metadata, using a file save option, *Save without metadata*, making it easy to quickly remove private or sensitive data that can be hidden, but easily extracted, from office productivity documents.

ETHICAL Perspective

STATE BAR OF SOUTH DAKOTA

Rule 1.6. Confidentiality of Information.

(a) A lawyer shall not reveal information relating to the representation of a client unless the client gives informed consent except for disclosures that are impliedly authorized in order to carry out the representation or the disclosure is permitted by, and except as stated in paragraph (b).

(b) A lawyer may reveal information relating to the representation of a client to the extent the lawyer reasonably believes necessary:

(1) to prevent the client from committing a criminal act that the lawyer believes is likely to result in imminent death or substantial bodily harm;

(2) to secure legal advice about the lawyer's compliance with these Rules;

(3) to establish a claim or defense on behalf of the lawyer in a controversy between the lawyer and the client, to establish a defense to a criminal charge or civil claim against the lawyer based upon conduct in which the client was involved, or to respond to allegations in any proceeding concerning the lawyer's representation of the client;

(4) to the extent that revelation appears to be necessary to rectify the consequences of a client's criminal or fraudulent act in which the lawyer's services had been used; or

(5) to comply with other law or a court order.

SPECIAL FEATURES OF WORD PROCESSOR PROGRAMS

Every software program has some special feature. Special features are what differentiate software programs. Even with the special differentiating features there are common features. Switching between programs or learning a new program requires learning where the basic features and the special features are found. In some cases it is a matter of terminology. For example, we have seen that WordPerfect refers to *metadata*, while Word refers to *personal information* in discussing removing both from final versions of documents.

Headers and Footers

Header
Items at the top of each page in the document.

Footer
Items at the bottom of each page in the document.

Another common feature is the ability to add **headers** and **footers** to documents. These are the items at the top or bottom of each page in the document, like page numbering in a footer or the location where the document is filed (path) in a header or a copyright notice in a header or footer. To add a header or footer: In Word 2003 use the View pulldown menu, and select Header and Footer (Exhibit 6.33); in Word 2007, from the Insert Tab select the Header, Footer or Page Number option (Exhibit 6.34), right mouse click in the selection options opens additional options that are context sensitive; in WordPerfect select the Insert pulldown menu, and select Header/Footer (Exhibit 6.35). Same feature, different terminology.

Track Changes

It is common practice in many offices for multiple parties to have input into the final version of a document. As each person makes changes, the revised document

Exhibit 6.33 Header and Footer menus in Word 2003

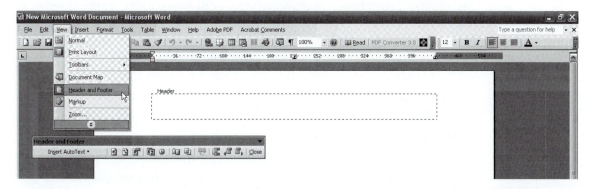

Exhibit 6.34 Choose Insert Tab, then Header or Footer in Word 2007

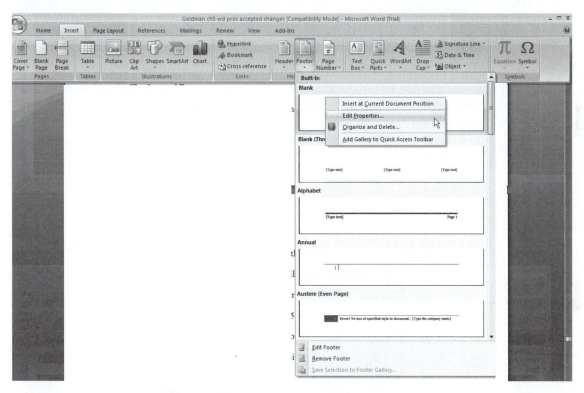

Exhibit 6.35 Header/Footer menus in WordPerfect X4

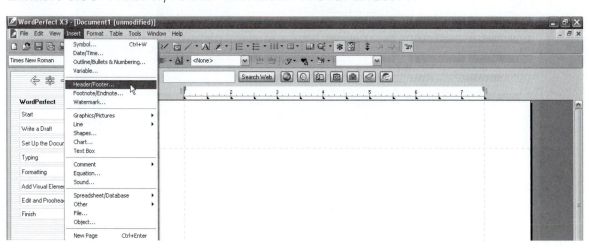

is sent to the others for review, additions, and corrections. This is usually done electronically, either over an office network or in some cases over the Internet as an attachment to an e-mail. It is easier and more productive to know what specific changes have been made, what has been deleted, and what has been added while looking at a single document and not digging up the old versions for comparison. MS Word provides a built-in feature called Track Changes that shows:

> the original text,
> the deleted text, and
> the new text

by a series of lines that show as a strike through the deleted text and by margin notes on the document. Exhibit 6.36 shows the Track Changes options.

Exhibit 6.37 shows the original Word file, the changes inserted, and old text with a strike through it, and the final version with the changes still showing in the margin of the document.

Document Comparison

Ever wonder what the differences were in the document you have and the one someone else has worked on? The document comparison tool (see Exhibit 6.38) allows the two documents to be compared and the differences shown, with the final version being a merger of the two documents.

Word processing is more than just typing documents. It is a collaboration tool with many features that can be used to enhance the productivity of the legal team. It can also be a source of ethical concern if the security features are not understood and used when appropriate.

Exhibit 6.36 Microsoft Word 2003 Track Changes options

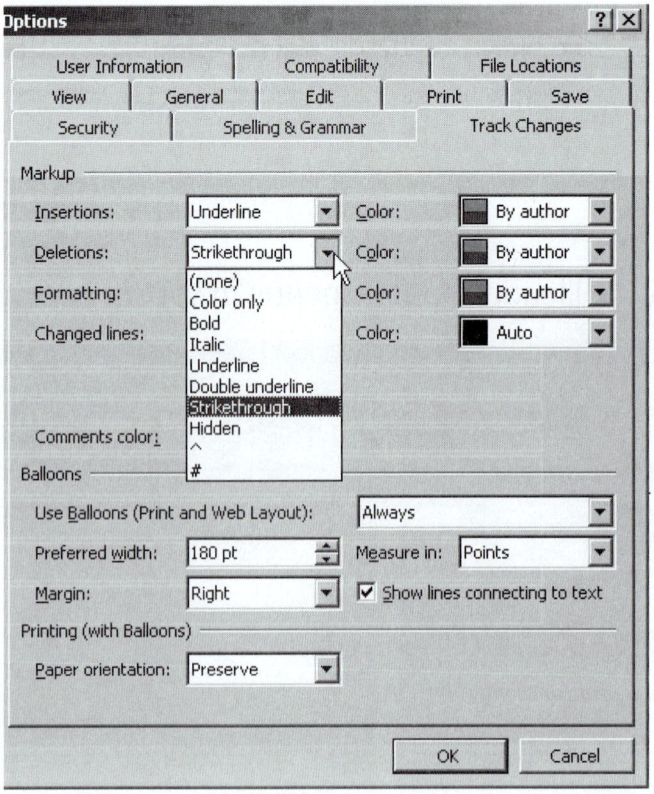

Exhibit 6.37 Track Changes document example in Word 2003

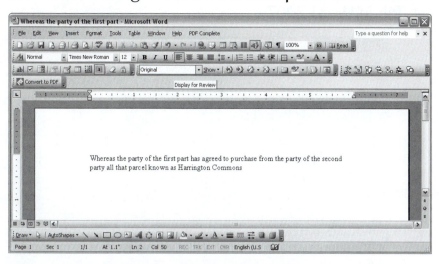

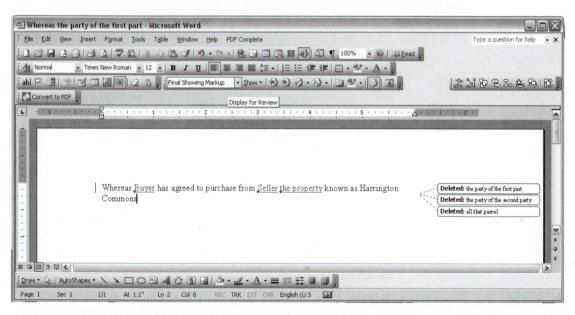

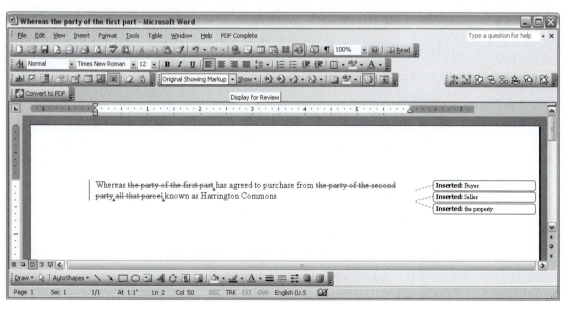

Exhibit 6.38 Document comparison group in the Review Tab in Word 2007

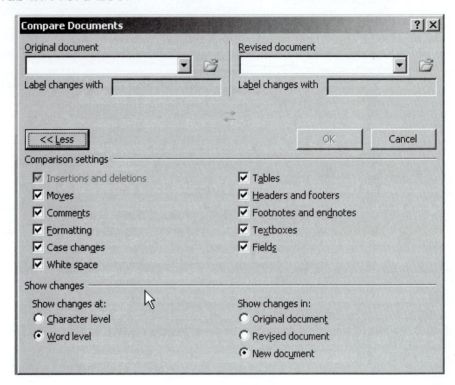

Mail Merge

Mail Merge
A macro that combines a document with a list of recipients.

Mail Merge is a macro, a program within a program, which automatically combines a document with a list of recipients. Each person on the list gets what appears to be a personalized letter. In MS Word, this may be complete using the Mail Merge Wizard shown in Exhibit 6.39

The creation of the document as well as the selection of the recipients is completed step-by-step making the appropriate selections in the Wizard's 6 steps, as shown in Exhibit 6.40. Wizards are a useful tool for using less frequently used features of a program.

Table of Authorities

Table of Authorities
A list of the references in a document and related page numbers where they are located.

A **table of authorities** is a listing of the citations or other references in a document and the page numbers where they are located. Each desired authority is first identified and marked by opening the Table of Authorities menu (pressing ALT + SHIFT + I) and organized by category, as shown in Exhibit 6.41. Each authority is marked and an identifier inserted in the document called a TA or Table of Authority Entry in MS Word. These marks are visible when the Hidden Marks button is selected, as shown in Exhibit 6.42

The table of authorities may be inserted using the Insert Table of Authorities selection in the Reference tab, as shown in Exhibit 6.43.

Changes in Word Processing Programs

Software is constantly updated and upgraded, sometimes multiple times in a year. These changes are to fix problems, called bugs, improve existing features, and add

Exhibit 6.39 Microsoft Word Mail Merge options menu

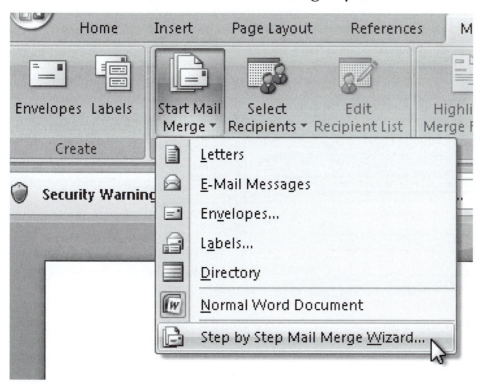

Exhibit 6.40 Word Mail Merge Wizard

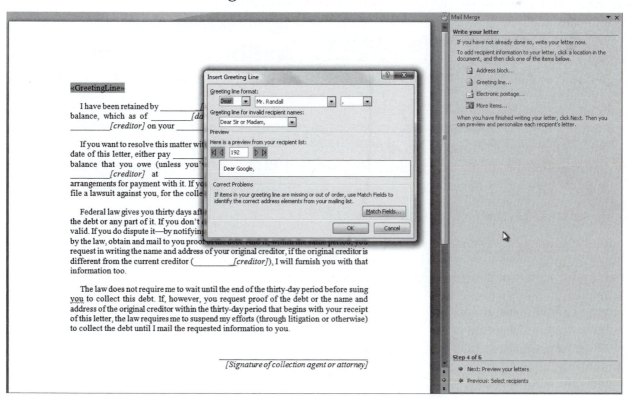

Exhibit 6.41 Table of Authorities selection menus

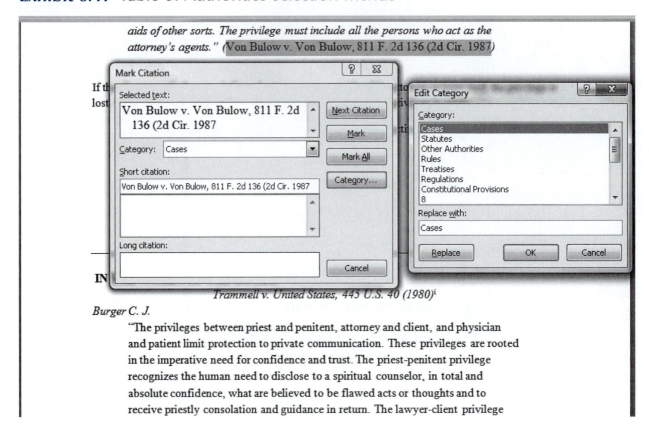

Exhibit 6.42 Table of Authorities hidden characters

new features. Generally, the changes made do not affect the use of files created and saved in previous versions. However, this is not always the case. Some older versions and features may not be supported. New versions may create files that cannot be opened or used with older versions that may still be in use. Most programs feature a What's New item as part of the Help feature. New releases of software are usually accompanied by press releases and special notations on the software package highlighting the changes.

Exhibit 6.43 Table of Authorities options menu

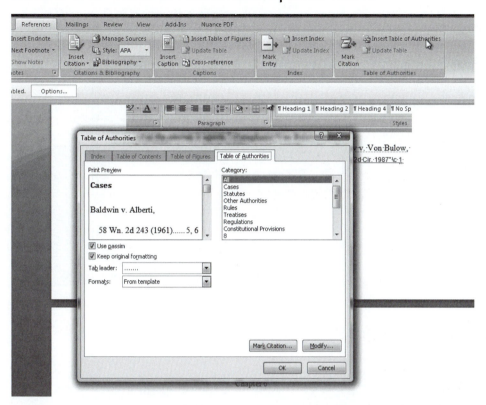

Web Exercise

Check for changes in software by using your Web browser and searching for changes, for example, WordPerfect X4 changes.

Word 2007

Not everyone will upgrade to the 2007 version of Office or the component programs. The decision in the workplace is often a combination of considerations. It is because of the different views of the issues involved that one often finds offices using programs two and three versions old such as Word 97 and WordPerfect 10. If you understand that the basic functions are the same, you can find the needed help to use them.

Some of the new features of Microsoft Office 2007 make the use of the programs for some users more efficient and time effective. Other features allow a level of collaboration not easily attained with older versions.

For the "power" law office user there are a number of items that make document preparation easier and reduce the number of keystrokes and mouse clicks to accomplish the desired result. For example, inserting a symbol, such as the § and ¶, is facilitated with the Insert tab Symbols group shown in Exhibit 6.44.

For anyone who prepares legal briefs or documents requiring footnotes, citations, and tables of figures, all of these functions are provided in the Reference tab shown in Exhibit 6.45. Each is quickly and easily accessed and used with minimal keystrokes.

Exhibit 6.44 Word 2007 Symbol Group Special Characters

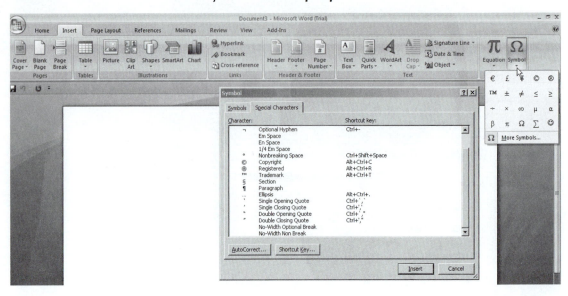

Exhibit 6.45 Reference tab and groups

Among other new features are:

- Quick styles and document themes that can change the appearance throughout a document.
- Live Word Count at the bottom of the word screen to track the length of documents when a limit exists as in some court filings.
- The ability to share documents in different electronic formats.

WordPerfect X4

Change is a part of productivity. WordPerfect has consistently added new enhancements to aid users in being more productive. With the increased use of PDF documents in every aspect of legal practice from internal document sharing to online forms on government websites, creation and use of PDF files is essential to being productive even when the Adobe Acrobat® is not installed on a user's computer. PDF is a file format created by Adobe that has become as common as some of the proprietary word processor formats from companies such as Microsoft. WordPerfect has addressed these isues in its X4 version.

PDF Support

- ***Import Scanned PDF Files***—Built-in features allow the import, edit, and export of PDF documents without use of Adobe Acrobat®.
- ***Add Password Protection***—PDF files aren't inherently secure. Text can be copied and pasted from PDF files. WordPerfect provides built-in

Exhibit 6.46 WordPerfect password control Security tab for PDF files

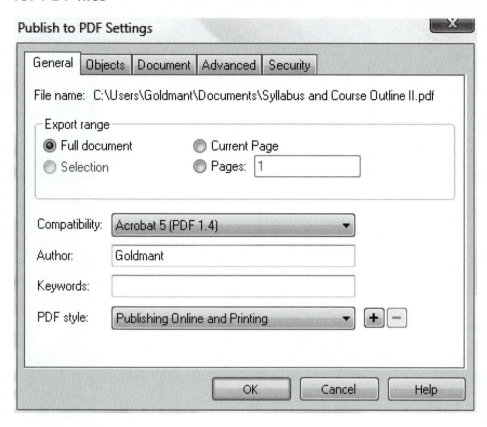

password controls for deciding who may view, copy, edit, or print the document. Two levels of password protection are provided: open and permission. "Open" password, the reader must know the password to view the contents. "Permission" password, what the recipient can do is controlled, see Exhibit 6.46 For example, you may want to allow someone to print the document, but not copy any of the text.

- *Automatic PDF Preview*—PDF files are automatically opened after creation for review of how they appear.
- *Format-neutral*—Over 60 file formats are supported including those of completive products to allow users to share documents created in other programs.
- *Redaction*—The need to protect confidential personal information in documents, such as those submitted as part of court filings, requires that names, addresses, social security numbers, account numbers or other confidential data be blacked out or redacted. You can open any file type that WordPerfect supports and replace sensitive or confidential information with a black bar in a way that ensures that the replaced text cannot be retrieved or revealed in the redacted version of the document, then output the redacted document to DOC, PDF, or WordPerfect, see Exhibit 6.47.

Exhibit 6.47 WordPerfect X4 Redaction tool save options

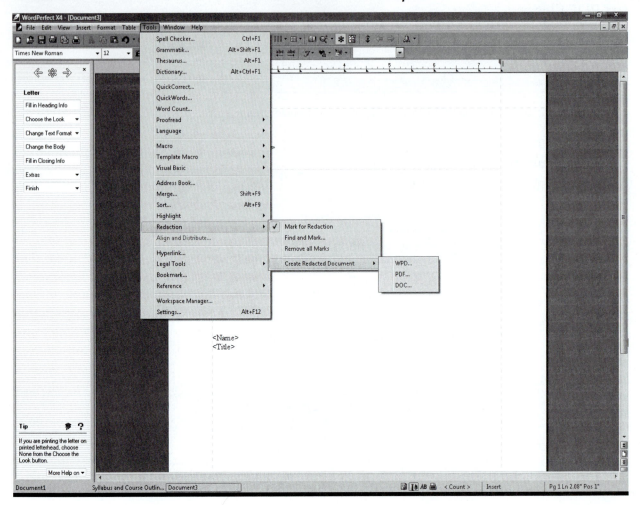

CHAPTER *6*
ETHICS, REGULATION, AND PROFESSIONAL RESPONSIBILITY

Introduction to Word Processing	Written communication and document preparation are at the heart of every law office. Changes or revisions are frequently made to electronic file copies by reviewers. Changes made to the original document, by each person on the legal team, may be monitored by using built-in features such as MS Word's Track Changes tool. All word processing programs have a set of basic word processing functions, like format, style, and saving options. Some programs offer additional features like document comparison. Microsoft Office 2007 offers the same traditional functions plus new features and a new user interface called the Ribbon.

Change	For the paralegal, legal assistant, lawyer, and members of the legal team, change is constant. With change are changes in the software used in the workplace. What is important is the ability to adapt, to recognize the common features and functions, and quickly learn, generally on one's own, the differences, the new features, and the new user interface.
Navigating in Word Processor Programs	Menus and toolbars are the traditional ways to access the features and information about the program. Office Suite 2007 uses the new Ribbon view. The principal difference in the traditional interface and the new Ribbon interface is the grouping of commands by tasks most frequently used in a tab format for the groups of tasks. Menus display a list of commands and are located on the menu bar, also called a toolbar, at the top of the page in the program. Toolbars can contain menus, buttons, or a combination of both. Microsoft Office 2007 does change the traditional appearance, but the basic functions of the programs are the same as in the previous version.
Resources for Learning and Using Word Processor Software	Every program has some level of instruction or help available for using the program. Resources include: information available over the Internet from the software vendors; guides, instructions, or formal documentation; built-in help function.
Starting a Document	The first step in creating a document is to select and start (launch) the desired program. The next step, in most cases, is opening the File menu, the Office Button in Office Suite 2007.
File Search Function	Each program has a search tool that performs a search of your computer and the file server for files with designated names, terms, or words.
Templates	A preset, predesigned page, such as a pleading layout with line numbers. A template may have predefined borders, margins, type font, and size.
Saving the File	Saving the new document requires the selection of an appropriate name for the file, a location in which it is to be filed or stored, and the selection of the format in which it is to be saved. The Save command saves the file with the same name and in the same location from which it was opened. The Save command effectively erases the previous file with the same name. The Save As command prompts the user to indicate the name and the location in which the file is to be saved before saving the file.
File Formats	A file format is the way the word processor files are saved with the document properties such as type font and type size, and document formatting details. A file extension (a period followed by characters) is added to the end of the file name that identifies the program or format in which the file has been saved.
Security Features	All programs allow for some degree of security in the process of saving the file or sharing the file.
Protect Documents	The Protect Documents options restrict how people may access the document.
Document Properties	Document properties are a part of the metadata for word processor documents. Metadata is the data or information about the document. One of the most basic items in the metadata is the date of creation and the author.

Special Features of Word Processor Programs	The items at the top or bottom of each page in the document, like page numbering in a footer or the location where the document is filed (path) in a header.
Headers and Footers	
Track Changes	A feature that shows: the original text, the deleted text, and the new text by a series of lines that shows as a strike through the deleted text and by margin notes on the document.
Document Comparison	Allows two documents to be compared and the differences shown, with the final version being a merger of the two documents.
Mail Merge	A macro that combines one document with information from another such as a letter with a list of recipients.
Table of Authorities	A macro that automates the creation of a list of authorities such as statutes or cases into a table that can be inserted into a document.
Changes in Word and WordPerfect	Some of the new features of Office Suite 2007 make the use of the programs for some users more efficient and time effective. Other features allow a level of collaboration not easily attained with older versions. WordPerfect X4 addresses the increased use of different file formats by providing file saving and conversion into over 60 formats, including some legacy formats and those of other word processing programs.

KEY TERMINOLOGY

Boilerplate   165
File extension   165
File format   165
Footer   172

Header   172
Macro   148
Mail Merge   176
Ribbon   148

Table of Authorities   176
Template   164

CONCEPT REVIEW QUESTIONS AND EXERCISES

1. Test your knowledge and comprehension of the topics in this chapter by completing the multiple-choice questions on the textbook Companion Website.
2. Test your knowledge and comprehension of the topics in this chapter by completing the True-False questions on the textbook Companion Website.
3. What are the advantages and the disadvantages in using passwords with word processor documents?
4. What are the security features available in Word or WordPerfect?
5. What steps may be taken to locate and use the resources for learning how to use specific software programs? Prepare a memo for new members of a law office.

6. Explain the functions of the word processing software as used by the legal team.
7. Describe what might be found in a word processor menu and toolbar.
8. Find online and program resources for learning how to use your word processor program and its features.
9. Write a step-by-step guide to create and save a document in your word processor program (Word or WordPerfect).
10. How can you identify the document format by reference to the file extension?
11. What are the ethical issues in saving word processing documents?
12. Prepare a step-by-step guide for how to protect word documents with a password.

13. What are the characteristics of a strong password?
14. How can you control the degree to which others can access and change specific areas of your documents and specify the types of changes, such as tracked changes, comments, and formatting? Why would you want to have different levels of access?
15. How can you find and remove hidden data, such as tracked changes, comments, and hidden text, from the documents you send to others?
16. Find information on Mail Merge in your word processor. Create a simple one-paragraph letter and a list of five recipients with addresses. Use the instructions to do the mail merge and print out the results.
17. How can you help control sensitive information in your documents?
18. Use Word to create a letter and Mail Merge to address it to any two or more people in your address book or create at least two new recipients.
19. Use Word to create a document with at least three case names and citations, you may copy information from this text. Create a table of authorities and place it at the end of the document.
20. How does the ethical duty of confidentiality affect the way word processor documents are saved?

INTERNET EXERCISES

1. View the demo "Create a legal team notebook" at http://office.microsoft.com/en-us/assistance/HA012190161033.aspx
2. Complete the online Microsoft training course on protecting Word documents.
3. Complete the Microsoft Office lesson on Security for Word.

PORTFOLIO ASSIGNMENTS

1. Prepare a presentation for the lawyers and support staff in a small office on the danger in using the word processing feature Track Changes.
2. Write a proposed policy for ensuring that metadata and earlier edits to the documents have been eliminated from the final version. Include a step-by-step procedure for Word or WordPerfect.

SCENARIO CASE STUDY

Use the opening scenario for this chapter to answer the following questions. The setting is a paralegal sitting alone in his office in a small suburban town after normal working hours, trying to make sense of the differences between the word processing program he used to use and the one that his new office uses.

1. Prepare a list of the three online tutorials you would recommend to someone switching from Word to WordPerfect, and from WordPerfect to Word, or from an older version to a newer version. Explain why.
2. Prepare a memo of not more than 200 words explaining how to find help in the software program used for word processing for a new employee, for the employee handbook.
3. Prepare a memo on the reason for having an office policy on document security.
4. Prepare a memo on the value and the dangers of using Track Changes for new employees and the procedures to be followed.

CONTINUING CASES AND EXERCISES

1. Use the Internet to locate a sample fee agreement letter and save it as a form or template.
2. Use the fee agreement form/template to prepare a fee agreement letter for the client in the case study for the services in preparing his wills and documents for his family trip. Activate Track Changes and print a copy showing the track changes for attorney review. Use the following billing rates:
   a. Attorney $200 per hour
   b. Paralegal $75 per hour
3. Prepare a contingent fee agreement for use with the clients involved in the accident described in the case study material in Appendix 1.
   a. The contingent fee is 30% of the net recovery, plus all out-of-pocket costs. Prepare the file to be sent to the clients electronically.
   b. Use the same contingent fee agreement but reduce the fee to 20% for the driver who brought the case into the office. Are there any issues with regard to hidden data that should be removed?

ADVANCED EXERCISES

1. Use the Table function to set up a table with the information on the office staff including names, address, social security information, and the other information required on the federal IRS forms W-4 and W-9.
2. Is the Sort function of any value in using the form created using the table?
3. Use the Table function to set up a table with the information on the clients in the accident case. Use the information on the sample client interview sheet for the headings.

Chapter 7 Digital Resources at **www.prenhall.com/goldman**

■ Author Video Introduction
■ Comprehension Quizzes and Glossary

Electronic Spreadsheets | CHAPTER 7

OPENING SCENARIO

Mr. Mason and Caitlin were preparing for a labor negotiating session the following day. They had been working on the different proposals and possible counterproposals for a number of days. There were at least a dozen different possibilities for how much each of the demands and offers would cost. He needed to be able to quickly calculate what the costs and benefits would be, based on any number the other side might throw out on the table. He needed to quickly assess whether the total costs and bottom-line benefits to the employees were within the negotiating authority and budgets, and basically if the proposal made any sense.

There were a fixed number of employees with current salary and hour information available. What he needed was the ability to quickly calculate what the cost for each proposal would be, based on the different percentage increases proposed, the individual fringe benefit cost, and a total per employee and total for all employees, during the negotiating session without having to leave to have the figures calculated. Caitlin had taken a course in preparing and using spreadsheets, which had saved a lot of time in doing calculations in a complex estate that required consideration of a number of alternative tax and estate planning strategies. Mr. Mason was hoping his paralegal could do the same thing in this case because without an electronic spreadsheet it would take hours to get through the session, and the other side always seemed to have the numbers at their fingertips.

LEARNING OBJECTIVES

After studying this chapter you should be able to:

1. Define the terms used to identify the parts of an electronic spreadsheet.

2. Find online and program resources for learning how to use the program and its features.

3. Create and save an electronic spreadsheet.

4. Use some of the special features of spreadsheets, including creating graphics.

INTRODUCTION TO ELECTRONIC SPREADSHEETS

Many areas of legal practice involve calculating and presenting financial information. In family law practice, the preparation of family and personal balance sheets and income and expense reports are routinely prepared for support and equitable distribution hearings. Wills, trusts, and estate practices frequently must calculate the financial impact of taxes on different estate plans, or prepare and submit an accounting to beneficiaries or to the court for approval, with details showing how the fiduciary handled the financial affairs of the estate or trust. Trial attorneys must account to clients for the proceeds of settlements, including details of the receipts and disbursements from the case and in some cases, like minors' compromises and class action cases, to the court for approval. The computerized spreadsheet, when laid out in the format acceptable to the court, can be printed without reentering the data, or copied into word documents.

For many applications in legal practice there are templates with formulas for calculating the information needed, such as an electronic spreadsheet version of the Housing and Urban Development (HUD) sheet used in real estate settlements or closings. Electronic spreadsheets have reduced the potential for error in manually calculating or retyping amounts or in using formulas for calculation. The tedium of manually completing a worksheet by hand to recalculate a small change is eliminated by instant reproduction of the template or spreadsheet and changing a number to determine its effect on the rest of the calculation. The use of computer spreadsheets reduces the errors associated with manual mathematical calculations and errors in retyping the information. Caution must be taken to make sure that the formula is accurate and performs the desired calculation. Even expert spreadsheet users use a set of sample numbers to test the formulas, knowing what the result should be, based on prior use or calculations.

CREATING AND WORKING WITH SPREADSHEETS

As you look at the following spreadsheet examples and at the templates provided online from Microsoft, Corel, and other sources you will note a number of different presentation styles and degrees of complexity. A spreadsheet in its most basic form is any two items with some relationship that is acted upon mathematically and the result presented in a third location (called a cell). Spreadsheets are frequently used in situations requiring many complex calculations, like in "what-if" tables in complex estate planning. Some people specialize in developing these complex spreadsheets using complex mathematical formulas and then designing a user-friendly appearance or format. With an understanding of what the spreadsheet can be used to accomplish, you will be able to express what you need to present and what the relationships of the data are to someone else, like the in-house IT person or outside computer consultant to get what you need.

NAVIGATING IN ELECTRONIC SPREADSHEETS

Spreadsheets use standard terms to describe the parts of the spreadsheet, such as **rows, columns, cells, formula bar,** active cell and formula, and **workbooks,** as shown in Exhibit 7.1.

Excel 2007 and its new Ribbon design changes the appearance of the user interface and some of the other items, including the menus and toolbar and layout,

Row
A horizontal set of cells in a spreadsheet.

Column
A vertical set of cells in a spreadsheet.

Cell
In a spreadsheet, the box at the intersection of a row and column for text or numerical data.

Formula Bar
In Excel, the area at the top of the spreadsheet for entering formula and data into spreadsheet cells.

Workbook
A collection of worksheets.

Exhibit 7.1 Names of parts of a spreadsheet, using Excel 2003 as a sample spreadsheet

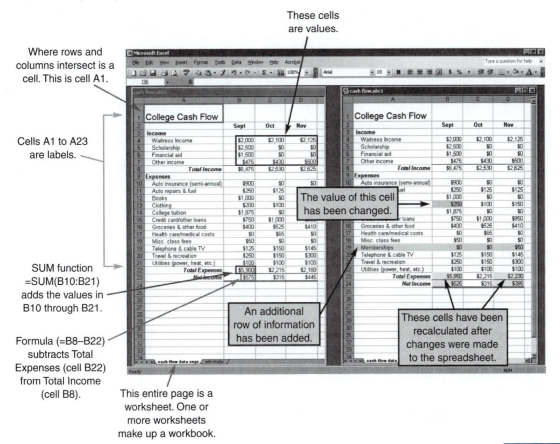

These cells are values.

Where rows and columns intersect is a cell. This is cell A1.

Cells A1 to A23 are labels.

SUM function =SUM(B10:B21) adds the values in B10 through B21.

Formula (=B8–B22) subtracts Total Expenses (cell B22) from Total Income (cell B8).

This entire page is a worksheet. One or more worksheets make up a workbook.

The value of this cell has been changed.

An additional row of information has been added.

These cells have been recalculated after changes were made to the spreadsheet.

as shown in Exhibit 7.1, but does not change the names of the basic parts of a spreadsheet, as shown in Exhibit 7.2, or change the basic functions for which a spreadsheet is used.

As with other Microsoft Office Suite 2007 programs, the 2007 version uses tabs, groups, and command buttons in the groupings to carry out a command or display a menu of options for access to the features and functions formerly accessed using the menus and toolbars.

RESOURCES FOR LEARNING AND USING ELECTRONIC SPREADSHEETS

As seen in Chapter 6 on word processing, most vendors of software provide help in learning and using the software. Microsoft offers a number of online tutorials, some of which are listed in Exhibit 7.3, which shows those for Excel 2003. An example is shown in Exhibit 7.4.

Corel's Quattro Pro provides tutorials within the program that can be used without the need for an Internet connection to a website. Exhibit 7.5 shows a partial list of the available tutorials and Exhibit 7.6 shows the contents of a tutorial, in this case on using the **property bar**. The property bar in Quattro Pro appears above the column letters and is a context sensitive set of commands. (Context sensitive means it changes according to what is being worked on.)

WWW MINI EXERCISE

The Excel 2003 courses from Microsoft available online may be accessed at http://office.micro soft.com/en-us/training/ CR071831141033.aspx

WWW MINI EXERCISE

The Excel 2003 Overview tutorial may be accessed at http://office. micro soft.com/training/ training.aspx?AssetID= RC011234971033

The Excel 2007 Overview tutorial may be accessed at http://of fice.microsoft.com/train ing/training.aspx?Asset ID=RC100720751033

Property Bar
In Quattro Pro, the area at the top of the spreadsheet for entering formula and data into spreadsheet cells.

Exhibit 7.2 Excel 2007 Ribbon view of Excel Spreadsheet (reproduced from the Excel tutorial Overview)

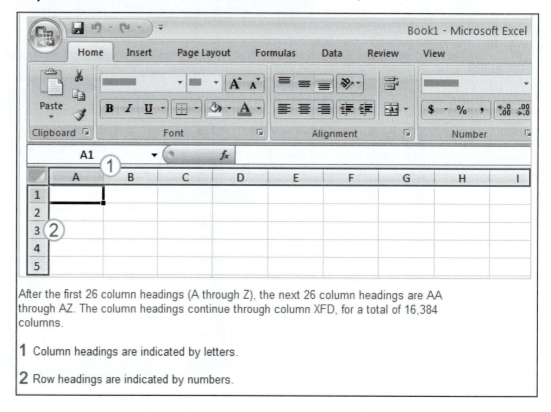

After the first 26 column headings (A through Z), the next 26 column headings are AA through AZ. The column headings continue through column XFD, for a total of 16,384 columns.

1 Column headings are indicated by letters.

2 Row headings are indicated by numbers.

Exhibit 7.3 Online tutorials available for learning Excel 2003

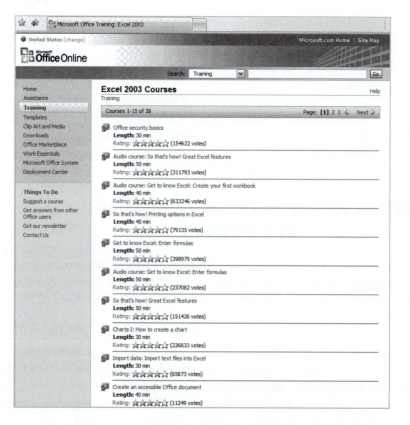

Exhibit 7.4 Excel online tutorial Overview

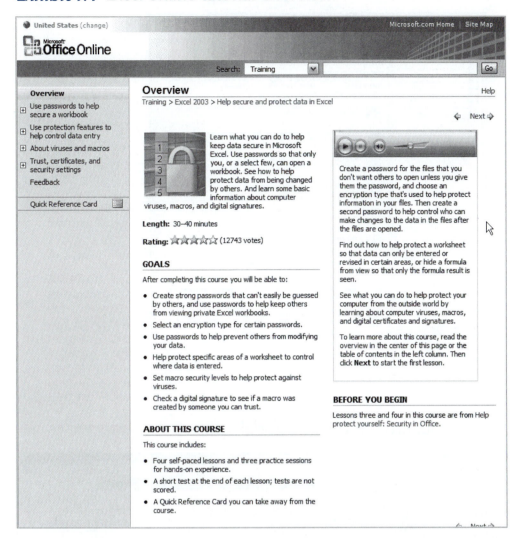

Excel 2007 offers a series of options, as shown in Exhibit 7.7, selected by a left mouse click on the question mark symbol in the top right of the Excel frame.

In addition to the global help, content specific help is offered in select program options as shown in Exhibit 7.8 for the Pivot Table feature.

CREATING A SPREADSHEET

As shown in Exhibit 7.9, in a decedent's estate, the calculation involved may be as simple as multiplying the number of shares owned by a decedent by the value on the date of death, and then calculating the profit or loss when the stock was sold. Without a computerized spreadsheet, all of the calculations would have to be done manually, using a multicolumn form known as a spreadsheet or accountant's working papers. The information then would have to be typed in a report format for submission to the court, the beneficiaries, and/or the taxing authorities.

Using a computerized spreadsheet such as Microsoft Excel or Corel Quattro Pro, the numbers are entered in cells, and a formula assigned to the cell in which the result is to be displayed, such as:

"multiply Column E [Number of Units] by Column F [Cost per Unit]"
and "display the result in Column G [Original Cost]"

Exhibit 7.5 Partial list of tutorials available in Quattro Pro

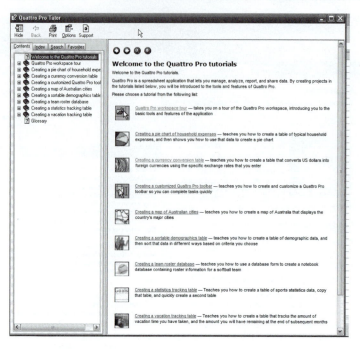

Exhibit 7.6 Quattro Pro online tutorial screen

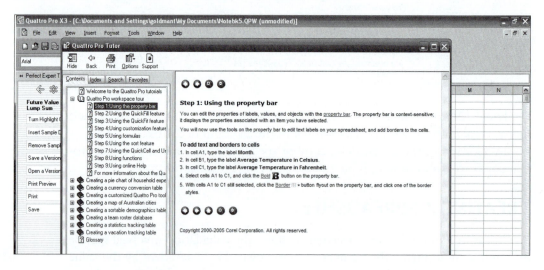

Creating a Basic Spreadsheet

First—Start with what you want the spreadsheet to show or calculate.
Creating a Spreadsheet Checklist

- What do you want to do?
- What are the inputs?
- What is the desired outcome?
- What are the formulas?
- What columns are needed?

Exhibit 7.7 Excel 2007 Help options

Exhibit 7.8 Pivot Table program Help

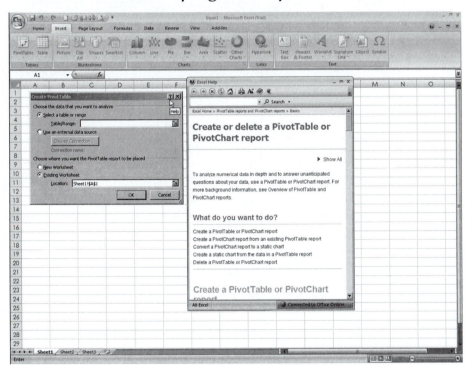

Exhibit 7.9 Estate Asset Ledger modified from an Excel 2007 template downloaded from the Microsoft Excel website

Investment type	Investment description	Purchase date	Number of units (shares)	Cost per unit (share)	Original cost (basis)	Date of Death Value	Unrecognized Gain (Loss)
Estate of Ethel Morris							
Asset Ledger							
Gray cells are calculated for you. You do not need to enter anything into them.							
Stocks	800 common shares-Fourth Coffee	5/4/03	1,800.00	$67.00	$120,600.00	$197,500.00	$76,900.00
					$0.00		0.00
					$0.00		0.00
					$0.00		0.00
Bonds	10-year treasury (4.76% yield)	5/20/03	1,500.00	$102.26	$153,390.00	$148,500.00	($4,890.00)
					$0.00		0.00
					$0.00		0.00
					$0.00		0.00
					$0.00		0.00
Mutual funds	Woodgroove Bank equity fund	6/30/03	2,000.00	$25.50	$51,000.00	$50,000.00	($1,000.00)
					$0.00		0.00
					$0.00		0.00
					$0.00		0.00
					$0.00		0.00
Minority interests	Litware, Inc. (20% ownership)	1/15/99	$1,000.00	$500.00	$500,000.00	$550,000.00	$50,000.00
					$0.00		0.00
					$0.00		0.00
Other					$0.00	$18,000.00	$18,000.00
					$0.00		0.00
					$0.00		0.00
					$0.00		0.00
					$0.00		0.00
					$0.00		0.00

For example:

Create a Dollar-Euro Conversion Chart, another chart where one item (column) will be multiplied (or divided, added, or subtracted) by another item (column) to arrive at a total.

What do you want to do?	Calculate the number of Euros I will get for a dollar.
What are the inputs?	Number of dollars Current value of Euro
What is the desired outcome?	Number of Euros
What are the formulas?	Dollars times Euro conversion rate
Example	$100 × 0.86 = 86 Euros

Second—Create the column labels.

Setting up an electronic spreadsheet is a little like setting up the columns in a table, with each column having a heading; in this example, Dollars, Conversion Rate, and Euros. The label can be in any row, but in this example it is in Row 1.

Third—Enter a formula.

The cell (row and column) in which the answer will be calculated must contain the desired formula.

In the example shown in Exhibit 7.10 it is Cell C2 (the intersection of Column C and Row 2).

Each time you place your cursor in a cell, a window opens for input of the formula in the property bar (Quattro Pro) or formula bar (Excel).

Exhibit 7.10 Dollar-Euro conversion spreadsheet. Note that the calculation resides in Cell C (intersection of Column C and Row 2)

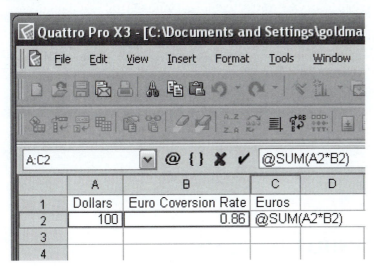

Electronic spreadsheets have many potential formulas that can be used from the very simple (add two numbers) to the complex (calculate the present or future value of a number). In Quattro Pro the *@sum( )* formula is the most basic and with a little effort can be used for most applications. The *@sum* symbol-word combination tells the program you want to calculate the information found between the parentheses ( ); in this example, to multiply the amount in Cell A2 times the amount in Cell B2 and put the result in Cell C2.

Note: In Microsoft Excel the = sign is used instead of the @ used in Quattro Pro.

Basic Mathematical Function Symbols Used in Spreadsheets
- Multiply   *
- Divide   ÷
- Add   +
- Subtract   −

To add a set of numbers you enter a formula, such as,
@sum(A1+B1+C1)

To multiply a series of numbers
@sum(A1*B1*C1)

To divide one number by another
@sum(A1/B1)

Note that there are no spaces between formula symbols, letters, and numbers. While the example shows the numbers in adjacent columns, they don't have to be. Any cell can be used from anywhere in the spreadsheet with any other cell in the spreadsheet, such as @sum(A1+C3+E40).

Editing a Label

Just as a formula can be entered or changed by editing it in the property bar, so can a label. A label can be entered by typing it in a cell, or by selecting the cell and typing it in the property bar (see Exhibit 7.11). Editing is easier if done in the property bar since all the letters do not have to be retyped. If you edit words in a cell, all of the letters have to be retyped.

Exhibit 7.11 To change a label in Quattro Pro, type the desired words in the property bar

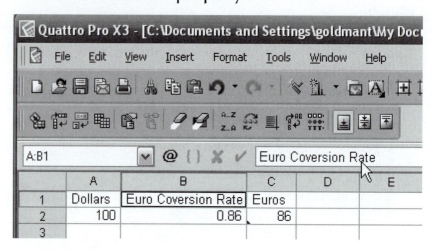

SPREADSHEET TEMPLATES

Many offices save spreadsheet templates in the same way that sample word processing documents are saved for future use. For example, a real estate settlement spreadsheet with formulas and headings may be saved without amounts. Because the formulas do not change and the form has proven accurate, it may be used as a template for other clients' real estate settlements.Exhibit 7.12 shows a HUD real estate settlement Excel spreadsheet with its parts identified. Notice the similarity in the menu bar and toolbar between Excel and MS Word.

Corel's Quattro Pro electronic spreadsheet is similar in function and appearance to Microsoft's Excel. As shown in Exhibit 7.13, Quattro also allows for personal customization in the way the program functions and displays items.

In most programs a selection from the active screen is made by using the mouse to point to it and left-clicking the mouse button.

Some readers may wonder what the right mouse button is for; the right mouse button usually brings up context sensitive options, like the Quattro Pro Options menu. Pointing at the top of the Quattro page in the bar with the name of the program and file name and location and right clicking brings up the Options menu for the program. Selections are then made using the left button.

Templates—Projects

Quattro provides the option when creating a new spreadsheet to use Project Templates or Projects (see Exhibit 7.14). These are similar to the templates provided in Excel for use in Excel.

One question often asked is, can Excel templates be used in Quattro Pro? As described in the following boxed insert, the answer is no.

Templates from Microsoft

A number of spreadsheet templates are available for download from the Microsoft website by selecting the template option when creating a new spreadsheet. Most of the templates will work with the more current versions of Excel; however, some will only work with a specific version, such as Excel 2007. Always check the compatibility before downloading.

FAQ—FREQUENTLY ASKED QUESTIONS

OPENING A MICROSOFT EXCEL TEMPLATE IN QUATTRO PRO

Question:
Can I open Microsoft Excel templates .xlt files in Quattro Pro?

Answer:
No, you can't open Microsoft Excel templates .xlt files in Quattro Pro because they are not supported.
   Microsoft Excel and Quattro Pro have similarities, but they are proprietary applications that are built using different architectures. This makes it difficult to successfully convert templates.

Exhibit 7.12 Excel spreadsheet template created for HUD real estate settlements

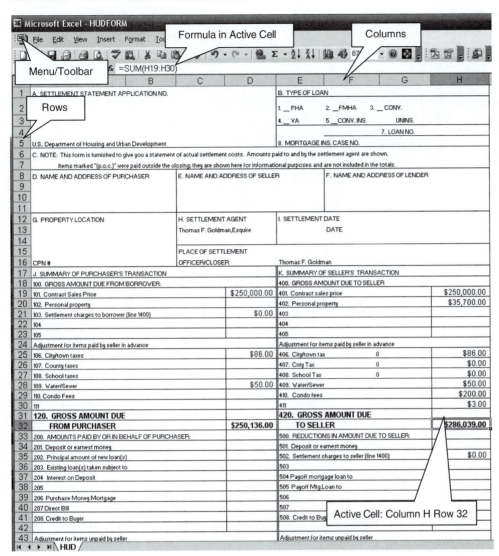

The spreadsheet in Exhibit 7.15 is a weekly timesheet template downloaded from the online Microsoft template resource.

Cell G24 has been selected and highlighted to show the formula in the formula bar (Excel) or property bar (Quattro) used to calculate the total of the entries that will be made in column G. Note that the references are to a total (SUM) of the cells G7 through G23 using this formula shortcut:

$$=SUM(G7:G23).$$

The same total could be calculated using the formula:

$$=SUM(G7+G8+G9+G10+G11+G12+G13+G14+G15$$
$$+G16+G17+G18+G19+G20+G21+G22+G23).$$

Note again that there are no spaces between symbols, numbers, and letters.

Exhibit 7.13 Options in Quattro Pro spreadsheet allow for personal customization

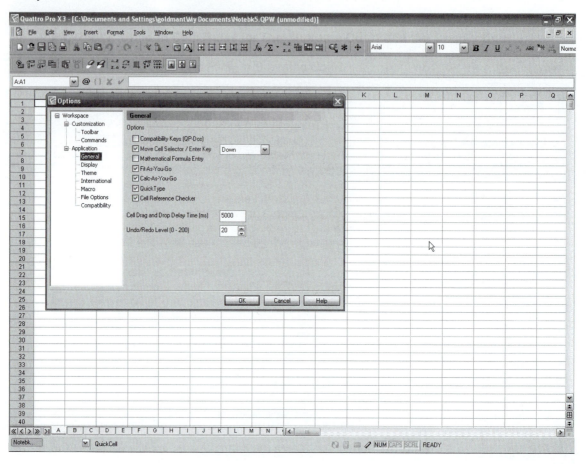

Exhibit 7.14 Selecting the project Legal from Quattro Pro's options menu

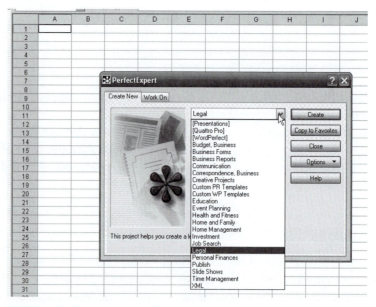

Exhibit 7.15 Weekly Timesheet Template in Excel 2007 showing formula for total hours

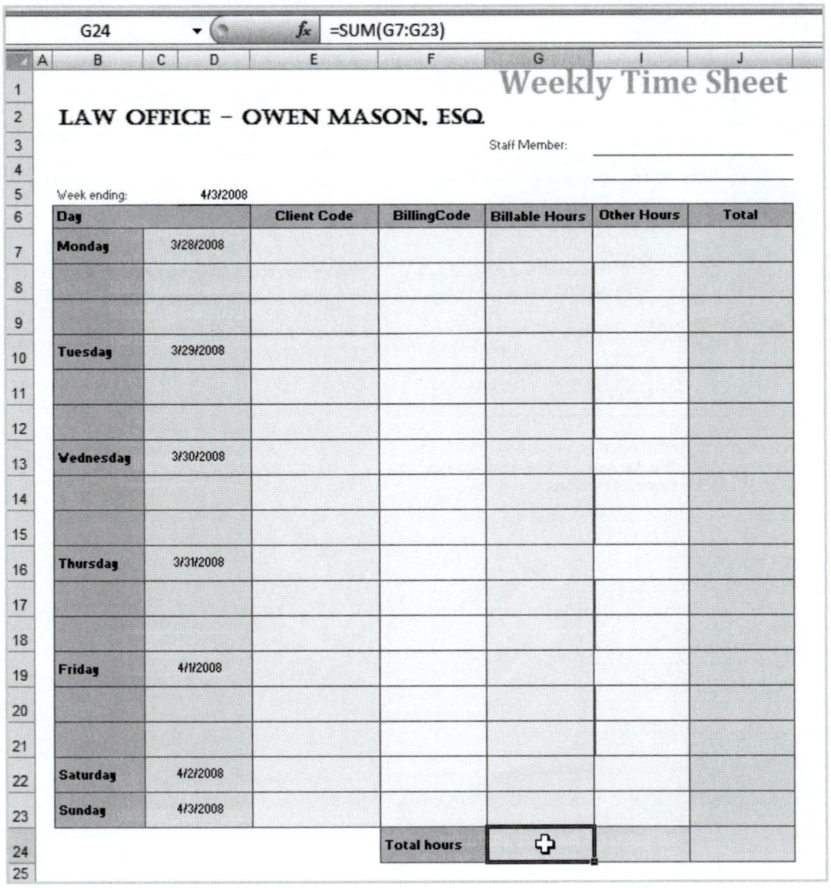

SPREADSHEET SECURITY

Most office suite applications can be password controlled for security. The example in Exhibit 7.16 from the Excel 2003 tutorial shows the method for limiting access to an Excel spreadsheet.

For comparison purposes Exhibit 7.17 shows the Review tab, Changes group options, and the Protect Workbook commands in Excel 2007.

As with other Office 2007 programs, an Office Button feature—Prepare—provides a number of security options, including inspections of the document for hidden metadata as shown in Exhibit 7.18, as well as the ability to encrypt the file with a password, or to restrict access similar to that shown in Exhibit 7.17.

SPECIAL FEATURES OF ELECTRONIC SPREADSHEETS

Each spreadsheet has a choice of tools and features that may be displayed on the toolbars for quick use. Exhibit 7.19 shows the Microsoft Excel standard buttons.

One of the more useful is the AutoSum button, shown as the Greek letter sigma (Σ) found in Excel 2007 (highlighted in Exhibit 7.20) in the Home tab and in the Formulas tab in the Function Library Group as shown in Exhibit 7.21. This applies the selected function; for example, Sum (add up), the selected cells in any row or column without typing any formula.

Exhibit 7.16 Limiting access in an Excel 2003 spreadsheet

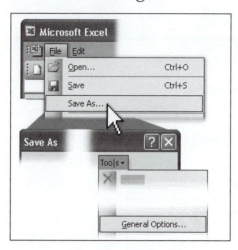

Imagine that you have a workbook that you don't want anyone else to open except for you, and perhaps a select few. To create a password, you can start from either of two places:

- On the **File** menu, click **Save As**. In the **Save As** dialog box, click **Tools**, and then click **General Options** to open the **Save Options** dialog box.

—or—

- On the **Tools** menu, click **Options**, and then click the **Security** tab.

We tell you about both places because where you enter passwords looks a little different at either location, but the passwords you create at either place are the same.

You can create a password when you save a workbook. On the **File** menu, click **Save As**. In the **Save As** dialog box, click **Tools**, and then click **General Options**.

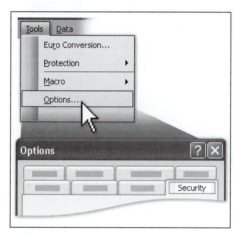

Or you can create a password another way: On the **Tools** menu, click **Options**, and then click the **Security** tab.

Exhibit 7.17 Excel 2007 Protect Workbook options

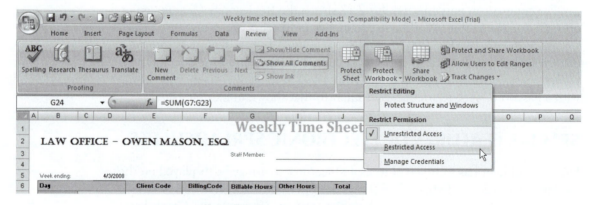

Graphing in Spreadsheets

Data in a spreadsheet are frequently better explained in the form of a graph. In Excel any selection of cells can be converted to a graph using the Chart Wizard button on the toolbar. The Chart Wizard automatically converts the information in

Exhibit 7.18 The Office Button shows security options in Excel 2007

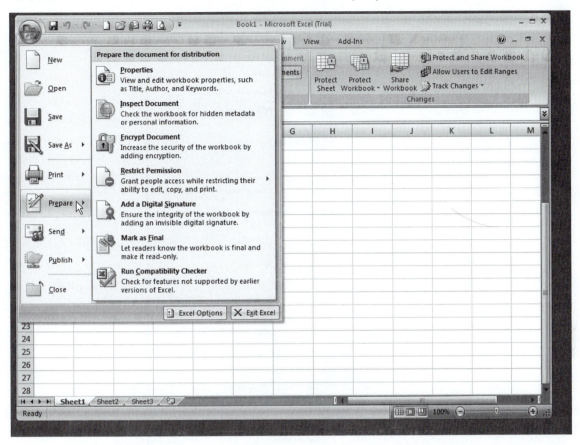

the cells into any one of a number of graphic representations, as shown in Exhibit 7.22. This is a graph of a portion of the information from a template downloaded from the Microsoft website.

The new Ribbon style screen view of Excel 2007 is shown in Exhibit 7.23.

Change

As mentioned in Chapter 6, change is as inevitable in software as it is in life. There have been significant changes in the functionality of the Quattro Pro and Excel spreadsheets from prior versions. What has not changed is the basic function to compute rows and columns of numerical data. The changes generally make the job easier, minimizing the number of keystrokes required, like the use of the sum function shown in Exhibit 7.20. Prior users will find the older functions, but possibly in a different location, and additional features.

Integrated Software Solutions

A number of specialty software programs provide practice-area–specific software. The real estate practice software such as that from SoftPro prepares all the necessary forms to complete a real estate transaction instead of using multiple individual software programs including spreadsheet, database, and word processing software. The Excel spreadsheet template in Exhibit 7.12 is an example of the individual spreadsheet templates created and used in many offices. The template provides spaces for the entry of the information and embedded formulas are used for automatic computations. Programs such as SoftPro use a series of input screens, as shown in Exhibit 7.24, to capture and calculate the necessary information that

Exhibit 7.19 Standard options available on Excel toolbar

Exhibit 7.20 Choose Σ for the AutoSum feature in Excel

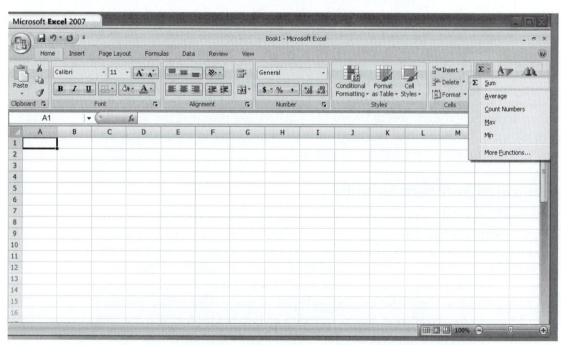

Exhibit 7.21 Excel 2007 Formulas tab

Exhibit 7.22 Choosing a graph template in Excel 2003

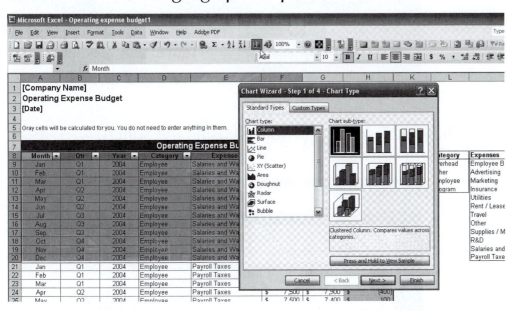

Exhibit 7.23 Excel 2007 Ribbon view of graphing options

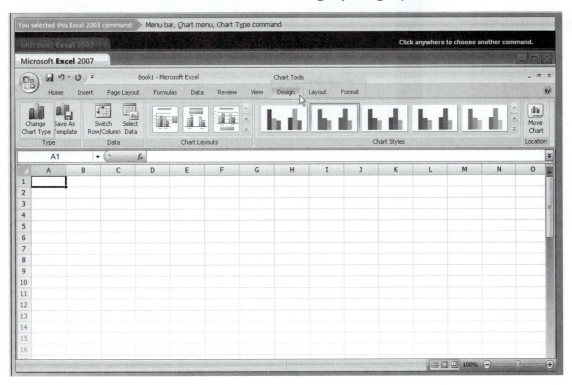

Exhibit 7.24 SoftPro Escrow Automation Solutions input screens

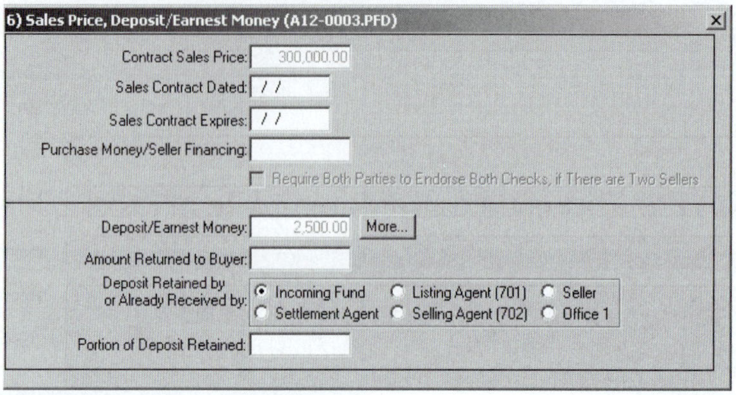

Exhibit 7.25 HUD-1 produced using the SoftPro ProForm software

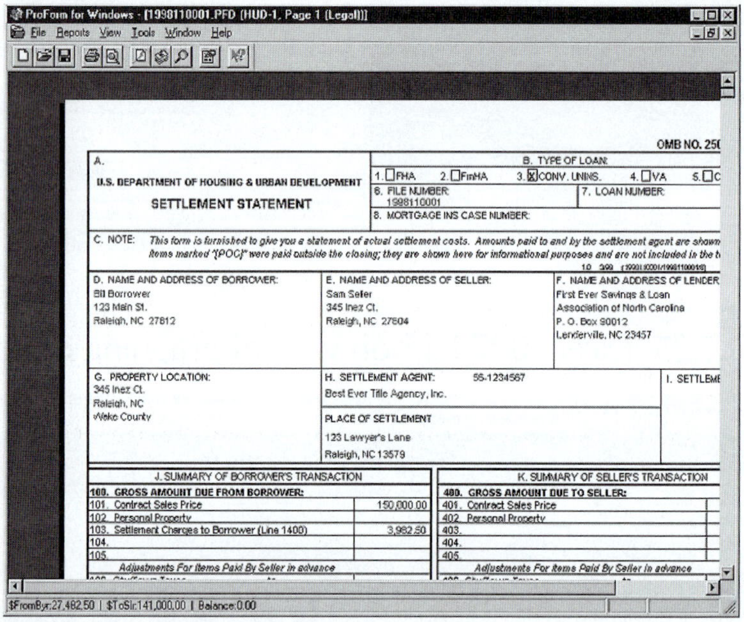

Source: Images courtesy of SoftPro, www.softprocorp.com.

is then transferred to the appropriate forms to create the Hud-1, as shown in Exhibit 7.25. The information is saved in a database for use in producing the other documents required for the real estate closing and title documents, including deed descriptions and tax reporting forms.

SUMMARY

CHAPTER 7
ELECTRONIC SPREADSHEETS

Introduction to Electronic Spreadsheets	Many areas of legal practice involve calculating and presenting financial information.
	The computerized spreadsheet, when laid out in the format acceptable to the court, can be printed without reentering the data, or copied into word documents.
	For many applications there are templates with formulas for calculating the information needed, such as an electronic spreadsheet version of the Housing and Urban Development (HUD) sheet used in real estate settlements.
	The use of computer spreadsheets reduces the errors associated with manual mathematical calculations and errors in retyping the information.
Creating and Working with Spreadsheets	A spreadsheet in its most basic form is any two items with some relationship that is acted upon mathematically and the result presented in a third location.
Navigating in Electronic Spreadsheets	Spreadsheets use standard terms to describe the parts of the spreadsheet, such as rows, columns, cells, formula bar, active cell and formula, and workbooks.
Resources for Learning and Using Electronic Spreadsheets	As seen in the chapter on word processing, most vendors of software provide help in learning and using the software. Microsoft offers a number of online tutorials.
Creating a Spreadsheet	Using a computerized spreadsheet such as Microsoft Excel or Corel Quattro Pro, the numbers are entered in cells, and a formula assigned to the cell in which the result is to be displayed.
	Start with what you want the spreadsheet to show or calculate.
	■ What do you want to do?
	■ What are the inputs?
	■ What is the desired outcome?
	■ What are the formulas?
	■ What columns are needed?
Editing a Label	Just as a formula can be entered or changed by editing it in the property bar, so can a label. A label can be entered by typing it in a cell, or by selecting the cell and typing it in the property bar.
Spreadsheet Templates	Many offices save spreadsheet templates in the same way that sample word processing documents are saved for future use.
Spreadsheet Security	Most office suite applications can be password controlled for security.
Special Features of Electronic Spreadsheets	Each spreadsheet has a choice of tools and features that may be displayed on the toolbars for quick use.
	AutoSum button, shown as the Greek letter sigma (Σ), applies the selected function; for example, Sum (add up) the selected cells in any row or column without typing any formula.
Graphing in Spreadsheets	Data in a spreadsheet are frequently better explained in the form of a graph.

KEY TERMINOLOGY

Cell 190	Formula bar 190	Row 190
Column 190	Property bar 191	Workbook 190

CONCEPT REVIEW QUESTIONS AND EXERCISES

1. Test your knowledge and comprehension of the topics in this chapter by completing the multiple-choice questions on the textbook Companion Website.
2. Test your knowledge and comprehension of the topics in this chapter by completing the True-False questions on the textbook Companion Website.
3. What are macros? What is the danger in using them?
4. What are the security features available in Excel?
5. Define the terms used to identify the parts of an electronic spreadsheet.
6. What steps may be taken to locate and use the resources for learning how to use Excel or Quattro Pro programs and their features?
7. List the steps in creating and saving an electronic spreadsheet.
8. Create a spreadsheet that shows your grades for a course, or a list of five numbers in the range of 1 to 100, including the average of all the grades or numbers listed. Use the graphics feature to prepare a graph.
9. What are the steps that can be taken to protect an Excel workbook?
10. Use the Euro to Dollar conversion chart as a guide to creating a spreadsheet to calculate total billing by multiplying a number of hours (try 27.4 hours) by a billing rate (try $125). What is the difference in billing if the rate is reduced to $90 per hour?
11. Prepare a spreadsheet for
   a. support calculations
   b. payroll computations
   c. time and billing worksheet

INTERNET EXERCISES

1. Download the Investment Ledger from the Microsoft website. Print out the graph "Investment Chart."
2. Complete the Microsoft Office online tutorial "Audio Course: Get to Know Excel: Create Your First Workbook."
3. Complete the Microsoft Office online tutorial "Get to Know Excel: Enter Formulas."

PORTFOLIO ASSIGNMENTS

1. Prepare a procedure and related forms for requesting the creation of a spreadsheet.
2. Prepare a presentation on the uses of an electronic spreadsheet as a productivity tool.

SCENARIO CASE STUDY

Use the opening scenario for this chapter to answer the following questions. The setting is an attorney and paralegal preparing for a labor negotiation session.

1. What should the attorney know about using a spreadsheet in the negotiation session? Prepare a memo for the attorney to use in preparing for the negotiation session.
2. What information should the attorney convey to the paralegal to enable the paralegal to prepare an electronic spreadsheet?
3. How much of the spreadsheet can be set up ahead of time? Explain fully with examples.
4. What hardware or software will the attorney need for the meeting? Be specific and explain the reasons.

CONTINUING CASES AND EXERCISES

1. Prepare a spreadsheet for recording the time slips for the office.
   a. What headings are needed?
   b. See the rates previously mentioned.
   c. Enter all of your time information accumulated since Chapter 1.
   d. Sort the information by the billing function performed.
2. Prepare a spreadsheet for calculating the payroll for the office.

ADVANCED EXERCISES

1. Copy the table created in Chapter 6 and paste it into a spreadsheet.
2. Modify the table to add the necessary formula to calculate billing and payroll information.
3. Identify the additional functions that the spreadsheet can perform.

Chapter 8 Digital Resources at www.prenhall.com/goldman

- Author Video Introduction
- Comprehension Quizzes and Glossary

Electronic Databases | CHAPTER 8

OPENING SCENARIO

Before taking the position with Owen Mason, Ethan had worked for a sole practitioner who had been practicing for thirty years who had finally hired a new associate. The attorney had maintained a set of 3-by-5 cards for each client with all the personal information about the client, a set of cards for each opposing counsel and those attorneys' clients, and copies with the name of the opposing party that could be checked for conflicts of interest. A separate file was kept by Ethan, with the important dates for each case that could be pulled out daily and the related file recovered from the file room and put on the attorney's desk. The system was increasingly difficult to maintain accurately. Unable to find a card that had been accidentally removed and not replaced, Ethan had made an appointment for one of the new associates in the office for an individual who was suing a current client. The associate, after asking Ethan if there was any conflict and being assured the name was not in the 3-by-5 card file, accepted the case, reviewed all the documents in the case, and received a substantial retainer. With a conflict between the clients and the information obtained from each it was almost a certainty that they would probably not be able to continue to represent either client.

LEARNING OBJECTIVES

After studying this chapter you should be able to:

1. Define the function of a database and the terms used to identify the components.

2. Explain how databases may be used by the legal team.

3. Find online and program resources for learning how to use the program and its features.

4. Explain how to plan and set up a database.

5. Explain what can be done to protect data and computers.

INTRODUCTION TO ELECTRONIC DATABASES

A database program is a repository of information of all types that can be sorted and presented in a desired, meaningful manner. Some offices use a manual card system to keep track of the names of clients and opposing parties. These cards are searched to determine possible conflicts of interest in representing new clients. For the small office, this system works. But for the larger office with multiple attorneys and possibly multiple offices, timely entry and searching of large amounts of information is not realistic. Computerized database software, such as Microsoft Access and Corel DB, will facilitate timely, accurate access to information by every authorized member of the legal team. For example, information may be stored on the law firm's server in an information database that includes the names, addresses, contact information, personal data such as birth dates of every client, every opposing party, every fact witness and expert witness, and every opposing counsel with whom any member of the firm has ever had contact in litigation, contract negotiations, or counseling sessions, or met in any business or legal setting. With a few keystrokes, a list can be prepared for manually checking for conflicts of interest or a computer search can be performed with a printout of any matter or litigation where a name appears.

In addition to the obvious use in avoiding accepting a client with a potential conflict of interest, the information frequently is used in maintaining client relations. Many firms use the information to send birthday and anniversary greetings and updates on specific changes in the law for which the client has consulted the firm previously.

THE REALITY OF USING DATABASES

The reality is that legal team members, lawyers, paralegals, and legal assistants rarely create their own databases. In some cases, a simple database of a single table might be used to sort or organize some information, such as the client list or conflict list.

So why do we care about learning about databases? While members of the legal team may not actually create their own databases, they do use them all the time. Virtually every law office specialty application program for managing the office, cases, or documents in litigation is a database. Software vendors have created applications for the legal community. They have custom designed the **Form Views** for input of information, query forms for generating the desired reports, and set up the search and presentation algorithms (formulas for searching). When special applications are required, many of the software vendors will create custom tables and report generators, such as one for a particular area of practice, like estates.

Form Views
An alternative way of viewing and presenting the information in a database.

Knowing what a database is and the associated terminology makes working with the software developer, in-house IT professional, or outside consultant easier and more productive in obtaining what is needed, wanted, and possible, Knowing how a database works and is organized makes using the applications software based on database designs easier to use and work with.

NAVIGATING ELECTRONIC DATABASES

Table
Data that is organized in a format of horizontal rows and vertical columns.

Field
Information located in vertical columns.

Electronic databases use standard terminology to describe parts of the database: table, field, cell, and record, as shown in Exhibit 8.1. Databases are collections of tables. **Tables** contain fields of information (data); a **field** is one type of information,

Exhibit 8.1 Names of parts of an electronic database (in Table Layout View)

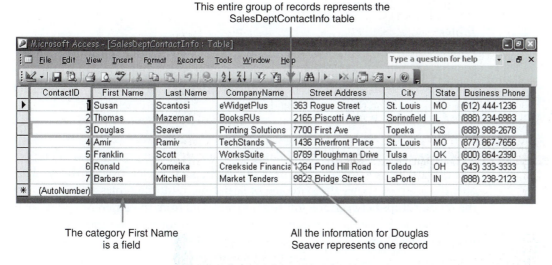

This entire group of records represents the SalesDeptContactInfo table

The category First Name is a field

All the information for Douglas Seaver represents one record

Exhibit 8.2 Access screen in Create Table in Design View

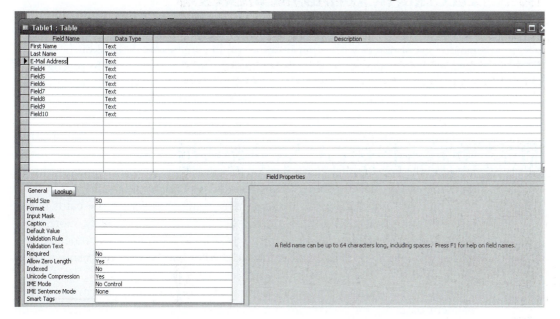

like last names. A **record** is all the information about one item or person; for example, Exhibit 8.3 shows a record of information for each employee. Note that the numeral 1 appears in the Record window at the bottom of the screen, indicating that the cursor is positioned to enter the first record. Think of the database as being a file cabinet; a table being a file drawer for a specific set of information like employees; the record being individual files for each employee; and the field being individual pieces of information about the employee.

The table layout shown in Exhibit 8.1 is one way of showing the basic elements of a database—the fields, records, and cells. The same elements may appear in a different layout, such as the Design View in Access shown in Exhibit 8.2.

In the Design View, the fields listed in a columnar or vertical fashion are the same fields as in Table Layout View, just a different way of looking at it. The Design View also permits more information to be supplied in designing the database.

Record
In a database, the information in a horizontal row.

This includes how many characters should be allowed for the fields, called field size or string length, and what kind of information or data will be entered, text or amounts. Text may include numbers used not in a mathematical way but as part of text data, like an address.

Tables

Databases can and frequently do contain two or more tables. For example, a database used in a legal office may have one table for employees of the firm, another for clients of the firm, a third for opposing attorneys, and a fourth for the opposing parties in cases the firm has handled.

Reports

Reports present the data from the database in an organized presentation. A report may present just the information from one table, such as employee birthdays. Frequently, a report shows the outcome of searching multiple tables and displaying the relationships between the information and data from the different tables, such as a report of the employees that have ever worked for an opposing counsel in a case against a client.

ELECTRONIC DATABASE BASICS

A database is just a collection of information. It may be names. Or it may be an expanded list of names with other information like addresses, dates of birth, occupation, children's names, or any other combination of information. In precomputer days, databases frequently were a box or boxes of cards with the information about a client or important dates. These were the heart of the conflict of interest or deadline databases. The dates database was checked daily and a list made up for the legal team of such things as deadlines, statutes of limitations, and appointments. Conflicts of interest were also checked in the same way, a search of the cards maintained in the boxes in alphabetical order. In some offices a card was prepared for all opposing parties. Each of these "decks of cards" was a database.

The electronic database is nothing more than a version of the cards in the boxes—except that more information can be checked more quickly, more accurately, and automatically. No more misfiled cards out of alphabetical order. It is essentially an electronic card with information that can be searched using a set of things to look for and present in a predefined manner.

Exhibit 8.3 shows a template for input of information into a contacts management database for one record, for Mike Danseglio. The contact information record for Mike Danseglio is one of any number of records in the contacts table in the database. Any field in the record can be searched and a report generated in one of the predefined reports, as shown in the View Reports options in Exhibit 8.4. The final report is shown in Exhibit 8.5.

One of the advantages of the modern database is the ability to search across a number of different sets of information and sort the data according to a predefined set of criteria. Some have likened the World Wide Web to a big database that can be searched using a search engine.

Resources for Learning Database Basics

Step-by-step tutorials for learning to create and use databases are provided on the Microsoft tutorial website. See Exhibit 8.6 for a list of tutorials that can be used to learn Microsoft's Access database program.

Exhibit 8.3 Contact management data input form in Microsoft Access

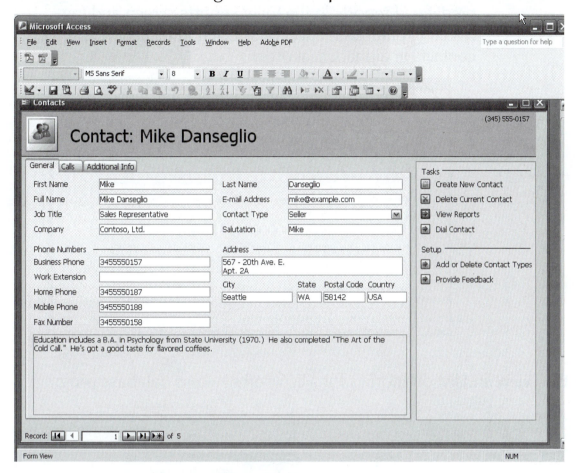

Exhibit 8.4 View Reports option

WWW MINI EXERCISE

For complete listing of available tutorials and the Access 2003 Overview, go to http://office. micro soft.com/en-us/training/CR061829401033 .aspx and http://office .microsoft.com/training/training.aspx?AssetID= RC061181381033 For the Access 2007 Overview, go to http://office. micro soft.com/training/training.aspx?AssetID= RC101933201033

SETTING UP A DATABASE

A database at its most basic is a set of records that contain fields of information. For example, in the card in Exhibit 8.7, all of the information on one card is a record. The individual pieces of information, like the last name and the first name, are called fields. There are different views of the same information in Access. The same information is shown in the Datasheet View in Exhibit 8.8 and partially completed for comparison purposes in the Design View in Exhibit 8.9. Both views contain the same basic field information (taken in part from the information shown in Exhibit 8.4). They are just different options for looking at

Exhibit 8.5 Contact management database screen showing predefined reports in the View Reports screen and the resulting database report of selected information about contacts in alphabetical order

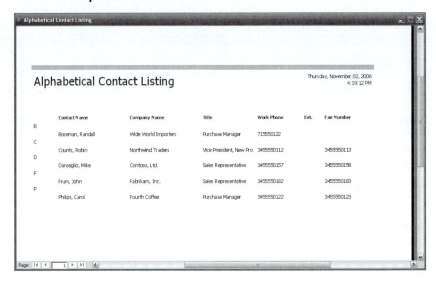

Exhibit 8.6 Overview and list of tutorials for Microsoft's Access database program

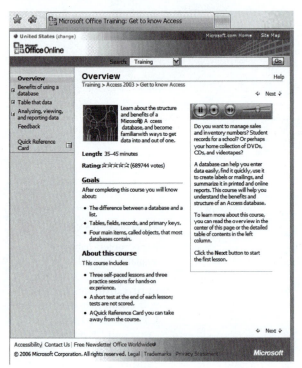

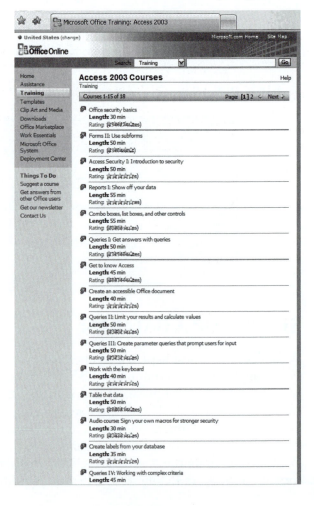

Exhibit 8.7 A Record: All fields are filled in

CLIENT	OPPOSING PARTY	CLIENT/MATTER NUMBER
Jonathan Leonard	Robert Howard	08-012

MATTER	
Leonard vs. Howard, et.al MV Accident	LITIGATION ☐ NON LITIGATION ☐ MATTER FILE FOLDER

CLIENT ADDRESS	PHONE
152 Timber Ridge Road, Peidmont,IL	555 432 2098

CLIENT CONTACT	HOME PHONE	OPPOSING COUNSEL
Jonathan Leonard	555 432 2098	Teven Rich

OPPOSING COUNSEL ADDRESS	PHONE
424 Michigan Ave. Marengo, IL	555 856 4267

RESPONSIBLE LAWYER	ASSIGNED LAWYERS	FEE BASIS	TICKLER DATES
Owen Mason		Contingent	

ENGAGEMENT RECEIVED BY	ENGAGEMENT RECEIVED FROM	ENGAGEMENT DATE	FILE DISPOSITION
Owen Mason	Website Referr	Oct 3	

CLIENT	OPPOSING PARTY	CLIENT/MATTER NUMBER

Exhibit 8.8 Datasheet View in Access 2003

Fields

Records

	Field1	Field2	Field3	Field4	Field5	Field6	Field7	Field8	Field9	Field10
▶	First Name	Last Name	Full Name	E-Mail Address	Job Title	Contact Type	Company	Salutation	Businesss Ph	Address

Table1 : Table

the same basic information for a database. The Design View also provides an opportunity for customization of the database in the same Page View.

Access 2007 makes the setup of a database relatively simple. A database may be created starting with a Blank database to which the desired fields are added as shown in Exhibit 8.10 with the use of the Add New Fields Templates.

A database may also be created using a Featured Online Template available in the opening Access screen or from a library of other sample templates available from Microsoft Office Online as shown in Exhibit 8.11.

Each of the available selections includes a tutorial on setting up and using the selected database, such as the Contacts database in Exhibit 8.12.

As with other Office suite programs, Wizards are provided for step-by-step operations such as that for collecting data through e-mail messages in the Issues database template shown in Exhibit 8.13. This Wizard is also part of the menu options in the External Data group Collect Data tab.

Creating a Database from External Data

A database in Access 2007 can also be created using a previously created spreadsheet. For example, Exhibit 8.14 shows a database created using the External Data

Exhibit 8.9 Design View in Access 2003. In a simple layout of a database, the fields are the columns and the rows are the records

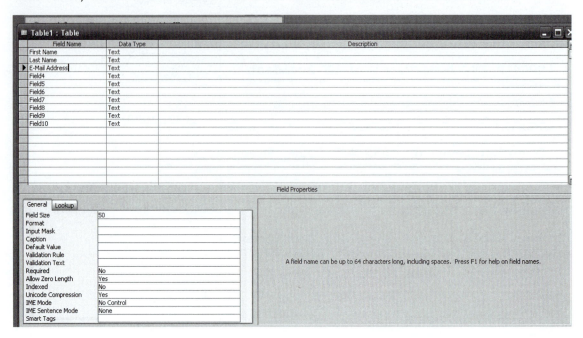

Exhibit 8.10 Create tab—Tables group option

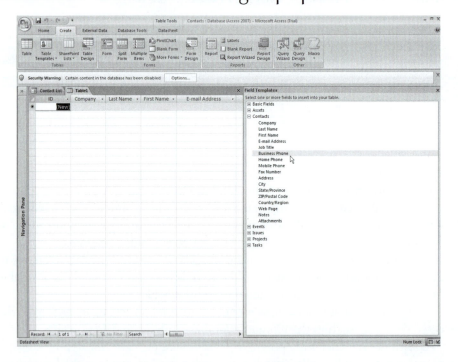

tab, Import group functions with an Excel spreadsheet as the source, in this case the Investment Ledger from Chapter 7 with the title information removed, as shown in Exhibit 8.15.

By removing the extra information in the first few rows of the spreadsheet, the top row of the spreadsheet can be set up automatically as the database Fields when imported into Access. Further entries of records for each investment can be made using the field headings shown at the top of the access database.

Exhibit 8.11 Access opening screen options

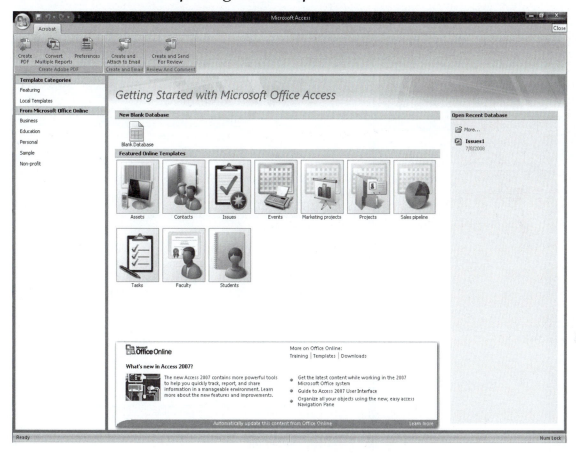

Each record from the database can be viewed in the Form View; for example, record 1, Stocks: 800 common shares, as shown in Exhibit 8.16.

THE USE OF DATABASES IN THE LAW OFFICE

The modern computer database is a very powerful tool, capable of performing complex searches and calculations. Fortunately, most of the functions for which a database is used are performed by the applications programs used in most law offices. Case management, client contacts, and billing and litigation management programs are basically databases. They are designed with input forms and preset reports that search the fields of data records to prepare predefined reports.

It is sometimes necessary to create a database for a customized application for which there is no readily available program. Regardless of the ultimate complexity of the database, its creation starts with knowing what data needs to be manipulated and deciding on the fields (the individual items of data, like last name and zip code) and the total collection of fields of a single type (like a record that contains all of the personal information—fields—of one person). Then a search can be made of any combination of fields that can be reported in any form, showing particular fields of information like last names, zip codes, dates of birth, or any other field from a record or sets of records that meet the search criteria.

From the legal team perspective, the actual design of the database is usually done by the IT staff or an outside database consultant. What the legal team must

Exhibit 8.12 Contact database template and instructions

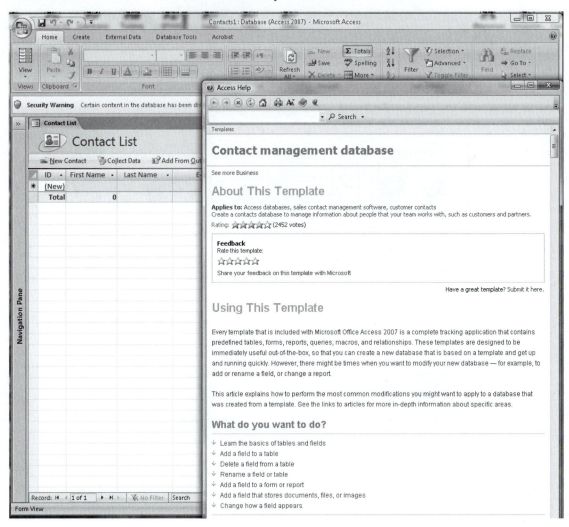

identify is what they need the database to show. When the IT person speaks in "database talk," it will be necessary for everyone concerned to know the difference between a record, a field, and a report.

SPECIAL FEATURES OF ELECTRONIC DATABASE PROGRAMS

Security

It is obvious that a database in a law office contains confidential information, like the list of clients, and may contain potentially privileged information, like the reason the client is consulting the law firm. Protecting this information becomes an ethical obligation. The question that must be considered is how to balance the need for access with the need to restrict access to those with a need to have the information.

Microsoft Access provides options for password and permissions level setup that can be used to restrict access (see Exhibit 8.17).

Password and security options are found on most programs used in the legal community. Typically offices use specialty applications programs that are

Exhibit 8.13 Collect Data Wizard through E-mail

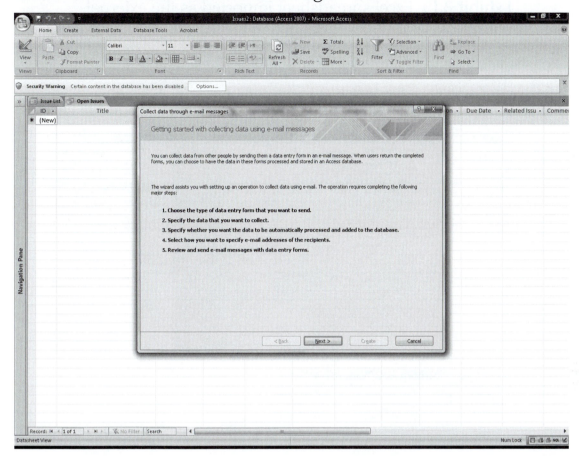

Exhibit 8.14 Access database in Design Sheet View created using external data, an Excel spreadsheet

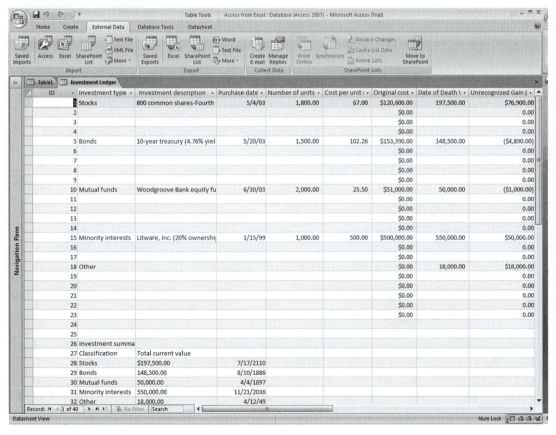

Exhibit 8.15 Excel spreadsheet imported as the external source of data

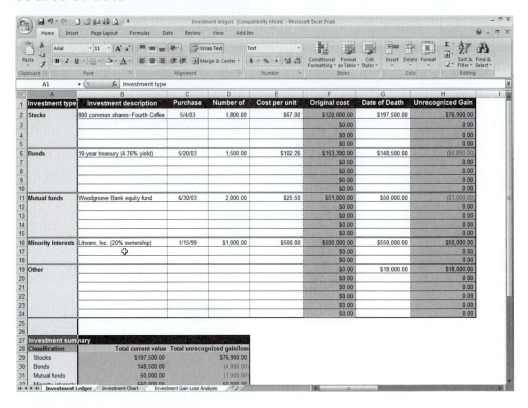

Exhibit 8.16 Record #1 from the Investment Ledger database

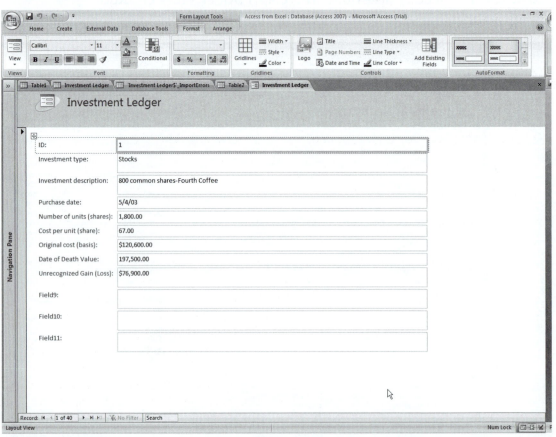

Exhibit 8.17 Security password setup in Microsoft Access

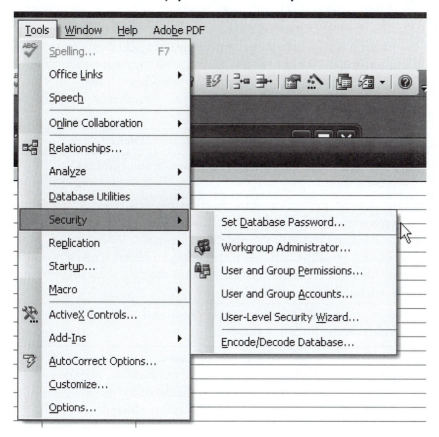

themselves database programs with input and report features. Where the data are of the same confidential or privileged nature, they should have a secure procedure for limiting access to those who need access to the particular functions or information.

SUMMARY

CHAPTER *8*
ELECTRONIC DATABASES

Introduction to Electronic Databases	A database program is a repository of information of all types that can be sorted and presented in a desired, meaningful manner.
The Reality of Using Databases	The reality is that legal team members, lawyers, paralegals, and legal assistants rarely create their own databases. Software vendors have created applications for the legal community with custom designed views for input of information, query forms for generating the desired reports, and set up the search and presentation formulas for searching for data. Knowing what a database is and the associated terminology makes working with the software developer, in-house IT professional, or outside consultant easier and more productive in obtaining what is needed, wanted, and possible.

Navigating Electronic Databases	Electronic databases use standard terminology to describe parts of the database: table, field, cell, and record. Databases are collections of *tables*. Tables contain *fields* of information (data) (called a column in a spreadsheet); a field is one type of information, like last names; a *record* is all the information about one item or person (called a row in a spreadsheet); the intersection of a row and a column in a spreadsheet is a cell, in the database it is one field in a record.
Tables	Databases can and frequently do contain two or more tables.
Reports	Reports present the data from the database in an organized presentation.
Electronic Database Basics	A database is a collection of information, essentially an electronic card with information that can be searched using a set of things to look for and present in a predefined manner. An advantage of the database is the ability to search across a number of different sets of information and sort the data according to a predefined set of criteria.
Resources for Learning Database Basics	Step-by-step tutorials for learning to create and use databases are provided on the Microsoft tutorial.
Setting Up a Database	A database at its most basic is a set of records that contain fields of information. The individual pieces of information, like the last name and the first name, are called fields. Databases may be set up using a blank form to which desired Fields are added or using a database template which may be modified to meet specific needs.
Creating a Database from External Data	A database in Access 2007 can also be created using a previously created spreadsheet.
The Use of Databases in the Law Office	The modern computer database is a very powerful tool, capable of performing complex searches and calculations. Creation starts with knowing what data needs to be manipulated and deciding on the fields and the total collection of fields of a single type.
Special Features of Electronic Database Programs	It is obvious that a database in a law office contains confidential information that ethically must be protected.
Security	Microsoft Access provides options for password and permissions level setup that can be used to restrict access.

KEY TERMINOLOGY

Field   212

Form Views   212

Record   213

Table   212

CONCEPT REVIEW QUESTIONS AND EXERCISES

1. Test your knowledge and comprehension of the topics in this chapter by completing the multiple-choice questions on the textbook Companion Website.
2. Test your knowledge and comprehension of the topics in this chapter by completing the True-False questions on the textbook Companion Website.
3. What security features are available in Access?
4. What steps may be taken to locate and use the resources for learning how to use the Access database program?
5. Explain the function of a database and define the terms used to identify the components.
6. Discuss how databases may be used by the legal team.
7. Explain how to plan and set up a database.
8. Explain what you can do to help protect your database and the reasons for doing so.
9. A database of information can be used in many ways by the legal team. Prepare a list of reports that could be prepared using a database.
10. How can a database be used to prevent a conflict of interest?
11. How can a properly maintained database be used for marketing the firm's services?
12. In a law office that has a network, everyone may have access to all the information on the network. If the firm's database is on the network, what, if anything, should be done to limit access? What levels of access should be set up and why?
13. Prepare a database of family and friends including important dates like birthdays and anniversaries. Sort the list by date.

INTERNET EXERCISES

1. Complete the Microsoft Office "Hands-On Training for Access 2003—Forms I: Create a form to enter and view your data."
2. Prepare a list of online tutorial topics for learning and using the Access database.

PORTFOLIO ASSIGNMENTS

1. Prepare a procedure and related forms for requesting the creation of a database.
2. Prepare a presentation on the uses of a database as a productivity tool.

SCENARIO CASE STUDY

Use the opening scenario for this chapter to answer the following questions. The setting is a law office with metal boxes full of 3-by-5 cards.

1. Prepare a memo stating the reasons why the attorney should switch to an electronic database.
2. Prepare a design for a database table or tables for a small office practice, listing the fields for each table.
3. Explain how the database designed in question 2 can be used in the future.
4. How could the database designed in question 2 have prevented the conflict in the opening scenario?
5. Prepare a memo for the employee handbook about the procedure to be followed using the database to avoid conflicts.

CONTINUING CASES AND EXERCISES

1. Prepare a database for the information in the case study in Appendix 1.
2. If you are using Access 2007, copy the table from Chapter 6 that was pasted into the spreadsheet in Chapter 7 so the column headings become the fields in the Access 2007 database.
3. Prepare a list of individual databases that should be set up with the records and fields to manage the case in Appendix 1.
4. Use the Contacts template in Access 2007 to create a database of the clients in the case study in Appendix 1.

Chapter 9 Digital Resources at www.prenhall.com/goldman

- Author Video Introduction
- Case Study Video: Signing Documents
- Comprehension Quizzes and Glossary

The Paperless Office | CHAPTER 9

OPENING SCENARIO

Everyone was talking about the paperless office in the bar association meeting, but the reality had not struck home until a call came from Ethan, asking his supervising attorney Mr. Mason, where they should file the twenty boxes of files from the litigation that had just been settled. There was no room left in the small storage area allotted to them in the basement of the office building. It looked like most of the documents in the file transfer boxes were already on the office file server. Only the documents received from the opposing side were still in paper form. The reality was that most of the files were paper copies of electronic files on the server. Scanning the paper was a chore, but with the high-speed scanner that was shown at the tech show it might not be a big issue. There was also the service bureau that would scan everything and reproduce it on a CD, like the electronic discovery in the recently closed case provided by the defendant. It seemed like a good time to discuss the costs of storage and new equipment with the other attorney with whom he was sharing office space. Maybe there was a solution and a chance to recover all the storage space, save money in the long term—and get the coffee room back.

LEARNING OBJECTIVES

After studying this chapter you should be able to:

1. Explain what is meant by the term "the paperless office."

2. Explain the need for a filing system for electronic documents.

3. Discuss the ethical considerations in the paperless environment.

4. Describe issues in court-related electronic filing.

5. Describe the types of electronic document formats.

6. Describe the hardware and software issues in scanning documents.

7. Explain the concept of the electronic notary.

229

INTRODUCTION TO THE PAPERLESS OFFICE

Paperless Office
Office where documents are created, stored, received, and sent electronically.

To some people the ideal office is one in which there are no paper documents, or hardcopy, as they are sometimes called. The office where documents are created, stored, received, and sent electronically is sometimes referred to as the **"paperless office"** or "electronic office." In the traditional office, documents are created electronically with word processing software, or received by fax or e-mail and then printed. Electronic portability requires inexpensive, portable computer memory to store and transport the documents, and small, lightweight computers to display them. Conversion of existing paper documents requires the availability of scanners and software that converts the documents to an acceptable format that cannot be easily changed.

The paperless law office is becoming a reality with the advent of modern scanning technology, secured methods for transmission of documents, accepted protocols for use of electronic replacements for paper documents, and rules of court permitting, and in some cases requiring, electronic submission of documents.

Difficult as it may seem to believe for some who have grown up in the paper world, the paperless office is rapidly approaching reality. In the paperless office, documents are created using computer-based word processor programs, such as Microsoft Word, or Corel WordPerfect. These electronic files are then sent electronically to the attorney for review. Changes or revisions are frequently made to the electronic file copy by the reviewer. Where multiple parties may be working on a document, changes made to the original document by each person on the legal team may be monitored by using built-in features such as Track Changes as found in MS Word. This feature shows the original text, the deleted text, and the new text by a series of lines that show as a strike through the deleted text and by margin notes on the document.

When the final document is completed it may be sent by e-mail, fax (frequently directly from the computer without any intermediate paper), and in some jurisdictions filed electronically with the court.

ORGANIZING THE OFFICE FOR STORING ELECTRONIC DOCUMENTS

Saving electronic documents is easy: press the save button. However, finding the electronic document may not be as easy unless there is a systematic method for saving these documents.

Files and Folders

Having a system for saving electronic document files is essential for finding and using them. In the traditional paper office, file cabinets, and file folders with sub-file folders (as holders for parts of the main file folder) form the basic structure. For example, a file cabinet may be set up to contain client material, and each client may have an individual folder with files in that folder for specific items like correspondence and billing information. A large client might have its own file drawer, file cabinet, or even its own file room. A filing structure for electronic files uses the same basic format, but with virtual folders and files.

In a network computer system, most if not all files from everyone on the network are filed on the central file server. See Exhibit 9.1 for an example of a typical filing hierarchy. Having a system in place and a standardized procedure for

Exhibit 9.1 Example of a typical filing hierarchy, which can be maintained whether files are paper or virtual

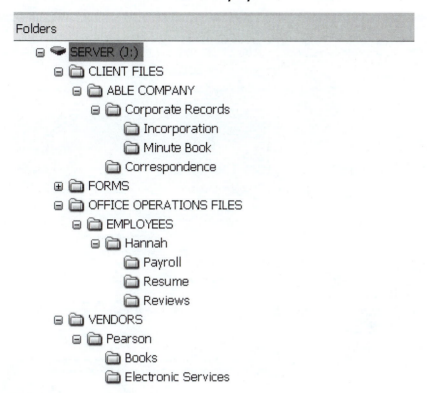

setting up and maintaining **files** avoids the potential of someone setting up a competing system that can result in only that person knowing where things are filed, or duplication of files when others can't find the file where they think it should be and, as a result, re-create and file it somewhere else.

Setting up and organizing documents in folders is simplified by the use of drop and drag tools and software such as ScanSoft PaperPort 11 that show thumbnails of the documents as shown in Exhibit 9.2.

Files
In the paperless office, single data documents.

SECURITY ISSUES

Access to Files and Folders—Ethical Considerations

Ethical issues must be considered when an electronic filing system is designed. Provisions must be made for protecting confidential and privileged documents. Consider protection like locking the file cabinet and restricting the key to only those with a need to have access. Electronic files must have the same ability to be "locked up," or access restricted electronically.

It is sometimes necessary to restrict access to information about a client or a case by building an **ethical wall** around case information. This may be because of a merger of firms, regulatory requirements, or new hires with contact with a party or firm with potential conflict of interest.

Ethical Wall
A restriction on access to information about a case or a client.

At the lowest security level, the document files may be saved with password-restricted access. At the highest security level, only those with the password can open the file. At a lesser security level, others may access the file but not make changes. At the highest level, access may be restricted to the network by password.

Exhibit 9.2 ScanSoft PaperPort 11 file organizer and document manager

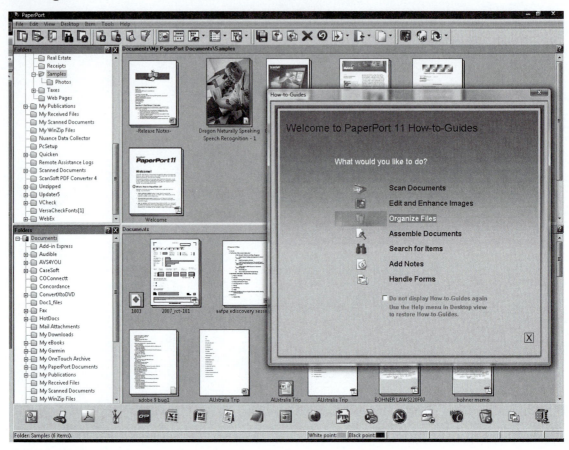

Again it may be a low-level access restricted to certain features of the network or full access generally granted only to the network administrator.

The network administrator is the person with the highest level of access to the network and the ability to add, delete, or change individual users' access rights and permissions to files, **folders,** and connection on the network. In the law office it must be a person that has the right to see and access everything on the office network. In many offices, the network administrator is a member of the IT staff. Similar rights as a network administrator may also be given to a high-level member of the firm such as the managing partner.

One method of restriction is to set up separate file servers for different clients or sensitive cases with access limited exclusively to those working on the case. In other cases it may be necessary to put an ethical wall around certain folders or files to avoid a conflict of interest, such as a member of the legal team who had worked for the opposing party and now works for the new firm.

Limiting Access to Electronic Files

Security and privacy issues require the use of controlling access, as just discussed. Various programs have different ways of limiting access. Exhibit 9.3A–D describe how access to electronic files can be limited, specific to the Microsoft Access database (MDB) program.

Folders
Collections of files.

ETHICAL Perspective

NEBRASKA RULES OF PROFESSIONAL CONDUCT

Terminology

Screened

8. This definition applies to situations where screening of a personally disqualified lawyer is permitted to remove imputation of a conflict of interest under Rules 1.11, 1.12 or 1.18. The definition, as well as Comments [9] and [10] to this rule, also generally apply to the screening of support persons pursuant to Rule 1.9(e)(2).

9. The purpose of screening is to assure the affected parties that confidential information known by the personally disqualified lawyer remains protected. The personally disqualified lawyer should acknowledge the obligation not to communicate with any of the other lawyers in the firm with respect to the matter. Similarly, other lawyers in the firm who are working on the matter should be informed that the screening is in place and that they may not communicate with the personally disqualified lawyer with respect to the matter. Additional screening measures that are appropriate for the particular matter will depend on the circumstances. To implement, reinforce and remind all affected lawyers of the presence of the screening, it may be appropriate for the firm to undertake such procedures as a written undertaking by the screened lawyer to avoid any communication with other firm personnel and any contact with any firm files or other materials relating to the matter, written notice and instructions to all other firm personnel forbidding any communication with the screened lawyer relating to the matter, denial of access by the screened lawyer to firm files or other materials relating to the matter and periodic reminders of the screen to the screened lawyer and all other firm personnel.

10. In order to be effective, screening measures must be implemented as soon as practical after a lawyer or law firm knows or reasonably should know that there is a need for screening.

WWW Mini Exercise

Review the terminology used in the Nebraska Rules of Professional Conduct at http://www.supreme court.ne.gov/rules/pdf/ rulesprofconduct-34 .pdf

ETHICAL Perspective

MISSISSIPPI RULES OF PROFESSIONAL CONDUCT

Rule 1.6 Confidentiality of Information

(a) A lawyer shall not reveal information relating to the representation of a client unless the client gives informed consent, the disclosure is impliedly authorized in order to carry out the representation, or the disclosure is permitted by paragraph (b). . . .

Web Exploration

Contrast and compare Mississippi Rules of Professional Conduct Rule 1.6 Confidentiality at http://www.mssc.state. ms.us/rules/msrulesofcourt/ rules_of_professional_con duct.pdf with the American Bar Association Model Rules of Professional Responsibility at http://www.abanet.org/cpr/ mrpc/mrpc_toc.html, and the ethical rule in your jurisdiction

ELECTRONIC FILING

A number of courts have established procedures for the **electronic filing** of documents. Each court is free to set up its own rules and procedures and must be consulted before attempting to use this service. The Internal Revenue Service and

Electronic Filing
Filing of documents in electronic format using the Internet or computer connection.

Exhibit 9.3A To set up user access security levels in Microsoft Access database, go to Tools, then Options, then Security, then Password Setup

User-Level Security
In Microsoft Access, the ability to limit access to the Access database tables, queries, forms, reports, and macros.

Permissions
A set of attributes that specifies what kind of access a user has to access files and folders.

Workgroup
A group of users in a multiuser environment who share data and the same workgroup information file.

Workgroup Information File
A file that contains information about the users in a workgroup. This information includes users' account names, their passwords, and the groups of which they are members.

About User-Level Security (MDB)

Note: The information in this topic applies only to a Microsoft Access database (.mdb).

Microsoft Access **user-level security** (user-level security: When using user-level security in an Access database, a database administrator or an object's owner can grant individual users or groups of users specific permissions to tables, queries, forms, reports, and macros) is very similar to the security mechanisms seen on server-based systems. By using passwords and **permissions** (permissions: A set of attributes that specifies what kind of access a user has to data or objects in a database), you can allow or restrict the access of individuals, or groups of individuals, to the objects in your database. Security accounts define the users and groups of users allowed access to the objects in your database. This information, known as a **workgroup** (workgroup: A group of users in a multiuser environment who share data and the same workgroup information file), is stored in a **workgroup information file** (workgroup information file: A file that Access reads at startup that contains information about the users in a workgroup. This information includes users' account names, their passwords, and the groups of which they are members.).

Under user-level security, users type a password when they start Microsoft Access. Access goes out and reads a workgroup information file, where each user is identified by a unique identification code. Within the workgroup information file, users are identified as authorized individual users, and as members of specific groups, by their personal ID and password. Microsoft Access provides two default groups: administrators (named the *Admins group (Admins group: The system administrator's group account, which retains full permissions on all databases used by a workgroup. The Setup program automatically adds the default Admin user account to the Admins group.)*) and users (named the *Users group (Users group: The group account that contains all user accounts. Access automatically adds user accounts to the Users group when you create them.)*), but you can define additional groups.

---

some states have combined in a joint effort to allow electronic filing of both the federal and state individual income tax returns in one step. The local or state tax authority retrieves the information from the Internal Revenue Service. A feature of this service, known as IRS e-file, is the return receipt when the federal and state governments receive the form. As with any emerging technology, it takes time for a standard to emerge. There is no universal standard for electronic filing in every instance. Each agency in the federal government and in the various states has its own requirements. Gradually software companies are addressing the need, and some software is available for multilocation filing, such as federal and state tax return filing. In other cases the specific agency requirements must be checked. Most agencies post their electronic filing policy and instructions on their websites, as shown in Exhibit 9.4 and Exhibit 9.5.

Exhibit 9.3B Word password option setup

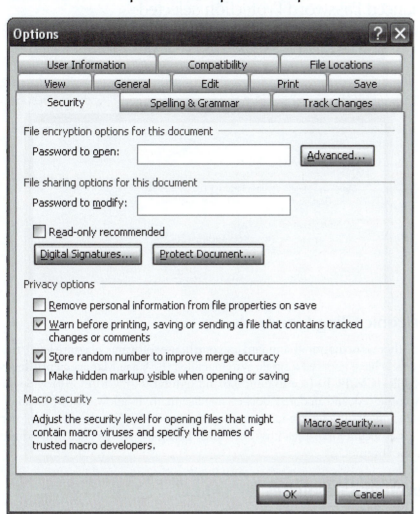

Exhibit 9.3C Note checkmark in "Password protect" box in lower left corner of WordPerfect "Save as" screen

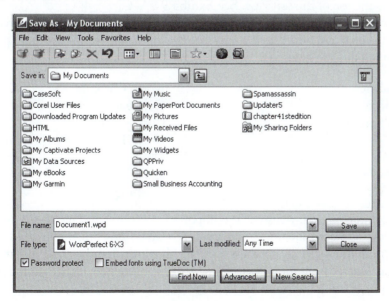

Exhibit 9.3D Two levels of password protection provided; Enhanced Password Protection selected

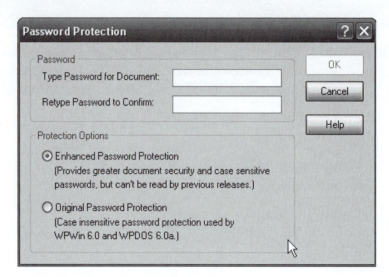

Electronic Filing Standards

Case Management/Electronic Case Files (CM/ECF)
The federal court's electronic access and filing system.

While there is no national standard for courthouse software on a state level, the federal courts have adopted a single system, called the **Case Management/Electronic Case Files(CM/ECF)** (see Exhibit 9.6 and Exhibit 9.7). CM/ECF provides courts with enhanced and updated docket management. It allows courts to maintain case documents in electronic form. And it gives each court the option of permitting case documents—pleadings, motions, petitions—to be filed with the court over the Internet.

WWW Mini Exercise

For complete information on CM/ECF go to http://pacer.psc.uscourts .gov/cmecf/

WWW Mini Exercise

Additional information on the federal system can be found at the following websites:

- http://www.uscourts .gov/cmecf/cmecf .html
- http://www.privacy .uscourts.gov/
- http://www.pacer .psc.uscourts.gov/

Educational Resources for CM/ECF

As we have seen, every software program has its own features and user interface screens. The federal CM/ECF system is no different than most other programs. It uses a familiar menu/toolbar, as shown in Exhibit 9.8.

A series of tutorials and videos is provided on the U.S. Courts website that describes the use of the software. See Exhibit 9.9A–C.

According to the American Bar Association Legal Technology Resource Center, as of 2008 a number of state courts (see the following list) are using State-Wide Electronic Filing Systems.

Alabama	North Carolina
Arizona	Colorado
California	Connecticut
Delaware	North Dakota (pilot program)
District of Columbia	Ohio
New-Jersey	Texas
New York	Washington

They note on their website: "It is important to note that some courts that have rules allowing electronic filing do not yet have an e-filing program in place." Electronic filing rules specific to each state are shown in Exhibit 9.10. Exhibit 9.11 shows an excerpt from the rules for New York State trial courts, where the process for electronic filing is termed filed by electronic means (FBEM).

Exhibit 9.4 The U.S. Patent and Trademark Office posts its electronic filing policy on its website

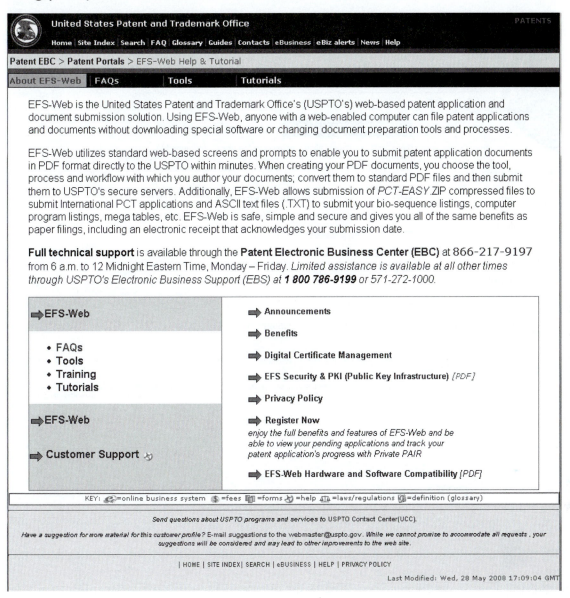

ELECTRONIC DOCUMENT FORMATS

With increasing frequency, the Internet is being used to obtain needed forms. These may be government agency forms, tax forms, or court forms. Even the best-equipped office will require one form or another that is not in the office supply room for completing a case. This may be an unusual federal tax form or a form from your state or another state.

The most popular format for the federal government forms is PDF, and many state agencies also use the PDF format for document delivery. Other options may be presented for selection.

WWW Mini Exercise

For a list of the courts in the process of implementing CM/ECF, go to

http://www.uscourts.gov/cmecf/cmecf_about.html

Exhibit 9.5 The Federal Election Commission offers its position on its website

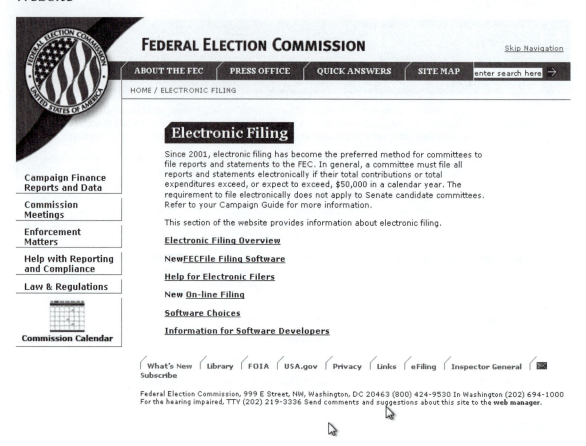

PDF Format

WWW Mini Exercise

View the video on CM/ECF at http://www.uscourts.gov/video/USCourts_HIGH.mov

The ability to save documents in a format that cannot be easily changed through the use of the computer is one of the basic requirements of a system that allows for electronic documentation. Anyone who has received a word processing document file knows that he or she may change it, save it, and present it as an original unless access has been restricted by use of password restriction. Documents may now be saved in a graphic image format or portable document format (PDF), developed by Adobe Systems. (PDF format is also discussed in Chapter 14 in the context of litigation support.) These graphic images may not be easily or readily changed by the recipient.

The creation of documents in PDF format requires specialty software such as Adobe Acrobat. However, everyone can download a free Adobe Reader to view these documents, adding to the acceptance of the PDF format. With the acceptance of this format has come a willingness to scan and store documents electronically and eliminate or return to the client the original paper copies. Companies like Adobe Systems frequently provide free, limited versions of their programs, downloadable from their website, that allow the opening and reading of files created using their proprietary software formats, such as Adobe's PDF file format. Many websites that provide programs using these proprietary formats, such as the Internal Revenue Service forms website, contain links to these programs. These programs are limited in that they allow the user to open and read files but do not

WWW Mini Exercise

Check the current list of states at www.abanet.org/tech/trc/efiling/home.html

Exhibit 9.6 U.S. Courts Case Management/Electronic case files

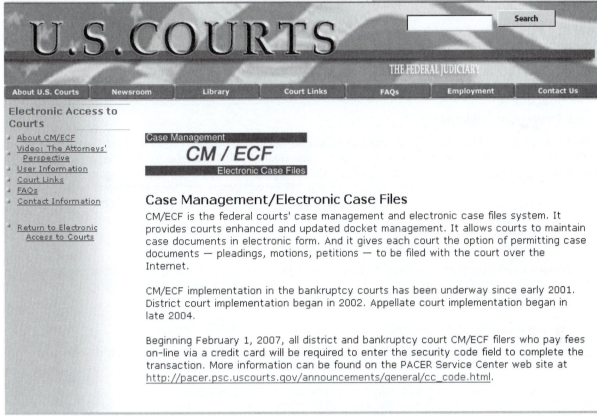

Case Management
CM / ECF
Electronic Case Files

Case Management/Electronic Case Files

CM/ECF is the federal courts' case management and electronic case files system. It provides courts enhanced and updated docket management. It allows courts to maintain case documents in electronic form. And it gives each court the option of permitting case documents — pleadings, motions, petitions — to be filed with the court over the Internet.

CM/ECF implementation in the bankruptcy courts has been underway since early 2001. District court implementation began in 2002. Appellate court implementation began in late 2004.

Beginning February 1, 2007, all district and bankruptcy court CM/ECF filers who pay fees on-line via a credit card will be required to enter the security code field to complete the transaction. More information can be found on the PACER Service Center web site at http://pacer.psc.uscourts.gov/announcements/general/cc_code.html.

About The U.S. Courts | Newsroom | Library | Court Links | FAQs | Employment Opportunities | Contact Us | Search

This page is maintained by the Administrative Office of the U.S. Courts on behalf of the U.S. Courts.
The purpose of this site is to function as a clearinghouse for information from and about the Judicial Branch of the U.S. Government.

Privacy and Security Notices

Source: http://pacer.psc.uscourts.gov/ecfcbt/dc/

allow the creation of new document files, which requires the full version of the program. See Exhibit 9.12 for more information about PDF format.

Adobe Acrobat

Adobe Acrobat has become a standard software tool in many paperless offices for creating PDF files. With each new version or update to the original program, additional features have been added to allow greater sharing of documents with a higher level of security and facilitating collaboration on document preparation.

In new versions of Acrobat the creator of a PDF document, using Adobe Acrobat (versions 5 and above) can limit the ability of the receiver of the PDF file to print, or not print, the document using a password to control the printing. This

WWW Mini Exercise
Review the complete rule at http://www.courts.state.ny.us/rules/trial courts/202.shtml#05b

WWW Mini Exercise
Check the current list of electronic filing rules at www.abanet.org/tech/trc/efiling/rules.html

Exhibit 9.7 Selected portions of CM/ECF FAQs

What is CM/ECF?

ANSWER: CM/ECF—the Case Management/Electronic Case Files project—is a joint project of the Administrative Office of the U.S. Courts and the federal courts to replace old case management systems with a new system based on current technology, new software, and increased functionality. This system gives federal courts the ability to maintain electronic case files and offer electronic filing of court documents over the Internet. . . .

Is CM/ECF currently available?

ANSWER: Yes, CM/ECF is currently available in most courts. The CM/ECF system for bankruptcy courts began implementation nationally in early 2001. The district court CM/ECF system began to roll out nationally in May 2002. Implementation of the CM/ECF system for appellate courts began in 2005. CM/ECF currently is in use in 99% of the federal courts. Millions of cases and tens of millions of documents are on CM/ECF systems and more than 320,000 attorneys across the country are filing documents electronically.

Will all federal courts offer electronic filing?

ANSWER: Almost all district and bankruptcy courts offer electronic filing. Most appellate courts will offer electronic filing, too. For information about whether your local court offers electronic filing, contact your local court.

What hardware and software are needed to file documents in CM/ECF systems?

ANSWER: Filing documents into CM/ECF electronic filing systems requires the following hardware and software:

- A personal computer running a standard platform such as Windows or Mac OS X.
- A PDF-compatible word processor like Mac OS X or Windows-based versions of Corel WordPerfect or Microsoft Word.
- Internet service.
- A Web browser. For district and bankruptcy CM/ECF, Mozilla Firefox 2 or 1.5, or Microsoft Internet Explorer 7.0 or 6.0 are recommended. Some users have had positive experiences with other Web browsers, but those listed here have been tested and certified for compatibility with CM/ECF. Mozilla Firefox is compatible with Mac and can be downloaded at no cost.
- For appellate CM/ECF, Firefox and Internet Explore are recommended, but users will need the Java 1.6 plug-in. The plug-in is available as a free download from www.java.com. The appellate software will operate on a Mac computer that has software that allows Windows to run on the Mac. The appellate software currently does not operate on a Mac using the Apple-supplied Java, because Apple has not yet released a port of the current version of Java (1.6).
- Software to convert documents from a word processor format to portable document format (PDF). Adobe Acrobat 8 Professional is recommended. Adobe Acrobat 7 Professional, Adobe Acrobat 6 Professional, and Acrobat Writer 5.0 adequately meet the CM/ECF filing requirements.
- Adobe Acrobat Reader, which is available for free, is needed for viewing PDF documents.
- A scanner may be necessary to create electronic images of documents that are not in your word processing system.

Who may file documents on CM/ECF systems?

ANSWER: Filing a document into CM/ECF requires a login and password. Each court determines for itself to whom it will issue filing logins and passwords. Courts offering electronic filing are providing document filing access principally to attorneys, U.S. Trustees, and bankruptcy case trustees. Some courts permit bankruptcy claimants and other pro se litigants to file electronically.

Who may view documents on CM/ECF systems?

ANSWER: Subject to court orders in individual cases, policy, or other individual court limitations, the public may view dockets and documents in CM/ECF systems through the Public Access to Court

Exhibit 9.7 Continued

Electronic Records (PACER) program. PACER logins are available to the public at: http:www.pacer.psc.uscourts.gov/register.html . Directed by Congress to fund electronic access through user fees, the federal judiciary has set the fee at the lowest possible level sufficient to recoup program costs. Information is currently available at a rate of eight cents per page, with a maximum cost per document calculated to be the equivalent of a 30-page document ($2.40). Transcripts of court proceedings are not subject to the fee limit.

Do documents that will be filed on CM/ECF systems need to be in a particular format?

ANSWER: CM/ECF systems are designed to accept only documents in PDF format. This format was chosen because it allows a document to retain its pagination, formatting and fonts no matter what type of computer is used to view or print the document. It is also an open standard format. Adobe developed the format, and offers software that allows conversion of documents created in most word processing systems into PDF. This software is recommended. Several word processing and other programs contain features that convert documents created in those programs into PDF.

Are there fees associated with CM/ECF?

ANSWER: There are no added fees for filing documents over the Internet using CM/ECF, although existing court document filing fees do apply. Electronic access to individual case docket sheets and filed documents is available through the Public Access to Court Electronic Records (PACER) program. Litigants receive one free copy of documents filed electronically in their cases through a link in the e-mailed Notice of Electronic Filing; additional copies are available to attorneys and to the general public for viewing or downloading at the current PACER cost of eight cents per page with a maximum cost per document calculated to be the equivalent of a 30-page document ($2.40). Transcripts of court proceedings are not subject to the fee limit. Directed by Congress to fund electronic access through user fees, the federal judiciary has set the fee at the lowest possible level sufficient to recoup program costs.

Are there procedural rules relating to electronic filing?

ANSWER: Rule 5(e) of the Federal Rules of Civil Procedure, Rule 5005(a) of the Federal Rules of Bankruptcy Procedure, Rule 25(a) of the Federal Rules of Appellate Procedure, and Rule 49(d) of the Federal Rules of Criminal Procedure authorize individual courts by local rule to permit or require papers to be filed by electronic means. Most courts that offer electronic filing have issued an authorizing local rule; most have supplemented the local rule with a general order and/or procedures that set forth the relevant procedures governing electronic filing in that court. Individual court rules and procedures are generally available on their Web sites. Rules 5(b) and 77 of the Federal Rules of Civil Procedure, Rules 25 and 26 of the Federal Rules of Appellate Procedure, Rules 45 and 49 of the Federal Rules of Criminal Procedure and Rules 7005, 9014 and 9022 of the Federal Rules of Bankruptcy Procedure also authorize service of documents by electronic means if parties consent. The amendments do not apply to service of process. For more information, click here. Individual court rules and procedures are generally available on their Web sites.

Are documents filed in CM/ECF secure?

ANSWER: Yes. There are two utility programs that verify documents. One program is used to verify the integrity of a PDF document as it is filed in CM/ECF. A second, separate program is run automatically at preset times to verify that the documents have not changed since they were filed. (Top)

This page is maintained by the Administrative Office of the U.S. Courts on behalf of the U.S. Courts.

The purpose of this site is to function as a clearinghouse for information from and about the Judicial Branch of the U.S. Government.

Exhibit 9.8 CM/ECF toolbar

Exhibit 9.9A Menu of training modules available for CM/ECF

DISTRICT COURT CM/ECF
COMPUTER-BASED TRAINING MODULES

Below is a series of generic training modules to help you become more familiar with the electronic filing aspects of the District Court CM/ECF product. In addition, most courts provide a separate CM/ECF database for training purposes. Links to information and training materials offered by the local courts are available by clicking here.

NOTE: These modules work only in supported web browsers. At this time that includes the following:

- Microsoft IE 5.5 SP1 and above
- Netscape 7.2 and above
- Firefox and other Mozilla-based browsers

Other browsers, including earlier versions of Netscape and IE, are not supported.

NOTE: These training modules are run in pop-up windows. You must allow pop-ups from this site or you will not be able to view these modules. If you have Service Pack 2 for Windows XP on your PC, the pop-up blocker may not allow you to see the training modules. To bypass the pop-up blocker, ctrl-click the links below.

The training modules may take a while to load.

An Introduction to CM/ECF
Logging in to CM/ECF
Converting Documents to PDF
Windows File Management Part 1
Windows File Management Part 2
Setting Up Automatic E-mail

Filing a Civil Answer
Filing a Civil Motion
Filing a Civil Response to Motion
Queries
Filing a Criminal Motion
Filing a Criminal Response to Motion

Source: http://pacer.psc.uscourts.gov/ecfcbt/dc/

Exhibit 9.9B CM/ECF tutorial screen of sample content of civil events options

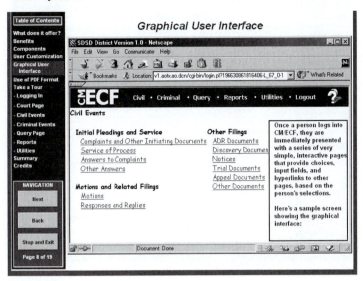

password feature allows the legal team to send documents that can be viewed by others on the legal team without permitting changes to the original document but allowing comments to be made and submitted to the originator of the document. The Acrobat 9 Help Viewer is shown in Exhibit 9.13.

In typical use the attorney or paralegal creates the document in a word processor such as Word or WordPerfect and uses Adobe Acrobat to convert the document to a PDF. The PDF format reduces the risk of sending the document metadata found in the native or original word processor document. See Exhibit 9.14.

PDF Converter 5

ScanSoft PDF Converter 5 by Nuance (see Exhibit 9.15) is a lower-cost alternative to the widely used Adobe Acrobat. In addition to creating PDF documents, it also provides a number of other options. The converter feature can be used to convert PDF files into fully formatted Word, WordPerfect, and Excel documents.

An interesting additional feature is the ability to convert documents into audio files that can be played back through a computer or on an MP3 player, like an Apple iPod. Anyone who has tried to proofread, by themselves, technical language in a document or the legal description in a real estate agreement or deed will appreciate the ability to have the language "read to them" while following the language in the document to verify accuracy.

As with Acrobat, ScanSoft PDF Converter 5 allows the same type of security settings for documents created with the program, including password limitations for changes and printing, as shown in the PDF Converter Help screen for security and the security menu options in Exhibit 9.16.

Exhibit 9.9C Sample pages from CM/ECF tutorial

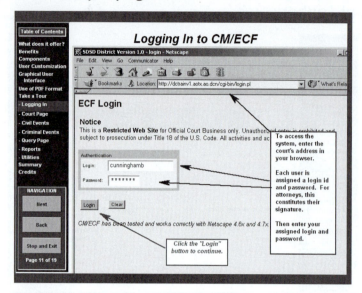

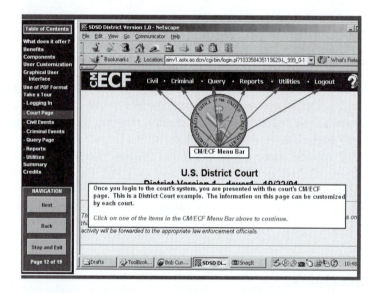

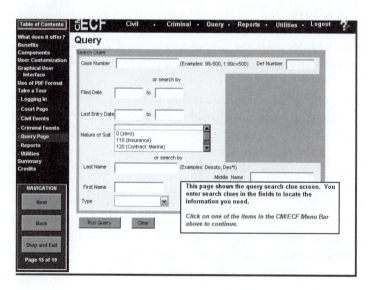

Exhibit 9.10 Examples of electronic filing rules in states

JURISDICTION	COURT	ELECTRONIC FILING RULES
Arizona	Arizona Supreme Court	Rule 124. Electronic Filing, Delivery and Service of Documents
Arizona—Maricopa	Maricopa County Superior Court	Administrative Order 2003-115 Court's e-filing rules, orders, and procedures (via LexisNexis)
Arizona—Pima	Pima County—Justice Courts Small Claims	Administrative Order 97-71 Administrative Order 99-20 Court's e-filing rules, orders, and procedures (via LexisNexis)
California	Administrative Office of the Courts	Electronic Filing Technical Standards Project
California—Alameda	Alameda County Superior Court	Local Rule 1.8: Facsimile Filing and Electronic Filing Court's e-filing rules, orders, and procedures (via LexisNexis)
California—Contra Costa	Contra Costa County Superior Court	Court's e-filing rules, orders, and procedures (via LexisNexis)
California—San Bernandino	San Bernardino County Superior Court	Local Rule-Chapter Eighteen: Electronic Filings and Service Court's e-filings rules, orders, and procedures (via LexisNexis)
California—Los Angeles	Los Angeles Superior Court	Local Rules-Chapter Eighteen: Electronic Filing and Service Court's e-filing rules, orders, and procedures (via LexisNexis)
California—San Diego	San Diego Superior Court	Court's e-filings and rules, orders, and procedures (via LexisNexis)
California—San Francisco	San Francisco Superior Court	Court's e-filings rules, orders, and procedures (via LexisNexis)
California—Santa Barbara	Superior Court of California Santa Barbara County	Court's e-filings rules, orders, and procedures (via LexisNexis)
California—Shasta County	Shasta County Superior Court	Court's e-filings rules, orders, and procedures (via LexisNexis)
Colorado	Statewide	Colorado Rules of Civil Procedure Rule 121 Court's e-filings rules, orders, and procedures (via LexisNexis)
District of Columbia	Superior Court of the District of Columbia	Court's e-filings rules, orders, and procedures (via LexisNexis)
Georgia—Dekalb County	Dekalb County Superior Court	Court's e-filings rules, orders, and procedures (via LexisNexis)

(Continued)

Exhibit 9.10 Continued

Georgia—Fulton County	State Court of Fulton County/ Asbestos and Mercury Poisoning Litigation	Court's e-filings rules, orders, and procedures (via LexisNexis)
Georgia—Fulton County	Fulton County Superior Court	Court's e-filings rules, orders, and procedures (via LexisNexis)
Illinois	Illinois Supreme Court	Policy for Implementation of an Electronic Filing Pilot Project in Illinois' Courts
Illinois—DuPage County	DuPage 18th Judicial Circuit Court	Article 5: E-Filing Court's e-filings rules, orders, and procedures (via LexisNexis)
Kansas	Kansas District Courts	Order Adopting Technical Standards
Maine	Pilot Project—Protection from Abuse Complaints	Administrative Order JB-01-05
Maryland	Supreme Court of Maryland	Rule 16-506
Maryland—Baltimore	Baltimore City Circuit Court	Court's e-filings rules, orders, and procedures (via LexisNexis)
Michigan—Ottawa County	Ottawa County, 20th Judicial Circuit Court	Court's e-filing rules, orders, and procedures (via LexisNexis)
Michigan—Washtenaw County	Washtenaw County Circuit Court	How to File Briefs Electronically
Nevada	Clark County District Court	E-File & Serve Information
New Jersey	Supreme Court of New Jersey	Supreme Court Rule Relaxation Order
New Jersey—Atlantic County	Atlantic County Superior Court	Court's e-filing rules, orders, and procedures (via LexisNexis)
New Jersey—Bergen County	Bergen County Superior Court	Court's e-filing rules, orders, and procedures (via LexisNexis)
New Jersey—Middlesex County	Middlesex County Superior Court	Court's e-filing rules, orders, and procedures (via LexisNexis)
New York	New York State Unified Court System	Uniform Civil Rules for the Supreme Court and the County Court
North Carolina	North Carolina Business Courts	General Rules of Practice and Procedure—Rule 5
Ohio	Supreme Court of Ohio	Ohio Rules of Court Rules of Appellate Procedure (Title III: Rule 13)
Ohio—Butler County	Butler County Court of Common Pleas	Court's e-filing rules, orders, and procedures (via LexisNexis)
Ohio—Cuyahoga County	Cuyahoga County Court of Common Pleas	Court's e-filing rules, orders, and procedures (via LexisNexis)

Exhibit 9.10 Continued

Ohio—Cuyahoga County	Garfield Heights Municipal Court	Local Rule 7—Electronic Filing The Electronic Court Project E-filing Frequently Asked Questions Electronic Document Type Information
Ohio—Hamilton County	Hamilton County Clerk of Courts	Local Rules of the First Appellate Judicial District [Hamilton County] RULE 16 Hamilton County Rules of Practice of the Court of Common Pleas RULE 34 Hamilton County Municipal Court (Local) Rules of Civil Procedure RULE XXVIII
Ohio—Lucas County	Lucas County Court of Common Pleas	Court's e-filing rules, orders, and procedures (via LexisNexis)
Oklahoma	Oklahoma Supreme Court	Oklahoma Statute Title 20, Chapter 40, Section 3004: Electronic Filing of Documents
Pennsylvania	First Judicial District of Pennsylvania	In Re: President Judge Administrative Order 2001–01
Pennsylvania—Philadelphia	Philadelphia Orphan's Court	Pa.O.C.R. 3.7 GCR 2004-01
Pennsylvania—Lancaster County	Lancaster County Court of Common Pleas	Court's e-filing rules, orders, and procedures (via LexisNexis)
Pennsylvania—Montgomery County	Montgomery County Court of Common Pleas	Rule 205. 4: Electronic Filing and Service of Legal Papers
Texas	Texas Supreme Court	Electronic Filing Rules Template
Texas—Dallas County	Dallas County District and County Court Asbestos Cases	Court's e-filing rules, orders, and procedures (via LexisNexis)
Texas—Jefferson County	Jefferson County District Courts	Court's e-filing rules, orders, and procedures (via LexisNexis)
Texas—Johnson County	Johnson County Courts	Court's e-filing rules, orders, and procedures (via LexisNexis)
Texas—Madison County	Montgomery County District Court and Courts of Law	Court's e-filing rules, orders, and procedures (via LexisNexis)
Texas—Nueces County	Nueces County District Court	Court's e-filing rules, orders, and procedures (via LexisNexis)
Utah	Utah State Courts	Utah State Court Rules of Civil Procedure: Rule 1. General Provisions
Washington	Washington State Courts	GR 30 Electronic Filing
Washington	Chelan County District Court	Local Rule 5 Court's e-filing rules, orders, and Procedures (via LexisNexis)
Wyoming	Statewide	Rule of Civil Procedure 5(e)

Exhibit 9.11 Sample pages from the Uniform Rules for New York State Trial Courts

PART 202. Uniform Civil Rules for The Supreme Court and the County Court

Section 202.05b Electronic Filing in Supreme Court.

(a) Application.

(1) There is hereby established a pilot program in which documents may be filed and served by electronic means in civil actions in Supreme Court. Documents may be filed or served by such means only to the extent and in the manner authorized in this section and only in the following actions: (i) tax certiorari actions (including small claims actions under Title 1-A of Article 7 of the Real Property Tax Law) and tort and commercial actions in the Supreme Court in Albany, Bronx, Essex, Kings, Livingston, Monroe, Nassau, New York, Niagara, Onondaga, Queens, Richmond, Suffolk, Sullivan and Westchester Counties; and (ii) actions in Supreme Court in Broome County and Erie County of any type designated by the appropriate Administrative Judge.

(2) For purposes of these rules:
(i) "electronic means" shall mean any method of transmission of information between computers or other machines, other than facsimile machines, designed for the purpose of sending and receiving such transmissions, and which allows the recipient to reproduce the information transmitted in a tangible medium of expression;
(ii) the "e-filing Internet site" shall mean the website located at www.nycourts.gov/efile;
(iii) "e-filing", "electronic filing" and "electronically filing" shall mean the filing and service of documents in a civil action by electronic means through the e-filing Internet site;
(iv) an "authorized e-filing user" shall mean a person who has registered to use e-filing pursuant to subdivision (c) of this section;
(v) an "action";
(vi) "hard copy" shall mean information set forth in paper form; and
(vii) "party" or "parties" shall mean the party or parties to an action or counsel thereto. . . .

SCANNING

The heart of the paperless office is the ability to create electronic files. With word processors the files created are stored in an electronic format and viewable on a computer monitor, eliminating the need for paper copies. Until the paperless office becomes a universal standard, there will still be paper documents. For example, the real estate area has been slow to adopt a paperless system for real estate purchases, mortgages, and documents for filing. A typical real estate transaction may involve hundreds of pages of documents, including agreements of sales, mortgagees, mortgage notes, title reports and supporting documents, receipts, and other miscellaneous sheets of paper collectively inches thick that to store take up valuable file space. Once originals have been recorded and sent to mortgage lenders, copies may be easily saved by scanning all the documents and saving them on a computer hard drive or CD easily searched and printed if necessary, and copies of the CD presented to the buyer and seller if required.

The same situation is true for most other closed files that are only taking up space in the storage area or file room. Copies can be scanned and archived or

WWW Mini Exercise

For an Introduction to How Scanners Work and the Scanning Process go to How Stuff Works at http://computer.howstuffworks.com/scanner.htm

Exhibit 9.12 How Do PDFs Work?

How do PDF files work?

PDF files display texts correctly wherever they are viewed because they carry their typographic information with them. Fonts in the document are embedded in the PDF file and are used after distribution to reconstruct the document. The display does not depend on the needed font files being available on the viewing machine, nor on the language of its operating system.

PDF documents present their pages as images. They can be marked-up and commented, but the ability to change the basic text is limited. Most PDF files can be searched, because the file has two layers. There is an image layer that is presented on-screen. Behind that there is usually a text layer that can be matched to the characters displayed on the screen.

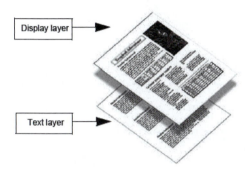

When the starting point for a PDF file is a set of images, or a scanning process, this text layer is not present and the result is an image-only PDF. When the starting point is an editable document, the text layer can be created and the PDF is called 'Normal' or 'Searchable'. The creator of a PDF can require provision of a password to allow access the text layer.

Source: PDF Converter 4 Professional Quick Reference Guide. © Nuance Communications, Inc. All Rights Reserved.

Exhibit 9.13 Screen of Adobe Acrobat 9 Professional Help Viewer

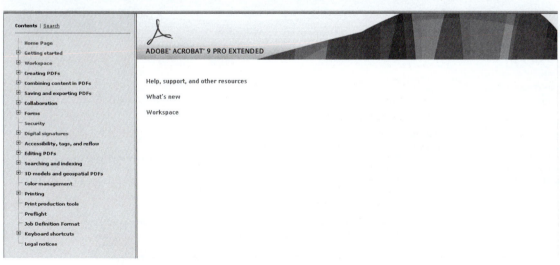

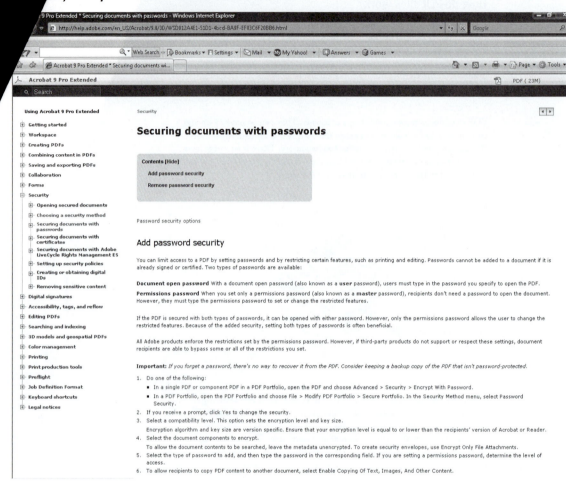

Sample of Acrobat 9 Help Instructions

Convert a file to PDF

1. In Acrobat, do one of the following:
   - Choose File > Create PDF > From File.
   - In the toolbar, click the Create button and choose PDF From File.
2. In the Open dialog box, select the file. You can browse all file types or select a specific type from the Files Of Type menu.
3. Optionally, click Settings to change the conversion options. The options available vary depending on the file type.
   Note: *The Settings button is unavailable if you choose All Files as the file type or if no conversion settings are available for the selected file type.*
4. Click Open to convert the file to a PDF.
   Depending on the type of file being converted, the authoring application opens automatically or a progress dialog box appears. If the file is in an unsupported format, a message appears, telling you that the file cannot be converted to PDF.
5. When the new PDF opens, choose File > Save or File > Save As; then select a name and location for the PDF.

   When naming a PDF that's intended for electronic distribution, limit the filename to eight characters (with no spaces) and include the .pdf extension. This action ensures that email programs or network servers don't truncate the filename and that the PDF opens as expected.

Exhibit 9.15 ScanSoft PDF Converter 5

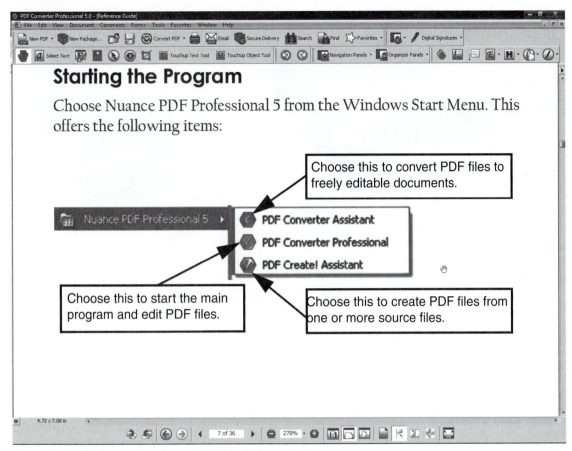

Exhibit 9.16 ScanSoft PDF Converter 5 Security Menus

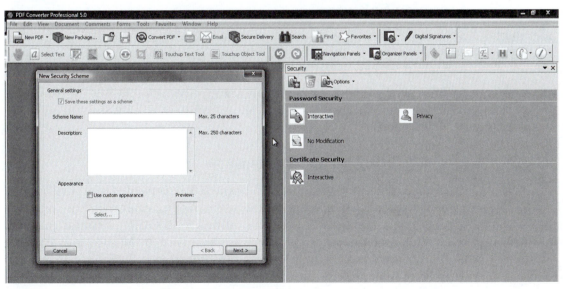

Exhibit 9.17 Scanner types

Flat Bed Scanner   Automatic Document Feed Scanner

saved until the appropriate time for destruction as set in the firm's destruction policy.

Scanning Hardware

Original scanning hardware was costly and frequently unreliable. Modern scanners provide double-sided (front and back) scanning of documents with a high degree of accuracy at a relatively low cost. Scanning today has become a common feature in office printers and copy machines. Double-sided scanning is found today in multifunction devices containing printing, scanning, copying, and faxing at prices under $100. These devices when coupled with applications software such as PaperPort allow virtually anyone to create electronic documents. An automatic document feed scanner allows for single or multiple sheet-fed scanning, which is a time-saver when scanning multiple-page documents. A flat bed scanner allows for scanning sheets as well as documents that can't be fed through a feeder, such as books or labels on packages (see Exhibit 9.17).

Scanning Software

Scanning and storing paper documents has become easier with the development of software such as PaperPort by Nuance. This software provides easy-to-use high-speed scanning and document capture. As a documents management software application, it allows for the organization, finding, and sharing of paper and digital documents, permitting the elimination of paper documents. See Exhibit 9.18.

Optical Character Recognition

Optical Character Recognition (OCR)
A technology that takes data from a paper document and turns it into editable text data. The document is first scanned, then OCR software searches the document for letters, numbers, and other characters.

There are obviously times when documents need to be converted from graphic image to a format that allows for editing or other use in an office suite of applications. These software applications have come to be referred to as **OCR,** or **optical character recognition** applications. Products such as Omni Page, by Nuance, provide document conversion solutions by permitting any scanned page, PDF file, or other image or document file to be converted quickly and accurately into one of a number of different editable formats, including Microsoft Word or Corel WordPerfect.

Exhibit 9.18 The scanning and converting process

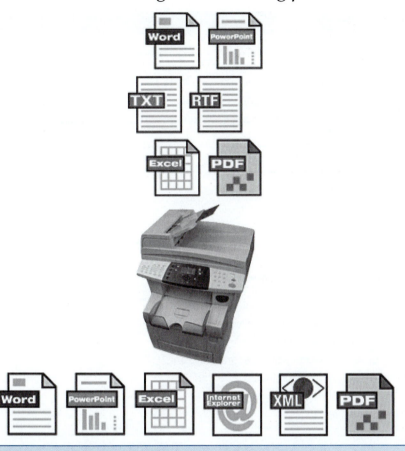

> **The Scanning and Conversion Process**
> Start with any printed page, any PDF File, or other image or document file.
>
> **Scan Any Page**
>
> **Perform the Conversion**
> Using the software program to perform the conversion.
>
> **Save and Edit Your File**
> Save the newly-created file for editing or distribution.

Many times there is a need to use the information in a PDF document in other than a word processor, such as a spreadsheet. ScanSoft PDF Converter 5 converts PDF files into documents, spreadsheets, and forms, complete with all formatting and graphics that can be edited.

Examine a PDF for Hidden Content

Every document has metadata—data about the document—as part of the document file. Acrobat is used to create PDF format documents, sometimes in the mistaken belief that the file does not have metadata. Exhibit 9.19 shows the basic metadata for a PDF copy of a chapter of this book, which is viewable by selecting the Document Properties tab. This is similar in appearance to the Document

Exhibit 9.19 Basic metadata shown in Document Properties

```
Document Properties                                              [X]

 Description | Security | Fonts | Initial View | Custom | Advanced
 ┌─Description────────────────────────────────────────────────────┐
 │     File:  CHAPTER ONE Introduction                             │
 │    Title:  [CHAPTER ONE- Technology in the Law Office         ] │
 │   Author:  [Thomas F. Goldman                                 ] │
 │  Subject:  [                                                  ] │
 │ Keywords:  [                                                  ] │
 │            [                                                  ] │
 │            [                                                  ] │
 │  Created:  11/7/2006 3:28:24 PM           [ Additional Metadata...] │
 │ Modified:  11/7/2006 3:32:36 PM                                 │
 │ Application:  Acrobat PDFMaker 8.0 for Word                     │
 └────────────────────────────────────────────────────────────────┘
 ┌─Advanced───────────────────────────────────────────────────────┐
 │ PDF Producer:  Acrobat Distiller 8.0.0 (Windows)                │
 │  PDF Version:  1.4 (Acrobat 5.x)                                │
 │     Location:  \\Server01\vol1\B\LAWS 260 SPRING 2007\          │
 │    File Size:  16.17 KB (16,560 Bytes)                          │
 │   Page Size:  8.50 x 11.00 in           Number of Pages:  2     │
 │  Tagged PDF:  Yes                        Fast Web View:  Yes    │
 └────────────────────────────────────────────────────────────────┘

 [ Help ]                                    [ OK ]   [ Cancel ]
```

Properties available in MS Word for files created using Word. Exhibit 9.20 shows the additional detailed metadata for the same file using the Advanced settings in Acrobat.

As shown in the Preference selections window in Exhibit 9.21, one of the options in Acrobat is to set preference to Examine Documents. Two options exist: 1) *before* sending the e-document electronically, and 2) examining before saving. Both practices might prevent information being sent that is not intended for the receipient.

THE ELECTRONIC NOTARY

The traditional role of a notary is to offer an independent validation of a person's act of signing a document. The notary is required to:

1. Require the signer to personally appear.
2. Scan the document to ensure it is complete.

Exhibit 9.20 Advance Metadata View in Acrobat

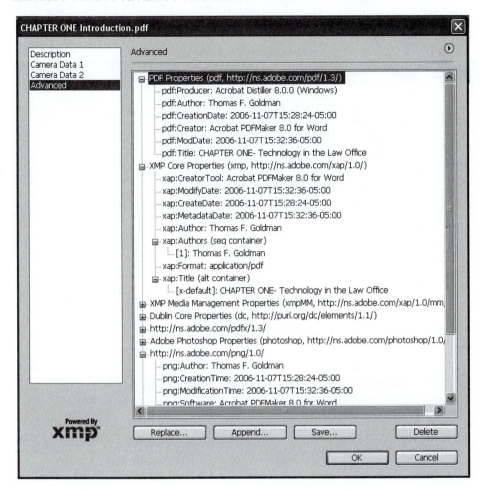

3. Screen the signer for awareness, willingness, and identity.
4. Record the notary in a journal.
5. Complete the certificate and affix the official signature and seal.

Traditionally, the affixing of the seal was done with a metal embossing seal. Some states have replaced the raised embossed seal with a rubber stamp seal that allows for photocopying for electronic recording.

The newest version of the notary is the Electronic Notary. The **electronic notary seal (ENS)**, is a form of electronic digital signature unique to the individual notary. When made a part of an electronic document, it encodes an electronic signature that makes any changes to the electronic document obvious to anyone viewing the document, with a message on the document indicating that a change, addition, or deletion to the original document has occurred.

Electronic Notary Seal (ENS)
A form of electronic digital signature unique to the individual notary.

WWW Mini Exercise

The Notary Public Code of Professional Responsibility can be viewed and downloaded at http://www.nationalnotary.org/UserImages/Notary_Code.pdf

Exhibit 9.21 Set Acrobat Examine Document Preferences option selection to prompt examining the document for metadata before it is sent to anyone

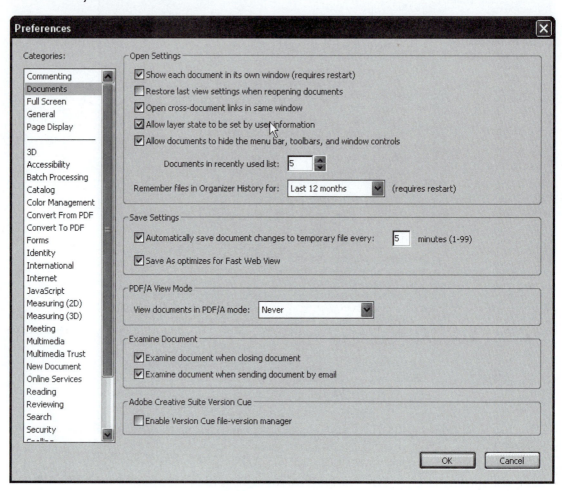

Among the early states to adopt provisions for permitting electronic notarizations are:

California
Colorado
Florida
Michigan
Pennsylvania
Texas

The National Notary Association requires that members of its profession adhere to a code of ethics as expressed in the Notary Public Code of Professional Responsibility (see Exhibit 9.22).

Exhibit 9.22 The Notary Public Code of Professional Responsibility

The Notary Public Code of Professional Responsibility

10 Guiding Principles

I. The Notary shall, as a government officer and public servant, serve all of the public in an honest, fair and unbiased manner.

II. The Notary shall act as an impartial witness and not profit or gain from any document or transaction requiring a notarial act, apart from the fee allowed by statute.

III. The Notary shall require the presence of each signer and oath-taker in order to carefully screen each for identity and willingness, and to observe that each appears aware of the significance of the transaction requiring a notarial act.

IV. The Notary shall not execute a false or incomplete certificate, nor be involved with any document or transaction that the Notary believes is false, deceptive or fraudulent.

V. The Notary shall give precedence to the rules of law over the dictates or expectations of any person or entity.

VI. The Notary shall act as a ministerial officer and not provide unauthorized advice or services.

VII. The Notary shall affix a seal on every notarized document and not allow this universally recognized symbol of office to be used by another or in an endorsement or promotion.

VIII. The Notary shall record every notarial act in a bound journal or other secure recording device and safeguard it as an important public record.

IX. The Notary shall respect the privacy of each signer and not divulge or use personal or proprietary information disclosed during execution of a notarial act for other than an official purpose.

X. The Notary shall seek instruction on notarization, and keep current on the laws, practices and requirements of the notarial office.

Source: Published by the National Notary Association, 9350 DeSoto Ave., Chatsworth, CA 91311-4926, and reprinted with permission. Contact the NNA at (800) 876-6827 or online at www.nationalnotary.org.

SUMMARY

CHAPTER 9
THE PAPERLESS OFFICE

Introduction to the Paperless Office	"Paperless office" or "electronic office": Office in which there are no paper documents, or hardcopy. Becoming a reality with the advent of modern scanning technology, secured methods for transmission of documents, accepted protocols for use of electronic replacements for paper documents, and rules of court permitting electronic submission of documents.
Organizing the Office for Storing Electronic Documents	A system for filing electronic documents is essential for finding and using them.
Files and Folders	A filing structure for electronic files uses the same basic format, but with virtual folders and files.

Security Issues	Electronic files must have the same ability to be "locked up," or access restricted electronically. It is sometimes necessary to build an ethical wall around case information. One method of restriction is to set up separate file servers for different clients or sensitive cases with access limited exclusively to those working on the case.
Limiting Access to Electronic Files	Limiting access can be achieved by using passwords and permissions. Permissions: A set of attributes that specifies what kind of access a user has to data or objects in a database. Permissions can allow or restrict the access of individuals or groups of individuals.
Electronic Filing	Each court is free to set up its own rules and procedures and must be consulted before attempting to use this service. Most agencies post their electronic filing policy and instructions on their websites. No national standard exists for courthouse software on a state level. The federal courts have adopted a single system, called the Case Management/Electronic Case Files (CM/ECF).
PDF Format	Documents may now be saved in a graphic image format or portable document format (PDF), developed by Adobe Systems. The creation of documents in PDF format requires specialty software such as Adobe Acrobat. However, everyone can download a free Adobe Reader to view these documents. Adobe Acrobat has become a standard software tool in many paperless offices for creating PDF files. PDF Converter 5 by ScanSoft is a lower-cost alternative to the widely used Adobe Acrobat. In addition to creating PDF documents, it also provides a number of other options. The converter feature can be used to convert PDF files into fully formatted Word, WordPerfect, and Excel documents.
Scanning	Copies of paper documents can be scanned and archived or saved until the appropriate time for destruction as set in the firm's destruction policy.
Scanning Hardware	Double-sided scanning is found today in multifunction devices containing printing, scanning, copying, and faxing, at prices under $100. These devices when coupled with applications software such as PaperPort allow virtually anyone to create electronic documents.
Scanning Software	Software provides easy-to-use high-speed scanning and document capture and allows for the organization, finding, and sharing of paper and digital documents, permitting the elimination of paper documents.
Optical Character Recognition	OCR (optical character recognition) applications provide document conversion solutions by permitting any scanned page, PDF file, or other image or document file, to be converted quickly and accurately into one of a number of different editable formats, including Microsoft Word or Corel WordPerfect.

Examine a PDF for Hidden Content	Every document has metadata—data about the document—as part of the document file. Metadata includes information about the document and its contents, such as the author's name, keywords, and copyright information, that can be used by search utilities.
The Electronic Notary	The traditional role of a notary is to offer an independent validation of a person's act of signing a document. The electronic notary seal (ENS) is a form of electronic digital signature unique to the individual notary. When made a part of an electronic document, it encodes an electronic signature that makes any changes to the electronic document obvious to anyone viewing the document, with a message on the document indicating that a change, addition, or deletion to the original document has occurred.

KEY TERMINOLOGY

Case Management/Electronic Case Files (CM/ECF)   236
Electronic filing   233
Electronic notary seal (ENS)   255
Ethical wall   231

Files   231
Folders   232
Optical character recognition (OCR)   252
Paperless office   230

Permissions   234
User-level security   234
Workgroup   234
Workgroup information file   234

CONCEPT REVIEW QUESTIONS AND EXERCISES

1. Test your knowledge and comprehension of the topics in this chapter by completing the multiple-choice questions on the textbook Companion Website.
2. Test your knowledge and comprehension of the topics in this chapter by completing the True-False questions on the textbook Companion Website.
3. Describe the features of the paperless office.
4. Define what is meant by the term *paperless office*.
5. Explain the need for an organized filing system for electronic documents.
6. Discuss the ethical considerations in the paperless environment.
7. Describe issues in court-related electronic filing.
8. Describe the types of formats used in electronic documents.
9. Describe the hardware and software issues in scanning documents.
10. Explain the concept of the electronic notary.
11. How can an ethical wall be "built" around documents in the paperless office?
12. What is meant by user-level security?
13. What are some of the advantages in using the PDF format?
14. What is the difference between Adobe Acrobat and Adobe Reader?
15. How is a scanner used in the paperless office?
16. What is OCR and what are its uses in the law office?
17. What system is used by the federal courts for electronic filing?
18. How can members of the legal team learn how to use the federal court's system for electronic filing?
19. How can PDF documents be made more secure?
20. Prepare a comparison list of features of software that can be used to create PDF documents.

INTERNET EXERCISES

1. Complete the federal court system tutorial for using the CM/ECF system for filing.
2. Find and download a copy of the Adobe Acrobat 9 for Legal Professionals white paper.
3. Use the Internet to determine if your state has an electronic filing system in place. What is the URL for the site for filing? Is there any online training? Is there any training available or required to use the system?

PORTFOLIO ASSIGNMENT

Prepare a policy and procedure for addressing the security issues that must be considered in a paperless office.

SCENARIO CASE STUDY

Use the opening scenario for this chapter to answer the following questions. The setting is a law office overwhelmed with years of paper files.

1. Prepare a memo to the partners of the firm about the advantages and disadvantages of the paperless office.

2. Prepare a list of suggested hardware and software that will be required if the firm implements a paperless office solution. Use the Internet to obtain a list of items ranked by speed and cost for consideration by the managing partner.
3. Prepare a memo to explain the issues in using an outside service bureau to scan the office files.

VIDEO SCENARIO: SIGNING DOCUMENTS

 The statute of limitation will run out at the close of the day, and the court office for filing documents is closing in minutes. The paralegal taking action to avoid missing the deadline asks if there is an alternative. Electronic filing is suggested by the clerk as a way to avoid having to rush to the court to file documents.

Go to the Companion Website, select Chapter 9 from the pull down menu, and watch this video.

1. Are there dangers in using electronic filing at the last minute?
2. Are there preliminary steps that must be taken to be able to use electronic filing?
3. What are the rules on electronic filing in your local state and federal courts?

Office Management Software

OPENING SCENARIO

Mrs. Hannah saw her role changing—from a paralegal actively working on cases and with clients, to managing the office, handling the accounting and payroll, and directing human resource functions. In the early days it took very little time, working for one attorney, to take care of the checkbooks, pay the bills, and prepare the payroll tax forms. However, as staff was added and Mrs. H took on the office management responsibilities for the other attorney in the office suite, the tasks were becoming overwhelming. Manual calculation of payroll alone took almost a full day. Then there was the time and billing issue, which involved getting everyone's time slips and preparing the bills for clients. In a good month, that alone could take days. Without some help she would not be able to manage it all.

LEARNING OBJECTIVES

After studying this chapter you should be able to:

1. Explain the basic functions of office management software.

2. Describe the function of calendaring software in the law office.

3. Explain the importance of timekeeping software.

4. Explain the importance of accounting records in a law office.

5. Find online and program resources for learning how to use a program and its features.

INTRODUCTION TO OFFICE MANAGEMENT SOFTWARE

There are certain administrative activities that are common to most, if not all, law offices. These are the functions that are necessary for the successful management of the business operation of the office. Timekeeping, calendar maintenance, and accounting are all critical administrative activities in a law office. Without adequate timekeeping, fees may be lost for hours worked and not billed. Missing a calendar date may result in missing a critical appointment, trial date, or worse, missing a statute of limitations. Tracking the expenses of any business is important. In a law office it is even more important because it may include the fiduciary responsibility of handling client funds in escrow accounts and accounting to the courts as well as clients.

The sole practitioner with only a secretary or paralegal and few clients can keep track of most important office information with a multiyear calendar and a checkbook. Appointments, deadlines, and statute of limitations dates can be entered and the calendar consulted on a daily basis. Any disbursements can be recorded in a checkbook and client funds deposited and disbursed using a separate checkbook.

When the number of clients increases and additional personnel are added it becomes increasingly difficult to record and extract the information. With busy schedules and more and more time spent out of the office the communication of critical information may be delayed or lost. The manual paper system requires someone to physically look at "the book"—inconvenient to do if the offices are separated on different floors, and impossible if out of the office in another town or courthouse. Electronic office management systems allow access from anywhere over a computer network or with an appropriate Internet connection. Important deadlines can be automatically sent to the responsible party by the software program without dependency on a staff person who might be out for the day.

OFFICE MANAGEMENT PROGRAMS

Most of the office functions can be divided into the following categories:

Calendar—Keeping the personal appointment, case deadlines, statutes of limitations, and important reminder dates.
Contacts—Keeping a current list of names, addresses, phone, e-mail addresses, and other information for clients, opposing counsel, vendors, networking contacts, and other people and firms.
Files—Keeping track of individual case files, projects, client matters, and related documents.
Accounting—Keeping track of time and billing information, client and firm funds and escrow accounts, and preparing bills, reports, and tax returns.

HOW DO OFFICE MANAGEMENT SYSTEMS WORK?

There are legal specialty office management programs and generic office management software programs. One of the generic programs used by many is Microsoft Outlook. Outlook does not offer the depth of features of specialty programs for managing the office functions. However, it does have a number of features

Exhibit 10.1 Microsoft Outlook personal organizer

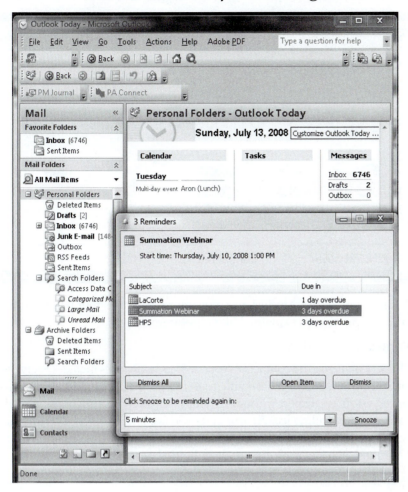

common to the specialized programs like calendaring, contact management, e-mail, and appointment reminder features, as shown in Exhibit 10.1. One of the advantages of Outlook for users of mobile systems like the BlackBerry, is the ease of synchronization of the information by use of software such as the BlackBerry Desktop Manager shown in Exhibit 10.2.

There are also a number of legal specialty office or practice management software programs available, of which AbacusLaw and Tabs3 are two of the most popular. These programs offer a number of **integrated functions** in a common package, like Office Suites. In the past, office managers have purchased and used one program for maintaining their calendars, another program for time and billing, and yet other programs for other functions like contact management. Today's programs integrate some or all of these functions into one **program shell.** These shells allow the use of one or more programs and the sharing of information across programs.

Office management software programs use a database or sets of databases to record information. This information can then be searched for specific items desired and assembled and reported as a response to a query, such as, what are the appointments for today? As previously described, a **database** is a collection of similar records such as your address book, which has a name, address, city, and phone number for each person in it.

Integrated Functions
The sharing of data between different functions in a software program.

Program Shell
A software program containing a platform for using different software programs. See integrated functions.

Database
A collection of similar records.

Exhibit 10.2 BlackBerry desktop manager

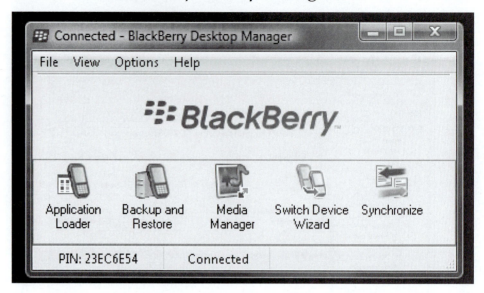

As an example, the AbacusLaw software program uses four main databases to store the information as explained in its literature:

Names

Think of names as the contacts in your address book. This includes every person with whom your firm has contact: clients, prospects, vendors, defendants, judges, attorneys, expert witnesses, friends, relatives, and anyone you might want on your mailing list. Abacus gives you fast and easy access to information on anyone in your Names database. Notes for names are kept in a linked database so you can keep essentially unlimited notes about your contacts.

Events

Events are any appointments, tasks, reminders, or things to do that are scheduled for specific dates. Events can be entered into Abacus by many different methods. The events window is the primary data window, while the Daily Organizer and various calendar windows give you different views of your events.

Matters

Matters refer to any matter, case, file, or project that you need to track. Once entered, matters can be attached to any number of names. Notes for matters are kept in a linked database so you can keep essentially unlimited notes about your files.

Documents

In Abacus, **documents** are any previously saved word processing files, scanned images, pleadings, correspondence, or Internet Web pages. They can be files on disk or just printed documents stored in a box. Abacus keeps a list of these documents in a database so you can find or edit them right from the client's Name or Matter window.

These databases can be searched individually, such as the Names databases for a list of clients presented alphabetically, or across all databases; for example, a list of all documents, for a client, sorted by individual matters being handled by the firm for the client and listing important dates and deadlines.

Events
Any appointments, tasks, reminders, or things to do that are scheduled for specific dates.

Matters
Any item, case, file, or project that you need to track.

Documents
In Abacus, documents are any previously saved word processing files, scanned images, pleadings, correspondence, or Internet Web pages.

CALENDAR MAINTENANCE PROGRAMS

The law office calendar is a source of information about:

Appointments with clients
Litigation deadlines
Filing deadlines
Court appearance dates
Statute of limitations dates
Routine reminders

The more traditional approach to calendar issues was maintaining a paper version master office calendar. In multiple attorney offices some of these calendars had multiple columns for the different attorneys. Frequently a task of the office assistant was to print out or photocopy the calendar on some regular basis, such as weekly, for each person in the office. Diary reminders including the statute of limitations dates were recorded on cards or multicarbon sets filed in a file box by date, usually a fixed period of time before the deadline to allow action on the file. The daily activities of the legal assistant or paralegal included pulling out the deadlines and reporting them to the responsible attorney, frequently with a reminder attached to the outside of the file.

The more contemporary approach to calendar matters is the use of a calendar database program. Calendar software is at its basic level a database of dates and related information. Preset reporting criteria allow for presentation of the data in a number of ways:

Office daily, weekly, monthly, or annual calendars
Individual daily, weekly, monthly, or annual calendars
Reports of important dates—like statute of limitations or reminders of deadlines

AbacusLaw Calendar Program Overview

Automatic Notification

A feature of many calendar programs is the alert or alarm feature that signals when a preset time occurs. Typically a specific time and date is set for a reminder or alert. (In programs like Microsoft Outlook, it is an automatic alert in a pop-up window of items set for alarm notice.) In programs like Abacus, it requires a specific time setting, which can be a fixed time of day, such as 8:00 A.M. for alerts or alarms of items for that day.

Rules-Based Calendars

A feature of some calendar programs is the automatic calculation of important calendar dates using rules-based calendaring. Programs like AbacusLaw, shown in Exhibit 10.3, automatically count the days and make entries in the calendar for such items as filing deadlines and hearing dates.

Calculating Deadlines. The rules of civil procedure of the court in which the complaint has been filed will include a provision describing how the time limits are calculated. Generally, counting begins the day after receipt of a pleading. If served with a complaint today, day 1 is tomorrow, and counting includes all calendar days that follow, including Saturday, Sunday, and holidays. The due date is the twentieth day. If the due date falls on a Saturday, Sunday, or holiday, the due date is the next regular business day of the court. The paralegal generally is

Exhibit 10.3 AbacusLaw rules-based calendaring

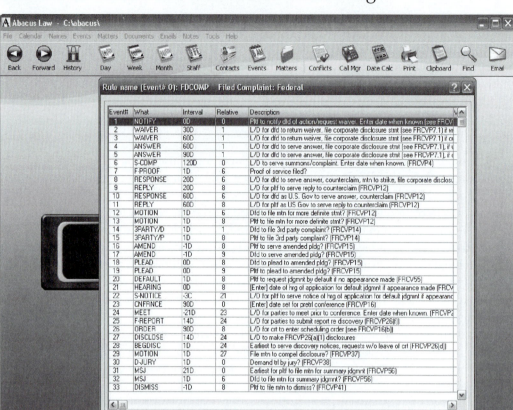

Source: Reprinted with permission from Abacus Data Systems Inc.

responsible for entering the due dates and sufficient reminder dates into the firm's central calendaring system.

Software for Calculating Deadlines. Calculating the important dates in a case requires a careful review of the specific court rules of the jurisdiction in which the case is filed. Within the same state there may be variations in the timetable for civil litigation proceedings. Some software programs provide rules of court-based automatic calendaring. In these programs, such as Abacus (Exhibit 10.3), the calendar dates for those jurisdictions selected are built into the program. Automatic calculation is based on the required interval in days after specific events, or a customized date calculation can be created.

The custom date calculation can be used to set deadlines or reminders based on a set of days after selected events, such as the time for sending reminders or follow-up letters or dates for routine case status conferences in the office. Where local rule books are available, the deadlines and timetables can be determined by consulting the court rules. Where the case is in a jurisdiction for which the rule book is not readily available, such as a case being handled by outside or out-of-state counsel, dates can be determined by online reference to the specific court, or by use of an automated, online, rules-based calendaring service such as Deadlines On Demand by Compulaw, which provides an online calendar creation of case-related dates based on individual jurisdictions.

ETHICAL Perspective

RULE 226

KANSAS RULES OF PROFESSIONAL CONDUCT

1.5 Client-Lawyer Relationship: Fees

(a) A lawyer's fee shall be reasonable. The factors to be considered in determining the reasonableness of a fee include the following:

   (1) the time and labor required, the novelty and difficulty of the questions involved, and the skill requisite to perform the legal service properly;

   (2) the likelihood, if apparent to the client, that the acceptance of the particular employment will preclude other employment by the lawyer;

   (3) the fee customarily charged in the locality for similar legal services;

   (4) the amount involved and the results obtained;

   (5) the time limitations imposed by the client or by the circumstances;

   (6) the nature and length of the professional relationship with the client;

   (7) the experience, reputation, and ability of the lawyer or lawyers performing the services; and

   (8) whether the fee is fixed or contingent.

(b) When the lawyer has not regularly represented the client, the basis or rate of the fee shall be communicated to the client, preferably in writing, before or within a reasonable time after commencing the representation.

(c) A lawyer's fee shall be reasonable but a court determination that a fee is not reasonable shall not be presumptive evidence of a violation that requires discipline of the attorney.

(d) A fee may be contingent on the outcome of the matter for which the service is rendered, except in a matter in which a contingent fee is prohibited by paragraph (f) or other law. A contingent fee agreement shall be in writing and shall state the method by which the fee is to be determined, including the percentage or percentages that shall accrue to the lawyer in the event of settlement, trial or appeal, and the litigation and other expenses to be deducted from the recovery. All such expenses shall be deducted before the contingent fee is calculated. Upon conclusion of a contingent fee matter, the lawyer shall provide the client with a written statement stating the outcome of the matter and, if there is a recovery, showing the client's share and amount and the method of its determination. The statement shall advise the client of the right to have the fee reviewed as provided in subsection (e).

(e) Upon application by the client, all fee contracts shall be subject to review and approval by the appropriate court having jurisdiction of the matter and the court shall have the authority to determine whether the contract is reasonable. If the court finds the contract is not reasonable, it shall set and allow a reasonable fee.

(f) A lawyer shall not enter into an arrangement for, charge, or collect:

   (1) Any fee in a domestic relations matter, the payment or amount of which is contingent upon the securing of a divorce or upon the amount of alimony, support, or property settlement; or

   (2) a contingent fee for representing a defendant in a criminal case; or

   (3) a contingent fee in any other matter in which such a fee is precluded by statute.

(g) A division of fee, which may include a portion designated for referral of a matter, between or among lawyers who are not in the same firm may be made if the total fee is reasonable and the client is advised of and does not object to the division.

(h) This rule does not prohibit payments to former partners or associates or their estates pursuant to a separation or retirement agreement.

Web Exploration

Contrast and compare Rule 1.5 of the Kansas Rules of Professional Conduct at http://www.kscourts.org/rules/Rule-Info.asp?r1=Rules+Relating+to+Discipline+of+Attorneys&r2=50 with the American Bar Association Model Rules of Professional Responsibility at http://www.abanet.org/cpr/mrpc/mrpc_toc.html, and the ethical rule in your jurisdiction

TIMEKEEPING SOFTWARE

Timekeeping
The recording of all time spent performing activities during the work day.

Timekeeping is one of the principal administrative functions in a law office. Timekeeping includes the recording of all time spent performing activities during the work day. In some offices only time spent doing work that may be billed to a client is recorded. In others, both billable and nonbillable, such as pro bono work or client development is also recorded. Keeping track of billable time becomes a critical function to ensure that the law firm will be properly compensated for its advice and efforts on behalf of clients. Timekeeping is not limited to just the attorneys but usually includes paralegals and in some cases secretaries and file clerks. Fortunately, the task has been automated by the use of software, such as Tabs3 by STI (Software Technology, Inc.), that accurately captures, stores, and processes this information and automatically prepares billing and timekeeping records (see Exhibit 10.4).

Time records may be created formally or informally by writing down the information for later recording in the timekeeping software program. One of the informal methods used by many lawyers and paralegals is to record the time spent and the activity on the case file folder either inside or outside. One issue with the recording of the information on the outside of the case folder is the possibility of a folder being left out where it may be read without opening it, allowing a client's potentially confidential information to be disclosed. Recording on the inside at least would require an unauthorized person to open the file to read what was done for the client. Exhibit 10.5 is a sample of a formal time recording form used by many noncomputerized firms and those looking for an intermediate recording method before formal entry into the time and billing software.

The more formal form shown in Exhibit 10.5 is similar in many ways to the input form used in programs such as Abacus Accounting, as shown in Exhibit 10.6, to which the information would be transferred when entered formally in the software program.

ETHICAL Perspective

PROOF OF SUPERVISION
Accurate, contemporaneously recorded time records for the paralegal and for the attorney may be used to show the level of supervision of the paralegal by the supervising attorney.

ETHICAL Perspective

Billing for Paralegal Time
The 11th Circuit Court of Appeals has said ". . . . we have held that paralegal time is recoverable as "part of a prevailing party's award for attorney's fees and expenses, [but] only to the extent that the paralegal performs work traditionally done by an attorney." Quoting from *Allen v. United States Steel Corp.*, 665 F.2d 689, 697 (5th Cir. 1982). . . . "To hold otherwise would be counterproductive because excluding reimbursement for such work might encourage attorneys to handle entire cases themselves, thereby achieving the same results at a higher overall cost." *Jean v. Nelson*, 863 F. 2d 759 (11th Cir. 1988).

Exhibit 10.4 Tabs3 time and billing screens

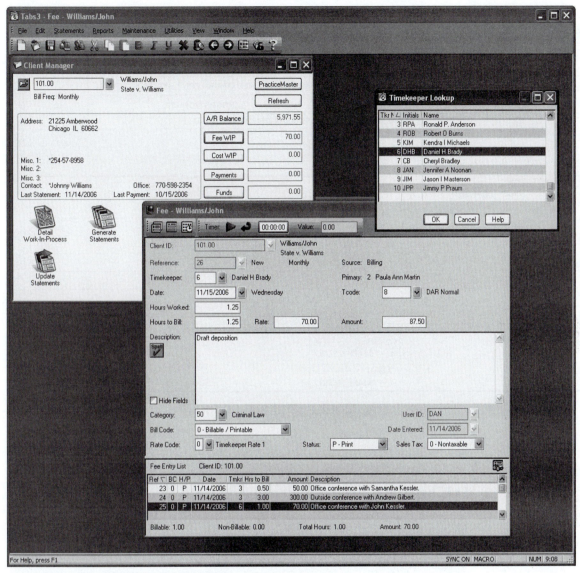

Source: Reprinted with permission from Software Technology, Inc.

ACCOUNTING SOFTWARE

Accounting software is specialty application software. General accounting software programs use the general rules of accounting for recording **assets, liabilities, equity, revenues,** and **expenses.** While every industry or profession uses the same five major classifications, each has its own industry or profession specific chart of accounts. A **chart of accounts** is a list of the individual categories under the five major classifications. For example, in a law firm, revenue would most likely be listed as Fees Received, where a retail business would use the description Sales. Accurate financial record keeping and reporting is an important part of the operation of the law office. Clients expect accurate billing and accounting for costs expended on their behalf. The courts expect accurate reporting of escrowed client funds, such as proceeds of settlements where court approval is needed. The employees and the federal, state, and local government expect payroll records to be maintained and reported accurately. Finally, vendors of goods and services to the firm expect accurate and prompt payment.

Assets
Things that have value.

Liabilities
Claims of outsiders to the assets of the entity.

Equity
The value of the assets of an entity reduced by the claims of outsiders.

Revenue
Increases in the owner's equity from the delivery of goods or services.

Expenses
Decreases in the owner's equity caused by an outflow of assets from the entity in the delivery of goods and services.

Exhibit 10.5 Weekly time report

ACCOUNT NUMBER	NAME OF CLIENT	HOURS WORKED								AMOUNT	
		MON.	TUE.	WED.	THUR.	FRI.	SAT.	SUN.	TOTAL		1
ACCOUNT NUMBER	NAME OF CLIENT	MON.	TUE.	WED.	THUR.	FRI.	SAT.	SUN.	TOTAL	AMOUNT	2
		HOURS WORKED									
DO NOT WRITE IN SHADED AREA BELOW											3
											4
											5

DATE	TIME			CODE	DESCRIPTION OF SERVICES PERFORMED	
	START	STOP	ELAPSED			
						6
						7
						8
						9
						10

CODE		NAME	
		CLIENT ──────► ◄── STAFF MEMB.	11
		CLIENT ──────► ◄── STAFF MEMB.	12

Exhibit 10.6 Abacus Accounting time ticket entry form

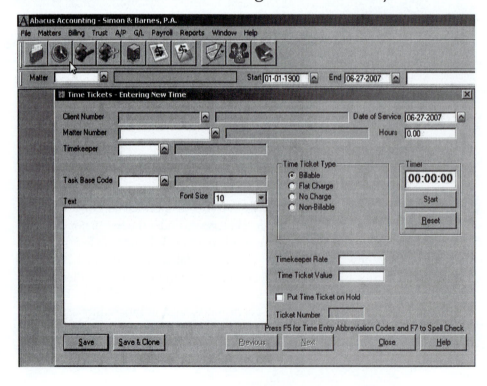

For many small offices, the checkbook in paper form or electronic form is the accounting system. In larger firms the paper form may involve the traditional ledgers and registers. Managing large volumes of accounting information may be more efficiently handled using electronic accounting software. While many computerized accounting programs are available, those with specialized input and output requirements of the law office may be easier to implement without modification.

A popular, basic, computerized checkbook program is Quicken. Generally used as a **check register,** it allows multiple bank accounts to be maintained in one program. For example, a firm generally will have an operating account, an escrow account for client funds, a petty cash account for small disbursements, a payroll account, and possibly an IOLTA account. While each may be in a different bank, all are managed through the same computerized program.

Where a computerized set of records is desired that more closely resembles the traditional accounting records, many firms use QuickBooks. This expanded version of Quicken provides subsidiary **ledgers** for **journals** such as accounts payable and accounts receivable.

Chart of Accounts
A listing of all the names of the accounts used in a particular financial entity.

Check Register
A chronological record of disbursements of checks and deposits.

Ledger
The individual account records for each account.

Journals
Chronological listings of financial transactions of a business.

ETHICAL Perspective

LOUISIANA RULES OF PROFESSIONAL CONDUCT

Rule 1.15. Safekeeping Property

(a) A lawyer shall hold property of clients or third persons that is in a lawyer's possession in connection with a representation separate from the lawyer's own property. Funds shall be kept in a separate account maintained in a bank or similar institution in the state where the lawyer's office is situated, or elsewhere with the consent of the client or third person. Other property shall be identified as such and appropriately safeguarded. Complete records of such account funds and other property shall be kept by the lawyer and shall be preserved for a period of five years after termination of the representation.

(b) A lawyer may deposit the lawyer's own funds in a client trust account for the sole purpose of paying bank service charges on that account, but only in an amount necessary for that purpose.

(c) A lawyer shall deposit into a client trust account legal fees and expenses that have been paid in advance, to be withdrawn by the lawyer only as fees are earned or expenses incurred. The lawyer shall deposit legal fees and expenses into the client trust account consistent with Rule 1.5(f).

(d) Upon receiving funds or other property in which a client or third person has an interest, a lawyer shall promptly notify the client or third person. For purposes of this rule, the third person's interest shall be one of which the lawyer has actual knowledge, and shall be limited to a statutory lien or privilege, a final judgment addressing disposition of those funds or property, or a written agreement by the client or the lawyer on behalf of the client guaranteeing payment out of those funds or property. Except as stated in this rule or otherwise permitted by law or by agreement with the client, a lawyer shall promptly deliver to the client or third person any funds or other property that the client or third person is entitled to receive and, upon request by the client or third person, shall promptly render a full accounting regarding such property.

(e) When in the course of representation a lawyer is in possession of property in which two or more persons (one of whom may be the lawyer) claim interests, the property shall be kept separate by the lawyer until the dispute is resolved. The lawyer shall promptly distribute all portions of the property as to which the interests are not in dispute.

(f) A lawyer shall create and maintain an interest-bearing trust account for clients' funds which are nominal in amount or to be held for a short period of time in compliance with the following provisions:

(1) No earnings from such an account shall be made available to a lawyer or firm.

(2) The account shall include all clients' funds which are nominal in amount or to be held for a short period of time except as described in (6) below.

(3) An interest-bearing trust account shall be established with any bank or savings and loan association or credit union authorized by federal or state law to do business in Louisiana and insured by the Federal Deposit Insurance Corporation or the National Credit Union Administration. Funds in each interest-bearing trust account shall be subject to withdrawal upon request and without delay.

(4) The rate of interest payable on any interest bearing trust account shall not be less than the rate paid by the depository institution to regular, non-lawyer depositors.

(5) Lawyers or law firms depositing client funds in a trust savings account shall direct the depository institution:

A. To remit interest or dividend, net of any service charges or fees, on the average monthly balance in the account, or as otherwise computed in accordance with an institution's standard accounting practice, at least quarterly, to the Louisiana Bar Foundation, Inc.;

B. To transmit with each remittance to the Foundation a statement showing the name of the lawyer or law firm for whom the remittance is sent and the rate of interest applied; and

C. To transmit to the depositing lawyer or law firm at the same time a report showing the amount paid to the Foundation, the rate of interest applied, and the average account balance of the period for which the report is made.

(6) Any account enrolled in the program which has or may have the net effect of costing the IOLTA program more in bank fees than earned in interest over a period of time may, at the discretion of the program's administrator, be exempted from and removed from the IOLTA program. Exemption of an account from the IOLTA program revokes the permission to use the administrator's tax identification number for that bank account. Exemption of a pooled clients' trust account from the IOLTA program does not relieve an attorney or law firm from the obligation to maintain the property of clients and third persons separately, as required above, in a non-interest-bearing account.

IOLTA Rules

Effective January 1, 1991

1. The IOLTA program shall be a mandatory program requiring the participation by attorneys and law firms, whether proprietorships, partnerships or professional corporations.

2. The program shall apply to all clients of the participating attorneys or firms whose funds on deposit are either nominal in amount or to be held for a short period of time.

3. The following principles shall apply to clients' funds which are held by attorneys and firms.

(a) No earnings on the IOLTA accounts may be made available to or utilized by an attorney or law firm.

(b) Upon the request of the client, earnings may be made available to the client whenever possible upon deposited funds which are neither nominal in amount nor to be held for a short period of time; however, traditional attorney-client relationships do not compel attorneys either to invest clients' funds or to advise clients to make their funds productive.

(c) Clients' funds which are nominal in amount or to be held for a short period of time shall be retained in an interest-bearing checking or savings trust account with the interest (net of any service charge or fees) made payable to the Louisiana Bar Foundation, Inc., said payments to be made at least quarterly.

Web Exploration

Contrast and compare Rule 1.15 of the Louisiana Rules of Professional Conduct at http://www.ladb.org/Publications/ropc2006-04-01.pdf with the American Bar Association Model Rules of Professional Responsibility at http://www.abanet.org/cpr/mrpc/mrpc_toc.html, and the ethical rule in your jurisdiction

Does your jurisdiction have an IOLTA program?

Specialized Legal Accounting Software

Abacus Accounting and Tabs3 are typical of programs designed specifically for the legal environment. They have preset input screens and output report functions for typical law office items, such as client fees and costs expended and received. In addition, they are designed to be integrated with their respective timekeeping programs (see Exhibit 10.7).

Exhibit 10.7 Abacus Accounting input screens

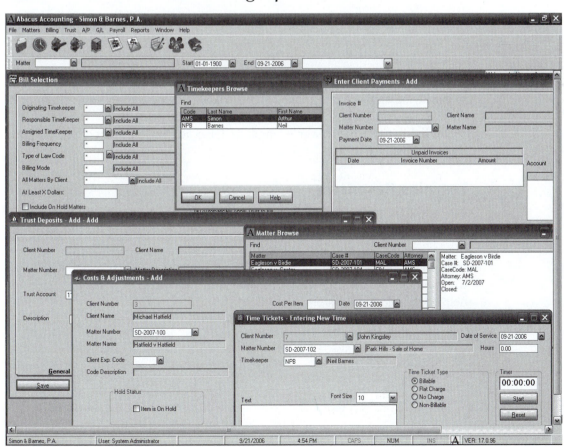

Source: Reprinted with permission from Abacus Data Systems.

Exhibit 10.8 Tabs3 Window with task folders displayed

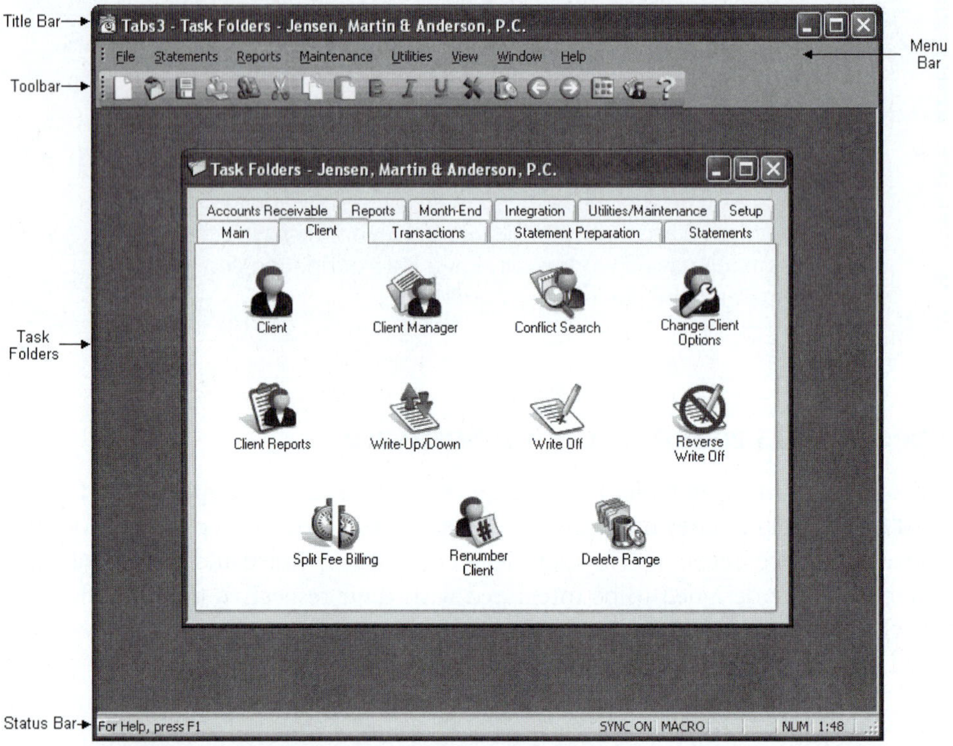

Source: Reprinted with permission from Software Technology, Inc.

As shown in Exhibit 10.8, Tabs3 software provides user-friendly screens, such as displaying icons of task folders. This makes it easy for the user at-a-glance to click on the task he or she needs, using icons instead of text.

In Exhibit 10.9, you see an example of Tabs3 accounting chart of accounts and input screens.

Learning Resources

The following examples are representative of the kinds of information that are available from most software vendors for use in learning to use the programs and the individual features. The availability of these resources from within the program and from online software vendor websites allows users to quickly start to use the programs and features without the need to attend classes or refer to the many help books sold in bookstores.

Exhibit 10.10 is an example of the resources available.

Exhibit 10.9 Tabs3 Accounting Chart of Accounts and input screens

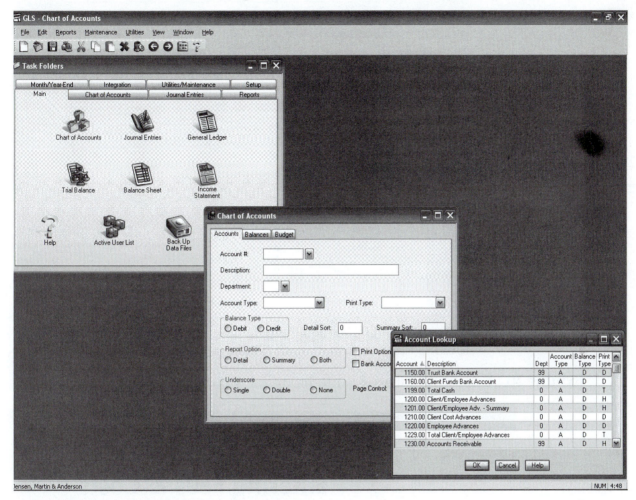

Source: Reprinted with permission from Software Technology, Inc.

Documentation

Exhibit 10.11 is a sample page of the Tabs3 tutorial available for download from the Tabs3 website. It offers keystroke by keystroke lessons in using different functions in the program.

In Exhibit 10.12, a tutorial screen shows the variety and depth of the training available from the basic to the advanced for each of the major functions in the software program for AbacusLaw.

Exhibit 10.13 shows a sample screen from the training materials using actual program screens.

Exhibit 10.10 Tabs3 online resources and tutorials

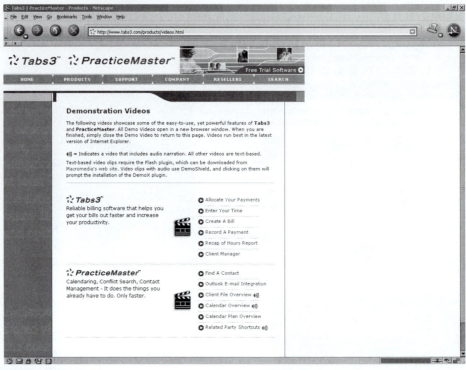

Source: Reprinted with permission from Software Technology, Inc.

Exhibit 10.11 Sample tutorial page from Tabs3 tutorial

Section 2
Entering Fees & Costs

Fee Entry

We are now ready to add fee transactions.

From the Tabs3 task folders,

Click: the **Main** tab	To select the **Main** task folder.
Click: the **Fee** icon	To select the Fee Entry program.

Notice that the default client number shown is 88.01. Tabs3 "remembers" the last client used during data entry and automatically uses this number as the default when you start another data entry program.

Press: **Tab**	To advance to the **Reference** field.
Press: **Tab**	When the cursor is in the **Reference** field to automatically assign a reference number. Each transaction is assigned a unique reference number so it can be accessed later for purposes of editing or deleting. The reference numbers for each client begin with "1".
Enter: **1**	In the **Timekeeper** field to assign the timekeeper for the fee transaction.

Notice that the **Date** field defaults to the system date, which is also the date that this transaction took place.

Press: **Tab**	To advance to the **Tcode** field.

Tabs3 Version 14 Tutorial   9

Source: Reprinted with permission from Software Technology, Inc.

Exhibit 10.12 AbacusLaw online lessons for Accounting Management Training

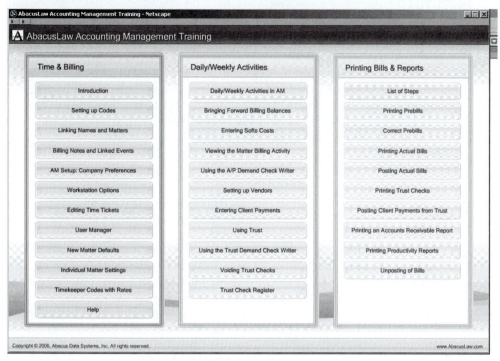

Exhibit 10.13 Sample AbacusLaw lesson

Abacus Accounting: How The Functions Fit Together

The best way to describe how the program can work for you is to give you an example. So picture the following:

You manage the law firm of Anderson, Bascombe, and Clark (ABC). On March 1, your firm took on its first (and, for this example, only) matter—a patent infringement matter for Xtrafine Yardgoods and Zippers, Inc. (XYZ). XYZ is to be billed at the end of each month until the matter is closed. The personnel from your firm who will be handling the matter are Joanne Brown, responsible attorney, Chris Umber, paralegal, and Nola Gray, researcher. Your firm has also hired Peter Sienna, a yardgoods specialist, as a consultant, and you will use CCC Printing to photocopy the exhibits.

First, you set up XYZ as a client, patent infringement as a matter, Peter Sienna as a vendor, and CCC Printing as a vendor. Joanne, Chris, and Nola are already set up in your system as timekeepers.

As Joanne, Chris, and Nola work on this matter, they record their time using the Time Ticket function. As invoices arrive from Peter and CCC Printing, you enter them in Accounts Payable and as a billable item for XYZ. At the end of March, you use the Print Prebills function to preview the information before printing their bill. When you activate this function, the program searches for all time tickets with the XYZ client code and patent infringement matter number. It locates all the time tickets entered by Joanne, Chris, and Nola and calculates their hours. Since Joanne, Chris, and Nola are billed at different rates, the program multiplies their hours by their billing rates to calculate the total billable hours amount. It then locates any other billable costs to be added to the bill. In this search, the amount billed for Peter and CCC Printing would be found. With all the calculations done, the system generates a prebill that shows the client billing address information and the hours billed along with the costs owed. (If you have set up your system to calculate a percentage of the billed time as administrative overhead, the program will perform that calculation and include that amount on the prebill.)

After you review the prebill and find everything is correct, you then activate the Print Bills function. The program will then print the bill for XYZ. It will also, when you post this bill, update the client's ledger (and all tables in the database that are affected by this transaction).

When you receive payment from XYZ, you enter the payment on the XYZ account. The program will update XYZ's account and your general ledger.

Now that your firm has money to pay Peter and CCC Printing, you activate the Print Check function in Accounts Payable and print the checks for Peter and CCC Printing. The system will then update your Accounts Payable and General Ledger tables in the database.

With a small number of entries, a few keystrokes, and very little time, you have completed all the financial transactions for this client.

SUMMARY

CHAPTER 10
OFFICE MANAGEMENT SOFTWARE

Introduction to Office Management Software	Certain administrative activities are necessary for the successful management of the business operation of the law office: timekeeping, calendar maintenance, and accounting.
What Do Office Management Programs Do?	Most of the office functions can be divided into: Calendar Contacts Accounting These programs offer a number of integrated functions in a common package. Office management software programs use a database or sets of databases to record information.
Calendar Maintenance Programs	The law office calendar is a source of information about: Appointments with clients Litigation deadlines Filing deadlines Court appearance dates Statute of limitations dates Routine reminders
Timekeeping Software	Timekeeping includes the recording of all time spent performing activities during the work day. Keeping track of billable time becomes a critical function to ensure that the law firm will be properly compensated for its advice and efforts on behalf of clients.
Accounting Software	Accounting software is specialty applications software for recording assets, liabilities, equity, revenues, and expenses.
Specialized Legal Accounting Software	Abacus Accounting and Tabs3 are typical of programs designed specifically for the legal environment. They have preset input screens and output report functions for typical law office items, such as client fees and costs expended and received.

KEY TERMINOLOGY

CONCEPT REVIEW QUESTIONS AND EXERCISES

1. Test your knowledge and comprehension of the topics in this chapter by completing the multiple-choice questions on the textbook Companion Website.
2. Test your knowledge and comprehension of the topics in this chapter by completing the True-False questions on the textbook Companion Website.
3. What steps may be taken to locate and use the resources for learning how to use office management software programs?
4. Explain what office management software does and how it works.
5. What is the function of calendaring software in the law office?
6. What is the importance of maintaining accurate accounting records in a law office?
7. What are some of the basic functions for which law office management software is used?
8. What are the obligations of a paralegal who, while inputting time records, sees that the same law firm employee is billing two clients for the same time (double billing)? Are there any ethical issues for the paralegal or the law firm?
9. What are the ethical issues in recording time spent on a case on the outside of the client's file folder?
10. How can legal specialty software ensure compliance with the ethical obligations related to client funds?
11. What is the purpose of the IOLTA account program? Is it in use in your jurisdiction?
12. What are the ethical implications of attorneys using client funds?
13. How do IOLTA programs help the administration of justice?

INTERNET EXERCISE

Prepare a list of companies offering law office management software. Prepare a comparison list of functions performed and the training resources available online.

PORTFOLIO ASSIGNMENT

Prepare a memo for the employee handbook on the procedures to be followed for using the software solutions proposed if purchased and implemented. Include an explanation of the reason for the procedures.

SCENARIO CASE STUDY

Use the opening scenario for this chapter to answer the following questions. The setting is that of a paralegal in an office that has grown from just her and one attorney to a large firm of partners, paralegals, and secretaries.

1. What are the tasks that can be automated in a firm of this size?
2. Use the Internet to find software solutions for performing the tasks listed in your answer to question 1. What are the costs for software licenses?

What are the recommended hardware requirements for the different software solutions?
3. What are the security and confidentiality issues that must be addressed? Explain fully with suggestions for resolving the issues.
4. What are the advantages that can be presented to the partners to justify the cost of implementing the solution you recommend?

CONTINUING CASES AND EXERCISES

1. Use the following information to set up a sample law office using AbacusLaw:
   a. You manage the law firm of Anderson, Bascombe, and Clark (ABC). On March 1, your firm took on their first (and, for this example, only) matter—a patent infringement matter for Xtrafine Yardgoods and Zippers, Inc. (XYZ). XYZ is to be billed at the end of each month until the matter is closed. The personnel from your firm who will be handling the matter are Joanne Brown, responsible attorney, Chris Umber, paralegal, and Nola Gray, researcher. Your firm has also hired Peter Sienna, a yard-goods specialist, as a consultant, and you will use CCC Printing to photocopy the exhibits.
   b. Set up:
      i. XYZ as a client: 2916 Princeton Avenue, Philadelphia, PA 19149, 215-555-5555.
      ii. Patent infringement as a matter.
      iii. Peter Sienna as a vendor: 721 Landis Street, Philadelphia, PA 19124, 215-555-6666.
      iv. CCC Printing as a vendor: 41 Euclid Street, Hartford, CT 06012, 860-555-1111.
      v. Joanne Brown, Chris Umber, and Nola Gray as attorney, paralegal, and researcher, respectively.
2. Complete the AbacusLaw tutorial available on the Companion Website www.prenhall.com/goldman.
3. Complete the Tabs3 tutorial available on the Companion Website www.prenhall.com/goldman.
4. Enter all of your calendar information and time slip information in AbacusLaw and Tabs3.
5. Enter the relevant information in each program from the case in Appendix 1.
6. Prepare an interim bill for your time spent in preparing for and attending class and print a draft copy for your instructor.

ADVANCED EXERCISES

1. What functions performed using Abacus and Tabs3 can be performed using the programs found in an Office Suite of programs? Explain the advantages and disadvantages.

2. What additional case management functions available in the applications software from Abacus and Tabs3 should be used, if any, for efficient management of the law office as it grows?

VIDEO SCENARIO: FEES AND BILLING–CONTEMPORANEOUS TIMEKEEPING

He must get his time records completed. He is trying to figure out how he has spent his day. Because he has trouble remembering what he did during a long day, he makes up time records to fillout his billable day.

Go to the Companion Website, select Chapter 10 from the pull down menu, and watch this video.

1. What are the advantages and disadvantages of computerized timekeeping?
2. Would use of computer software have prevented this ethical issue?
3. Can properly prepared time records be used to document proper supervision and diligent handling of a case?

Chapter 11 Digital Resources at www.prenhall.com/goldman

- Author Video Introduction
- Case Study Video
- Comprehension Quizzes and Glossary
- Video Software Introduction: LexisNexis® CaseMap®

Case Organization and Management Software

OPENING SCENARIO

Twenty people were injured when a small bus was struck by a tractor trailer. Preliminary investigation indicated that the truck driver claimed the cause of the accident was in part due to a defective brake system in the truck. The injuries to the bus passengers were partially the result of seats breaking loose from the bus floor. Though the injuries were regrettable, the scope of the case was something every lawyer dreams of. It was Mr. Mason's first big case.

From a casual review it was clear even if they only got a few of the passengers as clients, there would be thousands of documents; potentially twenty clients, each with multiple doctors alone represented a potentially overwhelming number of items to track. Then there were the investigation documents for the brake failure and the seat design issues. Mr. Mason, Mrs. Hannah, and Ethan could handle most of the organization of the file but clearly would need to enlist the help of other investigators, attorneys, and paralegals. Fortunately attorney Ariel Marshall had agreed to work on the case with Mr. Mason and the sole practitioner on the other side of town they had worked within another federal court case. With so many people needing access to the files, the danger was that documents, file folders, and boxes would be everywhere and not necessarily available to any one person when needed.

LEARNING OBJECTIVES

After studying this chapter you should be able to:

1. Explain the reasons for the use of software for managing litigation cases.

2. Describe the types of specialty applications software programs used in case management and organization.

3. Describe how case management programs are used.

4. Explain how case management software systems can enable the legal team to collaborate on cases more efficiently.

5. Describe the advantage of time lines in litigation.

INTRODUCTION TO CASE ORGANIZATION AND MANAGEMENT SOFTWARE

There is a close relationship between office management and case management functions. Some of the functions overlap; for example, contact management—maintaining information for contacting clients, parties, and others, like mailing and e-mail addresses, and home, work, and cell (telephone numbers)—is a part of office management *and* of case management. Many of the specific specialty applications software programs used to perform these functions duplicate the automation of these functions. Early versions of some software programs were individual applications, like calendar creation and maintenance programs, that are now incorporated in specialty applications suites with integrated modules that perform these functions.

There is a trend toward integrating all of the desired functions of office and case management and organization into a single master integrated program with modules for all the needed functions in running a law office. The advantages frequently mentioned are a single software vendor point of contact, reduced time for inputting information, and a single user interface for the user to learn.

Effectively managing a case may involve reviewing, sorting, and marking for identification hundreds or even thousands of documents, photographs, and other graphics. Careful tracking and handling of evidence should start at the beginning of the case. Good case management requires a thoughtful process for storing, handling, examining, evaluating, and indexing every page. In the computer age, case management includes making decisions on methods of acquiring and using electronically stored documents, and the appropriateness and potential use of electronic display technologies, as well as on traditional paper exhibit presentations. **Tangible evidence**—physical items such as defective products in a strict liability action or an automobile in a motor vehicle accident—may have to be obtained and preserved for examination by expert witnesses or for use at trial.

There are almost as many different approaches to setting up case files and managing cases as there are legal teams. One of the traditional approaches includes the case notebook, or case **trial notebook**. Summary information about the case is maintained in a notebook with tabs for each major activity, party, expert, or element of proof needed. With the use of a trial notebook comes the responsibility to maintain the case file and file boxes or file cabinets into which the hard copies of documents, exhibits, and physical evidence are maintained. If only one trial or case notebook is kept for the team, someone on the litigation team must take responsibility to be certain that there is no duplication of effort and that the most current activities are entered. When multiple copies are used, each trial notebook must be updated regularly, again to be sure that there is no duplication of effort and that current activity information is made available for all members of the legal team.

The use of computer systems can simplify the process. All of the file information may be maintained on a single computer, including copies of documents in electronic form. Each member of the litigation team may, with proper access rights, access the information.

CASE AND PRACTICE MANAGEMENT SOFTWARE

The legal team may work on a number of cases at the same time, and each case may be in a different stage of preparation for trial. With the team approach to handling cases, each member of the team must be able to access case information and

Tangible Evidence
Physical objects.

Trial Notebook
Summary of the case, usually contained in a tabbed three-ring binder with sections such as pleadings, motions, law, pretrial memo, and witness.

know what the other members of the team have done and what still needs to be done. In the traditional paper file case management approach, the physical file is the repository of everything from interview notes to pleadings and exhibits. As the team works on the case, members must locate the physical file and remove the needed folder. In the **paperless office**, everything, in theory, is available on the computer screen. Documents are scanned and saved in an electronic format on the computer, pleadings and notes are saved as word processor files, and transcripts of depositions and court hearings are stored in electronic form. For the case with voluminous paperwork and days- or weeks-worth of deposition transcripts, relevant documents or appropriate deposition notes can only be accessed quickly and efficiently by use of computer software. The creation of documents in electronic format and the scanning of existing paper documents into electronic format allow the storage of shared documents from any data storage device. In some cases, the files are stored on remote file servers of outside consultants and vendors, sometimes called *e-repositories* or *online document* repositories, with remote access permitted only by authorization. Exhibit 11.1 shows a model of a secure remote access for the legal profession.

Paperless Office
Office where documents are created, stored, received, and sent electronically.

A number of software programs can be used to manage the law office and the cases within the office. They generally provide what is sometimes referred to as *case management*, or *practice management*, programs. Practice management programs have evolved out of the early programs that tracked time spent on cases, sometimes with a calendar component that could be used to track deadlines such as the statute of limitations for a case. Modern programs may include practice management functions such as time and cost tracking, calendaring, conflict checking, scheduling, and contact management. Others allow for management of the individual cases, tracking of documents, parties, issues, and events.

Productivity and Cost Effectiveness

The pressure is on everyone to become more productive in a working environment. The increased cost of litigation imposes additional demands upon the litigation team to perform the desired representation of clients in the most cost-effective manner. One of the methods for increasing productivity is the use of computers to eliminate some of the manual and repetitive functions performed

Exhibit 11.1 Secure remote access for the legal profession

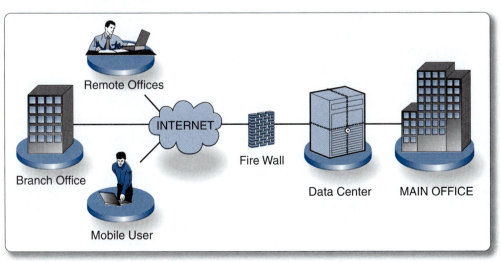

before the use of computers. With increased scrutiny by clients and by the courts, accurate detailed reporting adds to the burden of the litigation team.

For the litigation office representing corporate clients, an additional burden is imposed by the demands of the corporate in-house counsel for the most cost-effective representation with continual feedback and updating of progress on the case and the costs expended in the handling of the litigation. Many corporate clients utilize electronic communications for the interchange of information, including status reports, invoicing, and the transmission of documentation.

SPECIALTY APPLICATION SOFTWARE PROGRAMS

Every year, computers become more powerful—operating faster and with more operating and storage memory. Software programs are getting more powerful and capable of performing more complex functions on more data. Whereas older models of computers can perform only basic word processing and data management, newer, more powerful computers can perform complex functions seamlessly, thereby permitting management of law office functions and management of cases and litigation.

Legal Specialty Applications Software

Paper has long been the bane of the litigation attorney. Even simple cases can involve hundreds of pages of documents. Complex litigation may involve millions of documents and hundreds of witnesses and, in the case of class action litigation, potentially millions of clients. Keeping track of all of the documentation and parties is an overwhelming task even with a large staff of assistants and endless rows of organized file cabinets and file boxes.

Before the availability of fast computers with inexpensive memory-running case and litigation management software, most case management work was done manually, usually by a team of paralegals, junior associate attorneys, and teams of law students, some hired for multiyear positions, to read through and identify the documents, manually index them, and look for a document that would make the case (sometimes referred to as the "smoking gun" document).

The use of computers for e-mail and document storage by business and government has caused a massive increase in the number of potential documents that may have to be reviewed, tracked, and made available to opposing counsel in a case. Managing cases and litigation with the massive amount of data has become increasingly difficult. As the numbers of documents has increased and cases have become more complex, the number of members of the legal team working on a given case also has increased. These factors have led to greater use of the computer to manage the case files and the litigation process.

In precomputer days, attorneys frequently concentrated on one case, personally working on all of the documentation, pleadings, and discovery. They learned every detail of the case in anticipation of trying the case and had little backup support, except in the largest cases in the larger firms. The legal team approach to case management and litigation has allowed, in some ways, for specialization within the legal team. Some members of the litigation team may specialize in discovery of documents. Others may be concerned with locating, interviewing, and preparing witnesses. Still others concentrate on investigative matters and legal research.

The trial team frequently has to find a document or information on a specific issue from among potentially thousands of pages of documents. With a computer and the proper **specialty application program**, this is possible. Some of the

Specialty Application Program
Software that combines many of the basic functions found in software suites, word processing, database management, spreadsheets and graphic presentations to perform law office, case, and litigation management.

Exhibit 11.2 Case organization flowchart using LexisNexis CaseMap software

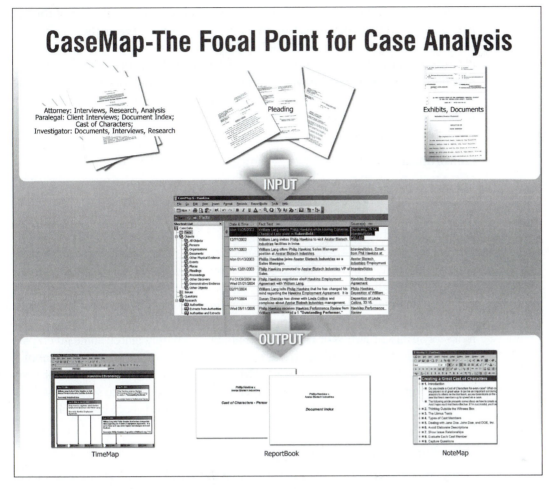

CaseMap-The Focal Point for Case Analysis

Attorney: Interviews, Research, Analysis
Paralegal: Client Interviews; Document Index; Cast of Characters;
Investigator: Documents, Interviews, Research

Pleading

Exhibits, Documents

INPUT

OUTPUT

TimeMap ReportBook NoteMap

litigation and case management specialty software programs found in the law office are discussed here.

CaseMap

CaseMap™ from LexisNexis® is a case management and analysis software tool that acts as a central repository for critical case knowledge. As facts are gathered, parties identified, and documents and research assembled, they may be entered into the program, allowing for easy organization and exploration of the facts, the cast of characters, and the issues by any member of the legal team.

It also allows for creating specialty reports and documents including trial notebook information. Exhibit 11.2 shows the flow of information in a typical case, using CaseMap as a case management tool.

Summation

The Summation family of products, from CT Summation Inc. (a Wolters Kluwer business), and similar software applications programs are classified as litigation support systems. As the number of documents increases in a case, the ability to locate relevant documents in a timely fashion becomes more and more critical. Managing the documents is critical to successful litigation outcomes. In cases involving potentially millions of documents, it is essential to be able to find the relevant information quickly, sometimes in the middle of the direct or cross-examination of a witness.

Summation-type programs allow for easy search and retrieval of all of the evidence, whether documents, testimony, photographs, or electronic files, with a single command. Documents associated with a case are stored on the computer in electronic folders. These folders may be set up to include transcripts, pleadings, text files (from OCR or otherwise), casts of characters, and core databases. Some versions of these programs are designed to work on stand-alone systems such as a laptop carried into court. Others permit concurrent use by many users over a network, and some permit remote access over the Internet.

Concordance

LexisNexis Concordance is a litigation support system program that provides document management. Early versions of Concordance were limited to storing and handling 4 gigabytes of data, or approximately 280,000 documents. The newer version allows the management of 128 times that amount, or more than 35 million documents. Like other document support tools, Concordance has a powerful search engine that allows searches by word, phrase, date, e-mail address, or document type, as well as Boolean, using the fuzzy and wildcard searches.

A Boolean search uses connectors between words such as AND, OR, or NOT to narrow the search. A fuzzy or fuzzy string search is the name for a search that looks for strings or letters or characters that approximately match some given pattern. A wildcard search allows the use of a "wild" character such as the symbol * to replace a letter in the search word. This allows you to search for plurals or variations of words using a wildcard character. It also is a good way to search if you do not know the spelling of a word—for example, book* finds booking, booked, and books.

Other Programs and Media Support

Sanction and similar trial presentation programs are electronic trial-presentation software applications. More and more courtrooms are providing, or allowing litigants to provide for their trial, computer-based electronic display systems. Some see this as nothing more than a logical outgrowth of the multimedia presentations that started with the use of chalkboards, movie clips, and slide projectors.

Modern trial presentations frequently include videotaped depositions and the presentation of images, photos, videos, and portions of documents. These may be on personal monitors or large-screen displays.

Managing the hundreds of individual components in the courtroom can be a trial nightmare unless they are organized and easily accessed for presentation. Sanction II and similar programs, like TrialDirector by inData, allow the legal team to organize and control the documents, depositions, photographs, and other data as exhibits for trial, and then display them as evidence as and when needed in depositions and trial.

MANAGING THE CASE

Case(s)
Issues that a client has presented to a legal team to handle and resolve.

Cases, or matters, to the law office, are issues that a client has presented to a legal team to handle and resolve. Cases are sometimes referred to in the office as the "client file" or the "client file on the [name of topic] matter." A case file in a simple case like the "Gordon Power of Attorney file," or the "Leonard Will file" may consist of only a few pages of information obtained from the client, a copy of an old document, and the final document prepared for the client's signature. In a more complex case like a tort claim involving a building under construction, or an employment discrimination class action, the case file may consist of thousands of documents with hundreds of people involved as parties (plaintiffs and defendants), witnesses, and experts—and a dozen or more members of the legal team who will work on the case and need access to the information.

It is possible to handle a complex case without computers. For hundreds of years lawyers have handled cases, pushed papers around, moved file boxes, and spent hours reviewing documents, creating indexes, catalogues, and writing notes to others working on the case.

Manual case management for the legal team may include the creation and use of a case notebook and a trial notebook. These are tabbed binders with a tab for each major element of the case. In some cases an entire binder may be devoted to one topic, like witnesses or documents.

The following is a representative listing of tabs and a sample of the form that might be used.

Things to Do

Date Due	What	Responsible Party
6-30-2007	Obtain accident report	J. L. Investigator
7-15-2007	Interview investigating police officer	J. L. Investigator

Parties-Witnesses

Name	Address	Home Phone	Work Phone	Comments
Nancy Smith	333 Main St	123-456-7890	987-654-3210	Passenger in other car
K. Lombardo	222 South St	555-111-2222	555-333-4444	School bus driver letting off passengers facing accident scene

Documents

Bates #	Document Name	Date	Comments	Author
P001–P003	Police accident report	5-15-2007	Shows citations issued to Def.	Officer Hannah
P002	Repair record	4-20-2006	Shows brake problem in Def. car	Newtown auto repair mechanic Ed

Research-Authorities

Name	Jurisdiction	Type	Citation	Description
Bell v. Farmers Insurance Exchange	Cal. Super. Ct	Case law	234 Cal. 456	Compensation issue
Driving too fast for conditions	Cal.	Statute	43 Ca. Code	Defines standards for. . .

A more complete list of tabs for the case notebook and the trial notebook is shown in Exhibit 11.3. Each of the pages in the case or trial notebook can be created using a word processing program and the table feature, with headings added as shown in previous samples. They could also be created using a spreadsheet or

Exhibit 11.3 Tabs for the case notebook and the trial notebook

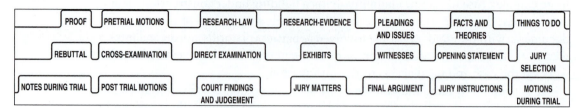

PROOF	PRETRIAL MOTIONS	RESEARCH-LAW	RESEARCH-EVIDENCE	PLEADINGS AND ISSUES	FACTS AND THEORIES	THINGS TO DO
REBUTTAL	CROSS-EXAMINATION	DIRECT EXAMINATION	EXHIBITS	WITNESSES	OPENING STATEMENT	JURY SELECTION
NOTES DURING TRIAL	POST TRIAL MOTIONS	COURT FINDINGS AND JUDGEMENT	JURY MATTERS	FINAL ARGUMENT	JURY INSTRUCTIONS	MOTIONS DURING TRIAL

database program depending on the need to sort information or extract information using database queries.

The manual method will work in smaller cases. In the days before computers, that was the only method available. Preprinted forms were substituted for the word processing table creation of forms. Database applications were accomplished by entering the information such as witness contacts on individual cards. In cases involving multiple members of the litigation team, constant questions heard in the offices were, "Who has the case file?" or "Who took home the evidence binder?" and similar pleas for the location of the missing portion of the file needed by another member of the team to enter data, review information, or prepare documents.

The advent of the computer has been both a blessing and a curse. It has been to some a curse because it is so easy to create electronic documents that may be relevant to a case. Consider the number of e-mails generated each day in large organizations that need to be reviewed to find relevant documents to prove that the large multinational financial institution created a hostile working environment or sexually harassed employees. The blessing is that computers can also be used to search for relevant terms in a document and automatically eliminate duplicates of the same e-mail.

Case management software can be used to organize the cast of characters in a case—the documents, the relevant time table, issues, legal authority, and other desired information. Good case management software does all of these organization functions and provides the information in an organized manner for everyone working on the case. Individuals are able to input information on the portions for which they are responsible, with data from others, and everyone has computer access to the information even over wide area networks.

The typical file or case starts with an interview with the client. In the precomputer days, in offices that had formalized their "paper system," this consisted of a client interview form completed by the person who conducted the initial interview. The system may have also included the use of additional forms for gathering and organizing information from fact witnesses and experts, and a system for recording the key information on the outside of the file folder or on a paper data sheet on the inside cover.

The forms you see in Exhibit 11.4, and others like them, are still used in many offices—not as a repository of the information but as the input documents for the computerized system used for case management. More aggressive users can even bypass the paper input forms and enter the information directly using a laptop or tablet PC or by keyboarding directly into a workstation. Some case management programs, like LexisNexis CaseMap (discussed next), have provisions for scanning in data directly from forms and templates. Exhibit 11.5 is a sample of the CaseMap form that is designed for importing directly into the program database.

Exhibit 11.4a Paper-based interview form—Accident fact sheet

Accident Fact Sheet ▄▄▄▄▄▄▄▄▄▄▄▄▄▄▄▄▄▄▄▄

CLIENT PERSONAL DATA

Client Name

Age, Date of Birth

Address

Home Phone

City, State, Zip

Work Phone

Place of Employment

Social Security No.

Job Description

Time Lost from Work

Date/Time of Accident

Location of Accident

Bodily Injuries

Name and Cost of Ambulance

Name and Address of Hospital

Names of Treating Physicians, including Physical Therapist

Exhibit 11.4b Paper-based interview form—Witness information

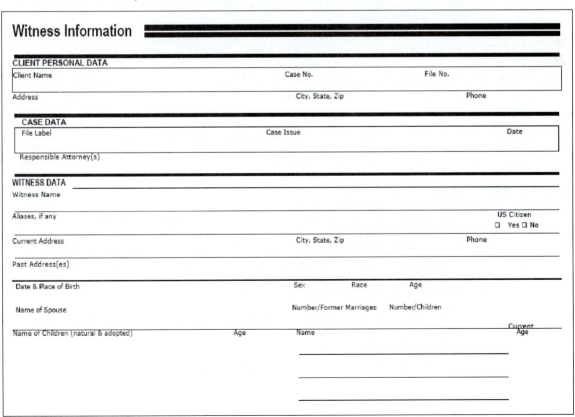

Witness Information ▄▄▄▄▄▄▄▄▄▄▄▄▄▄▄▄▄▄▄▄

CLIENT PERSONAL DATA

Client Name | Case No. | File No.

Address | City, State, Zip | Phone

CASE DATA

File Label | Case Issue | Date

Responsible Attorney(s)

WITNESS DATA

Witness Name

Aliases, if any | US Citizen ☐ Yes ☐ No

Current Address | City, State, Zip | Phone

Past Address(es)

Date & Place of Birth | Sex | Race | Age

Name of Spouse | Number/Former Marriages | Number/Children

Name of Children (natural & adopted) | Age | Name | Current Age

Exhibit 11.5 CaseMap input form with explanations of what is required for client use

Completing CaseMap Input Forms

Using CaseMap software, the attorney or someone on the legal team would ask plaintiffs and witnesses to complete the following information using a word processor or by hand to be transcribed later by the law firm staff.

Persons

- Please list all people related to the case—even people with a minor connection to it.
- List only one person in each row of the following.
- In the Description cell for each person, please explain who the person is and how they are connected to the case. Your description can be any length—the Description cells grow as you type in them.
- As mentioned, you may need more horizontal rows than we've provided by default. When you're in the last cell of the Description of Person table, pressing the TAB key on your keyboard creates a new row.
- Please do not add or remove the vertical columns in this or any of the following tables.

Name of Person	Description of Person

Organizations

- List all case-related organizations—even ones with a minor case connection.
- List only one organization in each row of the following table.
- Please describe the organization in the Description cell provided. Be sure to explain how the organization is connected to the case. Your description can be any length—the Description cells grow as you type in them.

Name of Organization	Description of Organization

Events/Facts/Rumors

- This is the most important step. Please take the time to read the directions carefully.
- Please list important case-related events, facts, and even rumors in the table below. You don't have to have to be 100% sure that what you tell us happened or is true. And you don't have to have direct personal knowledge of the items you list. We just need the widest possible list of items to thoroughly investigate.
- Here's how to deal with dates and times:

  - Don't worry about listing events in proper date sequence. We'll put them in order when we receive this document back from you.
  - Only use numeric dates. For example, list Monday, January 1, 2007, as 1/1/07.

- Only use complete dates when you're sure of the date. When you're unsure, use a partial date. For example, let's say you know a meeting took place in March of 2006, but you don't know what day. List the date as 3/06. If you're very unclear about the date, just put a question mark in the date cell.
- If the time of day when the event occurred is important, list it after the date. When you list times, please use 24-hour time (military time). This avoids confusion over a.m. versus p.m. In 24-hour time, 7 a.m. is listed as 0700, 2:30 p.m. is listed as 1430, and so on. If you don't know the exact minute when an event occurred, you can use question marks for the portion of the time about which you're unsure. For example, an event that occurred sometime between 8 and 9 in the morning would be listed as 08??.
- Some facts and rumors don't have dates associated with them (for example, "Greg has blue eyes"). When that's the case, just leave the Date cell for that row blank and enter the fact or rumor in the Description cell.

- After you've recorded what you know about the date of the event, type a brief write-up of the event itself in the Description cell. Don't worry about being super complete as we'll discuss each event you list during our next meeting.
- As you write up the events in the case, you'll probably think of people and organizations you did not list in the preceding tables. Be sure to back up and add them.

Date of Event	Description of Event

Documents

- Please gather up any case-related documents in your possession. Also take the time to print out copies of any case-related e-mails. Be sure to bring this material with you to our next meeting.
- After collecting the documents you do have, please think hard about other important case-related documents and e-mails of which you're aware but that you don't have copies of. Please describe these "missing" documents in the following table so we'll know to look for them during our investigation.
- Follow the guidelines for describing dates that appear in the previous Events/Facts/Rumors directions.

Date of Document	Description of Document

Questions

- As you organize information about the persons, organizations, facts, and documents, you'll probably think of questions you'll want to ask us about the case, about how we handle cases, and about many other topics. Please list these questions in the following table. List one question per row.

Questions

As the different members of the legal team—lawyers, paralegals, investigators, and secretaries—obtain the information, they can enter it into the case management software and update the case file as new information becomes available.

A typical case file contains documentation of the:

- interview of the client;
- interviews of fact and expert witnesses;
- investigation reports;
- expert reports;
- research memoranda;
- pleadings; and
- trial preparation material.

USING CASE MANAGEMENT SYSTEMS

Case Management System
Software for organizing the parts of a case in a central repository that can be shared by all members of a legal team.

Efficient use of a **case management system** provides all authorized members of the legal team access to all the case information day or night. Effective case management, therefore, requires some central repository of the information gathered by each of the team members, as well as the ability of each to access the case information input by others. Computer systems today even permit members of the legal team to access the same information from remote locations across town, across the country, and sometimes around the world.

A high level of collaboration among members of the legal team is becoming common practice, in even smaller law offices. In part it is a result of increased complexity of cases, shortened time to prepare for trial under court rules and procedures for getting the backload of cases reduced, and increasing the speed of justice. In many smaller, specialized practices, the resources or the expertise may not be available to handle the occasional large or complex case. For example, a small firm of tax attorneys who have the expertise in tax evasion issues but not the trial experience may collaborate with a small trial or litigation boutique, with each firm supplying the expertise in one area and sharing all the case files and information to better serve the client. One of the tools in collaborative situations is the individual assessment of the importance of items in the case, as shown in Exhibit 11.6.

Exhibit 11.6 Fact evaluation feature in CaseMap

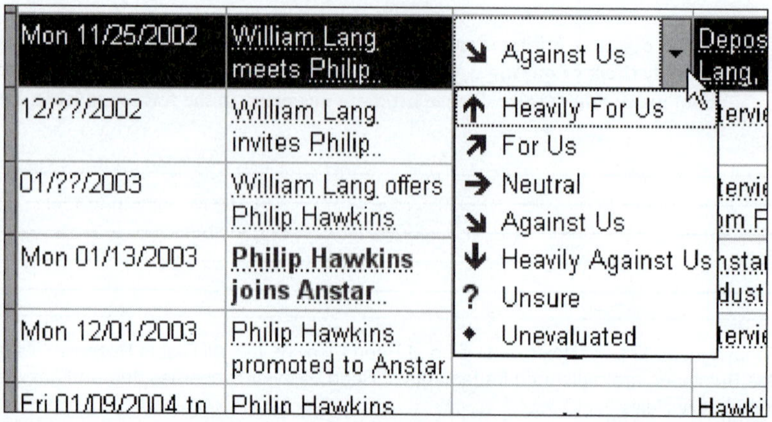

Source: Copyright 2008 LexisNexis, a division of Reed Elsevier, Inc. All Rights Reserved. LexisNexis and the Knowledge Burst logo are registered trademarks of Reed Elsevier Properties, Inc. and are used with the permission of LexisNexis.

12.

13.

14.

15.

16.

17.

IN THE WORDS OF THE COURT...

Fee Calculation

Berman v. Schweiker,

531 F. Supp. 1149 at 1155 (N.D.III. 1982), aff'd,

713 F.2d 1290 (7th Cir. 1983).

"... The application states that counsel's firm actually paid the second year law student who worked on this case $14.00 per hour for his services. We believe these payments constitute reasonable expenses of counsel. Moreover, denying compensation for a student law clerk would be counterproductive. As plaintiff's counsel points out, law firms frequently employ student law clerks to perform tasks under attorney supervision as one way of controlling the spiraling costs of litigation. Excluding compensation for fees incurred by employing student law clerks will force attorneys to handle the entire case themselves, achieving the same results but at a much higher cost."

Litigation can be very expensive. Part of the cost is related to the time the litigation team must spend processing, organizing, and sharing information and documents. Where the organization can be handled by a team member whose time is billed at a lower rate, the client saves money and the supervising attorneys and paralegals can work more productively. Clients and the courts prefer or even require members of the legal team, such as student law clerks and paralegals, to do work that does not require the skill of the higher-billing-rate attorney, as demonstrated in In The Words of the Court. Submitting a fee for court approval in some courts for work done by an attorney that could have been done by a paralegal will result in the fee being denied or reduced accordingly.

Allowing for the sharing of responsibilities in processing the information about a case requires collaboration. Each member of the team must have the ability to input and use information for the tasks assigned to him or her. For example, investigators input information on witness identifications and dates of importance, paralegals input information about parties and documentation, and lawyers evaluate the facts. To do their part, all must have the ability to share the information. Exhibit 11.7 shows a CaseMap object-event display screen ready for entry of a new item. In precomputer days, this was accomplished by taking the file folder (an expandable folder), or a part of the file, and working on it with an appropriate notice placed in the file or file cabinet to indicate who had the file.

Exhibit 11.8 shows a list of the documents in a case in CaseMap. As noted previously, with a computer and the proper specialty software program, it is possible to locate the document quickly.

Case Management Software

A case management software program, like the very popular LexisNexis CaseMap, offers a convenient method for organizing the parts of a case in a central repository.

Web Exploration

Find more information on central hosting servers at www.iqwestit.com

team can, based on prior experience or reported similar cases, put a potential value on a trial outcome. In many cases the decision to try a case or settle a case is a business decision. Is the cost of a trial outweighed by the potential recovery? With two well-prepared legal teams the evaluation is surprisingly close and settlement is more likely than not.

Preparing for Trial

Web Exploration

Contrast and compare Rule 3.4 of the Hawai'i Rules of Professional Conduct at http://www.state.hi.us/jud/ctrules/hrpcond.htm with the American Bar Association Model Rules of Professional Responsibility at http://www.abanet.org/cpr/mrpc/mrpc_toc.html, and the ethical rule in your jurisdiction

Properly completed discovery eliminates the potential for surprises in evidence presented at trial. In fact many of the "surprises" one sees on television dramas about trials are not possible under rules that are designed to prevent the introduction of surprise witnesses and evidence. Among the rules designed to prevent surprises is the ethical obligation of fairness to opposing counsel and parties. For example, the Hawai'i Rules of Professional Conduct state in part:

Rule 3.4. Fairness to Opposing Party and Counsel.

A lawyer shall not:
(a) unlawfully obstruct another party's access to evidence or unlawfully alter, destroy or conceal a document or other material having potential evidentiary value. A lawyer shall not counsel or assist another person to do any such act;

Facilitating Settlement

Properly conducted discovery facilitates settlements. Careful analysis of the evidence revealed through discovery enables the legal team to evaluate the client's case and that of the opposing side, their relative strengths and weaknesses. Both sides are in a better position to evaluate their chances of success before the trier of fact and the likelihood of success based on the weight of evidence and the perceived credibility of witnesses.

Rules of Court and Rules of Evidence

What is permitted and what is prohibited in litigation is set out in the procedural rules of court and the rules of evidence of the jurisdiction, with allowances for the style of counsel permitted by the trial judge. In the federal courts, the Federal Rules of Civil Procedure (Fed.R.Civ.P.) provide the framework for conducting litigation. Local court rules may supplement these rules as will the particular requirements and procedures, if any, of the assigned judge, such as those of U.S. District Judge Padova shown in Exhibit 12.1. The conduct of the trial is largely a matter of what evidence is and what is not permitted to be introduced and admitted at trial. The Federal Rules of Evidence (FRE) provide the guidelines for use of evidence in federal courts. As stated by Judge Grimm below, "admissibility of evidence is determined by a collection of evidence rules."

Civil litigation is serious business. The rules of court, ethical guidelines of the legal profession, and the rules of evidence provide a level playing field. Like a professional baseball or football game, both sides need to know what the rules are and have them fairly applied. The judge becomes the interpreter and enforcer of the rules similar to the role of the umpire or referee. With a well-understood set of rules evenly and fairly applied, justice may be served with each side feeling they have had their day in court.

Exhibit 12.1 Policies and procedures of United States District Judge Padova

The Honorable John R. Padova
United States District Judge
Room 17613, U.S. Courthouse
601 Market Street
Philadelphia, PA 19106
215-597-1178
Fax: 215-580-2272

Deputies: **Gerrie Keane (Civil Case Management and Scheduling)**
Jenniffer Cabrera (Criminal Case Management and Scheduling)
Policies and Procedures

(Revised August, 2005)

. . . .

Discovery Conferences and Dispute Resolution
Judge Padova normally does not hold discovery conferences, but encourages the use of telephone conferences in lieu of motion practice to resolve discovery disputes. When a **discovery** *default* occurs, Judge Padova encourages counsel to file a motion to compel, which he will usually grant upon presentation pursuant to Local Civil Rule 26.1(g). When a **discovery** *dispute* occurs, and counsel have been unable to resolve it themselves or with Judge Padova's assistance by telephone, he requires a motion to compel. Judge Padova expects discovery to be voluntary and cooperative in accordance with the Federal Rules of Civil Procedure and the Plan.

Confidentiality Agreements
Parties may agree privately to keep documents and information confidential. The Court may enter an Order of Confidentiality only after making a specific finding of good cause based on a particularized showing that the parties' privacy interests outweight the public's right to obtain information concerning judicial proceedings. See Pansy v. Borough of East Stroudsburg, 23 F.3d 772, 786 (3d Cir. 1994).

Expert Witnesses
Counsel are required to identify expert witnesses and provide curriculum vitae and, as to all experts, voluntarily exchange the information referred to in Federal Rule of Civil Procedure 26(a)(2)(B) by expert report, deposition or answer to expert interrogatory in accordance with the dates outlined in the Court's scheduling orders. Except for good cause, expert testimony will be limited at trial to the information provided.

DOCUMENTS AND ELECTRONIC DISCOVERY

For hundreds of years of legal practice, the traditional source of documentation in legal cases was in the form of paper documents. Documents were created by hand, with typewriters, and later word processors, fax machines, and other mechanical reproduction machines like blueprint machines. In a relatively short period of time the computer, and the use of other computerized devices, have enabled the creation of documents that formerly were created in paper form to be created and viewed solely in electronic form. Documents that were formerly printed and placed in file folders on computers, file servers, and filing cabinets are now created and saved in electronic files and folders. Documents that were sent in paper form are now sent electronically, in some cases to hundreds of recipients without anyone printing a paper copy.

IN THE WORDS OF THE COURT . . .

LORRAINE v. MARKEL AMERICAN INSURANCE COMPANY
(Md. 5-4-2007)

JACK R. LORRAINE AND, BEVERLY MACK Plaintiffs v. MARKEL AMERICAN INSURANCE

COMPANY Defendants.

CIVIL ACTION NO. PWG-06-1893.

United States District Court, D. Maryland.

May 4, 2007

Memorandum Opinion

PAUL GRIMM, Magistrate Judge

. . . Whether ESI is admissible into evidence is determined by a collection of evidence rules that present themselves like a series of hurdles to be cleared by the proponent of the evidence. Failure to clear any of these evidentiary hurdles means that the evidence will not be admissible. Whenever ESI is offered as evidence, either at trial or in summary judgment, the following evidence rules must be considered: (1) is the ESI **relevant** as determined by Rule 401 (does it have any tendency to make some fact that is of consequence to the litigation more or less probable than it otherwise would be); (2) if relevant under 401, is it **authentic** as required by Rule 901(a) (can the proponent show that the ESI is what it purports to be); (3) if the ESI is offered for its substantive truth, is it **hearsay** as defined by Rule 801, and if so, is it covered by an applicable exception (Rules 803, 804 and 807); (4) is the form of the ESI that is being offered as evidence an **original** or **duplicate** under the original writing rule, of if not, is there admissible secondary evidence to prove the content of the ESI (Rules 1001-1008); and (5) is the probative value of the ESI substantially outweighed by the danger of **unfair prejudice** or one of the other factors identified by Rule 403, . . .

Interrogatories
Formal written discovery requests, seeking the identification and physical location of relevant documents and requesting copies.

In the paper world, **interrogatories**, formal written discovery requests, sought the identification and physical location of relevant documents and requesting hard copies with the answers to the interrogatories. The results frequently were poor reproduction photocopies of the paper documents. In the electronic document world, the questions center on the sources, format, and location of the electronically stored documents.

In many cases counsel demanded delivery of documents that the opposing counsel considered confidential or work product. The documents not supplied in response to the request often became the subject of motions to compel disclosure of the documents. Before delivering requested documents, lawyers, paralegals, and law clerks routinely scanned every document to find anything considered confidential, subject to the attorney–client privilege, or the result of preparation for trial and protected from disclosure under the work product doctrine. Increasingly in litigation involving technology, additional protections were sought and delivery of documents refused in response when counsel or a party considered the information a trade secret or a proprietary process.

ADVICE FROM THE FIELD

ROLE APPRECIATION & PERSPECTIVE
Litigators, Litigation Support Professional and the Electronic Discovery Review Model
By Charlotte Riser Harris and Don Swanson

In the world of e-discovery there are two distinct teams—the legal team and the technical team—with two distinct perspectives. The technical team includes litigation support personnel and legal technology providers. The legal team includes attorneys and paralegals. These teams share goals. The goals are to get through the discovery stage of litigation as completely, quickly, efficiently, and painlessly as possible, while achieving the best possible result for their litigation client.

Members of each team often face challenges when they work together to collect, process, review, and produce electronically stored information (ESI) in litigation. These challenges create frustrations that are widely discussed in litigation support circles. There seems to be no dispute that technology is here to stay, that many legal teams are in the beginning stages of the transition to the full use of technology, and that this transition is painful for both the technical and the legal teams.

The difficult and frustrating management of this transition has become part of the job description of litigation support personnel, often implicitly. And many in this position are not trained or prepared to manage change and transition. Given this reality, taking the time to understand the differences in perceptions of each team might make the e-discovery process and the integration of technology into the practice of law easier.

ELECTRONIC DISCOVERY REFERENCE MODEL

The Electronic Discovery Reference Model (EDRM) is a flow chart and series of definitions designed to create a standard approach and common language for measuring the full range of electronic discovery activities. It was placed in the public domain in May 2006 after about three years of development. One of the goals of the EDRM was to codify the best practices and procedures for the e-discovery industry. The EDRM is widely accepted as a credible model for understanding the e-discovery process, and it is now included in many presentations regarding e-discovery. It has continued to be expanded upon and improved since its first public release.

Work on the EDRM is continuing under the auspices of the "Evergreen Project," which is examining other aspects of the e-discovery process towards the goal of creating an even better understanding and standardization of additional aspects of e-discovery. Matters currently under consideration include metrics, an XML schema, and a code of conduct. Metrics refers to standardized methods to measure the time, effort and expenses associated with various electronic discovery activities. XML schema refers to the development of a standardized way to facilitate the movement of electronically stored information from one step of the electronic discovery process to the next, from one software program to the next and from one organization to the next; and the code of conduct effort focuses on the development of voluntary ethical guidelines for providers and consumers concerning electronic discovery.

Interestingly, the EDRM may provide a vehicle for understanding the perspectives of the technology and legal teams.

THE TECHNICAL TEAM AND PERSPECTIVE

The EDRM describes the technical team's role in and view of the litigation process. Those working in the e-discovery industry understand the EDRM, and many who contributed to it are using it. It defines their scope of work and provides standards that can be followed to deliver services to legal teams.

However, it is unlikely that the content of the EDRM projects will reach—or should reach—the complete understanding and appreciation of most legal teams.

THE LEGAL TEAM PERSPECTIVE

The EDRM represents a small and largely unknown aspect of the legal team's role in and view of the litigation process.

To most legal teams, discovery is a small part of the litigation process and ESI is a small part of discovery. This is partly because most pending legal actions do not have a smoking gun anywhere, much less lurking in the slack space of a hard drive. Many legal

(Continued)

team members don't yet know what ESI is—except they know that email, Word, Excel and other electronic documents have to be produced. They have attended enough CLEs and read enough articles to be generally informed, but the terminology and process of e-discovery is not yet part of the legal team's daily jargon and instant recall.

UNDERSTANDING THE DIFFERENCES

Much of the litigation work done by legal teams is not included in the EDRM chart of the e-discovery process. Although the steps outlined in the EDRM are critical and lay the foundation for the rest of the litigation process, they are but a small part of the litigation process from the legal team's perspective.

Between the production and presentation stages, and after the presentation stage, legal teams are focused on other phases of a litigation matter. For example, after a party has produced their documents, the legal team must create a privilege log; receive opposing party and non-party productions; incorporate those productions into the existing review application; review and analyze those productions; identify issues and fully address each one from both sides; prepare briefs, motions, and other legal materials; identify, hire and prepare expert witnesses; prepare witnesses; take and defend depositions; and much more.

While technical teams are focused on and have embraced litigation support applications and processes as modeled by the EDRM, many legal teams are still struggling in their daily practice to manage huge volumes of email and to use collaborative tools to share documents.

ESI has changed the landscape of discovery, and legal teams, for the most part, are over-whelmed by the change. When one is overwhelmed, often avoidance and denial are the first reactions. It is probably safe to say that many legal teams are actively avoiding and denying e-discovery!

THE PRACTICE OF LAW DOES NOT REQUIRE TECHNOLOGY BUT

The legal team's struggle is understandable. Think about it. . . . the practice of law does not require technology. True, in today's world, technology provides tools of the trade that are required to get the job done. But if all electrical power was permanently lost,

lawyers could and would continue to practice law. To litigate one only needs knowledge of the law with the appropriate licenses to practice, law books, a client, an opposing party with counsel, and a judge. In fact, there are probably many attorneys today who would welcome a return to that simplicity. Contrast that perspective with the technical team's love of technology—indeed, technology is the technical team's lifeblood and reason for being—at work anyway!

The reality is that technology is required in all phases and types of legal work. Legal teams who embrace and leverage the use of technology have a competitive edge, and the day is soon coming when legal teams simply will not be able to compete without the integration of technology into their practice. Because of the volume, complexity and nature of e-discovery, without the proper use of technology, it will be impossible to produce ESI of any significant volume, much less within the deadlines required by the courts.

That reality contrasts greatly with most legal teams' acceptance, understanding and use of computer technology today.

TECHNOLOGY IN LAW SCHOOLS AND PARALEGAL SCHOOLS

Attorneys, especially litigators, generally attend law school because they love to debate and analyze, and want to change the world. This is also true for paralegals attending paralegal school. Few, if any, study the law in order to develop their use of computers and databases, or even consider the two to be linked.

The need for technology in the legal workplace has moved forward faster than most legal practitioners are ready, and traditional formal education programs have not kept up with the realities of the workplace. Consider the fact that most law school and paralegal school curricula do not include courses on the use of technology (other than computer-aided legal research) nor do they incorporate the use of applicable software tools into courses (other than perhaps the use of word processing and spreadsheet applications). The study of the production of ESI is certainly not universally included in coursework.

Many attorneys and paralegals are entering the workplace with little or no training and skill in the use of litigation technology, much less an awareness of the e-discovery process.

RESPONSIBILITIES OF EACH TEAM

It is not necessary for technical team members to obtain law degrees or paralegal certificates; likewise, it is not necessary for legal team members to understand how the technology they use is programmed or all of the technical aspects of e-discovery. However, each team must have some basic knowledge about the work of the other team for projects to be successful. And the legal team must have a high level of trust in the technical team and the tools being used.

Each team has responsibilities in this process. However, the technical team can, and perhaps should, take the lead in managing the transition to the full use of technology by legal teams. By understanding the attorney or paralegal's level of acceptance of and comfort with technology, and gearing their interaction and information to that level, the technical team can

be more effective. Attorneys and paralegals must take the time and make the effort to gain the knowledge necessary to enable them to make informed decisions throughout the most visibly appealing and interactive timeline presentations. Either way, any of these tools can be used to create useful timelines so that the trial lawyer can effectively walk a jury or audience through the story and the evidence of their case.

About the Authors: Charlotte Riser Harris is a Managing Consultant with Five Star Legal and Compliance Systems, Inc. Previously, she was the Manager of Practice Support at Vinson & Elkins LLP. Don Swanson is the President and Founder of Five Star Legal and Compliance Systems, Inc. Don is a recognized expert in litigation support computer systems and works with law firms and corporate and government clients across the country.

Even in the small-scale litigation, which is the majority of litigation, with a limited number of documents, the process is time consuming and costly, at least from a document handling and duplication standpoint. In some jurisdictions local rules provide a formula or specify which party has the obligation to pay the cost of duplication and delivery. For example, a discovery request of a medical record from a medical provider or hospital may be shared with each party paying half the total cost or paying for any copies they request.

With increasing use of electronic alternatives for creation and storage of documents of all types, the number of paper copies has been reduced. For example, e-mails are becoming the dominant form of communications. Rarely are the messages reproduced in hardcopy. In a large organization, such as international business organizations, the number of e-mails created and received daily in the organization may be in the thousands or tens of thousands, particularly if you consider all the persons that are copied on e-mails, all of which may be discoverable. Exhibit 12.2 shows the e-mail routing at Enron before its collapse.

In major construction litigation, the traditional rolls of blueprints and construction documents are being replaced by electronic files created with computer graphics programs and sent electronically to architects, builders, subcontractors, suppliers, and clients. When written documentation, in the form of e-mails and other word processor documents, is added the number and location of individual documents needed in the litigation process may number in the thousands or more.

Discovery in Transition

Computer usage in business and in the law office has created a number of changes in the practice of law and in litigation. The practice of law has long been based on tradition, with change coming slowly and only as needed. Computers have, to some in the profession, "burst" upon the scene. Suddenly everyone is using word

Exhibit 12.2 E-mail patterns in the Enron Corporation

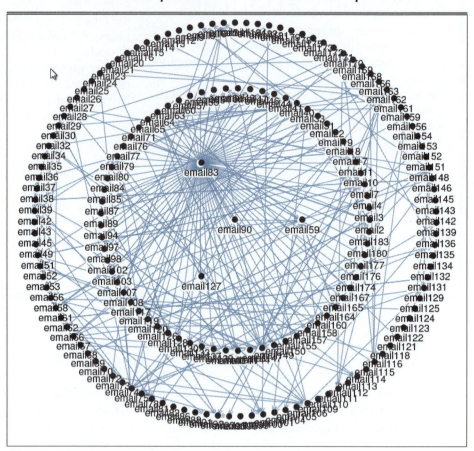

Source: Scan Statistics on Enron Graphs
Carey E. Priebe
Johns Hopkins University, Baltimore, MD
John M. Conroy
IDA Center for Computing Sciences, Bowie, MD
David J. Marchette
NSWC B10, Dahlgren, VA
Youngser Park
Johns Hopkins University, Baltimore, MD

processing, sending e-mails, converting to paperless offices, and being required to file documents electronically. For many practitioners the need to recognize the role of electronic documents has come slowly and with great reluctance. Many lawyers who have not grown up in the computer age have resisted the change to electronic documentation and the impact on their practice of law and how they handle and try cases in court. It may seem to some that the changes have been overnight. In reality, it has evolved, but admittedly at an increasing pace and over a relatively short period of time. A few major cases have thrust the profession into a position of forced acknowledgment that electronics have replaced hardcopies and the procedures, policies, and methods have changed. Businesses have come to depend on the computer for virtually every aspect of operations. E-mails have replaced traditional paper for most written communication in-house and with the outside. With inventory systems, order placement and purchasing is done electronically, frequently without any paper being generated including payments that are handled electronically by wire or electronic transfers between banks. The courts have had to face the issue of electronic discovery to maintain the orderly administration of justice and case management.

AMENDMENTS TO THE FEDERAL RULES OF CIVIL PROCEDURE

The changes, effective December 2006, amended six rules and provided one new form:

Rule 16 Pretrial Conferences; Scheduling; Management

". . . amendment to Rule 16(b) is designed to alert the court to the possible need to address the handling of discovery of electronically stored information early in the litigation if such discovery is expected to occur . . ."[1]

Rule 26 General Provisions Governing Discovery; Duty of Disclosure

". . . amended to direct the parties to discuss discovery of electronically stored information if such discovery is contemplated in the action . . ." a party must disclose electronically stored information as well as documents that it may use to support its claims or defenses . . ."[1]

Rule 33 Interrogatories to Parties

". . . recognizing the importance of electronically stored information. . . . the Rule 33(d) option should be available with respect to such records as well."

". . . Special difficulties may arise in using electronically stored information, either due to its form or because it is dependent on a particular computer system. Rule 33(d) allows a responding party to substitute access to documents or electronically stored information for an answer only if the burden of deriving the answer will be substantially the same for either party . . ."[1]

Rule 34 Production of Documents, Electronically Stored Information, and Things and Entry Upon Land for Inspection and Other Purposes

". . . amended to include discovery of data compilations, anticipating that the use of computerized information would increase . . ."[1]

Rule 37 Failure to Make Disclosures or Cooperate in Discovery; Sanction

". . . absent exceptional circumstances, sanctions cannot be imposed for loss of electronically stored information resulting from the routine, good-faith operation of an electronic information system."[1]

Rule 45 Subpoena

". . . amended to recognize that electronically stored information, as defined in Rule 34(a), can also be sought by subpoena. . . ."[1]

Form 35 Report of Parties' Planning Meeting

". . . a report to the court about the results of this discussion."[1] (under Rule 26)

WWW MINI EXERCISE
View the full text of the new rules and the comments of the Advisory Committee on Civil Rules of the Judicial Conference Committee on Rules of Practice and Procedure at www.uscourts.gov/rules or www.law.cornell.edu/rules/frcp/overview.htm. The committee notes give insight to the intent and reasons for the changes.

Note: The original December 2006 rules were restated effective December 2007.

---

[1] Comments of the Advisory Committee on Civil Rules of the Judicial Conference Committee on Rules of Practice and Procedure

Revised Process and Procedure

The new Federal Rules of Civil Procedure provide a framework for requesting and satisfying requests for documents in electronic format, like e-mails, electronically stored word processor documents, and information in electronic databases.

Scope of Discovery

Under the Federal Rules of Civil Procedure everything is discoverable that is not privileged and is relevant or may lead to relevant evidence. Documents and information that may be obtained through the discovery process are considerably broader than that which may be used or admissible at trial under the Federal Rules of Evidence. Everything is discoverable that is not privileged, or attorney work product, and is relevant or may lead to relevant evidence. An item or information is **relevant** for purposes of discovery where it has a relationship to evidence about the litigation and is likely to lead to admissible evidence. That an item or information meet the requirement of the Rules of Evidence is not required for admission at trial.

Relevant
Has a relationship to or is likely to lead to admissible evidence.

Production of Documents or Things

Production of documents or things makes available for discovery documents and other physical objects, like defective products, relevant to the lawsuit. The process of production of documents is a written request addressed to a party to the litigation. The party must respond in writing to each request. The response may also include a paper (hardcopy) or electronic copy (e-discovery) of the documents or the items requested. Examples include medical records of an injured plaintiff, a copy of a liability insurance policy, a police accident report, or an employee personnel file.

Where the "thing" is not capable of delivery, such as a building or other large object, this discovery tool includes the right to entry onto the land of another for purposes of inspection. This discovery tool may also be used in cases where the volume of documentary evidence or electronic records is too large for practical delivery, such as a warehouse with thousands of cartons of paper files.

Example: The parties dispute the contents of the hard drive of the defendant. The plaintiff may believe that relevant information may have been erased or not

FRCP 26 (b) Discovery Scope and Limits

(b) Discovery Scope and Limits

(1) Scope in General

Unless otherwise limited by court order, the scope of discovery is as follows: Parties may obtain discovery regarding any nonprivileged matter that is relevant to any party's claim or defense—including the existence, description, nature, custody, condition, and location of any documents or other tangible things and the identity and location of persons who know of any discoverable matter. For good cause, the court may order discovery of any matter relevant to the subject matter involved in the action. Relevant information need not be admissible at the trial if the discovery appears reasonably calculated to lead to the discovery of admissible evidence. All discovery is subject to the limitations imposed by Rule 26(b)(2)(C).

Note: The December 2006 rules were restated effective December 2007.

delivered. Inspection of the computer hard drive by a forensic expert would be permissible under the rules.

FEDERAL RULES TIME LINE AND DISCOVERY

The Federal Rules provide a time line and a set of obligations the attorneys must follow as part of the discovery process starting with an attorney conference and culminating with a meeting with the judge. Insight to the rule change may be found in the comments to the rules as shown in Exhibit 12.3.

Attorney Meet and Confer

The Federal Rules provide an initial time line for pretrial procedures as shown in Exhibit 12.4. Discovery may not begin until the lawyers for the parties have conferred and developed a proposed discovery plan, as required in Fed. R. Civ. P. 26(f). (Fed. R. Civ. P. 26(d)). This meet and confer step is required before the required scheduling conference with the assigned judge.

Discovery Timing

The scheduling conference occurs within 90 days after the **entry of appearance** by the attorney who will represent the defendant (or 120 days after the defendant is served with the complaint). The meet and confer must occur at least 21 days before the scheduling conference with the judge, therefore allowing 99 days for the meet and confer session. Following the meet and confer conference between counsel, a written statement memorializing the items discussed is required to be submitted to the court within 14 days.

The required meet and confer conference is between the attorneys without a judge. It affords them the opportunity to amicably agree on a discovery schedule that can be submitted to the trial judge. This process of discussing and planning discovery is particularly important in complex litigation and in those cases involving large volumes of electronically stored documentation.

The conference of the attorneys is linked in time and responsibility to the Rule 16(b) scheduling conference with the judge. Under the Federal Rules, a judge

Entry of Appearance
A formal written notice by an attorney that he or she is representing one of the parties to the action.

Exhibit 12.3 Comments of the Advisory Committee on Civil Rules of the Judicial Conference Committee on Rules of Practice and Procedure

The Advisory Committee on Civil Rules of the Judicial Conference Committee on Rules of Practice and Procedure comments explain the reason for the change:

"The amendment to Rule 16(b) is designed to alert the court to the possible need to address the handling of discovery of electronically stored information early in the litigation if such discovery is expected to occur. Rule 26(f) is amended to direct the parties to discuss discovery of electronically stored information if such discovery is contemplated in the action. Form 35 is amended to call for a report to the court about the results of this discussion. In many instances, the court's involvement early in the litigation will help avoid difficulties that might otherwise arise."

Exhibit 12.4 Time line from the filing of the complaint to the scheduling conference

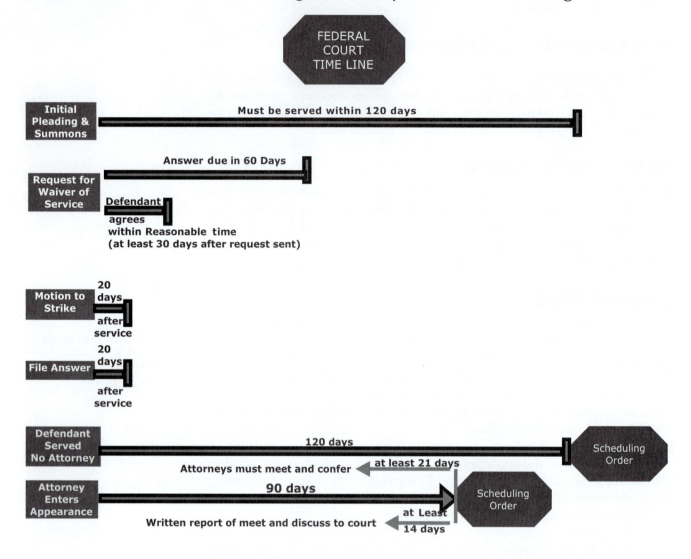

is assigned to the case from the time of filing the complaint. The judge will usually take an active role in setting a time line for discovery and trial. The attorneys have an opportunity to participate in that process by issuing the report of their conference and participating in the scheduling conference with the judge. The judge will usually give great deference to the recommendation of the attorneys in scheduling deadlines for discovery.

The goal of the conference between counsels is to discuss the nature of the claims, the likelihood of settlement, arrange for mandatory disclosure under Rule 26(a), and develop a discovery plan in the event one is necessary.

Meet and Confer Issues

The meet and confer is supposed to result in a discovery plan. In a case not involving electronic documents, the attorney would prepare by reviewing the client's records and the investigative file and come prepared with a list of parties to be deposed and records sought from the other side that could be produced in paper form, or occasionally in the form of X-rays or other similar forms.

In the electronic document cases, preparation is not as simple. Critical commitments and demands for access and delivery of electronic data require a technological skill set that many lawyers do not possess. Lawyers for the most part are trained in the procedural and substantive areas of law, not in the science of computer data storage. Without the knowledge of the technology, methods of storage used by the client, location and format of the files, and other technical issues, they may find themselves agreeing to a document production plan that is not physically possible, or extremely costly. A growing number of skilled litigators will take with them, to the meet and confer, a member of the IT or litigation support staff knowledgeable in the procedures and methods of e-discovery to ensure proper requests are made and realistic agreement given.

Mandatory Disclosure Requirements

Rule 26(a) makes mandatory the disclosure of certain information that for years was available only after a formal written discovery request was issued. For many cases, no action was taken on a file until one side moved the case forward with a formal discovery request. Under current rules everything the legal team intends to rely upon to prove its claims must be disclosed early in the litigation. Insufficient time to investigate the claim is not a valid excuse for failure to comply. The benefits of mandatory disclosure are twofold:

1. The early evaluation and settlement of claims
2. The reduction in the amount, nature, and time necessary to conduct formal discovery

From a practical standpoint, the plaintiff's legal team must be prepared for disclosure at or shortly after filing the complaint.

While the new rules contemplate a specific time frame for disclosure, they do permit the attorneys to agree to some other time frame for the disclosure. Although the attorneys may agree to extend that time, the judge at the scheduling conference may encourage them to conclude the disclosure at a faster pace.

The investigation that might have occurred under prior rules must now be completed before filing suit. For the defense team, the time to investigate and comply is very short. There is no time for procrastination in investigating and establishing the grounds to defend the claims.

Information Subject to Mandatory Disclosure

Almost anything relied upon in developing the claim, regardless of whether it is admissible at trial must be disclosed. This disclosure includes the identity of witnesses, copies of documents, a computation of damages, and a copy of any insurance policy that may be used to satisfy a judgment obtained in the litigation.

The computation of damages information traditionally represents the plaintiff attorney's thought process and was typically not released as part of discovery under the work product privilege. Under the current rule the attorney's value on the case is made known within months of the complaint being filed.

From the defense standpoint the disclosure of insurance coverage, which is not admissible at trial, is a significant change from traditional discovery. A key element in settling most cases is the existence of and limitations on insurance coverage. With both the plaintiff's calculation of damages and the defendant's ability to pay based upon insurance being known within months of filing the lawsuit, the chances for fruitful settlement discussions are enhanced.

Experts and Witnesses

Expert Witness
A person qualified by education, training or experience to render an opinion based on a set of facts that are outside the scope of knowledge of the finder of fact.

Expert witnesses expected to be called at trial must also be identified and accompanied by a copy of the expert's qualifications as an expert, including a list of publications from the preceding ten years, a statement of compensation, and a list of other cases in which they have testified. The most critical element to be shared is the written report of the expert's opinion. The report represents what the expert is expected to say at trial. The written report must include the opinion of the expert, the basis of that opinion including the information relied upon, and any assumptions made. The disclosure of the expert and his or her report must be made at least 90 days prior to trial. Some courts require the disclosure of the expert at the time of the initial disclosure or within 30 days of receipt of the expert's report. Many lawsuits become a battle of the experts. The early disclosure of the expert and opinion will often lead to early resolution of the case.

DOCUMENT RETENTION

E-discovery
Discovery of documents created, disseminated, and stored via electronic means.

E-discovery is used to describe discovery of documents created, disseminated, and stored via electronic means. Until adoption of the new Federal Rules, lawyers and the courts relied on the traditional Request for Production of Documents to obtain paper copies to also obtain electronic documentation. From a practical standpoint a request to produce all copies of a document that may exist in electronic format could be problematic. The new rules address three specific concerns, namely: (1) preserving electronic materials, (2) producing electronic materials, and (3) destruction of electronic materials.

Lawyers and paralegals are concerned about their responsibilities and how to advise clients of the impact of the rules on business practices, like retention policies for electronic data. This concern extends to small-scale litigation that represents the majority of litigation and to any client who creates and maintains documents electronically. For example, in a typical construction case, blueprints and construction documents are being replaced by electronic files created with computer graphics programs and sent electronically to architects, builders, subcontractors, suppliers, and clients. When written documentation in the form of e-mails and other word processor documents is added, the number and location of individual documents needed in the litigation process may number in the thousands or more. How do the client and the legal team know how long to keep these documents, how do they review documents in response to a request for production, and who bears the cost of retrieval?

Litigation Hold

At what point should an individual or business save materials about a particular matter? This unique issue arises out of the concern over destruction of electronic materials with a single keystroke, whether intentional or inadvertent. A company that is concerned about a potential lawsuit could easily destroy evidence contained in electronic files. The amendments to the Rules seem to suggest that once a client has a reasonable belief that litigation may arise from a dispute, a duty to preserve all documents related to that dispute arises. Note that the requirement is not that a lawsuit has been filed or a complaint served, but only that a reasonable belief that litigation may arise. An emerging line of cases suggests that there may be a requirement if the party knows or should have known of the possibility of litigation. Preservation may require placing a matter and all documents related to it on

ADVICE FROM THE FIELD

FEDERAL COURTS IN FOUR STATES LOOK TO "E-DISCOVERY COORDINATORS" TO ASSIST WITH DISCOVERY OF ELECTRONICALLY STORED INFORMATION

Qubit *a monthly publication on computer forensic and e-discovery issues Volume I, Issue 5*
by Susan Ardisson, J.D.

The federal courts in Ohio, Delaware, Pennsylvania and Maryland recognize the growing complexity of ESI discovery. When the parties cannot reach agreement on e-discovery issues, the courts have directed them to designate an e-discovery coordinator or liaison to act on their behalf and aid in the resolution of e-discovery disputes. It can be expected that judges will have little patience with parties who are uninformed about the technical aspects of their cases such as the types of computer systems, media systems and servers in use, the technology used historically to store electronic information and the availability of and cost to restore electronic data. These issues will be discussed at length at the Rule 16 and Rule 26(b) conferences. Reasonably accessible electronic evidence could mean that parties will be ordered to bear substantial burdens in its production. Counsel should be prepared to back up statements at these conferences with affidavits from key IT personnel and e-discovery coordinators because the ultimate responsibility for conducting e-discovery rests with counsel. Thorough preparation will be the means to successful e-discovery.

The United States District Court for the Northern District of Ohio established local "Default Standards for Discovery of Electronically Stored Information ("E-Discovery")." Theses default standards permit the e-discovery coordinator to be an attorney, third party consultant, or employee of the party.

Regardless of who is selected, he or she "must be familiar with the party's electronic systems and capabilities in order to explain these systems and answer relevant questions. knowledgeable about the technical aspects of e-discovery, including electronic document storage, organization and format issues. prepared to participate in e-discovery dispute resolutions."

E-discovery coordinators are "responsible for organizing each party's e-discovery efforts to insure consistency and thoroughness and, generally, to facilitate the e-discovery process." The court was, however, careful to point out that, at all times, the attorney of record shall be responsible for responding to e-discovery requests and that the "ultimate responsibility" for complying with e-discovery rests on the parties.

Source: Adapted and edited from the July 2007 issue of *Qubit*. The complete article may be viewed at www.bit-x-bit.com.

---

litigation hold. This term, or some equivalent, serves as a red flag to the company and its employees not to destroy or alter, but instead to save, in their present condition, all documents related to the dispute.

Producing Electronic Materials

The production of documents created and stored electronically falls under the traditional Production of Documents discovery tool. The unique issue that arises with production of electronic documents is the review for privileged information, and the costs of that privilege review and retrieval. Legal teams use search engines to locate and review documents containing key terms. But if 100 employees have received a single e-mail containing those key words, all 100 e-mails will be part of the search result. The amendments to the Rules attempt to address the time and cost of sifting through thousands of documents. When opposing counsels meet and confer, under Rule 26(f), they must discuss electronic discovery and how they intend to address documents produced that may include privileged information.

Litigation Hold
A process whereby a company or individual determines an unresolved dispute may result in litigation, and, as a result, electronically created and stored documents should not be destroyed or altered.

Web Exploration

Issues of *Qubit* are available at
www.bit-x-bit.com

Claw Back Provision
Any agreements the parties reach for asserting claims of privilege or of protection of trial-preparation material after production.

Most will include a **claw back provision,** which requires return of inadvertently disclosed privileged communications.

Cost of Producing Electronic Materials

A major concern in the production of electronic materials is the cost associated with review and production as well as the cost of retrieval and restoration of archived, corrupted, or deleted computer files. Traditionally, the costs of production of records were the responsibility of the party producing the records unless it was an extraordinary item for which the cost would be shifted to the requester. The same appears to apply in e-discovery. However, where the costs become excessive due to retrieval and recovery costs of corrupted and deleted files, the court may reassess the costs. If corrupted or deleted files exist because a litigant intentionally and without good faith destroyed or altered them, the court will assign the cost to reconstruct and resurrect that data to that litigant.

An example of the cost is outlined in the *Laura Zubulake v. UBS Warburg, LLC., UBS Warburg, and UBS AG.* case, UBS was billed:

31.5 hours for restoration services at an hourly rate of $245 ($7,717.50), 6 hours for the development, refinement, and execution of a search script at $245 an hour ($1,470), 101.5 hours of "CPU Bench Utilization" time for use of the forensic consultants computer systems at a rate of $18.50 per hour ($1,877.75), plus a five percent "administrative over-head fee" of $459.38.

Thus, the total cost of restoration and search was $11,524.63. In addition, UBS incurred the following costs:

$4,633 in attorney time for the document review (11.3 hours at $410 per hour) and $2,845.80 in paralegal time for tasks related to document production (16.74 hours at $170 per hour).

The total cost of restoration and production from the five backup tapes was $19,003.43 less $432.60 in photocopying costs, paid by Zubulake and not part of the cost. The cost of additional production was estimated by UBS to be $273,649.39, based on the cost incurred in restoring five tapes and producing responsive documents from those tapes, the total figure including $165,954.67 to restore and search the tapes and $107,694.72 in attorney and paralegal review costs [*Zubulake v. UBS Warburg*, (S.D.N.Y. 2003) 216 F.R.D. 280, July 24, 2003].

Destruction of Electronic Records

Spoliation
Spoliation is the destruction of records that may be relevant to ongoing or anticipated litigation, government investigation, or audit. Courts differ in their interpretation of the level of intent required before sanctions may be warranted.

Destruction of evidence when the party knows there is litigation is called **spoliation** of evidence and is punishable by sanctions against the party who destroyed the evidence. Typical sanctions include advising the jury of the destruction, which may be interpreted negatively or as denying the party an opportunity to defend the claims that arise out of the destroyed document. With such serious consequences for destruction of information the question becomes "Must we save everything?" The legal team working with electronic materials must advise a client to put in place a procedure that will allow the destruction of records without penalty.

First, the client must institute a standard operating procedure for the retention and destruction of records. In a perfect world, clients would have some system in place long before a dispute arises or a lawsuit filed. For example, the requirements of HIPAA, notwithstanding, state that in a medical practice all files with no activity for a period of three (3) years are destroyed. Instituting and observing this

Exhibit 12.5 Page 1 of sample letter to client to preserve electronic evidence

SAMPLE PRESERVATION LETTER—TO CLIENT

[Date]

RE: [Case Name]—Data Preservation

Dear:

Please be advised that the Office of General Counsel assistance believes electronically stored information to be an important and irreplaceable source of discovery and/or evidence in [description of event, transaction, business unit, product, etc.]. The lawsuit requires preservation of all information from [Corporation's] computer systems, removable electronic media and other locations relating to [description of event, transaction, business unit, product, etc.]. This includes, but is not limited to, email and other electronic communication, word processing documents, spreadsheets, databases, calendars, telephone logs, contact manager information, Internet usage files, and network access information.

[Corporation] should also preserve the following platforms in the possession of the [Corporation] or a third party under the control of the [Corporation] (such as an employee or outside vendor under contract): databases, networks, computer systems, including legacy systems (hardware and software), servers, archives, backup or disaster recovery systems, tapes, discs, drives, cartridges and other storage media, laptops, personal computers, internet data, personal digital assistants, handheld wireless devices, mobile telephones, paging devices, and audio systems (including voicemail).

Employees must take every reasonable step to preserve this information until further notice from the Office of General Counsel. *Failure to do so could result in extreme penalties against [Corporation].*

All of the information contained in the letter should be preserved for the following dates and time periods: [List dates and times].

PRESERVATION OBLIGATIONS

The laws and rules prohibiting destruction of evidence apply to electronically stored information in the same manner that they apply to other evidence. Due to its format, electronic information is easily deleted, modified or corrupted. Accordingly, [Corporation] must take every reasonable step to preserve this information until the final resolution of this matter.

This includes, but is not limited to, an obligation to:

- Discontinue all data destruction and backup tape recycling policies;
- Preserve and not dispose of relevant hardware unless an exact replica of the file (a mirror image) is made;

Source: Sample Forms and Pleadings © 2007 Kroll Ontrack Inc. Visit (www.krollontrack.com) for the latest version. Page 1 of 6 Last Revised 1/1/07.

retention policy will demonstrate the good faith and ordinary course of business destruction the court views favorably. Where there is good faith, it is unlikely sanctions will be imposed. In some professions and businesses, the retention and destruction policies may be dictated by the laws regulating that industry, such as the obligations imposed by the Securities laws and Federal regulation of the pharmaceutical industry and the health care community.

Second, and in conjunction with the retention policy, is adopting a litigation hold policy. The client needs to establish a set of rules for determining which matters may result in litigation and not destroy those records under the standard retention policy. In a medical practice this might include patients who have complained about their medical treatment or have failed to pay their bills. Files that meet either of these criteria would be placed on a litigation hold and not destroyed until some later date, usually after the statute of limitations expires. Exhibit 12.5 is the first page of a sample letter to a client to preserve electronic evidence.

General Provisions

Additionally there are some general limitations on discovery that are imposed by the Rules. The Rules seek to eliminate duplicative, burdensome, and oppressive discovery requests. Requests are duplicative or burdensome when the information sought has already been provided or is more easily obtained from another source.

Another obligation that continues throughout the litigation is the duty to supplement or revise responses should additional or different information become known. A typical example is an answer to an interrogatory that indicates the identity and address of a witness. At some later point in time it is learned that the witness has relocated. That information must be shared with opposing counsel.

COMPLIANCE AND COURT INTERVENTION

Theoretically, the process of discovery should be accomplished in a cooperative fashion without court intervention. Often that is not the case. Whatever the reason, the legal team's response to discovery requests is often delayed, or worse, forgotten. The paralegal and supervising attorney must be sure they have a system in place to comply with discovery deadlines. That means establishing an internal calendaring system and obtaining client cooperation. There will be times when it is not possible to comply and the paralegal needs to know the steps to take to obtain an extension of time to comply. Alternatively, the paralegal must also know the manner in which to use court intervention to have the opposing party come into compliance.

Most judges disfavor involvement in the discovery process. The mindset of the bench is that counsel should be able to resolve these issues without court intervention. Many practitioners find court intervention is like a trip to the principal's office after a disagreement on the school bus, unpleasant and leaving a bad impression with the authority figure. The litigation teams should anticipate problems that might arise in the discovery process, resolve them during the Rule 26(f) conference, and document their agreement as to discovery issues via the scheduling order.

Seeking Compliance

As the Recipient of Discovery Requests

The litigation paralegal or support staff will have primary responsibility for preparation of responses within the specified time frame. Developing a procedure that ensures client participation and cooperation in the preparation of responses is crucial. The meeting with the client in a case involving e-discovery should be used to determine the sources, locations, types, and formats of electronic documents. Sufficient information must be obtained about the methods of storage of electronic files and the retention policies to allow the attorney to go to the meet and confer with enough information to properly work out a meaningful discover plan and timetable.

As the Issuer of Discovery Requests

It may be necessary to seek relief from the court when the responding party is not cooperative. It may be a matter of recalcitrance or a response to not being able to comply with an agreement made at the meet and confer because of a lack of knowledge of the client's system by the attorney in making the initial agreement. The court will almost always ask if a good faith attempt was made to secure the information before granting any orders compelling compliance. A sample Motion to compel and order is shown in Exhibit 12.6.

Exhibit 12.6 Sample motion to compel on order

UNITED STATES DISTRICT COURT NORTHERN DISTRICT OF NEW YORK

B.K., a minor by her

Parents and Guardians,
Janice Knowles and
Steven Knowles,   Plaintiff

v.

Harry Hart,
Kinnicutt Bus Company,
Charles Stanley, and
MVF Construction Company,
                    Defendants

No.: _____

PLAINTIFF'S MOTION TO
COMPEL DEFENDANT
KINNICUTT BUS COMPANY
ANSWERS TO INTERROGATORIES

Attorney ID No. 124987

Plaintiff in the action files this Motion for relief and alleges as follows

1. On May 15, 2008, Plaintiff served by first class mail Interrogatories addressed to the Defendant Kinnicutt Bus Company.

2. Answers to the Interrogatories were due on June 17, 2008.

3. On June 20, 2008 counsel for plaintiff contacted defense counsel by telephone and follow-up letter to ascertain the reason for delay in response and to obtain a time frame within which answers would be provided. Defense counsel indicated an additional 30 days was required. A true and correct copy of the letter dated June 20, 2008 is attached as Exhibit A.

4. On July 25, 2008 more than 30 days had passed and still answers to Interrogatories were outstanding. Plaintiff counsel attempted to telephone and left numerous messages for defense counsel, none of which were returned.

5. On August 1, 2008 plaintiff's counsel issued a letter advising defense counsel of the intention to file the within Motion to compel. A true and correct copy of the letter dated August 1, 2008 is attached as Exhibit B.

6. To date, Defendant has neither answered nor objected to the Interrogatories.

7. To date, Defendant has filed neither a Motion for Enlargement of Time to Respond nor a Motion for a Protective Order.

8. Plaintiff has incurred costs in conjunction with seeking the compliance of Defendant Kinnicutt. Attached as Exhibit C is an affidavit of the time expended in informal means of contacting defendant as well as for the preparation, filing, service of the within motion.

WHEREFORE, it is respectfully requested this Honorable court enter an order compelling defendant to issue answers to interrogatories within 10 days and prohibiting objection to answer and awarding attorneys fees and costs in a reasonable sum.

Respectfully submitted,
Mason, Marshall and Benjamin
ATTORNEYS FOR PLAINTIFF

_____
Ethan Benjamin, Esquire
Attorney ID #
Mason, Marshall and Benjamin
Address,
Albany,
New York
Phone
Fax
Email

(Continued)

Exhibit 12.6 Continued

UNITED STATES DISTRICT COURT NORTHERN DISTRICT OF NEW YORK

B.K., a minor by her
Parents and Guardians,
Janice Knowles and
Steven Knowles,   Plaintiff

v.

Harry Hart,
Kinnicutt Bus Company,
Charles Stanley, and
MVF Construction Company,
                    Defendants

No.: _____

PLAINTIFF'S MOTION TO
COMPEL DEFENDANT
KINNICUTT BUS COMPANY
ANSWERS TO INTERROGATORIES

Attorney ID No. 124987

ORDER

AND NOW this _____ day of _____, 2008 the matter having been brought before the court on Plaintiff's Motion to Compel and after consideration of the Reply and the hearing on this matter it is hereby

ORDERED that Defendant KINNICUTT Bus Company shall within ten (10) days of the date hereof answer completely, fully and without objection the Interrogatories served upon it by the Plaintiff on May 15, 2008. Failure to comply with the terms of this order will result in the imposition of sanctions in accordance with Fed. R. Civ. P. 37;

FURTHER ORDERED Defendant Kinnicutt shall within ten (10) days of the date hereof pay to plaintiff the sum of $500, the reasonable attorney's fees and costs associated with obtaining compliance with the discovery request.

BY THE COURT

_____

ETHICAL Perspective

RULES GOVERNING THE MISSOURI BAR AND THE JUDICIARY— RULES OF PROFESSIONAL CONDUCT

Rule 4-1.6: Confidentiality of Information

(a) A lawyer shall not reveal information relating to the representation of a client unless the client gives informed consent, the disclosure is impliedly authorized in order to carry out the representation, or the disclosure is permitted by Rule 4-1.6(b).

ETHICAL Perspective

RHODE ISLAND RULES OF PROFESSIONAL CONDUCT

Rule 3.4 Fairness to Opposing Party and Counsel

A lawyer shall not:

. . . .

(c) knowingly disobey an obligation under the rules of a tribunal except for an open refusal based on an assertion that no valid obligation exists;

Web Exploration

Contrast and compare Rule 4-1.6 of the **Missouri Bar and the Judiciary–Rules of Professional Conduct** at: http://www.courts.mo.gov/page.asp?id=707 with the American Bar Association Model Rules of Professional Responsibility at http://www.abanet.org/cpr/mrpc/mrpc_toc.html, and the ethical rule in your jurisdiction

(d) in pretrial procedure, make a frivolous discovery request or fail to make reasonably diligent effort to comply with a legally proper discovery request by an opposing party;

(e) in trial, allude to any matter that the lawyer does not reasonably believe is relevant or that will not be supported by admissible evidence, assert personal knowledge of facts in issue except when testifying as a witness, or state a personal opinion as to the justness of a cause, the credibility of a witness, the culpability of a civil litigant or the guilt or innocence of an accused; or

(f) request a person other than a client to refrain from voluntarily giving relevant information to another party unless:

    (1) the person is a relative or an employee or other agent of a client; and

    (2) the lawyer reasonably believes that the person's interests will not be adversely affected by refraining from giving such information.

Web Exploration

Contrast and compare Rule 3.4 of the **Rhode Island Rules of Professional Conduct** at http://www.courts.ri.gov/supreme/pdf-files/Rules_Of_Professional_Conduct.pdf with the American Bar Association Model Rules of Professional Responsibility at http://www.abanet.org/cpr/mrpc/mrpc_toc.html, and the ethical rule in your jurisdiction

PROTECTING CONFIDENTIAL OR PRIVILEGED MATERIALS

As previously discussed, the attorney has an obligation to preserve the confidences of clients (see Rule 1.6 of the ABA Model Rules of Professional Conduct).

The FRCP in Rule 26 specifically recognizes that parties may withhold information, otherwise discoverable, and it provides within the rule a framework for the process as shown in Exhibit 12.7.

When vast numbers of electronic files are delivered as part of the discovery process, it may not always be possible, within the limited time frames required for compliance, to check every document before handing them over to opposing counsel. Many times the documents will be part of an answer to a request for electronically stored documents that will be delivered on computer tape, CD, DVD, or other computer storage media. In the electronic documents delivered may be confidential material, like e-mails between attorney and client, work product materials, or a client's proprietary information or trade secret.

The new rules provide for a "claw back" provision as part of the discovery plan. A "claw back" provision is under FRCP Rule 16 (6) "any agreements the parties reach for asserting claims of privilege or of protection as trial-preparation material after production;" In theory, if privileged or confidential material is inadvertently disclosed, the material may be recovered. Different courts have applied different interpretation and rules regarding the inadvertent disclosure of confidential material. State courts are still split in their approaches from those courts barring its use, to the courts allowing it as if the disclosure were intentional and therefore the privilege waived. Under the new federal rules at the least, the legal team must include a "claw back" clause to prevent a potential claim of malpractice for not attempting to protect the material. The use of the claw back agreement alone does not relieve the attorney of his or her obligations regarding confidential client information. The legal team must still take necessary steps to protect the confidences of clients. The claw back is only a safety device for inadvertent disclosure after reasonable methods, under the circumstance, have been used to otherwise protect and preserve confidential material.

WWW MINI EXERCISE

Review Rule 1.6 of the ABA Model Rules of Professional Conduct: http://www.abanet.org/cpr/mrpc/rule_1_6.html

WWW MINI EXERCISE

Find the complete version of FRCP Rule 26 at Cornell Law School Legal Information Institute at www.law.cornell.edu/rules/frcp/rule26.htm

Exhibit 12.7 Fed. R. Civ. P. 26(5)(A) and (B) procedures for claiming protection for privileged on work product materials

---

Rule 26. General Provisions Governing Discovery; Duty of Disclosure

(5) Claims of Privilege or Protection of Trial Preparation Materials.

(A) Information Withheld.
When a party withholds information otherwise discoverable under these rules by claiming that it is privileged or subject to protection as trial-preparation material, the party shall make the claim expressly and shall describe the nature of the documents, communications, or things not produced or disclosed in a manner that, without revealing information itself privileged or protected, will enable other parties to assess the applicability of the privilege or protection.

(B) Information Produced.
If information is produced in discovery that is subject to a claim of privilege or of protection as trial-preparation material, the party making the claim may notify any party that received the information of the claim and the basis for it. After being notified, a party must promptly return, sequester, or destroy the specified information and any copies it has and may not use or disclose the information until the claim is resolved. A receiving party may promptly present the information to the court under seal for a determination of the claim. If the receiving party disclosed the information before being notified, it must take reasonable steps to retrieve it. The producing party must preserve the information until the claim is resolved.

Committee Notes to Rule 26 indicate the intention to recognize "that a party must disclose electronically stored information as well as documents that it may use to support its claims or defenses." The Committee Notes to Rule 16 indicate recognition of the need in electronic discovery to protect privileged and confidential material, which the parties can do by agreement as part of the discovery plan. Under Rule 16 the intention is to cause the parties to alert the court to the possible need to address the handling of electronically stored information early in the litigation as part of the case management.

SUMMARY

CHAPTER *12*
ELECTRONIC DISCOVERY–THE FUNDAMENTALS

Introduction to Discovery in the Technological Age	Discovery is a step in the litigation process where the parties share information. The Federal Rules of Civil Procedure (FRCP), effective December 2006, created a sudden interest and concern in some segments of the legal community about electronic document discovery. Lawyers and paralegals are concerned about their responsibilities and how to advise clients of the impact of the rules on business practices like retention policies of electronic data. Information technology (IT) staffs for law firms are concerned about making available the needed computer and technology resources.
Purposes of Discovery	Among the purposes of discovery are understanding and evaluating the client's case, including focusing the legal team on the strengths and weaknesses of their case; understanding and evaluating the strengths and weakness of the other side; preserving testimony; potentially facilitating settlement; learning information that may be used to impeach a witness such as showing inconsistencies in testimony.

Case Evaluation	Case Evaluation. Each side is able to eva^l meet burdens of proof.
Preparing for Trial	Preparing for Trial. Properly conducte evidence at trial.
Facilitating Settlement	Facilitating Settlement. Each side ca weaknesses and better determine cl
Rules of Court and Rules of Evidence	Rules of Court and Rules of Evidence. Ti provide a level playing field to hopefully
Documents and Electronic Discovery	For hundreds of years of legal practice, the traditio documentation in legal cases was in the form of paper The computer, and the use of other computerized devices, has c creation of documents that formerly were created in paper form to created and viewed solely in electronic form. In the paper world, interrogatories, formal written discovery requests, sought the identification and physical location of relevant documents and requesting hard copies. With increasing use of electronic alternatives for creation and storage of documents of all types, the number of paper copies has been reduced. Paper documents are being replaced by electronic files. The number of e-mails created and received daily in the organization may be in the tens of thousands, thousands of which may be discoverable.
Discovery in Transition	Suddenly everyone is using word processing, sending e-mails, converting to paperless offices, and being required to file documents electronically. The courts have had to face the issue of electronic discovery to maintain the orderly administration of justice and case management.
Amendments to the Federal Rules of Civil Procedure	Federal Rules of Civil Procedure provide a framework for requesting and satisfying requests for documents in electronic format. New rules to address the increased use of electronically stored documents were effective in December 2006. ■ Rule 16 Pretrial Conferences; Scheduling; Management ■ Rule 26 General Provisions Governing Discovery; Duty of Disclosure ■ Rule 33 Interrogatories to Parties ■ Rule 34 Production of Documents, Electronically Stored Information, and Things and Entry Upon Land for Inspection and Other Purposes ■ Rule 37 Failure to Make Disclosures or Cooperate in Discovery; Sanction ■ Rule 45 Subpoena ■ Form 35 Report of Parties' Planning Meeting
Federal Rules Time Line and Discovery	The Federal Rules mandate a time line for pretrial discovery and impose certain obligations on the attorneys.
Attorney Meet and Confer	In federal court counsel are required to meet and confer about a discovery issue and propose a discovery schedule to the trial judge.
Discovery Timing	The federal rules provide a time line for meeting, submitting a report to the trial judge, and scheduling a conference with the judge.
Meet and Confer Issues	Attorneys without sufficient knowledge of electronic data systems or of the client's record keeping practices may agree to a discovery schedule and delivery of documents that is not possible or very costly.

CHAPTER 12

Mandatory Disc
Requirements
Information
Mandator
Exper

...osure	Fed. R. Civ.P. Rule 26(A) mandates the disclosure of information without formal request.
...Subject to ...Disclosure	Information must generally be revealed even if not admissible at trial, including identity of witnesses, documents, insurance policies, and damage computations.
...s and Witnesses	Expert witnesses expected to be called at trial must be identified and accompanied by a copy of qualifications, including a list of publications from the preceding ten years, a statement of compensation, and a list of other cases in which they have testified.
Document Retention	Parties must preserve evidence when a lawsuit has been instituted or when they know or have reason to know of potential litigation.
Litigation Hold	When litigation is commenced the parties must cease any destruction of documents related to the claim.
Producing Electronic Materials	The same rules apply for paper and electronic document discovery. The issues with electronic delivery include review for privileged information and the costs associated. Part of the agreement between counsels should include a provision agreeing to return inadvertently produced privileged documents. This is called a "claw back" provision.
Cost of Producing Electronic Materials	A major issue in e-discovery is the cost of discovery, the cost to recover and produce a tape backup.
Destruction of Electronic Records	Spoliation is "the destruction or significant alteration of evidence or the failure to preserve property." If no litigation is contemplated or is pending, there is some support for the position that if a regular destruction policy is in place the company may destroy the files safely. Once a case is filed or pending, the duty exists to preserve evidence.
General Provisions	The Rules seek to eliminate duplicative, burdensome, and oppressive discovery requests.
Compliance and Court Intervention	It is usually the litigation support or paralegal staff who have to ensure client compliance with discovery.
Seeking Compliance as the Recipient of Discovery Requests	Requires a procedure to ensure client cooperation. Sufficient information about clients systems must be had to allow attorney to go to meet and confer.
As the Recipient of Discovery Requests	
As the Issuing Request	Must be able to satisfy court a good faith effort has been made.

Protecting Confidential or Privileged Materials	The attorney has an obligation to preserve the confidences of clients under Rule 1.6 of most Model Rules of Professional Conduct. It may not always be possible, within the limited time frames required for compliance, to check every document before handing them over to opposing counsel. The new rules provide for a "claw back" provision as part of the discovery plan. A "claw back" provision is under FRCP Rule 16 (6) "any agreements the parties reach for asserting claims of privilege or of protection as trial-preparation material after production;" State courts are still split in their approaches from those courts barring its use, to the courts allowing it as if the disclosure were intentional. The use of the claw back agreement alone does not relieve attorneys of their obligations regarding confidential client information.

KEY TERMINOLOGY

Claw back provision 328	Entry of appearance 323	Litigation hold 327
Discovery 312	Expert witnesses 326	Relevant 322
E-discovery 326	Interrogatories 316	Spoliation 328

CONCEPT REVIEW QUESTIONS AND EXERCISES

1. Test your knowledge and comprehension of the topics in this chapter by completing the multiple-choice questions on the textbook Companion Website.
2. Test your knowledge and comprehension of the topics in this chapter by completing the True-False questions on the textbook Companion Website.
3. What is the role of the discovery in litigation?
4. Have the methods for discovery changed because of technology? Explain.
5. Has the purpose of discovery changed in the technology age?
6. How have the costs of discovery changed the thinking of clients on litigation?
7. How can proper discovery aid in evaluating a case?
8. How can discovery be used to facilitate settlement?
9. Can a party demand physical possession of the opposing party's computer? Explain fully?
10. What is the time frame that the litigation team must follow in federal court?
11. What information must be turned over without a formal request?
12. What is the impact of the new Federal Rules of Civil Procedure on the timetable for discovery requests?
13. What types of electronic information might be requested in litigation today that did not exist twenty years ago?
14. What is meant by "spoliation of evidence?"
15. What are the possible sanctions for spoliation of evidence?
16. What are the 2006 Amendments to the Federal Rules of Civil Procedure that apply to electronic discovery?
17. What are the possible costs associated with electronic discovery?
18. What are the ethical issues in protecting confidential or privileged information in an age of electronic documents?
19. What is meant by a "claw back provision" in a discovery plan? How important is it ethically?
20. What is the role of the information technologist on the legal team in the area of electronic discovery?
21. What role does cost play in electronic discovery plans?
22. May a firm or client regularly destroy files and records? Explain fully.
23. What is the purpose of a "litigation hold"?
24. What are the penalties for not maintaining a litigation hold?

INTERNET EXERCISES

1. Use the Internet or a library to find copies of the most current version of Federal Rules of Civil Procedure, Rules 16, 26, 33, 34, 37, and 45 and the comments to the Rules.
2. Locate and download a current case on spoliation of evidence. What were the circumstances that the court decided were cases of "spoliation" and what was the penalty imposed?
3. Use the Internet to prepare a list of software and vendor resources for the legal community for electronic discovery. List the services offered and the contact information.

PORTFOLIO ASSIGNMENT

Prepare a memo from the litigation support and IT staff to the trial attorneys who are preparing to attend a meet and confer for the first time explaining what issues they should be aware of and suggestions for obtaining and protecting needed data.

SCENARIO CASE STUDY

Use the opening scenario for this chapter to answer the following questions. The setting is a paralegal and attorney discussing pending litigation in which e-mail evidence may be critical to the case.

1. Prepare a summary for the attorney of the major changes in the Federal Rules of Civil Procedure (FRCP) on electronic discovery.
2. Prepare the discovery plan required under the Federal Rules of Civil Procedure.
3. Prepare a memo to the IT staff or outside consultant explaining what is needed by the trial team in a case of this type.
4. Prepare a memo from the litigation support staff to the trial team explaining what issues they should be aware of and suggestions for obtaining and protecting the needed data.

CONTINUING CASES AND EXERCISES

1. Prepare an electronic document discovery request, under the applicable Federal Rules of Civil Procedure for the accident case in Appendix 1.
2. As defense counsel, draw a document discovery agreement for plaintiff's counsel. Is the language the same for both plaintiff and defendant? Explain.

VIDEO SCENARIO: MEET AND CONFER

The attorneys are meeting as required under the Federal Rules of Civil Procedure. The defense counsel has recently taken over the case from another attorney. He wants more time to complete discovery. The meeting is conducted without anyone experienced in electronic discovery.

Go to the Companion Website, select Chapter 12 from the pull down menu, and watch this video.

1. What is the purpose of the meet and confer under the Federal Rules of Civil Procedure?
2. How should trial counsel prepare for the meet and confer under the federal rules?
3. How important is it to have someone in the meet and confer who is knowledgeable in electronic discovery?
4. Is there any time limit on the completion of the meet and confer?

Chapter 13 Digital Resources at www.prenhall.com/goldman

- Author Video Introduction
- Case Study Video
- Comprehension Quizzes and Glossary
- Video Interview: Role of Paralegal in Litigation with Charlotte Riser Harris

Electronic Discovery—Rules and Procedures

OPENING SCENARIO

Attorneys Owen Mason and Ariel Marshall weighed filing the lawsuit involving multiple plaintiffs injured as a result of what appeared to be defective brakes in the various courts with jurisdiction and venue. Procedurally they wanted the case to get to a jury as quickly as possible. A concern was the time it might take in state court where they felt the rules were not as rigid as in the federal system. It was hoped the new discovery rules in federal court would bring out all the discoverable evidence that might be used in court. After attending a continuing legal education program, the partners came away with a number of questions about the time lines and actual implementation of the rules on discovery. They worked out what they thought was a discovery timetable for the case and had an uneasy feeling about the apparent shortness in time for taking action before meeting with the judge assigned to the case. Since neither of them had ever taken part in a meet and confer under the new federal rules, they were uncertain as to what would happen and how to prepare. No one in the office had any extensive technology training and there were some doubts about the requests for electronically stored documents and the production of documents to the other side.

LEARNING OBJECTIVES

After studying this chapter you should be able to:

1. Discuss the reason for the lack of absolute standards in the e-discovery rules.

2. Describe the use of case law on answering e-discovery procedural questions.

3. Define *spoliation* of evidence.

4. Explain some of the issues in e-discovery as a result of the new Federal Rules of Civil Procedure that apply to electronic discovery.

5. Explain the duty and issues in protecting privileged or confidential information.

6. Explain the process for claiming a privilege.

7. Explain the reason for having the correct witness in a Rule 30(b) deposition.

INTRODUCTION TO E-DISCOVERY PROCEDURES

The adoption of the e-discovery rules to the Federal Rules of Civil Procedure (Fed. R. Civ. P.), effective December 2006, created a sudden interest and concern in some segments of the legal community. It appeared to them that a dark cloud suddenly descended on the handling of litigation, with new terminology and concepts to be grasped, and a little uncertainty that comes with anything new in the law.

It might seem from the reaction in the legal community that electronic storage of documents had suddenly burst on the scene. In reality it has been coming for some time. As technology has advanced, paper has been replaced with electronic documents. E-mails, text messages, and instant messages have replaced written memos and in some cases invitations, announcements, and greeting cards. When everyone wrote letters, there was a single document and maybe a copy. With e-mail, as the new standard form of communications in business and in personal life, multiple copies frequently are sent to a list of recipients contained in an electronic address book with a single keystroke. Where paper copies could be destroyed by shredding, fires, and floods, electronic documents can be destroyed by a few keystrokes. As in any emerging area of the law, there is a lack of any absolute standard or long history of cases to look to for guidance. Until enough lawyers and judges have analyzed enough cases the rules will not be clear. A framework is emerging from a few of the cases that have been reported on some of the duties and procedures that must be followed and the potential penalties for not conforming to good practices and procedures. Rules for obtaining, retaining, preserving, and restoring electronic documents are becoming clearer and are a new area the legal team must address, whether representing a plaintiff, a defendant, or just a client seeking advice on keeping or destroying electronic documents.

EMERGING CASE LAW AND COURT RULES

The new Federal Rules of Civil Procedure provide a framework for requesting and satisfying requests for documents in electronic format, like e-mails, electronically stored word processor documents, and information in electronic databases. There are few cases to look to that offer guidance on the issues surrounding electronic storage and electronic discovery. A case that stands out is *Laura Zubulake v. UBS Warburg, LLC., UBS Warburg, and UBS AG*. In a series of opinions the court addressed many of the issues in this area.

Zubulake I May 13, 2003	
Zubulake II May 13, 2003	217 F.R.D. 309
Zubulake III July 24, 2003	216 F.R.D. 280
Zubulake IV October 22, 2003	220 F.R.D. 212
Zubulake V July 20, 2004	229 F.R.D. 422
Zubulake VI February 2, 2005	
Zubulake VII March 16, 2005	

The *Zubulake* case was initially filed in the Federal District Court for the Southern District of New York, February 2002 (02civ. 1243) after Zubulake had received a right to sue letter from the EEOC based on her initial filing with the

EEOC on August 16, 2001. The issues raised, primarily concerning electronic discovery, have resulted in a number of notable opinions, decisions, and orders by Judge Shira Scheindlin:

Laura Zubulake sued her former employer, UBS Warburg LLC, for sex discrimination, including disparate treatment and wrongful termination, and retaliation in violation of Title VII of the Civil Rights Act of 1964. As with many cases the needed proof was in electronically stored documents and e-mails. The court in the case was required to address the significance of electronically stored documentation, the required procedures for disclosure, and to whom the costs associated with production should be assessed (see Words of the Court).

SCOPE OF DISCOVERY

As previously discussed, under the Federal Rules of Civil Procedure everything is discoverable that is not privileged or attorney work product, and is relevant or may lead to relevant evidence under FED. R.CIV. P. 26 (b).

IN THE WORDS OF THE COURT . . .

ZUBULAKE v. UBS WARBURG LLC, (S.D.N.Y. 2004) *229 F.R.D. 422*

LAURA ZUBULAKE, Plaintiff, v. UBS WARBURG LLC, UBS WARBURG, and UBS AG, Defendants.

02 Civ. 1243 (SAS).

United States District Court, S.D. New York.

July 20, 2004

Shira Scheindlin, District Judge

VI. Postscript

The subject of the discovery of electronically stored information is rapidly evolving. When this case began more than two years ago, there was little guidance from the judiciary, bar associations or the academy as to the governing standards. Much has changed in that time. There have been a flood of recent opinions—including a number from appellate courts—and there are now several treatises on the subject. . . . In addition, professional groups such as the American Bar Association and the Sedona Conference have provided very useful guidance on thorny issues relating to the discovery of electronically stored information. . . . Many courts have adopted, or are considering adopting, local rules addressing the subject. . . . Most recently, the Standing Committee on Rules and Procedures has approved for publication and public comment a proposal for revisions to the Federal Rules of Civil Procedure designed to address many of the issues raised by the discovery of electronically stored information. . . .

Now that the key issues have been addressed and national standards are developing, parties and their counsel are fully on notice of their responsibility to preserve and produce electronically stored information. The tedious and difficult fact finding encompassed in this opinion and others like it is a great burden on a court's limited resources. The time and effort spent by counsel to litigate these issues has also been time-consuming and distracting. This Court, for one, is optimistic that with the guidance now provided it will not be necessary to spend this amount of time again. It is hoped that counsel will heed the guidance provided by these resources and will work to ensure that preservation, production and spoliation issues are limited, if not eliminated.

SO ORDERED.

IN THE WORDS OF THE COURT . . .

ZUBULAKE v. UBS WARBURG LLC, (S.D.N.Y. 2004) *229 F.R.D. 422*

LAURA ZUBULAKE, Plaintiff, v. UBS WARBURG LLC,
UBS WARBURG, and UBS AG, Defendants.

02 Civ. 1243 (SAS).

United States District Court, S.D. New York.

July 20, 2004

Shira Scheindlin, District Judge

In sum, counsel has a duty to effectively communicate to her client its discovery obligations so that all relevant information is discovered, retained, and produced. In particular, once the duty to preserve attaches, counsel must identify sources of discoverable information. This will usually entail speaking directly with the key players in the litigation, as well as the client's information technology personnel. In addition, when the duty to preserve attaches, counsel must put in place a litigation hold and make that known to all relevant employees by communicating with them directly. The litigation hold instructions must be reiterated regularly and compliance must be monitored. Counsel must also call for employees to produce copies of relevant electronic evidence, and must arrange for the segregation and safeguarding of any archival media (e.g., backup tapes) that the party has a duty to preserve.

Once counsel takes these steps (or once a court order is in place), a party is fully on notice of its discovery obligations. If a party acts contrary to counsel's instructions or to a court's order, it acts at its own peril.

UBS failed to preserve relevant e-mails, even after receiving adequate warnings from counsel, resulting in the production of some relevant e-mails almost two years after they were initially requested, and resulting in the complete destruction of others. For that reason, Zubulake's motion is granted and sanctions are warranted.

SPOLIATION OF EVIDENCE

Spoliation

Spoliation is the destruction of records that may be relevant to ongoing or anticipated litigation, government investigation, or audit. Courts differ in their interpretation of the level of intent required before sanctions may be warranted.

Many court opinions have addressed the issue of spoliation of evidence. **Spoliation** is "the destruction or significant alteration of evidence or the failure to preserve property for another's use as evidence in pending or reasonably foreseeable litigation" [*West v. Goodyear Tire & Rubber Co.*, 167 F.3d 776, 779 (2d Cir. 1999)].

It may be the destruction of the physical evidence such as the disposal, crushing, or other destruction of a motor vehicle showing evidence of the accident. It may be the shredding or burning of a letter or handwritten note confirming the existence of a promise or other obligation. In the electronic world it may be the deleting of electronically stored documents on a computer or the erasing of the backup tapes of e-mails and documents.

Preservation

One of the questions legal counsels are often asked is, How long do I have to keep the records or documents? With paper or other physical evidence the issues frequently were ones of space with file cabinets or boxes of paper taking up valuable

IN THE WORDS OF THE COURT . . .

IN RE: TELXON CORPORATION SECURITIES LITIGATION,
(N.D.Ohio 2004)

IN RE: TELXON CORPORATION SECURITIES LITIGATION. *WILLIAM S. HAYMAN, et al., Plaintiffs, v. PRICEWATERHOUSECOOPERS, LLP, Defendant.*

Case Nos. 5:98CV2876, 1:01CV1078.

United States District Court, N.D. Ohio,

Eastern Division.

July 16, 2004

. . . Finally, the magistrate judge has considered, but cannot recommend, any lesser sanction than the entry of default judgment against PwC. lesser sanctions would result in "unwinding" over three years of litigation. This would require the re-taking of many depositions and the taking of new depositions, the conduct of additional expert analyses and the production of new reports, and the propounding of new interrogatories. But four considerations militate against this solution to the problem.

First, beginning discovery again would mean additional lengthy delay before the case reaches a resolution. Telxon and plaintiffs have already suffered sufficient delay because of PwC's bad-faith conduct; to allow PwC's misbehavior to impose substantial new delays to reaching a resolution of this litigation would be unfair to Telxon and plaintiffs.

Second, because PwC failed to archive the 1998 work papers which are at the heart of this case until late January of 1999, those work papers were vulnerable to undetectable alteration while the Telxon litigation was pending. The Ennis case in particular creates strong suspicions that this has been done to at least one document. Third, PwC's production of still more documents after April 21, 2004 undercuts any belief that PwC has now or will ever produce all relevant material in its possession. Fourth, and most critical, there is strong evidence that documents have been destroyed, placing plaintiffs and Telxon in a situation which cannot be remedied.

Because PwC's conduct has made it impossible to try this case with any confidence in the justice of the outcome, PwC should bear the burden created by its conduct. For this reason the magistrate judge recommends that the court grant Telxon's and plaintiffs' motions and enter default judgment against PwC and in favor of Telxon and plaintiffs in cases 5:98CV2876 and 1:01CV1078.

and costly storage space and the constant concern for the flammability if not stored in fireproof or sprinklered areas. The electronic era has changed some of the issues. Paper is still important, but electronic documents and e-mails are becoming more prevalent as the source of business records. With tape and CD storage of electronic documents, thousands of documents can be saved and stored in the space formerly taken up by a few sheets of paper. So the question then becomes, How long should these be saved? *Forever* is one answer, but what about the potential document, such as an e-mail, hidden in the old files that would conclusively impeach or destroy the credibility of a witness or be evidence that conclusively determines an issue—the "smoking gun"? And what are the consequences if the old files are stored on a tape or other storage media for which the original device used to write and read the information is no longer available? For example, in the past some companies used floppy disks to store documents, or other forms of magnetic tape using proprietary tape formats and drives to write and read the information. As the technology has improved some computers no longer have floppy drives. Additionally, older tapes are subject to deterioration, and some of the companies that made the tape drives have gone out of business, rendering the tapes costly to recover and convert to a readable format on more technologically advanced computers.

Litigation Hold

If no litigation is contemplated or is pending, there is some support for the position that if a regular destruction policy is in place the company may destroy the files safely. Plaintiff counsel may argue differently, hoping to find a smoking gun somewhere in the mass of e-mails or other electronic documents in some case in the future. But once a case is filed or pending, the duty exists to preserve evidence. Case law clearly imposes on the attorney an affirmative duty to not only instruct the client to cease further action destroying documents but to also follow up and verify that the client has followed the instruction. See Words of the Court for examples of cases in which spoliation of evidence was critical. The Court in *Residential Funding v Degeorge Financial* discusses the potential sanctions for not delivering discoverable material, (See Words of the Court).

ETHICAL Perspective

COMPETENCY IDAHO RULES OF PROFESSIONAL CONDUCT SELECTED PORTIONS OF RULE AND COMMENTS

Rule 1.1: Competence

A lawyer shall provide competent representation to a client. Competent representation requires the legal knowledge, skill, thoroughness and preparation reasonably necessary for the representation.

Commentary

Legal Knowledge and Skill

[1] In determining whether a lawyer employs the requisite knowledge and skill in a particular matter, relevant factors include the relative complexity and specialized nature of the matter, the lawyer's general experience, the lawyer's training and experience in the field in question, the preparation and study the lawyer is able to give the matter and whether it is feasible to refer the matter to, or associate or consult with, a lawyer of established competence in the field in question. In many instances, the required proficiency is that of a general practitioner. Expertise in a particular field of law may be required in some circumstances. . . .

Thoroughness and Preparation

[5] Competent handling of a particular matter includes inquiry into and analysis of the factual and legal elements of the problem, and use of methods and procedures meeting the standards of competent practitioners. It also includes

adequate preparation. The required attention and preparation are determined in part by what is at stake; major litigation and complex transactions ordinarily require more extensive treatment than matters of lesser complexity and consequence. An agreement between the lawyer and the client regarding the scope of the representation may limit the matters for which the lawyer is responsible. See Rule 1.2(c).

Maintaining Competence

[6] To maintain the requisite knowledge and skill, a lawyer should keep abreast of changes in the law and its practice, engage in continuing study and education and comply with all continuing legal education requirements to which the lawyer is subject.

Web Exploration

Contrast and compare Rule 1.1 of the Idaho Rules of Professional Conduct at http://www.isc.idaho.gov/irpc0304_cov.htm with the American Bar Association Model Rules of Professional Responsibility at http://www.abanet.org/cpr/mrpc/mrpc_toc.html, and the ethical rule in your jurisdiction

ISSUES IN E-DISCOVERY

The opinions written in the *Zubulake* case raise many of the issues surrounding the emerging issues of e-discovery: duty to preserve evidence, duty to produce, cost of production, and the need for early awareness in the case of potential e-discovery issues. The new Federal Rules of Civil Procedure (FRCP) effective December 2006 address many of these issues as indicated by the comments of the Advisory Committee on Civil Rules of the Judicial Conference Committee on Rules of Practice and Procedure as shown in Exhibit 13.1.

WWW Mini Exercise

Review Rule 1.6 of the ABA Model Rules of Professional Conduct: http://www.abanet.org/cpr/mrpc/rule_1_6.html

PROTECTING CONFIDENTIAL OR PRIVILEGED MATERIALS

As previously discussed, the attorney has an obligation to preserve the confidences of clients (see Rule 1.6 of the ABA Model Rules of Professional Conduct).

Exhibit 13.1 Comments of the advisory committee on civil rules of the judicial conference committee on rules of practice and procedure

The Advisory Committee on Civil Rules of the Judicial Conference Committee on Rules of Practice and Procedure comments explain the reason for the change:

"The amendment to Rule 16(b) is designed to alert the court to the possible need to address the handling of discovery of electronically stored information early in the litigation if such discovery is expected to occur. Rule 26(f) is amended to direct the parties to discuss discovery of electronically stored information if such discovery is contemplated in the action. Form 35 is amended to call for a report to the court about the results of this discussion. In many instances, the court's involvement early in the litigation will help avoid difficulties that might otherwise arise."

IN THE WORDS OF THE COURT . . .

RESIDENTIAL FUNDING CORP. v. DEGEORGE FINANCIAL,
306 F.3d 99 (2nd Cir. 2002)

RESIDENTIAL FUNDING CORPORATION, Plaintiff-Appellee, v. DeGEORGE FINANCIAL CORP., DeGeorge Home Alliance, Inc. and DeGeorge Capital Corp, Defendants-Appellants.

No. 01-9282.

United States Court of Appeals, Second Circuit.

Argued: August 8, 2002.

Decided: September 26, 2002.

Appeal from the United States District Court for the District of Connecticut, Arterton, J.

. . . [T]his is not a typical spoliation case. It does not appear that RFC *destroyed* the e-mails on the back-up tapes. Rather, RFC failed to produce the e-mails in time for trial. Accordingly, this case is more akin to those in which a party breaches a discovery obligation or fails to comply with a court order regarding discovery.

. . . Where, as here, the nature of the alleged breach of a discovery obligation is the non-production of evidence, a district court has broad discretion in fashioning an appropriate sanction, including the discretion to delay the start of a trial (at the expense of the party that breached its obligation), to declare a mistrial if trial has already commenced, or to proceed with a trial and give an adverse inference instruction. *See Reilly v. Natwest Markets Group Inc.,* 181 F.3d 253, 267 (2d Cir. 1999)

. . . Where a party destroys evidence in bad faith, that bad faith alone is sufficient circumstantial evidence from which a reasonable fact finder could conclude that the missing evidence was unfavorable to that party. *See, e.g., Kronisch,* 150 F.3d at 126 ("It is a well-established and long-standing principle of law that a party's intentional destruction of evidence relevant to proof of an issue at trial can support an inference that the evidence would have been unfavorable to the party responsible for its destruction."). Similarly, a showing of gross negligence in the destruction or untimely production of evidence will in some circumstances suffice, standing alone, to support a finding that the evidence was unfavorable to the grossly negligent party. *See Reilly,* 181 F.3d at 267–68. Accordingly, where a party seeking an adverse inference adduces evidence that its opponent destroyed potential evidence (or otherwise rendered it unavailable) in bad faith or through gross negligence (satisfying the "culpable state of mind" factor), that same evidence of the opponent's state of mind will frequently also be sufficient to permit a jury to conclude that the missing evidence is favorable to the party (satisfying the "relevance" factor) . . .

. . . In this case, the District Court stated that the only evidence DeGeorge had adduced "suggesting that [the unproduced e-mails] would likely have been harmful to RFC" was the non production itself. Trial Tr. at 1377. It also stated, however, that RFC's actions after it retained EED, "including representation that e-mails would be produced, without mentioning the absence of any from the critical time period, a missed Federal Express deadline for sending backup tapes so they could be forwarded to DeGeorge's vendors, and resistance to responding to technical questions about the tapes, suggest *a somewhat purposeful sluggishness on RFC's part.*" Trial Tr. at 1376 (emphasis added).

. . . In sum, we hold that:

1. where, as here, the nature of the alleged breach of a discovery obligation is the non-production of evidence, a District Court has broad discretion in fashioning an appropriate sanction, including the discretion to delay the start of a trial (at the expense of the party that breached its obligation), to declare a mistrial if trial has already commenced, or to proceed with a trial with an adverse inference instruction;

2. discovery sanctions, including an adverse inference instruction, may be imposed upon a party that has breached a discovery obligation not only through bad faith or gross negligence, but also through ordinary negligence;

3. a judge's finding that a party acted with gross negligence or in bad faith with respect to discovery obligations is ordinarily sufficient to support a finding that the missing or destroyed evidence would have been harmful to that party, even if the destruction or unavailability of the evidence was not caused by the acts constituting bad faith or gross negligence; . . .

ADVICE FROM THE FIELD

SAILING ON CONFUSED SEAS:
Privilege Waiver and the New Federal Rules of Civil Procedure
John M. Facciola*

. . .

VII. THE FUTURE

Lawyers and judges face a difficult future in dealing with privileged information stored in a computer's memory. As server space increases and the cost of memory decreases, the tendency of computer users to save everything and organize none of it will increase. As noted earlier, the new Federal Rules justify extremely limited relief in one situation, the "claw back," and leave other solutions, including "sneaking a peek" or agreements as to waiver, where it found them. Furthermore, waiver agreements cannot bind the rights of strangers to the litigation and, therefore, are full of peril where third-person litigation against one of the parties to the agreement is even a remote possibility. Indeed, the Tenth Circuit recently rejected a claim that disclosure to a government agency of computer information, pursuant to a confidentiality agreement, was not a waiver of the privilege as to third parties.[16] That result is sobering not only for its rejection of any notion of the legitimacy of any kind of "selective waiver," but also for its insistence that the attorney-client privilege not be extended an inch further than necessary to accomplish its purposes and its niggardly

reading of the circumstances under which waiving it can be avoided. Thus, it can be said that, without the dramatic intervention of a new rule adopted by Congress providing that disclosure pursuant to court-ordered agreements is not a waiver, lawyers will have to confront the reality that their clients either (1) authorize what may be a king's ransom to do a full-scale privilege review or (2) permit them to enter into an agreement that eliminates the need for such a detailed review and take the risk that the agreement will not prevent a third party from seeing privileged information.

Perhaps an answer may lie in the technology. Word processing is now dominated by two companies and one wonders why they have not sought to market a program that would prevent a user from saving a document unless the user indicated that it was privileged. Electronic marking of such documents and their segregation into a privileged file would, at least, narrow what must be reviewed.

Absent the technology, one wonders when American corporations will adopt records retention policies that are reasonable, applicable without exception in all departments, and enforced by a corporate

(*Continued*)

manager with real power to discipline those employees who refuse to follow them. It is hard to imagine a greater waste of money than paying a lawyer $250 an hour to look at recipes, notices of the holiday party, and NCAA Final Four pool entries while doing a privilege review. A company that permits that situation to occur is wasting its shareholders' money as surely as if it were burning it in the parking lot.

In the meantime, the staggering costs of a privilege review will grow, driving the costs of litigation ever upward and probably increasing the tendency of parties to avoid the federal courts for other *fora* to resolve their disputes. One thing is certain: without relief from somewhere, that associate will never sail on the Chesapeake Bay.

About the Author: *John M. Facciola, is a United States Magistrate Judge. In the United States District Court for the District of Columbia.

[16]In re Qwest Comm. Int'l, Inc., 450 F.3d 1179 (10th Cir. 2006).

Source: Federal Courts Law Review September 2006.

See the Advisory Committee on Evidence Rules Proposed Amendment: Rule 502, available at http://www .lexisnexis.com/applieddisco very/lawlibrary/Rule502.pdf.

Exhibit 13.2 FRCP Rule 26 (5) (A) and (B) procedures for claiming protection for privileged or work product materials

Rule 26. General Provisions Governing Discovery; Duty of Disclosure (5) Claims of Privilege or Protection of Trial Preparation Materials.

(A) Information Withheld.

When a party withholds information otherwise discoverable under these rules by claiming that it is privileged or subject to protection as trial-preparation material, the party shall make the claim expressly and shall describe the nature of the documents, communications, or things not produced or disclosed in a manner that, without revealing information itself privileged or protected, will enable other parties to assess the applicability of the privilege or protection.

(B) Information Produced.

If information is produced in discovery that is subject to a claim of privilege or of protection as trial-preparation material, the party making the claim may notify any party that received the information of the claim and the basis for it. After being notified, a party must promptly return, sequester, or destroy the specified information and any copies it has and may not use or disclose the information until the claim is resolved. A receiving party may promptly present the information to the court under seal for a determination of the claim. If the receiving party disclosed the information before being notified, it must take reasonable steps to retrieve it. The producing party must preserve the information until the claim is resolved.

The FRCP in Rule 26 specifically recognizes that parties may withhold information, otherwise discoverable, and it provides within the rule a framework for the process as shown in Exhibit 13.2.

When vast numbers of electronic files are delivered as part of the discovery process, it may not always be possible, within the limited time frames required for compliance, to check every document before handing them over to opposing counsel. Many times the documents will be part of an answer to a request for electronically stored documents that will be delivered on computer tape, CD, DVD, or other computer storage media. In the electronic documents delivered may be confidential material, like e-mails between attorney and client, work product materials, or a client's proprietary information or trade secret.

The new rules provide for a "claw back" provision as part of the discovery plan. A "claw back" provision is under FRCP Rule 16 (6) "any agreements the parties reach for asserting claims of privilege or of protection as trial-preparation material after production;" Exhibit 13.3 is a sample claw back agreement.

Exhibit 13.3 Sample "claw back" agreement from Kroll Ontrack, Inc.

NON-WAIVER AND CONFIDENTIALITY AGREEMENT ("Agreement")

WHEREAS, the parties have agreed to produce all documents deemed discoverable under the Federal Rules of Civil Procedure, including Electronically Stored Information ("ESI"), that are responsive to each other's discovery requests and not privileged or otherwise exempted from discovery under the Federal Rules of Evidence, Federal Rules of Civil Procedure or other applicable source of law;

WHEREAS, some of the ESI and other documents produced in this matter may contain attorney-client privileged communications or other information protected as "privileged" under the Federal Rules of Evidence ("Privileged Material") and not subject to discovery under the Federal Rules of Civil Procedure or the Federal Rules of Evidence ("Privileged Material");

WHEREAS, some of the produced ESI and other documents in this matter may contain protected attorney work-product material prepared or compiled in anticipation of litigation and not subject to discovery under the Federal Rules of Civil Procedure of the Federal Rules of Evidence ("Work-Product Material");

WHEREAS, the parties acknowledge that, despite each party's best efforts to conduct a thorough pre-production review of all ESI and other documents, some Work Product Material and Privileged Material ("Protected Material") may be inadvertently disclosed to the other party during the course of this litigation;

WHEREAS, the volume of potentially discoverable ESI may substantially increase the total volume of documents that will be produced by the parties, thereby exacerbating the risk of inadvertent disclosure of Protected Material;

WHEREAS, in the course of this litigation, the parties may—either inadvertently or knowingly—produce information that is of a confidential, private, personal, trade secret, or proprietary nature ("Sensitive Material");

WHEREAS, the undersigned parties desire to establish a mechanism to avoid waiver of privilege or any other applicable protective evidentiary doctrine as a result of the inadvertent disclosure of Protected Material; and (b) keep disclosed Protected Material and Sensitive Material confidential to the maximum extent possible;

IT IS HEREBY STIPULATED AND AGREED by the parties that the following clauses of this Agreement shall govern the disclosure of Protected Material and Sensitive Material in this action.

NON-WAIVER OF PRIVILEGE OR OTHER PROTECTIVE DOCTRINE BY INADVERTENT DISCLOSURE

1. The inadvertent disclosure of any document which is subject to a legitimate claim that the document should have been withheld from disclosure as Protected Material shall NOT waive any privilege or other applicable protective doctrine for that document or for the subject matter of the inadvertently disclosed document if the producing party, upon becoming aware of the disclosure, promptly requests its return and takes reasonable precautions to avoid such inadvertent disclosure.

2. Except in the event that the requesting party disputes the claim, any documents which the producing party deems to contain inadvertently disclosed Protected Material shall be, upon written request, promptly returned to the producing party or destroyed at the producing party's option. This includes all copies, electronic or otherwise, of any such documents. In the event that the producing party requests destruction, the requesting party shall provide written certification of compliance within thirty (30) days of such written request. In the event that the

(Continued)

Exhibit 13.3 Continued

requesting party disputes the producing party's claim as to the protected nature of the inadvertently disclosed material, a single set of copies may be sequestered and retained by and under the control of requesting party for the sole purpose of seeking court determination of the issue pursuant to Federal Rule of Civil Procedure 26(b)(5)(B).

3. Any such Protected Material inadvertently disclosed by the producing party to the requesting party pursuant to this Agreement, shall be and remain the property of the producing property.

4. To the extent there may be inconsistency between the aforementioned stipulations in this Agreement and Federal Rule of Civil Procedure 26(b)(5) and the accompanying Committee Note, Rule 26(b)(5)(B) and the Committee Note shall control.

CONFIDENTIAL TREATMENT OF SENSITIVE MATERIAL

5. Any Protected Material or Sensitive Material disclosed in this litigation is to be considered confidential and proprietary to the producing party and the requesting party shall hold the same in confidence and shall not use any disclosed Protected Material or Sensitive Material other than for the purposes of this litigation. To that end, the parties shall limit the disclosure of all Protected Material and Sensitive Material only to those persons with a need to know the information for purposes of supporting their position in this litigation. Moreover, Protected Material and Sensitive Material will not be disclosed, published or otherwise revealed to any other party in this litigation except with the specific prior written authorization of the producing party.

6. If Protected Material or Sensitive Material is disclosed through inadvertence or otherwise to any person not authorized under this Agreement, the party causing such disclosure shall inform the person receiving the Protected Material or Sensitive Material that the information is covered by this Agreement, make its best efforts to retrieve the Protected Material or Sensitive Material, and promptly inform the producing party of the disclosure.

7. The requesting party shall have no confidentiality obligations with respect to any information which:
   a. is already known to the requesting party without restriction;
   b. is or becomes publicly known otherwise than by the requesting party's breach of this Agreement;
   c. is received by the requesting party without restriction from a third-party who is not under an obligation of confidentiality;
   d. is independently developed by the requesting party;
   e. is approved for release by written authorization of the producing party; or
   f. is disclosed by the requesting party pursuant to judicial action, provided that producing party is notified at the time such action is initiated.

8. Any Protected Material or Sensitive Material disclosed by the producing party to the requesting party pursuant to this Agreement shall be and remain the property of the producing property.

9. This Agreement terminates and supersedes all prior understandings or agreements on the subject matter hereof.

10. This Agreement shall be binding on the parties hereto when signed regardless of whether or when the court enters its Agreement thereon.

11. Nothing herein shall prevent any party from applying to the court for a modification of this Agreement should the moving party believe the Agreement, as originally agreed upon, is hampering its efforts to prepare for trial; or from applying to the court for further or additional protective Agreements; or from an Agreement between the parties to any modification of this Agreement, subject to the approval of the court.

Exhibit 13.3 Continued

12. This Agreement shall survive the final termination of this case regarding any retained documents or contents thereof.

13. The effective date of this Agreement shall be _____.

DATED: _____   DATED: _____

LAW FIRM NAME   LAW FIRM NAME

_____   _____
ATTORNEY NAME, BAR #   ATTORNEY NAME, BAR #
ADDRESS   ADDRESS
CITY, STATE   CITY, STATE
PHONE NUMBER   PHONE NUMBER

Source: Visit **www.krollontrack.com** for latest version Last Revised 12/1/06

In theory, if privileged or confidential material is inadvertently disclosed, the material may be recovered. Different courts have applied different interpretation and rules regarding the inadvertent disclosure of confidential material. State courts are still split in their approaches from those courts barring its use, to the courts allowing it as if the disclosure were intentional and therefore the privilege waived. Under the new federal rules at the least, the legal team must include a "claw back" clause to prevent a potential claim of malpractice for not attempting to protect the material. The use of the claw back agreement alone does not relieve the attorney of his or her obligations regarding confidential client information. The legal team must still take necessary steps to protect the confidences of clients. The claw back is only a safety device for inadvertent disclosure after reasonable methods, under the circumstance, have been used to otherwise protect and preserve confidential material.

Committee Notes to Rule 26 indicate the intention to recognize "that a party must disclose electronically stored information as well as documents that it may use to support its claims or defenses." The Committee notes to Rule 16 indicate recognition of the need in electronic discovery to protect privileged and confidential material, which the parties can do by agreement as part of the discovery plan. Under Rule 16 the intention is to cause the parties to alert the court to the possible need to address the handling of electronically stored information early in the litigation as part of the case management.

Web Exploration

For additional *e*-discovery information, sample forms, and case list go to the Kroll Ontrack website at http://www.krollontrack.com/legalresources/

WWW Mini Exercise

Find the complete version of FRCP Rule 26 at Cornell Law School Legal Information Institute at www.law.cornell.edu/rules/frcp/rule26.htm

ETHICAL Perspective

PROPOSED AMENDMENT TO THE FEDERAL RULES OF EVIDENCE

The Judicial Conference submitted a new Evidence Rule 502 on Waiver of Attorney-Client Privilege and Work Product in September of 2007. Public law 110-322 was signed into law by President Bush on September 19, 2008 making the propal a New Rule of Evidence 502.

Rule 502. Attorney-Client Privilege and Work Product; Limitations on Waiver

The following provisions apply, in the circumstances set out, to disclosure of a communication or information covered by the attorney-client privilege or work-product protection.

(a) **Disclosure made in a federal proceeding or to a federal office or agency; scope of a waiver**—When the disclosure is made in a federal proceeding or to a federal office or agency and waives the attorney-client privilege or work-product protection, the waiver extends to an undisclosed communication or information in a federal or state proceeding only if:
   (1) the waiver is intentional;
   (2) the disclosed and undisclosed communications or information concern the same subject matter; and
   (3) they ought in fairness to be considered together.

(b) **Inadvertent disclosure**—When made in a federal proceeding or to a federal office or agency, the disclosure does not operate as a waiver in a federal or state proceeding if:
   (1) the disclosure is inadvertent;
   (2) the holder of the privilege or protection took reasonable steps to prevent disclosure; and
   (3) the holder promptly took reasonable steps to rectify the error, including (if applicable) following Fed. R. Civ. P. 26(b)(5)(B).

(c) **Disclosure made in a state proceeding**—When the disclosure is made in a state proceeding and is not the subject of a state-court order concerning waiver, the disclosure does not operate as a waiver in a federal proceeding if the disclosure:
   (1) would not be a waiver under this rule if it had been made in a federal proceeding; or
   (2) is not a waiver under the law of the state where the disclosure occurred.

(d) **Controlling effect of a court order**—A federal court may order that the privilege or protection is not waived by disclosure connected with the litigation pending before the court—in which event the disclosure is also not a waiver in any other federal or state proceeding.

(e) **Controlling effect of a party agreement**—An agreement on the effect of disclosure in a federal proceeding is binding only on the parties to the agreement, unless it is incorporated into a court order.

(f) **Controlling effect of this rule**—Notwithstanding Rules 101 and 1101, this rule applies to state proceedings and to federal court-annexed and federal court-mandated arbitration proceedings, in the circumstances set out in the rule. And notwithstanding Rule 501, this rule applies even if state law provides the rule of decision.

(g) **Definitions**—In this rule:
   (1) "attorney-client privilege" means the protection that applicable law provides for confidential attorney-client communications; and
   (2) "work-product protection" means the protection that applicable law provides for tangible material (or its intangible equivalent) prepared in anticipation of litigation or for trial.

IN THE WORDS OF THE COURT . . .

VICTOR STANLEY, INC., Plaintiff vs. CREATIVE PIPE, INC., et al.,
Defendant

CIVIL ACTION NO. MJG–06–2662

UNITED STATES DISTRICT COURT FOR THE DISTRICT OF
MARYLAND

2008 U.S. Dist. LEXIS 42025

May 29, 2008, Decided

. . . the Defendants initially sought to enter a non-waiver agreement such as discussed in *Hopson,* but then abandoned this effort). Should the issue of privilege waiver by inadvertent production of voluminous ESI be considered by the Fourth Circuit at some time in the future, it may be hoped that the court will be cognizant of the unique problems presented with regard to avoiding privilege waiver presented by ESI discovery, as well as the fact that the approval of Proposed Evidence Rule 502 by the Committee on the Rules of Evidence, as well as the Judicial Conference, recognizes a need to provide relief in this difficult area. The substantive law of privilege is not rigid and inflexible, *Hopson, 232 F.R.D. at 240*(citing *Jaffee v. Redmond, 518 U.S. 1, 8, 116 S. Ct. 1923, 135 L. Ed. 2d 337 (1996)),* [*23] but is governed by principles of the common law as interpreted "by the courts of the United States in the light of reason and experience." *Fed. R. Evid. 501.* Experience has now shown that ESI discovery presents unique, heretofore unrecognized, risks of waiver of privilege or work-product protection even when the party asserting the privilege or protection has exercised care not to waive it. The approval of Proposed Evidence Rule 502 by the Judicial Conference, is a reasoned response to this new experience, but still pending in Congress. For those courts that have yet to decide which approach to follow regarding the inadvertent disclosure of privileged material during ESI discovery, the commentary to the proposed rule is worthy of consideration.

6 As noted in *Continental Casualty Co. v. Under Armour, Inc., 537 F. Supp. 2d 761 (D. Md. 2008),* if documents qualify as both attorney-client privileged and work-product protected, separate analysis is required to determine whether inadvertent production constitutes waiver. However, the majority view is that disclosure of work-product material in a manner that creates a substantial risk that an adversary will receive it waives the protection. *Id. at 772–73* [*24] (citing *Restatement (Third) of the Law Governing Lawyers § 91* (2000)). In this case, Defendants' voluntary, though inadvertent, production of the 165 documents directly to counsel for the Plaintiff waived any work-product protection they may have had. *Id.* . . .

PRIVILEGE IN ELECTRONIC DISCOVERY

Withholding the document claimed to be a privileged document sounds like a simple matter of not giving it to anyone. With paper this may be true. However, in the age of electronics it is easy to accidentally send a privileged document by e-mail or fax. Just push the wrong speed dial or address book entry. With vast quantities of data transferred electronically the matter becomes even more complicated. Which of the thousands of potential documents is privileged.

Claim of Privilege

Privilege is not automatically invoked. The person claiming the privilege—usually the client—has the burden to establish its existence, called **claim of privilege.**

> "To sustain a claim of privilege, the party invoking it must demonstrate that the information at issue was a communication between client and counsel or his employee, that it was intended to be and was in fact kept confidential, and that it was made in order to assist in obtaining or providing legal advice or services to the client" *SR International Bus. Ins. Co v. World Trade Center* Prop No 01 Civ 9291 (S.D.N.Y. 2002), quoting *Browne of New York City, Inc v. Ambase Corp.*

IN THE WORDS OF THE COURT . . .

Ruling on Plaintiff's Motion to Compel and Motion for Protective Order

BREON v. COCA-COLA BOTTLING COMPANY OF NEW ENGLAND, (Conn. 2005)

Civil No. 3:04-CV-00374(CFD)(TPS).

United States District Court, D. Connecticut.

November 4, 2005

Thomas Smith, Magistrate Judge

. . . B. Attorney-Client & Work-Product Claims

To protect from abuse, discovery must have limiting principles aside from the low threshold of relevance. One of these principles is that matters are not discoverable, under certain circumstances, if they are privileged. Fed.R.Civ.P. 26(b)(1). Here, the defendant claims that a number of requests for production are inappropriate because they ask for information protected by either the attorney-client privilege or work-product doctrine.[fn3]

The attorney-client privilege prevents disclosure of a communication from a client to a lawyer, where that communication relates to a fact of which the attorney was informed (a) by his client (b) without the presence of strangers (c) for the purpose of securing primarily either (i) an opinion on the law or (ii) legal services or (iii) assistance in some legal proceeding, and not (d) for the purpose of committing a crime or tort; and (4) the privilege has been (a) claimed and (b) not waived by the client. *United States v. United Shoe Machinery Corp., 89 F.Supp. 357, 358* (D. Mass. 1950); *Colton v. United States, 306 F.2d 633, 637*(2d Cir. 1962). The rationale behind the privilege is to foster open and honest communication between a client and his lawyer. *United States v. Schwimmer, 892 F.2d 237, 443* (2d Cir. 1989). Because of this underlying rationale, communication running from the lawyer to the client is not protected unless it reveals what the client has said. *SCM Corp. v. Xerox Corp., 70 F.R.D. 508, 522* (D. Conn. 1976); *Clute v. Davenport Co.,* 118 F.R.D 312, 314 (D.Conn. 1988).

Completely distinct from the attorney-client privilege is the work-product doctrine. The work-product doctrine, as codified in the Federal Rules states: a party may obtain discovery of documents and tangible things otherwise discoverable . . . and prepared in anticipation of litigation or for trial by or for another party or by or for that other party's representative (including the other party's attorney, consultant, surety, indemnitor, insurer, or agent) only upon a showing that the party seeking discovery has substantial need of the materials in the preparation of the party's case and that the party is unable without undue hardship to obtain the substantial equivalent of the materials by other means.

Fed.R.Civ.P. *26*(b)(3). "The work-product doctrine ... is intended to preserve a zone of privacy in which a lawyer can prepare and develop legal theories and strategy with an eyetoward litigation, free from unnecessary intrusion by his adversaries." *United States v. Adlman, 134 F.3d 1194, 1196* (2d. Cir. 1998) (internal quotations omitted). As the rule itself makes clear, work-product enjoys only limited immunity from discovery. For "fact" work-product, that is work-product that does not contain legal opinions or conclusions, the party seeking discovery must meet the "substantial burden" and "undue hardship" tests outlined in Rule 26. *Maloney v. Sisters of Charity Hosp., 165 F.R.D. 26, 30* (W.D.N.Y. 1995). Opinion work product, on the other hand, constitutes thoughts, strategies, legal opinions and conclusions by an attorney. *See Loftis v. Amica Mut. Ins. Co., 175 F.R.D. 5, 11* (D. Conn. 1997). Opinion work-product is given stronger protection and only discoverable in rare circumstances where the party seeking discovery can show extraordinary justification. *Id.; S.N. Phelps & Co. v. Circle K. Corp.,* 1997 U.S. Dist. LEXIS 713, No. 96 CV 5801 (JFK), 1997 WL 31197, at *7 (S.D.N.Y. 1997).

Under both the attorney-client privilege and work-product doctrine the party asserting the claim has the initial burden of showing it applies. *See Cornelius v. Consolidated Rail Corp., 169 F.R.D. 250, 253* (N.D.N.Y. 1996) (party claiming work-product protection must show three elements, "[f]irst, the material must be a document or tangible thing. Second, it must have been prepared in anticipation of litigation. Third, it must have been prepared by or for a party or its representative."); *In re Horowitz, 482 F.2d 72, 82* (2d Cir.), *cert denied,* 414 U.S. 867 (1973) ("the person claiming the attorney-client privilege has the burden of establishing all essential elements").

To assist the court and counsel, both the Federal and Local Rules require that the party asserting a privilege provide the court with a privilege log. Fed.R.Civ.P. *26*(B)(5); D. Conn. L.Civ. R. 37(a)(1) When a party withholds information otherwise discoverable under these rules by claiming that it is privileged or subject to protection as trial preparation material, the party shall make the claim expressly and shall describe the nature of the documents, communications, or things not produced or disclosed in a manner that, without revealing information itself privileged or protected, will enable other parties to assess the applicability of the privilege or protection.

Fed.R.Civ.Pro. *26*(B)(5). A party seeking to avoid discovery cannot hide behind bald statements of "privilege" and "work-product" and expect the court to supply the rational to support the claims. *See Obiajulu v. City of Rochester Dep't of Law, 166 F.R.D. 293, 295* (W.D.N.Y. 1996). At the very least, the log should identify each document's author and recipient, as well as reasons why the information is claimed to be privileged. *See United States v. Construction Prod. Research, 73 F.3d 464, 473* (2d Cir. 1996). The privilege log is not simply a technicality,it is an essential tool which allows the parties and the court to make an intelligent decision as to whether a privilege or immunity exists. *See Bowne v. Ambase, 150 F.R.D. 465, 474* (S.D.N.Y. 1993). Preparation of a privilege log is a critical step in discharging one's burden of establishing the existence of a privilege.

Privilege Logs

A **privilege log** is a list of documents claimed by the submitting party to contain material subject to privilege or work product exclusion. Exhibit 13.4 shows a sample privilege log.

Privilege log
A list of documents claimed by the submitting party to contain material subject to privilege or work product exclusion.

Exhibit 13.4 Sample privilege log

Public Records Request			Privilege Log	July 18, 2008
			Ivy Frye's and Frank Bailey's February 2008 E-mails	
Date	Author	Recipient	Document Description	Privilege
02/01/08	C. Fredeen. PDC Eng.	F. Bailey, GOV	6:59 am *E-mail re Request for Reappointment for Craig Freeden to AELS Board	Deliberative Process/Executive
01/24/08	D. Ogg	F. Bailey, GOV	9:21 am *E-mail re Education	Deliberative Process/Executive
02/01/08	D. Ogg	F. Bailey, GOV	8:32 am *E-mail re Education	Deliberative Process/Executive
02/01/08	S. Leighow, GOV	F. Bailey, GOV	8:46 am *E-mail re Appointment of member to the state Board of Game	Deliberative Process/Executive
02/01/08	S. Parnell, GOV	S. Palin, GOV	7:41 am *E-mail re Andrew Halcro	Deliberative Process/Executive
02/01/08	S. Parnell, GOV	F. Bailey, GOV K. Perry, GOV T. Palin	8:22 am *E-mail re Andrew Halcro	Deliberative Process/Executive
02/01/08	S. Palin, GOV	F. Bailey, GOV K. Perry, GOV T. Palin	8:28 am *E-mail re Andrew Halcro	Deliberative Process/Executive
02/01/08	S. Palin, GOV	F. Bailey, GOV K. Perry, GOV T. Palin	8:30 am *E-mail re Andrew Halcro	Deliberative Process/Executive
02/01/08	I. Frye, GOV	S. Palin, GOV F. Bailey, GOV K. Perry, GOV T. Palin	8:42 am *E-mail re Andrew Halcro	Deliberative Process/Executive
02/01/08	S. Palin, GOV	I. Frye, GOV K. Perry, GOV F. Bailey, GOV T. Palin	10:10 am *E-mail re Andrew Halcro	Deliberative Process/Executive
02/01/08	I. Frye, GOV	S. Palin, GOV F. Bailey, GOV K. Perry, GOV T. Palin	10:23 am *E-mail re Andrew Halcro	Deliberative Process/Executive

ADVICE FROM THE FIELD

PRODUCING METADATA IN E-DISCOVERY—WHAT YOU NEED TO KNOW
(Continued from Chapter 4)
By Leonard Deutchman and Brian Wolfinger

. . . LEGAL ISSUES

Now that we have reviewed the technical issues in gathering and producing metadata, we will review legal issues arising from metadata requests and production. By understanding the technical and legal issues regarding metadata, you can diminish the occasions upon which you will have to produce metadata and insure that when it is produced it is done so properly.

PRESERVATION

Since gathering untrustworthy discovery leads only to producing untrustworthy metadata, the initial question is how and when Electronically Stored Information ("ESI") must be preserved. Rule 37(1) governs the preservation of ESI, and it is very confusing. On the one hand, the Rule prohibits a court from sanctioning a party for failing to preserve ESI "lost as a result of the good-faith, routine operation of an electronic information system," and the Committee Note and Advisory Committee Report acknowledge that metadata falls within this category. Thus, it would seem metadata lost as a result of automatic computer functions (as opposed to a user's conscious decision to remove it) is permitted.

However, the Committee Note goes to great length to emphasize that when ESI is destroyed after the duty to preserve potential discovery information is triggered, that is not considered "good faith." The duty to preserve can be triggered by receiving a request for preservation from the requesting party, but it can also arise from events themselves (e.g., an oil spill or a fired employee who is escorted out of the building screaming, "You'll be hearing from my lawyer"). The practice point for the requesting party is to render formal notification as soon as possible, and for the requesting party not to ignore events that would lead a reasonable person to recognize that litigation could ensue.

REQUESTS

Rule 34(a) allows a requesting party to request ESI in discovery, and Rule 34(b) allows the requesting party to request the form of discovery and the responding party to object. Rule 26(f) requires that the parties confer to resolve disputes, and unresolved objections go before the court at the pretrial conference under Rule 16(b). Two consequences pertaining to metadata arise from these Rules changes. The first is that the requesting party must specifically request metadata. There are some circumstances, such as in Williams v. Sprint, supra, where the nature of the request presumes a request for metadata. In Williams, plaintiffs claimed that spreadsheets had been revised to conceal age discrimination and sought comments, deletions and other metadata regarding prior iterations of the spreadsheets; the court held that the metadata sought was relevant to the important issue of intent and should be produced. Williams, however, is the exception. Far more common is Wyeth v. Impax Labs, Inc., 2006 U.S. Dist. LEXIS 79761 (D.DE. 10/26/2006), where the court held that metadata was properly not produced where it had not been requested. The court reasoned that there was a general presumption that metadata need not be produced, which presumption was not rebutted either by a general argument for production or the demonstration of "a particularized need for the metadata." So, beware that metadata need not be produced if it is not requested or if the requesting party cannot meet an objection by demonstrating a particularized need for it.

FORM OF PRODUCTION

Wyeth, in addition, also illustrates the second consequence of the Rules changes to requests for metadata: if the requesting party does not request ESI production in the right form, they lose their opportunity to view metadata. In Wyeth, the requesting party did not request a specific form of production, and the producing party produced in TIFF which, as we discussed, does not allow access to metadata. Rule 34(b) states that when no form of production is specified by the requesting party, the producing party may produce in the form in which the ESI is normally kept or in any reasonable form, which includes TIFFs. The practice point for requesting parties, then, is to request the form of production that gives you what you want, while the practice point for responding parties is that the form requested, or not requested, will dictate what you have to produce.

(Continued)

UNDUE BURDEN OR COST

Even assuming that a requesting party has made the proper request for and shown a particularized need to inspect metadata, that request is still subject to the objection under Rule 26(b)(2)(B) that such information is not "reasonably accessible due to undue burden or cost," and so seek either not to produce the metadata or to shift the cost of production to the requesting party. The usually sought metadata is generally provided as part of routine e-discovery production. However, if Track Changes, deleted materials, comments and other less common metadata are sought, the producing party must review such metadata for privilege, which will add greatly to the cost of production.

Moreover, after review, the producing party can choose either to produce the files in TIFF with a link to the file in its native format, which would allow the requesting party to see all metadata or, much more commonly, to TIFF such metadata and redact what it deems to be privileged. Linking the TIFFed image to a file in native form adds a field to and increases the complexity of the database, which will increase cost; as well, if you choose to have a vendor host the data, where vendors charge by the gigabyte of hosted data, adding the native files to the data set will drastically increase the cost of hosting. If you choose to TIFF the metadata, that choice will also substantially increase the cost of production. The producing party should be aware of these costs when responding to discovery requests and, where appropriate, seek relief under Rule 26.

CONCLUSION

A Lit Support Professional who understands the importance of how ESI is preserved, gathered and produced, and the legal issues and requirements of each step of EDD production, will be in the best position to "get all the metadata." He or she will know what can and must be produced, how to shape and respond to production requests, and how to comply and discharge the firm's duty to represent its client consistent with the recent Federal Rules changes and emerging case law.

Note: The first part of this article appears in Chapter 4.

About the Author: Leonard Deutchman, Esquire is General Counsel and Managing Partner, and Brian Wolfinger, CIFI is Vice President of Electronic Discovery and Forensic Services LegisDiscovery, LLC, a firm based in Fort Washington, PA and McLean, VA that specializes in electronic digital discovery and digital forensics. You may contact them at ldeutchman@legisdiscovery.com and bwolfinger@legisdiscovery.com.

Source: Originally published in *Litigation Support Today* May 2007.

CHAIN OF CUSTODY

Chain of custody
Steps taken to ensure that evidence is properly collected, preserved, and that the possession of the evidence is properly documented and accounted for at all steps in the processing, pretrial, and trial phases.

Many people who watch the current crime and forensic television shows know the term **chain of custody** and have some idea of what it means. In the criminal case it starts with the use of paper or plastic bags for the collection and storage of evidence. Steps are taken to ensure that evidence is properly collected, preserved, and the possession of the evidence is properly documented and accounted for at all steps in the processing, pretrial, and trial phases. The point is generally made that any failure to follow a prescribed protocol can result in the evidence lacking credibility at the time of trial. The same may be said for electronic evidence. Computer sources such as hard disk drives and other storage media and the electronic documents they contain must be properly handled, accessed, and preserved to ensure the reliability of the electronic files. Every time an electronic file is opened or accessed the metadata (file information or history) changes electronically to reflect that information unless proper steps are taken to ensure it is not changed. For example, each time you open a word document on your computer and then save it, even if no changes are made in the content of the document, the metadata such as the date of last access changes to reflect the latest date of access. If the original words and the original date of creation are important to a case, the original version must be preserved to avoid changes of any type in the underlying metadata. Where the physical storage devices are critical the same procedures including the use of sealed evidence bags, such as that shown in Exhibit 13.5, may be used. In

Exhibit 13.5 Evidence bag sample

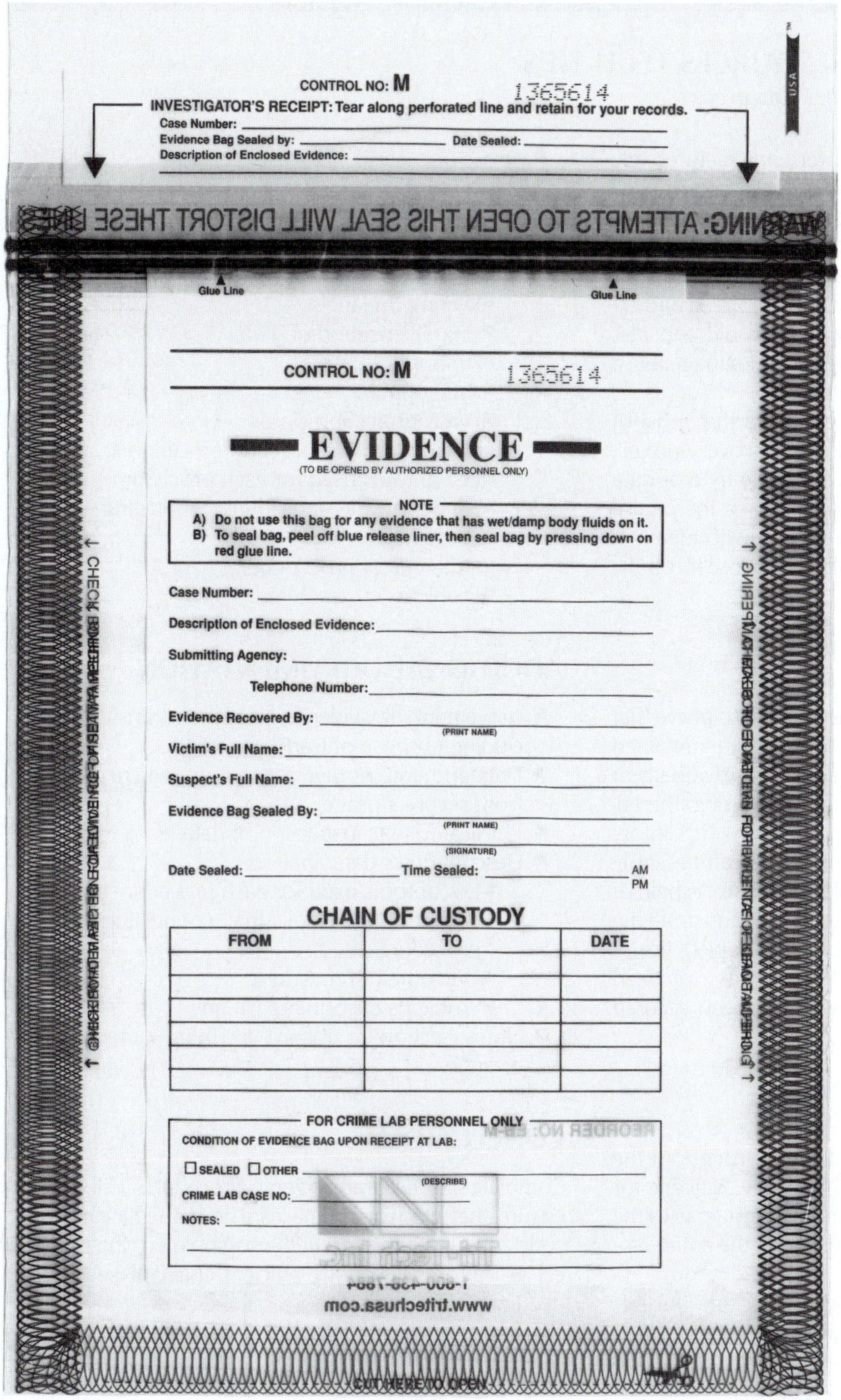
CONTROL NO: M 1365614

INVESTIGATOR'S RECEIPT: Tear along perforated line and retain for your records.

Case Number: ____

Evidence Bag Sealed by: ____ Date Sealed: ____

Description of Enclosed Evidence: ____

WARNING: ATTEMPTS TO OPEN THIS SEAL WILL DISTORT THESE LINES

Glue Line Glue Line

CONTROL NO: M 1365614

EVIDENCE

(TO BE OPENED BY AUTHORIZED PERSONNEL ONLY)

NOTE

A) Do not use this bag for any evidence that has wet/damp body fluids on it.

B) To seal bag, peel off blue release liner, then seal bag by pressing down on red glue line.

Case Number: ____

Description of Enclosed Evidence: ____

Submitting Agency: ____

Telephone Number: ____

Evidence Recovered By: ____ (PRINT NAME)

Victim's Full Name: ____

Suspect's Full Name: ____

Evidence Bag Sealed By: ____ (PRINT NAME) ____ (SIGNATURE)

Date Sealed: ____ Time Sealed: ____ AM PM

CHAIN OF CUSTODY

FROM	TO	DATE

FOR CRIME LAB PERSONNEL ONLY

CONDITION OF EVIDENCE BAG UPON RECEIPT AT LAB:

☐ SEALED ☐ OTHER ____ (DESCRIBE)

CRIME LAB CASE NO: ____

NOTES: ____

CUT HERE TO OPEN

Source: Courtesy of Tri-Tech, Inc., *www.tritechusa.com.*

this way a chain of custody is maintained in case the original must be accessed to prove no changes have occurred. If a claim is made of spoliation, that forensic examination is properly conducted.

ADVICE FROM THE FIELD

LEXISNEXIS CLIENT RESOURCES TECH TIPS
Preserving Chain of Custody in E-Discovery

As the field of electronic discovery has matured, attorneys have enjoyed the benefits of electronic document review. They realize that the actual discovery and review processes have not changed—only the tools and the storage media are different. Review teams have become accustomed to the speed and efficiency of electronic discovery and would consider even a small-sized document review unmanageable if forced to use paper review methods.

Veteran review teams have learned that most of what it takes to make an electronic discovery project successful must happen before a single byte of data is gathered. This article discusses one of the crucial components of a discovery project: how to maintain a chain of custody log for all data gathered throughout the life of the case.

PURPOSE

The purpose of a chain of custody log is to prove that the integrity of the evidence has been maintained from seizure through production in court. Chain of custody logs document how the data was gathered, analyzed, and preserved for production. This information is important, as electronic data can be easily altered if proper precautions are not taken. A chain of custody log for electronic data must demonstrate the following: the data has been properly copied, transported, and stored; the information has not been altered in any way; and all media has been secured throughout the process.

PROCEDURES

Documentation must be maintained throughout the life of the evidence and must be readily available for review at any time. Every instance of contact with the data must be documented throughout the entire discovery process.

A chain of custody log should include the following items in the documentation:

INITIAL DATA COLLECTION

- Name of individual who received the evidence
- Date, time and place of collection or receipt

- Name of custodian
- Description of data obtained, including media-specific information:
  - Media type, standard and manufacturer
  - Serial numbers and/or volume names
  - Writing on labels
  - Characterization of data
  - Amount of data
  - Type of data
  - Write-protection status
- Description of data collection procedures
  - List of tools used for each procedure
  - Name of the individual conducting each procedure
  - Outcome of procedures
  - Problems encountered, if any

ADDITIONAL DOCUMENTATION

- Movement of evidence (evidence transfer), including purpose of transfer
- Date and time of media check-in and check-out from secure storage
- Physical (visual) inspection of data
- Description of data analysis
  - List of tools used for each procedure
  - Name of the individual conducting each procedure
  - Outcome of procedure
  - Problems encountered, if any
- Notes section to record anything out of the ordinary

CONCLUSION

Complete and accurate logging procedures will help ensure that electronic data can be authenticated in court. A little extra effort at the beginning of the project will afford a smooth, efficient chain of custody documentation process.

RULE 30 (b) DEPOSITION

Depositions have historically allowed parties the out-of-court opportunity to spontaneously question parties and witnesses, under oath, without the limitation of carefully prepared written answers to interrogatories. Depositions are, within the confines of court rules and procedures, opportunities to ask open-ended questions, obtain spontaneous responses, and follow up with additional questions. The costs of taking depositions can be significant. In addition to the cost for counsel and their assistants, there is a cost for the court reporter to transcribe the testimony. In videotaped depositions this may include a court reporter and one or more videographers or technicians, and in some cases the cost of videoconferencing connections.

Deposing the correct person with the needed information is important. As stated in the *Heartland Surgical* case, "For a Rule 30(b)(6) deposition to operate effectively, the deposing party must designate the areas of inquiry with reasonable particularity, and the corporation must designate and adequately prepare witnesses to address these matters. If the rule is to promote effective discovery regarding corporations the spokesperson must be informed."

Failure to properly present a properly responsive witness for a company who can answer the questions about the company electronic filing systems can result in sanctions for the costs incurred by the requesting party. In cases where electronically stored documents are involved, the proper person may be a technical person and not necessarily the traditional custodian of documents, which in more traditional paper-based document cases might be an office manager.

 IN THE WORDS OF THE COURT . . .

HEARTLAND SURGICAL SPECIALTY HOSPITAL, LLC, Plaintiff, v. MIDWEST DIVISION, INC. d/b/a HCA MIDWEST DIVISION, et al., Defendants.
Case No. 05-2164-MLB-DWB
UNITED STATES DISTRICT COURT FOR THE DISTRICT OF KANSAS
2007 U.S. Dist. LEXIS 26552
April 9, 2007, Decided
April 9, 2007, Filed

OPINION BY: Donald W. Bostwick

Memorandum and Order

Before the Court is Defendants' Joint Motion to Compel Heartland Surgical Specialty Hospital LLC ("Heartland") to Produce a Rule 30(b)(6) Witness with Knowledge of Its Production of Documents and Data. . . .

Discussion

The procedure for taking an oral deposition of an organizational entity is governed by FED. R. CIV. P. 30(b)(6):

A party may in the party's notice . . . name as the deponent a[n] . . . association . . . and describe with reasonable particularity the matters on which [*10] examination is requested. In that event, the organization so named shall designate one or more officers, directors, or managing agents, or other persons who consent to testify on its behalf, and may set forth, for each person designated, the matters on which the person will testify. . . . The persons so designated shall testify as to matters known or reasonably available to the organization. . . .

. . . Judge Rushfelt has set out the general guidelines with respect to Rule 30(b)(6) depositions:

For a Rule 30(b)(6) deposition to operate effectively, the deposing party must designate the areas of inquiry with reasonable particularity, and the corporation must designate and adequately prepare witnesses to address these matters. If the rule is to promote effective discovery regarding corporations the spokesperson must be informed. A notice of deposition made pursuant to Rule 30(b)(6) requires the corporation [*13] to produce one or more officers to testify with respect to matters set out in the deposition notice or subpoena. A party need only designate, with reasonable particularity, the topics for examination. The corporation then must not only produce such number of persons as will satisfy the request, but more importantly, prepare them so that they may give complete, knowledgeable and binding answers on behalf of the corporation . . .

Rule 30(b)(6) implicitly requires the designated representative to review all matters known or reasonably available to it in preparation for the Rule 30(b)(6) deposition. This interpretation is necessary in order to make the deposition a meaningful one and to prevent the sandbagging of an opponent by conducting a half-hearted inquiry before the deposition but a thorough and vigorous one before the trial. This would totally defeat the purpose of the discovery process. The Court understands that preparing for a Rule 30(b)(6) deposition can be burdensome. However, this is merely the result of the concomitant obligation from the privilege of being able to use the corporate (or other organizational) form in order to conduct business. A party does not fulfill [*14] its obligations at the Rule 30(b)(6) deposition by stating it has no knowledge or position with respect to a set of facts or area of inquiry within its knowledge or reasonably available. . . .

SUMMARY

CHAPTER 13
ELECTRONIC DISCOVERY—RULES AND PROCEDURES

Introduction To E-Discovery Procedures	The Federal Rules of Civil Procedure (FRCP), effective December 2006, created a sudden interest and concern in some segments of the legal community.
	Lawyers and paralegals are concerned about their responsibilities and how to advise clients of the impact of the rules on business practices like retention policies of electronic data.
	Litigation support and information technology (IT) staffs for law firms are concerned about making available the needed computer and technology resources.

Emerging Case Law and Court Rules	Federal Rules of Civil Procedure provide a framework for requesting and satisfying requests for documents in electronic format. As a relatively new area of procedure there are few cases to look to for guidance.
Spoliation of Evidence	Spoliation is "the destruction or significant alteration of evidence or the failure to preserve property." In the electronic world it may be the deleting of electronically stored documents on a computer or the erasing of the backup tapes of e-mails and documents.
Preservation	If no litigation is contemplated or is pending, there is some support for the position that if a regular destruction policy is in place the company may destroy the files safely.
Litigation Hold	Once a case is filed or pending, the duty exists to preserve evidence.
Protecting Confidential or Privileged Materials	The attorney has an obligation to preserve the confidences of clients. It may not always be possible, within the limited time frames required for compliance, to check every document before handing them over to opposing counsel. The new rules provide for a "claw back" provision as part of the discovery plan. A "claw back" provision is under FRCP Rule 16 (6) "any agreements the parties reach for asserting claims of privilege or of protection as trial-preparation material after production;" State courts are still split in their approaches from those courts barring its use, to the courts allowing it as if the disclosure were intentional. The use of the claw back agreement alone does not relieve attorneys of their obligations regarding confidential client information.
Privilege in Electronic Discovery	Withholding privileged material in electronic form is not a simple matter. With potentially thousands or more documents it is not always possible to review every document and avoid inadvertent disclosure.
Claim of Privilege	Privilege is not automatically invoked. The party claiming the privilege must make the claim. Federal Rules of Civil Procedure Rule 26 (5) (A)(B) provides a procedure for claiming the privilege.
Privilege Log	A list of documents claimed to contain privileged material.
Chain of Custody	A protocol for handling evidence to ensure its integrity and reliability at the time of trial.
Rule 30 (b) Deposition	A deposition of a person from an organization who has knowledge of the production and data storage.

KEY TERMINOLOGY

CONCEPT REVIEW QUESTIONS AND EXERCISES

1. Test your knowledge and comprehension of the topics in this chapter by completing the multiple-choice questions on the textbook Companion Website.
2. Test your knowledge and comprehension of the topics in this chapter by completing the True-False questions on the textbook Companion Website.
3. What is the impact of the new Federal Rules of Civil Procedure on the procedural practice of law?
4. Where can the litigation team look for guidance on the procedure for trying cases involving electronic documentation?
5. What is discoverable under the Federal Rules?
6. Define spoliation. Give examples of spoliation.
7. What is the duty to preserve documents?
8. Has the introduction of electronically stored documents changed the duty to preserve documents?
9. Explain what some of the emerging issues are in electronic discovery.
10. What is the legal team's duty to preserve client confidences?
11. How is the claim of privilege made?
12. What is the purpose of a privilege log?
13. How important is maintaining a chain of custody in a civil case?
14. What are the judicial views on inadvertent disclosure of privileged material?
15. Why is it important to have the correct person available for a Rule 30 (b) deposition?
16. What are the possible sanctions for failure to produce the correct witness for a Rule 30(b) deposition?
17. What are the possible costs associated with electronic discovery?
18. What are the ethical issues in protecting confidential or privileged information in an age of electronic documents?
19. What is meant by a claw back provision in a discovery plan? How important is it ethically?
20. May a firm or client regularly destroy files and records? Explain fully.
21. Does an attorney have a duty to learn about the issues in e-discovery?

INTERNET EXERCISES

1. Use the Internet to locate a current version of the Federal Rules of Civil Procedure, Rules 16, 26, 33, 34, 37, and 45.
2. Locate and download a current case on privilege.
3. Locate a case on privilege logs under the new Federal Rules.

PORTFOLIO ASSIGNMENT

Prepare a protocol for the litigation team to follow in order to preserve the chain of custody of electronic data.

SCENARIO CASE STUDY

Use the opening scenario for this chapter to answer the following questions. The setting is a paralegal and attorney discussing pending litigation in which maintenance and repair record evidence may be critical to the case.

1. Prepare a motion that might be used if it is found that the opposing side has not preserved vital evidence after notice of the lawsuit.
2. Prepare a discovery plan proposal for use at the meet and confer.
3. Prepare a memo outlining the potential sanctions that can be requested from the judge in the intitial meeting with the court if it is decided that the opposing party has not honored all the mandatory and other discovery requests.
4. Prepare a memo from the IT staff to the trial team explaining what issues they should be aware of and suggestions for obtaining and protecting the needed data in the meet and confer.

CONTINUING CASES AND EXERCISES

1. Prepare a protocol for the litigation team to use in reviewing documents for a claim of privilege for the accident case in Appendix 1.

2. As defense counsel, who would be on a list for expert and factual witness that you would call at trial? What other mandatory disclosures must be made under the Federal Rules?

VIDEO SCENARIO: SCHEDULING CONFERENCE

The trial attorneys are meeting with the Judge assigned to the case in a scheduling conference. Significant discovery issues are raised by both sides and a request for sanctions. The judge mentions violation of the hold order as a reason for granting sanctions.

Go to the Companion Website, select Chapter 13 from the pull down menu, and watch this video.

1. Is the granting of sanctions a real threat?
2. What would be the impact of a negative inference instruction to the jury?
3. How important is a "litigation hold" under the Federal Rules of Civil Procedure?

Chapter 14 Digital Resources at www.prenhall.com/goldman

- Author Video Introduction
- Case Study Video
- Comprehension Quizzes and Glossary
- Video Interview: Working with I.T. with Charlotte Riser Harris

Litigation Support

OPENING SCENARIO

The senior attorney on the second floor of the office building had been a big help in advising attorneys Owen Mason and Ariel Marshall, based on his years of experience as a lawyer, and frequently was found in their coffee room telling war stories. He rarely tried any cases, at least not in the past ten years.

He approached Caitlin and Owen to personally request Caitlin's help with a case that had been filed in federal court. He had just received a discovery request involving Product Guild Limited, one of his biggest international clients. PGL, as everyone called them, was a paperless organization that stored everything electronically. He admitted to her he had no idea how to handle a case like this where there was a request for all the e-mails from the client for the past two years and all the corporate correspondence and a time deadline imposed by the rules of court. He asked if Caitlin could work for him as a part-time, independent paralegal and prepare a plan and e-mail it to him while he was out of the country on business for the next few weeks.

She suspected he had asked because it would involve working with the same outside IT support staff company they used, and as he had said many times, "I don't seem to speak their language." The last time he had talked to them they had said something about a "picnic," a geek term she knew was not a compliment, which referred to the problem being "in the chair," not "in the computer." She knew there would be hundreds of thousands of documents, and she was not sure how they could identify, gather, and review them all and still meet the deadline. She was also concerned about the costs. The case involved a simple warranty claim, but the attorney suspected that it was a fishing expedition to obtain privileged contents of the legal opinions that he had provided electronically to PGL, for which normally a nondisclosure agreement would be required in order to protect PGL's confidential trade secrets and process material.

LEARNING OBJECTIVES

After studying this chapter you should be able to:

1. Explain the issues in processing documents as part of the discovery process.

2. Explain the e-discovery process and the mechanics of document processing.

3. Explain what metadata is and how it impacts e-document disclosure.

4. Describe the use of software for managing documents in litigation.

5. Explain the ethical issues in document delivery.

INTRODUCTION TO LITIGATION SUPPORT

As the number of documents in litigation has increased, the use of technology has become essential for the administration of files in case management. Many file documents are still in paper form, but increasingly the documents are in electronic form located on computers and electronic backup file media, such as tape, CDs, DVDs, and similar electronic storage devices. The discover process in theory is simple; identify the potential evidence, organize it, verify it, and review it. The reality is not as simple. As more documents are created and kept in electronic format, manual processing of documents in litigation is not realistic. Because of the skills necessary in electronic processing of discovery a new and growing support group has been created, litigation support. Litigation support personnel are those who possess not only the legal skills, such as paralegals and lawyers, but also the technology skills in the use of litigation support software and understand the technical aspects of computer storage and retrieval. Litigation support software, such as Summation and Concordance, provide specialty application software programs for managing electronically stored documents. Among the features of these software programs is the ability to search among potentially millions of pages to find relevant documents quickly. As with all technology, litigation support technology in the form of software changes frequently. New versions are a constant factor of litigation support life. Methods and approaches change almost as often. Only a few years ago documents were routinely sent out to a vendor for processing from scanning and coding to production for delivery to opposing counsel and for use at trial. Today, an increase in the amount of electronic documents and a decrease in the need to process paper allow for in-house processing of many cases. With advances in interconnectivity and high-speed access, the availability of data repositories is coming into wider use. With data repositories, access is permitted by Internet access to anyone with authority anywhere an Internet connection can be found. For the novice in the field, learning a particular litigation support tool may not be as important as fully understanding the process and the available tools. Even in the same law firms, different solutions may be used, for which training is available on the job to ensure current knowledge of the particular solution selected.

Launched on May 24, 2006, the EDRM Metrics project is intended to provide a standard approach and a generally accepted language for measuring the full range of electronic discovery activities, as shown in Exhibit 14.1.

Exhibit 14.1 Identification–steps in determining scope of responsive data from EDRM

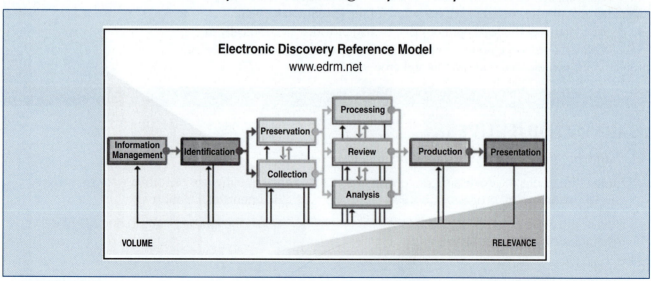

Exhibit 14.1 Continued

Contents

Additional Data Sources

Beyond the servers in the organization, there are many other devices and options that provide the ability to store active data. Examples include:

Ability to store files/e-mail archives on local workstations or laptop hard drives;
A Storage Area Network (SAN) where data from multiple servers is centrally stored;
Ability to store information on removable media (floppies, CD-Roms, DVDs, zip drives, thumb drives, etc.);
Digital voice mail stores and/or VOIP(voice over internet protocol) stores. Personal Digital Assistants (Palm Pilot, Blackberry, etc.);
Information on company intranet/extranet and the ability to export from these sources;
Employee use of their home computers for business matters and the storage of business information on them;
Any information cached in the e-mail gateway;
Do users cell phones cache business data such as text messages or e-mails;
Does the company phone switch maintain relevant records;
Failed drives from which a forensic recovery might be possible;
Former employee computers prior to being recycled. Are any PC's currently pending recycling; and
Any collaborative systems (e.g. Groove Technologies, eRoom, SharePoint) that might contain relevant data.

Determining Whether Forensic Data Capture Will be Needed

Have any types of activities occurred that would require the forensic copying of hard drives and servers? Have files been deleted or written over that may be potentially relevant? Deleted files generally require a burden of proof that documents have not been produced (see Zubalake). Some states have restrictions on whether deleted files come into play (e.g. TxCivR 196.4). When deleted files become involved, its imperative that a forensic bit by bit/sector by sector duplicate, otherwise known as a forensic image, be made. A forensic image preserves the information as it existed at the time of the acquisition. Spoliation of the data is always a major concern when hard drive data is involved in litigation. Data is routinely overwritten and purged from hard drives as part of their standard operating procedures. Potentially hundreds of files or residual fragments of files that may be relevant, such as e-mail, word processing documents, Internet usage files, and spreadsheets are constantly being deleted from an active computer. Preserving the data in a forensically sound manner by creating a forensic image makes an unalterable snapshot of the data, including potentially recoverable deleted information, partial instant message conversations, metadata, Internet e-mail, swap files and temporary files.

Forensic processes can be discussed at the meet and confer to determine their necessity (and expense) to the project.

Source: EDRM at http://edrm.net

REVIEWING ELECTRONIC DOCUMENTS

Not every lawsuit will require the use of all of the tools available for electronic discovery. Many cases may involve limited numbers of documents, in paper and electronic form. Knowing what documents may be in electronic form and the issues of securing them may be enough. For example, it may be enough to know the different formats used when requesting medical records for a case from a doctor's office that maintains records in a paperless form. In the uncomplicated case, just asking for the files in a PDF format may be enough, or agreeing to the delivery on a DVD in the original MS Word format (native format) knowing this might require a copy of MS Word to view them or with a PDF viewer like Adobe Reader.

In more complex cases, like one involving a concern that records may have been intentionally erased or "lost," the costs of the use of the electronic discovery tools may be an issue in whether to accept or pursue a case. Corporate clients will frequently be sophisticated enough to ask for a discovery budget as part of a cost-benefit analysis. Clients less knowledgeable or experienced in litigation need to be properly advised as to the costs associated with the potential discovery issues. It will frequently be the role of the paralegal to determine what outside discovery experts and vendors, like forensic experts, will charge. Clients do not like surprises when it comes to the costs that they will be expected to pay. Good client relationship management requires a discussion of the discovery budget.

One of the biggest costs in electronic discovery is incurred in reviewing the electronic material to find relevant items, and to identify privileged, confidential, or protected documents. In small cases, making copies of the files using the original programs used to create the files, like the process for making a backup copy, may be the easiest method for delivery. The client just copies and delivers the files by copying them from the computer onto a portable storage device, like a CD, DVD, or tape. File review is completed by using a program like the one used to create the file, such as Word, Excel, or Access, and viewing the material on a computer screen or printing it out.

When documents are delivered in a number of different formats, such as word processor, database, or spreadsheet formats, review usually requires multiple programs to view the originals. When the number of documents is in the thousands or tens of thousands, this process can be very time consuming. One solution is to convert the documents into a common format that may be searched and indexed using one program to view all documents.

ELECTRONIC DISCOVERY—THE PROCESS

Electronic or e-discovery should be thought of as a process and not a single event, see the EDRM Chart in Exhibit 14.1. The initial step in the e-discovery process is determining what documents are wanted, who has those documents, what format the documents are in, the value of those documents, and the potential costs of retrieving them. As discussed in the *JICARILLA APACHE NATION v. U.S.* case (see Words of the Court), many different types of documents are considered a "record" by the court and may be part of the discovery request. A properly prepared electronic document request, based on the federal or local rules, can then be prepared.

After obtaining the documents, decisions must be made about how to process the material supplied. Nearly all business documents will be computer generated and stored. These will be in many formats: e-mails, spreadsheets, word processing documents, database documents, graphic images, and a number of electronic file

IN THE WORDS OF THE COURT ...

JICARILLA APACHE NATION v. U.S., (Fed.Cl. 2004)
JICARILLA APACHE NATION, formerly JICARILLA APACHE TRIBE,
Plaintiff, v. THE UNITED STATES, Defendant.
No. 02-25L.
United States Court of Federal Claims.
Filed: April 19, 2004

a. "Record" Defined
As used in this Order, "record" means any book, bill, calendar, chart, check, compilation, computation, computer or network activity log, correspondence, data, database, diagram, diary, document, draft, drawing, e-mail, file, folder, film, graph, graphic presentation, image, index, inventory, invoice, jotting, journal, ledger, machine readable material, map, memo, metadata, minutes, note, order, paper, photograph, printout, recording, report, spreadsheet, statement, summary, telephone message record or log, transcript, video, voicemail, voucher, webpage, work paper, writing, or worksheet, or any other item or group of documentary material or information, regardless of physical or electronic format or characteristic, and any information therein, and copies, notes, and recordings thereof.

format variations within each category. The good news is that electronic files, as opposed to paper documents, lend themselves to electronic or computer processing.

The response to the discovery request may be hundreds, thousands, or millions of individual electronic documents, some or most of which have little value in the litigation. **Filtering** is the process used to scan or search the documents for relevant terms in an attempt to narrow the focus, such as a filter to eliminate documents created before or after a certain date. Another step in the process is eliminating duplicates. **De-duplication,** or **de-duping,** is the term used to describe the process of electronically eliminating the duplicates of the same document. For example, you need only one copy, not thousands, of the same e-mail that was sent to the entire corporate mail list. The same is true for the copy (cc) of the letter sent to many recipients, unless you are trying to show knowledge or republication or similar issues.

Obtaining Documents via Paper Discovery

Not all documents are in electronic form. For instance, many public agencies, like police and fire departments, still file paper-based reports. Another example is litigation that involves a time frame when documents were not prepared electronically. These may still involve a large volume of material that must be processed by the legal team. Converting them to electronic forms may be a solution.

CONVERTING DOCUMENTS

The typical response to a paper document request is the delivery of a photocopy of the requested items. As with electronic discovery, the number of documents can be in the thousands or even millions (for example, a class action suit involving tobacco companies). Before the computer era, these documents had to be reviewed manually, which provided work for many law students and paralegals. Computer

Filtering
The process used to scan or search the documents for relevant terms in an attempt to narrow the focus, such as a filter to eliminate documents created before or after a certain date.

De-Duplication (De-Duping)
The process of comparing electronic records based on their characteristics and removing duplicate records from the data set.

Native File Format

Electronic documents have an associated file structure defined by the original creating application. This file structure is referred to as the "native format" of the document. Because viewing or searching documents in the native format may require the original application (e.g., viewing a Microsoft Word document may require the Microsoft Word application), documents are often converted to a standard file format (e.g., TIFF) as part of electronic document processing.

TIFF File Format

Short for tagged image file format. It is one of the most widely used formats for storing images. TIFF graphics can be black and white, gray-scaled, or color.

PDF (Portable Document Format)

An Adobe technology for formatting documents so they can be viewed and printed using the Adobe Acrobat reader.

technology allows these paper documents to be converted into electronic files that may be processed like other electronic files. Typically the documents are copied or scanned and saved in some electronic file format.

File Formats for Electronic Documents

In the e-discovery phase of litigation, the terms you will hear most often are *native file*—meaning the document is saved in the same format in which it was created—and *PDF* and *TIFF*, which are the formats most frequently used in converting documents.

Native file format is the format used by a program to save the data produced by the program; for example, *.doc* for Microsoft Word or *.wpd* for WordPerfect.

"Delivery documents in native format" refers to delivering the files in the same format as created and saved originally.

TIFF is short for tagged image file format. It is one of the most widely used formats for storing images. TIFF graphics can be black and white, gray-scaled, or color. Files in TIFF format often end with a .tif extension.

PDF is short for portable document format. It was created by Adobe, who had previously invented the TIFF format.

ADVICE FROM THE FIELD

AUTOMATIC DOCUMENT CODING
By Lisa Rosen

Document coding has historically been the most expensive and time-intensive step of the entire process required for creating document production databases. On average, a coding professional can manually code approximately 20 documents (based on a five-page document) and 10 bibliographic fields per hour. In order to reduce the time and cost associated with manual coding, a movement began to send documents offshore to areas of cheap labor. However, many law firms and government agencies cannot or will not send their documents offshore for security reasons. The cost and time associated with manual document coding is significantly reduced with the use of document coding software, such as ALCoder, which allows the case team to focus efforts on the case at hand. The new federal rules pertaining to ESI (Electronically Stored Information) has created an increased awareness of the need for coding and the need for auto-coding. ESI or native files/emails are often processed and imported into existing databases such as CT Summation and LexisNexis Concordance. During the extraction process, metadata (or data about the data) is identified and populated into those databases for searching and sorting purposes. Many believe that the metadata is accurate or complete, when that is often not the case. The metadata reflects the "profile" of a document, not the bibliographic information contained within the document. ALCoder goes into the native files, emails and attachments and extracts the bibliographic information from the document, supplementing the metadata with accurate bibliographic information. The improvement in Optical Character Recognition (OCR) technology in quality and price (through the availability of off-the-shelf software) has resulted in OCR frequently replacing slower and often prohibitively expensive manual document coding. The problem with searching databases limited to OCR is that critical information such as document dates and authors are not able to be searched and sorted. For example, if the documents need to be assembled in chronological order, they must be coded. Automatic coding software, like ALCoder, solve the problem.

Source: Reprinted with permission. Lisa Rosen is President of Rosen Technology Resources, Inc. and may be contacted at lisa.rosen@rosentech.net or through the website at www.rosentech.net

DOCUMENT PROCESSING

Coding

Each document must be identified by certain characteristics to allow it to be effectively sorted, retrieved, and identified for further review. This process is known as coding. **Coding** is the process of capturing case-relevant information (e.g., author, date authored, date sent, recipient, date opened, etc.) from a paper document.

The most basic type of coding is **objective coding**, also referred to as bibliographic indexing. This includes the author, type of document, recipient, and date. Additional coding may include **subjective coding**, which identifies keywords within the document or other criteria not related to bibliographic information.

Obviously the manual coding of this information is time consuming and costly. As an attempt to reduce costs for coding, some companies offer outsourcing to services in foreign locations where the labor rates are less than in the United States. With modern scanning techniques and high-speed scanners, some companies provide **auto coding.** Auto coding is the electronic scanning and coding of documents by selected key terms and dates. In some cases the documents are first auto coded and then selected documents manually coded.

Redaction

In cases of documents containing privileged information, privileged material may be redacted. **Redaction** is the removal of confidential information, or at least that which is claimed to be confidential or material prepared for trial under the work product doctrine. With paper documents the process has usually been to use a black marker to block out the desired material before copying. With electronic documents the process is not as easy. It may include deletion of material or use of a program that electronically blacks out the material and then allows for a copy to be made either electronically or in hardcopy. Claims of improper redaction or non-delivery of documentation frequently result in motions to the court for orders to disclose. As discussed, the federal rules specifically address the process for the protection of this type of information.

Production Numbering

In a delivery of paper documents, in response to interrogatories, the pages were frequently numbered sequentially to aid in the review and identification in pleadings and at trial, plaintiff using a letter *P* before the document number, and the defense a *D*. The sequential numbering of documents was and still is referred to as **Bates production numbering**. Previously added to paper documents with a mechanical numbering device, computer document management programs sometimes have a feature to add the numbers to the documents.

Metadata

Every electronic document has *metadata*, which is simply information about the document. This information may include information about the location of the file, referred to as **resource or system metadata,** and **content or application metadata,** information about the content and author. The method used to create the electronic file can have an impact on the metadata delivered. As described in *WILLIAMS v. SPRINT/UNITED MANAGEMENT COMPANY* (see Words of the Court), if the document is delivered in its native format, the

WWW MINI EXERCISE

The full definition of TIFF can be found at http://www.webopedia.com/TERM/T/TIFF.htm

Coding
The process of capturing case-relevant information (e.g., author, date authored, date sent, recipient, date opened) from a document.

Objective Coding
Also referred to as bibliographic indexing. This includes the author, type of document, recipient, and date.

Subjective Coding
Identifies keywords within the document or other criteria not related to bibliographic information.

WWW MINI EXERCISE

For more information about coding, or to find a coding service company, go to http://www.compulit.com/services/coding/

Auto Coding
The electronic scanning and coding of documents by selected key terms and dates.

Redaction
The removal of confidential information, or at least that which is claimed to be confidential or material prepared for trial under the work product doctrine.

Bates Production Numbering
A tracking number assigned to each page of each document in the production set.

System (or Resource) Metadata
Data such as file names, size, and location.

Content (or Application) Metadata
Information about the contents of a document.

metadata is part of the document. However, if delivered in a copied format, such as TIFF, which is a document *image*, the hidden data or metadata cannot be seen. This may be an advantage or disadvantage depending on whether you are the sender or the recipient.

IN THE WORDS OF THE COURT …

WILLIAMS v. SPRINT/UNITED MANAGEMENT COMPANY,
(Kan. 2005)
SHIRLEY WILLIAMS et al., Plaintiffs, v. SPRINT/UNITED MANAGEMENT COMPANY, Defendant.
Civil Action No. 03–2200–JWL–DJW.
United States District Court, D. Kansas.
September 29, 2005

1. Emerging standards of electronic discovery with regard to metadata

a. What is metadata?

Before addressing whether Defendant was justified in removing the metadata from the Excel spreadsheets prior to producing them to Plaintiffs, a general discussion of metadata and its implications for electronic document production in discovery is instructive.

Metadata, commonly described as "data about data," is defined as "information describing the history, tracking, or management of an electronic document."

Appendix F to *The Sedona Guidelines: Best Practice Guidelines & Commentary for Managing Information & Records in the Electronic Age* defines metadata as "information about a particular data set which describes how, when and by whom it was collected, created, accessed, or modified and how it is formatted (including data demographics such as size, location, storage requirements and media information.)" Technical Appendix E to the *Sedona Guidelines* provides an extended description of metadata. It further defines metadata to include "all of the contextual, processing, and use information needed to identify and certify the scope, authenticity, and integrity of active or archival electronic information or records."

Some examples of metadata for electronic documents include: a file's name, a file's location (e.g., directory structure or pathname), file format or file type, file size, file dates (e.g., creation date, date of last data modification, date of last data access, and date of last metadata modification), and file permissions (e.g., who can read the data, who can write to it, who can run it). Some metadata, such as file dates and sizes, can easily be seen by users; other metadata can be hidden or embedded and unavailable to computer users who are not technically adept.

Most metadata is generally not visible when a document is printed or when the document is converted to an image file. Metadata can be altered intentionally or inadvertently and can be extracted when native files are converted to image files. Sometimes the metadata can be inaccurate, as when a form document reflects the author as the person who created the template but who did not draft the document. In addition, metadata can come from a variety of sources; it can be created automatically by a computer, supplied by a user, or inferred through a relationship to another document.

Appendix E to *The Sedona Guidelines* further explains the importance of metadata: Certain metadata is critical in information management and for ensuring effective retrieval and accountability in record-keeping. Metadata can assist in proving the authenticity of the content of electronic documents, as well as establish the context of the content. Metadata can also identify and exploit the structural relationships that exist between and within electronic documents, such as versions and drafts. Metadata allows organizations to track the many layers of rights and reproduction information that exist for records and their multiple versions. Metadata may also document other legal or security requirements that have been imposed on records; for example, privacy concerns, privileged communications or work product, or proprietary interests.

The Microsoft Office Online website lists several examples of metadata that may be stored in Microsoft Excel spreadsheets, as well as other Microsoft applications such as Word or PowerPoint: author name or initials, company or organization name, identification of computer or network server or hard disk where document is saved, names of previous document authors, document revisions and versions, hidden text or cells, template information, other file properties and summary information, non-visible portions or embedded objects, personalized views, and comments.

It is important to note that metadata varies with different applications. As a general rule of thumb, the more interactive the application, the more important the metadata is to understanding the application's output. At one end of the spectrum is a word processing application where the metadata is usually not critical to understanding the substance of the document. The information can be conveyed without the need for the metadata. At the other end of the spectrum is a database application where the database is a completely undifferentiated mass of tables of data. The metadata is the key to showing the relationships between the data; without such metadata, the tables of data would have little meaning. A spreadsheet application lies somewhere in the middle. While metadata is not as crucial to understanding a spreadsheet as it is to a database application, a spreadsheet's metadata may be necessary to understand the spreadsheet because the cells containing formulas, which arguably are metadata themselves, often display a value rather than the formula itself. To understand the spreadsheet, the user must be able to ascertain the formula within the cell.

Due to the hidden, or not readily visible, nature of metadata, commentators note that metadata created by any software application has the potential for inadvertent disclosure of confidential or privileged information in both litigation and non-litigation setting, which could give rise to an ethical violation. One method commonly recommended to avoid this inadvertent disclosure is to utilize software that removes metadata from electronic documents. The process of removing metadata is commonly called "scrubbing" the electronic documents. In a litigation setting, the issue arises of whether this can be done without either the agreement of the parties or the producing party providing notice through an objection or motion for protective order.

Scanning Documents

Paper documents may be scanned to convert them to an electronic form. The format into which they are saved may vary depending on the use and the purpose of the scanning process. Most scanners have a software program that allows a choice of format. One of the most popular graphic image scanning formats is the PDF

Exhibit 14.2 Considerations for scanning documents in-house versus using a service bureau

Consider Scanning In-House When:

- The case documents comprise a small quantity or are received piecemeal.

- The law firm owns scanning software and equipment.

- The firm can allocate internal personnel to scanning, coding, and/or loading.

- All coding (objective AND subjective) will be performed in-house.

- The majority of case documents are already in an image format, such as TIFF or PDF, and do not require scanning.

Consider Using a Service Bureau When:

- The case documents comprise a large quantity.

- The firm either:

  - Does not own scanning software and equipment or owns scanning software and equipment that are limited in capacity.

  - The firm does not have internal personnel to allocate for scanning, coding, and/or loading.

  - The firm wants objective coding (for example, document date, type, author, and so on) to be done prior to the firm's internal document review.

  - The majority (or all) of the case documents must be scanned and coded.

Source: User's Guide for Loading Documents and Other Data into Summation, p. 15. Reprinted with permission of CT Summation.

format, which permits easy portability and sharing of the resulting electronic file. Modern scanners in conjunction with the use of such software programs as Nuance PaperPort allow documents to be scanned and converted using optical character recognition (OCR) into a native format that can be processed as a word processing file. OCR is a technology used to create a full-text, searchable version of an image document. Using the full-text OCR document, you can search for words and phrases within its body.

Consideration for using a service Bureau or scanning in-house are shown in Exhibit 14.2

DUPLICATE DOCUMENT ISSUES

As previously discussed, one of the initial steps in processing electronic documents is the potential elimination of duplicate documents by the de-duplication process. The initial thought would be to ask, if all of the e-mails say the same thing, is it necessary to have all of the copies in the discovery material? Normally the answer might be no, probably one is enough. But what might still be needed are the names of the parties to whom it was sent. Consider the need to prove a branch manager was sending harassing or defamatory comments; the names of recipients of the

IN THE WORDS OF THE COURT . . .

WIGINTON v. CB RICHARD ELLIS, INC., (N.D.Ill. 2004)

AMY WIGINTON, KRISTINE MORAN, NORMA PLANK FETHLER, ANDREA COREY and OLIVIA KNAPP, individually and on behalf of all persons similarly situated, Plaintiffs, v. CB RICHARD ELLIS, INC., Defendant.

Case No. 02 C 6832.

United States District Court, N.D. Illinois, Eastern Division.

August 9, 2004

. . . Plaintiffs filed this class action complaint against CBRE alleging a nationwide pattern and practice of sexual harassment at the CBRE offices. As evidence of the hostile work environment prevalent at the offices of CBRE, Plaintiffs seek discovery of pornographic material that they claim was distributed electronically (i.e., via e-mail) and displayed on computers throughout the offices.

CBRE initially produced 94 monthly e-mail backup tapes from 11 offices. The backup tapes consist of the e-mails that existed on a given server at the time the backup is made. They are not a complete depiction of every e-mail that existed on the CBRE system during a month.

. . . At this point, we note that discussing documents in terms of numbers is somewhat inexact. For example, an e-mail containing a search term that exists in a user's outbox, and also exists in another user's inbox, counts as two hits, even though it is really one document. A document containing a search term that is sent from one user to another, and returned under the "reply with history" option available on CBRE's e-mail system counts as two hits. But, because of de-duplication, an e-mail that is present multiple times in one user's mailbox is not counted multiple times. So although talking about documents in terms of numbers is not entirely accurate, the search system was designed to get an idea of how frequently the documents containing search terms were being passed around by CBRE users within or between the offices. Because spam was eliminated, it means the picture does not present an entirely accurate view of any other pornographic e-mails that maybe have been available on the CBRE e-mail system, or how often users are opening such documents in view of other people. The numbers also do not reflect e-mails that were not captured on backup tapes.

---

messages and those to whom they had forwarded the same message would be important. The same situation may be true for invoices, letters, and similar documents. The metadata on each e-mail or document might in some cases be important, if there is a need to show changes, recipients, or similar information. See *WIGINTON v. CB RICHARD ELLIS, INC.,* for one court's view of e-mail metadata.

Preferred Document Formats

There is a range of opinion regarding which format is required or preferred. As the field of e-discovery advances, the current relative freedom to choose the format may be impacted by the rules of court or of governmental agencies who desire to standardize document format for ease of use or convenience.

Comparison of PDF and TIFF

The two formats competing for use as a common format for large-scale case use are the TIFF and PDF formats. The up-front cost to process from the native file format to TIFF or PDF is about the same. Many programs used to create the original documents, like WordPerfect and Word, have a built-in feature allowing files to be saved automatically as PDF files. In addition, most litigation support software programs, such as Summation and Concordance, support both TIFF and PDF formats. The advantage of conversion to either format is that the new files can be searched across the different file types and indexes prepared.

TIFF was developed in the 1980s as a format for scanning paper documents by Aldus and Microsoft Corp, and the specification was owned by Aldus, which in turn merged with Adobe Systems, Inc. Consequently, Adobe Systems now holds the copyright for the TIFF specification. Many lawyers latched onto this format and continue to prefer it. Adobe invented PDF in 1992 as a replacement for the TIFF format. Adobe has not supported any new activity for TIFF since then. PDF files have the advantage of being usable across many different platforms (computer systems) and software programs regardless of how they were originally created.

One of the differences between TIFF and PDF is the amount of memory required to store one document. Because of the built-in file compression in the PDF format, PDF files are normally about one-tenth the size of TIFF files. The actual file size will vary depending on which of the many compression methods is used in saving the TIFF file. If you have ever sent an e-mail with an attachment, consider the additional time it took to send a TIFF file instead of a PDF file of the same document.

Some attorneys prefer TIFF format because TIFF files:

- Cannot be altered.
- Can be redacted.
- Can be Bates numbered.
- Can be searched easily.

The disadvantage from the receiving party point of view is that hidden data or metadata cannot be seen.

According to Adobe, "Adobe PDF files look exactly like original documents and preserve source file information—text, drawings, 3D, full-color graphics, photos, and even business logic—regardless of the application used to create them." Adobe Acrobat Version 8 allows for redaction and Bates page numbering.

Both PDF and TIFF formats are generally preferred over any other because they lock the document into a format that cannot be changed easily, as opposed to the possible changes that could be made if saved as a Word or WordPerfect format file.

In summary, Exhibit 14.3 compares the two formats.

WWW MINI EXERCISE

More information on Adobe and Adobe Acrobat can be found at www.Adobe.com.

RESOURCES THAT SUPPORT E-DISCOVERY

Service Companies

In many cases a consultant, service bureau, or company may be retained to help in the electronic discovery process. There are many reasons for using an outside consultant—possibly a lack of in-house expertise or a workload that will not permit another case to be handled in-house. Some full-service companies offer a range of services from the basic, like scanning paper documents into electronic form, to complex, like forensic recovery and investigation of lost, destroyed, or missing

Exhibit 14.3 Comparison of PDF and TIFF format features

PDF Format	TIFF Format
Adobe invented PDF in 1992 and still supports it.	Adobe invented TIFF in the late 1980s and no longer supports it.
Locks the document into a format that cannot be easily changed.	Locks the document into a format that cannot be easily changed.
PDF documents are searchable.	TIFF documents are searchable.
Up-front costs of converting to PDF about the same as converting to TIFF.	Up-front costs of converting to TIFF about the same as converting to PDF.
Supported by most litigation support software.	Supported by most litigation support software.
Word and WordPerfect have built-in "Save to PDF format" features.	Word and WordPerfect do not have built-in features of saving to TIFF format, but saving to TIFF format is an easy process.
Memory required to save to PDF is about one-tenth of what is required for TIFF.	Memory required to save to TIFF is about ten times what is required for PDF.
Version 8 and above can be Bates numbered and can be redacted.	Can be Bates numbered and redacted.
Hidden data or metadata can be seen.	Hidden data or metadata cannot be seen.

files. In some cases, allowing a specialist to prepare and deliver the documents in a form for attorney review and use at trial may be a better allocation of resources and costs. This might include delivery in a format for use in a document management litigation program like Summation or Concordance.

Litigation Support Software

LexisNexis Concordance™ and CT Summation™ families of software are two of the most widely used software packages for electronic litigation support. These software programs provide the capability of searching and organizing electronic documents including transcripts and notes. Each provides a basic stand-alone version as well as networked versions and data repository services.

In theory the process is one of identifying and finding potential evidence, organizing it in a useful manner, and reviewing it for relevancy. In practice this may include converting documents from one form to another such as paper to electronic form or nonsearchable images to searchable text. It may also include reviewing vast quantities of documentation for privileged and confidential information.

In smaller cases all of this may occur in-house in the law firm. As cases become more complex and include multidistrict litigation or cooperation with other law firms, the litigation support function may be set up using a central data repository.

Centralized data repositories use a centralized site for the document databases which can be accessed over the Internet, allowing everyone access regardless of location.

As cases progress to the deposition and ultimately trial phases, litigation support software may be used for the management of transcripts. Transcripts may be searched using any number of criteria to find relevant passages, such as references to a person, place, or item. Exhibit 14.4 shows the CT Summation iBlaze search screen.

Exhibit 14.4 CT Summation iBlaze search screen

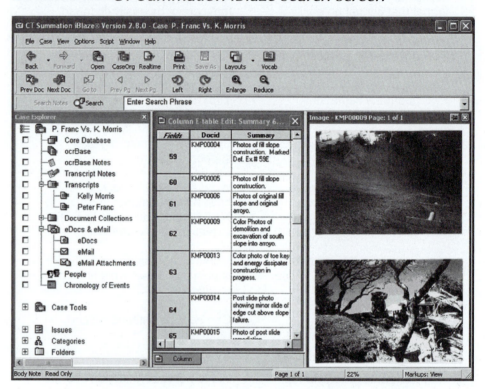

Exhibit 14.5 Concordance getting started guide

Concordance®

Benefits | Features | Ordering | Brochures | Case Studies | Our Partners

Getting Started Guide
Learn How to Use Concordance and Concordance Image — Without Leaving Your Desk

The Concordance team has put together an instructive Getting Started Guide to help you master Concordance 2007 and Concordance Image at your own pace. This easy to follow guide will walk you through the basics of using our award-winning software. Topics covered include:

1. Concordance Document Viewing
2. Searching
3. Case Organization
4. Managing Transcripts
5. Printing Reports
6. Concordance Image Document Viewing
7. Navigating
8. Redlines and Markups
9. Image Production
10. Printing Images

Download the Getting Started Guide. (Viewing this file requires Acrobat Reader®. Get a free download now.)

WWW MINI EXERCISE

Look at the Concordance Quick Help Guides at http://law.lexisnexis.com/concordance/quick-help-guides

Obtain a full copy of the Concordance Getting Started Guide at http://law.lexisnexis.com/concordance/getting-started-guide

Each of the major litigation software companies provides similar types of programs. As with all software they are constantly being updated to add new features and capability. At the basic level they allow stand-alone systems and at the higher end provide data repository services with remote secure access. These concepts are discussed in the following Advice from the Field. These software programs offer extensive training and help resources for the novice who wants to obtain an overview to the experienced users who want to learn the newest feature. Examples of the online help from Concordance are shown in Exhibits 14.5 and 14.6. A partial list of tutorials from CT Summation is shown in Exhibit 14.7.

WWW MINI EXERCISE

Obtain a tutorial from the Summation website at: http://www.summation .com/Support/tutorials .aspx

WWW MINI EXERCISE

To learn more about Concordance, go to http:// law.lexisnexis.com/ concordance

WWW MINI EXERCISE

For the latest information on Summation software, go to http://www .summation.com

Exhibit 14.6 Concordance quick help guides

Concordance®

Benefits | Features | Ordering | Brochures | Case Studies | Our Partners

Quick Help Guides

Quick Help Guides provide helpful instruction for completing common tasks in Concordance. Download these handy PDF documents here:

- Adding Menu Items
- Alias Fields
- Authority List
- Concatenating Databases
- Concordance 2007 Installation Guide
- Configuring IPRO View
- Creating a Replica Database
- Creating an Email Database
- Creating EDocs Database
- Embedded Punctuation
- Export to Delimited Text File
- Export OCR CPL
- FYI Reviewer Manual
- Gap Check
- New! Hosting Your Own FYI Reviewer Web Page
- ImageCheck CPL
- Importing a Delimited ASCII (DAT) File
- Importing eDiscovery Email
- Importing Multi-page OCR Text Files
- Importing Single-page OCR Text Files
- Linking Images in Concordance
- Merging Tags
- Most Recently Opened Setting
- Organizing Testimony
- Overlay a Database
- Producing Docs in Concordance Image
- Registering an Imagebase Using Register-Load
- Registering an Imagebase Using Register-Scan
- Reindexing Daemon
- Searching
- Security Overview
- Tag History and Store It
- Tag Tips
- Text File to Query
- Tracking Changes in Concordance
- Troubleshooting-Regeneration and Sync TAG and TRK Files

Exhibit 14.7 Summation support materials online

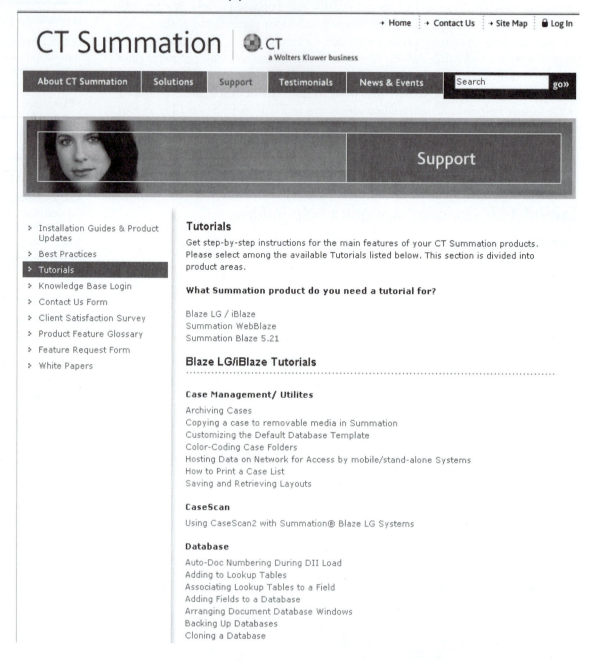

Home
Contact Us
Site Map
Log In
CT Summation
CT
a Wolters Kluwer business
About CT Summation
Solutions
Support
Testimonials
News & Events
Search
go»
Support
Installation Guides & Product Updates
Best Practices
Tutorials
Knowledge Base Login
Contact Us Form
Client Satisfaction Survey
Product Feature Glossary
Feature Request Form
White Papers
Tutorials
Get step-by-step instructions for the main features of your CT Summation products. Please select among the available Tutorials listed below. This section is divided into product areas.
What Summation product do you need a tutorial for?
Blaze LG / iBlaze
Summation WebBlaze
Summation Blaze 5.21
Blaze LG/iBlaze Tutorials
Case Management/ Utilites
Archiving Cases
Copying a case to removable media in Summation
Customizing the Default Database Template
Color-Coding Case Folders
Hosting Data on Network for Access by mobile/stand-alone Systems
How to Print a Case List
Saving and Retrieving Layouts
CaseScan
Using CaseScan2 with Summation® Blaze LG Systems
Database
Auto-Doc Numbering During DII Load
Adding to Lookup Tables
Associating Lookup Tables to a Field
Adding Fields to a Database
Arranging Document Database Windows
Backing Up Databases
Cloning a Database

ETHICAL ISSUES IN DOCUMENT DELIVERY

Federal rules and case law provide sanctions for failing to properly deliver documents under a discovery request. The sanctions ordered or imposed by the court may be as slight as an extension of the date for trial, or as extreme as a negative jury instruction that the inference to be drawn from the failure to produce the evidence is that the information was not favorable to the side not delivering the information or, worse, a charge of contempt or criminal charges against the client and possibly the attorney for destruction of evidence.

The legal team under appropriate rules of ethics has a duty to protect the documents and comply with the discovery request in compliance with court discovery orders. A major issue is the clients' handling of the documents before

ADVICE FROM THE FIELD _____

SUPPORTING LITIGATION EFFORTS WITH CONCORDANCE™ FYI™

by Mark Lieb, *Ad Litem Consulting, Inc.*

ON LITIGATION SUPPORT

Today's litigation support department provides project management and technical services for hundreds of cases and thousands of databases. The work is fast paced and intense, requiring both organization and diplomacy. At any given time, there are dozens of active matters, all with their own needs, personalities and deadlines. When litigators and paralegals change review teams, litigation support must immediately update access rights for all associated databases. Clients, counsel and experts, all of whom need remote access to specific databases, also require their time and attention.

Litigation support professionals load databases, generate productions and address other ad hoc needs throughout the entire discovery lifecycle. In tandem to these case-specific efforts, they also manage ongoing operational factors that impact the quality of support for all cases. These include monitoring critical indexes such as server capacity, CPU utilization and network bandwidth. There is also the ever-growing inventory of files, folders and case-related materials to manage.

In an effort to organize discovery and databases for all cases in a uniform manner, litigation support often employs a client-matter hierarchy of folders and subfolders. However, simply locating the right folders is not enough. Administrators need a powerful central data repository which clearly displays the relationships between the clients, matters, databases, and user access rights, while making overall management fast and simple.

In the litigation environment, success requires a powerful, yet flexible software solution that organizes information, anticipates how both the attorneys and litigation support staff will use it to achieve their goals, and helps facilitate the entire process. The faster litigation support can load data or update passwords, the more time attorneys have to review documents and prepare their cases. The fewer people needed by the firm to successfully maintain this overall system, the better.

A question facing law firms today is how they can use their existing litigation support department to successfully support an ever-increasing load of complex, electronic discovery-intensive cases. The right software can address the long term problems of how

to expedite review and minimize tedious administrative work, thereby helping existing staff to successfully support a larger case load. . . .

SECURE, REMOTE DOCUMENT REVIEW

Today's users require secure, instant access to their own data from any location. They also require restricted access for those who are outside of the firm, such as the client's in-house counsel, outside experts and co-counsel. Litigation support can use FYI and Concordance security to allow co-counsel access to certain client-matter databases but remove necessary fields (e.g., "internal notes") from view.

Meanwhile, firm team members enjoy total access.

FYI Server incorporates a dual-level firewall to separately limit both administrative and user access to specific internal and external locations. In this manner, litigation support can restrict administrative logins to workstations in a secured area. As attorneys and paralegals log in, the application's field-level security controls which fields each user can view and modify. Because users may connect from unsecured locations, FYI encrypts all communications between the FYI Server and the remote client.

This blocks third parties from eavesdropping on Internet communications.

Hackers can, and do, target unsecured Internet traffic for potentially valuable information. Banks, law firms and insurance companies are good examples of prime targets. All FYI related communications—login name, password, images, attachments and queries—are encrypted using a protocol known as "SSL." Online banking Web sites use SSL security so customers can safely access their accounts. FYI and Concordance offer a flexible and safe way for the litigation team to review case-critical discovery while the litigation support department oversees all ongoing activity from a single tool. . . .

THE FUTURE OF LITIGATION SUPPORT

Electronic discovery changed the scale, complexity and responsibilities of litigation support work forever.

Litigation-related files have grown from hundreds of GBs to thousands. New federal rules only reinforce this trend. Firms need to address the

(Continued)

increased workload for litigation support. For every client matter there are multiple databases, some of which reference hundreds of thousands of "native" files and millions of images. The number of collections and potential caches of discovery continues to grow, making management more complex. The days of the simple ten box project are gone. As the scale of cases continues to grow firms must provide greater resources to the litigation support department and litigation teams.

Whether litigation teams work from a single office or multiple locations around the world, it requires secure, powerful tools that will help organize and manage each client matter in a consistent fashion. Otherwise the department risks losing control of current and historical data. The software must also expedite the review process by enabling team access to case-critical documents from anywhere and at anytime. Firms need to make the investment in software which will aid in the overall management and operations of the litigation support department, in addition to helping attorneys find, produce and exhibit key documents. The Concordance FYI software is a logical step for firms seeking to achieve a long term, scalable solution.

About the Author: Mark R. Lieb is the President of Ad Litem Consulting and author of the books, *Litigation Support Department* and *Litigation Support Technical Standards.* Mr. Lieb consults on case, department and firm level initiatives ranging from software upgrades to mentoring. To learn more, please visit Ad Litem Consulting at http://www.AdLitem.net/ or call 866-477-4523.

Web Exploration

Contrast and compare Rule 3.4 of the Washington State Court Rules at: http://www.courts. wa.gov/court_rules/?fa= court_rules.list&group=ga& set=RPC with the American Bar Association Model Rules of Professional Responsibility at http://www.abanet.org/cpr/ mrpc/mrpc_toc.html, and the ethical rule in your jurisdiction

ETHICAL Perspective

WASHINGTON STATE COURT RULES: RULES OF PROFESSIONAL CONDUCT

RPC Rule 3.4

FAIRNESS TO OPPOSING PARTY AND COUNSEL
    A lawyer shall not:

(a) Unlawfully obstruct another party's access to evidence or unlawfully alter, destroy or conceal a document or other material having potential evidentiary value. A lawyer shall not counsel or assist another person to do any such act;

(b) Falsify evidence, counsel or assist a witness to testify falsely, or offer an inducement to a witness that is prohibited by law;

(c) Knowingly disobey an obligation under the rules of a tribunal except for an open refusal based on an assertion that no valid obligation exists;

(d) In pretrial procedure, make a frivolous discovery request or fail to make reasonably diligent effort to comply with a legally proper discovery request by an opposing party; or

(e) In trial, allude to any matter that the lawyer does not reasonably believe is relevant or that will not be supported by admissible evidence, assert personal knowledge of facts in issue except when testifying as a witness, or state personal opinion as to the justness of a cause, the credibility of a witness, the culpability of a civil litigant or the guilt or innocence of an accused.

(f) [Reserved.]

they are produced to the legal team. Clients must be advised under a litigation hold to preserve evidence and not destroy it. But, what about before litigation is pending? There may be legitimate reasons to purge files and to strip out metadata from electronic files. Improperly removing or changing metadata can lead to court-ordered sanctions. If there is a legitimate reason, and a standing policy on document retention and destruction, it is unlikely any sanctions will be imposed. But, as soon as notice of impending litigation is given, clients must be advised to cease all scrubbing, or removing, of metadata and suspend the destruction or erasing of applicable electronic files. There are no hard and fast rules on preservation and retention; each case must be reviewed on its own unique facts. The problem is properly advising the client of the action permitted. The general rule is if one knows or has reasonable grounds to know of the pendency of litigation, documents should be preserved.

SUMMARY

CHAPTER *14*
LITIGATION SUPPORT

Introduction to Litigation Support	The use of technology has become more critical as the volume of documents has increased as a result of the use of computer technology to create and store documents.
Reviewing Electronic Documents	Biggest costs in electronic discovery are incurred in reviewing the electronic material. Use of different formats often requires multiple viewers or copies of all the programs used to create the originals.
Electronic Discovery—the Process	E-discovery is a process and not a single event. Determining: what documents are wanted, who has them, what format they are in, their value in the case, and the cost of retrieving them. Defined by courts as virtually any document. *De-duping* is the term used to describe the process of electronically eliminating the duplicates. *Filtering* is the process used to scan or search the documents for relevant terms. Not all documents are in electronic form, but they must still be processed.
Converting Documents	Paper documents may be converted into electronic files and processed the same as electronic files.
File Formats for Electronic Documents	*Native file format:* Format used by a program to save the data produced by the program. *TIFF file format:* Tagged image file format. *PDF file format:* Portable document format.

Comparison of PDF and TIFF	Same cost. Both supported by most programs. Can be searched across different file formats. File metadata cannot be seen in TIFF format.
Metadata	Information about the document.
Scanning Documents	Paper documents may be scanned to convert them to an electronic form.
Optical Character Recognition (OCR)	A technology used to create a full-text, searchable version of an image document.
Coding Documents	Identify and capture relevant, objective data.
Resources That Support E-Discovery	
Service Companies	Service bureau or company retained to help in the electronic discovery process.
Summation Software and Concordance Software	Software application programs used for litigation support. Advantage to litigation support software: Allows for easy search and retrieval of all of the evidence, whether documents, testimony, photographs, or electronic files, with a single command.
Ethical Issues in Document Delivery	The legal team, under appropriate rules of ethics, has a duty to protect the documents and still properly comply with the discovery request in compliance with court discovery orders.

KEY TERMIMOLOGY

Auto coding   375

Bates production numbering   375

Coding   375

Content (application) metadata   375

De-duplication (de-duping)   373

Filtering   373

Native file format   374

Objective coding   375

Portable document format (PDF)   374

Redaction   375

Resource (system) metadata   375

Subjective coding   375

TIFF file format   374

CONCEPT REVIEW QUESTIONS AND EXERCISES

1. Test your knowledge and comprehension of the topics in this chapter by completing the multiple-choice questions on the textbook Companion Website.
2. Test your knowledge and comprehension of the topics in this chapter by completing the True-False questions on the textbook Companion Website.
3. What is the impact of court rules on the use of software and trial practice?
4. Why is e-discovery referred to as a process? Explain the mechanics of the process.
5. Describe the differences in file formats used in e-discovery.
6. What are the advantages and disadvantages of TIFF format, PDF format, and native format?
7. What is metadata and how does it impact e-document disclosure?
8. What is coding?
9. What is meant by de-duplication?
10. Explain the use of software for managing documents in litigation.
11. What are the ethical issues in document delivery?
12. What are the issues in the clients' handling of the documents before they are produced to the legal team?

INTERNET EXERCISES

1. Locate litigation support service companies on the Internet. List the services each performs.

2. Locate free electronic discovery update information. Who is the provider and what services does each offer the legal community?

PORTFOLIO ASSIGNMENT

Explain in a memo to the attorney the different formats that can be used to satisfy the discovery requests, describing the advantages and disadvantages of each.

SCENARIO CASE STUDY

Use the opening scenario for this chapter to answer the following questions. The setting is an attorney seeking help from a litigation support paralegal in a case involving electronic documents and discovery.

1. Explain in a memo the role of the IT staff in a case of this type.
2. Prepare a plan listing the information that will be needed by the trial team and how they should handle the discovery request from the opposing side.

3. How can the legal team protect the client's confidential and privileged information?
4. In a situation like this of potentially working as a freelance paralegal, can the paralegal discuss the case with her twin sister who works in the same office but has not been asked by the outside attorney to work on the case?

CONTINUING CASES AND EXERCISES

1. Download the demo version of Summation from the Summation website. Complete the Summation tutorial available from the CT Summation website.

Chapter 15 Digital Resources at **www.prenhall.com/goldman**

- Author Video Introduction
- Case Study Video
- Comprehension Quizzes and Glossary
- Video Software Introduction: SmartDraw

Presentation and Trial Graphics | CHAPTER 15

OPENING SCENARIO

The legal team had worked hard for the past six months preparing the case for trial. It was a big case for a small firm. A lot of the young firm's resources in time and money had been invested in the case, and success was essential. The firm was notified by the court that trial was scheduled in three weeks. Everyone agreed it was a great case if they could just show the jury the facts and evidence that they had prepared and get the jury's attention. They had been assigned to the new electronic courtroom that was equipped with individual monitors and large projection screen. The legal team all agreed that the photos they had would make everyone take notice of where and how it all happened. Good quality graphics would be essential to showing the jury what happened and gain their sympathy and hopefully a good verdict. Owen Mason, the lead attorney, and his partner were concerned that they not make the mistakes they had seen other lawyers make with poor graphics that did not help the case or which the trial judge excluded for lack of veracity. With limited additional resources, they knew they had to prepare the graphics in-house.

LEARNING OBJECTIVES

After studying this chapter you should be able to:

1. Explain how presentation graphics programs may be used in litigation.

2. Create a basic PowerPoint presentation.

3. Create an accident scene graphic exhibit using a graphic software program.

INTRODUCTION TO PRESENTATION AND TRIAL GRAPHICS

It has been said that one picture is worth ten thousand words. Properly prepared graphics are an excellent way of telling a story and making a point whether to a jury, a client, or to a group of concerned residents in a public meeting. Poorly prepared graphics can be boring and can distract from the main message. Everyone has seen a PowerPoint presentation used as part of a presentation. Some hit home and everyone in the audience wishes they had copies. Others convey a confused message at best or offer a few minutes of sleep to the audience at worst. More and more people use graphics in presentations as the software to create them becomes easier to use and more affordable.

Among the most available presentation graphics software programs are those included as part of the office suites of programs from Microsoft, PowerPoint (see Exhibit 15.1), and WordPerfect, Presentation X4. Already included in the software

Exhibit 15.1 Microsoft PowerPoint 2003

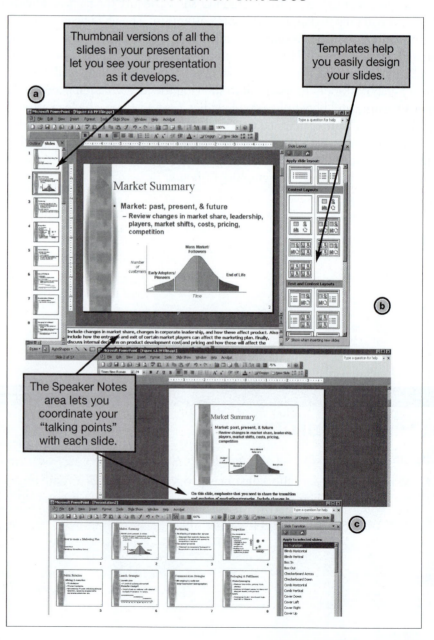

ADVICE FROM THE FIELD _____

THE "BUM" RULE—HOW TO CREATE EFFECTIVE DEMONSTRATIVE EVIDENCE
by John Cleaves

Remember Justice Potter Stewart's famous observation: "I shall not today attempt further to define the kinds of material I understand to be embraced . . . [b]ut I know it when I see it. . . ."? This statement applies to effective demonstrative evidence just as well as it does to the original subject Justice Stewart had in mind.

What is effective demonstrative evidence? Nearly anything. Physical items, such as weapons, car bumpers, and computer chips; video shot at the scene of an accident, or showing the process by which an item is manufactured are typical examples. Other demonstratives include graphics illustrating events along a timeline, animation of a patent drawing, or diagrams of a medical procedure.

Attorneys occasionally fall into the trap of using bullet points to list their facts and arguments. But bullet points rarely help explain the facts and seldom convince jurors of the merits of the case. They do, however, bore everyone to tears as the attorney reads one after another. Bullet points are not effective demonstrative evidence.

As a Litigation Support professional you may be called upon to assist or manage the creation of demonstratives within your firm or corporate legal department. As trial time approaches the attorney team may be focusing on finalizing their exhibits and preparing witnesses. The creation of demonstratives may fall through the cracks or be a last minute detail left to you or your staff. Follow these tips to ensure you or you're (sic) staff create demonstratives that capture the attention of the jury and/or judge.

BELIEVE, UNDERSTAND AND REMEMBER

When considering that demonstrative evidence can be nearly anything (bounded by the rules of evidence, of course)—and often is an "I know it when I see it" type of thing—how do you as a litigation support professional come up with a demonstrative that is truly effective? One way is by using the "BUM" criteria: is the demonstrative believable, understandable and memorable? A demonstrative is believable if it appeals to the jurors' common sense, is straightforward, and is honest. For example, in a case where a company was accused of fraud for selling "vaporware," the defense attorney used the product in opening. Not an image or photograph, but the actual item, putting it to the use it was intended. It is difficult to argue an item does not exist when it is sitting in court on counsel's table doing what it was supposed to do.

A demonstrative is understandable if it makes sense to the jurors without a long explanation. Attorneys often use clichés, logic and fundamentals (such as $2 + 2 = 4$) to create understandable demonstratives. For example, in a breach of contract case a graphic showing a man with his fingers crossed behind his back was used to demonstrate that one of the parties had ulterior motives. By referencing the simple childhood cliché of crossing one's fingers when making a promise the jury immediately understood the point made in the demonstrative.

An exhibit is memorable when it sticks with the jurors throughout the trial and deliberations. Unfortunately it is difficult to know what jurors will find memorable; jury research often shows jurors remembering items the attorneys find insignificant and missing points the attorneys stress repeatedly. One method to overcome this problem is to force the jurors to use several senses to process the information. Jurors typically rely on sight and sound, but adding touch to the mix helps fix the information in their minds. For example, in a patent infringement case involving the manufacture of computer chips, counsel distributed silicon wafers to the jurors as the expert explained the process by which they were made. . . .

OVERCOMING THE PROBLEMS AND PITFALLS OF DEMONSTRATIVES

Two kinds of problems tend to come up when using demonstratives. The first is procedural: are they legally relevant, was a proper foundation laid, or are they argumentative? These are important questions to keep in mind as they consider and use the demonstratives.

The second type of problem is substantive. Demonstratives work best when they are straightforward, clear of piles of money saved by the defendants by not enacting safety measures are often used to sway jurors feelings.

Another good source of demonstratives is to give jurors visual displays of the sheer volume of

(Continued)

evidence, on the theory that a lot of evidence on one side probably means that is the party that should prevail, even if the small amount of evidence on the other side is very effective.

SEEING FROM THE JURORS' POINT OF VIEW

When selecting physical items as demonstrative evidence, consider if the item is relevant, if it adds to the story, or if it is something a layperson would be curious to see. In civil cases it may be difficult to come up with an item, often and concise. When full of information, perhaps lots of text or images, they can become confusing and even intimidating to jurors. If jurors are overwhelmed with a tidal wave of data they may simply tune out. At the same time, it can be difficult for attorneys to avoid this pitfall because they are so intimately informed about every aspect of the case and have only a short time to teach and convince the jurors about a case they have been working on for months or years.

There are several ways to avoid these risks. One is to be very conscientious about limiting the number of words in a graphic. Most billboards ads are effective because they have very few words. The same is true of demonstratives—the fewer words the better.

Next, remove all extraneous information. This can be as simple as removing the decimal points if every number in a chart ends in .00, or cropping a photo to center it on the primary subject, or showcasing only the portion of a machine that's at issue rather than an entire piece of equipment. When jurors are first exposed to a new demonstrative they do not necessarily know what is most important. If it is cluttered with extra information, they may be distracted or confused and miss your crucial point.

Finally, build slowly. Introduce the components of the demonstrative one at a time so they can be explained individually. If the jurors are presented with information in small bites it is more likely they will understand and follow along. Even though it may be tempting to put the multi-variable formula or the hyper-detailed flowchart up all at once, if it causes even one juror to stop paying attention it has not helped the case.

There are rewards for the attorney who effectively uses demonstrative evidence. In addition to showing common sense is on their side—which is one of the keys to consistent success in trial—effective demonstratives help entertain, and therefore engage the jurors in the proceedings. Think back to those warm spring days in high school science class when the professor would show a video instead of dryly lecturing. Weren't those classes more interesting and memorable? Demonstrative evidence can also speed up the trial by teaching the jury the facts in a more concise and therefore quicker way. One example is a timeline which ties together various facts into a chain of events. Another could be a theme signpost which can help add structure to the disjointed way in which facts are presented in a case and can help jurors fit the facts together in a way that is logical and makes sense.

Finally, demonstrative evidence can be a very effective way of showing the other sides' motive. This is a key piece of information for jurors. Whether it is a physical item, as in a criminal case, or a smoking gun document in a civil case, showing the item or document repeatedly and reminding the jurors of the motive again and again will help cement it in their memories. Andy Warhol once said, "I'm afraid that if you look at a thing long enough, it loses all its meaning." The same can be true of the evidence in a case. Documents, testimony and other exhibits can be spun one way or the other. They can be forgotten or ignored by a jury. Or, worst of all, they can be misinterpreted in favor of the opposition. But by using demonstratives the jurors will believe, understand and remember to add meaning to the evidence, the chances of success are dramatically improved.

About the Author: By John Cleaves, Director, Forensic and Litigation Consulting, FTI Consulting

Source: The full article first appeared in *Litigation Support Today* May/July 2007.

used in many offices, they are being used to create high-quality slide shows and drawings, including text, data charts, and graphic objects.

One of the advantages of these programs is their flexibility. They can be used to prepare and present the graphic presentation electronically, using a computer, with or without a projector, and to print out paper copies for distribution. Presentation programs typically provide stock templates of graphics, artwork, and layout as a sample that the user can easily modify. More advanced users can add sound clips to the presentation, include still photos, and incorporate custom graphics from other programs, as well as video clips.

ELECTRONIC GRAPHIC CREATION

It used to be that when you walked into a courthouse you knew who was trying a case by the armload of poster-board graphics and easels being carried by the legal support staff. The use of photographs has always been a common form of exhibit. Use of photographs is a good lesson in what is appropriate for a presentation graphic. While some lawyers carry snapshot-size photos (4 × 5 in.) and others larger photos (8 × 10 in.) it is good to remember the words of a wise old judge to an novice trial attorney: If it's important enough to use a photo, make sure the last person in the jury box and the judge can see it at the same time. Many wiser trial attorneys, with the introduction of overhead projectors and slide and computer projectors, have given up larger (30 × 40 in.) blow-ups of photos in favor of computer projected versions (where size is limited only by the screen or wall). The same is true of drawings and diagrams. But always remember the advice about poorly prepared graphics—do not use them.

Graphic creation programs are used to create graphics for presentations either as stand-alone graphics or as part of a graphic presentation, such as part of a PowerPoint presentation. One of the newer classes of graphic software programs that offers templates is SmartDraw. Exhibit 15.2 shows examples of graphics prepared using SmartDraw Legal Version.

The obvious advantage to this class of software is the ability of the legal team to create their own graphics without the need of graphic artists and outside consultants. It is possible to create trial graphics in court, on a laptop computer, to

Exhibit 15.2 Graphics created using SmartDraw Legal Version

Accident Reconstruction Diagrams
10 Examples

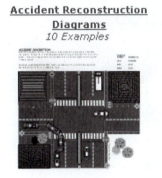

Crime Scene Diagrams
8 Examples

Estate Planning & Family Law
9 Examples

Legal Timelines
5 Examples

Personal Injury, Insurance, Medical Malpractice
8 Examples

Source: Reprinted with permission of SmartDraw.

meet an unexpected factual twist and display the image using the laptop and projection unit. Even when the graphics are printed out it provides an electronic backup if the large display boards are delayed in transit or damaged or destroyed by an overzealous cleaning staff. Exhibit 15.3 shows a sample graphic created for trial using SmartDraw Legal Version.

Users of PowerPoint 2007 and SmartDraw Legal Version will notice a similarity in the user interface as shown in Exhibit 15.4 and Exhibit 15.5. Commands for creating presentations are grouped by function in a series of tabs.

Exhibit 15.3 Intersection of accident scene created with SmartDraw Legal Version

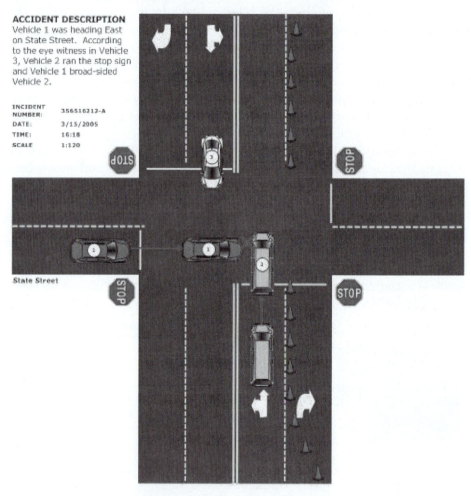

Source: Reprinted with permission of SmartDraw.

Exhibit 15.4 PowerPoint 2007 Ribbon design tab

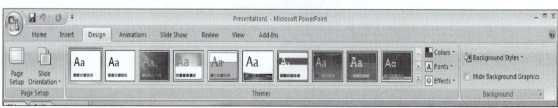

Exhibit 15.5 SmartDraw Legal Version user interface design tab

Source: Reprinted with permission of SmartDraw.

Exhibit 15.6 Microsoft tutorials available online for PowerPoint

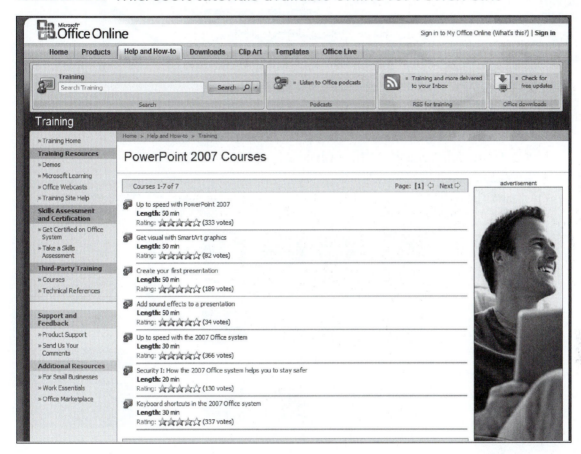

PowerPoint has become a standard for making electronic presentations of all types to all types of audiences, from grade school (Exhibit 15.7) to corporations and in courtrooms.

Creating slide presentations in PowerPoint is made easier with the wide variety of templates and content slides available for download from the Microsoft website when creating a new presentation from the Office Button New command, Exhibit 15.8.

A new presentation starts with a blank slide from the slide formats available to which may be added text or graphics. Exhibit 15.9 shows a possible first slide for a trial presentation. The text of the first slide tells the potential jury and judge what the presenter is going to tell them, Facts of the Case. Depending on the audiences and the approach to the case, a graphic might be added, in this case the scales of

WWW MINI EXERCISE

For more PowerPoint training options, see Roadmap to PowerPoint 2003 training at http://office.microsoft.com/en-us/assistance/HA011206091033.aspx

PowerPoint 2007 courses are available at http://office.microsoft.com/en-us/training/CR100654571033.aspx

Exhibit 15.7 PowerPoint sample slide

Exhibit 15.8 PowerPoint 2007 templates and content slide from Microsoft Office Online

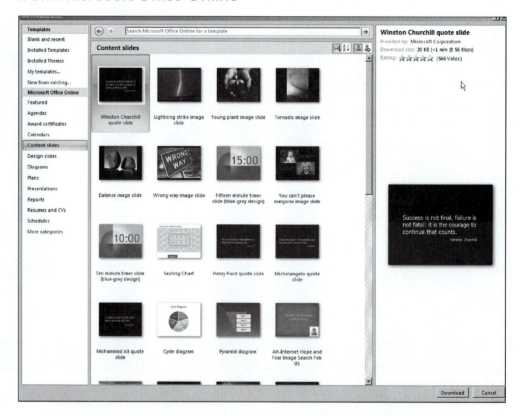

justice. Graphic images can be found using the Insert tab, Clip Art command in the Illustrations groups as shown in Exhibit 15.9. A search of "scales of justice" in all collections produces many options in many styles, from modern art to classic black and white. The selected art can be "dragged and dropped" by a left click of the mouse pointer on the graphic and sliding it over while holding the left button and releasing the button when the graphic is positioned on the PowerPoint slide. Additional adjustments to size are possible by using the mouse pointer on one of the

Exhibit 15.9 PowerPoint 2007 first slide using the clip art search feature

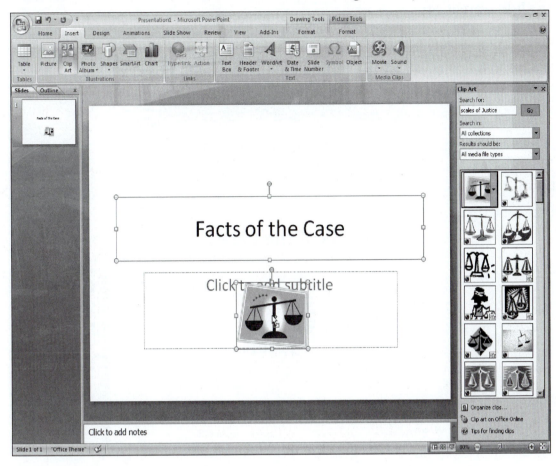

circles or boxes surrounding the image or any place on the slide and dragging the mouse while holding the left button, a standard technique in many programs.

PowerPoint allows many enhancements to a slide presentation, from slide transitions—like fading in and fading out and the addition of sounds during a slide transition. The standard transitions are selectable from the Animations tab on the PowerPoint Ribbon, such as the sounds that may be used that are found on the Transition to This Slide group sounds as shown in Exhibit 15.10.

A good PowerPoint presentation can reinforce and highlight the speakers' ideas and concepts. A poor presentation can undermine all the hard work of a presentation. While some presentations are designed for unattended viewing, in the legal community they are typically used to reinforce ideas, concepts, and thoughts the presenter wants to make to the audience.

A few pointers on presentations using PowerPoint:

- **Viewability**—Use background and text color combinations that can be read by everyone in the room. Be aware of the issue of colorblindness and the effect of some colors, like soothing pastel colors and vivid wake-up colors like red.
- **Density**—Slides should support ideas in as few words as possible; no one wants to read a full page of text.
- **Sounds**—Sounds can be very effective, when used appropriately. Overdo it and the impact is lost. Inappropriate sound effects, like gunshots, used in a courtroom may not be acceptable or permitted.
- **Stand aside**—Even the best presentation is lost if the presenter is standing in front, blocking the viewers' ability to see it.

Exhibit 15.10 PowerPoint 2007 sounds selections for enhancing a slide transition

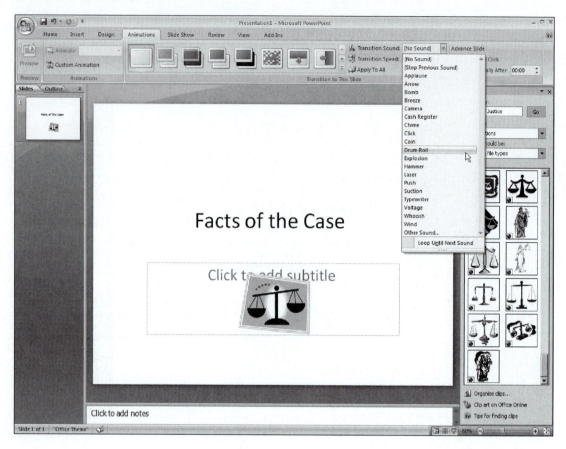

■ *Imagery*—As quoted elsewhere, one good picture is worth ten thousand words, but choose the picture wisely. What is the lasting impression you want to leave in the mind of, say, the jury, when it goes into deliberations? Among the most effective pictures in a personal injury case may be of the victim sitting in a wheelchair or lying in a hospital bed; no words are necessary.

Microsoft PowerPoint

PowerPoint can be used to present graphics and documents created using other programs as well as those created within PowerPoint. Graphics and document files may be imported from such programs as LexisNexis TimeMap, SmartDraw, Adobe Acrobat, and Nuance PDF Converter 5. Many of these programs provide a link or option in a menu choice to import or export files. Some of these links are added automatically to other programs when the software is installed on a computer on which the other program is already installed. For example, the PDF Converter 5 Pro link used in Exhibit 15.11 was added to PowerPoint (a previously installed program on the computer) when PDF Converter 5 Pro was installed. Exhibit 15.11 shows the result of using the Import/Export link. Each page of the original document, saved as a single PDF file with many pages, has first been converted into a usable format by PDF Converter 5, then imported into PowerPoint as individual pages, each a separate screen or slide.

Exhibit 15.11 PDF images created from a single PDF file using PDF Converter 5

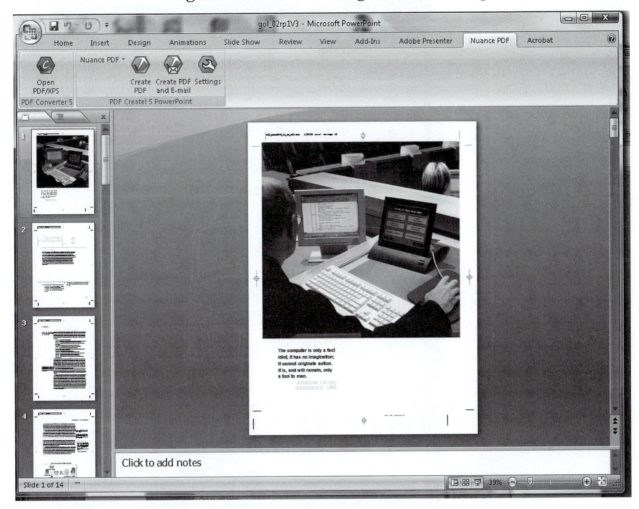

Program integration is a time-saver when using different presentation and case management tools. Integration allows a single mouse or keystroke to start a process that would otherwise require the start-up of multiple programs and the use of multiple functions in each program to achieve a common end, the transfer in a usable format of information from one program to another. This is similar to the integration features previously mentioned in suites of office programs, like Microsoft Office Suite or Corel WordPerfect Suite. Exhibit 15.12 shows another example. This is a time line created using LexisNexis TimeMap directly exported from TimeMap to PowerPoint with a single mouse click. The user has a choice of showing a separate slide per entry, or a combined single-entry slide showing multiple time points all with one keystroke, a saving of many keystrokes.

Creating a PowerPoint presentation starts with the New command in the Power-Point menu. This command creates a new working window and a single slide. Text, graphics, sound, video, and animation can be added to the slide. The Insert menu option displays a number of options for inserting graphics. A popular method of inserting graphics is from clip art. The Clip Art search menu opens as a panel with a search feature for finding available clip art and sounds that can be used by the drag and drop method. Exhibits 15.13 to 15.17 show a PowerPoint presentation being created using clip art for a presentation of an accident. The search results of available clip art using the term "accident" provide a number of choices.

Exhibit 15.12 TimeMap send to options

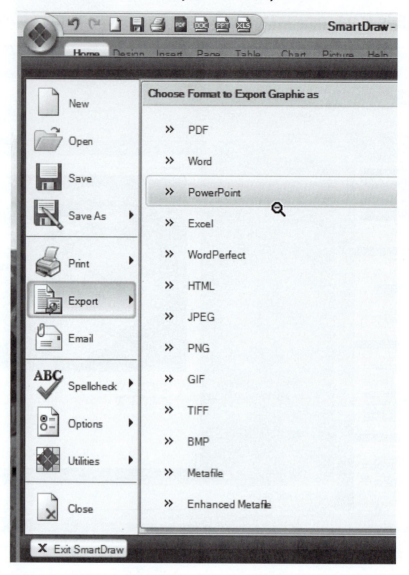

Exhibit 15.13 First step—clip art

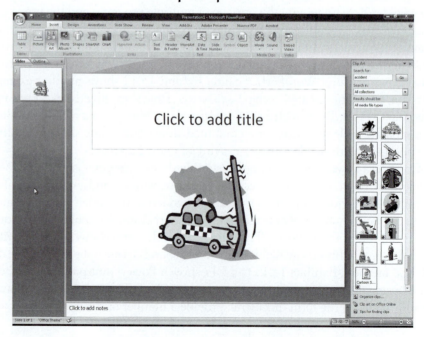

Exhibit 15.14 Second step—Sound plays automatically

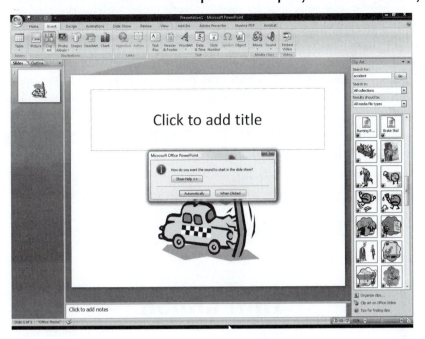

Exhibit 15.15 Presentation slide showing two sound clips are part of the presentation

Presentations may be enhanced, when appropriate, by the introduction of sound. Sound clips may also be found in the Clip Art panel. The sounds may be added by clicking on the Insert selection that is part of the items options menu or by the drag and drop method. Sounds may be added to play automatically when the slide opens or upon the user clicking the mouse or keyboard as shown in Exhibit 15.14. The presence of the sound clip is represented by the speaker icon as shown in Exhibit 15.15, which shows that two separate sounds were added.

Presentation Graphic Elements

Multiple graphic elements may be used in single slides such as the taxi accident graphic and the arrow shape added from the Home tab Drawing options as shown in Exhibit 15.16. Any graphic element can be moved in front of or in back of another graphic in the slide to allow one graphic to appear to overlay another as shown in Exhibit 15.17, where the Send to Back option from the Home tab Design menu has been selected after the arrow graphic was selected as the object to which it would apply.

Exhibit 15.16 Menu for presentation options and addition of graphic feature

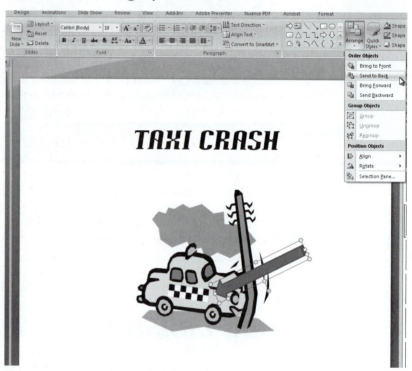

Exhibit 15.17 Graphic feature, the arrow sent to back

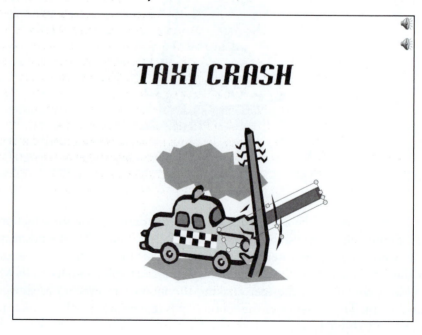

Exhibit 15.18 PowerPoint 2007 demo

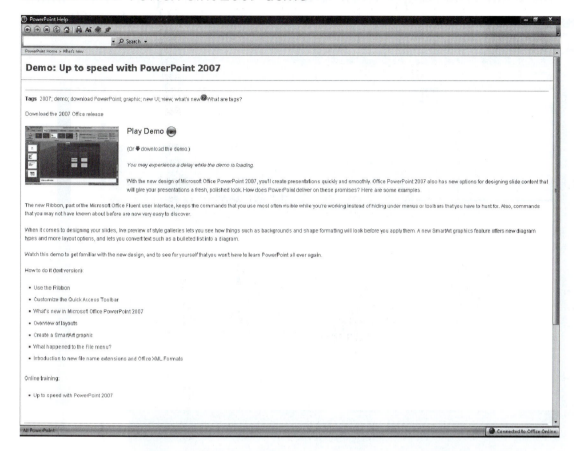

When an object has been selected, a dotted line appears around the selected object as shown in the arrow in Exhibit 15.16. Notice the corner and midline markers that also appear. These may be used to expand or contract the size of the selected object by a left mouse click on the desired point and moving the mouse in or out while holding the left mouse button. The marker in the middle of the line below the arrow in Exhibit 15.16 may be used in the same way to rotate the object.

There are many options available that may be used for a particular presentation depending on the situation and the audience. Microsoft makes available online tutorials and demos for learning about the program and the features desired. A demo about the 2007 version of PowerPoint is available from the Help menu as shown in Exhibit 15.18.

Microsoft Visio

Microsoft Visio is a popular graphic drawing program. It provides many of the traditional engineering and architectural design elements frequently used in courtroom presentations for drawings of buildings and roadway diagrams. It also provides many of the elements necessary for the creation of business graphics and times lines. A sample of the work screen is shown in Exhibit 15.19.

First Tort Claim—Automobile Rear-Ender

The practice is continuing to grow as Owen Mason and Associates is contacted by a new client who was injured in a rear-end automobile accident case. Typical of these types of personal injury cases, the firm accepts the case on a contingent fee basis.

Using information supplied below:

1. Create a form for obtaining the information necessary for use with a client who has had a minor automobile accident.
2. Set up the new client file, and determine the headings or folders that you would use in an electronic filing system for this case.
3. Locate a template for a contingent fee agreement for this client, and save the form as a template for future use.
4. Use the Internet to obtain an aerial photograph or diagram of the intersection where the accident occurred.
5. Prepare a diagram of the accident using graphics preparation software.

Client Information

Gordon Martin
82801 Heavenly Way
Sugarland, Your State
555-975-3197

Interview Notes

Mr. Martin was driving south on Central Park South in New York City, at 2:30 P.M. As he slowed 15 feet before the intersection of 64th Street, trying to decide if he should go straight or turn, on his way to Columbus Circle, he was struck in the rear of his 1999 Isuzu Trooper, sufficient to cause the vehicle to be irreparable. His car was spun around and came to rest facing north on the opposite side of the street parallel to the curb with his front bumper in the northside crosswalk. The other driver, Sal Cartage, was driving a 2006 Hummer. The Hummer stopped in the southbound lane in the curb lane with its front bumper along the Southside crosswalk. Mr. Cartage was cited for following too close and ordered to appear for a hearing on the following Monday but did not appear. He lives at 23 Boca Drive, Hollywood, Florida, and was on his way home to start a new job and was not able to return.

VIDEO SCENARIO: FINAL PRETRIAL EVIDENTIARY ISSUES

Trial counsel are meeting with the judge prior to the trial. Counsel have opposing views of the use of graphic pictures. The court agrees to take the use under consideration.

Go to the Companion Website, select Chapter 14 from the pull down menu, and watch this video.

1. How important are the use of photographs and graphics in a trial?
2. Are there any issues that should have been reviewed about the use of video-tape depositions?
3. Is the final pretrial conference an appropriate time to determine the judge's willingness to allow Multimedia presentations?

Chapter 16 Digital Resources at www.prenhall.com/goldman

- Author Video Introduction
- Case Study Video
- Comprehension Quizzes and Glossary
- Video Software Introduction: Sanction II

The Electronic Courthouse | CHAPTER 16

OPENING SCENARIO

It had been a very event-filled six months preparing the big truck-bus collision case, with twenty-five clients seeking damages for their injuries. The facts were not in great dispute, but the challenge remained in how to show the physical evidence, or at least a good representation and how the product defects in the truck and the bus contributed to the severity of the injuries. The court's technical support person told them all they had to do was bring a laptop and hook it up. The lead attorney, Owen Mason, was nervous and not sure he could handle presenting the case and working the laptop with the graphics. There was a lot of documentation, including the electronically stored documents they had discovered during discovery that contained the "smoking gun" language that proved a big part of the case. They all thought they were lucky to get the case into a federal court that had an electronic courtroom, unlike the state court where they did not even have TV monitors for video depositions. The question that had yet to be answered was whether to present the case electronically or use large photographic blow-ups. The multimedia tools were all available, if a little costly, but what would make the best impression on the court and the jury? A major problem was that the engineering expert they were counting on would be out of the country the week the trial was scheduled. Getting the individual treating physicians to appear at the last minute was also a major issue. In planning for the trial, the firm had anticipated the problem of getting all the medical experts away from their practices to attend a trial at the last minute. The firm incurred considerable expense in taking videotaped depositions of all the medical experts and the plaintiffs. The hope was that using a high-technology electronic courtroom in federal court, the entire case could be presented with graphics and videotape.

LEARNING OBJECTIVES

After studying this chapter you should be able to:

1. Describe how courts are implementing technology.

2. Describe the elements of an electronic courtroom.

3. Explain the use of trial presentation programs.

4. Describe the process of working with the court staff and issues of using electronic equipment in the courthouse.

INTRODUCTION TO THE ELECTRONIC COURTHOUSE

Computer technology is changing the way law offices and court systems perform traditional functions. The ease of creating electronic documents, including traditional letters and contracts, and electronic communications in the form of e-mails, has resulted in a document explosion. At the same time, cases are coming to trial faster because of the demand for "quicker justice," which allows less time to prepare and present a case in court. The result has been growth in the use of electronic documentation, computerized case management, and the use of computers in litigation.

THE ELECTRONIC COURTROOM

Increasingly, judges are embracing the use of electronics and computer-based systems in the courts. The initial reluctance to allow the "newfangled" technology is giving way to acceptance of tools that enhance the speedy administration of justice. One of the earliest uses of technology in the courtroom was the playing of videotaped depositions of expert witnesses on TV monitors in court.

Getting experts to testify is difficult when the time and day for presenting their testimony is uncertain because of the uncertainty of trial schedules. Many experts, such as noted surgeons and medical forensics experts have active, lucrative practices, and demand compensation that can range to the thousands of dollars per hour for the time lost waiting to testify. The average litigant can rarely afford this litigation cost. A videotape or electronic recording of a deposition can be used in trial as a cost-effective method of presenting expert witnesses, or for witnesses, who for reasons of health or distance would not otherwise be available to testify personally at a trial.

As judicial budgets allow, courtrooms are being outfitted with computers and audiovisual presentation systems. Exhibit 16.1 shows the U.S. Tax Court's

Exhibit 16.1 U.S. tax court electronic (north) courtroom

UNITED STATES TAX COURT ELECTRONIC (NORTH) COURTROOM

Exhibit 16.2 Sanction presentation of videotape deposition

electronic courtroom in Virginia. Computerized courtrooms can be seen frequently on Court TV televised trials, in which computer terminals are present at each lawyer's table, the judge's bench, for each of the court support personnel, and monitors for the jury.

Litigation support software is used in trial to display documentary evidence, graphic presentations, and simulations of accident cases. Relevant portions of documents can be displayed as the witness testifies and identifies the document for everyone in the courtroom to see at the same time, without passing paper copies to everyone. Lawyers can rapidly search depositions and documents, sometimes in the tens of thousands of pages, on their laptop computer to find pertinent material for examination or cross-examination of witness. Exhibit 16.2 shows another way in which litigation support software, in this case Sanction II, is used to display part of a transcript and the video presentation at the same time.

Electronic courtroom
Courtroom equipped with electronic equipment for use in trial presentations.

THE WIRED COURTROOM

The extent to which courtrooms are set up for technology ranges from the basic, wall outlets for power, to the advanced, installed wiring and equipment. Some courts have started the process toward the wired courtroom by eliminating the traditional court reporters, replacing them with an audio wired courtroom with microphones at each needed location—witness box, counsel table, judge's bench—and a recording system located either in the courtroom or at a remote location. For example, the Delaware County courthouse in Pennsylvania has wired all of its courtrooms with microphones and playback equipment monitored from a separate location in the courthouse. Requests to repeat what was said are handled by a request to the audio operator to play back an audio segment. Examples of basic and advanced layouts are shown in Exhibits 16.3 and 16.4.

ELECTRONIC TRIAL PRESENTATION PROGRAMS

More and more courtrooms are providing, or allowing litigants to provide for their trial, computer-based electronic display systems. Some see this as nothing more than a logical outgrowth of the multimedia presentations that started with the use of chalkboards, movie clips, and slide projectors.

Exhibit 16.3 Example of basic courtroom layout

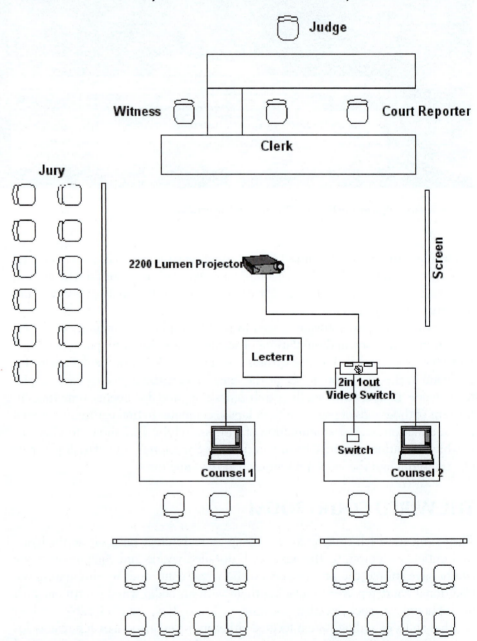

Exhibit 16.4 Example of advanced courtroom layout

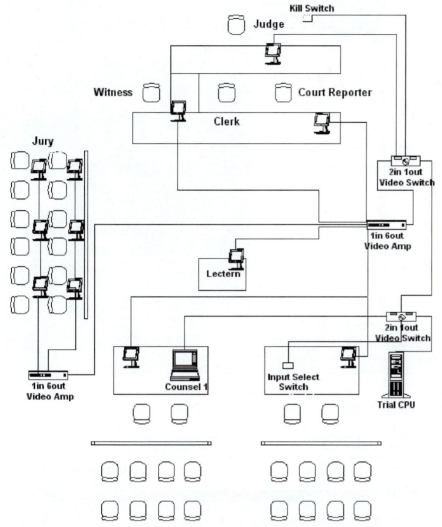

Modern trial presentations frequently include videotaped depositions and the presentation of images, photos, videos, and portions of documents. These may be on personal monitors or large-screen displays.

Managing the hundreds of individual components in the courtroom can be a trial nightmare unless they are organized and easily accessed for presentation. Sanction II, TrialDirector, and similar trial presentation programs allow the legal team to organize and control the documents, depositions, photographs, and other data as exhibits for trial, and then display them as evidence when needed in depositions and trial. Exhibit 16.5 shows a sample screen from Sanction II.

TrialDirector, from inData Corporation, and similar trial presentation programs are electronic trial presentation software applications. Exhibit 16.6 shows the TrialDirector layout. Extensive help is provided with the program and online for learning to use the program and its features.

Exhibit 16.5 Sample screen from Sanction II

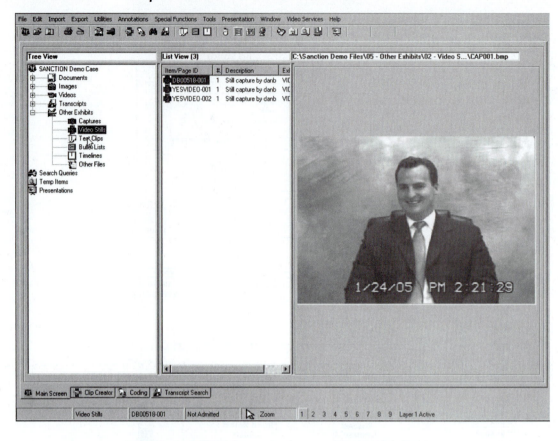

Exhibit 16.6 TrialDirector screen layout

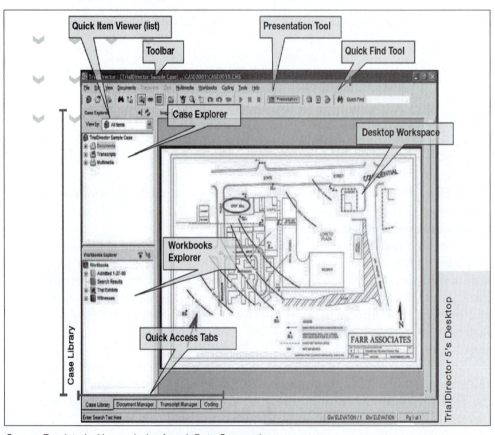

Source: Reprinted with permission from inData Corporation.

Supported Formats

Not all native formats can be used in all trial presentation programs, just as not all music files can be played on every brand of portable music player. It is wise to check the formats supported by the **trial presentation program** selected for trial early in the preparation process to ensure compatibility and avoid a rush near trial to convert or find suitable replacements.

Trial presentation program
Computer program that organizes and controls documents, depositions, photographs, and other data as exhibits for trial, and displays them as evidence.

USING TECHNOLOGY TO PRESENT THE CASE

Litigation presentation programs, like Sanction II by Verdict Systems and TrialDirector by inData, are multifaceted trial presentation programs that offer a comprehensive approach to presenting all types of exhibits in the courtroom, including documents, photographs, graphic images, video presentations, and recorded depositions. Unlike PowerPoint, which requires the creation of individual slides, these programs allow existing documents and files to be presented without any more effort than copying them into the program data file and making a selection for presentation. Trial presentation programs, like Sanction, are databases of the documents in either a case file or on a computer.

Sanction II like some other presentation programs uses familiar Windows Explorer Tree view with a panel showing the Folders and another showing the files within the folders as shown in Exhibit 16.7. Transfer of content is also made using the familiar "drag and drop" method. As shown in Exhibit 16.8, Sanction II uses three panels allowing a preview of the file, like the Windows Explorer thumbnail views.

The final presentation is usually previewable on the computer or laptop screen using the dual monitor mode before being projected, as shown in Exhibit 16.9.

The advantage of these higher-level presentation programs, apart from their relatively intuitive functionality, is the ability to work with a variety of file types including video, an increasingly popular tool in the courtroom. Video presentations allow a convenient method of showing prerecorded depositions of witnesses, particularly experts who might not be available on short notice to appear in a trial when called from the trial list. It is also used for elderly and very young witnesses who cannot travel or for whom the trial itself might be too emotionally upsetting. As shown in Exhibit 16.10, the video may be edited to show only the desired questions and answers allowing for the exclusion of objectionable questions as determined by the trial judge in the pretrial conference. The video and sound may also be presented with the written transcript on the screen as shown in Exhibit 16.2.

WWW MINI EXERCISE

For further information on the Wisconsin court system or to read the full report, go to www.wicourts.gov/

WWW MINI EXERCISE

More information on Courtroom 21 is available at http://www.legaltechcenter.net/

Bringing It All Together

Presentation programs like Sanction II and TrialDirector allow the legal team to assemble all of the electronically storable evidence in one program. Photographs, video, document images, transcripts, and sound files can all be preloaded into the program for use in trial. In courtrooms equipped with display equipment it is as simple as hooking the laptop to the system.

With everything stored electronically it is not a problem to find and show almost anything on a moments notice when testimony or strategy changes. With a coordination between the trial attorney and the litigation support team running the equipment the presentation to the court and the jury may appear flawless.

Using presentation software, as with any software requires some training and practice. When the use is a public forum like the courtroom, it is best to be up to

Exhibit 16.7 Windows Explorer view in Sanction II

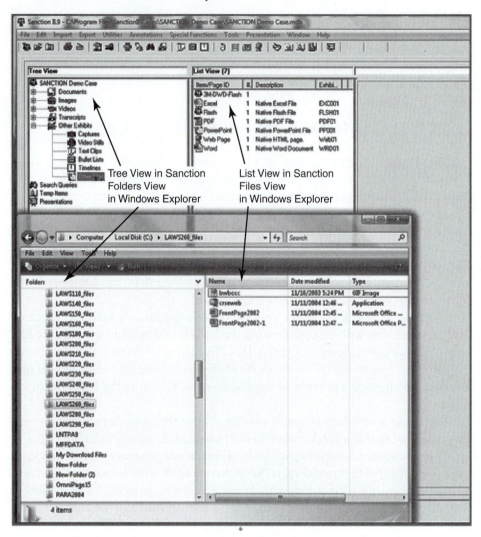

Source: © Verdict Systems 1999–2007. Reprinted with permission.

Web Exploration

Try out a training module for Sanction II at www.sanction .com/training/online 9020module

speed and take advantage of available training and refresher courses. Sanction II by Verdict Systems provides a series of self-guided online training modules available for access 24/7 to allow initial training or to update and refresh the user's skills on using the program and its features. A list of the available topics is shown in Exhibit 16.11.

Limitations on Presentation Graphics

The limitation on using presentation graphics is determined by the equipment in the courtroom. If the courtroom is not set up with appropriate power sources, screens, or monitors, computer presentations will not work, and print exhibits may still be needed. A key issue for the legal support staff is to determine well in advance the availability of technical resources in the courtroom in which the trial will take place. If not equipped for computer presentations, will the court allow the installation and use of equipment? And, if all of the equipment must be supplied, will the client be willing to pay for the costs associated with acquiring or renting and installing the needed hardware? In cases like the notorious O.J. Simpson case, if the courtroom

Exhibit 16.8 Sanction II three-panel view

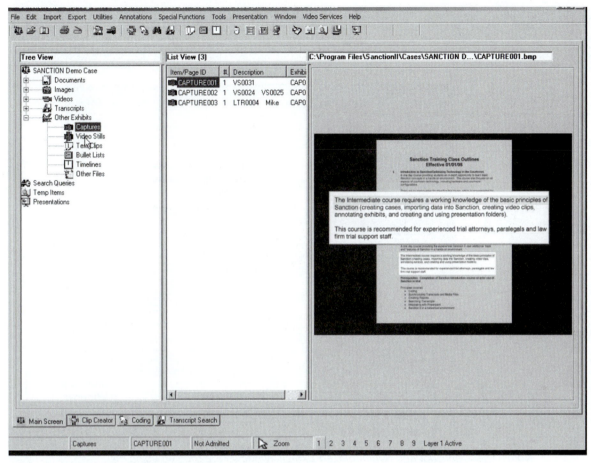

Exhibit 16.9 Sanction Dual Monitor Mode for Courtroom Presentation allows the trial team to see the image before it is projected on the courtroom and individual monitors

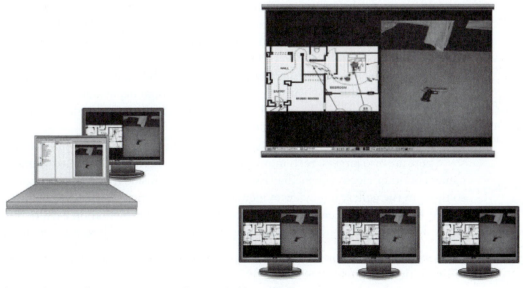

Exhibit 16.10 Sanction II transcript–video editing screen

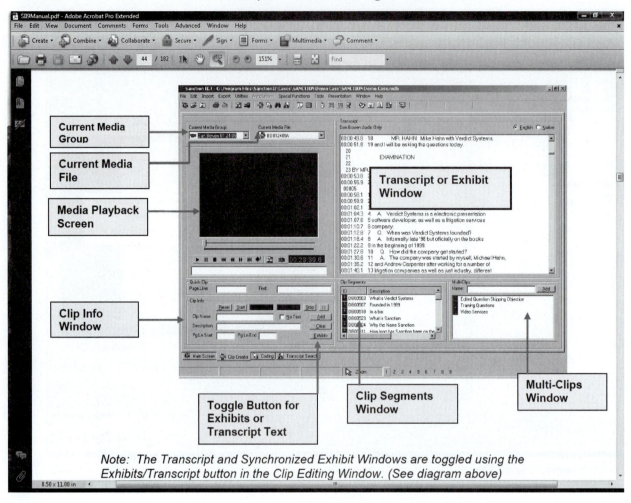

Note: The Transcript and Synchronized Exhibit Windows are toggled using the Exhibits/Transcript button in the Clip Editing Window. (See diagram above)

Large screen monitor
Video monitor conveniently located in the courtroom and large enough for all to see the graphics displayed.

Visual presentation cart
Media center located in courtroom.

Annotation monitor
Monitor that allows a witness to easily make on-screen annotations with the touch of a finger.

Document camera
Portable evidence presentation system equipped with a high resolution camera.

were not wired for computer use, the defendant certainly could have afforded the associated cost if advised of its benefits by counsel and allowed by the court.

The following information and photographs are from the online material available from the U.S. District Court for the District of South Carolina, which opened its first fully electronic courtrooms at the Matthew J. Perry, Jr. Federal Courthouse in Columbia, South Carolina. It offers a glimpse into the features and equipment that may be found in other courtrooms and courthouses.

Video monitors are strategically placed around the courtroom. The judge's bench (Exhibit 16.12), the witness stand, the courtroom deputy, and each of the counsel tables (Exhibit 16.13) and the jury box (Exhibit 16.14) have a video monitor to view the display of evidence.

The jury box has one flat-panel monitor placed between every two juror chairs.

There are also **large-screen monitors** for display of evidence using a document camera or other electronic media (Exhibit 16.15) just inside the well of the court, so those in the gallery may view evidence displayed through the system.

At the heart of the electronic courtroom is the **visual presentation cart,** or media center, which contains most of the presentation electronics. These items include:

Annotation monitor–Allows a witness to easily make on-screen annotations with the touch of a finger.
Document camera–A portable evidence presentation system. This unit is equipped with a high-resolution camera.

Exhibit 16.11 Sanction II online training topics

Sanction II Online Training

Overview
- [ ] Overview

Adding Case Items
- [ ] Add Data – Drag and Drop Individual Item
- [ ] Add Data – Drag and Drop Multiple Items to Individual Groups
- [ ] Add Data – Drag and Drop Multiple Items to Single Group
- [ ] Add Data – Add by Browsing
- [ ] Add Media Files – Single File
- [ ] Add Media Files – Multiple Files
- [ ] Add & Associate Transcripts

Managing Case Items
- [ ] Rename/Renumber – Single
- [ ] Rename/Renumber – Multiple
- [ ] Assign Exhibit Number – Single
- [ ] Assign Exhibit Number – Multiple
- [ ] Create Grouping
- [ ] Create User Folders
- [ ] Case Editor to Change Exhibit Info
- [ ] Verify File Locations

Working with Media Files
- [ ] Clip Creator Overview
- [ ] Create Clip – From Transcript
- [ ] Create Clip – No Transcript
- [ ] Create Multi Clip
- [ ] Edit Clip
- [ ] Convert Clip to Windows Media File
- [ ] Create Duration List
- [ ] Create Video Still

Presenting Case Items
- [ ] Create/Manage Presentation Folder
- [ ] Display Exhibits
- [ ] Basic Annotation Tools
- [ ] Basic Annotation Settings
- [ ] Basic Presentation Mode Settings
- [ ] Create Bullet List
- [ ] Present Bullet List
- [ ] Add Annotation Layers
- [ ] Present Annotation Layers

Working with Transcripts
- [ ] Search Transcript
- [ ] Create Video Clip
- [ ] Create Text Clip
- [ ] Convert to Tif

Coding Case Items
- [ ] Coding Overview
- [ ] Coding Design
- [ ] Coding Entry
- [ ] Coding Query

Printing Case Items
- [ ] Basic Exhibit Printing
- [ ] Print Image w/ Field Info
- [ ] Apply Batestamps
- [ ] Print Image w/Footer
- [ ] Print Exhibit List Report
- [ ] Print Barcode
- [ ] Print Thumbnail Report
- [ ] Print Slip Sheet
- [ ] Apply Exhibit Stamp
- [ ] Print Image w/ Watermark

Finding Lost Files
- [ ] Browse Files via Filepath
- [ ] Edit File Info
- [ ] Find Files

Exporting Case Data
- [ ] Create SDT
- [ ] Create SCL
- [ ] Export Transcripts

Importing Case Data
- [ ] Field Import
- [ ] Create OCR
- [ ] Import Load File

Supplemental Concepts
- [ ] Optimal Explorer View Settings
- [ ] Windows Color Theme
- [ ] Enabling Dual Monitors

Exhibit 16.12 The judge's bench

Exhibit 16.13 Counsel tables

Exhibit 16.14 The jury box

Exhibit 16.15 Counsel lectern with document camera and large-screen display

ADVICE FROM THE FIELD

TRIAL SUPPORT
LONE STARS: Enron trial support and the SPECIALISTS who made it happen
By Hillary Easom

Anyone who's stepped onto a dance floor knows that a waltz, a tango, and a two-step all require partners to move in sync. Working together, partners move smoothly and gracefully, creating a perfect rhythm. The relationship between attorneys and trial support specialists is another dance, demanding careful choreography, smooth movements, and excellent communication both before and during the trial.

In recent years, technology has helped make the trial dance less cumbersome. At the same time, glitches with technology can trip up one or both partners, creating awkward moments in the courtroom. The job of trial technology specialists is to develop a method of seamless presentation, supporting the attorneys without the need to count out each and every step.

A classic example of this vital "choreography" was the recent Enron criminal trial (U.S. vs. Kenneth Lay and Jeffrey Skilling). Over the course of several months, attorneys and support personnel had to practice their moves so as not to step on each other's toes during trial. One misstep in the litigation support process on either side could have been a serious factor in the trial's outcome.

Similar to a dance, the key to courtroom success can be summed up in one word: Preparation.

EXPECT THE UNEXPECTED

Scott Parreno knows the importance of careful pretrial groundwork. Parreno, from the Los Angeles office of O'Melveny & Myers, was the lead defense paralegal in the Enron case. He and four other paralegals acted as middlemen between the defense attorneys and other support personnel, ensuring that witness preparation binders and exhibits were complete and reproduced for relevant parties.

A 16-week trial with 56 witnesses inevitably presents surprises. "One thing that was constantly changing was the witnesses that were going to testify," says Parreno. This could be frustrating, as the team would put in a lot of time and effort in preparation to cross-examine a witness called by the prosecution, and suddenly the witness would be dropped and replaced by an alternate. "We'd be right back at square one preparing for a witness. The Judge maintained that each side had to know five witnesses ahead of time who the other side planned to call, but how important that witness was to either side really affected how much work we all would put into preparing."

In addition, preparations had to be made in advance for witnesses the defense believed might possibly be called further into the case. "For instance," says Parreno, "we thought that the government would be calling Richard Causey at some point during the trial, so we not only had to compile prep materials for him in case he was called, but we also had to work on the other five witnesses that the government had already disclosed."

Sounds pretty high-stress. But Parreno maintains that the team got along famously. "Sort of like sailors in a submarine, we learned to depend on each other," he says. "We really did have a great crew, and we all thought of each other as family."

One of those "family" members was Pam Radford, a trial consultant with Houston-based Legal Media Inc. Radford and her colleague Trevor Brock ran all of the trial presentations for the defense.

A STITCH IN TIME

Skilling's attorneys required more help with preparation than Lay's due to the greater number of securities and wire fraud counts being tried—28 versus 6. On a typical day, Radford and Brock arrived at Skilling's office at 6:30 AM. By 7:45 or 8:00 they were in the courtroom preparing for the day's events. After a full day of presenting evidence, they adjourned to Skilling's office to prepare for the next day. Despite the long hours, the attorney-support relationship was positive. "They were some of the best attorneys in the country, by far," says Radford. . . .

Similarly, the Legal Media Inc. team was structured so that they could take over for each other if necessary. This alleviated some of the stress that could otherwise come with such a long, drawn-out trial. Radford and Brock were able to take turns meeting late into the night with the attorneys, preparing for the next day's proceedings.

The pair created all demonstratives for the Skilling team and a small portion for the Lay team. Thanks to technology's growing presence in the courtroom, Radford and Brock needed only two laptop computers. Radford used Trial Director to organize document, and Brock used Sanction to present video and audio evidence in court.

Exhibits included between 800,000 and 1 million pages of documents, stored on two external hard drives. Almost a terabyte of video evidence was stored on additional hard drives. Every day during this trial, some 200 documents were added to the cache.

COURTROOM TECH 101

Technology in the courtroom was limited. "Judge Lake was very strict about not bringing additional monitors in," says Radford. The courtroom had one large monitor, and at the Judge's insistence the federal courts brought their own additional monitors. *Legal Media Inc. needed only to provide additional audio mixers and filters, equipment to help regulate sound in the courtroom.*

"We did have some glitches with their system because of the way it was wired," says Radford. For example, sometimes the audio would get out of sync after a recess. However, learning how the system functioned made these problems easy to fix.

The Enron Broadband case, which tried five former Enron Broadband Services executives, presented a different set of technological hurdles. Unlike the one used in the criminal trial, this courtroom was not equipped for technology, and cables had to be installed for video distribution during the trial. This was no easy task, as there were almost 20 video outputs used in the trial.

Arizona-based Verdict Systems (Sanction) handled technology support for this case under the direction of Dan Bowen, acting COO of the company. "The source set of data was somewhere in excess of 100 million pages," Bowen recalls. "At the trial site, we had access to 25 million pages of paper. We ultimately went into trial every day with over 4700 exhibits that made up almost 75,000 pages of paper, and over 500 video clips. And that was a subset."

Whereas in the past these documents would have to be lugged back and forth each day to court, modern technology helps prevent countless backaches: a single laptop with additional external hard drives is all that's needed. This was unheard of as recently as 5 or 6 years ago. . . .

"In a case of this complexity, there was literally so much volume that things got pushed right up until almost the day of trial," Bowen says. "We were doing a lot of data management trying to not just identify from the client what their exhibit lists were going to be, but then convert those lists down into usable electronic data so that it could be used in Sanction for the electronic presentation." This required months of pre-trial preparation. "We literally worked around the clock writing custom applications to strip out the pertinent data and create it into a usable format."

The efforts proved worthwhile, however, once the trial started, allowing the attorneys to think about the law and not have to worry about the technology. "Because of the way that the [Enron Broadband trial] database was structured, with very simple naming conventions," says Bowen, "the attorneys were able to

(*Continued*)

say something as simple as, 'Let me show you Exhibit 4000," and the technology support specialist was able to quickly pull up the document. A labeling system that used the defendant's initials followed by a 4-digit number simplified the process; Exhibit 4000 was labeled "JH4000" and could be retrieved by typing 6 keys and hitting "Enter." This, in addition to prepping with the attorneys and trial team, helped greatly facilitate communication in court.

ROOM FOR ERROR

Still, no matter how well a team prepares, there is always room for a glitch. "We had hard drives fail," says Bowen, stressing that backups are essential in any trial situation. Radford agrees and adds, "Always have it somewhere else inside the courtroom with you."

Experienced support personnel know to have extra hard drives on hand with backups of all documents and video or audio evidence, in case the primary computer should fizzle. But what good does this equipment do if it's not there when an emergency strikes?

During the Lay/Skilling Enron trial, Radford tried to power up her computer with the opening statements, and the machine refused to boot. Fortunately, she was prepared with another machine containing the same information, and when she pulled out the mirrored backup everything went smoothly.

In another instance during the trial, an attorney accidentally kicked a plug out under a table. "When we went to test the audio, it wasn't playing," says Radford. "It had been playing 30 minutes before." This emphasizes the importance of testing equipment ahead of time; Radford and Brock were able to troubleshoot before the trial resumed. They also had backup speakers and computers on hand in case of emergency; fortunately, none of these had to be used.

For Radford and Brock, working the Enron case required stopping work on all other cases 2-1/2 months before the trial began. . . .

Most pre-trial work was done via e-mail between the support specialists and the attorneys. Pre-trial work for Brock included digitizing and synchronizing video and audio evidence—a daunting task—and organizing all media exhibits. Radford's time was spent meeting with attorneys to work on demonstrative ideas, exhibit structure, and graphic design.

AND IN THIS CORNER. . .

Technology in the courtroom, for the prosecutors, was a new bag. This required some special choreographing by CACI, Inc.–Commercial, the firm providing litigation support for the government, to facilitate communications between the person in the hot seat and the attorneys.

Brian Katz was CACI, Inc.–Commercial's Technical Support Services Manager at the time of the trial. "Some of these attorneys had never used technology or used it very little," he says. "This was a technology-driven case. Some attorneys would turn to the person in the hot seat and say, 'Could you zoom in to paragraph 2?'" Others simply mention an exhibit, and the technology support specialist must take the cue.

It is critical, notes Katz, to understand how each attorney operates. "They're going to blame you at the end of the day if a document didn't come up quick enough."

Chris Sasso, Michael Denault, and Matthew Mehler made up Katz's team, working with attorneys and running presentations during the trial. Katz's job was to ensure that the other three were able to get into a rhythm.

Sasso and Denault were in the hot seat running trial presentations, while Mehler worked behind the scenes, preparing and scanning documents and exhibits to be passed on for review. He essentially built the case in the "war room" and passed it on to his teammates to present in the courtroom. . . .

The team prepared for over a year before the trial began, processing e-mails and documents for exhibits. This came to a head about 2-1/2 weeks before the trial, as they honed in on detailed preparations. Though another company prepared and presented opening statements, CACI, Inc.–Commercial, continued to work with the prosecution for the extent of the trial. . . .

About the Author: Hillary Easom is a freelance writer and photographer whose work has appeared internationally in various print and online publications including Better Investing, Marie Claire, Cruise Magazine, and American Fitness. Ms. Easom lives in Bethesda, Maryland, with her husband, son, and lop-eared rabbit. Her interests include travel, yoga, and pop culture.

Source: Edited from the original article originally published in *Litigation Support Today* August 2006.

Infrared headphones–Used as an assisted listening device for the hearing impaired.

Laptop port–A connection into which a laptop may be plugged.

Interpreter box–Routes language translations from an interpreter to the witness/defendant's headphones or the courtroom's public address system.

VCR and dual cassette player–For video and audio playback

In addition to the electronic courtroom capabilities, videoconferencing technology is available in any courtroom at the Matthew J. Perry, Jr. Courthouse.

ELECTRONIC EQUIPMENT IN THE COURTROOM

Document Camera

The document camera (Exhibit 16.16) is an easy-to-operate, portable evidence presentation system. This unit is equipped with a high-resolution camera and features a 12:1 magnification zoom lens with a high accuracy auto focusing system. The document camera can present evidence (e.g., 3-D objects, paper documents, transparencies, X-rays, etc.) for display on monitors throughout the courtroom.

Annotation Monitor

Annotation monitors (Exhibit 16.17) allow a witness to easily make on-screen annotations with the touch of a finger. Annotations can be made by pressing lightly and dragging your finger as you would a pen.

Interpreter Box

The interpreter box (Exhibit 16.18) routes language translations from an interpreter to the witness/defendant's headphones or the courtroom's public address system.

Infrared headphones
Assisted listening device for the hearing impaired.

Laptop port
Connection into which a laptop can be plugged.

Interpreter box
Routes language translation from an interpreter to the witness/defendant's headphones or the courtroom's public address system.

VCR
Equipment that plays back audio and video.

Dual cassette player
Equipment that plays back audio.

WWW MINI EXERCISE

For complete information and documentation on the Matthew J. Perry, Jr. Courthouse in Columbia, South Carolina, go to http://www.scd.uscourts.gov/

Exhibit 16.16 Document camera

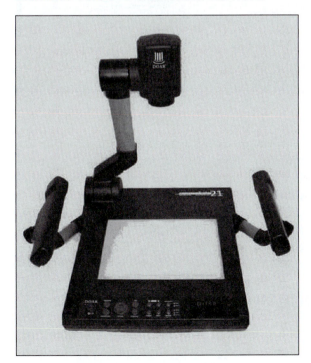

Exhibit 16.17 Annotation monitor

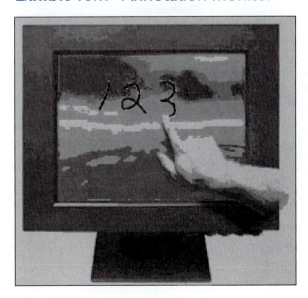

Exhibit 16.18 Interpreter box

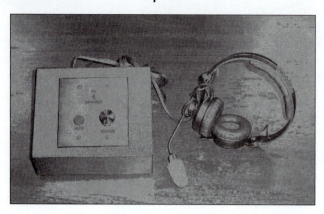

Exhibit 16.19 Infrared headphones

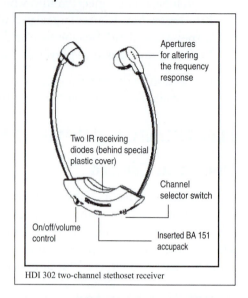

Apertures for altering the frequency response

Two IR receiving diodes (behind special plastic cover)

Channel selector switch

On/off/volume control

Inserted BA 151 accupack

HDI 302 two-channel stethoset receiver

Exhibit 16.20 Electronic courtroom of U.S. District Court for the Eastern District of California website

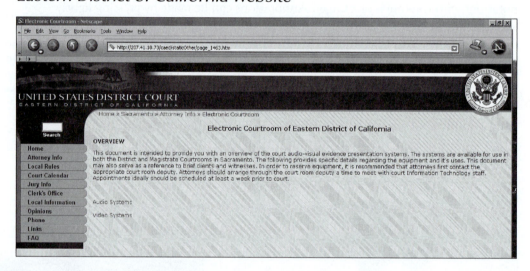

Infrared Headphones

Infrared headphones (Exhibit 16.19) are used as an assisted listening device for the hearing impaired. The Americans with Disabilities Act requires that this type of device be available for any individual needing it. It can also be used in conjunction with the interpreter box, for language interpretations.

Typical of the information available online about the electronic courtrooms is that on the U.S. District Court for the Eastern District of California website (Exhibit 16.20), which can be viewed at http://207.41.18.73/caed/staticOther/page_1463.htm.

WORKING WITH COURTHOUSE TECHNOLOGY STAFF

Within each courthouse and each courtroom are numerous people more than willing to help the legal team if properly approached and consulted. The people working in these areas have specialty knowledge developed from working in their area on a daily basis that occasional users of the services like members of a litigation trial team cannot expect to have unless they also spend considerable time learning the ropes. And even then, courthouse technology staff can make the process flow smoothly and help solve the problems inevitably incurred at some point because they are familiar with the idiosyncrasies peculiar to their own installation.

Exhibit 16.20 shows an example of how the U.S. District Court for the Eastern District of California invites users to become familiar with electronic support in the courtroom. The IT or technical support office should be the first place to go or contact if any technology will be needed or used in the courthouse, whether in a deposition or a trial. Find out what the procedures are first. Members of the support staff are usually the ones who also know how the different judges feel about the use of technology. Some may not approve of large-screen displays, while others may think a single large-projection screen is appropriate. Some may have individual monitors all over the courtroom and yet not want them used for things like presenting a video deposition, preferring instead a single monitor placed for the judge and the jury to view.

The technical support person may also be the one to help clear the hardware through security, saving time and stress on the day of trial by getting everything into the building in time to set it up and try it out beforehand. Remember, courtroom IT staff are usually the ones with the master keys to unlock the courtroom. It is also an advantage for the legal team to have someone who speaks the same technical jargon and can interface at the same knowledge level. A little goodwill can go a long way.

Clearing the Right to Bring in the Equipment Beforehand

Anyone who has been in a courthouse in the past few years knows of the increased security measures in place: metal scanners, X-ray machines, and briefcase searches. Anything out of the ordinary, particularly electronic equipment, can result in special scrutiny. In the ideal setting the only thing the legal team needs to bring is the CD, videotape, or other electronic storage media—all the equipment is provided by the courthouse.

Rarely does everything work so smoothly as the ideal. Most attorneys carry the electronic files on their laptops. The trial presentation plan may be to use the software and files on a laptop by connecting it to the courtroom equipment with a cable. Where the court system is not compatible or the equipment is not provided, the legal team must bring the needed equipment into the courthouse. It is highly recommended that the security office be contacted ahead of time to learn the policy and procedures for bringing everything into the courthouse and setting it up. In a number of courthouses it means using the loading dock of the courthouse or other alternate entrance and waiting for clearance. Preclearing equipment can save valuable time on the day of trial, not to mention stress and concern that everything will work as planned.

WHAT HAPPENS WHEN THE LIGHTS GO OUT

Even the best plans can be sidetracked when the equipment fails or when the power needed is not available. In many parts of the country the reaction to excess power demand is to reduce the power, sometimes called a brownout, when the voltage is reduced. Some equipment will work at a lower than optimum voltage while other items must have a constant power supply. For example, many homeowners have found their refrigerators not working after a brownout because the motors could not operate at the lower voltage supplied by the power company, and the motors burn out. While there are options like battery-powered backup systems, these may not be practical. In anticipation of "when all else fails," it is always good to have backup hardcopies of graphs and charts.

Many legal teams bring a backup of important files and software on extra laptop computers, just in case. Particularly well-prepared or overly concerned legal teams check the equipment in advance and bring extra projection bulbs for the computer projector, and even bring backup projectors, monitors, and in some cases printers. To paraphrase an old adage, if anything can go wrong, it will, at the worst possible moment—and in the middle of trial.

SUMMARY

CHAPTER *16*
THE ELECTRONIC COURTHOUSE

Introduction to the Electronic Courthouse	Technology is changing the way that courts perform their traditional function of recognizing the demand for swift justice.
The Electronic Courtroom	Electronics and court-based systems are increasingly being used in the courts. As budgets allow, courtrooms are being outfitted with computers and audiovisual presentation systems.
The Wired Courtroom	Courtrooms are being wired with technology ranging from the very basic to high technology with monitors and computers at every workstation for lawyers, the judge, and the jury.
Electronic Trial Presentation Programs	Courtrooms are providing, or allowing litigants to provide for their trial, computer-based electronic display systems. Trial presentations frequently include videotaped depositions and the presentation of images, photos, videos, and portions of documents. Trial presentation programs allow the legal team to organize and control the documents, depositions, photographs, and other data as exhibits for trial, and then display them as evidence when needed. ■ Sanction Trial presentation programs are electronic trial presentation software applications. ■ Supported formats Not all native formats can be used in all trial presentation programs. It is wise to check the formats supported by the trial presentation program selected for trial early in the preparation process to ensure compatibility.
Working With Courthouse Technology Staff	Courtrooms generally have support personnel who are available to assist the members of the litigation team in the use of the technology available in the courtroom or the courthouse. They are also the key contact for obtaining a right to bring equipment into the courthouse on the day of trial. Good working relations with the technical support staff can be invaluable when everything goes wrong and backup equipment is needed on an emergency basis.

KEY TERMINOLOGY

Annotation monitor   426

Document camera   426

Dual cassette player   431

Electronic courtroom   419

Infrared headphones   431

Interpreter box   431

Large-screen monitor   426

Laptop port   431

Trial presentation program   423

Visual presentation cart   426

VCR   431

CONCEPT REVIEW QUESTIONS AND EXERCISES

1. Test your knowledge and comprehension of the topics in this chapter by completing the multiple choice questions on the textbook Companion website.
2. Test your knowledge and comprehension of the topics in this chapter by completing the True-False questions on the textbook Companion website.
3. List and explain some of the advantages to the use of technology in litigation.
4. What are the functions for which the litigation team uses the litigation presentation programs?
5. How can PowerPoint be used as a litigation presentation program?
6. How may the legal team use presentation graphics programs? Give examples of both litigation and nonlitigation legal teams.
7. Explain the use of trial presentation programs.
8. What can you do when the power fails?
9. List and explain considerations in the creation of presentation graphics.
10. List and explain limitations on presentation graphics used at trial.
11. Why is the courthouse technology team important to the legal team?

INTERNET EXERCISES

1. Use the Internet to locate resources for learning how to use Microsoft PowerPoint. List the topics available and the Web address for accessing this information.
2. What Internet resources are available for obtaining maps and aerial views of locations that might be used for trial preparation?

PORTFOLIO ASSIGNMENTS

1. Prepare a memo for the attorneys of the firm on the issues involved in using outside sources for the preparation of trial graphics.
2. Create an accident scene graphic exhibit using a graphics software program.
3. Create a basic PowerPoint presentation on the use of PowerPoint in litigation.
4. Create a basic PowerPoint presentation on the use of PowerPoint by the legal team, including an explanation of how to make a slide.

SCENARIO CASE STUDY

Use the opening scenario for this chapter to answer the following questions. The setting is a discussion among the legal team about the upcoming big case.

1. What are the possible methods of presenting expert testimony and the advantages and disadvantages of each?
2. How can graphics be used in the trial?
3. What cautions should the trial attorney consider in using graphics at trial?
4. What pretrial measures should be taken if trial graphics are going to be used?

CONTINUING CASES AND EXERCISES

1. Obtain information on the electronic capabilities of the courtrooms for the federal and state courts in your jurisdiction.
2. Complete the SmartDraw tutorial available from the Companion Website at www.prenhall.com/goldman.
3. After completing the tutorial for SmartDraw Legal Version, prepare a diagram of the comprehensive case study accident scene for the case, using SmartDraw Legal Version, showing the vehicles:
   a. Before the impact.
   b. After the collisions and all of the vehicles had come to rest.
4. Prepare a diagram of the comprehensive accident case study in Appendix 1, showing the vehicles at the time of the first impact.
5. Prepare a PowerPoint presentation for use in trial using the exhibits in the comprehensive accident case study in Appendix 1 and the graphics prepared using SmartDraw Legal Version and TimeMap.
6. Create a presentation for use in court using Sanction II for the comprehensive accident case study in Appendix 1.

VIDEO SCENARIO: VIDEO DEPOSITION OF EXPERT

 The expert witness whose testimony is critical may not be available at the time of trial. Arrangments are made to take a video deposition of his testimony that can be used in trial. With only one opportunity to take the deposition, a court reporting service is contracted to take the video deposition and record the testimony using a Real Time reporting system, providing a standard word processor document simultaneously to insure accuracy.

Go to the Companion Website, select Chapter 3 from the pull down menu, and watch this video.

1. What computer hardware and software does the law firm need to use the video-tape deposition and read the text version of the transcript?
2. Should the legal team have any special training before taking a video deposition?
3. What arrangement will the legal team need to make in order to use the video deposition at the time of trial?
4. Can the legal team edit the video-tape deposition and only show the part it wants the jury to see?

CASE STUDIES

Data are provided for use in various end-of-chapter exercises throughout the book. These data are based on the information within the chapter opening scenarios and the case study material provided in Appendix 1. The factual scenarios and parties are semifictional; some of the scenarios are based very loosely on facts and situations from a number of sources woven together to provide a feel of a growing law office.

■ OPENING SCENARIOS

Each chapter has an opening scenario to help focus on the issues in the chapter. The scenarios follow the career of Attorney Owen Mason. Attorney Mason, a former law clerk to a federal judge, hires Mrs. Hannah, an experienced paralegal from a prestigious downtown law firm. To defray costs they sublet space to Ariel Marshall, a former prosecution attorney, and her litigation support paralegal, Emily Gordon. With the growth of both practices, as Mrs. Hannah becomes overwhelmed with managing the practice and taking care of the administrative functions, Mr. Mason hires Emily's sister Caitlin as an additional paralegal. When a client is involved in a major lawsuit and brings in an additional dozen clients, they all agree to work on the case together, with the assistance of a new paralegal IT support person, Ethan Benjamin.

■ LAW OFFICE INFORMATION

Law Office of Owen Mason
2 South State Street
Newtown, Your State and Zip
Office Phone 555 111-2222

Owen Mason, Esquire
138 South Main Street
Newtown, Your State and Zip
Social Security Number 123-45-6789
Office Phone 555 111-2222
Home Phone 555 345-3333
Date of Birth 08-19-1980

Mrs. Hannah
43 Washington Avenue
Newtown, Your State and Zip
Social Security Number 123-45-6790
Home Phone 555 453-3134
Date of Birth 1-12-1960

Ariel Marshall, Esquire
621 Merion Road
Old Station, Your State and Zip
Social Security Number 123-45-6792
Office Phone 555 222-2224
Home Phone 555 432-5673
Date of Birth 7-26-1978

Emily Gordon
2916 Boulevard Avenue
Forest Park, Your State and Zip
Social Security Number 123-45-6793
Home Phone 555 468-3335
Date of Birth 1-28-1994

Caitlin Gordon
76 Medford Road
Lawnview, Your State and Zip
Social Security Number 999-11-0000
Home Phone 555-444-8888
Date of Birth 1-28-1994

Ethan Benjamin
12 Schan Drive
Richboro, Your State and Zip
Social Security Number 555-22-7890
Home Phone 555 987-6543
Date of Birth 6-23-1995

Billing Rates

Owen Marshall, attorney $175 hour
Mrs. Hannah, paralegal $75 hour
Ariel Marshall, attorney $200 hour
Emily Gordon, litigation paralegal $90 hour
Caitlin Gordon, paralegal $65 hour
Ethan Benjamin, paralegal IT support $50 hour

YOUR HOURLY RATE, $20 hour

Contingent Fee Cases

Thirty (30) percent of the net recovery if settled before trial, forty (40) percent
if settled after trial commences, plus all out-of-pocket expenses.

COMPREHENSIVE CASE STUDIES

The comprehensive case studies are based on actual facts as reported in a National
Transportation Safety Board (NTSB) Report. Content has been edited and reproduced in the words of the report to provide as much authenticity as possible. Figures
are reproduced from the same report. Some liberty has been taken with the identity
of the parties, and no names used represent or are actual parties involved in
the tragic accident. The use of actual incidents is to allow you to perform basic legal and factual research that will present actual information that would be found
in a real case on which you may work in the future.

■ CASE A

Multi-vehicle Collision
Interstate 90
Hampshire–Marengo Toll Plaza
Near Hampshire, Illinois
October 1, 2003

Abstract

On October 1, 2003, a multi-vehicle accident occurred on the approach to an Interstate 90 toll plaza near Hampshire, Illinois. About 2:57 P.M., a 1995 Freightliner
tractor-trailer chassis and cargo container combination unit was traveling eastbound on the interstate, approaching the Hampshire–Marengo toll plaza at mile-
post (MP) 41.6, when it struck the rear of a 1999 Goshen GC2 25-passenger
specialty bus. As both vehicles moved forward, the specialty bus struck the rear of
a 2000 Chevrolet Silverado 1500 pickup truck, which was pushed into the rear of a
1998 Ford conventional tractor-box-trailer. As its cargo container and chassis be-

gan to overturn, the Freightliner also struck the upper portion of the pickup truck's in-bed camper and the rear left side of the Ford trailer. The Freightliner and the specialty bus continued forward and came to rest in the median. The pickup truck was then struck by another eastbound vehicle, a 2000 Kenworth tractor with Polar tank trailer. Eight specialty bus passengers were fatally injured, and 12 passengers sustained minor-to-serious injuries. The bus driver, the pickup truck driver, and the Freightliner driver received minor injuries. The Ford driver and co-driver and the Kenworth driver were not injured.

Interview Notes

Our Client

Jonathan Leonard,
152 Timber Ridge Road
Piedmont, Your State and Zip
Phone 555 432-1098
Social Security Number 111-22-3333

> **NOTE TO FILE:** I agreed to a contingent fee for the personal injury case. Usual rates unless he brings in other passengers as clients, then reduced to 20%.
>
> **NOTE:** Someone needs to check if that reduction is allowed under our state law and ethics rules.
>
> O.M.

Passengers

Refer to seat numbers on National Transportation Safety Board (NTSB) seating chart

1A Alice Bates
1B Betty Charles
1C Clara Donald
1D Donna Edwards

2A Amy Francs
2B Allan Gordon
2C Clarisa Howard
2D Doris Issacs

3A Agnes Jones
3B Beth Kaye
3C Callie Leonard
3D Delia Masons

4A Ariel Nathan
4B Barbara Osgood
4C vacant
4D vacant

5A Ashley Peters
5B Bently Quist
5C Colleen Roberts
5D vacant

6A vacant
6B Beula Victors
6C vacant
6D Davia Thompson
6E Elisabeth Stein

■ OTHER DRIVERS AND PARTIES

Chevrolet Silverado
    Robert Howard
Freightliner Tractor-Trailer
    Stephen Blanca
Kenworth Tractor-Trailer
    Glen Davids
Ford Tractor-Box-Trailer
    Sigmund Curtis

DETAILS

Freightliner Tractor-Trailer

The Freightliner driver reported that on the morning of the accident, about 6:00 A.M., he picked up his tractor at a rental space in Chicago, Illinois, and completed a 10- to 15-minute pretrip inspection, verifying that the lights, tires, brakes, and other equipment were in safe operating condition. Before picking up the accident chassis, he picked up another chassis trailer and cargo container and delivered both to a rail yard. He then drove to the Hamilton rail yard, where he picked up the accident chassis and empty cargo container. He reported conducting a 14-minute inspection of the chassis trailer and container—including the brakes, tires, and lights—and also said that he inspected the cargo container for cleanliness and damage. From the Hamilton yard, he drove to Midwest Recycling in Rockford, Illinois, where the cargo container was loaded with bundled recycling paper. He then departed for the return trip to Chicago.

The Freightliner driver reported that he was traveling at a speed of 40 to 45 mph in the right lane of I-90 East, following a specialty bus by about two car lengths. He stated that he routinely maintained this vehicle separation distance to prevent other vehicles from changing lanes into his path. He reported that he remained in the right lane from the time he departed Rockford until he reached the accident location and that he experienced difficulty pulling the loaded container because of the small engine in his truck. The driver said that traffic was moving normally into the toll plaza and that the sun was high and to his rear, without glare or reflection. He stated that he maintained a constant view ahead and was startled when he saw the specialty bus stopped just in front of his vehicle. According to the Freightliner driver, the bus was not displaying brake lights. The driver stated that he braked hard and turned the steering wheel to the left in an unsuccessful attempt to avoid a collision. He said that he felt the truck brakes "grab," but the braking action was insufficient to stop the truck, and the trailer shifted to his left and went out of control; the trailer overturned and the truck came to a stop in the median. The driver remained in his truck until the police arrived and asked him to exit the vehicle.

Goshen Specialty Bus

On October 1, 2003, about 9:25 A.M., the 25-passenger specialty bus left Chicago, with 20 passengers on board, for a round-trip sightseeing charter to Rockford. About 2:15 P.M., the bus departed Rockford for the return trip to Chicago. The bus driver stated that he was in the left lane while on I-90 East and switched to the right lane 1 to 1.5 miles prior to the accident location. He reported that he was traveling at a speed of approximately 45 mph about 1 mile west of the Hampshire–Marengo toll plaza when he observed a line of vehicles approaching the plaza and gradually began to reduce speed to ensure passenger comfort. The driver stated that the line of traffic was a little longer than usual and that only one manual toll booth appeared to be in operation. According to the driver, this toll plaza does not operate an automatic toll lane for commercial vehicles.

The bus driver reported that the sun was above and behind him at the time of the accident and that he did not experience adverse sun glare or reflection. He said that he was driving 10 mph about 0.5 mile from the toll plaza, when he observed in his left side mirror a red tractor-trailer approaching in his lane at a high rate of speed. The driver reported feeling the impact of the tractor-trailer and feeling his vehicle hit a vehicle ahead of him in the right lane. The driver's air bag deployed, the bus was pushed into the median, and the driver reported steering to the right to avoid entering the westbound traffic lanes. The driver said that he unbuckled his seat belt and stepped out of the bus to call for emergency assistance.

Chevrolet Pickup, Ford Tractor-Box-Trailer, and Kenworth Tractor-Tank-Trailer

When the specialty bus was struck by the Freightliner, it was pushed forward and struck a 2000 Chevrolet Silverado pickup truck equipped with a bed-mounted camper. The pickup truck driver stated that he had been traveling eastbound in the right lane at a constant speed of 50 mph when he suddenly heard a loud crash and was simultaneously forced back into his seat by the impact of something striking his vehicle from behind. The driver reported that he had been looking forward and did not observe the traffic behind him and had no recollection of the vehicles ahead of him. He stated that he heard no other sounds prior to the collision and had not braked, changed lanes, or made any other maneuver before the accident. He remembered that his vehicle came to rest beneath a large truck and that he was trapped in the driver's seat. He had been wearing his three-point seat belt, and his air bag deployed.

When the pickup truck was struck from behind by the specialty bus, the truck was pushed forward into the rear of a 1998 Ford tractor pulling a box trailer. The driver of the Ford combination unit stated to Safety Board investigators that he had been traveling in the right lane at a speed of 30 to 35 mph while approaching the toll plaza. He recalled following another tractor-semi-trailer that was about two truck-lengths ahead of him and said that he had not noticed the traffic to his rear. He reported hearing a loud "explosion" and feeling a simultaneous impact involving the rear of his vehicle, followed by two other impacts, and immediately brought his truck to a stop. After departing his vehicle, he said that he talked to the driver trapped in the cab of the pickup truck until emergency personnel arrived.

The fifth vehicle involved in this accident was a 2000 Kenworth tractor-tank-trailer. The driver reported that he drove the same route weekly and, on the day of the accident, was traveling eastbound in the right lane after reducing his speed from 62 mph in the posted 45-mph work area speed zone, anticipating slower traffic on the approach to the toll plaza. He stated that he was following a pickup truck, which was 50 to 100 feet ahead of his vehicle, and the pickup truck was closely following a Ford tractor-box-trailer, when the specialty bus and the Freightliner tractor-trailer passed him in the left lane and then merged back into the right lane in front of him. He reported that, as he approached the toll plaza, he did not notice whether a line of vehicles was waiting to go through the manual toll booth. The Kenworth driver said that he observed the Freightliner in the left lane, braking hard with brake lights illuminated, and then watched it collide with the Ford tractor-box-trailer and overturn. According to the Kenworth driver, he saw the pickup truck collide with the Ford and then lost sight of it as his vehicle skidded forward. During this sequence, he reported that he braked hard in an attempt to avoid becoming involved in the accident and later realized that the front of his vehicle had collided with the pickup truck.

■ DRIVER INFORMATION

Freightliner Driver

Certification and Experience. The 49-year-old Freightliner driver held a valid Illinois Class A commercial driver's license (CDL), with a corrective lenses restriction and an expiration date of January 5, 2006. He possessed a valid medical certificate issued August 6, 2003, approximately 2 months prior to the accident, with an expiration date of August 6, 2005. The driver had 13 years of truck driving experience and had been employed full time by Frontline Transportation Company for 6 weeks at the time of the accident.

Medical. According to the Freightliner driver, he did not take any prescription medications, was wearing his prescription eyeglasses at the time of the accident, and was not fatigued.

Duty Status. The Freightliner driver reported that he picked up his tractor about 6:00 A.M.; picked up and delivered a chassis trailer and cargo container; and then picked up the accident chassis and cargo container and traveled to Midwest Recycling in Rockford, Illinois, where the container was loaded. He said that he had driven the Chicago–Rockford route on four or five previous occasions.

Class-A license classification includes any combination of vehicles with a gross combination weight rating (GCWR) of 26,001 pounds or more, provided that the gross vehicle weight rating (GVWR) of the vehicle(s) being towed exceeds 10,000 pounds. (Holders of a Class A license may, with appropriate endorsements, operate all vehicles within classes B, C, and D.)

Bus Driver

Certification and Experience. At the time of the accident, the 57-year-old bus driver held an Illinois Class B9 CDL, with a passenger endorsement and an expiration date of September 27, 2007. The bus driver did not possess a valid medical certificate in accordance with 49 CFR 391.41. His medical certificate had been issued in 1999 and had expired in 2001. While working for Leisure, the bus driver had accumulated 6.5 years of experience driving buses similar to the accident bus. He said that he was very familiar with the I-90 route, having traveled it many times. He had previously worked as a professional firefighter with the Great Lakes Naval Training Center, where he operated heavy fire department vehicles and served as a driving instructor.

Medical. During an interview with Safety Board investigators, the bus driver stated that he was a Type II diabetic and used prescribed medications to control the condition. The driver reported that he was taking the prescription medications Lotensin, Actose, Amaryl, and Metformin daily; monitored his blood sugar and diet; and had undergone cataract surgery on his right eye during the year prior to the accident. On October 10, 2003, following the accident, the bus driver passed a complete physical examination for commercial driver fitness and was issued a valid medical certificate. The medical examination report indicated that the driver's Type II diabetes was well controlled through the use of prescribed oral medication.

Duty Status. The bus driver reported for duty at 7:00 A.M. on October 1, 2003. He then drove the accident bus 35 miles from the company headquarters in Lake Bluff, Illinois, to downtown Chicago, where he arrived at 9:15 A.M. He loaded his passengers and departed on a round-trip route from Chicago to Rockford at 9:25 A.M. At 2:15 P.M., he departed Rockford for the return trip to Chicago.

The bus driver was not required to keep driver logs due to the local nature of his operations.

Class B license classification includes any single vehicle with a GVWR of 26,001 pounds or more, or any such vehicle towing a vehicle not exceeding 10,000 pounds GVWR. (Holders of a Class B license may, with appropriate endorsements, operate all vehicles within class C, which includes any vehicle weighing 26,000 pounds [GVWR] or less designed to transport 16 or more people.)

The bus driver's operations fell within the 100-air-mile exemption. See <www.fmcsa.dot.gov/rulesregulations/administration/fmcsr/395.1.htm#e>, January 31, 2006.

■ OTHER DRIVERS

Chevrolet Pickup Truck

The 67-year-old pickup truck driver was traveling eastbound on I-90 from Beaver Dam, Wisconsin, to Bartlett, Illinois. The evening prior to the accident day he had been camping in Horicon, Wisconsin, and reported that he slept from 11:00 P.M. until 8:00 A.M. in his camper, which was mounted in the bed of his truck.

Ford Tractor-Box-Trailer

The 56-year-old Ford driver had 27 years of truck driving experience as an employee of Penner International, Inc. At the time of the accident, he was driving eastbound on I-90 en route to Durham, North Carolina, from Steinbach, Manitoba, Canada, transporting a box trailer containing 25 pallets of prescription medication. His co-driver was asleep in the sleeper berth.

Kenworth Tractor-Tank-Trailer

The 59-year-old Kenworth driver was an employee of Carl Klemm, Inc., and had 36 years of truck driving experience. At the time of the accident, he was transporting a tanker load of ink dye capsule liquid and was traveling eastbound on I-90, en route to West Carrollton, Ohio, from Portage, Wisconsin. The driver said that he had been on vacation for several days before returning to work on the day of the accident.

■ HIGHWAY INFORMATION

General

The accident occurred on I-90 east at MP 41.6, approximately 2,600 feet west of the Hampshire–Marengo toll plaza. I-90—a divided, straight, and level four-lane asphalt roadway—is classified as an urban principal arterial road. As part of the Illinois State Toll Highway, this section of roadway is referred to as the "Northwest Tollway," 76.5 miles stretching from I-294 in Chicago northwest to the Wisconsin state line. At the accident location, the 41-foot-wide paved portion of roadway comprised two main travel lanes (25 feet total width), an 11-foot-wide right shoulder, and a 5-foot-wide left shoulder. A 50-foot-wide depressed grassy median separated the eastbound and westbound lanes. Because of a construction work zone that extended from MPs 25.5 to 62.5, the posted speed limit for I-90 at the accident site was 45 mph. The signage for the reduced speed limit began 5.3 miles prior to the accident site, and toll information signage began 0.5 mile prior to the accident site (at MP 42.1).

Hampshire–Marengo Toll Booth Configuration

Figures 14 and 15 show the Hampshire–Marengo approach view and toll booth and toll lane configuration at the time of the accident. Lanes 1–3 (from right to left) were manual cash lanes with toll collectors for all vehicles, and lanes 4–6 (from right to left) were automatic coin lanes for cars only. At the time of the accident, the only manual lane available for commercial traffic was lane 3. Lane 1 was open weekdays during peak commercial hours, from 6:00 A.M. to 2:00 P.M., and closed the rest of the day. At the time of the accident, the toll collector for lane 2 was on break, and this lane was closed. The lane 3 toll collector stated that he observed no unusual queuing of traffic in lane 3 before the accident; he said that four or five tractor-semi-trailers were in line to pass through the toll plaza.

■ METEOROLOGICAL INFORMATION

The National Weather Service at DeKalb-Taylor Municipal Airport, 21 miles south of the accident site, reported the weather at 3:00 P.M. on October 1, 2003, as mostly sunny and clear, with a temperature of 50 degrees Fahrenheit, 23 percent humidity, and winds northwest at 15 mph.

■ TOXICOLOGICAL INFORMATION

Toxicological specimens were collected from the Freightliner driver at a local hospital following the accident. The ISP laboratory tested the specimens and found the driver's blood and urine to be negative for alcohol and other drugs of abuse. The Safety Board also had the specimens tested and determined that no carbon monoxide, cyanide, ethanol, or other drugs were present.

Toxicological specimens were collected from the bus driver 2 days after the accident, on October 3, 2003. The specimens were evaluated locally and were found to be negative for drugs of abuse. No alcohol testing was conducted. According to 49 CFR 382.303, the employer of a driver of a commercial motor vehicle operating on a public road in commerce is required to conduct alcohol and controlled substance testing on that driver if the vehicle is involved in a fatal accident. Safety Board investigators found no evidence that Leisure completed any post-accident alcohol testing on the bus driver, as required.

Figure 1 Regional map of accident location

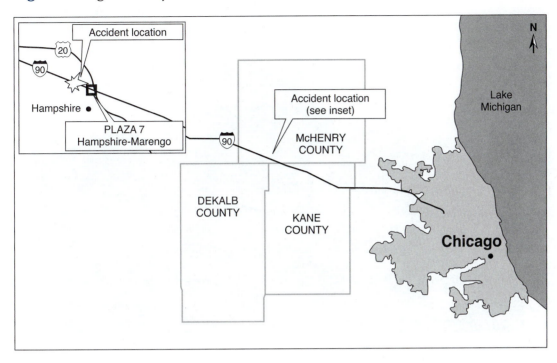

Figure 2 View of accident location, I-90 eastbound

Figure 3 Damaged Freightliner tractor-trailer

Courtesy of Illinois State Police

Figure 4 Damaged Goshen specialty bus

Figure 5 Damaged pickup truck

Courtesy of Illinois State Police

Figure 6 Damaged Ford tractor-box trailer

Figure 7 Damaged Kenworth tractor-tank trailer

Figure 8 Accident scene diagram

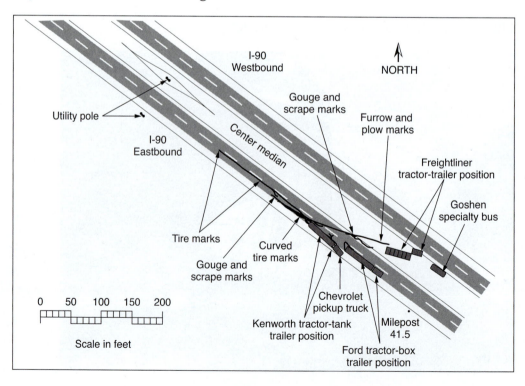

Figure 9 Specialty bus seating diagram

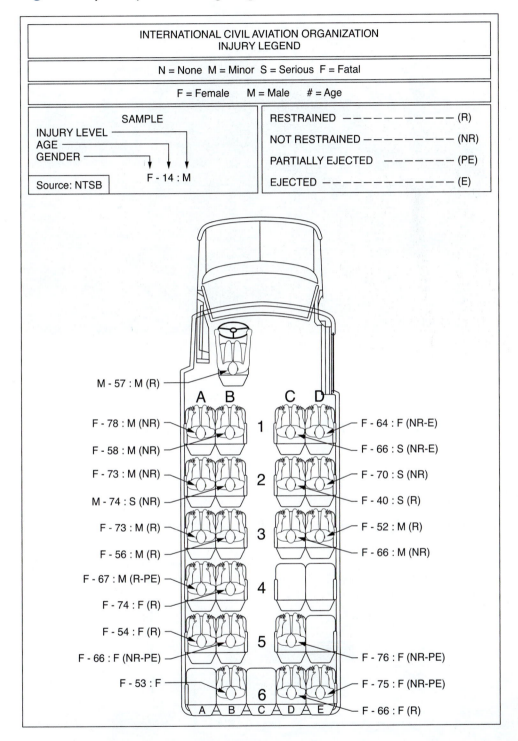

INTERNATIONAL CIVIL AVIATION ORGANIZATION
INJURY LEGEND

N = None M = Minor S = Serious F = Fatal

F = Female   M = Male   # = Age

SAMPLE

INJURY LEVEL
AGE
GENDER

F - 14 : M

Source: NTSB

RESTRAINED — — — — — — — — — (R)

NOT RESTRAINED — — — — — — — (NR)

PARTIALLY EJECTED — — — — — — (PE)

EJECTED — — — — — — — — — — — (E)

M - 57 : M (R)

A B   C D

F - 78 : M (NR)   1   F - 64 : F (NR-E)

F - 58 : M (NR)   F - 66 : S (NR-E)

F - 73 : M (NR)   2   F - 70 : S (NR)

M - 74 : S (NR)   F - 40 : S (R)

F - 73 : M (R)   3   F - 52 : M (R)

F - 56 : M (R)   F - 66 : M (NR)

F - 67 : M (R-PE)   4

F - 74 : F (R)

F - 54 : F (R)   5

F - 66 : F (NR-PE)   F - 76 : F (NR-PE)

F - 53 : F   6   F - 75 : F (NR-PE)

A   B   C D E   F - 66 : F (R)

449

Figure 10 Specialty bus rear-impact damage

Note: Figures 11, 12, and 13 have been omitted from the orginal report.

Figure 14 Approach view of accident toll plaza

Figure 15 Accident scene toll plaza lanes

Figure 16 Graphic depiction of open road toll system

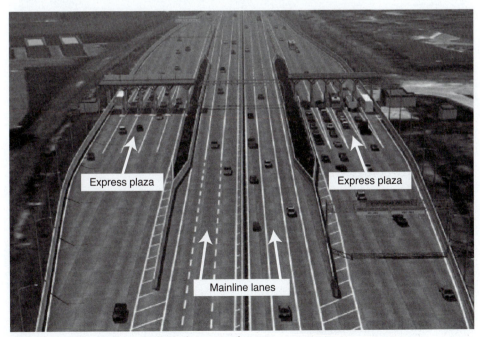

Courtesy of Illinois State Toll Highway Authority

Acronyms and Abbreviations

AAMVA	American Association of Motor Vehicle Administrators
ABS	antilock brake system
ADT	average daily traffic
ASA	automatic slack adjuster
ASE	National Institute for Automotive Service Excellence
ATA	American Trucking Associations, Inc.
Blossom Valley	Blossom Valley Farms, Inc.
CCMTA	Canadian Council of Motor Transport Administrators
CDL	commercial driver's license
CFR	*Code of Federal Regulations*
CVSA	Commercial Vehicle Safety Alliance
EDSMAC4	Engineering Dynamics Simulation Model of Automobile Collisions, 4th revision
FHWA	Federal Highway Administration
FMCSA	Federal Motor Carrier Safety Administration
FMCSRs	*Federal Motor Carrier Safety Regulations*
GVWR	gross vehicle weight rating
HVE	Human, Vehicle, Environment
ISS-2	Inspection Selection System
MCMIS	Federal Motor Carrier Management Information System
NHTSA	National Highway Traffic Safety Administration
NPRM	notice of proposed rulemaking
OOIDA	Owner-Operator Independent Drivers Association
PennDOT	Pennsylvania Department of Transportation
psi	pounds per square inch
SafeStat	Safety Status Measurement System
SIMON	Simulation Model Non-linear
SRPD	Southern Regional Police Department
THC	tetrahydrocannabinol
UMTRI	University of Michigan Transportation Research Institute
USDOT	U.S. Department of Transportation

CASE B

Collision Between a Ford Dump Truck and Four Passenger Cars
Glen Rock, Pennsylvania
April 11, 2003
Highway Accident Report
NTSB/HAR-06/01. Washington, DC.

Abstract

About 3:36 P.M. on April 11, 2003, in the Borough of Glen Rock, Pennsylvania, a 1995 Ford dump truck owned and operated by Blossom Valley Farms, Inc., was traveling southbound on Church Street, a two-lane, two-way residential street with a steep downgrade, when the driver found that he was unable to stop the truck (Figure 1). The truck struck four passenger cars, which were stopped at the intersection of Church and Main Streets, and pushed them into the intersection. One of the vehicles struck three pedestrians (a 9-year-old boy, a 7-year-old boy, and a 7-year-old girl), who were on the sidewalk on the west side of Church Street. The

Figure 1 Accident truck

Source: Southern Regional Police Department

truck continued across the intersection, through a gas station parking lot, and over a set of railroad tracks before coming to rest about 300 feet south of the intersection. As a result of the collision, the driver and an 11-year-old occupant of one of the passenger cars received fatal injuries, and the three pedestrians who were struck received minor-to-serious injuries. The six remaining passenger car occupants and the truck driver were not injured.

Narrative

The 21-year-old accident truck driver worked for Blossom Valley Farms, Inc., (Blossom Valley) an agricultural nursery, making deliveries of landscaping materials, including mulch, dirt, and stone. He had been working for Blossom Valley for 10 days when the accident occurred. According to the accident driver, on the day of the accident, he started work about 8:00 A.M., and his first delivery in the 1995 Ford dump truck consisted of 8 yards of mulch to an address in Parkton, Maryland. (See Figure 2.) He also made his second and third deliveries, of 4 yards of mulch and 2 yards of Red Mountain Stone, respectively, to Parkton. On the way back from the third delivery, he stopped at a fast-food restaurant in Shrewsbury, Pennsylvania, where he picked up food and then returned to Blossom Valley. He ate lunch in the truck while topsoil was loaded into the truck. The fourth delivery of the day was a load of 14 yards of unscreened topsoil, which was being delivered a day late. The driver indicated that he knew it should take three trips to complete the topsoil delivery because the truck's capacity was limited to 5 scoops of wet topsoil (it was raining at the time). The employee who loaded the truck told the driver he had loaded 7 scoops and that the driver should go on with the delivery.

The driver indicated that he followed the directions printed on the delivery invoice given to him by his employer. He traveled north on the Susquehanna Trail and turned left on Church Street toward Glen Rock. He said he saw the "3/4 ton limit, Except Local Deliveries" signs at the beginning of Church Street

Figure 2 Map of the general region of the accident site

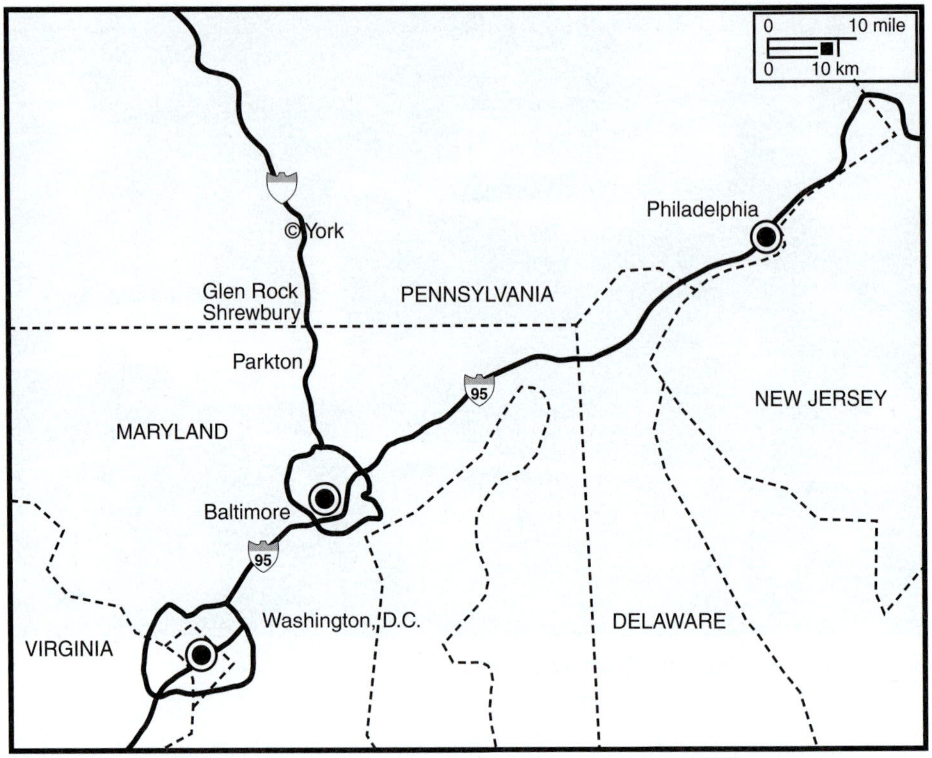

but continued anyway because the directions given him by Blossom Valley told him to use that street and he thought he was making a local delivery. (See Figures 3 and 4.) He said that he was traveling 25 to 35 mph on Church Street and stopped at the top of the hill near a water tower and electrical substation. (A witness following the truck indicated in a police interview that the accident truck did not stop.)

The accident driver stated that as he started down the hill (see Figure 5), he did not select a lower gear. He said that at some point during the descent, he pumped his brakes and the truck began to speed up. He also stated that about a quarter of the way down the hill, he lost his brakes and the brake warning light in the truck began to flash. He said he knew then that he had brake problems because his boss and a coworker had told him that if the brake light flashed, he did not have enough pressure [air pressure]. He said he could not stop the truck, and he saw children and cars at the bottom of the hill. He indicated that he leaned out the window and yelled, "No brakes, get out of the way" as the truck neared Center Street (about 3 blocks from the accident site). He said he struck the back of a black car and thought he "went airborne." He said that he did not sound the horn and that he was not wearing a seat belt. He stated that his recollection of the events after the initial impact was "vague."

Witnesses reported that just before the accident, a school bus had unloaded students on Main Street. After exiting the bus, the students crossed Church Street and, as the bus began to leave, they walked up the sidewalk on the west side of Church Street. Witnesses also reported that four passenger cars were stopped at the "STOP" sign for southbound traffic on Church Street, where it intersects with Main Street. The first car in the queue was a 1997 Pontiac Grand Prix, occupied by a driver and three passengers; the second was a 1996 Mazda Protégé, occupied by a driver; the third was a 1987 Chevrolet Nova, occupied by a driver and a front seat passenger; and the fourth was a 1993 Chevrolet Camaro, occupied by a driver.

Figure 3 Map of the accident area, showing the Borough of Glen Rock (shaded area), the location of Blossom Valley Farms, and the intended delivery destination. The large arrows show the direction of the accident truck's travel

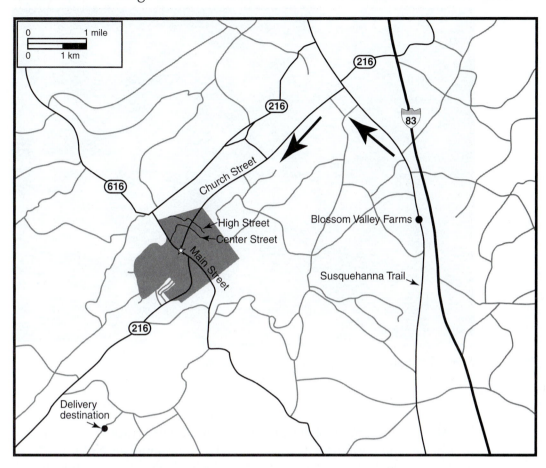

Figure 4 Weight prohibition signs at the beginning of Church Street

Source: Pennsylvania Department of Transportation

Figure 5 Descending grade on southbound Church Street

Source: Pennsylvania Department of Transportation

About 107 feet north of the intersection, the accident truck struck the rear of the Camaro, causing it to rotate clockwise and pushing it into the Nova. The Nova rotated counterclockwise; the rear of the vehicle climbed the 6-inch-high curb and struck three children on the sidewalk and a metal post on a fence on the west side of the sidewalk. The Nova continued to rotate counterclockwise and struck the Mazda, pushing it forward into the rear of the Pontiac. The truck pushed the passenger cars into the intersection.

The Camaro came to rest near the northwest corner of the intersection of Church and Main Streets, facing south. The Nova came to rest with its front wheels on the southern sidewalk in front of the gas station, facing south. The Mazda and Pontiac came to rest in the parking area of the gas station, west of the Nova by about 25 feet and facing southeast. The accident truck proceeded across Main Street, through the western portion of the gas station parking lot, onto Water Street, across the railroad tracks, and then west into an alley, coming to rest about 130 feet west of the intersection of the alley and Water Street. The truck traveled about 407 feet from its initial point of impact with the Camaro to its point of rest. (See Figures 6 and 7.)

Emergency Response

SRPD, Glen Rock Fire and Ambulance, and Loganville Fire Company responders were dispatched at 3:36 P.M. Glen Rock Ambulance responders were on scene within a minute, Glen Rock Fire Department personnel were on scene by 3:39 P.M., and SRPD officers arrived on scene about 3:44 P.M. In addition, the Shrewsbury and New Freedom, Pennsylvania, fire companies responded to the accident. Glen Rock, Rose Fire Company, and Jacobus ambulance services transported patients to Penn State Hershey Medical Center and York Hospital.

Figure 6 Intersection of Church Street and Main Street looking southbound on Church Street

Source: Southern Regional Police Department

Figure 7 At-rest positions of the vehicles at the accident scene

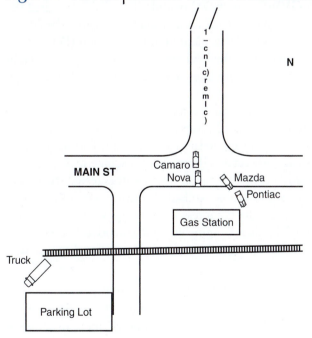

Driver Information

The 21-year-old truck driver lived in White Hall, Maryland, and had been working for Blossom Valley as a truck driver since April 1, 2003. He possessed a Maryland Class "C" noncommercial driver's license. This license permitted the driver to operate an automobile, station wagon, light truck, or any motor vehicle, except a motorcycle, with a gross vehicle weight of 26,000 pounds or less. A commercial driver's license (CDL) is required to drive a single vehicle weighing 26,001 pounds or more.

On the day of the accident, the driver was operating a commercial truck with a gross vehicle weight rating (GVWR) of 26,000 pounds that was equipped with an air brake system, which does not operate in the same way that hydraulic brake systems for automobiles do. (This report will discuss operation of air brake systems in a subsequent section.) According to the accident driver, he had no experience driving an air-braked truck before Blossom Valley hired him, and the largest vehicle he had previously driven was a pickup truck. According to the driver and his employer, he received no air brake training. He said that he had been shown how to operate the lift on the accident truck. At the time of the accident, he had been driving the accident truck for less than a week. Postaccident, he told investigators that he did not know that pumping an air brake-equipped truck's brakes depleted the brakes' air pressure.

Three days before the accident, on April 8, 2003, the driver had a minor accident in the same truck, which he stated was due to loss of braking. (The driver's truck rolled into the back of a stopped passenger car. Neither vehicle suffered substantial damage.)

Truck Information

The accident truck was a 1995 Ford Motor Company, F-800 Series, 2-axle truck with a dump body. It was equipped with a Ford FD-1060 6-cylinder diesel engine that produced 175 horsepower at 2,500 rpm, an Allison model AT-545 4-speed automatic transmission, air brakes, and a hydraulic dump bed. It did not have an antilock brake system (ABS). The truck had an odometer reading of 145,095 miles. According to the manufacturer, the truck's GVWR was 26,000 pounds. The SRPD weighed the truck during the postaccident investigation and found the total weight to be 26,600 pounds. In July 2003, the Pennsylvania Department of Transportation (PennDOT) weighed the truck on portable scales with the load removed, and the empty weight was 15,540 pounds. The wheelbase was 207 inches, and the overall truck length was 25 feet, 5.5 inches.

The truck was equipped on the front and rear axles with standard S-cam drum foundation air brakes with automatic slack adjusters (ASAs). A Bendix model 2150 single-cylinder, gear-driven compressor supplied air to the system. The air governor was a Bendix model D-2, permanently set at 110 pounds per square inch (psi).

As part of the Safety Board's normal protocol, investigators tested the brakes postaccident. The diesel engine was operable, and all air testing was done with air supplied by the engine-mounted Bendix compressor, using the vehicle foot valve (brake pedal) for brake testing. The diesel engine was started and full brake applications were made at about 90 psi of air pressure. No air leaks were discovered in the air brake system.

Note: Table 1 from the original report has been omitted.

The brake testing results, summarized in Table 2, indicated that the pushrod stroke for both rear brakes exceeded the adjustment limit by 1/2 inch, resulting in little or no brake force for the rear wheels.

The truck was equipped with Gunite ASAs on all four brakes. After the accident, Safety Board investigators removed the automatic adjusters from the rear brakes, along with the quick-connect devises and clevis pins, and took them to the Gunite facility for testing. The quick-connect devises had wear in the clevis holes, where they attached to the slack adjusters, and some flexing was observed where

Table 2 Accident truck brake test results summary

Axle	Air chamber size	Slack arm length"	Pushrod stroke	Adjustment limit[B]	Rated stroke
Left front	T-16	5 1/2 in.	1 1/2 in.	1 3/4 in.	2 1/4 in.
Right front	1-16	5 1/2 in.	1 1/2 in.	1 3/4 in.	2 1/4 in.
Left rear	1-30	5 1/2 in.	2 1/2 in.	2 in.	2 1/2 in.
Right rear	1-30	5 1/2 in.	2 1/2 in.	2 in.	2 1/2 in.

"The distance from the center of the splined camshaft to the center of the clevis pin, which secures the pushrod to the slack adjuster; also known as the "lever arm length."

[B]The maximum pushrod stroke permitted. The values utilized for the "brake adjustment limit" are those stated in the *Commercial Vehicle Safety Alliance (CVSA) North American Standard Out-of-Service Criteria*. (Revised edition, April 2003.)

"The total length the pushrod can travel inside the air chamber." (When the "pushrod stroke" is equivalent to the "rated stroke," generally no braking forces are obtained when the brakes are applied.)

the two parts met. The combination of wear in the clevis pin holes and flexing of the joints rendered the automatic feature of the ASAs inoperative. When tested with the devises and clevis pins from the accident truck, the pushrod stroke would not go below 2 1/2 inches, at which point it produced little or no brake force. When the two rear adjusters were tested at the Gunite facility with new devises and clevis pins, the adjusters worked correctly and kept the adjustment well under 2 inches.

All four brake drums were removed, examined, photographed, and measured. The front axle had 15-inch drums and the rear axle had 16.5-inch drums. Heat cracks were present in all the drums, and some discoloration (bluing) was found on the front drums, which were smooth. The drum diameters were measured with a calibrated Central Tool digital brake drum gauge, and all were within manufacturer's tolerances. The brake shoe widths were 4 inches for the front wheels and 7 inches for the rear wheels. The brake shoes had no observable cracks and exhibited no anomalies All the shoes were measured and found to be within CVSA-established tolerances.

The truck was equipped with a dash-mounted red brake warning light, which illuminated when the air pressure went below 70 psi. An audible alarm accompanied this illumination. The spring brakes (parking brakes) were automatically fully applied on the rear axle when the system air reached about 40 psi. Investigators installed air gauges in all the air chambers, or in the service air line just outside the chamber, to check the amount of air going into the chamber during a service brake (foot pedal) application. When a forceful application was made at 90 psi, the chamber gauge pressure read about 75 psi on all four wheel positions (about 15 pounds less than the applied pressure).

The parking brake test was conducted by pulling the parking brake valve that applied the spring brakes. The engine was started and the transmission was moved into "DRIVE" in an attempt to move the vehicle forward on a concrete floor. The truck moved forward with only a slight increase in engine rpm. The truck was then placed in "REVERSE" and, with minimal engine acceleration, it went backward, even with the parking brake applied.

Highway Information

Church Street (State Route 3008) is a two-lane, two-way rural road 27 miles long between the Susquehanna Trail (State Route 3001) to the north and Main Street

(State Route 216) to the south. The Susquehanna Trail is a two-lane, north/south roadway, which parallels Interstate Highway 83 on the west between Harrisburg and the Pennsylvania/Maryland State Line. The topography of the surrounding area is rolling hills.

As Church Street enters the Borough of Glen Rock, the downgrade becomes increasingly steep, from 3.4 percent near the top of the hill to 13 percent at the base of the hill (intersection with Main Street). According to PennDOT, the roadway width varies from 20 feet before entering the borough to 26 feet inside the borough. There is an 8-foot-wide parking lane on the west side of Church Street in the borough, next to housing, and the travel lanes are 9 feet wide. Solid, double, yellow lines separate the north/south lanes.

Main Street is a two-lane, two-way, east/west roadway traversing the Borough of Glen Rock. Immediately to the east of the intersection between Main Street and Church Street, a painted pedestrian crosswalk traverses Main Street. A gas station is located on the south side of the T-intersection of Church Street and Main Street.

The speed limit on Church Street traveling south from the Susquehanna Trail is 55 mph. The speed limit changes 1.2 miles south of the intersection to 40 mph and again 1.8 miles south of the intersection, as Church Street enters the Borough of Glen Rock, to 25 mph. The speed limit at the accident site (intersection of Church Street and Main Street) is 25 mph.

According to PennDOT, the average daily traffic (ADT) on Church Street in 1998 was 3,213, of which 8 percent was trucks and buses. In 2001, the ADT was 3,915, of which 9 percent was trucks and buses.

PennDOT data indicated that from January 1999 to December 2002, 11 traffic accidents occurred on Church Street within the Borough of Glen Rock. Of the 11 accidents, 1 involved a fatality, 1 a major injury, 4 moderate injuries, and 5 minor injuries. Two of the 11 accidents involved trucks.

According to PennDOT, in 1965, after a fatal accident involving a truck at or near the April 11, 2003, accident intersection, the Borough of Glen Rock requested and obtained a weight restriction of 1,500 pounds (load capacity) on Church Street, and the street was so posted. At the intersection of the Susquehanna Trail and Church Street are R5-2 signs conforming to the *Manual on Uniform Traffic Control Devices* indicating that Church Street is a weight-restricted street. The signs indicate that the load weights are limited to 3/4 ton (1,500 pounds), except for local deliveries. The weight restriction applies only in the Borough of Glen Rock. (Refer to Figures 3 and 4.) For traffic traveling northbound on the Susquehanna Trail, an additional sign reads, "Trucks over 1 ton use [Pennsylvania State Route] 216 to Glen Rock." (See Figure 8.)

Additional signs and updated signs have periodically been erected in an effort to keep vehicles with weights in excess of the restriction from using Church Street. The borough ordinance reads (in part)

> It shall be unlawful for any person to operate a motor vehicle, trailer, or semitrailer, as defined in The Vehicle Code, having a load capacity in excess of fifteen hundred (1,500) pounds, on Church Street . . . .[except] (a) Delivering goods or supplying services to any location on said street or accessible only by the use of said street; and (b) Moving any such vehicle to the residence of the owner of such vehicle or to the customary place of parking such vehicle at any location on said Street or accessible only by the use of said Street.

PennDOT officials indicated that the restriction applies to vehicles "having a load capacity" in excess of 1,500 pounds; many of today's vehicles, including many

Figure 8 Intersection of Susquehanna Trail and Church Street. (Note the weight restriction sign directing trucks over 1 ton to use Pennsylvania State Route 216)

Source: Pennsylvania Department of Transportation

pickup trucks, have a load-carrying capacity in excess of 1,500 pounds. According to PennDOT and the SRPD, enforcement of the weight restriction on Church Street is sporadic and complicated due to the wording of the ordinance and a local magistrate's interpretation of the ordinance to allow use of this street for local deliveries to addresses that are not on or intersecting the street.

Motor Carrier Information

General

At the time of the accident, Blossom Valley was a private interstate carrier located in New Freedom, Pennsylvania. It was registered as a motor carrier with the U.S. Department of Transportation (USDOT). The carrier began operations in 1987; it transported building and construction materials, agricultural and farm supplies, and nursery stock. Blossom Valley trucks covered about 16,000 miles a year, including about 2,500 interstate miles. The majority of the interstate miles involved delivery of mulch, topsoil, stone, and nursery items. According to Blossom Valley's owner, before the accident, he was unaware of many of the Federal regulations and requirements concerning motor carrier operations.

The Blossom Valley fleet consisted of five trucks—two straight trucks, a 1994 Chevrolet dump truck, a 1995 Ford utility dump truck (the accident truck), and a 1990 International truck tractor with a 1997 Reit flatbed semitrailer. The tractor-semitrailer combination truck was the only vehicle in the fleet that required a driver with a CDL. It had a combined GVWR of 80,000 pounds and, like the accident truck, was air brake-equipped. The Chevrolet dump truck was equipped with hydraulic brakes. The carrier employed two drivers, one with a CDL and one without (the accident driver). The driver with a CDL drove the two straight trucks and the tractor-semitrailer.

According to statements made during Safety Board interviews with the accident driver, the motor carrier owner, and the other driver, Blossom Valley did not give the accident driver a road test. Title 49 CFR 391.31-33, "Road test," specifies that "a person shall not drive a commercial motor vehicle unless he/she has first successfully completed a road test and has been issued a certificate of driver's road test. . . ." Title 49 CFR 390.5 defines a commercial motor vehicle as "any self-propelled motor vehicle. . . used on a highway in interstate commerce. . . [with] a gross vehicle weight rating of. . . 10,001 pounds or more. . . ." The road test certificate or a copy of a valid CDL is to be retained in the driver's qualification files.

The accident driver operated within a 100-mile radius of the home terminal and returned to that location every night, so, according to 49 CFR 395.1(e), he was not required to keep a record of duty status. However, as a motor carrier, Blossom Valley was required to maintain driver time records. After the accident, Blossom Valley was unable to provide investigators with the required time records. The accident driver's actual hours of service are unknown.

On March 10, 2004, another Blossom Valley truck, driven by a different driver, was ticketed for traveling down Church Street, because the vehicle was in violation of the weight restriction.

Accident Truck Maintenance History

At the time of the accident, Blossom Valley did not have a regular, scheduled vehicle maintenance program in place as required by 49 CFR 396.3. Safety Board investigators obtained maintenance records from four facilities that serviced Blossom Valley's vehicles: RG Group and Beasley Ford, both in York, Pennsylvania; Truck Specialties, Inc., in Shrewsbury, Pennsylvania; and C & T Transport in Parkton, Maryland. The service facilities did not have preventative maintenance agreements with Blossom Valley. Rather, they serviced the carrier's vehicles when Blossom Valley brought them in for repairs.

Truck Specialties completed Pennsylvania State inspections of the accident truck in 2001 and 2002. The facility had last serviced the truck in May 2002 for non-brake-related repairs.

On April 10, 2002, about 1 year before the accident, the accident truck was stopped in Maryland and subjected to a CVSA level 1 inspection, which included checking the brakes for adjustment. At that time, the pushrod stroke for the left rear brake was 2 1/4 inches and the pushrod stroke for the right rear brake was 2 1/2 inches. The adjustment limit is 2 inches, so the brake condition resulted in the truck being placed out of service. Safety Board investigators interviewed the driver who was operating the truck at the time of this inspection. (Blossom Valley no longer employs this driver.) He stated that he [manually] adjusted the brakes before departing the inspection site. He also indicated he had adjusted the accident truck's brakes three or four times during his seasonal employment with Blossom Valley during 2002. He further stated that he had worked full-time as a mechanic for a construction company, was a Pennsylvania State-certified truck inspection mechanic, and had been a truck mechanic for more than 20 years.

On January 20, 2003, the accident truck underwent a Pennsylvania State annual inspection performed by the Beasley Ford dealership in York, Pennsylvania. According to the service manager, the truck mechanics at Beasley are certified by the National Institute for Automotive Service Excellence (ASE). (For more information, see the section in this report on "Inspector and Mechanic Certification

Table 3 Glen Rock accident vehicle inspection history

Date	Type of inspection	Comments
August 2, 2001	Pennsylvania State annual	Inspection and subsequent repairs performed by Truck Specialties mechanics; no brake problems noted
March 27, 2002	Pennsylvania State annual	Inspection and subsequent repairs performed by Truck Specialties mechanics; no brake problems noted
April 10, 2002	Roadside, CVSA level 1	Placed out of service for out-of-adjustment brakes; driver adjusted brakes and left inspection site
January 20, 2003	Pennsylvania State annual	Inspection and subsequent repairs performed by Beasley Ford; rear brakes out of adjustment
April 15–18, 2003	Postaccident inspection (CVSA level 1)	Placed out of service for out-of-adjustment brakes, a loose brake component, and an inoperative turn signal

Requirements" under "Other Information.") The dealership pays the expenses of acquiring and maintaining certification. The mechanic who performed the annual inspection was a Pennsylvania State-certified truck inspector. He told Safety Board investigators that the rear brakes were out of adjustment and that he had [manually] adjusted them.

According to the dealer's service manager, ASAs, which work "pretty well," still require inspection and manual adjustment, particularly if the vehicle operates in hilly or mountainous areas, or in dirt, gravel, or mud. The Ford owner's manual for a year 2003 model F650/750 (a vehicle similar to the accident truck) states

Inspect standard air brakes equipped with automatic slack adjusters for proper brake adjustment every 4 months or 20,000 miles, and more frequently if operated in hilly or mountainous regions or in mud.

At the time of the January 2003 inspection, the recorded mileage on the truck was 142,810. The accident occurred less than 3 months later, at which time the odometer read 145,095 miles No manual adjustments are known to have been made to the brakes between the January 20 inspection and the April 11 accident. The truck had traveled a total of 2,285 miles during that period. Table 3 summarizes the inspection history of the accident truck, indicating the date of each inspection, the type of inspection performed, and whether the brakes were adjusted.

Motor Carrier Oversight

General

At the time of the accident, Blossom Valley had not undergone a Federal Motor Carrier Safety Administration (FMCSA) compliance review or been assigned a safety rating, so it was considered an unrated carrier. Because the carrier had been involved in this multiple-fatality accident, the FMCSA conducted a compliance review of Blossom Valley's safety management controls on May 2, 2003. The compliance review revealed discrepancies in the areas of drug/alcohol testing, driver qualification files, records of duty status, vehicle inspection record-keeping, and driver/vehicle inspection reports. The compliance review resulted in a safety rating of "Conditional" for Blossom Valley. As of October 13, 2005, the FMCSA safety rating had not changed.

Table 4 Factors for FMCSA safety compliance and the results of Blossom Valley's compliance review

Factors	Applicable FMCSRs and other criteria	Results of May 2, 2003, Blossom Valley compliance review
1—General	Parts 387 and 390	Satisfactory
2—Driver	Parts 382, 383, and 391	Satisfactory
3—Operational	Parts 392 and 395	Satisfactory
4—Vehicle	Parts 393 and 396 and out-of-service rate	Unsatisfactory
5—Hazardous materials	Parts 107, 171, 172, 173, 177, 180, and 397	Not applicable
6—Accident	Recordable accident rate	Satisfactory

Table 5 Other Blossom Valley vehicle inspections

Date	Type of inspection	Comments
June 3, 2003	Roadside	Chevrolet pickup with a trailer: trailer brakes inoperative (no actuator switch); breakaway brake device not connected; vehicle placed out of service
June 27, 2003	Roadside	International tractor with Reit trailer: 4 of 10 brakes out of adjustment; vehicle placed out of service

FMCSA standards require a motor carrier to have adequate management controls in place to comply with applicable safety requirements. The FMCSA uses a rating formula to determine a motor carrier's safety fitness. The safety fitness rating methodology begins with an FMCSA-conducted compliance review, applying the six factors shown in Table 4 that rate the carrier's compliance with the *Federal Motor Carrier Safety Regulations* (FMCSRs).

Factors 1—General, 2—Driver, 3—Operational, 4—Vehicle, and 5—Hazardous Materials are rated "Satisfactory," "Conditional," or "Unsatisfactory." Factor 6—Accident is rated either "Satisfactory" or "Unsatisfactory"; a "Conditional" rating is not given. The ratings are defined as follows:

- "Satisfactory"—Carrier has not violated any acute regulations or shown a pattern of noncompliance with critical regulations for that factor.
- "Conditional"—Carrier has violated an acute regulation or had a pattern of noncompliance with critical regulations.
- "Unsatisfactory"—Carrier has violated two or more acute regulations or has patterns of noncompliance with two or more critical regulations.

After the FMCSA May 2003 compliance review, two other vehicles in Blossom Valley's fleet underwent roadside inspections and were placed out of service. (See Table 5.)

Toxicological Information

The accident truck driver told police that he began using illicit drugs in October 2002 (about 6 months before the accident). He acknowledged use of cocaine, marijuana, heroin, rock cocaine, and hydrocodone. (The driver did not have a prescription for the prescription medication hydrocodone.) He admitted using marijuana 2 days before the accident and estimated that he had last used cocaine about 2 weeks before the accident. He denied use of any controlled substance on the day of the accident.

Blood and urine specimens were collected from the driver at 6:33 P.M. and 6:55 P.M., respectively (about 3 and 3 1/4 hours postaccident). At the request of the York County, Pennsylvania, District Attorney, National Medical Services of Willow Grove, Pennsylvania, conducted postaccident toxicological testing of the truck driver's blood and urine. Postaccident urinalysis showed the presence of methylecgonine and benzoylecgonine (both metabolites of cocaine), morphine, and A^9-carboxy-tetrahydrocannabinol, an inactive metabolite of A^9-tetrahydrocannabinol (THC, the active hallucinogenic compound in marijuana). Blood was tested only for THC and metabolites; test results were negative. Urinalysis testing results for ethyl alcohol and cocaethylene were also negative.

Tests and Research

To evaluate the effectiveness of the truck's brakes, the Safety Board conducted computer simulations of the truck's descent on Church Street to the accident site and its impact with the four passenger cars. Investigators used a Human, Vehicle, Environment (HVE) system that employed two physics modules, the Simulation Model Non-linear (SIMON) for the truck descent and EDSMAC4 for the impact. The driver estimated his speed at the time of impact at 40 to 45 mph but stated that when he last looked at the speedometer, the truck was going 25 mph. The speed at impact was needed to determine a target speed for the truck at the bottom of the hill.

SIMON uses Brake Designer to assess the effects of temperature on the brake drums and linings. The HVE system has a Ford F-800 truck in its vehicle library. The size and adjustment of the brakes, the engine power curve, the transmission ratios, the differential ratio, and the load of the vehicle were set to replicate the accident truck in the simulation. Using the simulation tools, the brakes could be applied and released at different intervals as the vehicle descended the hill. SIMON does not model the compressor output and determine the available air pressure, but the force applied to the brake pedal can be varied. SIMON does model aerodynamic drag and rolling resistance. For the simulation, the downgrade was modeled as one grade that was 3,350 feet long at an average grade of 7.7 percent. This is equivalent to the grade at the accident site hill, which varied continuously. Based on the physical evidence (including tire marks and final vehicle positions) and HVE default vehicles for the 1993 Chevrolet Camaro, 1996 Mazda Protégé, 1987 Chevrolet Nova, and 1997 Pontiac Grand Prix, the EDSMAC4 simulations of the vehicle collisions near the intersection indicated that the speed of the truck at impact with the Camaro was about 35 mph.

The impact speed of 35 mph was used as a target for the SIMON downhill final speed. Witness statements concerning the speed of the truck on the hill varied. The driver stated that he stopped near the water tower and electrical substation at the top of the hill. He indicated that he pumped the brakes and that a quarter of the way down the hill, he lost the brakes. He said that as he was traveling about 25 mph, the brake warning light on the dashboard began to flash. A witness following the truck, however, stated that the truck did not stop and was traveling 25 to 30 mph at the top of the hill and then increased speed as it went down the hill. Numerous scenarios were simulated, including having the accident truck stop at the top of the hill and having it crest the hill at 25, 35, 45, and 55 mph. Simulations were made with and without sufficient brake pressure, for a total of 35 simulation runs. The simulations showed that the front brake drums could have heated from 615°F to 1,441°F. (At temperatures in excess of 900°F, brakes fade rapidly.) See appendix B (pages 469–70) for information on the simulations.

The simulations showed that if the driver had pumped the brakes rapidly and depleted the truck's air pressure to below 50 psi, the truck would not have been able to stop. If the driver had applied the brakes too late on the descent, the front brakes would have overheated, and the driver would not have been able to stop. If the driver had allowed the speed of the truck to exceed 38 mph on the descent, the front brakes would have overheated and faded. The simulations showed that the lowest brake drum temperatures occurred when the brakes were continually snubbed on and off as the truck went down the hill. The simulations indicated that the front brakes would have slowed the truck somewhat, keeping the truck to about 35 mph at the time of impact.

Other Information

Commercial Driver's License

The majority of States (32) have a classified license system, which is one in which the State issues different licenses for specific classes of vehicles. Before the CDL program was instituted (see below), in States that did not have a classified license system, any person licensed to drive an automobile could drive a commercial motor vehicle.

The CDL requirement was established under the Commercial Vehicle Safety Act of 1986 and became effective nationwide in 1992. It established testing and license requirements for drivers of commercial motor vehicles. The main purpose of the act was to reduce or prevent truck and bus accidents and fatalities by disqualifying unsafe commercial motor vehicle drivers. The classifications of CDL, by vehicle group descriptions, are

- Combination Vehicle (Group A)—Any combination of vehicles with a gross combination weight rating of 11,794 kilograms or more (26,001 pounds or more) provided the GVWR of the vehicle(s) being towed is in excess of 4,536 kilograms (10,000 pounds).
- Heavy Straight Vehicle (Group B)—Any single vehicle with a GVWR of 11,794 kilograms or more (26,001 pounds or more), or any such vehicle towing a vehicle not in excess of 4,536 kilograms (10,000 pounds) GVWR.
- Small Vehicle (Group C)—Any single vehicle, or combination of vehicles, that meets neither the definition of Group A nor that of Group B as contained in this section, but that either is designed to transport 16 or more passengers including the driver, or is used in the transportation of materials found to be hazardous for the purposes of the Hazardous Materials Transportation Act and which require the motor vehicle to be placarded under the Hazardous Materials Regulations.

Any CDL driver operating a commercial motor vehicle equipped with air brakes must pass an air brake test indicating that the driver has specific knowledge about air brake systems, inspection of the brakes, and "implications of low air pressure warning." If a CDL driver has not passed the air brake test, the CDL will display an "L" restriction, meaning the driver is prohibited from driving air brake-equipped vehicles. A CDL driver may have this restriction removed by passing a State air brake test at a later date.

Canadian Air Brake Endorsement

Since 2001, Transport Canada has required all drivers to have an air brake endorsement to drive any vehicle equipped with air brakes. According to the Canadian

National Safety Code #4, "Classified Driver's Licence Program," a driver must possess a valid driver's license of an appropriate class to operate the assigned vehicle, including an air brake endorsement when the vehicle is equipped with air brakes. Transport Canada reports that Canada has experienced a reduction in brake-related accidents since the adoption of this requirement. Also, between September 1999 and September 2004, Canada experienced a 25-percent reduction in brakes found to be out of adjustment to the point of being out of service.

Brake Systems

Passenger cars are usually equipped with hydraulic brake systems. Trucks are equipped with either hydraulic brakes or air brakes. The two brake systems operate differently. A hydraulic brake system is filled with hydraulic fluid. When the brake pedal is depressed, a proportional force is applied to the fluid, which in turn forces the brake shoes against the drums, creating friction, which stops the vehicle. When the brake is released, the pressure is released, and the brakes release. Hydraulic brake systems are closed systems, so there is no depletion of the brake fluid. Also, hydraulic systems have little discernible lag time between pedal depression and brake application.

An air brake system converts compressed air into a linear force that acts upon a number of components, including the pushrod, slack adjuster, and camshaft, to apply the brake shoes against the brake drum, creating friction, which stops the vehicle. The compressor provides a supply of air to the holding tanks (also known as air supply reservoirs). When the brakes are applied, the stored air is distributed in the system through relay valves to the brake chambers, which convert the air pressure to a linear force. Using this force, the pushrod moves a slack adjuster that is attached to a camshaft, which rotates and causes the brake shoes to expand and contact the brake drum. When the brakes are released, the air used to activate the brakes is exhausted to the atmosphere.

The air brake system is an open system, in that the air used to apply the brakes is lost, and the air supply must be replenished before the brakes can operate. Repeated brake applications in succession (pumping the brakes) may prevent an air brake system from resupplying the air expended during braking quickly enough to maintain a supply of air sufficient to stop the vehicle.

Another distinct characteristic of an air brake system is the mechanical lag time, that is, the interval between the depression of the brake pedal and the application of the brakes. The lag time varies from about 0.20 to 0.55 second and may

Figure 9 Brake schematic

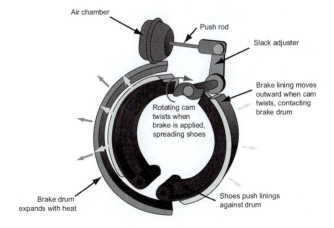

be longer in poorly maintained systems. The mechanical lag time adds to the overall stopping distance. For instance, at 50 mph, a vehicle travels at 73.30 feet per second. In a typical air brake system for which the lag time is 0.50 second, the vehicle will travel an additional 36 feet from the moment of brake pedal depression until the brakes are fully applied.

Vehicles that are typically equipped with air brakes include dump trucks, large transport trucks, and many types of buses. Some motor homes also have air brakes. Air brakes are optional on many trucks in the 19,501- to 33,000-pound weight classes. Hydraulic brakes typically wear out faster. In addition, air brake replacement parts are generally cheaper and more readily available than hydraulic brake system parts.

Automatic Slack Adjusters

ASAs, which are components of air brakes and are also known as automatic brake adjusters, have been offered as optional equipment on some commercial vehicles since the late 1960s. In 1992, the Safety Board noted, "The majority of truck tractors and about half the trailers currently being manufactured are equipped with automatic adjusters." When the rule requiring automatic adjusters on all air brake-equipped vehicles built on or after October 20, 1994, was enacted, most heavy vehicles were already in compliance. The primary purpose of ASAs is to maintain brake adjustment levels without a mechanic or driver having to adjust the brakes manually. (See Figure 10.)

The accident truck was equipped with Gunite ASAs. The Gunite service manual states (bold print in original), **"An automatic slack adjuster should not have to be manually adjusted except for initial installation and at the time of brake reline."** This manual also explains how to troubleshoot to find the cause of excessive pushrod stroke. It does not suggest that manual adjustment is a way to correct excessive pushrod stroke.

Figure 10 Schematic of a Gunite automatic slack adjuster

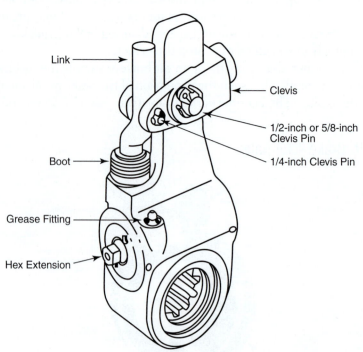

Source: Adapted from a figure that appears in the *Gunite Corporation Automatic Slack Adjuster Service Manual,* June 1994 edition.

Inspector and Mechanic Certification Requirements

The ASAs on the accident truck were manually adjusted at different times by at least two individuals—a former Blossom Valley driver, who was a truck mechanic with 20 years' experience, and the mechanic from the Beasley Ford dealership in York, Pennsylvania. Both individuals were Pennsylvania State-certified truck inspection mechanics; the Ford dealership mechanic was also ASE certified.

Knowledge and Skills Needed to Drive Air Brake-Equipped Vehicles

Although the Glen Rock accident driver said that he slowed the truck before starting down the hill, he did not select a lower gear, which would have provided engine braking, an action recommended by the AAMVA model *Commercial Driver License Manual* and experienced truck drivers. Had he used a lower gear, the vehicle would have slowed due to normal engine compression. In addition, he pumped the brakes, reducing the capability of the front brakes and exacerbating the loss of braking capability in the out-of-adjustment rear brakes. Until recent widespread use of ABS brakes, drivers of hydraulically braked vehicles (passenger cars, sport utility vehicles, and pickups and other light-duty trucks) were taught to pump their brakes in emergencies. But in an air-braked vehicle, pumping the brakes depletes the air pressure, thereby drastically reducing the brakes' capability.

				Appendix B								
			Results of Safety Board computer simulations of accident events									
Sim. no.	Initial speed (mph)	In gear (Y/N)	Brake forces (drag or pulse)	Time 10 to 15 (psi)	Time 30 (psi)	Time 50 (psi)	Highest speed (mph)	Lowest speed (mph)	Able to stop (speed end)	Length sim. (sec.)	Brake drum temp. (°F)	Brake lining temp. (°F)
1	1	Y	Drag	12	75.2	77.7	27	0	Y	92.7	737	485
2	1	Y	Drag	12	65.2	67.7	26	0	Y	82.4	676	438
3	1	Y	Drag	12	65.2	67.7	26	0	Y	81.7	669	430
4	1	Y	Drag	22	85.2	—	26	1	N (30)	86.2	588	399
5	1	Y	Drag	32	80.5	—	27	1	N (33)	81.8	546	358
6	1	Y	Drag	32	—	—	37	1	N (37)	73	540	323
7	1	Y	Drag	32	—	72	37	1	N (36)	73	516	320
8	25	Y	Drag	3	79.3	81.8	27	16	N (16)	87.7	761	500
9	25	Y	Drag	3	69.3	71.8	26	0	Y	85.1	763	506
10	25	Y	Drag	3	59.3	61.8	27	0	Y	75.2	707	458
11	25	Y	Drag	3	50.5	53	27	0	Y	66.6	656	417
12	25	Y	Drag	3	40.5	43	27	0	Y	56.6	595	370
13	25	Y	Drag	21	55.3	57.8	37	21	N (21)	67.4	768	408
14	25	Y	Drag	39.5	50.5	53	48	25	N (40)	58.2	550	259

(Continued)

Appendix B

Results of Safety Board computer simulations of accident events (Continued)

Sim. no.	Initial speed (mph)	In gear (Y/N)	Brake forces (drag or pulse)	Time 10 to 15 (psi)	Time 30 (psi)	Time 50 (psi)	Highest speed (mph)	Lowest speed (mph)	Able to stop (speed end)	Length sim. (sec.)	Brake drum temp. (°F)	Brake lining temp. (°F)
15	25	Y	Drag	38	49	51.5	47	25	N (35)	59.1	638	289
16	35	Y	Drag	3	40.5	43	40	0	Y	54.7	918	552
17	35	Y	Drag	3	30.5	33	38	0	Y	53.9	838	489
18	35	Y	Drag	3	20.5	23	38	0	Y	42.9	733	415
19	35	Y	Drag	3	50.5	53	39	27	N (27)	60.6	850	474
20	35	Y	Drag	3	53.5	56	39	34	N (34)	59.8	746	446
21	45	Y	Drag	3	38	40.5	53	45	N (47)	45.4	771	401
22	45	Y	Drag	3	28	30.5	51	17	N (17)	53.2	1170	642
23	45	Y	Drag	3	34.5	37	52	34	N (36)	46.7	1012	489
24	55	Y	Drag	3	34.5	37	59	53	N (53)	39.2	817	402
25	55	Y	Drag	3	25.5	28	58	34	N (34)	42.1	1177	549
26	55	Y	Drag	3	26	28.5	58	35	N (35)	41.8	1158	536
27	25	N	None	—	—	—	70	25	N (70)	46.6	150	150
28	1	N	None	—	—	—	67	1	N (67)	63.9	150	150
29	1	Y/N	None	Neutral at 11.6 sec			67	1	N (67)	61.9	150	150
30	1	Y	Pulse	12	32	—	28	0	Y	80.1	570	416
31	1	Y	Pulse	12	32 (pump down)		31	1	N (31)	119.6	573	504
32	1	Y	Pulse	12	32 (pump down)		30	1	N (30)	118	543	480
33	1	Y	Pulse	12	32 (pump down)		36	1	N (36)	111.4	488	431
34	25	Y	Pulse	3	Pumped down to 0		36	25	N (36)	75.6	466	356
35	25	Y	Pulse	3	Pumped down to 0		35	25	N (35)	75.6	456	349

FREQUENTLY ASKED QUESTIONS (FAQ) ABOUT INSTALLING SOFTWARE

■ SOFTWARE INSTALLATION

Installing or setting up software on a computer is a relatively simple process. In many cases it is automatic, requiring minimal user effort. A few of the issues that you may find are discussed here.

Firewall Issues

A firewall is a program designed to limit access to a computer or server on a network. In some installations a firewall limits access from outside sources such as Internet downloads, e-mail from unknown sources, or personal computers not authorized for access. This limitation may include access from the companion website or from a software vendor website. In some locations your ability to *send* files may also be restricted by a firewall.

Permission to override these limitations must come from the network administrator. If you are working in a law office, corporate facility, or governmental agency, check with the network administrator before starting the exercises in the text.

Restricted Computer Use

Many schools, libraries, and public locations restrict the users' ability to download and install software programs on their computers. In many locations anything that might be saved on the computer, such as a data file, is deleted when the computer is turned off or restarted.

If you use this type of computer access, be sure you have appropriate media for saving your work, such as a USB memory device, floppy disk, or memory card. Many newer computers only provide the ability to use the USB devices. Check the computer to determine what can be saved and the type of storage devices allowable.

In some educational settings, software may have been installed to allow you to use the program. Generally you can save your personal data files on external memory devices. However, in some locations the software may be a network version that will not allow independent use of separate memory. Always check with your instructor before starting work to avoid disappointment when you cannot save your work product.

Antivirus Software Issues

Antivirus software is designed to prevent malicious software code (the virus) from entering your computer system or to isolate it from running on your computer.

One of the ways these programs work is to look for programs that are self-executing or have the power to install themselves. The software applications will typically have as the extension .exe or .com. When you install one of the demo programs used with this text your virus software may try to block these programs and ask for your confirmation that you do wish to install them. Other programs as part of the installation want to write entries into the Registry of the operating software you are using. The Registry is like a command center for computer operations. As a result, the antivirus program blocks writing needed entries, in some cases without advising users it is doing this. You will know if this happens because the software will not work properly. If you are SURE the software to be installed is from a reliable trusted source, turn your antivirus software OFF when installing the program and turn it back ON after you finish with the installation.

Remember. Antivirus software is only of value if it is kept up to date. Be sure to update the antivirus software regularly—there are new viruses created every day.

Downloading

The process of downloading software is fairly routine: go to a trusted source, click a Download button. The software will either automatically download and install itself, or it will ask you where you want to save the program on your computer and then ask you to install it after it is downloaded.

Preliminary issues:

- Will the computer you are using allow downloading of software?
- Is it a restricted computer?
- Is there a firewall?
- Is it a trusted site?

Assuming there are no preliminary issues, then determine if your computer has the needed resources. For example, downloading Microsoft Office 2007 Trial Version requires a minimum set of resources:

Things to know before you download	How to set-up and install your trial	Licensing	System requirements	May we recommend

Computer and processor	500 megahertz (MHz) processor or higher.
Memory	256 megabyte (MB) RAM or higher. 512 MB RAM or higher recommended for Instant Search.
Hard disk	1.5 gigabyte (GB); a portion of this disk space will be freed after installation if the original download package is removed from the hard drive.
Drive	CD-ROM or DVD drive
Display	1024 × 768 or higher resolution monitor
Operating system	Microsoft Windows (R) XP with Service Pack (SP) 2, Windows Server (R) 2003 with SP1, or later operating system.
Other	Connectivity to Microsoft Exchange Server 2000 or later is required for certain advanced functionality in Outlook 2007. Connectivity to Microsoft Windows Server 2003 with SP1 or later running Microsoft Windows SharePoint Services is required for certain advanced collaboration functionality. Microsoft Office SharePoint Server 2007 is required for certain advanced functionality. PowerPoint Slide Library requires Office SharePoint Server 2007. Microsoft Internet Explorer 6.0 or later, 32 bit browser only. Internet functionality requires Internet access (fees may apply). * Instant Search requires Microsoft Windows Desktop Search 3.0.
Additional	Actual requirements and product functionality may vary based on your system configuration and operating system. For complete requirements visit http://www.microsoft.com/office/products.

Some programs, like the Microsoft downloads, may require validation of the existence of authorized or properly licensed software on the computer (see the following validation screen from Microsoft) or may require the use of a specific Web browser such as Internet Explorer.

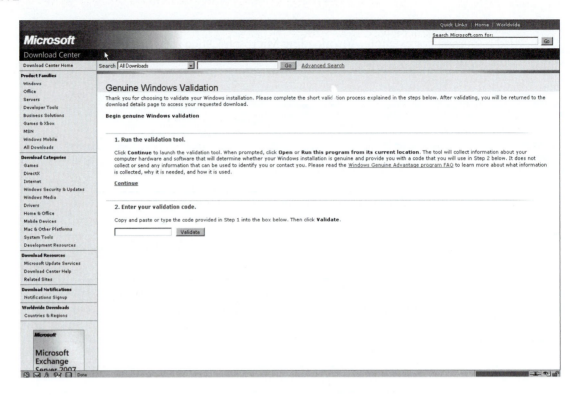

If you are using a download manager, after the program download is saved on your computer you will need to launch the program (install it). This may be done using the Launch button on the download manager or finding where the program was saved and double left clicking the mouse button when it is on the icon to the left of the program name. Clicking on the program name may bring up the rename option and not launch the program as desired.

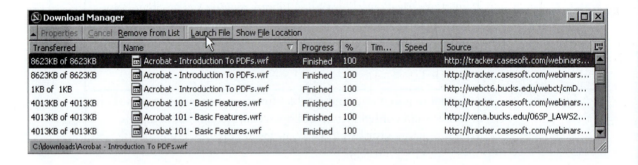

The time it takes to download a program depends on the size of the program and the speed of the Internet connection. See Exhibit A.1 for what speeds to expect from different types of Internet connections.

It is essential that the Internet connection be kept open until the download is complete. With a large program and slow-speed connections it is not unusual to lose the connection and have to start over.

Automatic Installation

Many programs supplied on a CD will automatically launch and install the program when the CD is inserted in the computer's CD player.

Exhibit A.1 Connection type and speed comparison

Internet Speed Comparison	
TYPE CONNECTION	**SPEED RANGE**
Dial-up	2400 bps to 56 Kbps
DSL (Digital Subscriber Line)	1.5 to 9 Mbps when receiving
	16 to 640 Kbps when sending
Cable	512 Kbps to 20 Mbps
T-1	1.544 Mbps
Fiber Optic	up to 30 Mbps

Manual Installation

Some software will not automatically launch and install itself. The user must find the necessary file to install the software manually. The file to install the software is usually labeled SETUP.EXE, or INSTALL.EXE, or in some cases LAUNCH.EXE.

To find the file, insert the CD in the computer CD drive.
Click on the START icon:

Then click the RUN selection:

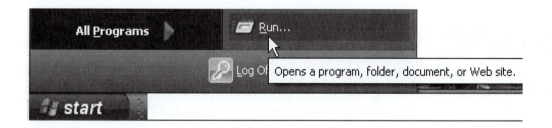

From the Run interface screen, select Browse and look for the files on the CD using the CD drive letter designation for your computer:

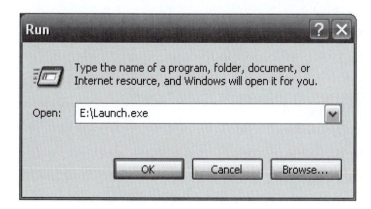

Exhibit A.2 Bytes in sizes of storage

Name	Symbol	Number of Bytes	Equal to
kilobyte	KB	1,024	1,024 bytes
megabyte	MB	1,048,576	1,024 KB
gigabyte	GB	1,073,741,824	1,024 MB
terabyte	TB	1,099,511,627,776	1,024 GB
petabyte	PB	1,125,899,906,842,624	1,024 TB
exabyte	EB	1,152,921,504,606,846,976	1,024 PB
zettabyte	ZB	1,180,591,620,717,411,303,424	1,024 EB
yottabyte	YB	1,208,925,819,614,629,174,706,176	1,024 ZB

Source: http://www.webopedia.com/quick_ref/FileSizeConversionTable.asp.

You may need to look in one of the folders to find the correct program. Look for the program name Setup, or Install, or Launch with the extension of .exe (which means execute) or .com.

With the desired program name in the Open window, click on OK.

File-Size Conversion Table

Exhibit A.2 shows the relationship among the file storage sizes that computers use. Binary calculations are based on units of 1,024, and decimal calculations are based on units of 1,000. It should be noted that decimal calculations are based on units that have been rounded off to the nearest 1,000 and therefore differ from the actual number of bytes used in binary calculations.

■ PLUG-INS, VIEWERS, AND OTHER ADD-ONS

Plug In

A plug-in allows you to view a file saved in a specific format, such as a Quicktime for viewing video files, or a PDF viewer like ScanSoft PDF Converter, Adobe Reader, or Adobe Acrobat to view a PDF file.

Adobe

Adobe Reader allows you to view files saved in PDF format.
Adobe Reader download site:
http://www.adobe.com/products/acrobat/readstep2.html

QuickTime

Quicktime allows you to view files, usually streaming video.
Quicktime viewer download site:
http://www.apple.com/quicktime/products/qt/

Windows Media Player

A Windows XP plug-in for digital media, music, video, and pictures.
Windows Media Player download site:
http://www.microsoft.com/windows/windowsmedia/download/

■ BROWSERS

A browser is a program that allows you to view Internet sites.

Microsoft Internet Explorer

Microsoft Internet Explorer download site:
http://www.microsoft.com/windows/products/winfamily/ie/default.mspx

■ UTILITY

A utility is a program that performs a function such as compressing or uncompressing a file.

WinZip

WinZip Demo Version download site:
http://www.winzip.com/ddchomea.htm

Webinex

This is a plug-in that allows you to view the Webinars in the course.

Webinex download site:
http://www.casesoft.com/student.asp

■ FIREWALL

A program that blocks intruders from access to a computer. It is not a virus protection program, but merely blocks access over the Internet to sites that try to access a computer.

ZoneAlarm

ZoneAlarm offers a full range of firewalls, including a basic demo version and trial period for their upgraded versions.
ZoneAlarm download site:
www.zonealarm.com

Adapters Devices for changing the connection on a connector to a different configuration.

Agent A person authorized to act on behalf of another.

Annotation monitor Monitor that allows a witness to easily make on-screen annotations with the touch of a finger.

Antivirus software Programs that scan the computer to identify the presence of viruses; the better programs eliminate the virus.

Applications software A collection of one or more related software programs that enables a user to enter, store, view, modify, or extract information from files or databases. The term is commonly used in place of "program" or "software." Applications may include word processors, Internet browsing tools, and spreadsheets.

Assets Things that have value.

Attachment An attachment is a record or file associated with another record for the purpose of storage or transfer.

Attachments A popular method of transmitting text files and occasionally graphic images, by attaching the file to an e-mail.

Attorney–client privilege A rule of evidence permitting an attorney to refuse to testify as to confidential client information.

Auto coding The electronic scanning and coding of documents by selected key terms and dates.

Backup To create a copy of data as a precaution against the loss or damage of the original data.

Bates production numbering A tracking number assigned to each page of each document in the production set.

Boilerplate Standard language used in other documents.

Bookmarks Netscape term for saved URLs.

Browser A software program that allows a person to use a computer to access the Internet.

Cable Operates over cable TV lines.

Candor Ethical obligation to not mislead the court or opposing counsel with false statements of law or of facts which the lawyer knows to be false. Without prejudice or malice, presented honestly. The ethical duty to not mislead the court or tribunal.

Capacity, with regard to computers The technical specifications such as CPU speed and computer memory.

Case management program Software for organizing the parts of a case in a central repository that can be shared by all members of a legal team.

Case Management/Electronic Case Files (CM/ECF) The federal court's electronic access and filing system.

Case(s) Issues that a client has presented to a legal team to handle and resolve.

Cell In a spreadsheet, the box at the intersection of a row and column for text or numerical data.

Central processing unit (CPU) Central processor unit, the computer chip, and memory module that performs the basic computer functions.

Chain of custody Steps taken to ensure that evidence is properly collected, preserved, and that the possession of the evidence is properly documented and accounted for at all steps in the processing, pretrial, and trial phases.

Chart of accounts A listing of all the names of the accounts used in a particular financial entity.

Check register A chronological record of disbursements of checks and deposits.

Claim of privilege Preventing the disclosure of confidential communications as evidence based on a recognized privilege. The person claiming the privilege has the burden to establish its existence.

Claw back provision Any agreements the parties reach for asserting claims of privilege or of protection of trial-preparation material after production.

Coding The process of capturing case-relevant information (e.g., author, date authored, date sent, recipient, date opened etc.) from a document.

Column A vertical set of cells in a spreadsheet.

Compatibility In software usage, designed to work on a particular type of computer or operating system.

Competent Having the requisite knowledge and skill thoroughness and preparation necessary for representation.

Computer hardware A tangible or physical part of a computer system.

Computer system A combination of an input device, a processor, and an output device.

Computer virus Programs that attack and destroy computer programs, internal computer operating systems, and occasionally the hard drive of computers.

Concept searching Using a list of terms statistically related to the words in a query.

Confidentiality In the law, any information with regard to a client, learned from whatever sources, that is to be kept in confidence by the legal team. An obligation to not reveal information which is based on a relationship of trust placed in one person by the other.

Conflict of interest Representing one client that will be directly adverse to the interest of another client, the attorney, or another third party not a client.

Connections The way in which workstations, file servers, and other peripheral devices are joined to the network.

Connectors Instructions in a search query on how to treat the combinations of words in the query.

Content metadata Information about the contents of a document.

CPU Central processor unit, the computer chip, and memory module that performs the basic computer functions.

Database A collection of similar records.

De-duplication (de-duping) The process of comparing electronic records based on their characteristics and removing duplicate records from the data set.

Dial-up access Uses a modem connected to a PC to connect to the Internet by dialing a phone number.

Digital format A computerized format utilizing a series of 0's and 1's.

Discovery A step in the litigation process where the parties exchange information.

Document camera Portable evidence presentation system equipped with a high resolution camera.

Documents In Abacus, documents are any previously saved word processing files, scanned images, pleadings, correspondence, or Internet Web pages.

Domain nomenclature Part of the URL naming protocol.

DSL Digital subscriber line that is always connected using existing telephone lines.

Dual cassette player Equipment that plays back audio.

Due process An established course of judicial proceedings or other activity designed to ensure the legal rights of an individual.

E-discovery Discovery of documents created, disseminated, and stored via electronic means.

E-mail archiving The continuous saving of e-mail data.

Electronic courtroom Courtroom equipped with electronic equipment for use in trial presentations.

Electronic filing Filing of documents in electronic format using the Internet or computer connection.

Electronic notary seal (ENS) A form of electronic digital signature unique to the individual notary.

Electronic repository An off-site computer used to store records that may be accessed over secure Internet connections.

Encryption Scrambling documents using algorithms (mathematical formulas).

Entry of appearance A formal written notice by an attorney that he or she is representing one of the parties to the action.

Equity The value of the assets of an entity reduced by the claims of outsiders.

Ethical wall A restriction on access to information about a case or a client.

Ethics Minimally acceptable standards of conduct in a profession.

EULA–end user license agreement The contract between the software company and the user authorizing the use and setting limitations for use of the program.

Events Any appointments, tasks, reminders, or things to do that are scheduled for specific dates.

Expenses Decreases in the owner's equity caused by an outflow of assets from the entity in the delivery of goods and services.

Expert witness A person qualified by education, training or experience to render an opinion based on a set of facts that are outside the scope of knowledge of the finder of fact.

Factual research Determining the facts about a case.

Favorites Internet Explorer term for saved URLs.

Federal rules of evidence The rules governing the admissibility of evidence in federal court.

Fiduciary relationship A relationship where one is under a duty to act for the benefit of another under the scope of the relationship.

Field Information located in vertical columns.

File In the paperless office, a single data document.

File extension A tag of three or four letters, preceded by a period, which identifies a data file's format or the application used to create the file.

File format The internal structure of a file, which defines the way it is stored and used.

File server A computer in a network that controls the flow of information in the network.

Filtering The process used to scan or search the documents for relevant terms in an attempt to narrow the focus, such as a filter to eliminate documents created before or after a certain date.

Firewalls Programs designed to limit access to authorized users in an application.

Folder A collection of files.

Footer Items at the bottom of each page in the document.

Form views An alternative way of viewing and presenting the information in a database.

Formula bar In Excel, the area at the top of the spreadsheet for entering formula and data into spreadsheet cells.

Freeware Software distributed, generally over the Internet, at no charge to the user.

Full service online providers Those providing a broad range of legal materials, including cases, statutes, and regulations.

Full text retrieval A search of every word except "stop words."

Graphic user interface (GUI) A set of screen presentations and metaphors that utilize graphic elements such as icons in an attempt to make an operating system easier to use.

Hardcopy Paper copies of documents.

Header Items at the top of each page in the document.

Host Every computerized device, like a computer, printer, or fax machine that is connected to a network.

Hot spots A wireless access point, generally in a public area.

Hub A device used for sharing a signal among multiple computer devices.

Information technologist A member of the legal team who has legal and technology skills and primarily supports electronic discovery activities.

Infrared headphones Assisted listening device for the hearing impaired.

Integrated functions The sharing of data between different functions in a software program.

Internet The interconnecting global public network made by connecting smaller shared public networks. The most well-known is the Internet, the worldwide network of networks, which uses the TCP/IP protocol to facilitate information exchange.

Internet browser A program that allows the user to access the Internet.

Interpreter box Routes language translation from an interpreter to the witness/defendant's headphones or the courtroom's public address system.

Interrogatories Formal written discovery requests, seeking the identification and physical location of relevant documents and requesting copies.

IP Internet protocol address. A string of four numbers separated by periods used to represent a computer on the Internet.

ISDN Integrated services digital network; uses digital telephone lines.

ISP Internet service provider, a company that provides users with local access to the Internet.

IT Information technology, the technology support staff within organizations.

Journals Chronological listings of financial transactions of a business.

Laptop Smaller, portable computer.

Laptop port Connection into which a laptop can be plugged.

Large screen monitor Video monitor conveniently located in the courtroom and large enough for all to see the graphics displayed.

Ledger The individual account records for each account.

Legal specialty software Programs that combine functions found in software suites for performing law office management functions.

Liabilities Claims of outsiders to the assets of the entity.

Limited service search providers Those specialized in providing limited access to cases and additional items.

List servers An automatic mailing list, usually for specific topics.

Litigation hold A process whereby a company or individual determines an unresolved dispute may result in litigation, and, as a result, electronically created and stored documents should not be destroyed or altered.

Local area network (LAN) Usually refers to a network of computers in a single building or other discrete location.

Logical address Addresses for delivering messages.

Macro A set of instructions or keystrokes (a program within a program).

MAC address A physical address that is unique that is stored in a special memory location in a computerized device.

Macros Small programs that execute software functions when activated.

Mail merge A macro that combines a document with a list of recipients.

Mailbox An electronic storage location for e-mail messages.

Mainframe A large computer system used primarily for bulk processing of data and financial information.

Matters Any item, case, file, or project that you need to track.

Metadata Information about a particular data set, which may describe, for example, how, when, and by whom it was received, created, accessed, and/or modified, and how it is formatted.

Minimum requirements The minimum computer requirements in terms of memory, speed, and other characteristics necessary for software to run properly.

Mobile operate system The software that controls the functions of mobile operating devices.

Model rules of professional conduct The American Bar Association set of proposed ethical standards for the legal profession.

Modem A piece of hardware that lets a computer talk to another computer over a phone line.

Multi-user license Authorizes the installation of software on multiple computers.

Municipal area network (MAN) A network in a specific geographic municipality, usually a wireless network.

Native file format Electronic documents have an associated file structure defined by the original creating application. This file structure is referred to as the "native format" of the document. Because viewing or searching documents in the native format may require the original application (e.g., viewing a Microsoft Word document may require the Microsoft Word application), documents are often converted to a standard file format (e.g., tiff) as part of electronic document processing.

Netiquette Rules of behavior for using the Internet.

Network A group of computers or devices that is connected together for the exchange of data and sharing of resources.

Network administrator The person with the highest level of access or authority to the network.

Network file server A computer that controls the flow of information over the network.

Network license Authorizes the use of the software on a computer network with a specified number of simultaneous users on the network.

Network operating system Computer software that controls the functions and flow of information over the network.

Network rights and privileges Rights to access the different information on the network.

Networked A group of computers or devices that is connected together for the exchange of data and sharing of resources.

Networked computer Any combination of workstations (stand-alone computers) electronically connected, usually with a central computer that acts as a server on which files and data are stored for access to all other computers and shared software programs.

Objective coding Also referred to as bibliographic indexing. This includes the author, type of document, recipient, and date.

Office software suites The software consists of commonly used office software programs that manage data and database programs; manipulate financial or numeric information, spreadsheet programs; or displayed images and presentation graphics programs.

Online collaboration Using the Internet to conduct meetings and share documents.

Operating system The software that the rest of the software depends on to make the computer functional. On most PCs this is Windows or the Macintosh OS. Unix and Linux are other operating systems often found in scientific and technical environments.

Optical character recognition (OCR) A technology that takes data from a paper document and turns it into editable text data. The document is first scanned, then OCR software searches the document for letters, numbers, and other characters.

Outsourcing Use of persons or services outside of the immediate office staff.

Palm OS A proprietary computer operating system for personal digital assistants and smartphones.

Paperless office Office where documents are created, stored, received, and sent electronically.

Passwords Combinations of letters, numbers, and symbols to restrict access to files and computers.

PC Personal computer.

PDA Personal digital assistant: Handheld digital organizer.

PDF (portable document format) An Adobe technology for formatting documents so they can be viewed and printed using the Adobe Acrobat reader.

Permissions A set of attributes that specifies what kind of access a user has to access files and folders.

Physical address The physical address is the media access control, or MAC, address.

Principal One who authorizes another to act on his or her behalf.

Privilege A rule of evidence that protects certain forms of communication from disclosure at trial. The attorney–client privilege provides that communication between the attorney and client in obtaining legal advice may not be required to be revealed in court.

Privilege log A list of documents claimed by the submitting party to contain material subject to privilege or work product exclusion.

Program shell A software program containing a platform for using different software programs. See integrated functions.

Property bar In Quattro Pro, the area at the top of the spreadsheet for entering formula and data into spreadsheet cells.

Random access memory (RAM) Temporary computer memory that stores work in progress.

Read only memory (ROM) A type of nonvolatile memory that does not require power to retain its contents.

Recommended computer requirements Computer system configuration of memory, speed, and other characteristics for the maximum utilization of the software.

Record In a database, the information in a horizontal row.

Redaction The removal of confidential information, or at least that which is claimed to be confidential, or material prepared for trial under the work product doctrine.

Relevant Has a relationship to or is likely to lead to admissible evidence.

Remote access Accessing a file server or computer from a remote location using the Internet.

Remote collaboration Working on a common document utilizing remote access by two or more parties.

Revenue Increases in the owner's equity from the delivery of goods or services.

Ribbon A term used to describe the new user interface in Microsoft Office 2007 suite of products.

Router A piece of hardware that routes data from a local area network (LAN) to a phone line.

Row A horizontal set of cells in a spreadsheet.

Rules of court Rules governing the practice or procedure in a specific court.

Search engines Services for searching the World Wide Web using words or phrases.

Search query Specific words used in a computerized search.

Security protocols Software programs that limit access to the file server and peripherals such as printers or other workstations.

Self-defense exception The right to reveal a client confidence when necessary to defend oneself against a claim of wrongful conduct.

Server Any computer on a network that contains data or applications shared by users of the network on their client PCs.

Shareware Software that the author has chosen to make available free to the using public on the honor system.

Shepardizing The process of using Shepard's, an electronic compilation of legal citations, to update research.

Single-user license Authorizes the installation of software on one computer.

Smartphone Generally a wireless telephone with features such as camera and Internet connection.

Smoking gun Document, such as an e-mail, hidden in the old files that would conclusively impeach or destroy the credibility of a witness or be evidence that conclusively determines an issue.

Social bookmarking Sharing of bookmarks or favorites.

Software Coded instructions (programs) that make a computer do useful work.

Software compatibility Software for the type of computer on which it is to be used.

Software integration Direct input from one program into another program.

Specialized search engines Search engines that use highly developed algorithms to search for relevant information and return a listing in order of relevancy with amazing accuracy.

Specialty application programs Specialty programs combine many of the basic functions found in software suites, word processing, database management, spreadsheets, and graphic presentations to perform law office case and litigation management.

Spoliation Spoliation is the destruction of records that may be relevant to ongoing or anticipated litigation, government investigation, or audit. Courts differ in their interpretation of the level of intent required before sanctions may be warranted.

Stand-alone computer A computer on which all of the software used is installed and on which all of the data or files are electronically stored.

Static files A file that contains only data.

Stop words Words used too commonly to be used in a search.

Subjective coding Identifies keywords within the document or other criteria not related to bibliographic information.

Supervising attorney The attorney managing or supervising the legal team members.

Switch A high-performance alternative to a hub.

System metadata information Data such as file name, size, and location.

Table Data that is organized in a format of horizontal rows and vertical columns.

Table of authorities A list of the references in a document and related page numbers where they are located.

Tablet PC Laptop that allows input from a pen device instead of a mouse or keyboard.

Tangible evidence Physical objects.

Teleworkers People who work from remote locations, typically from home.

Template A form or standard document.

Thin client A computer system where programs and files are maintained on a centralized server.

TIFF file format Short for tagged image file format. It is one of the most widely used formats for storing images. TIFF graphics can be black and white, gray-scaled, or color.

Time line Chronological listings of the facts of a case.

Timekeeping The recording of all time spent performing activities during the work day.

Trial notebook Summary of the case, usually contained in a tabbed three-ring binder with sections such as pleadings, motions, law, pretrial memo, and witness.

Trial presentation program Computer program that organizes and controls documents, depositions, photographs, and other data as exhibits for trial, and displays them as evidence.

Type-ahead feature This feature completes the address after a few letters of the address are typed.

Uninterruptible power supply (UPS) A battery system that can supply power to a computer or computer peripheral for a short period of time.

URL (uniform resource locator) The Internet address for a website.

User-level security In Microsoft Access, the ability to limit access to the Access database tables, queries, forms, reports, and macros.

Utility software Programs that perform functions in the background related to the operation of the computer.

VCR Equipment that plays back audio and video.

Videoconferencing Conferencing from multiple locations using high-speed Internet connections to transmit sound and images.

Visual presentation cart Media center located in courtroom.

Voice recognition Computer programs for converting speech into text or commands without the use of other input devices such as keyboards.

VoIP Voice over Internet Protocol is a computer Internet replacement for traditional telephone connections.

Webex viewer A plug-in software program that allows use of webinars.

Webinar A program produced and presented over the Internet for viewing at the user's computer.

Wide area network (WAN) Network generally covering a large geographic area and made up of other networks; a network of networks.

Wireless computer networks A wireless network uses wireless technology instead of wires for connecting to the network.

Wireless network Computers on the network communicate over the airwaves wirelessly instead of through wired connections.

Work product In the law, material prepared in preparation for trial that is protected from disclosure.

Work product doctrine The rule of evidence that allows the attorney to treat as confidential and not make available work product to the opposing side.

Workbook A collection of worksheets.

Workgroup A group of users in a multi-user environment who share data and the same workgroup information file.

Workgroup information file A file that contains information about the users in a workgroup. This information includes users' account names, their passwords, and the groups of which they are members.

Workstation A computer connected to a network that is used for access consisting of a monitor, input device, and computer.

World wide web The WWW is made up of all of the computers on the Internet that use HTML-capable software (Netscape, Explorer, etc.) to exchange data. Data exchange on the WWW is characterized by easy-to-use graphical interfaces, hypertext links, images, and sound. Today the WWW has become synonymous with the Internet, although technically it is really just one component.

ZIP file An open standard for compression and decompression used widely for PC download archives. ZIP is used on Windows-based programs such as WinZip and Drag and Zip. The file extension given to ZIP files is .zip.

INDEX